BILLION DOLLAR
BATMAN

ALSO BY BRUCE SCIVALLY

Superman on Film, Television, Radio & Broadway

James Bond: The Legacy

The Special Effects & Stunts Guide

BILLION DOLLAR

BATMAN

A HISTORY OF THE CAPED CRUSADER ON FILM AND TELEVISION FROM 10¢ COMIC BOOK TO GLOBAL ICON

BRUCE SCIVALLY

HENRY GRAY

HG

PUBLISHING

Wilmette, IL

Published by Henry Gray Publishing

Set in 11 point Baskerville

Publisher's Cataloging-in Publication Data

Scivally, Bruce.
Billion dollar Batman : a history of the Caped Crusader
on film and television from 10¢ comic book to global icon
/ Bruce Scivally.
p. cm.
ISBN: 978-0-615-30641-4
1. Batman (Fictitious character). 2. Comic books, strips,
etc. —United States—History and criticism. 3. Popular
culture—United States.   I. Title.
PN6728.B363 S25 2011
741.5`973—dc22
                                        2011939945

HENRY GRAY

HG

PUBLISHING

Henry Gray Publishing
PO Box 397
Wilmette, Illinois 60091

To my brother, Rock Scivally,
a lifelong Batfan,
and my mother, Aileen Scivally,
who indulged our battiness.

Acknowledgments

Just as Batman wouldn't be as effective without his support network—Alfred, Lucius Fox, Commissioner Gordon, Barbara Gordon, Robin, etc.—I wouldn't have been able to write this book without mine. I must first thank the people who took time out of their busy schedules to grant me interviews, including Michael Uslan, Michael G. Wilson, Lorenzo Semple, Jr., Bob Hanks, Deborah Dozier Potter, Ed Begley, Jr., Sharmagne Leland-St. John, and Jane Adams. I also want to give a special thanks to Tom Mankiewicz, who gave me a lengthy interview about his tenure with the Batman movie, and then sadly passed away before I was able to complete the book.

Next, I want to thank those who helped with research, including Boyd and Donna Magers of Serial World, Tim Gardner, Dana Lucas Timmerman, Scott McIsaac, and a big shout out to Andy Mangels, who provided a treasure trove of rare magazine articles.

I also must give a tip of the cowl to my volunteer proofreaders—Marc Tyler Nobleman, whose own book on comic book writer Bill Finger will soon be published, and Bill Ramey of the Batman-On-Film website, which is an invaluable resource on all things Batman. John Cork not only proofread the book, but also provided insightful editorial assistance.

For helping with the design of the book, I must thank Siena Esposito for her typography expertise, and Photofest, Deborah Dozier Potter, Fred Wostbrock and Adam West for providing photos.

Thanks also go to Anagnostis Karras, Tony Radick and Paul Scrabo, for "coming to the aid of the party," as Ian Fleming once wrote. Also, I want to thank all the researchers and reporters who laid the groundwork on which this book is based. It was their trailblazing that made my journey possible.

And lastly, a huge thank you to Sandra Bogan. Now that the book is finished, it's time for me to emerge from my Batcave and repay her for two-and-a-half years of postponed social obligations. With the patience she's shown during the writing of this book, she is, undoubtedly, the real superhero.

Bruce Scivally
November 2011

Table of Contents

Introduction

A young boy leaves a movie theater with his parents. As they pass through an alley, they're accosted by a gunman. The boy's father leaps to defend his family, but a shot rings out, and the father falls dead. The mother screams; another shot and she, too, is silenced forever. The gunman runs away, leaving the boy kneeling between his dead parents. This boy, whose life is irrevocably shattered, will grow up possessed by a burning desire for vengeance, a desire that will motivate him to devote his life to becoming a crime fighter, a masked avenger whose name strikes fear into the hearts of the city's criminals—Batman.

In the superhero universe, Batman is often portrayed as a polar opposite of his literary predecessor, Superman. Superman came to earth from the planet Krypton with powers and abilities far beyond those of earthlings, was raised in humble rural surroundings and chose to use his god-like powers to fight a never-ending battle for truth, justice and the American way. We associate Superman with daylight; his powers are renewed by the sun, and he is such an all-American boy scout that he stands as an unswerving symbol of hope and goodness. Superman speaks to the best in all of us.

Batman was created from a tragedy, an urban character who grew up in great wealth but was driven by dark impulses. His wealth, as much as his drive and intellect, was his superpower; he used it to create the array of gadgets and vehicles he needed to carry on his mission. We associate Batman with night-time; he moves in darkness, a denizen of the shadows, in a film noir city where the moon seems always to be full and sliced by clouds. Though he fights for justice, he is motivated by vengeance. Batman speaks to our darker impulses, our wish to be powerful enough to beat our enemies, if not our demons, into submission.

In short, Superman is who we aspire to be; Batman is who we are.

Like Superman, Batman captured the imaginations not only of comic book readers but also of film and television producers who saw the character's moneymaking potential. Through the years, he evolved in the comic books from dark avenger to wisecracking father-figure and back. In film and TV, he progressed from kiddie matinee hero to camp cult figure to Dark Knight. Over the course of seven decades, he graduated from the pulp pages of comic books—thought to be cheap, disposable entertainment—to become one of the largest assets of a multinational conglomerate.

In a 1947 *World's Finest* comic book, Batman faced an adversary named Joe Coyne, a/k/a the Penny Plunderer. Coyne once sold newspapers for a penny on street corners, but he began keeping pennies from the distributor. He eventually created a vast criminal empire centered on pennies; he was obsessed with keeping every cent. After defeating Coyne, Batman kept a trophy of the encounter in the Batcave—a giant penny.

Like Coyne, many people connected with bringing Batman to life in film and television were obsessed with keeping every possible penny. As the money generated by the character grew into the millions and eventually into the billions, the real-life penny plunderers fought for their slice of the giant coin. Some became millionaires themselves; some were corrupted and consumed. Herein are their stories.

Now a brief word about this book. When I set out to write it, I had originally intended to cover not only the live-action interpretations of Batman but also the animated versions. Once I began writing about the *Batman* animated series and feature films, however, I realized that if I continued, my book would balloon to the size of a Tolstoy novel. Consequently, I decided to drop coverage of the animated *Batman* and concentrate solely on the live-action versions.

Also, though I briefly recount the plots of the screenplays on which the films were based, I chose to forego recitations of the plots of the films themselves. After all, the *Batman* films, including the 1943 and 1949 serials, are available for purchase from Warner Bros. Home Video, Sony Home Entertainment and Twentieth Century Fox Home Entertainment, so I am assuming that anyone reading this book has probably seen the movies, and if not, can easily find them for rent or purchase. The focus of this book, therefore, is how the character developed as he journeyed from comic books to TV to films, and the histories of the individual productions and key figures involved.

So atomic batteries to power, turbines to speed—and off we go!

Chapter One:
BOB KANE'S GHOSTS

"Batman is what I always wanted to be but never could."
—*Bob Kane[1]*

It all began with Zorro.

In their August 9, 1919 issue, *All Story Weekly*, the same pulp magazine that had published *Tarzan of the Apes* seven years earlier, ran the first installment of Johnston McCulley's serialized novel, *The Curse of Capistrano*. The main character was wealthy Don Diego Vega, "a fair youth of excellent blood and twenty-four years" who, unlike other young men, abhorred action, was polite to women, and who generally seemed bored with the world. In the end, it is revealed that Don Diego Vega is secretly Zorro, a dashing hero regarded as a bandit by the corrupt government against which he fights. The following year, the story became a film starring, co-written and executive produced by Douglas Fairbanks, Sr., the pre-eminent action film star of the silent era. As Zorro, Fairbanks was clad in black from head to toe, with a flowing black cape and a mask that covered the top half of his face and head. The movie scored a hit with audiences, but it held a special resonance for a Jewish kid from the Bronx named Robbie Kahn, who was all of five years old when it was released.

As he matured, Robbie Kahn would develop an alter-ego of his own, a character as dashing as Don Diego Vega, whose public feats would mask his private secrets, and whose actions would call his private ethics into question. The alter-ego Kahn created was not Batman, but rather Bob Kane, whose life and morals laid the groundwork for the empire that Batman would spawn. To fully understand the darkness of the Dark Knight, one must explore Robert Kahn's journey to becoming Bob Kane, one of the most ruthlessly successful entrepreneurs of the Golden Age of comic books.

The son of Herman Kahn, a Jewish engraver and printer for the *New York Daily News*, and his wife, Augusta, also known as Gussie, Robert Kahn was born on October 24, 1915. As young Robbie grew up in the tough East Bronx neighborhood at Freeman Street and Westchester Avenue, he discovered that he had a talent for drawing. He doodled constantly, and his father encouraged him, bringing home newspaper comic strips hot off the presses. Robbie would sit down with them and reproduce them exactly. "I used to be a copycat," he said in an interview years later. "I'd copy everything. And I doodled on the sidewalks of New York since I was about 8 years old. I drew on everything—schoolbooks, school walls, buses. I'd black out the teeth of girls on subway posters. Luckily it was with chalk and you could wipe it away."[2]

In the evenings, after dinner, Robbie would get together with other kids in his neighborhood. They formed a gang that met in a vacant lot near a lumberyard, in a shack made of stolen lumber. At Robbie's suggestion, the gang was called the Zorros, after Robbie's idol, but instead of fighting a corrupt government, they fought turf wars with other local gangs.

At age 15, Robbie won a second-place prize for replicating the newspaper comic strip *Just Kids*. He took it as an omen that he was destined to become a comic strip artist, but his aspirations seemed doomed when, a short time later, he was beaten up by neighborhood bullies from a rival gang. Separated from the rest of the Zorros, Robbie was cornered by the young toughs. They broke his drawing arm and stepped on his hand, crushing it. His parents paid for physical therapy, and in time Robbie regained use of his hand, but for the rest of his life he was unable to twist his arm around to show his palm. Unnerved by the incident, his parents decided to move to the safer environs of the Grand Concourse in the West Bronx.

By the time he attended DeWitt Clinton High School, the skinny, handsome, dark-eyed boy who now called himself Bob Kahn had a reputation as a lady-killer. He sometimes double-dated with classmate Will Eisner, whom he met when both were competing to have their cartoons published in the school newspaper, *The Clinton News*. Kahn's teachers, noting his interest in drawing, arranged a scholarship that allowed him to take a two-year course at the Commercial Illustration Studio's School of Art in Manhattan's Flatiron Building. The seventeen-year-old became an eager student, especially enjoying the life drawing classes, where pupils made sketches of nude female models. "It was better than *Playboy*," he would say years later.[3] Kane later attended the Cooper Union School of Art, graduating in 1933, and then followed his old high school friend Will Eisner to the Art Students League in Times Square.

Once out of school, Kahn and Eisner often ran into each other as they made the rounds of publishers, hawking their drawings and cartoons. Knowing that it would be tough for Jewish kids from the Bronx to break into the slick magazines, they set their sights lower, on the just-beginning comic book business. Kahn also decided he'd have more success with a less Jewish-sounding name, and legally changed his name to Bob Kane. He soon sold a few strips featuring his character Hiram Hick, a country bumpkin sheriff who goes to New York to fight crime, to publisher Jerry Iger's comic book *Wow, What a Magazine!* Eisner also sold some strips to Iger, and when *Wow, What a Magazine!* ceased publication, Eisner teamed with Iger to produce the magazine *Jumbo Comics*.

While waiting for his big break, Bob Kane took a job in his uncle's garment factory. In his autobiography, he wrote, "It's difficult to put into words the loathing I felt for this type of operation, for I knew in my heart that it was not to be my destiny. I received ten dollars a week for working in a sweatshop where the factory squalor and the din of the sewing machines was enough to drive me to a psychiatrist, if I could have afforded one."[4] He eventually quit the job, and pounded the pavement for six months before landing a job at the Max Fleischer Studios, home of the popular *Betty Boop* cartoon series. He now earned more than twice as much as he had at his uncle's garment factory, but he still found the work—mostly "in-betweening," doing the drawings that would come between one pose and another to give the illusion of movement when projected—routine and boring. More determined than ever, he again tried to sell his work to comic books. But while Kane's skills as an artist were improving, he realized he had a deficit—he wasn't a storyteller. Not one to let that drawback stand in the way of his success, he began searching for a collaborator. He found one at a party where he ran into another DeWitt Clinton High School alumnus named Bill Finger.

A little more than a year older than Kane, Bill Finger, a bright and articulate writer, wanted to be a novelist, but married young and now had a wife to support. To make ends meet, he'd taken a job as a shoe salesman. Kane, with the din of the sewing machines from his uncle's factory still echoing in his ears, understood how Finger felt. He offered Finger a job, agreeing to pay him to help come up with stories for his comic strips. Finger quickly agreed, but it was a Faustian bargain. He would help brainstorm and develop ideas, while Kane would do the drawing and deal with the comic book editors. Finger would receive a paycheck from Kane, but Kane would receive all the credit.

With Finger as silent collaborator, Kane began finding success. In 1937, his 7-page detective story, "The Case of the Missing Heir," was published in *Detective Picture Stories* Vol. 1 #5. The following year, he sold two juvenile features to *Circus Comics*, and began drawing the Walt Disney-inspired strip *Peter Pupp* for *Jumbo Comics,* published by his high school friend Will Eisner. By 1938, Kane was working for National Periodical Publications, doing fill-in work. Kane and Finger created a *Terry and the Pirates*-style strip he called *Rusty and His Pals* and sold it to National's editor Vin Sullivan, who published it in *Adventure Comics*. They followed that up with another strip, *Clip Carson,* about the escapades of a globetrotting adventurer.

Around the time that *Rusty and His Pals* made their debut, so did a character that would forever change the comic book industry. In the spring of 1938, National published *Action Comics* #1, with a cover featuring Superman, a character created by two young boys from Cleveland, Jerry Siegel and Joe Shuster. Superman quickly became a roaring hit, initiating a never-ending stream of superhero successors.

One Friday in 1939, Kane went for a drink with Vin Sullivan, who told him that National was looking for another superhero character. Sullivan added that as a result of *Superman's* success, Siegel and Shuster were earning $800 a week each. Kane, at the time, earned between $35 and $50 a week. Kane told Sullivan he would come up with a character over the weekend. And here's where the story gets cloudy...

Kane often maintained that he alone created the Batman character, inspired by a combination of Zorro, sketches of Leonardo da Vinci's bat-like flying machine, the pulp character *The Shadow* and a movie called *The Bat Whispers* (1930). Kane said he had been toying with the idea since he was 13, when he drew a sketch (which he later published in his autobiography) that showed the back view of a figure with outstretched arms, a scalloped cape and pointed ears that was labeled "a hawk-man?" and "Batman?" In the opposite corner was another crude sketch of a human figure free-falling with what appear to be two wings sticking out of his back, labeled "an Eagle-man." The middle of the page featured a very crude sketch of a man in a form-fitting costume with bat wings, a cowl that looked like the head of a bat, and a bat symbol on his chest. There was also a quote from da Vinci: "Remember that your bird should have no other model than the bat." It was signed "Robert Kane 1/17/34"—a date when Kane would have actually been 18. Most comic book scholars believe this sketch is a forgery done by Kane at a much later date in an effort to convince the public that he was the originator of the Batman concept. It *is* rather suspicious, to say the least, that he signed it "Robert Kane" at a time when he was still going by the name Robert Kahn. There is also Kane's own autobiography—published in 1989, years after Finger's death—in which Kane admits that it was Finger who suggested changing the character into something more bat-like.

Bill Finger insisted that when Bob Kane came to him on that fateful weekend, the Bat-man sketch Kane showed him was of a figure in a red union suit with black trunks, black bat-like wings coming out of his back and a little black domino mask—and Kane's autobiography, surprisingly, confirms this, a few pages after having made the contradictory claim of having created the character on his own. Finger felt the hero looked too much like Superman. In an interview years later, he said, "I got *Webster's Dictionary* off the shelf and was hoping they had a drawing of a bat, and sure enough it did. I said, 'Notice the ears, why don't we duplicate the ears?' I suggested he draw what looked like a cowl...I had suggested he bring the nosepiece down and make him mysterious and not show any eyes at all...I didn't like the wings, so I suggested he make a cape and scallop the edges so it would flow out behind him when he ran and would look like bat wings. He didn't have any gloves on. We gave him gloves because naturally he'd leave fingerprints."[5] Finger also suggested changing the color of the hero's suit from black and red to black and gray, to make it easier for him to conceal himself in the shadows.

Unlike other *Superman* imitators, Kane and Finger's creation was not an alien or imbued with some amazing special power. Instead, he was just a regular mortal, albeit one with a keen intellect and admirable physique. "I didn't want to emulate Superman and imitate it because I thought maybe they wouldn't want that, and I wanted to come up with something original," Kane said in a 1990 interview with National Public Radio's Terry Gross. "And secondly, I felt that every person that doesn't have super powers could relate to Batman a lot easier than they could to Superman. In other words, you didn't have to come from another planet to be a superhero; all you had to do was be born rich and build your body up to perfection and have the urge to go out and fight crime."[6] A character that wore a skin-tight costume and fought criminals actually pre-dated Superman. *The Phantom,* created as a newspaper strip character by Lee Falk, made his debut February 17, 1936. *The Phantom* was the first comic strip hero with a mask drawn so that the eyes appeared as white slits, with no pupils. Falk got the idea from Greek busts, whose eyes were carved without pupils, which Falk felt gave them an awe-inspiring look. Finger, a voracious reader whose knowledge extended from the classics to pulps and comics, had apparently seen Falk's comic strip.

When Kane showed the final Bat-Man concept to Vin Sullivan, Sullivan felt the character would be a natural for his publication *Detective Comics.* To make him a detective character, Finger wrote the initial Bat-Man stories to emphasize the hero's sleuthing abilities as well as his athleticism. "My idea was to have Batman be a combination of Douglas Fairbanks, Sherlock Holmes, the Shadow, and Doc Savage as well," said Finger.[7]

In developing the look of the comic, Finger and Kane were also influenced by two films by writer-director Roland West, *The Bat* (1926) and *The Bat Whispers* (1930). *The Bat,* based on a 1920 stage play by Mary Roberts Rinehart and Avery Hopwood, was an "old dark house" mystery where characters in a mansion look for a hidden stash of money while a thief who calls himself "the Bat" murders them one by one. In the silent film, the Bat dressed in an all-black outfit with a cape and a grotesque mask that looked like the head of a bat, and was seen deftly scaling the exterior of the mansion with a rope. There was also a scene where a beacon projected a bat silhouette on a wall, but it's a red herring—it's actually the outline of a moth stuck on an automobile headlight. When sound films arrived, Roland West remade the film as *The Bat Whispers*, but now changed the Bat's mask to a simple black hood. In the remake, which featured innovative model work and a fluid, moving camera, there were shots of the Bat lurking above his victims, casting a bat-like shadow over them—a clear inspiration on Kane's later artwork.

The Bat-Man, with a hyphen in his name that would be dropped after his first three appearances, debuted in *Detective Comics* #27 in May, 1939, in a story written by Finger called "The Case of the Chemical Syndicate." In this initial six-page story, the Bat-Man is first seen in the title panel in silhouette, appearing like a giant bat against a full moon. A caption reads, "The 'Bat-Man,' a mysterious and adventurous figure fighting for righteousness and apprehending the wrong doer, in his lone battle against the evil forces of society...his identity remains unknown." We are then introduced to Commissioner Gordon, entertaining pipe-smoking socialite Bruce Wayne in his home. When Gordon is called to a murder scene, Wayne tags along, but excuses himself when Gordon receives a phone call from Steven Crane, who fears he will be the next victim. The action then moves to Crane's home, where Crane is shot and killed by thieves who make off with a paper from his safe. The thieves climb up onto the roof of Crane's house and encounter the Bat-Man, who knocks one of the men out and throws the other off the roof. Gordon arrives with the police, who shoot at the escaping Bat-Man, whom they consider an outlaw. The Bat-Man drives away in his car—a bright red sedan—and speeds to the home of a scientist named Stryker, who is the mastermind behind the murders of his business partners. The Bat-man saves another scientist from being killed, knocks out Stryker's hulking assistant, and struggles with Stryker, who falls through a rail into a vat of acid—"A fitting ending for his kind," says the Bat-Man, clearly a proponent of vigilante justice. The next day, Bruce Wayne again visits Commissioner Gordon, who tells him of the latest exploit of the Bat-Man. Wayne remarks, "A very lovely fairy tale, Commissioner, indeed." After Wayne has gone, Gordon comments that his young friend "must lead a boring life." But in the final panels, we are shown a door in Bruce Wayne's home, which opens slowly to reveal the Bat-Man. "I thought it would be more exciting for Batman to work outside the law rather than inside it," said Kane. "I guess growing up in the Bronx, we used to be vigilantes to survive."[8]

Finger cribbed the plot of the debut story from a pulp magazine. "My first script was a take-off on a Shadow story," he said.[9] It was, in fact, borrowed from the story "Partners of Peril," published a few years earlier in *The Shadow* pulp magazine. In writing the Batman stories, Finger came up with names for all the major characters, including Bruce Wayne, the millionaire playboy who dresses as the Batman to fight crime. Finger said in an interview that the name came from Robert Bruce, the Scottish patriot, and Revolutionary War general "Mad" Anthony Wayne, though Bob Kane claimed that it was a name meant to invoke his own similar-sounding name. Finger also came up with the name for police commissioner James Gordon and decided to call the location of the stories—clearly modeled after New York—Gotham City.

Like all comic creators in those early days, when Kane sold the idea to National, he signed away his copyright to the character. But Kane had an advantage other comic book creators did not—a protective father who knew from working in the newspaper business that publishers were not to be trusted. The elder Kane made sure that National did not entirely take advantage of his son. In return for Bob Kane giving up his copyright, National struck a deal that guaranteed that Kane's name would always appear on comic book stories featuring "his" creation. "Being that they owned the copyright, I did the best I could at the time by compromising and getting a good piece of the action and a perpetuity contract," said Kane. "So therefore, I did rather well compared to some artists who sold it away and didn't get very much out of it."[10] Bill Finger and his contributions in creating the character were kept very much in the shadows, where they would remain for four decades; though some professionals working in the comics industry were aware of his contributions, fans were not.

It was Finger who helped insure that Batman used his brains as much as his brawn, as Bob Kane admitted when he said, "I made him a super-hero vigilante when I first created him; Bill made him into a scientific detective."[11] Finger's signature motif was to have Batman confront the villains on oversized props, like a giant pistol or a giant typewriter or giant bowling ball and pins, creating a fantastic world where miscreants like the Joker and the Penguin could seem credible. Finger also gave the artists research to help guide them; if a story took place on a battleship, he would clip photos of battleships to his pages. But Finger's thoroughness came with a price: he developed a reputation for being a slow writer. Bob Kane said, "He was a little tardy in getting things in on deadline." It was said that when a writer turned in the script of a story to National Comics, the editor immediately thumbed through it before signing the writer's check. The reason? Finger has once turned in a "script" with one completed page stapled to the top of a stack of blank pages.[12]

Batman artist Dick Sprang, in an interview with Joe Grant and Frank Squillace for *Amazing Heroes* magazine, said, "You know, Bill Finger was a funny guy. He almost never got his work in on time and he was the best writer they had—in my opinion. He was one of those fellows who couldn't meet a deadline. But he was tops. Really tops."[13] Finger's son, Fred Finger, told *Comics Interview's* Dwight Jon Zimmerman, "My parents separated when I was four-and-a-half so I wasn't too sure what it was all about. But I would stay with Bill on the weekends and he would be up all night, and I'd hear the typewriter going all night and then in the morning there'd be a stack of white originals and yellow carbons...I just knew that my father was crazy because he would be typing until three or four o'clock in the morning all the time in order to get something in by Monday...which, in subsequent years, I found out was supposed to be due the previous Monday."[14]

To maintain the illusion that he was the sole creative force behind the Bat-Man, Kane did all his work outside of the National offices, in his studio in his parent's apartment on the Grand Concourse. He already had a ghostwriter, Bill Finger, in his employ. Now, with the added workload of a monthly comic character, he added a ghost artist. Kane told a friend that he was looking to hire an assistant, and the friend recommended Sheldon Moldoff, a young artist just out of high school who lived in the Bronx. Moldoff went to Kane's parent's apartment, and told Kane that he had already sold some filler pages to National Comics. Kane hired him on the spot, and Moldoff soon began doing pages and covers for the Bat-Man, as well as inking, lettering and logos. Kane met with his artist and writer daily, usually over lunch or dinner, and then they would split up and go to their homes to do the work.

After the first couple of stories featuring the Bat-Man appeared, Kane hired yet another ghost artist, Jerry Robinson. Like Sheldon Moldoff, Robinson was a recent high school graduate. He was preparing to go to journalism school at Syracuse when his mother, who feared that he was underweight, suggested he spend a little time at a health spa. On the day of his arrival, Robinson, a tennis player, went out to the spa's tennis court wearing a white painter's jacket covered with illustrations. "That was a fad then, kids would get these linen jackets with all the pockets and personalize them with all this razzmatazz," said Robinson. "I was wearing mine as a warm-up jacket and someone tapped me on the shoulder and asked, 'Hey, who drew that stuff?' It was Bob Kane, who had just finished the first issue of *Batman*. I didn't even know what that was. He showed me the issue that was on sale there at the local village. I wasn't very impressed."[15] Nonetheless, Kane offered the young illustrator a job. Robinson switched from Syracuse to Columbia University, and went directly from the health resort to New York, where he began working for Kane. He started by inking Kane's artwork and eventually took over illustrating some of the stories. In an interview with Vincent Zurzolo of World Talk Radio's *The Comic Zone*, Robinson said, "We lived and dreamed and ate and slept Batman, and by working over and over again and of course studying what was around and observation, I gradually improved quite a bit over the first year until I was actually drawing and inking Batman."[16]

In 1940, another artist joined the stable—George Roussos. Orphaned as a child, Roussos and his sisters lived at the Brooklyn Orphan Asylum until graduating from Public School 125 in the Woodside neighborhood of Queens. A self-taught artist who entered the comics business lettering the Spanish-language version of *Ripley's Believe It or Not!*, Roussos was hired to assist Jerry Robinson with inking, drawing backgrounds, and lettering. Roussos and Robinson now worked out of an office Kane rented for them in the Times Building in Times Square.

Not all of Kane's co-creators worked outside of the National Comics offices. Helping to shape the early Batman mythos was Gardner Fox, a Brooklyn native whose imagination had been fired by the Mars novels of Edgar Rice Burroughs in his youth. Fox passed the New York bar and practiced as a lawyer for nearly two years, but as the Great Depression deepened and his clients evaporated, he began freelancing as a fantasy writer, contributing stories to pulp science-fiction magazines and to National Comics. In July 1939, he was asked to write the third Bat-Man story. In pitting the crime-fighter against a mad scientist named "Dr. Death," Fox made significant innovations to the Bat-Man character. For instance, he showed where the Bat-Man kept his crime-fighting costume—in a trunk. His yellow belt now had glass pellets of "choking gas" attached, a precursor of the "utility belt" to come, and besides a lasso, the Bat-Man used "suction gloves and knee pads" to help him scale a building. Fox immediately wrote a sequel, in which the Bat-Man again encountered Dr. Death, apprehending him at the end of the tale and leaving him bound with a note for the police to find.

In the fifth story, co-written by Bill Finger and Gardner Fox, readers were introduced to Julie Madison, Bruce Wayne's fiancée. His gloves were now lengthened into gauntlets that covered his forearms, and he had more gadgets, including a boomerang called the Batarang, and a bat-shaped autogiro called, naturally, the Bat-Gyro. In this odd two-part story, the Batman—now with no hyphen—traveled to Paris and Hungary to save his fiancée from the clutches of the Monk, who was revealed to be a vampire. To release Julie from the Monk's spell, the Batman melted down a silver statue to make bullets and, finding the coffin of the Monk, shot him.

The Batman seen on the cover of *Detective Comics* # 33 was an anomaly, with a costume that included a gun holster on the utility belt. In a prologue written by Bill Finger, the seventh story in the series finally revealed the Batman's origin. Millionaire Thomas Wayne was walking home from a movie with his wife and their young son, Bruce, when a crook emerged from the shadows with a gun. He reached for Mrs. Wayne's necklace. Thomas tried to stop him, and the crook gunned him down. Mrs. Wayne yelled for help, and the crook shot and killed her, too. Days later, young Bruce knelt by his bed by candlelight and swore, "by the spirit of my parents to avenge their deaths by spending the rest of my life warring on all criminals." As the years passed, Bruce became a master scientist and trained his body to physical perfection. Years later, in his father's mansion, which he inherited, the adult Bruce Wayne sat by the fireplace and pondered what sort of disguise he should use in his self-appointed mission. "Criminals are a superstitious, cowardly lot," he said, "so my disguise must be able to strike terror into their hearts. I must be a creature of the night, black, terrible...a...a..." At that moment, a bat flew in through the open window. "A bat!" exclaimed Bruce. "That's it! It's an omen. I shall become a bat!" The next panel showed the Batman crouching atop a building, against the backdrop of a full moon. The continuation of the story, "The Dirigibles of Doom," written by Gardner Fox, involved yet another mad scientist character, this one with a literal Napoleon complex (he looked and dressed like the Gallic general). Although the Batman carried a gun in this story, he never shot anyone with it. By the next story, the sidearm was gone. He'd also ditched the red sedan by the ninth story, replacing it with a blue "high-powered roadster" convertible.

Batman continued as a solo character until April 1940, when *Detective Comics* # 38 introduced his teen-aged sidekick, Robin, the Boy Wonder, "the sensational character find of 1940." Bob Kane said Robin was inspired by his childhood fantasies of imagining himself fighting alongside his idol, Douglas Fairbanks Sr., as well as a desire to "lighten up" Batman. Bill Finger maintained that Robin was invented to give Batman someone to talk to, so he wouldn't always be talking to himself.

"Adding a kid was Bill's idea," said Jerry Robinson, who said the Batman creative team "had a big session of the names, and we couldn't agree on the name."[17] Finger favored mythological names like Mercury, but Robinson felt that since Batman was a real person, his sidekick had to be a real person, too. Robinson remembered a book he'd read as a child, a volume of Robin Hood stories with illustrations by N.C. Wyeth. Robinson quickly drew a rough sketch of a boy in a domino mask and outfit that featured a Robin Hood-like tunic and shoes, a short cape, and trunks. Kane agreed that this was the way to go; it helped that Robin Hood was portrayed in

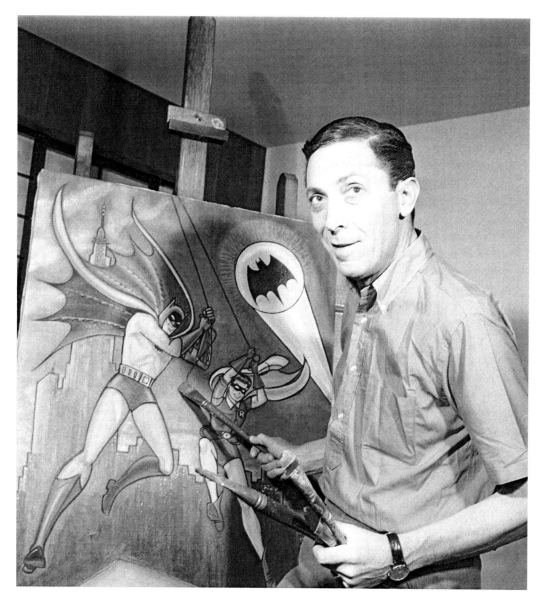

Bob Kane in the mid-1960s, with one of his Batman oil paintings (Photofest).

silent movies by Douglas Fairbanks, Sr., his childhood favorite. "I thought that every young boy would want to be like Robin," wrote Kane. "A laughing daredevil— free, no school, no homework, living in a mansion over the Bat Cave, riding in the Batmobile—he appealed to the imagination of every kid in the world."[18] Bill Finger said the name Dick Grayson, Robin's alter ego, came from a combination of the pulp magazines and a novel. "Frank Merriwell had a half brother, Dick," said Finger, "and Grayson came from a book I was reading, edited by Charles Grayson, Jr."[19]

Kane and Finger gave Robin an origin story similar to Batman's. A member of the circus acrobat troupe the Flying Graysons, young Dick watched his parents fall to their deaths after a criminal put acid on their trapeze ropes. The young orphan was taken in by Bruce Wayne, who taught him boxing and jiu-jitsu and made him a partner in crime-fighting.

Immediately after Robin's introduction, Batman—now having dropped the article "the" as well as the hyphen—was given his own magazine. Just one year after his introduction, the character became almost as popular as Superman, and like Superman, spawned a number of imitators. The success of Batman showed that costumed heroes didn't need to have special powers or come from another planet, they just needed a nifty costume, a Type-A personality and a pathological desire to wipe out evil. After Robin's debut, almost all of them also acquired a wise-cracking young sidekick, as well.

The first issue of *Batman* reprised the origin story of Batman and then introduced one of the serie's most intriguing villains, the Joker. With a clown-white face, red lips, green hair, demonic smile, and homicidal nature, the original Joker was a nasty piece of work, killing his victims with a gas that left their faces contorted in a maniacal smile. Jerry Robinson claimed that he came up with the idea for the Joker after bringing a joker playing card to Kane and Finger. Kane claimed that he and Finger jointly created the Joker, with Kane coming up with the idea of a villain who played deadly practical jokes and Finger suggesting they base the look of the character on the striking make-up worn by actor Conrad Veidt in the 1928 silent film *The Man Who Laughs*.

Finger also laid the foundation for another classic character when he created a female cat burglar for whom Batman felt an irresistible attraction. In her first appearance, the Cat disguised herself as an old lady on a yacht to steal a priceless diamond. Batman trapped her, rubbed off her make-up as he admonished "Quiet or papa spank," and revealed a raven-haired beauty with a face inspired by actress Jean Harlow. As Batman and Robin took the Cat back to shore, Batman purposefully allowed her to escape and said to Robin, "Lovely girl! What eyes! Say—mustn't forget I've got a girl named Julie! Oh well—she still had lovely eyes! Maybe I'll bump into her again sometime." Kane thought of Catwoman, as the feline felon would come to be called, as a female counterpart to Batman. "We came up with the idea of associating her with cats because they were kind of the antithesis of bats," said Kane.[20]

The December 1941 issue of *Detective Comics*, issue # 58, introduced the Penguin, another memorable recurring Batman villain. According to Kane, the character was inspired by the penguin mascot on a pack of Kool cigarettes, whom Kane thought looked like a fat little man in a tuxedo. The inspiration for Two-Face, an attorney who became a criminal after one side of his face was horribly scarred by acid, was *Dr. Jekyll and Mr. Hyde*. The MGM version of the Robert Louis Stevenson classic, starring Spencer Tracy, hit theaters in 1941. Posters for the film showed Tracy with one half of his face normal, and the other half monstrously contorted—almost a blueprint for Two-Face, who made his first appearance in *Detective Comics* #66 in August 1942.

As word spread through the industry that Kane was not the sole creative force behind Batman, other comic book publishers began approaching his ghosts. Sheldon Moldoff was the first lured away. "I wanted to do my own characters," said Moldoff. "I started to do Hawkman and other characters. Then I did *The Black Pirate* for Sheldon Mayer down at *All-American Comics*."[21] Jerry Robinson, George Roussos and Bill Finger also decided to leave Kane's shop and strike out on their own. "When we began to get offers from all over, and the publishers began to realize that there was a staff, not just Bob, but there was Bill and myself, and we were leaving, then the publisher hired us directly," said Robinson. "Really after the first year and a half perhaps, Bill and I were going to leave, and we were hired to continue *Batman* but directly for the publisher, so we were no longer responsible to Bob. So I began to do my own stories, my own covers, as well as to work on the ones that he worked on. We rarely saw each other after that."[22]

Kane continued hiring ghost writers and artists, whom he paid out of his earnings of nearly a thousand dollars a week—a lot of money in the early 1940s. But having learned from his experiences with Moldoff, Robinson and Finger, Kane now kept the ghosts separate, each working out of his own home, not knowing that other ghosts existed—or how much they were paid. "There were two kinds of Bob Kane ghosts," said writer and comics historian Mark Evanier. "Bob contracted with DC to provide a certain number of pages per month and he hired men like Sheldon Moldoff and Lew Sayre Schwartz to draw them. But DC needed more pages of Batman art than that number and so the DC editors hired men like Dick Sprang, Jim Mooney, Winslow Mortimer and Curt Swan to draw stories that never went anywhere near Kane or his studios. As per Kane's deal with DC, no one else's name could appear on them but his, but it would be wrong to suggest that Mooney, for example, was a Kane assistant. Or Sprang or [Carmine] Infantino or any of about two dozen others who did Batman art for DC."[23]

Kane was not only earning money from the three comic books regularly featuring Batman—*Batman, Detective Comics* and *World's Finest*—but also from a daily syndicated newspaper comic strip featuring the caped crusader that debuted in March 1944. The money he earned from Batman allowed him to live a Bruce Wayne lifestyle. In 1943, when Columbia Pictures began work on a *Batman* movie serial, Kane traveled to Los Angeles to observe the filming. He returned in 1949 for filming of the second serial, and that same year, became a married man at the age of 34.

Kane's original Batman contract came up for renewal in 1949, around the same time that Jerry Siegel and Joe Shuster were planning to sue National over the rights to Superman. They encouraged Kane to join the proceedings, figuring National would be more likely to buckle if the creators of their two biggest properties mutinied at the same time. Kane, however, responded by going to National and telling them of Siegel and Shuster's plan, indicating that it would be better if National cut a deal with him to keep him out of the lawsuit. When National countered that they felt the ownership of the Batman rights were indisputable, Kane pulled an audacious stunt—he lied about his age. According to Gerard Jones's book *Men of Tomorrow*, Kane told National that his original contract with them was invalid because he was a minor at the time he signed it. Although he was about 23 when he signed his deal, he now indicated that he had actually been under 21. His birth certificate, he said, had disappeared, and his parents would testify that he was born in 1919, not 1915. Rather than engage him in a messy lawsuit, National returned legal ownership of Batman to Kane, guaranteed him a certain number of pages per month at a high page rate, and a percentage of subsidiary rights. The only condition was that Kane keep quiet about the deal. Kane, who had kept his ghost writers and artists secret for years, had no problem with that caveat. He then told Siegel and Shuster that they were on their own.[24]

In his book, Kane relates that after an "important artist"—no doubt he was referring to both Siegel and Shuster—lost a lawsuit with National, Kane joined editor Whitney Ellsworth for a drink at the local bar. "It was January," wrote Kane, "and I said, 'Whit, it looks like it's going to be a very cold winter for so-and-so.' He touched my martini glass with his hand and answered sardonically, 'I'm not cold, are you?' Somehow in that terse remark, Whit summed up the self-preservationist philosophy of most people, and that is: 'Better him than me.'"[25]

Sheldon Moldoff, the first ghost artist to leave Bob Kane's studio, returned to the *Batman* comics in the 1950s. "When I met Bob again in '53, he said he needed a ghost," said Moldoff. "He wanted someone to do his *Batman*. Would I be interested? I said, 'Yeah, let's talk about it.' We came to an agreement, shook hands, and that was it." Unlike his previous tenure, when he just assisted with the comics, Moldoff now actually drew them. "When you're a ghost, you do it, and you don't say anything," said Moldoff. "He did very little. He would look at it, and then he would fool around with a nose or a chin or something like that. I picked up the script from him and then laid out the eight or ten pages or whatever it was. I did the whole thing from beginning to end."[26]

Moldoff, his wife and daughter socialized with Kane, his wife Beverly and their daughter Debbie for the next several years, while Moldoff continued working on the *Batman* comic books. During that time, Kane's womanizing ways brought an end to his marriage. In 1957, while getting a divorce, Kane once again traveled to Los Angeles, where he pitched an idea for an animated TV series called *Courageous Cat and Minute Mouse*, a kiddie take-off on Batman and Robin, with main characters that lived in the Cat Cave and were summoned by the Cat Signal. They fought an adversary named the Frog using an array of devices such as the Cat Mobile, Cat Plane and Cat Boat. 130 five-minute episodes were produced and put into syndication in 1960. Sheldon Moldoff later revealed that he actually wrote the stories and sketched the storyboards for Kane's animated series.

After his divorce, Kane moved east to Sutton Place in Manhattan. Moldoff handed in his Batman work to Kane, who presented it to DC Comics (as National came to be known; DC was an abbreviation of "Detective Comics"). Meanwhile, Moldoff also drew other DC titles like *Mr. District Attorney* and *Blackhawk*, and sometimes inked Curt Swan's *Superman* art. Charles Paris inked *Batman*, but when Paris got behind, *Batman* editor Jack Schiff sometimes asked Moldoff if he could do it—and handed Moldoff artwork that Moldoff had just turned in to Bob Kane a couple of days earlier. Still, Moldoff kept Kane's secret. "I never told anybody," he said. "The way I saw it at the time, they knew he had a ghost. As long as the work was there on time, they didn't really care. I've read recent articles where it's said it was the 'worst kept secret,' and everybody knew it. I don't buy that. Back in the '50s and '60s, I don't think too many people knew about it."[27]

Moldoff didn't mind doing the work and letting Kane get all the glory, so long as Kane's checks cleared the bank. He felt it was a trade-off; many comic book assignments only lasted a year or two, until the titles were cancelled. *Batman* was a steady thing, with no end in sight. "I would have liked to have had my name up there. I would have liked him to give me a mention or credit. That would have been nice. But Bob wasn't that type of person," said Moldoff.[28]

By the early 1960s, Bob Kane had become like Batman—a wealthy playboy harboring a dark secret. While he lived a life in the limelight, Moldoff toiled away on various *Batman* projects. "I was doing the *Batman* for Bob, and he had also started the Sunday and daily strip for the *Newark Star Ledger*, which I was also doing. I was loaded to the gills with work. And on top of that, he kept coming up with ideas for games and merchandising. Bob was always thinking up something. Then he would give it to me and say, 'Work this up into a presentation. I'm going to bring this around and see if I can sell a card game with the Batman and Joker.' Things like that. I was always doing extra stuff. I was really working my head off."[29]

Though actually drawing very little of Batman, Kane felt compelled to perpetuate his claim of being the sole creator of the Caped Crusader. In a September 1965 response to the fanzine *Batmania*, which had previously published an interview with Bill Finger in which Finger candidly spoke of his involvement with *Batman*, Kane wrote, "The Myth: Bob Kane is not the sole creator of 'Batman.' (I've heard this a thousand times in my lifetime), that 'Batman' was really created by Bill Finger, Jerry Robinson, Carmine Infantino, Jack Schiff, Julie Schwartz, my publisher, etc., etc., and my housekeeper!

"The Truth: All hogwash! I, Bob Kane, am the sole creator of 'Batman.' I created 'Batman' in 1939, and it appeared, if memory serves me correctly, in *Detective Comics* as a six or eight page story, and I signed the first strip, 'Robert Kane.'" Kane goes on to write, "It seemed to me that Bill Finger has given out the impression that he and not myself created the Batman, as well as Robin and all the other leading villains and characters. This statement is fraudulent and entirely untrue...let me state that I still draw about ninety percent of all Batman stories. I do all the stories for *Batman* Bimonthly, and share *Detective Comics* with Infantino, who draws every other one. Infantino now does all the covers for *Batman* and *Detective Comics*. As for inking and lettering, I am not too sure myself who finishes my pencils. However, the results are good, so I don't care.

"I do know one thing though, that in the 'Golden Age' of *Batman*, I penciled, inked, and lettered my strip by myself."[30]

Around this time, of course, *Batman* exploded on television as a live-action prime-time series. The success of the TV show couldn't have come at a more fortuitous time for Kane. Sales of the *Batman* comics, which had been steadily declining to the point that it was rumored the title might be canceled, suddenly went through the roof. The deal he'd made with National to credit him as the sole creator of Batman paid off, as Kane was featured on magazine covers and invited to appear on talk shows. More importantly, his deal was now up for renewal. Moldoff, who was secretly doing all the heavy lifting, was overwhelmed with work. "It was too much," said Moldoff. "Finally I gave up. I said, 'I just can't handle it all, Bob.' He said, 'I'm working on a new contract [with DC]. You're going to get a lot of money when this thing is settled. Just try to keep going.' But I just couldn't keep it all up, so finally he said that someone else would do the newspaper strip, and I would just concentrate on the magazine."[31] With *Batman* suddenly more popular than ever, Kane struck a sweet deal with DC. Able to increase his percentage of the take while at the same time retiring from the comic book, he decided to let his secret art studio go. "Bob owed me a lot of money," said Moldoff, "because he said he couldn't afford to pay me for all the extra work, but that I would get it eventually. Then one day he called me and said, 'I've signed my contact.' And I said, 'that's great! When do I start collecting?' He replied, 'the only problem is that the office is going to do all the drawing from now on, and I have nothing to do with it. They're going to handle it.' I said, 'Where does that leave me?' He said, 'I feel terrible, but there won't be any work.' That was the end of it! It ended just like that! It was all over."[32] Moldoff never saw Kane again, nor did he ever work on any other *Batman* comics from that time forward.

Kane also earned licensing income from the *Batman* TV series, and in 1967, his ship came in again. There was a change in ownership at DC Comics, and since Kane now legally owned the rights to Batman, he was able to negotiate the sale of the character. He ended up with an even larger slice of subsidiary income, not to mention a million dollar fee.

At the same time the *Batman* TV series went into production, Kane created another animated kids show. Inspired by the success of the James Bond films, he developed *Cool McCool*, a bumbling secret agent character, in 1965. The cartoon debuted on NBC in September 1966 and ran until August 1969, though only twenty shows featuring three 10-minute adventures each were produced.

Bill Finger, meanwhile, was barely scraping by. Although he branched out into writing some scripts for the TV series *77 Sunset Strip* with co-writer Charles Sinclair in 1961, his primary income still came from writing comic book stories. "When they did the *Batman* TV series, Bill was offered the position of going out to the coast and doing creative consultation on the initial pilot and the first season," recalled his son, Fred Finger. "And he didn't pick up on it. Which was his loss—for whatever reason, he was beating himself up."[33] Finger did co-write one two-part episode of the *Batman* TV series ("The Clock King's Crazy Crimes" and "The Clock King Gets Crowned," written with Sinclair), but otherwise work dried up for him. He and Sinclair penned the script for the English-Japanese co-production *The Green Slime* (1968), a sci-fi thriller, but the movie was a box-office dud. The year of its release, Finger joined other longtime DC comic book freelancers Gardner Fox, Otto Binder, and Arnold Drake in asking for health insurance and other benefits. The company's response was to stop giving them assignments.[34] Afterwards, the comic book writer who helped shape Batman's world and who'd dreamed of becoming a great novelist was unable to find work. Only near the end of his life did he receive any credit for *Batman*. DC editor Julius Schwartz named Finger as a writer of *Batman* stories in a Letters column in the 1960s, and beginning in the early 1970s, when DC began reprinting the early *Batman* stories, they carefully researched and credited the original writers. But fame and fortune passed Bill Finger by, while Bob Kane was celebrated, perhaps recalling the words of Whitney Ellsworth—"I'm not cold, are you?"

For Finger, the end came on January 18, 1974. "Unfortunately Bill died unheralded, uncredited and broke," said Jerry Robinson, "with a wife and child he didn't provide for, so that's one thing I never forgave Bob for, for not acknowledging Bill and including him in the rewards that came. I went on to other things and had other careers and it wasn't as vital to me. Bill stayed in the comics, and it really destroyed him, the lack of self-esteem when he was so mistreated. It was tragic."[35]

After Finger's death, Kane became more conciliatory about giving his former collaborator credit for the early Batman stories, but Kane's own autobiography is filled with contradictions. On page 41, he gives an account of how he and Finger created Batman, including Finger's suggestion of giving the hero a cowl instead of a domino mask and making the colors of his uniform black and gray instead of black and red. Then, a few pages later, he writes, "Now that my long-time friend and collaborator is gone, I must admit that Bill never received the fame and recognition he deserved. He was an unsung hero. Because he came into the strip after I had created Batman, he did not get a by-line."[36]

Speaking about Bill Finger, Kane was once quoted as saying, "I often tell my wife, if I could go back 13 or 14 years before he died, I would like to say, 'I'll put your name on it now. You deserve it.' I feel a slight sense of guilt that I didn't do it. I really loved the guy...My editor felt that only the creator's name should be on it."[37] Blaming the editors for Finger's lack of a creator's credit seems like a cop-out, especially given Kane's statement to cartoonist Shel Dorf in a mid-1970s interview, "I basically feel that Batman is my alter-ego. I abhor injustice in the world. I abhor the big bureaucracy stepping on the little man. I feel that I am Batman, underneath it all. A champion for justice and against injustice. I've fought for my own rights, and I try to fight for the rights of the little man. Definitely, I feel like Batman is me." Later in the same interview, Kane said, "You have to live with yourself and the only way you can sleep at night is to feel that you have done the right thing, that you fought for your own best interests; if you let people step all over you in life, you can't sleep very well because it's really a terrible shame to be exploited ruthlessly and not fight back."[38]

By 1975, Bob Kane was living in Las Vegas, where he partnered with Russ Gerstein to build a television center where they planned to produce TV shows and movies. Kane pursued the notion of doing an animated cartoon series based on the Marx Brothers, and had a meeting with Groucho Marx to discuss the idea, but dropped it when Erin Fleming, Marx's girlfriend and business agent, asked for $100,000 upfront. Kane eventually gave up on the TV center and returned to New York.

After a dozen years of doing Batman paintings as a hobby, Kane began exhibiting them around the globe. "Finally I decided to take them out of mothballs and sell them to the world," he said. "Batman has now graduated from comic strips to the world of fine art." Kane's Batman paintings and drawings were exhibited at St. John's University, Pace University and New York's Museum of Art. On October 31, 1978, he held a charity fundraiser exhibit in New York to benefit the American Cancer Society, motivated by the death of his father from cancer. Prices for his Batman art ranged from $150 for an unframed lithograph to $30,000 for an acrylic painting on canvas. "I wanted to do some spiritual good for the world," said Kane. "It's my way of repaying society for all the good things they have given to me."[39]

In 1979, reflecting on his career, Kane said, "Every author has one great book that can't be topped. I had figured in my mature years I could do better, something more artistic. It'll never happen." Still, Kane had no regrets about Batman, adding, "I'm happy. I'm satisfied. I'll just get by on his mighty wings."[40] He didn't have to get by alone. In 1980, he met an acting teacher named Elizabeth Sanders, and the two were soon wed. *Batman* was now in the works as a major motion picture, and Kane acted as a consultant, basking in the limelight once again.

"Bob was a guy who really enjoyed being Bob Kane," said screenwriter Tom Mankiewicz. "I remember he had some assistant, this babe, who was a lot younger than he was, and he would do promos for himself, where he was in a smoking jacket with a pipe and talking, and he would send me these things. He loved being Bob Kane. In fact, he very much enjoyed being a celebrity, of sorts."[41] As the 1989 *Batman* feature film spawned three sequels, Kane wrote his autobiography and continued touring the world with exhibitions of his Batman artwork—much of it rumored to have been painted by ghost artists. He died in Los Angeles on November 3, 1998.

When Kane died, Jenette Kahn, the president and editor-in-chief of DC Comics, said in a statement, "Bob Kane is a giant in the field of pop culture, one of a handful of people who launched the comic book industry and who gave the world a group of characters so colorful and inventive they continue to captivate every new generation. Bob will be greatly missed, but he has left a legacy that will keep his memory alive."[42] Kane himself, in 1995, said, "All the ghostwriters are forgotten. My imprint is left on the sands of time, and I'm very proud of that."[43]

1   Skow, John, "Has TV Gasp! Gone Batty??" *The Saturday Evening Post*, May 2, 1966

2   Markoutsas, Elaine, "For 40 years, Kane has gone to bat for justice," *The Chicago Tribune*, November 8, 1979, p. A1

3   Ibid.

4   Kane, Bob with Tom Andrae, *Batman & Me*, © 1989 Eclipse Books, Forestville, California, p. 24

5   Steranko, Jim, *The Steranko History of Comics*, © 1972 Crown Publishing Group

6   Interview with Bob Kane, *Fresh Air with Terry Gross*, © 1990 National Public Radio

7   Steranko, Jim, *The Steranko History of Comics*, © 1972 Crown Publishing Group

8   Benton, Mike, *Superhero Comics of the Golden Age*, © 1992 Taylor Publishing Co., Dallas, TX, p. 69

9   Steranko, Jim, *The Steranko History of Comics*, © 1972 Crown Publishing Group

10 Interview with Bob Kane, *Fresh Air with Terry Gross*, © 1990 National Public Radio

11 Barr, Mike W., "Bill Finger: The Man Way Behind The Batman," *Amazing Heroes* # 167, June 15, 1989, p. 8

12 Ibid.

13 Grant, Joe and Frank Squillace, "An Interview With Dick Sprang," *Amazing Heroes* # 167, June 15, 1989, p. 50

14 Zimmerman, Dwight Jon, "Fred Finger," *Comics Interview Super Special: Batman*, © 1989, Fictioneer Books, Ltd., New York, p. 22

15 Boucher, Geoff, "Hero Complex: Breaking Comic Book News and the Offshoots They Inspire—For Your Inner Fanboy." *The Los Angeles Times*, May 6, 2009

16 Interview with Jerry Robinson, *The Comic Zone*, © 2005 World Talk Radio

17 Ibid.

18 Kane, Bob with Tom Andrae, *Batman & Me*, © 1989 Eclipse Books, Forestville, California, p. 46

19 Ibid.

20 Ibid., p. 108

21 Thomas, Roy (editor), "My Years With Batman: An Interview With Sheldon Moldoff" conducted by Bill Schelly, transcribed by Sam Gafford, *Alter Ego: The Comic Book Artist Collection*, © 2001, TwoMorrows Publishing

22 Interview with Jerry Robinson, *The Comic Zone*, © 2005 World Talk Radio

23 Reed, Robby, "The Haunting of Robert Kane," *Dial B for Blog*, http://www.dialbforblog.com/archives/391/, accessed July 18, 2009

24 Jones, Gerard, *Men of Tomorrow: Geeks, Gangsters and the Birth of the Comic Book*, © 2004, Basic Books New York, pgs. 246-247

25 Kane, Bob with Tom Andrae, *Batman & Me*, © 1989 Eclipse Books, Forestville, California, p. 123

26 Thomas, Roy (editor), "My Years With Batman: An Interview With Sheldon Moldoff" conducted by Bill Schelly, transcribed by Sam Gafford, *Alter Ego: The Comic Book Artist Collection*, © 2001, TwoMorrows Publishing

27 Ibid.

28 Ibid.

29 Ibid.

30 Kane, Bob, "An Open Letter to All 'Batmanian's Everywhere," *Batmania*, 1965, reprinted at http://twomorrows.com/comicbookartist/articles/03kane.html, accessed July 18, 2009

31 Thomas, Roy (editor), "My Years With Batman: An Interview With Sheldon Moldoff" conducted by Bill Schelly, transcribed by Sam Gafford, *Alter Ego: The Comic Book Artist Collection*, © 2001, TwoMorrows Publishing

32 Ibid.

33 Zimmerman, Dwight Jon, "Fred Finger," *Comics Interview Super Special: Batman*, © 1989, Fictioneer Books, Ltd., New York, p. 22

34 Morrissey, Rich, "Gardner Fox: An Appreciation," *Amazing Heroes* # 167, June 15, 1989, p. 12

35 Interview with Jerry Robinson, *The Comic Zone*, © 2005 World Talk Radio

36 Kane, Bob with Tom Andrae, *Batman & Me*, © 1989 Eclipse Books, Forestville, California, p. 44

37 Barr, Mike W., "Bill Finger: The Man Way Behind The Batman," *Amazing Heroes* # 167, June 15, 1989, p. 8

38 Dorf, Shel, "Bob Kane: The Man Whose Name Means 'Batman,'" *Amazing Heroes* # 167, June 15, 1989, p. 28

39 Slavin, Stewart, "Batman Moves From Comics to Museums," *The Los Angeles Times*, August 6, 1978, p. D7

40 Markoutsas, Elaine, "For 40 years, Kane has gone to bat for justice," *The Chicago Tribune*, November 8, 1979, p. A1

41 Interview with Tom Mankiewicz, conducted July 26, 2009.

42 Radford, Bill, "Batman creator was unafraid to share credit," *The New Mexican*, November 22, 1998, p. E-5

43 Seiler, Andy, "Batman: Forever Bob Kane's," *USA Today*, Jul 6, 1995, p. 8

Chapter Two:
BATMAN COMES ALIVE

"Batman kind of killed my chances for playing Hamlet."
—Lewis Wilson[1]

Lewis Wilson always enjoyed a good joke. He didn't just enjoy jokes, he collected and catalogued them, remembering them by writing down their punchlines. A recent arrival in Hollywood, he had been toiling away in bit parts at Columbia Pictures, waiting for his big break. And now, it had arrived—a starring role. But it wasn't in a sophisticated, adult feature film; it was in a kid's serial, playing a costumed vigilante named Batman. Wilson was familiar with the character; he'd read some of the comic books featuring the crime fighter. But now, dressed in a Batman costume with a cowl that severely restricted his vision, he wondered if the joke might be on him.

The home of Frank Capra and the Three Stooges, Columbia was a minor studio in the 1930s. Whereas other studios like Paramount and Universal produced between 40 and 60 features per year, about a dozen of which were budgeted at $500,000 or more, Columbia only produced about two dozen annually, with most of them budgeted under $150,000. The studio was situated at the corner of Sunset Boulevard and Gower Street, where the first movie set in California was built in 1911. Within months, as more independent producers from the east migrated west to escape Thomas Edison and his Motion Picture Patents Corporation, Sunset and Gower became the nexus of Hollywood. During the teens and early twenties, so many fly-by-night studios sprang up along Gower that it became known as Poverty Row, or—because of the large number of Westerns made there—Gower Gulch.[2] Among the companies to locate there was Columbia Pictures, which arrived in 1926.[3] The company was formed six years earlier by the brothers Harry and Jack Cohn and their partner, Harry Brandt.[4] It was originally called CBC Studios after their initials, but the partners changed the name because they worried it could be an acronym for "corned beef and cabbage."[5] Brandt retired in 1931, leading to a power struggle between the two brothers; Harry, with backing from Bank of America, won.[6] Over the years, Columbia gobbled up more and more of the surrounding studios, until their facilities covered an entire city block.[7]

As the 1940s dawned, German dictator Adolph Hitler's push through Europe effectively cut off many of the foreign territories that American film distributors relied upon for a great share of their profits. One of the ways the studios responded to this challenge was by an increased reliance on pre-sold properties to increase their domestic revenues, looking to hit stage plays, bestselling books, and the new medium of comic books for inspiration.[8]

Comic books were particularly popular after the Japanese attack on Pearl Harbor resulted in America's entry into the war. With so many men in uniform causing a labor shortage, three million schoolchildren became wage earners, and were spending their money on comic books and movies. In his book *Superhero Comics of the Golden Age*, Mike Benton reports that during the early 1940s, 95 percent of all eight- to eleven-year-olds and 84 percent of all teenagers were regular comic book readers. But kids weren't the only comic book readers; 35 percent of all 18- to 30-year-olds also read them.

The majority of the adult readers were servicemen. Forty-four percent of all the men in training camps read comics regularly. At the PXs, more comic books were sold than issues of *The Saturday Evening Post, Life* and *Reader's Digest* combined. By 1944, one out of every four magazines that the government sent to troops overseas was a comic book, including a special overseas edition of *Superman* that shipped 35,000 copies every month. *Newsweek* reported that 25 million comic books were rolling off the presses each month, and retail sales in 1943 equaled nearly $30 million.[9]

Many of those comic-book reading kids went to the movies on Saturday, where the entertainment generally consisted of a cartoon, a newsreel, a serial chapter, and a feature. The serials had been around since 1912, when Thomas Edison—a restless genius and master of marketing who had been producing short films in his New Jersey studio for two decades—hit upon a new idea. Popular magazines of the day regularly published book-length stories one chapter at a time so that readers who became involved in the story would be hooked into buying the next month's issue to see how it progressed. Edison thought he could replicate this with films. In July of 1912, he released the first chapter of *What Happened to Mary?* Subsequent chapters were released one per month over the course of the next year. While each chapter was more or less a self-contained story, the overall question of who would win the battle over the heroine's inheritance was unanswered until the resolution of Chapter 12. As Edison hoped, once audiences were hooked, they kept coming back regularly month after month to see how the story resolved itself, providing him with a steady, predictable income stream.

Other motion picture producers took notice and began making serialized stories, or serials, of their own. Within a couple of years, the serials became a distinct entertainment form, characterized by stories of intense action and melodrama, with chapters that ended with "cliffhangers"—the hero or heroine in dire peril, metaphorically if not literally dangling from a cliff. As more serials were produced, the time between the exhibitions of successive chapters decreased, dropping from one month to one week. Now, an audience could find out the resolution of a 12-chapter serial over the course of three months instead of having to wait a whole year.

The movie serial survived the coming of sound, but by the mid-1930s, most serials were aimed at juvenile audiences. Consequently, the plotlines of serials became extremely simple. The characters were clearly defined as being either "good" or "evil." Once the goals of the characters were set in the first chapter, the next ten or more kept the protagonists and antagonists at a virtual stalemate. The good guy would generally win some minor victory over the evil mastermind in the middle of each chapter, but by the end, the villain had placed the hero's life in danger. How would he or she escape? Viewers had to come back the next week to find out. With each chapter lasting about 15 minutes, there was no time for deep character development or romantic subplots. Serials were all about action.

Moreover, serials based on newspaper comic strip and comic book characters were big business. When *Flash Gordon* (1936), a Universal Pictures serial starring Olympic champion Larry "Buster" Crabbe as Alex Raymond's intergalactic hero, became so popular that it began playing in the major movie houses on Broadway, Columbia took notice. At that time, only Universal and Republic Pictures were producing movie serials; beginning in 1937, they would have competition from Columbia.

Initially, Columbia hired independent producers to make their serials, with the studio handling the distribution. Their first entry, *Jungle Menace*, starring Frank "Bring 'em Back Alive" Buck, a big-game hunter turned action star, was produced by Adventures Serials, Incorporated, a company established by the Weiss Brothers, who produced a number of low-budget serials the previous decade. The Weiss Brothers produced two more serials for the studio, *The Mysterious Pilot* and *The Secret of Treasure Island*, before Columbia appointed Jack Fier to oversee serial production. Fier's first two serials were the Western *The Great Adventures of Wild Bill Hickock* starring Gordon Elliott (who would soon change his name to Wild Bill Elliott) and *The Spider's Web*, starring Warren Hull. The latter, the first serial ever produced using a character from the pulp magazines, became the most popular serial of 1938. The following year, the studio brought Lee Falk and Phil Davis's comic strip hero *Mandrake the Magician* to serial audiences, with Warren Hull again playing the lead.

Despite Fier's success, in 1940 Columbia turned serial production over to Larry Darmour, who had his own small studio nearby on Santa Monica Boulevard, across from the Hollywood Cemetery. Darmour delegated the job to his right-hand man, production manager Rudolph C. Flothow. Born in Frankfurt, Germany in 1895, Flothow came to Hollywood in the 1920s, where he worked as a dialogue director and production manager for Tiffany-Stahl Productions. By 1934, he had moved to Liberty Pictures, where he was production manager for a year before doing the same duties for Republic's Ellery Queen feature, *The Spanish Cape Mystery* (1935). Then, in August of 1936, he went to work for Larry Darmour Productions, primarily on B-movies starring Jack Holt that were made for Columbia Pictures to release.[10] Darmour and Flothow turned to pulp and comic strip characters as inspirations for Columbia serials, including *The Shadow* (1940), and *Terry and the Pirates* (1940), and made *The Spider Returns* (1941), a sequel to the studio's earlier hit.

As 1942 began, Darmour, feeling unwell, turned more of the production responsibilities over to Flothow. Harry Cohn, to protect Columbia's interests in the company, installed his nephew, screenwriter Ralph Cohn, as the head producer of the unit. During this time, the rights to their *Ellery Queen* mystery series lapsed, so Columbia went after the film rights to the popular radio series *The Crime Doctor*, as a new series for actor Warner Baxter. In March, after a three-month illness said to be a heart condition, Darmour died at the young age of 47.[11] His death left Larry Darmour Productions and the low-budget pictures they were working on in jeopardy. Acting quickly, Harry Cohn brought the company under the Columbia roof. Both Flothow and Ralph Cohn jockeyed to take over the Darmour projects, and after a couple of weeks, Harry Cohn decided to bet his fortunes on the more experienced Flothow rather than his nephew. Ralph Cohn was ousted. Exiting the company, he told *Daily Variety* that he resigned his post. When pressed to make a comment, he said any statement would have to come from Harry Cohn, who was out of town.[12]

Though still working out of the Darmour Studios, Flothow now reported directly to Harry Cohn. As the man in charge of Columbia's B-movie and serial units, Flothow became responsible for the studio's *Crime Doctor, Boston Blackie, Lone Wolf* and *The Whistler* series, as well as the cliffhangers. To kick off his serial program, he optioned one newspaper comic strip hero, Lee Falk's *The Phantom*, and one comic book hero, *Batman*.

The idea of doing a Batman serial originated at Republic Pictures. In 1940, Republic began negotiations with National Comics to bring their number one character, Superman, to the screen. Four weeks before shooting was to commence, the deal fell through when National insisted on creative control and more money for the rights than the serial's meager budget would allow. Republic then went to National's rival, Fawcett Publications, and made a deal for their Superman-like character Captain Marvel. The end result was one of the most popular serials ever produced, 1941's *The Adventures of Captain Marvel*, starring Tom Tyler. Republic also showed interest in Batman, but National was skittish, afraid the studio would not be faithful to their character. Instead, they made a deal with Columbia Pictures. On June 16, 1942, the studio announced its 1942-1943 production slate. Among the titles listed were four serials, including *The Batman*.[13]

The script for *Batman* was written by Victor McLeod, Leslie Swabacker and Harry Fraser. McLeod was a veteran of the Walter Lantz studios, where he wrote numerous *Oswald Rabbit* and *Andy Panda* cartoons. In 1940, he graduated to scripting features with the Johnny Mack Brown Western, *Boss of Bullion City*. He subsequently scripted several other Westerns for Brown, as well as a couple of action films for Richard Arlen. His first serial assignment came in 1942, with Universal's *Gangbusters*, co-authored with Morgan Cox, Al Martin and George H. Plympton. The story featured a police detective, Lt. Bill Bannister, who is assigned to stop Professor Mortis and his League of Murdered Men, criminals who are presumed dead after seemingly committing suicide on death row. Leslie Swabacker had a much slimmer resume, having earned his first credit as one of the writers of 1936's *The Vigilantes are Coming!*, one of the initial serials released by Republic. The Zorro-inspired tale revolved around the exploits of The Eagle, who leads a group of ranchers fighting against Cossacks who are trying to turn California into a Russian colony. Yes, you read that correctly— Cossacks trying to turn California into a Russian colony (I did mention these were for kids, right?). He next contributed to the script of Universal's *Secret Agent X-9*, a serial based on a Dashiell Hammett character. The veteran among the *Batman* scriptwriters was Harry Fraser, who entered films as an actor in 1916 and by the 1920s had become an amazingly prolific writer and director of low-budget Westerns, which he continued to churn out into the 1930s and '40s.

As with many serial adaptations, the final script turned in by McLeod, Swabacker and Fraser took liberties with the source material. Whereas in the comics Batman became a duly deputized police officer in 1941, in the serial he is still considered an outlaw by the police. Unknown to them, however, he is an agent of the federal government, who presumably know his secret identity of Bruce Wayne. Robin still fights by his side, but there is no Batmobile, Batboat or Batplane, due to budgetary considerations. Instead, Bruce Wayne and Dick Grayson are chauffeured around by their butler, Alfred, in a 1939 Cadillac Series 61 Convertible (the first car called a "Batmobile" in the comic books was a red 1936 Cord convertible that appeared in *Detective Comics* # 48 in February 1941, so the serial version isn't really that far off the mark; for more info on the various Batmobiles, visit www.batmobilehistory.com).

The plot begins with the kidnapping of Linda Page's Uncle Warren. Linda Page became Bruce Wayne's girlfriend in the comic books beginning with *Batman* # 5 (Spring 1941). In the comic books, Linda was a society girl whose father was an oil magnate; she eventually left high society and became a war nurse. She made her final appearance in *Detective Comics* # 73 (March 1943), but in *Batman* # 32 (Dec 1945/Jan 1946), Bruce Wayne mentioned that he had purchased a sapphire for her birthday. After that, she was never mentioned again. In the serial, Linda was a nurse who worked in Dr. Borden's office at the Gotham City Foundation. Just as in the comic books, the serial's scriptwriters had Linda scold Bruce for being a wastrel. Also, as often happened in the comic books, she was eventually captured by the villains, necessitating a rescue by Batman.

The writers borrowed a couple of ideas from an earlier Columbia serial, *The Spider's Web*. In Chapter 1, when Batman leaves a couple of crooks handcuffed to a light pole for pick-up by the police, there's a little bat symbol stamped in ink on their foreheads, similar to the spider silhouette tattoos of the earlier film. Later, in Chapter 9, Bruce Wayne disguises himself as hoodlum "Chuck White" to infiltrate the villain's gang, just as Richard Wentworth—a/k/a the Spider—disguises himself as underworld lowlife Blinky McQuade. As Chuck White, a Damon Runyon-esque character with "dese," "dem" and "dose" delivery and a slouching walk, the change in Bruce's demeanor, plus a cigarette in his mouth and a liberal use of nose putty, is enough to fool Linda Page and the members of the villain's gang.

Since serials were basically comprised of lots of good old-fashioned fisticuffs, the live-action Batman wasn't nearly as formidable a fighter as his comic book counterpart. He gets beaten up, knocked about, and—at the conclusion of the first chapter—shoved off a rooftop (Chapter 2 begins with him landing on a window washer's scaffold). And though he wears a big, thick metallic belt that appears to have secret compartments, he never pulls out any exploding gas capsules or other gadgets from it as he did with his utility belt in the comics. Stranger still is that aside from Batman, Robin, Alfred and Linda, there are no other characters from the comic books. Instead of Commissioner Gordon, Batman turns the crooks over to Captain Arnold. The colorful villains from the comic book are woefully absent, replaced by the inscrutably evil Japanese agent, Dr. Tito Daka, occasionally referred to as Prince Daka.

Part of Daka's plan involves turning men into living zombies by way of a brainwashing machine and special headgear with a wire that is attached to their spine. Daka, who has a prototype ray gun powered by radium capable of causing a concrete block to crumble into rubble, plans to steal enough radium to build a much larger-scale ray gun capable of toppling buildings. Over the course of 15 chapters, his plans are continually interrupted by Batman and Robin, so often, in fact, that at one point

Daka speculates that maybe there is more than one Batman (an idea that comic book writer Grant Morrison would use nearly seventy years later in his "Batman, Inc." stories in which Bruce Wayne franchises Batman).

With a phone-book sized script in hand, Flothow hired Lambert Hillyer to direct *Batman*. Hillyer had been writing and directing since 1917, when he worked on a couple of William S. Hart Westerns. By the time he picked up the script to *Batman*, the South Bend, Indiana native had over 100 films under his belt, including two moody horror thrillers for Universal, *Dracula's Daughter* and *The Invisible Ray*, both made in 1936. Those were the exceptions, however; most of his films were Westerns.

When Flothow and Hillyer turned their attention to casting, the first role they filled was that of Linda Page, the female lead. On May 8, 1943, *The Los Angeles Times* announced that Shirley Patterson, formerly a star of Westerns, had been selected to play Bruce Wayne's fiancée.[14] Born Shirley Bodette in Winnipeg, Manitoba, Canada on December 26, 1922, Patterson was the winner of the 1939 Southern California archery championship and was chosen as Miss California 1940 at the Venice Beach Mardi Gras in August 1940, in a competition whose judges included Sir Cedric Hardwicke.[15] She entered films immediately after graduating from high school in Eagle Rock, California in 1940. Columbia placed her under contract and co-starred her opposite Wild Bill Elliott and Tex Ritter in *North of the Rockies*, directed by Lambert Hillyer. The studio continued to give her featured roles in Westerns, as well as smaller bits in their A-list films such as the Joan Crawford romantic comedy *They All Kissed the Bride* (1942) and the Jean Arthur-Joel McCrae comedy *The More the Merrier* (1943). She also played a small part in the Three Stooges short *Spook Louder*.

On May 29, 1943, *The Los Angeles Times* announced "Serial Called 'Bat Man' Projected at Columbia." The newspaper noted that Lewis Wilson has been chosen to play the lead, "and will have a sort of dual role, concealing his more or less classic features under the camouflage much of the time."[16] Wilson, like Patterson, was a new arrival at the studio. The New Hampshire-born son of a Boston minister, Lewis Gilbert Wilson was born January 28, 1920; he was only 23 years old when he was tapped to play the Caped Crusader, making him the youngest actor ever to take on the role.

Wilson was a graduate of Worcester Academy, where he distinguished himself as a long-distance swimmer. He next attended Cecil Clovelly's Academy of Dramatic Arts at Carnegie Hall. While there, he met another young actress named Dana Natol who would soon become his wife. The couple had a son, Michael, born January 21, 1942. In November of 1942, Wilson was cast in a revival of Karel Capek's *R.U.R.*, a play about robots, at the Ethel Barrymore Theatre in New York. Directed by Lee Strassberg, the play began its run on December 3, 1942.[17] Though it closed soon afterwards, Wilson was spotted by a talent scout from Columbia, who encouraged the young actor to go to Hollywood. Wilson took his advice, and upon arriving in Los Angeles was placed under contract by the studio. On December 16, gossip columnist Hedda Hopper reported that Wilson would make his screen debut opposite Merle Oberon at Columbia under Dorothy Arzner's direction.[18] The eventual film, *First Comes Courage*, starred Oberon and Brian Aherne.[19] Along with another New York actor, Jess Barker, Wilson was next tapped to appear in *Our Friend Curley* with Humphrey Bogart and Rita Hayworth. The two leads eventually dropped out of the film, which was made as *Good Luck, Mr. Yates* with Claire Trevor and Edgar Buchanan in the leading roles. On December 29, Wilson was once again mentioned in Hedda Hopper's column. "Lupe Velez will move her bits and pieces over to Columbia for *Redhead from Rio*," wrote Hopper, "with newcomer from Broadway, Lewis Wilson, as leading man."[20] Filming began on January 18, 1943. Again, the film underwent a title change before its release, to *Redhead From Manhattan*. *The Chicago Tribune* called it "a story of a shipwreck, comedy and music. The stars find themselves in many funny and harrowing experiences, as they get mixed up with some Nazi-cached funds and FBI agents."[21]

In February 1943, Wilson was cast in Columbia's *Right Guy*, which was released as *Klondike Kate* with Ann Savage and Tom Neal.[22] For an actor who had been in Hollywood less than a year, his career seemed on the upswing. Then came *Batman*. By the end of May, the promising young actor with the handsome features and upper-crust accent was being fitted for Batman's cape and cowl; *Daily Variety* announced his hiring on June 1, 1943.[23] Wilson was happy to take the role, as his long-time friend Frank Hunt told Boyd Magers of *Serial Report*. "Lew had read the comics," said Hunt. "In fact, he was interested in cartooning as a young man. He enjoyed working on the serial but felt the production was greatly under-funded."[24]

To portray Robin, the Boy Wonder, the studio hired a young actor who made a career of playing the younger versions of other actors on-screen. Douglas Malcolm Wheatcroft was born in Seattle on August 12, 1925 and brought to Los Angeles when he was only two weeks old. According to studio publicity, which may very well be apocryphal, he was discovered while trying to crash a Knox Manning radio broadcast at Los Angeles Radio City. A man with an extra ticket noticed him and invited him to be his guest. Conversing with Wheatcroft, the man learned that the boy liked hunting, fishing, archery, basketball and miniature golf, and that his hobby was building model boats and airplanes. In private school, his favorite subjects were history and science, and he hoped to make the baseball team. The man, it turned out, was talent agent Lew Kramer, who saw Wheatcroft as the ideal American boy. He asked the young man to come and see him the next morning, and bring his mother. Though he didn't have any immediate work for the youngster, he signed him to a contract, and shortened his last name to Croft. What probably appealed to Kramer was that Croft was a slightly-built teenager who could convincingly play characters years younger than his actual age; publicity notices said that he signed his contract on his 12th birthday, but in fact, Croft was 16.

A few days later, Kramer was contacted by 20th Century-Fox, who were calling 46 boys to test for a role in *Remember the Day* with Claudette Colbert and John Payne. Kramer sent Croft to the audition. He was sixth in line for a screen test, and after seeing him, the studio sent the other boys home.[25] In the film, Colbert played a schoolteacher in a small Midwest community. Croft was the schoolboy whose appreciation for his teacher lasted through the years, so that when he grew up and became a presidential candidate (and was played by John Shepherd), he turned to her for counsel when he was faced with a critical decision.[26]

In his next film, 1942's *Kings Row*, Croft played Drake McHugh, who grows up to become Ronald Reagan. It was a pattern he continued in *Yankee Doodle Dandy*, where he played the 13-year-old George M. Cohan (James Cagney played the adult entertainer), *Flight Lieutenant,* where his character, Danny Doyle, grows up to be Glenn Ford, and *Pride of the Yankees*, where he was the young Lou Gehrig (Gary Cooper played the older baseball legend). In October 1942, he was quoted as saying, "I've been in only four pictures, but in every one I grow up and become someone played by a movie star. Then everyone forgets me and remembers the fellow I grew up to be. I'd like just to be in a picture—and that's all."[27] This quote was probably a publicist's concoction, given that he had a plum role in 1942's *Not a Ladies' Man* as a young boy who is embarrassed when his divorced father (Paul Kelly) begins to fall for his schoolteacher (Fay Wray). Croft was also featured in 1942's *George Washington Slept Here*, a Jack Benny comedy adapted from a stage play by Moss Hart and George S. Kauffman. According to poet Sharmagne Leland-St. John, Croft and her father, actor Jerry St. John, used to sit on the porch of the Andy Hardy set at MGM and chat. A couple of writers would sometimes join them and make notes on the slang terms the boys used, working it into the dialogue of the Andy Hardy films as typical teenage jargon.[28]

Batman's nemesis, Dr. Daka, was played by veteran character actor J. Carroll Naish, in yellowface make-up with heavy-lidded eyes and dark lipstick. A master of dialects, Naish was Hollywood's all-purpose ethnic. The swarthy, dark-haired actor played Latinos, Italians, Arabs, American Indians and Asians on-screen. Naish was born into an Irish family in New York City on January 21, 1896. As a young boy, he ran away from home to join a vaudeville troupe, but was sent home. The young man kept trying, however, and at age 12 he worked as a song plugger for Irving Berlin. Though he was only 16 as World War I began, he dropped out of school and enlisted in the Navy. Serving as a naval aviator in France, he still found time to form a song-and-dance team to entertain the soldiers. After the war, he remained in Europe, acquiring a knowledge of languages and dialects that would serve him well in his later career. In 1926, he was taking a trip to Shanghai when the ship he was on developed engine trouble. It docked in San Diego, and Naish debarked and made his way to Hollywood, where he played a Japanese prince for the first time in *The Shanghai Gesture*. He developed a relationship with the actress playing opposite him, Gladys Heaney. They married two years later.[29]

Naish was having a rough time of it until his fortunes were changed by another man's ill fate. When William Fox, the head of Fox Films, was severely injured in an auto accident in July 1929, the call went out for a blood donor who shared Fox's rare blood type. Naish responded, and when the film mogul recovered, he put the actor under contract. From the time Naish signed his Fox contract in December 1929, he would never again be an out-of-work actor.

With his penchant for dialects and chameleon features, Naish quickly became one of Tinseltown's busiest character actors, appearing in such prestigious films as *The Lives of a Bengal Lancer* (1935), *Captain Blood* (1935), *Anthony Adverse* (1936), *The Charge of the Light Brigade* (1936), *Beau Geste* (1939), *Blood and Sand* (1941) and *The Pied Piper* (1942). In 1940, while filming *Down Argentine Way*, Naish spoke to gossip columnist Paul Harrison about how audiences sometimes thought he was Eurasian because he played so many Asian characters. "Naturally, the studio never would want the heavy identified as a Chinese or Japanese," said Naish, "so when they'd begin worrying about accents I'd give 'em Chinese with a few extra r's and they'd say, 'that's swell—what is it?' I'd tell 'em it was a rare Malaysian dialect and everybody'd be happy." He went on to say, "Those pictures maybe didn't make for good acting, because nobody can be easy and convincing in a phony part, but they were a lot of fun as long as we didn't take 'em seriously."[30] He could have been speaking about *Batman*...

To appreciate the 1943 *Batman*, you must understand the world as it was at that time. Following the attack on Pearl Harbor, anti-Japanese hysteria gripped the nation. With Americans fearing another Japanese attack on American soil, President Franklin D. Roosevelt signed an executive order on February 19, 1942 that resulted in 120,000 citizens of Japanese descent being removed from their homes and placed in internment camps. It was against this background that *Batman* went into production, designed to be a nifty piece of propaganda as well as kiddie entertainment. The underlying message of *Batman*—and numerous other films of the time—was that the inscrutable Orientals could not be trusted, and would destroy our American way of life given half a chance. Coming so soon after the attack on Pearl Harbor, the atrocities the Japanese visited on Nanking, and the Bataan Death March, these assumptions did not seem so far-fetched to a populace consistently fed virulent anti-Japanese images. Also, it has to be remembered that the comic books of the time had a similar patriotic fervor; one *World's Finest* cover (No. 7, Fall 1942) featured Superman, Batman and Robin sitting astride the big phallic guns of a battleship, erect and pointing out at the viewer in a clear show of American superiority. As many reviewers have noted, the irony of the *Batman* serial is that the plot involves Dr. Daka trying to create a radium-powered weapon. Just two years later, the U.S. unleashed such weapons on Japan, with the atomic bombs dropped on Hiroshima and Nagasaki.

It is the portrayal of Daka that makes the serial so hard to watch in modern times. Even when one considers the propagandistic fervor of the time, the voice-over and dialogue in the serial are still shocking. In Chapter One, when Linda's Uncle, Martin Warren, is taken by Daka's men to Little Tokyo, a narrator intones, "This was part of a foreign land transplanted bodily to America and known as Little Tokyo. Since a wise government rounded up the shifty-eyed Japs it has become virtually a ghost street where only one business survives, eking out a precarious existence on the dimes of curiosity seekers." That business is a waxworks, the Japanese Cave of Horrors, which serves as a front for Daka's headquarters. There are only a few exhibits inside the cave, one showing Japanese soldiers forcing an American soldier to dig his grave, another showing Japanese soldiers about to bayonet a white woman whose hands are bound behind her back, and a third showing Japanese soldiers guarding an American soldier in a cage. Presumably, these are meant to show the consequences of not wisely rounding up the shifty-eyed yellow devils. Once inside a secret chamber in the Cave of Horrors, Warren is confronted by Dr. Tito Daka, who introduces himself as the head of the League of the New Order, composed of men who have been "dishonored." We can tell Daka is evil by the way he holds his cigarette holder, and because he is the only character in the serial who wears a string bow-tie. "I am Dr. Daka," says the villain, "humble servant of his majesty Hirohito, heavenly ruler and prince of the rising sun. By divine destiny my country shall destroy the Democratic forces of evil in the United

States to make way for the New Order, an order that will bring about the liberation of the enslaved people of America." Pretty much every Caucasian who encounters Daka, including Linda Page, exclaims, "A Jap!' upon seeing him. Daka responds, "Please to say Nipponese. That is the courteous way of addressing one of the future rulers of the world." Batman goes one better; when Daka orders a brainwashed Linda to slap the Caped Crusader, Batman exclaims, "You Jap devil!"

Like other Columbia serials, the *Batman* serial was filmed at the Larry Darmour Studios on Santa Monica Boulevard. In a 1966 interview, Lewis Wilson recalled, "We were so scorned by everyone at Columbia Studio that the executives rented other facilities for us so we wouldn't be seen on the main lot."[31] As filming got underway, Wilson found himself working long hours—he was in practically every scene. No wonder that when he appears as Bruce Wayne, whom the screenwriters have written to be lazy and prone to nearly lying down in chairs that normal people would simply sit in, he really does seem exhausted. Nonetheless, he has a natural insouciance that shines through despite the wooden dialogue. "He was charming and funny, especially when he was playing Bruce Wayne," recalled his son, Michael Wilson. "I think he in a way created that idea that Bruce Wayne was a sort of Scarlet Pimpernel type. And then he would become Batman."[32]

As Batman, Wilson was more vigorous, but still had a carefree air about him, as though he really enjoyed getting into fights with crooks wearing fedoras. This is no brooding Dark Knight vigilante, but rather the living personification of the wise-cracking Batman of the comic books of the time. He's also the only Batman with a blue-blood accent, pronouncing yard "yahd," can't as "cahn't" and "stand guard" as "stand gahd." Yet although he is obviously rich, he's more like the richest man in the city, not one of the richest men in the nation (with each new film incarnation, Bruce Wayne becomes richer; by the time of *Batman Begins*, he's in the Bill Gates league). In another nod to the times, Bruce Wayne explains that the reason he's not in the Army is because he's 4-F, but we later learn that he's actually on special assignment to the federal government. In Chapter 5, he receives his first special assignment when a coded message arrives, addressed not to Gotham City but to 1918 Hill Road, Los Angeles, Calif. The envelope contains what appears to be a blank page, but it's actually a coded message from Uncle Sam, so one wonders if the government knows that Batman and Bruce Wayne are one and the same, or if they've only enlisted wealthy playboy Bruce Wayne as an operative.

The biggest challenge Wilson faced as Batman wasn't battling the bad guys, but battling the Bat-suit. Capturing the sharp lines of the hyper-muscular comic book Batman proved difficult for costumers who, for the first time, were tasked with the challenge of creating a real-life Batman outfit. Unlike the Batman suit in the comics, the real-life version was baggy and sagging and prone to everyday nuisances, like visible seams, zippers and wrinkles. Furthermore, in making the transition from page to screen, Batman's cape was shortened, and his cowl, though reproduced as accurately as possible, fit loosely around the lower part of his head, with protuberances that looked more like devil horns than bat ears. Also, in some chapters, the cape and cowl are made from lighter colored material than the trunks and boots. The real-life outfit also featured a very thick utility belt that rode high on Batman's hips, obscuring

Lewis Wilson's slender waist and making him look pudgy, a problem exacerbated by the use of barrel-chested stuntman Eddie Parker, who doubled Wilson for the fight scenes and dangerous stunts like leaping out of vehicles before they went over cliffs. Parker, who doubled Buster Crabbe in the *Flash Gordon* serials and both Lon Chaney and Bela Lugosi in *Frankenstein Meets the Wolf Man,* seemed to have trouble dealing with the cape. In Chapter 2, when Batman climbs a rope, his tunic rides up over his belt, exposing his white undershirt. In the fight scene that follows, after Batman and Robin crash through a window and begin fighting Daka's minions, the cape first wraps itself around his arm, then comes off completely. Parker keeps fighting sans cape. After a quick cutaway to Alfred waiting down below, the cape is magically back on, though in many subsequent fight scenes the two sides are drawn to the middle and pinned together to keep them from getting entangled in the stuntman's mitts. After the fight, when Lewis Wilson is back in the costume, it looks like the side seam of Batman's trunks have split.

Robin's outfit is a very close facsimile of the one in the comic books, except that his mask is obviously a cheap dime-store Halloween half-mask. When the Dynamic Duo go into action, skinny, pencil-legged Douglas Croft is replaced by a much more stout and muscular stuntman. The serial showed why certain concepts just don't translate well from one medium to another. While, in the stylized universe of the comic books, Robin is drawn and presented as a credible adversary to the various thugs he faces, seeing a live-action teenager getting punched in the face by a grown man is a little hard to stomach—which is probably why in subsequent screen adaptations, Robin always looked closer to 20 than 13.

While Shirley Patterson didn't have a strange outfit to contend with, she did have trouble with one scene. When her character is captured by Dr. Daka, the sinister villain brainwashes her with a glass dome-like device that fits over her head and has special effects smoke pumped into it. "It made me sick to my stomach," she later told film historian Boyd Magers. "I don't know what they shot into that helmet...it might have looked effective on screen, but it made me quite ill."[33]

Though the budget restraints limited the film's fidelity to the comic books, the serial nonetheless had an impact on its source. The screenwriters apparently decided that the natural lair for a bat was a cave. Consequently, the first shot in the serial is a moody, shadowy depiction of Batman's headquarters, called the Bat's Cave. In the original comics, there was only a secret underground tunnel that connected Wayne Manor to an old barn where the Batmobile and Batplane were stored. By *Batman* #12 (August–September, 1942), comic book writer Bill Finger had changed it to secret underground hangars. After visiting the film set, Bob Kane mentioned the cave idea to Finger, who was scripting the first *Batman* daily newspaper strip. When the strip debuted in October 1943, so did the Batcave. It was introduced in the comic books in *Detective Comics* #83 the following January. The comics also adopted the way Bruce Wayne and Dick Grayson entered and exited the Batcave in the serial—through a secret door in a grandfather clock in the mansion.

In April 1943, a new character was introduced in the comic books, Alfred Pennyworth, Bruce Wayne's butler. In his first comic book appearances, as in the serials, Alfred was played for comic relief. He fancied himself an amateur detective, but to the extent that he actually solved crimes, he did so by accident. He was clean-shaven and portly in the comic books, but when slender, mustachioed William Austin won the role in the serial, the editors at National decided their Alfred should look like the one on-screen. Consequently, in *Detective Comics* #83 (January 1944), the comic book Alfred was sent to a health resort, where he slimmed down and grew a mustache. Though Austin may not have looked physically like the original Alfred of the comics, when he's first introduced, he's seen in the study of Wayne Manor reading a lurid detective novel, and in the course of the serial he twice disguises himself and goes undercover to help Batman and Robin. This is an Alfred who is played strictly for comic relief, a far cry from the more dignified butler of the later serial and the 1960s TV series. In Chapter 3, when Batman and Robin burst in on several of Daka's men who are confronting Alfred, a fight ensues. Alfred, hiding behind an overturned desk, picks up the phone and says, "Get me Scotland Yard! Give me the police! Oh, give me anything! Please, hurry! Yes, I'm being murdered here!"

Lee Zahler provided the music for the serial, choosing Richard Wagner's "Rienzi Overture" to set the proper mood of mystery. The theme song plays at the head of each chapter, under a logo of a bat with Batman's face. Zahler was an old

Douglas Croft as Robin and Lewis Wilson as Batman in Columbia Pictures' 1943 serial, Batman (Columbia Pictures/Photofest, © Columbia Pictures).

hand at providing music for serials; he scored *The King of the Kongo* for Mascot in 1929, the first serial to feature a synchronized musical score with sound effects.[34] In the 1930s, Zahler served as a musical director at the Larry Darmour Studios. By 1933, he was credited with having over 250 of his original compositions adapted for the movies. But the 1940s were rough years for the composer; as the decade began, his son Gordon, while performing a gymnastic feat at a junior high school, broke his neck. Gordon was left a paraplegic, and Zahler was left with medical bills that eventually ruined him financially and caused the break-up of his marriage. He died in 1947, at age 53.[35]

It is difficult to say how well *Batman* performed at the box-office in its original 1943 release. Unfortunately, when Columbia Pictures moved from its Gower Street location in Hollywood to Burbank in 1972, joining Warner Bros. to become The Burbank Studios, nearly all of Columbia's production records and office files were destroyed.[36] Thus, in writing about Columbia, film historians are left with what little they can glean from newspapers and trade papers of the time, and movie serials were never deemed worthy of much serious press attention.

When *Batman* was finished, the only featured actor in the cast whose career continued on an upward trend was J. Carrol Naish. In the same year that he appeared in *Batman*, he played Giuseppe opposite Humphrey Bogart in the WWII drama *Sahara*, a role that won Naish an Academy Award nomination for Best Actor in a Supporting Role. He received a second Oscar nomination and won a Golden Globe three years later for his supporting role in *A Medal for Benny*. He continued playing ethnic characters, starring as an Italian immigrant in Chicago in the TV series *Life With Luigi* in 1952, and as Earl Derr Biggers's Chinese detective in TV's *The New Adventures of Charlie Chan* (1957-58; *Chan* was produced by Rudolph Flothow, producer of the *Batman* serial, who scored an earlier hit as producer of the popular TV series *Ramar of the Jungle*). For horror fans, however, Naish's most memorable role was as Daniel the hunchback in the Universal monster-fest *House of Frankenstein* (1944). He remained busy in TV and film until 1971, and passed away in 1973.

Douglas Croft suffered the common fate of child stars—he grew up, losing the feature that made him most bankable, his youthfulness. After *Batman*, he played a small role as "Davey" in the Judy Garland-Van Heflin musical *Presenting Lily Mars* (1943), and an even smaller part in the mystery *River Gang* (1945). He entered the Army near the conclusion of World War II, and upon his return had a role sparring with Mickey Rooney, whom he knew from his days of hanging around the Andy Hardy set, in *Killer McCoy* (1947). By 1950, he was no longer acting, and was instead working as a short order cook at a restaurant owned by his friend Jerry St. John.[37] He died on October 24, 1963, at the young age of 38.

In the same year that she made Batman, Shirley Patterson appeared in four more films with Lewis Wilson, *Redhead From Manhattan*, *Good Luck, Mr. Yates*, *Klondike Kate* and *My Kingdom for a Cook*, though both she and Wilson only had small roles in each film. She costarred in Westerns with Charles Starrett and Eddie Dean and took bit parts in Lana Turner vehicles and the Judy Garland musical *The Harvey Girls* (1946) before taking a break from films in 1948 to raise her son. When she returned in 1953, she was acting under a new name, Shawn Smith. She found a little TV and film work, most notably in two science fiction films, *The Land Unknown* (1957), where she and Jock

Mahoney encountered dinosaurs, and *It! The Terror From Beyond Space* (1958), where she was menaced by Ray "Crash" Corrigan in a rubber monster suit. She then retired from films for good. In later life, she became ill with cancer, and passed away at age 72 in April 1995 in Fort Lauderdale, Florida.

Lewis Wilson's career also had a downward trajectory after *Batman*. On June 17, 1943, while still filming the serial, he renewed his Columbia contract.[38] He played small roles in a number of films through the rest of 1943 and 1944, but his career was interrupted by the war. "He got drafted and had to go into the Army," said his son, Michael G. Wilson. Lewis Wilson reported as a private at Fort MacArthur on June 27, 1944. Before the war's end, he would serve in Europe and in the front lines at the Battle of the Bulge. "He didn't get back until 1946," recalled his son.[39] When Wilson returned from the war, so did all the big-name studio actors whose absence left open a small door of opportunity for lesser-known performers. "Everybody came back, and he came back, and mother and I were living in New York," said Michael Wilson. "They started doing theater work, summer stock in New England and then they came out to the Pasadena Playhouse."[40] In August of 1948, Lewis Wilson had a small role as Marine Sgt. O'Hara in a production of *Rain* at the Laguna Beach Playhouse, with Gladys George as Sadie Thompson and Victor Killian as the missionary, Alfred Davidson.[41] Films roles were harder to come by. When Columbia made a sequel to *Batman* in 1949, they hired other actors to play the Caped Crusaders.

In 1950, the Weiss Brothers, producers of the very first Columbia serials, made a pilot for a TV Western called *Trigger Tales*. Wilson had a small role, but the pilot didn't sell. His next film job didn't come until 1951, when he played the male lead in writer/director Norman Dawn's *Wild Women*, which costarred his wife, Dana. The jungle adventure, about a trio of hunters who are held captive by the "white sirens of Africa," was filmed on a budget so low it makes the *Batman* serial look like *Gone With the Wind*. As Queen Bonga Bonga, Dana Wilson is reduced to purring lines like "Ulama throw weak man to fire god, Ulama make strong man husband." Their marriage ended soon afterward.

Wilson fared much better in the 1952 TV series *Craig Kennedy, Criminologist*, based on a character created by Arthur B. Reeve that first appeared in the December 1910 issue of *Cosmopolitan*. Kennedy was a scientific detective at Columbia University who used his knowledge of physics and chemistry to solve crimes. The show, produced by the Weiss Brothers, starred Donald Woods as Kennedy and Wilson as a wisecracking, womanizing newspaperman, Walt Jameson. Wilson seemed to have fun with the role, which allowed him to display his natural easy-going charm. It should have opened doors for him, but the series lasted for only 26 episodes. Several of the programs were directed by Harry L. Fraser, one of the writers of the *Batman* serial.

Wilson's final film appearance was an uncredited role in *Naked Alibi*, starring Sterling Hayden and Gloria Grahame, in 1954. With that, his career was effectively over. He had remarried in 1953, and now in his mid-30s, began concentrating on raising a family. With his new wife Vyola, he had two boys and two girls. "He never really got back into acting again," said Michael Wilson. "It never quite worked for him."[42] When the *Batman* TV series was being developed in 1965, Lewis Wilson was 45 years old, only 8 years older than Adam West. If he was galled at seeing another actor have success in a role he originated, he seldom showed it, though when interviewed in May 1966, Wilson said of West, "He's a fine fellow. He's a credit to the uniform. He makes a lot of money. I'm not envious." His wife added, "Maybe not envious, perhaps 'agonized' would be a better word." Of his children, then ages 3, 5, 8 and 9, Wilson joked, "When I ask them if they want the original Batman's autograph, they tell me to put it on a check."[43] He told *Newsweek* magazine that he'd like to play a villain on the *Batman* TV series. "I'm a ham and a heavy at heart," he said. "I'm heavier and I could take him."[44]

"I guess it was something that he was somewhat embarrassed about, because he wanted to be a serious actor," said Michael Wilson. "And then I think as he mellowed out in age he took a kind of tongue-in-cheek view of it."[45] By the mid-1960s, Lewis Wilson was firmly out of the business, working at General Foods. "He worked at a plant in Hollywood," recalled Michael Wilson. "They made pectin out of orange peels. He worked there until he was in his early 50s, and then he had a heart condition and retired. He had open heart surgery twice."[46] When the nostalgia boom hit America in the 1970s, serial *Superman* Kirk Alyn and other stars of yesteryear reemerged into the limelight and reconnected with fans at conventions around the globe. Lewis Wilson shunned such attention, preferring to live out his final years in peace. "I think he'd gotten over being an actor and he was just a family man, living an appropriate life," said Michael Wilson. "I kept on seeing him over the years all the time. I'd bring my kids around to see him on the holidays if we were in Los Angeles. He was always a good storyteller, full of jokes. Loved telling jokes. He told me at one time that he had 400 jokes, and he had the opening line and then the punch line—that's why he remembered them—on note cards."[47]

By that point, although Lewis Wilson was himself no longer interested in movies, his son was deeply involved in one of the biggest film franchises in cinema history. Lewis Wilson's ex-wife, Dana, married producer Albert R. "Cubby" Broccoli in 1959. Three years later, Broccoli teamed with Harry Saltzman to produce the first James Bond film, *Dr. No*. The Bond movies became a sensation, and are now produced by Dana Wilson Broccoli's children, Barbara Broccoli and Michael G. Wilson—so Batman's son is 007's producer.

Lewis Wilson died on August 9, 2000, at age 80. After he was gone, Michael Wilson wondered about that boxful of jokes on note cards. "I asked my sister to go and see if we could find that," he said. "No one could ever find it."[48] Had Lewis Wilson's career gone differently, he might have become a reliable actor in A-budget features, and had a career more befitting of his talents. But although starring in a kiddie serial like Batman may have seemed like a joke at the time, the fact that Wilson was the movies' first live-action Batman assures that he will never be forgotten. So, in the end, Lewis Wilson had the last laugh.

---

1   Reilly, Sue, "Original batman to Play Villain Role in PTA Play," *The Los Angeles Times*, May15, 1966, p. SF_B6

2   Wallace, David, *Lost Hollywood*, © 2001 L.A. Weekly Books/St. Martin's Press, p. 12

3   *Ibid.*, p. 13

4   Schatz, Thomas, *Boom and Bust: American Cinema in the 1940s*, © 1999 University of California Press, p. 62

5   Wallace, David, *Lost Hollywood*, © 2001 L.A. Weekly Books/St. Martin's Press, p. 13

6   Schatz, Thomas, *Boom and Bust: American Cinema in the 1940s*, © 1999 University of California Press, p. 62

7   *Ibid.*, p. 61

8   *Ibid.*, p. 64

9   Benton, Mike, *Superhero Comics of the Golden Age*, © 1992 Taylor Publishing Co., Dallas, TX, p. 53

10   — "Flothow as Darmour's Production Aide," *Daily Variety*, Aug. 17, 1936, p. 1

11   —, "Larry Darmour Rites Friday; Dies After 3-Month Illness," *Daily Variety*, March 18, 1942, p. 1, 4

12   — "Cohn Out As Producer; 'Crime' to Flothow," *Daily Variety*, April 5, 1943, p. 6

13   —, "Film Popularity Spurs Production," *The New York Times*, June 17, 1942, p. 26

14   Schallert, Edwin, "Marcy McGuire Lead in 'Seven Days Ashore,'" *The Los Angeles Times*, May 8, 1943, p. 7

15   —, "Schoolgirl, 17 and Blond, Chosen as Miss California," *The Los Angeles Times*, Aug 12, 1940, p. A1

16   Schallert, Edwin, "Serial Called 'Bat Man' Projected at Columbia," *The Los Angeles Times*, May 29, 1943, p. 9

17   —, "Revival Tonight for Capek's 'R.U.R.'" *The New York Times*, Dec. 3, 1942, p. 34

18   Hopper, Hedda, "Looking at Hollywood," *Chicago Daily Tribune*, Dec. 16, 1942, p. 28

19   —, "Film Houses Set Holiday Records," *The New York Times*, Dec. 29, 1942, p. 27

20   Hopper, Hedda, "Looking at Hollywood," *The Chicago Daily Tribune*, Dec. 29, 1942, p. 17

21   —"A Little About the Movies on City's Screens," *The Chicago Daily Tribune*, May 9, 1943, p. D7

22   Jone, Isabel Morse, "Screen and Stage: Pianists Provide Music Treat at Philharmonic," *The Los Angeles Times*, Feb. 24, 1943, p. A9

23   —, "Wilson To 'Bat,'" *Daily Variety*, June 1, 1943, p. 4

24   Magers, Boyd, "The Batman," *Serial Report* Chapter 52, Jan.-Mar. 2005, p. 2

25   —, "Typical American Boy Steps Into Movie Role," *Panama City News-Herald*, Sept. 21, 1941, p. 1

26   —, "Seattle Lad New 'Find' In Fox Film," *The Salt Lake Tribune*, Feb. 6, 1942, p. 8

27   —, "Boy Actor Tires of Growing Up," *Oakland Tribune*, Oct. 11, 1942, p. B-11

28   Leland-St.John, Sharmagne, email correspondence, July 29, 2009

29   Rawitch, Robert, "J. Carrol Naish, Master Ethnic Character Actor, Dies at 76," *The Los Angeles Times*, January 27, 1973, p. B1

30   Harrison, Paul, "Paul Harrison in Hollywood: J. Carrol Naish, Tired of Playing Creepy Roles, Now Writes Bed-Time Stories," *The Burlington, N.C. Daily Times-News*, Thursday, July 25, 1940, p. 2

31   Reilly, Sue, "Original batman to Play Villain Role in PTA Play," *The Los Angeles Times*, May 15, 1966, p. SF_B6

32   Interview with Michael G. Wilson, conducted July 17, 2009

33   Magers, Boyd, "The Batman," *Serial Report* Chapter 52, Jan.-Mar. 2005, p. 2

34   Lahue, Kalton C., *Continued Next Week: A History of the Moving Picture Serial*, © 1964, University of Oklahoma Press, Norman, Oklahoma, p. 147

35   Barlow, John F., "Lee Zahler," *The Internet Movie Database*, http://www.imdb.com/name/nm0006343/bio, accessed Oct. 21, 2011

36   Dick, Bernard F., *The Merchant Prince of Poverty Row: Harry Cohn of Columbia Pictures*, © 1993, The University Press of Kentucky, Lexington, Kentucky, p. 2-3

37   Leland-St.John, Sharmagne, email correspondence, July 29, 2009

38   Schallert, Edwin, "Grant Will Play Sub Commander in 'tokyo,'" *The Los Angeles Times*, June 17, 1943, p. 14

39   Interview with Michael G. Wilson, conducted July 17, 2009

40   *Ibid.*

41   —, "Gladys George Wins Ovation as 'Rain' Star," *The Los Angeles Times*, August 19, 1948, pg. 21.

42   Interview with Michael G. Wilson, conducted July 17, 2009

43   Reilly, Sue, "Original batman to Play Villain Role in PTA Play," *The Los Angeles Times*, May 15, 1966, p. SF_B6

44   —, "Where Are They Now?" *Newsweek*, April 25, 1966

45   Interview with Michael G. Wilson, conducted July 17, 2009

46   *Ibid.*

47   *Ibid.*

48   *Ibid.*

Chapter Three:
BATMAN ON THE AIR

"Ah, radio! You just had to be sober enough to read—
and not too much time was taken up, either."
—Gary Merrill[1]

Visitors to the New York World's Fair in 1940 were able to take home a special comic book prepared especially for the fair-goers, called *New York World's Fair Comics*. The cover featured Superman with Batman and Robin, though the stories inside had Superman and Batman in separate adventures. The one-off comic book would inspire a new comic book series for National Comics. In Spring of 1941, the company introduced *World's Best Comics* # 1 with the Man of Steel and the Dynamic Duo on the cover. For the second issue, the comic book's name was changed to *World's Finest Comics*, the title it would carry until its last issue, # 323, in January 1986. Initially, as in *New York World's Fair Comics*, the heroes would appear in separate, individual adventures. But the editors at National would eventually have them working together, first in a story that appeared in *Superman* # 76 in May/June 1952, and then in *World's Finest* beginning with issue # 71 in 1954. On radio, however, they had been working in tandem for nearly a decade.

Superman was the first of National's heroes to become a radio star. *The Adventures of Superman* debuted on Monday, February 12, 1940 as a syndicated series; it would later find a permanent home on the Mutual network. The show starred Clayton "Bud" Collyer as the Man of Steel for most of its run. It was very popular with children, so it would seem that a spin-off Batman series would be a natural idea. Consequently, sometime after Batman arrived on movie screens in a Columbia serial in 1943, a pilot for a possible *Batman* radio series was produced, with Scott Douglas voicing Bruce Wayne and Batman. The actual recording of the pilot broadcast has been lost to history, but the script remains, though it indicates no date and it is unclear who authored it. Called "The Case of the Drowning Seal," it based its interpretation of the character more on Columbia's movie serial than the comic books. The World War II story had Bruce Wayne as a government agent, on the trail of the Nazi spies that killed Robin Grayson's parents, who were FBI agents (yes, Dick Grayson's name was changed to Robin Grayson in the pilot). When Wayne donned the "black horned mask and cape" of Batman, he disguised his identity by adopting a British accent. Scott Douglas played another comic book hero, MLJ (Archie) Comics' *The Black Hood*, on a short-lived radio series that same year.

Though the Batman series was never sold and never aired, Batman did eventually come to radio, but as a guest star rather than a featured attraction. On Wednesday, February 28, 1945, *The Adventures of Superman* concluded with the Man of Steel saving not only Lois Lane and Jimmy Olsen from drowning in the bay, but also a boy in a capsized rowboat wearing a cape and a red leather vest with the letter 'R' on it. Superman recognized the boy as Robin, Batman's companion. Once revived, Robin told Superman that Batman, working on "the biggest case of his life," had disappeared. Thus began "The Mystery of the Waxmen," in which a villain named Zoltan was turning people into wax statues. Stacy Harris provided the voice of Batman for the broadcasts, while a young but seasoned radio actor named Ronald Liss played Robin. Alfred the butler was voiced by Jackson Beck, the show's narrator, with a British accent.

Born in Big Timber, Quebec, Stacy Harris worked as a sports reporter and cartoonist before becoming an actor. He appeared in five Broadway plays, including a starring role in 1941's *Song Out of Sorrow*, in which he played the lead role of Victorian poet Francis Thompson, and as one of the soldiers in the ensemble cast of *A Sound of Hunting*, a 1945 play in which a young Burt Lancaster made his debut. In between, Harris was very active in radio, appearing five afternoons a week in the NBC radio serial *Pepper Young's Family* in 1943, and later joining the cast of the popular *Gangbusters* program. He also served a stint as a merchant seaman during World War II.

Ronald Liss was a real-life boy wonder. In 1933, at age of 3, he was part of the New York Baby Orchestra, a 26-piece ensemble composed of children whose ages ranged from 2 to 7. When they made their debut at the Greenwich Presbyterian Church on 145 West 13th Street in New York, with their ranks cut to 16 due to a measles outbreak, Liss took the conductor's baton for part of the 90-minute show and also played and sang "Lightly Row."[2] When he was old enough to properly speak, he became a popular child performer on radio, appearing on the *Bright Horizons* series with a young Skip Homier.

The teaming of Superman and Batman was popular enough that the Dynamic Duo returned to the Man of Steel's radio program six months later, with Stacy Harris and Ronald Liss reprising their roles. In an adventure called "Dr. Blythe and the Confidence Gang," which began broadcasting on September 5, 1945, Lois Lane was made to take the fall for a moll named Dixie Lamar, whom she resembled, who faced the electric chair for having murdered a federal agent. In this adventure, it became apparent that Clark Kent knew Batman's secret identity, but Batman, whom the comic books called "the world's greatest detective," couldn't see past Kent's eyeglasses to recognize him as Superman. However, when Lois was put on trial for murder, with circumstantial evidence planted by Blythe mounting against her, it was Batman's detective skills that helped locate the real murderess and clear Lois. For the final episodes of the adventure, Batman's voice changed—after a brief absence, he was played by another actor, Matt Crowley.

Crowley, who was born June 20, 1904, was no stranger to comic book heroes. He was radio's *Jungle Jim* beginning with the show's debut on November 2, 1935. After three years, he left the series, succeeded by Gerald Mohr. He was also the second actor to play the title role in radio's *Buck Rogers in the 25th Century* (with Ronald Liss as his side-kick, Buddy), and was Paul Drake in radio's *Perry Mason* series. Like Harris, Crowley also appeared on Broadway; in October of 1942, he had a role in Maxwell Anderson's play, *The Eve of St. Mark*, one of the first serious dramas inspired by America's involvement in World War II.[3] In the same year that he appeared on *The Adventures of Superman*, Crowley also made his TV debut, playing Walter Burns in a broadcast of the popular Charles MacArthur-Ben Hecht play, *The Front Page*.

Batman next appeared near the end of a long multi-part story that pitted Superman against Atom Man, a German soldier that a Nazi scientist, Der Tuefel (the German name for the Devil; interestingly, the character was played by Matt Crowley with a heavy Teutonic accent), had turned into a weapon of mass destruction by injecting Kryptonite into his veins. After Superman defeated Atom Man, the remains of the Nazi spy ring that helped fund his creation came into possession of still more Kryptonite. In programs broadcast beginning December 6, 1945, Clark Kent looked to Batman for help in locating the Scarlet Widow, who had obtained some of the deadly substance. When Kent arrived at Bruce Wayne's mansion, he goofed by addressing Wayne as Batman, making Wayne instantly suspicious. To gain his confidence, Kent had to reveal his own identity, which he shared with Bruce Wayne on the following day's program. However, when Dick Grayson entered the room, Bruce and Kent chose not to reveal the secret to Robin.

Batman and Robin helped Superman find the remaining Kryptonite and round up the Nazi spies, appearing on almost all of the programs until the story wrapped up on January 8, 1946. In this adventure, Ronald Liss again played Robin, but the Caped Crusader was now played by yet another actor, Gary Merrill. While Crowley's smooth, somewhat soft voice had a slight air of sophistication befitting a millionaire playboy, Merrill's Batman and Bruce Wayne sounded more blue collar than blueblood. His voice had a tinge of gruffness, and in these episodes, Batman and Robin were written as hard-boiled characters that traded sarcastic wisecracks when in dire jeopardy. At the conclusion of the 26-episode story, Batman and Robin rescued Superman, after the Man of Steel was trapped in a cyclotron and bombarded by kryptonite radiation.

A graduate of Bowdoin College, Gary Merrill was born in Hartford, Connecticut on August 2, 1915. He began as an actor in summer stock plays, until he joined the Army Air Force and was cast in *Winged Victory*, a play created by the military as a morale booster and fundraiser for the Army Emergency Relief Fund. The Moss Hart drama opened on Broadway on November 20, 1943, its run ending only so that the cast could travel to Hollywood to make the film version in 1944. When it went before the cameras, Merrill made his movie debut, along with Red Buttons, Kevin McCarthy, Judy Holliday, Jeanne Crain, and Martin Ritt (who would later become a noted director). The cast also featured George Reeves, several years before he became TV's Superman. Returning to New York, Merrill stayed busy with radio work, which he felt offered a special kind of freedom. "I could dress as I pleased," he wrote in his autobiography. "Forget about wardrobe, fittings and make-up—just be the voice."[4] He also joined the cast of Broadway's *Born Yesterday*. "During the day I performed on radio doing the early version of the soap operas *Young Dr. Malone, The Second Mrs. Burton,* and *The Right to Happiness*—and appeared in *Born Yesterday* in the evening," wrote Merrill, adding, "We spent one hour in rehearsal for a fifteen-minute show. Except for *Superman*, which I played occasionally. That took even less time."[5]

Merrill returned as Batman on January 29, 1946, in the first of a 13-part adventure called "Is There Another Superman?" that concluded on February 14. The plot involved an Eastern European strongman who had been duped into impersonating Superman by a gang of resourceful robbers. When Superman, who was having blackouts after being bombarded by Kryptonite radiation in the previous adventure, feared that he was, in fact, robbing banks, he turned to Batman to help him solve the case. During the adventure, Robin disappeared while chasing the villains. Batman, fearing that he had been killed, was beside himself. As episode 10 began, Clark Kent and Bruce Wayne paid a visit to Inspector Henderson, asking for his help in finding Dick Grayson. Bruce, his "eyes red-rimmed and his cheeks etched with deep lines of fatigue," made an impassioned plea, saying, "That kid means

Bette Davis and Bruce Wayne? Gary Merrill, one of several actors who played Batman on radio, strikes a pose with Bette Davis, his All About Eve co-star, who later became his wife. (20th Century Fox/Photofest, © 20th Century Fox).

everything to me...Oh, you can't know how I feel about him." This was a much more emotional Bruce Wayne/Batman than was ever seen in the comics. While it is easy, in this post-Frederic Wertham world of cynicism, to listen to the broadcast and chuckle at what appear to be homosexual undertones, one must remember that at the time, such emotionality would have been considered the appropriate reaction of a parent who had lost a child, which is no doubt how the radio writers saw the Bruce Wayne/Dick Grayson relationship, and how they expected it to be interpreted by the show's young listeners.

A few months later, on April 5, Batman returned in part 6 of "The Story of the Century," a trifling bit of nonsense that had Batman cooperating with Lois Lane, Perry White and Jimmy Olsen to create an unsolvable April Fool's puzzle to trick Clark Kent. When Kent eventually figured out what was going on, he turned the tables on them, pulling some pranks of his own. As Superman, he made Perry White's house disappear and convinced the *Daily Planet* staffers that they were about to be killed by pirates. He meant to teach his coworkers that practical jokes aren't funny, but basically ended up teaching them that the Big Blue Boy Scout couldn't take a joke.

Batman also came in near the end of a 22-episode adventure called "Horatio F. Horn, Detective." During the course of the adventure, an ex-Scotland Yard detective named Herbert Caulkins suspected that Clark Kent was Superman, and began setting traps to prove it. In the 19th episode, Superman was scheduled to speak at the World Peace Federation. Caulkins was determined to accompany Kent to the rally, because even Superman couldn't be in two places at once. He didn't count on Bruce Wayne, in a Superman uniform and rubber mask, masquerading as the Man of Steel. In these episodes, Batman/Bruce Wayne was played by a new actor—Dan McCullough, the commercial announcer for *The Adventures of Superman* who usually spent the episode's commercial breaks hawking Kellogg's Pep cereal.

The origin of Robin was presented—after a fashion—in the final episode of the adventure called "George Lattimer, Crooked Political Boss" that aired on September 25, 1946. It began with Clark Kent being called to Bruce Wayne's home, where Wayne told him how Dick Grayson became Robin. In the radio version of the story, Bruce Wayne was a good friend of John Grayson, patriarch of the Flying Graysons. When John Grayson and his wife Mary were performing their wire-walking act, the wire snapped. Mary was killed instantly, but John Grayson lived long enough to ask Bruce to take care of his son, Dick. Grayson also tells Bruce that he and his wife are not the victims of an accident, but of murder. Wayne immediately investigated the steel wire and saw that it had been weakened by being partly sawn through. Wayne knew who the murderer was—a man named George Larson, the circus ringmaster. At the beginning of the war, he had found out that Mrs. Grayson was French, and had a sister and brother living in Paris who were members of the French underground. He threatened to report them to the Nazis unless he was paid off. For five months, he blackmailed the Graysons until they had no more money. Then, they told him they were going to the District Attorney to have him arrested for extortion and blackmail. The following night, the wire broke. This was the beginning of "The Dead Voice," an adventure that ran for fifteen episodes, ending October 16, with Batman/Bruce Wayne once again played by Matt Crowley.

During the adventure, Robin once again goes missing and Batman, fearing that he's dead, bemoans the loss of his young aide. Superman says, "This isn't at all like you, Batman." In fact, it's exactly like Batman was several episodes previously; in these later radio shows, Batman is not only emotional, he's also prone to bouts of extreme worry and hysteria.

Crowley played the Caped Crusader again in an adventure called "The Secret Letter" that began broadcasting on November 25, 1946. The plot involved Batman helping Superman track down a letter which revealed Superman's secret identity that had fallen into the hands of two small-time crooks.

Batman next appeared in "The Monkey Burglar," which ran for 10 episodes beginning February 25, 1947. The title referred to an acrobatic burglar who scaled up the sides of buildings to rob luxury apartments. Inspector Henderson shocked Clark Kent and Batman by revealing the identity of the burglar as Robin, the Boy Wonder. He believed the burglar was Robin based on descriptions by some of the victims, who described him as a youngster about five feet tall, weighing about a hundred and ten pounds, wearing a skin-tight costume and red jacket with a bat-like hood and half-mask. Robin was unable to give the police an alibi without revealing his secret identity, so Batman asked Superman to help him find the real culprit. With this adventure, Gary Merrill returned as the Caped Crusader.

Merrill was back in "Superman Versus Kryptonite," broadcast from May 14 to June 27, 1947, in which crooked political boss and unrepentant bigot Big George Lattimer, released from prison, poisoned Superman with kryptonite, causing Superman to lose his memory. Superman—dressed in overalls—escaped from Lattimer in his men, but still had amnesia. He ended up joining a minor-league baseball team, becoming their star pitcher under the name Bud Smith. After breaking numerous pitching and hitting records, he was traded to the big-league Metropolis Titans. With Batman's help, Superman eventually recovered his memory and defeated Lattimer.

With the conclusion of "Superman Versus Kryptonite," the Superman radio program went on summer break, returning to the air three months later. On November 27, 1947, an adventure began which again featured Gary Merrill as the Caped Crusader, helping Superman and Perry White defeat Joe Solitaire's "vicious pinboard racket," which preyed on school kids.

At the end of an episode broadcast on February 2, 1948, Dick Grayson summoned Clark Kent to Wayne Manor and announced that Batman was gone, and he was afraid they'd never see him again. Thus began "Batman's Great Mystery," in which Batman was kidnapped and replaced by an imposter. It took the Man of Steel to set things right, which he had done by the broadcast of February 17, 1948. In this adventure, Batman was again played by Merrill, with Liss as Robin.

"The Mystery of the Stolen Costume," broadcast from March 10 to April 1, 1948, began with Clark Kent returning to his apartment to find that someone has opened the secret panel where he kept a spare Superman outfit and stolen it. He immediately sought help from the only person who knew his secret identity— Batman. These programs were later adapted into an episode of the *Adventures of Superman* television show starring George Reeves, but the story was heavily rewritten and condensed, with Batman and Robin being written out completely.

In the final episode of "The Crossword Puzzle Mystery," broadcast May 3, 1948, after Superman rounded up gold hijackers out West, Clark Kent went to Inspector Henderson's office to tell him the identity of the brains of the outfit—a crook who ran a small time syndicate out of Metropolis, tipping off his accomplices with clues in crossword puzzles. But instead of Henderson, Kent found Batman (again voiced by Gary Merrill) in Henderson's office. Batman told Kent that he and Robin were working the case from another end, and had put the man in the city jail, thus bringing the case to a conclusion.

"The Secret of Meteor Island," broadcast from June 14 to July 6, 1948, began with Jimmy Olsen being slipped a package by a man named the Count. Jimmy was later kidnapped by gangsters who saw the Count slip Jimmy the package, which they expected to contain diamonds. In Episode 4, Batman and Robin arrived and attempted to rescue Jimmy. They found themselves outnumbered, but Superman showed up and lent a hand.

On an episode broadcast July 7, 1948, Clark Kent was awakened by a phone call from Bruce Wayne, who whisked him off in the Batmobile to a sonic laboratory where experiments were being conducted with high-speed sound waves, beginning an adventure titled "The Voice of Doom." Superman helped Batman defeat Butcher Stark, a criminal accidentally bombarded by a sonic ray gun, which gave him the ability to project a sound with his voice that could cripple those nearby and even collapse walls.

In 1950, there was another attempt to bring Batman to radio in his own series. A pilot was produced called *The Batman Mystery Club*. The show had a peculiar premise—each week, Robin would call a meeting of the Batman Mystery Club to order, presenting Batman, who would regale the assembled group of young kids with a ghost story designed to debunk the supernatural—a precursor, of sorts, to *Scooby-Doo*. A pilot episode, "The Monster of Dumphrey's Hall," basically a locked-room mystery, was produced in September 1950, with Liss again playing Robin and John Emery, radio's *Philo Vance*, as Batman. As Les Daniels notes in his book *Batman: The Complete History*, the pilot was penned by comic book writer Don Cameron, who was authoring a book on the occult when he died, age 48, in 1954.[6] The pilot never aired.

Emery was born into show business, the son of actors Edward Emery and Isabel Waldron, though some believed that he was the illegitimate son of John Barrymore, since the two bore a strong resemblance to each other. Born May 20, 1905, Emery attended Long Island's LaSalle Military Academy. His first film role came in 1937, in director James Whale's *The Road Back*. That same year, he married Tallulah Bankhead in Jasper, Alabama, only to divorce her four years later in Reno, Nevada. Throughout the 1940s, he continued to appear in films, including *Here Comes Mr. Jordan* (1941), *George Washington Slept Here* (1942), and Alfred Hitchcock's *Spellbound* (1945).

After his one Batman pilot, John Emery remained very active in films and television, appearing on episodes of *I Love Lucy*, *Alfred Hitchcock Presents* and *Wagon Train*, among many others, though science fiction fans will remember him for his role as Dr. Karl Eckstrom in 1950's *Rocketship X-M*. He died in New York on December 16, 1964.

Ronald Liss appears not to have had an acting career beyond the demise of radio dramas. He became a production manager of TV's *The Jimmy Dean Show* in 1958, then turned to writing. He was a writer on the ABC children's series *Director '62*, which began broadcast in October 1962,[7] and later wrote and performed voices on MGM/Leo the Lion records featuring characters such as Flash Gordon, Superman, the Flash, Aquaman, the Green Hornet, the Green Lantern and, of course, Batman. Liss died at the young age of 39, during the first week of October, 1969.

The actors who played Batman fared much better. Stacy Harris had a steady role on radio from 1948 to 1953, as agent Jim Taylor on ABC Radio's *This is Your FBI*. He became a close friend of Jack Webb, who cast him in numerous episodes of TV's *Dragnet* and named his eldest daughter, Stacy, after him. One of his last roles was as Leslie Harrington on the 1972 TV series *Return to Peyton Place*. Harris died of a heart attack in Los Angeles on March 13, 1973, at the age of 54.[8]

Matt Crowley played Dr. Brent on radio's *Road of Life* for several years until one day when he left for a two-week vacation. Since his character did not appear in every episode, he waited until the last few days of his rest in the country to call his agent for the next week's schedule. He learned that the network was holding auditions, but was told they were for another series. When he returned to New York on a Friday, he was informed that Don McLaughlin had been assigned Crowley's role of Dr. Brent.[9] Despite a barrage of letters from angry listeners, Crowley was not invited back and was never told why the change was made.[10] Not that he needed to worry about work—the much in-demand radio performer became radio's *Dick Tracy*, adding to his résumé of comic book heroes. In the 1950s and early 1960s, Crowley became a busy character actor in movies and TV, including a recurring role as the Lakeview Chief of Police on the daytime TV serial *The Edge of Night*. He died March 10, 1983.

As for Gary Merrill, when he returned to Hollywood in the early 1950s, he had high-profile roles in *Twelve O'Clock High* (1949) and *All About Eve* (1950), among other films. On the set of *All About Eve*, he met Bette Davis, with whom he began an affair. He and Davis soon divorced their respective spouses and were married, a union that lasted a decade, ending in 1960. He had a starring role in the short-lived TV series *The Reporter* in 1964, then settled into a long career of guest starring roles. With his distinctively rich voice, he also worked regularly doing voice-overs for radio and TV commercials until his death from lung cancer at age 74, on March 5, 1990.

RADIO REBORN

Though the Golden Age of radio serials faded out in the 1950s as television became the dominant entertainment medium in American homes, there have nonetheless been more recent audio adaptations of Batman. In 1988, BBC-4 producer Dirk Maggs, best known for his radio adaptation of *The Hitchhiker's Guide to the Galaxy*, produced a 50th anniversary Superman radio drama, *Superman on Trial*. The response to the program was so positive that the following year, he produced a 50th anniversary tribute to Batman, *Batman: The Lazarus Syndrome*. Written by Maggs and Simon Bullivant, the radio drama drew inspiration from the comic book stories *The Killing Joke*, *A Death in the Family*, *Batman: Year Three* and *Batman: Son of the Demon*.

The storyline featured Ra's al Ghul, having made himself look like Bruce Wayne through plastic surgery, imprisoning Batman and taking Wayne's place.

The 45-minute production featured Michael Gough, who had just been seen as Alfred the butler in a Batman motion picture, reprising his role for the radio drama. Batman/Bruce Wayne was played by Bob Sessions, an actor who had been performing on British television since 1968, when he appeared in an episode of *Sexton Blake*. Over the years, he popped up in episodes of *Journey to the Unknown*, *The Protectors*, *Rumpole of the Bailey* and *The Case-Book of Sherlock Holmes*. His deep voice, with just the slightest hint of a British accent, sounded convincingly authentic. "Funnily enough casting Batman was a no-brainer," said Dirk Maggs. "Back in 1988 Bob Sessions had come in to audition for the part of Superman when we made the 50th birthday Supes docudrama *Superman on Trial*. As soon as he walked in and said hello the voice was obviously Batman. Not the gravelly pseudo-tough guy Michael Keaton thing, but a rich deep Cary Grant with a bit of gravel. And he had the integrity too. As Batman was also in the docudrama—called upon to give 'evidence' at the trial (rather ambiguous evidence that nearly had Supes dispatched to the Phantom Zone!)—he was cast as Batman then and there. The following year we made the Batman 50th birthday tribute, *Batman: The Lazarus Syndrome*, and Bob really got his teeth into the part."[11]

A second Batman radio drama followed. In 1993, Matthew Bannister took over BBC Radio 1 and approached Dirk Maggs for a daytime serial. Maggs decided to do a more long-form Batman serial, and produced 65 three-minute episodes called *Batman: Knightfall*, which were aired as part of *The Mark Goodier Show*. Once again, Michael Gough appeared as Alfred, and Bob Sessions took on the role of the Dark Knight. As in the comic book arc that inspired it, the plot involved Batman taking on a villain named Bane, who escaped from Arkham Asylum, releasing numerous other villains in the process. Batman tracks down the villains one-by-one, exhausting himself in the process, until he eventually faces Bane. His confrontation with the steroid-enhanced giant ends with Bane breaking Batman's back. Another hero, Azrael, takes over as the new Batman while Bruce Wayne recovers. When Azrael/Batman becomes increasingly reckless and violent in his pursuit of criminals, a rejuvenated Batman eventually has to subdue him. In 1997, BBC Audiobooks edited the programs together and released them as a three-hour and forty minute CD set, which shot to the top of the Spoken Word charts in the U.K.[12]

"With 65 episodes of action featuring a lot of the big Batman criminals, it was necessary to use a lot of actors on *Knightfall*," said Maggs. "It helped that this was Radio 1's first daily drama and they were prepared to make the budget available! In fact there was still quite a bit of 'doubling', I could have wished for more but it worked very well. The feedback was very positive from both the industry and fans, thank goodness. DC Comics were very pleased with the result. Batman chief writer Denny O'Neil sent me a signed copy of the *Knightfall* novel which I still treasure, and generally speaking the press were very supportive. *The Daily Telegraph* said it 'struck just the right balance between Gothic horror, gung-ho heroism and camp humor, and maintained it', which is a fair enough comment on what we were trying to achieve. Favorable comparisons were made to the Tim Burton movies, which I was pleased about. Fans on the whole seem to think it is an accurate portrait of the Batman existing in the comics of the early 90s." Sessions died after the release of *Knightfall*. "I cannot imagine who I'd get to play Batman now," said Maggs. "Funny thing about Bob, he had the matinee idol dark good looks, and he was actually a song and dance man! He'd come to the UK years before from the USA and played in all the big West End musicals. A lovely person, a true gentleman, I miss him to this day. We always wanted to try and do Frank Miller's *The Dark Knight Returns* together, but sadly it wasn't to be."[13]

After the turn of the century, Batman surfaced in original audio productions created for free internet download. Pendant Productions, an internet-based audio theater group founded by Jeffrey Bridges, got its start when it created a *Star Trek* fan show in 2004. In January 2005, it began producing *Superman: The Last Son of Krypton* as a monthly 15-minute show. Given the popularity of the Superman broadcast, Pendant produced other shows based on DC Comics characters, *Batman: The Ace of Detectives, Wonder Woman: Champion of Themyscira* and *Supergirl: Lost Daughter of Krypton. Batman: The Ace of Detectives* began podcasting February 7, 2006, with Batman helping Superman stop a Bizarro clone who appears in Gotham. In the ongoing monthly series, Seth Adam Sher starred as Batman/Bruce Wayne and Scott Vinnacombe as Robin/Tim Drake. Dick Grayson, the previous Robin, now called Nightwing, was played by Mike Winters. As of this writing, the Pendant Productions series is still ongoing.

While Batman never managed to secure his own series during radio's Golden Age, his frequent appearances on *The Adventures of Superman*, along with the Batman comic books and syndicated newspaper strip, helped keep the character thriving into the late 1940s. Soon, he would be back on movie screens, in a second action-packed serial.

---

1   Merrill, Gary, with John and Jean Cole, *Bette, Rita, and the Rest of My Life: An Autobiography*, © 1988 Lance Tapley Publisher, Augusta, Maine, p. 78

2   —, "Baby Orchestra Makes Debut Here," *The New York Times*, May 17, 1933, p. 15

3   —, "The Openings", *The New York Times*, Oct. 4, 1942, p. X1

4   Merrill, Gary, with John and Jean Cole, *Bette, Rita, and the Rest of My Life: An Autobiography*, © 1988 Lance Tapley Publisher, Augusta, Maine, p. 68

5   Ibid., p. 78

6   Daniels, Les, *Batman: The Complete History*, ©1999 DC Comics, Chronicle Books, San Francisco, p. 59

7   —"Resolution Signed by President to Give Bob Hope a Gold Medal," *The New York Times*, June 14, 1962, p. 67

8   —"Stacy Harris, 54, Actor On Radio, Stage and TV," *The New York Times*, Mar 14, 1973, p. 46

9   Luther, Paul, "Inside Radio," *Evening Times*, Cumberland, Maryland, Monday, August 18, 1947

10   Luther, Paul, "Inside Radio," *Evening Times*, Cumberland, Maryland, Wednesday, March 24, 1948

11   Power, Ty, "It's Going to Be a Hot Time in Ol' Gotham Tonight!," http://freespace.virgin.net/ty.po/Knightfall.html, accessed Aug. 2, 2009, 10:11 AM

12   Ibid.

13   Ibid.

Chapter Four:
BATMAN AND BOSSMAN

*"Accepting a role in Batman may not have been financially lucrative,
but typical of my dad, the role probably amused him."[1]*
—Bob Hanks, son of Robert Lowery

"To me, the greatest all-time producer of serials was Sam Katzman," said Pierce Lyden, an actor who racked up hundreds of film credits playing villains in Westerns. "The 'Bossman,' as Sam was known to his friends, was the most prolific serial producer around," added Lyden. "He kept the wolf from my door many years. He was loyal and easy to work for. He always remembered the supporting actors, his stock company."[2]

Sam Katzman was the best at what he did, which was to produce movies so cheaply and quickly that it would be nearly impossible for them to lose money. Born into a poor Jewish family in New York City on July 7, 1901, Katzman first became involved in the film industry at age 13. He started at Fox Studios in Fort Lee, New Jersey as an errand boy. Working his way up through the ranks, he eventually became an assistant director, but was let go in 1933 when Fox instituted cutbacks. Undeterred, Katzman set out to make a film on his own. He enlisted his friend John Wayne to star, promising to pay him after the film was distributed. He also rounded up studio space the same way. He made *His Private Secretary*, which he also wrote, in six days. It turned a quick profit, earning the $13,000 it cost to make and allowing Katzman to pay off Wayne, the other actors, and the studio.[3] Katzman was now a producer. Throughout the rest of the 1930s, he made a number of films—mostly Westerns—for poverty row companies. In the 1940s, he landed at Monogram, where he developed the popular East Side Kids series and produced mystery and horror films starring Bela Lugosi.

Katzman began producing serials at Columbia in 1945, while still also working for Monogram. His first serial for Columbia was *Brenda Starr, Reporter*, starred Joan Woodbury as the comic strip heroine. In typical Katzman fashion, the 13-chapter serial completed filming in just 21 days.[4] That same year, Rudolph Flothow—who first brought Batman to the screen—produced his final Columbia serial, *The Monster and the Ape*. Once Katzman began producing for Columbia, Flothow concentrated on producing low-budget installments of the *Crime Doctor, Boston Blackie* and *The Whistler* series. Katzman, meanwhile, produced low-budget features, the *Jungle Jim* series (starring ex-Tarzan Johnny Weissmuller), and all of the studio's serials. Katzman churned out 32 serials from 1945 to 1956, with the chapter plays appearing on 6,500 movie screens in the U.S. every weekend.[5] The serials and programmers were good for Katzman; by the end of the 1940s, his yearly income consistently topped $100,000.[6] While others might have had ambitions to make more artistic A-pictures, Katzman was content to crank out his B-movies, saying "Let the other guy get ulcers."[7]

In 1948, Katzman succeeded where others had failed when he brought the popular comic book hero Superman to movie screens as a live-action hero. Starring Kirk Alyn as the Man of Steel, *Superman* became one of the top-grossing chapter-plays of all time. Flush with success, Katzman contacted National Comics to secure the rights to their next most popular comic book character, Batman. Negotiations with National's Harry Donenfeld began in October 1948, and the producer and Donenfeld soon reached a deal.[8]

Many of the principals of the *Superman* serial were also involved with the new Batman production. Spencer Gordon Bennet, who had a reputation as the ace of serial directors, was hired to helm the picture, while *Superman* writers Royal K. Cole and George Plympton wrote the script, from an adaptation by Joseph F. Poland. As with the 1943 *Batman* serial, the writers chose not to use any of the villains familiar to readers of Batman comic books, and instead came up with a new nemesis, the Wizard, a black-hooded mastermind of a criminal gang out to steal a remote-control device developed for the government by Professor Hammil. Unlike the earlier serial, however, this script did include Commissioner Gordon, as well as a Lois Lane-type character recently introduced into the comic books, Vicki Vale. Bob Kane maintained that he based Vicki Vale, who made her debut in *Batman* # 49 (October/November 1948), on Marilyn Monroe, whom Kane reportedly met at the wrap party for the 1943 serial and ran into again when he came to Hollywood for the 1949 serial. However, like all Kane stories, this has to be taken with a grain of salt; Monroe would have been all of 17 years old in 1943, and wouldn't make her film debut until four years later. While it is possible that Dick Sprang, who drew the Batman comics in the '40s, could have used photos of Monroe for reference while drawing Vicki Vale, truthfully, the character bears no resemblance to the actress.

When Kane came to Los Angeles for Batman's sophomore cinematic outing, he involved himself more directly in the casting of the dynamic duo, having been disappointed with the choice of Lewis Wilson for the first serial. He was pleased when he learned that Katzman had given the role of Batman to Robert Lowery, an actor who had just starred in a musical Katzman produced at Columbia, *Mary Lou* (1948). According to his book *Batman & Me*, Kane thought the 35-year-old Lowery was more athletic and had better acting skills than Wilson.[9]

With his dark, wavy hair, Cupid's-bow lips, heavy-lidded eyes, and a sonorous voice, Robert Lowery did seem like a good choice to play the dual roles of Bruce Wayne and Batman. Like the comic book hero, Lowery was tall (6'1") and athletic, and had a light, joking demeanor that masked a history of personal tragedies. Born Robert Larkin Hanks in Kansas City, Missouri on October 17, 1913, he was a descendant of Abraham Lincoln's mother, Nancy Hanks. His father, Roscoe Hanks, was a Kansas City attorney and oil investor, and his mother, Leah Thompson, was a concert pianist and organist.

As a teen, Robert showed great promise as an athlete. Following high school, he became a boxer, a baseball player for the minor-league Kansas City Blues team, and even a football star. Football proved to be one sport too many; a play gone wrong left him with a broken pelvis, effectively ending his athletic career. When his injury healed, he took a physically challenging job in a paper factory. Not long after, his father died. It was the height of the Great Depression, and Robert was now responsible for taking care of his mother. Despite the lost opportunities and dashed dreams, Robert remained hopeful. His mother felt that his good looks and pleasant singing voice would open doors for him. She took her son to Hollywood, where he began singing with local dance bands and studying acting at the Lila Bliss studio. It wasn't long before a talent scout spotted him and put him under contract to 20th Century Fox.[10]

When he arrived at Fox in 1936, the studio changed his name first to Steven Randall and then to Robert Lowery. He showed up in a succession of bit parts, including playing a juror in John Ford's *Young Mr. Lincoln* (1939); the studio's publicity department got mileage out of having an actual descendant of Abraham Lincoln appearing in a Lincoln biopic. Ford was pleased enough with him to cast him in his next picture, *Drums Along the Mohawk*. He had better roles in Fox's programmers, like *Charlie Chan on Broadway* (1937) and *Charlie Chan's Murder Cruise* (1940). He also became friends with one of Fox's biggest stars, Tyrone Power, with whom he was featured in five films, beginning with 1938's *Alexander's Ragtime Band* and including the classic 1940 remake of *The Mark of Zorro*. Lowery's son Robert Hanks recalled, "Tyrone and my dad were best friends and spent virtually every waking second together playing tennis, racing their cars (Power had a Cord, my father a beautiful Darrin convertible) and eating my grandmother's Texas chili. Dad lived in Laurel Canyon on Wonderland Avenue at the time and I understood from him that they'd have a few drinks and act out their respective roles. I don't think, however, my dad's take as Bruce Wayne/ Batman was influenced by Power's Zorro. My dad had a more relaxed approach to acting, whereas Power was far more intense in his interpretation of roles—no question about that."[11]

While Power's career soared in the 1940s, Lowery worked steadily in films of varying quality, with his most notable roles occurring in *Tarzan's Desert Mystery* (1943) with Johnny Weissmuller and *The Mummy's Ghost* (1944) with Lon Chaney, Jr. "Dad was not particularly busy in the late 1940's," said Robert Hanks, "doing a series of actioners for PRC and Republic as well as Monogram, trying to pay off his debts and a big mortgage on a house in Laurel Canyon." He also had alimony payments from his first marriage to Vivian Wilcox, which lasted from 1941 to 1944, and his second marriage to Rusty Farrell, which lasted 17 months, ending in 1948. By the time he was approached to play Batman, Lowery was apparently not worried about the possible effect playing the role would have on his career; he was just interested in working. "My take on this is that he was offered the role principally, and took it on a lark," said Hanks.[12]

Casting Robin proved more difficult. Kane suggested that they should find a young boy of 18 who looked 16 for the role, but Katzman had already decided on an actor—Johnny Duncan. Duncan was born December 7, 1923 on a farm in Centre, Kansas, not far from Robert Lowery's hometown of Kansas City, Missouri. As a child, Duncan danced for pennies at a local bar, saving enough—he claimed—to help his family make payments on their farm during the dark days of the Depression. He eventually opened a dance studio, teaching tap dancing to the local youngsters. One night, while performing a tap dance act at Kansas City's Tower Theater, he was approached by a scout from 20th Century Fox who offered to sign him to a contract at $50 a week—more money than the farm generated. The family sold everything and moved west, arriving at Fox just two years after Robert Lowery and his mother. Like Lowery, Duncan found himself in a steady stream of programmers, occasionally landing a small part in a big film, such as the radio operator in *Action in the North Atlantic* (1943), a war film starring Humphrey Bogart, or as "Jitterbug" in *Thirty Seconds Over Tokyo* (1944). While he was visiting a friend at the Hal Roach Studios, Sam Katzman saw him and offered to pay him more money than Fox. When Duncan's Fox contract ran out, he went to work for Katzman at Monogram, appearing in the producer's East Side Kids comedies. He also made a film with Robert Lowery at Monogram, 1943's *Campus Rhythm*.[13]

At 26, Duncan was nearly a decade older than Kane's ideal. When Katzman first mentioned Duncan to Bob Kane, the Batman creator felt the actor would be too old to play Robin. He pressed Katzman into issuing a casting call for the part. Over the next couple of weeks, Kane and Katzman saw over three hundred juvenile actors, but still felt none were suitable. Finally, Katzman called Duncan—who was on his honeymoon—and told him to come in for an audition wearing slacks with cuffs rolled up, an open shirt, and uncombed hair, so he would look as young as possible. Then Katzman revealed that the call was for the role of Robin in a Batman serial. Duncan, a fan of the *Batman* comic books, was thrilled.[14]

"So I walked in the casting office to meet Bob Kane," said Duncan. "I opened the office door and Sam and Bob Kane were there. Sam was sitting behind his desk as usual, smoking his big old cigar, and he didn't tell Bob Kane who I was. He said, 'Here's the guy you might want to see.' Before I could close the door, Bob Kane got up, walked over to me quickly and grabbed my hand, and said, 'I don't know your name, but you're Robin from now on.' Sam Katzman sat there and laughed."[15] Duncan signed his contract on January 31, 1949—just two days before shooting was due to begin.[16]

Duncan wasn't the only late addition to the cast. Two days before his signing, *The Los Angeles Times* announced that Jane Adams had been cast in the role of Vicki Vale.[17] Like Duncan and Lowery, Adams had come to Hollywood from the heartland after first pursuing a musical career. Born Betty Jane Bierce in San Antonio, Texas on August 7, 1921, Adams had been offered a full scholarship to study violin at Juilliard, but she had other ideas. First she went to California. "I got my training at the Pasadena Playhouse for four years," said Adams. "I took stage design, stage makeup, French, voice and diction. We performed in everything from Greek tragedy to classic comedies."[18]

Next, Adams went to New York. "I just took some little pictures with me and I thought well, I'll just see what happens," recalled Adams. She took her photos to the Harry Conover Modeling Agency, though at 5'3" she was deemed too short for a modeling career. "I went in and all the girls were six-foot-two and fashion models," she said. "And so I did head modeling. And I worked every day. I mean, I had more work than the fashion models, because there were so few head models. And I did a lot of the ads in the magazines for soap and all kinds of things." Adams found a place to live in a hotel for women. "It was a very respectable place for very young actresses to live, and it was at 62nd and Lexington, I think. And I did one color photo for a very famous photographer there, and he asked me if I'd care to work on spec. And I said yes, I'd be happy to. And he took this picture." The picture ended up being a double-page spread in *Esquire* magazine. "And through that," said Adams, "Walter Wanger called me to California to test and I got a very nice contract." Adams tested for the lead role in *Salome, Where She Danced*, but she was not a dancer; the part eventually went to Yvonne De Carlo.[19] Instead, Adams ended up with an uncredited bit part and a Universal Pictures contract. "The fact that I'd been on the stage and could remember lines and took everything seriously was to my benefit," said Adams. "So, I got stuck in Westerns for a while because I could learn the scripts quickly. But I did sixteen Westerns at Universal and a few elsewhere. That was fun. I liked it. The only girl with two hundred men—what young woman wouldn't like that, you know? I got a lot of attention."[20]

Adams had also experienced tragedy in her life. During World War II, she married a Navy pilot who, sadly, was killed in action on his first mission. After appearing as Nina the hunchback in Universal's *House of Dracula* in 1945, she wed Tom Turnage, an Army Major General. His career kept the couple on the move, so she retired from acting until he was sent to Korea. *Batman and Robin* marked one of her first roles upon her return to Hollywood.[21] "I suppose they looked at some of my rushes and things, and they must have thought I was right for the part," she said.[22]

For the role of Commissioner Gordon, Katzman cast Lyle Talbot. One of the busiest character actors then working, Pittsburg, Pennsylvania-born Talbot had already appeared in over 100 movies, including playing the title role in the Katzman-produced serial *Chick Carter, Detective* (1946) and a supporting role in the Katzman serial *The Vigilante: Fighting Hero of the West* (1947), which was adapted from a comic book hero appearing in National's *Action Comics*.

Another accomplished character actor, Eric Wilton, played Alfred, the butler. Tall, thin and distinguished, Wilton had made a career of playing assorted butlers, chauffeurs, waiters and desk clerks in nearly 200 films since his screen debut in 1928. However, this *Batman* serial gave Alfred much less to do than the previous one.

Shooting began February 2, 1949.[23] For Lowery and Duncan, as for Lewis Wilson and Douglas Croft before them, the costumes were a nuisance. The new Batman uniform sported a simple cloth belt instead of the previous film's more authentic-looking utility belt, and the cowl, though tighter fitting around the lower part of Lowery's head, still featured devil horns affixed to it instead of bat-like ears. Robin's cape now appeared to be black instead of the traditional yellow. In reality, both Robin's cape and Batman's cape and cowl were made of crimson cloth, which would photograph better on black-and-white film stock. Robin's domino mask was still of the dime-store variety. Lowery, according to his son, found his outfit "uncomfortable, badly tailored, hot and airless."[24] In an interview with Jan Alan Henderson for *Filmfax* magazine, Johnny Duncan said, "The tights would keep stretching out and drooping, because they were cotton tights. We were always pulling the tights up...The cowl dropped down over Bob's nose, and had little slits for eyes holes. For the ears, they had two tubes of cotton to keep them standing up. Well, the damn ears would start flopping like a dog's, so they had to put scotch tape on them. Every day we had to put new Scotch tape on those ears, sometimes three or four times a day."[25] The only bright spot, according to Duncan, was their boots; a Hollywood boot maker had fashioned six pairs each for them, and they were "comfort beyond belief."[26]

Lowery had other struggles with the form-fitting costume, according to his son. "He did have a weight problem of sorts. He often went without eating for days and worked out strenuously at the Hollywood Athletic Club and YMCA to get the pounds off so he'd look great."[27]

For a scene of Robin running across the top of some train cars, Johnny Duncan was dissatisfied to see that his stunt double was a balding, pot-bellied 50-year-old, so he recommended a buddy of his, Howard Kaiser, to be his stunt double. With his blonde hair dyed and curled, Kaiser did all of Duncan's stunts from then on. Paul Stader doubled Robert Lowery. The previous year, Stader doubled Kirk Alyn in the *Superman* serial, and also worked steadily as Johnny Weissmuller's stuntman in the Katzman-produced *Jungle Jim* programmers.[28]

House Peters, Jr., part of the Katzman stock company, played Earl, one of the Wizard's henchmen, in the final eight installments. He recalled, "Some of the exteriors for *Batman and Robin* were filmed on the site of an old oil refinery in the vicinity of 125th Street and Western Avenue in south L.A. We used this locale for at least two different chapters in the serial: a synthetic diamond factory and a research plant. There were catwalks and metal steps along the outside of the buildings; ideal for an action serial. We also did location filming in the industrial section of downtown L.A. Columbia leased a vacant multi-story building to serve as the interior of the gang's hideout. Inside were hallways and offices which the director, Spence Bennet, put to good use. This quiet-spoken director had made many serials by then and generally was ahead of schedule."[29]

Bennet earned a reputation for not shooting second takes unless critically necessary, a condition partly forced on him by the financial restrictions. "Budgets were usually around $8,000 an episode," said Bennet, who usually did one rehearsal and a single take. "The minute I would finish a scene, I knew exactly what the next setup was going to be. I would have it all mapped out. I kept the crew busy. I don't know any other director who cut in the camera as I did. I said to Katzman, 'You aren't paying me anything on these pictures. I'm saving you my salary on the lab bill.' And I did."[30]

Johnny Duncan claimed that on an average day, the *Batman and Robin* crew would shoot an astounding 55 set-ups, about ten times more than what was shot daily on an A-list feature. "Remember, a 15-chapter serial had a script as thick as three phone books," said Duncan. "Bob Lowery and I would get to the set at 5:30 in the morning. It was so damn cold, because we shot it in the wintertime, and we'd get in these tights. When you wear tights and a mask for two or three months, and you're supposed to think L.A. is Gotham City and make a movie-going audience believe it through your acting, and you don't take off the mask and tights 'til 8:00 or 9:00 at night—you start to believe it!" According to Duncan, he ended up making $1,100 a week in overtime, enough for him to buy a new 1950 Cadillac Coupe de Ville with just his overtime pay.[31]

The Bossman kept a close eye on the production. "Sam Katzman was a character," said House Peters, Jr. "He was always on the set, smoking a cigar—he was a great one for visiting and sitting around the set and chewing the fat. And he had a walking stick with an electric battery in it. He got a great kick out of using that on

The Wizard's henchmen get the drop on Batman (Robert Lowery) and Robin (Johnny Duncan) in this scene from producer Sam Katzman's 1949 Batman and Robin serial (Columbia Pictures/Photofest, © Columbia Pictures).

people, especially girls. He'd approach them with it and jab their knee or their leg in the back!"[32]

The crew completed filming on February 28, 1949, after a whirlwind 26 days.[33] Soon, the studio set up a local publicity tour for Lowery and Duncan. "We went to places like North Hollywood and Torrance—little outlying towns of Los Angeles County," said Duncan. "They would announce us at the theater a week before we would make the appearance. We wouldn't go in our costumes because, hell, we never wanted to see those things again. All we wore was sport clothes. The kids would line up for two or three blocks, and they used to have traffic cops to control the crowds."[3]

Robert Lowery did make at least one personal appearance in the Batman costume, at least momentarily. His son Robert Hanks said, "In New Orleans, my dad made a personal appearance as Batman on behalf of his studio. My mother and dad stayed in the French Quarter, and had a small wrought iron veranda overlooking Bourbon Street from their apartment. One night, my father was pretty much in his cups—well, drunk—and he decided to don his Batman uniform and step out on the veranda. He did, to much applause from a group of very young African-American kids on the street. Well, he decided to take it one step further and remove the costume altogether, and stepped out on the veranda naked. My mother tried to stop him, but she was laughing so hard, and he was so solid and strong, like a tree, that she couldn't stop him. I understand that he pantomimed wearing his costume and cape while bare naked, which further delighted the residents. True—at least according to my mother and a friend of his who also witnessed this spectacle."[35]

In his book *Batman & Me*, Bob Kane wrote that when he ran into Lowery at a party in Hollywood several years later, Lowery didn't seem too pleased to see him. When Kane asked why, Lowery reportedly said that the serial had been so successful that he had been typecast as Batman and couldn't get another role.[36] Upon hearing the anecdote, Robert Hanks said, "No truth to that at all. He had a great time and enjoyed it. We never talked at length about his role, but what he did share with me sounded like fun."[37]

Jane Adams continued acting for another four years after *Batman & Robin*, appearing in Westerns and TV series such as *The Cisco Kid, Adventures of Wild Bill Hickock, The Adventures of Kit Carson* and *Adventures of Superman*. Lyle Talbot added another hundred credits to his resume after completing his role as Commissioner Gordon, including playing the villain, Luthor, in the 1950 serial *Atom Man vs. Superman*. He is best remembered by baby-boomers as Ozzie's friend "Joe Randolph" in *The Adventures of Ozzie and Harriet*. He retired after appearing in a 1987 episode of *Newhart*, and passed away in San Francisco on March 2, 1996, at age 94.

After playing Robin, the Boy Wonder, Johnny Duncan had an amazing career. How many actors can claim to have worked with both Stanley Kubrick and Ed Wood? Besides appearing in Wood's *Plan 9 From Outer Space* (1959), which has earned a reputation as one of the worst films ever made, he performed a role in *Spartacus* (1960), which would have been his final onscreen appearance, if it hadn't ended up on the cutting room floor. The filmmakers needed someone to get beheaded by Kirk Douglas in a battle scene. Duncan, wearing a fake torso and fake head, played the soon-to-die solder. But the effect, which drenched Douglas in stage blood, proved too bloody for the censors, so out it came. It was Duncan's last work in the film industry, in a career whose highpoints included appearances with future president Ronald Reagan in *Bedtime for Bonzo* (1951) and with Humphry Bogart in *The Caine Mutiny* (1954), as well as showing off his dancing skills in *Running Wild* (1955), *Rock Around the Clock* (1956) and *Juke Box Rhythm* (1959).

Robert Lowery's superhero career didn't end with Batman. In 1956, he starred in an episode of *Adventures of Superman*, "The Deadly Rock," where he played a friend of Clark Kent's who fainted when confronted with Kryptonite, yet acquired all of Superman's powers while he was unconscious. Throughout the 1950s, Lowery was a reliable actor in low-budget films such as 1950's *I Shot Billy the Kid*, in which he played Pat Garrett opposite Don "Red" Barry as the infamous outlaw. Branching out into TV, he appeared on episodes of *Cowboy G-Men, My Little Margie, The Gene Autry Show, Death Valley Days* and *Judge Roy Bean*, as well as prestigious anthology series like *General Electric Theater* and *Playhouse 90*. In the 1956-57 season, he starred in his own series, *Circus Boy*, with a pre-*Monkees* Mickey Dolenz. He alternated between roles in TV shows and movies in the 1960s, including a part in the John Wayne Western *McClintock!* (1963). After appearing in another short-lived TV series, *Pistols 'n' Petticoats* (1966-1967), he retired from acting. The day after Christmas, 1971, Lowery spoke on the phone with the woman who had brought him to Hollywood thirty-five years earlier—his mother. During the call, Lowery suffered an apparent heart attack. His mother called for an ambulance, but by the time it arrived, Lowery lay dead in his Yucca Avenue apartment.[38]

Asked for his best memories of his father, Robert Hanks said, "His sense of humor and his vast intelligence and knowledge of just about everything."[39] His father's legacy, said Hanks, was "not to take the world so seriously as to be an asshole to others. Enjoy life, find something you love doing, and do it well. He never took acting as a serious career as compared to his father's career as an oil attorney. He lived humility and kindness to all."[40]

As for the Bossman, Sam Katzman continued producing low-budget fare for the next two decades. He was profiled for *Time* magazine in December 1952, in an article titled "Jungle Sam" in which he made no apologies for his low-brow legacy, saying, "If you were to X-ray every Oscar, you'd find every one of them has an ulcer inside."[41] After making a slew of sci-fi potboilers, crime dramas and Jungle Jim films in the 50s, he produced a couple of movies starring Elvis Presley and several hot-rod films in the 1960s. His last film was 1972's *The Loners*, a biker flick starring Dean Stockwell. A year later, on August 4, 1973, the Bossman passed away.

---

1 Interview with Bob Hanks, conducted June 4, 2009

2 Magers, Boyd, "Sam Katzman," *Western Clippings Serial Report*, Western Clippings website, http://www.westernclippings.com/sr/serial report_2009_08.shtml, accessed Aug. 2, 2009

3 Wiener, Willard L., "The Happiest Man in Hollywood: Sam Katzman, King of the Cliffhangers, May be Small Potatoes, but His Serials are Every Man's Meat," *Collier's* magazine, Dec. 30, 1950, p. 69

4 Magers, Boyd, "Sam Katzman," *Western Clippings Serial Report*, Western Clippings website, http://www.westernclippings.com/sr/serial report_2009_08.shtml, accessed Aug. 2, 2009

5 Wiener, Willard L., "The Happiest Man in Hollywood: Sam Katzman, King of the Cliffhangers, May be Small Potatoes, but His Serials are Every Man's Meat," *Collier's* magazine, Dec. 30, 1950, p. 32

6 *Ibid.*, p. 69

7 *Ibid.*, p. 32

8 Schallert, Edwin, "Hollywood Will Assist Israel Studio Project; Video Filmers Organize," *The Los Angeles Times*, Oct. 11, 1948, pg. A7

9 Kane, Bob with Tom Andrae, *Batman & Me*, © 1989 Eclipse Books, Forestville, California, p. 129

10 Interview with Bob Hanks, conducted June 4, 2009

11 *Ibid.*

12 *Ibid.*

13 Henderson, Jan Alan, "Robin Unmasked! Secrets From a Low-Budget Batcave with Johnny Duncan," *Filmfax No. 103*, July/Sept. 2004, p. 61

14 *Ibid.*, p. 64

15 *Ibid.*, p. 65

16 —, "Duncan Into Serial," *Daily Variety*, Feb. 1, 1949, p. 3

17 Schallert, Edwin, "Preston Incorporates for Baseball Feature; Mary Wickes Returns," *The Los Angeles Times*, Jan. 29, 1949, pg. 9

18 Fitzgerald, Mike, "An Interview with Jane Adams," *Western Clippings* website, http://www.westernclippings.com/interview/jane adams_interview.shtml, accessed Aug. 2, 2009

19 *Ibid.*

20 Interview with Jane Adams, conducted August 6, 2009.

21 Schallert, Edwin, "Preston Incorporates for Baseball Feature; Mary Wickes Returns," *The Los Angeles Times*, Jan. 29, 1949, pg. 9

22 Interview with Jane Adams, conducted August 6, 2009.

23 Schallert, Edwin, "Preston Incorporates for Baseball Feature; Mary Wickes Returns," *The Los Angeles Times*, Jan. 29, 1949, pg. 9

24 Interview with Bob Hanks, conducted June 4, 2009

25 Henderson, Jan Alan, "Robin Unmasked! Secrets From a Low-Budget Batcave with Johnny Duncan," *Filmfax No. 103*, July/Sept. 2004, pgs. 65 and 134

26 *Ibid.*, pg. 65

27 Interview with Bob Hanks, conducted June 4, 2009

28 Henderson, Jan Alan, "Robin Unmasked! Secrets From a Low-Budget Batcave with Johnny Duncan," *Filmfax No. 103*, July/Sept. 2004, pg. 134

29 Peters, Jr., House, *Another Side of Hollywood*, © 2000, Empire Publishing, Madison, N.C.

30 Magers, Boyd, "Sam Katzman," *Western Clippings Serial Report*, Western Clippings website, http://www.westernclippings.com/sr/serialreport_2009_08.shtml, accessed Aug. 2, 2009

31 Henderson, Jan Alan, "Robin Unmasked! Secrets From a Low-Budget Batcave with Johnny Duncan," *Filmfax No. 103*, July/Sept. 2004, pg. 65

32 Weaver, Tom, "The Serials of House Peters, Jr.," *Western Clippings* website, http://www.westernclippings.com/sr/serialreport_2009_07.shtml, accessed Aug. 2, 2009, 10:32 PM

33 —, "Data for Bulletin of Screen Achievement Records," filed March 16, 1949

34 Henderson, Jan Alan, "Robin Unmasked! Secrets From a Low-Budget Batcave with Johnny Duncan," *Filmfax No. 103*, July/Sept. 2004, pg. 134

35 Interview with Bob Hanks, conducted June 4, 2009

36 Kane, Bob with Tom Andrae, *Batman & Me*, © 1989 Eclipse Books, Forestville, California, pg. 129

37 Interview with Bob Hanks, conducted June 4, 2009

38 —, "Robert Lowery, Veteran Film, TV Actor, Dies," *The Los Angeles Times*, Dec. 27, 1971, p. A27

39 Interview with Bob Hanks, conducted June 4, 2009

40 *Ibid.*

41 —, Cinema: Jungle Sam, *Time Magazine*, Dec. 1, 1952

Chapter Five:
KNIGHT LITE

*"The main thing I strive for is to overlay with style what is
basically a pretty square character. You might say I'm trying
to invest Dickensian surroundings with an Oscar Wilde flavor."*
—*Adam West*[1]

CAMPING

In the early morning of March 16, 1966, astronauts Neil Armstrong and David Scott boarded their spacecraft, Gemini VIII, atop a Titan II rocket on a launch pad at Cape Kennedy, Florida. At 11:41 A.M., 101 minutes after another rocket carrying an unmanned spacecraft called Agena had lifted off, the Titan roared to life and launched the men into space. Their mission was to rendezvous with the Agena, which had entered a circular orbit 185 miles above the earth, and dock with it in space.

About six-and-a-half hours after lift-off, Gemini VIII acquired a radar lock on Agena, 181 miles distant. The spacecraft closed on the Agena, with Armstrong reducing speed to steer Gemini's sloping nose into Agena's docking collar. The first orbital docking in history was accomplished.

Then things got interesting.

After being linked to Agena for about 30 minutes, the combined spaceships suddenly started to pitch and buck. Armstrong tried to back the Gemini away from Agena, but couldn't. Coupled together, the two spacecraft rolled continuously—a situation the astronauts had never faced in pre-flight simulations. They finally undocked from Agena, but one of the eight thrusters that controlled Gemini VIII's movements was now stuck. The ship spun even faster, making one revolution per second, a motion so violent the men faced possible blackout. Armstrong hit the reentry thruster system, normally used to control descent back into earth's atmosphere. The gambit worked; stability was restored. After that harrowing experience, NASA terminated the flight. Armstrong and Scott were ordered to come home. Their spaceship splashed into the ocean off the coast of Japan at 7:23 P.M. Pacific Standard Time.[2]

TV networks NBC and CBS cancelled their regular evening programs (including *The Virginian* on NBC and—appropriately enough—*Lost in Space* on CBS) to devote airtime to news coverage of the emergency splashdown. ABC was more cautious. Between 7:30 and 8 P.M., the network interrupted their programming only three times, for a total of 11-1/2 minutes.[3] The result? Their switchboard lit up with three hundred angry phone calls during the half hour, growing to more than a thousand by 10 P.M.[4] And why were ABC viewers so upset?

Because the network had cut into *Batman*.

Roger Arm, a 20-year-old from Queens, complained, "I was plenty mad because I missed out on Batman finding the clues and I missed out on the fighting."[5]

One man, calling from Detroit, said, "What are you trying to do? I've got seven kids and they're all howling and screaming."[6] Commenting on the outcry in *The Los Angeles Times*, humorist Art Buchwald, with tongue in cheek, wrote, "It gives one great faith in the American people, and shows the power of entertainment over news in TV programming."[7]

It took more than a run-of-the-mill TV series to provoke this kind of outcry. *Batman* exploded onto television screens in 1966 as a cultural phenomenon, a merchandising bonanza, and—one might say—a work of art, born out of a perfect storm of influences.

The first was the dominance of television in the 1960s. By 1949, when the *Batman and Robin* serial was released, the movie theater and radio were no longer the pre-eminent hubs of pop culture in the lives of Americans. In 1949, for the first time, the four television networks (NBC, CBS, ABC and DuMont) covered a majority of American households with their signals. The dominance of TV was just beginning. In 1946, less than half of one percent of Americans owned televisions, but by 1955, over half of all households owned at least one. Now, Americans no longer had to go to their local cinema and pay to be entertained—they could watch TV for free.

Television was a death knell for the movie serials. The last one made was 1956's *Blazing the Overland Trail*, produced by Sam Katzman and directed by Spencer Bennet. In typical Katzman threadbare fashion, it mined footage from three previously produced Western serials. The kind of entertainment for children that the serials once afforded migrated to the new medium of television, where Superman, portrayed by George Reeves, thrived in the 1950s.

Besides being blamed for the demise of movie serials, television was also thought to be the primary cause of declining comic book sales. Whereas estimates of National Comics' annual comic book sales stood at over 8 million in 1951, by 1962 sales dropped to 6,650,058 comics.[8] The drop in sales was also exacerbated by the anti-comics fervor spurred by Dr. Frederick Wertham. In 1954, Wertham published *Seduction of the Innocent*, a book that pointed out the violent nature of many comics, the seemingly amoral content and the advertising that often promoted guns, knives and other weapons kids could order through the mail. Wertham blamed comic books for a nationwide rise in juvenile delinquency while labeling Wonder Woman a lesbian and Batman and Robin homosexuals.

After Wertham testified before Estes Kefauver's Senate Subcommittee on Juvenile Delinquency, the comic book industry, fearing censorship, adopted the self-regulatory Comics Code. The Code provided that "good shall in all cases triumph over evil," and that "females shall be drawn realistically without exaggeration of any physical qualities." Within three years of the Code's enactment, 24 of the original 29 subscribing members went out of business.[9] The controversial horror and crime comics of EC disappeared, and the type of superhero comics published by National Periodical Publications became even more simplistic. During the 1950s and early 1960s, the Batman comics became less like film noir crime thrillers and more like sci-fi tinged fairy tales, with Batman and Robin time traveling, turning into aliens, becoming giant-sized, or presented as crime-fighting mummies. There were also additions to Batman's crime-fighting family, in the form of Ace the Bat-Hound, Bat-

Woman, Bat-Girl, and Bat-Mite, a Batman fan who just happened to be an alien from another dimension. The Comics Code erased all traces of Batman as a revenge-driven vigilante. Comics were now sanitized, homogenized, and safe for kids.

The consequences of these changes did not bode well for the Caped Crusader. Sales dropped steadily each year. Editors struggled to find ideas that could inspire covers that would compel kids to purchase the comics. The more absurd the cover, the higher the sales. This led to a vicious circle: someone needed to come up with a story to match the cover, and the stories rarely lived up to the ludicrous cover art. As a result, the attempt to gain short-term sales led to more and more steady readers getting fed up and abandoning the character because of what they saw as silliness. By 1964, it looked as though National Periodical Publications might pull the plug on its *Batman* comic book title, leaving the Caped Crusader as the star of only one monthly title, *Detective Comics* (Batman was still also continuing in *World's Finest Comics*, where he teamed with Superman).

The live-action series *Adventures of Superman* had ended its television run in 1958, but the show remained a huge success in syndication, often broadcast daily during the afternoon hours when kids returned home from school. Ed Graham, an ex-advertising executive who became a producer of Saturday morning cartoon fare such as *Linus the Lionhearted*, saw the appeal of superheroes in the kids market. He optioned the TV rights to Batman from National Periodical Publications in the early 1960s. Graham envisioned Batman as a live-action show that he hoped would have an extended life in syndication, like *Adventures of Superman*. He struck a deal with CBS to produce a *Batman* TV series for kids that would run on Saturday mornings, and cast 6'2" Los Angeles Rams linebacker Mike Henry as the Caped Crusader. Reportedly, National Periodical Publications arranged for publicity photos of Henry in a Batman outfit, but these have never been made public.

As months passed, CBS failed to put the show into production. Meanwhile, Batman comic sales continued to fall across all three Batman titles, leading some to wonder why the network would even consider making a show with a character that seemed to be fading. With the project stalled, Mike Henry moved on at the end of January 1964, when producer Sy Weintraub tapped him to play Tarzan for a proposed CBS TV series;[10] instead, Weintraub produced three Ape Man movies starring the former linebacker. After the abrupt dismissal of CBS president Jim Aubrey on February 27, 1965, the *Batman* Saturday morning series was scuttled. Graham then took it to NBC, but they passed. Graham's attempts to bring Batman to TV had reached a dead end.

Simultaneously with the near-miss activity in television, Batman experienced a remarkable transformation. In early 1964, with sales falling, Julius Schwartz became the editor of *Detective Comics* and its sister publication, *Batman*. He engineered an overhaul that instituted "the new look." Gone was the angular artwork of Bob Kane's ghost artists; Batman's new lead artist, Carmine Infantino, drew the Caped Crusader in a more realistic way, with a modified costume that enclosed the bat silhouette on his chest in a yellow oval. Schwartz jettisoned Bat-woman, Bat-Girl, Bat-Mite, and Bat-Hound. Time travel and sci-fi fantasies disappeared from the pages; detective stories returned. The first "new look" Batman appeared in *Detective Comics* #327,

Between April and May 1964, Batman underwent a transformation in the comic books. The "new look" not only brought Batman's artwork up to date, but also changed the direction of the stories. Detective Comics #326 artwork by Sheldon Moldoff and Joe Certa; Detective Comics # 327 artwork by Carmine Infantino and Joe Giella. (© 1964 National Periodical Publications/DC Comics).

featuring a new red banner. Robin looked 16-years-old rather than 12, and—in order to introduce a female presence in Wayne Manor and, hopefully, stave off further charges of homosexuality—Alfred the butler died valiantly saving the dynamic duo, soon to be replaced by Dick Grayson's Aunt Harriet.

During this time, another force developed that was beginning to shape the world of comics, a force that would ultimately shape the fate of the industry—collectors. The Academy of Comic Book Arts and Sciences was formed in 1962, changing its name to The Academy of Comic Book Fans and Collectors by the time its charter was ratified by 92 fans in 1963. The Academy began giving an annual Alley Award for comic books and published the fanzine *The Comic Reader*. By 1965, the Academy's membership had grown to two thousand.[11] Like stamps and coins, comic book values rested on their rarity and the demand for them. Wastepaper collection drives during World War II destroyed many comics from the "golden age" of the 1940s. As a result, just over twenty years after they first hit newsstands, early editions of *Batman* and *Superman* fetched as much as $100 apiece.[12] Speaking to *The New York Times* in 1965, National Periodical Publications president Jacob S. Liebowitz said the upsurge in comic book trading grew from pure nostalgia, adding, "Many men in their twenties and thirties are having a rebirth of interest in their costumed fantasy heroes."[13]

As comic book collecting came of age, so did the influence of pop art. A movement that began in Britain in the mid-1950s and in the United States a few years later, pop art was predicated on the idea that the images and items of common culture—comic books, advertising, even cigarette packs and toilet seats—could be considered works of art. Roy Lichtenstein's paintings inspired by comic book panels and Andy Warhol's screen prints of movie stars and Campbell's soup cans became the most famous examples. By the mid-1960s, the influence of pop art could be seen in magazine and billboard advertising.

The Camp movement also gained media attention in the mid-1960s. In the fall 1964 issue of *Partisan Review*, Susan Sontag wrote an article called "Notes on 'Camp'" that was briefly recapped in the "Modern Living" section of *Time* magazine, and later appeared in the Sontag collection *Against Interpretation and Other Essays* (1966). Though some considered Camp—which seemed to revel in things considered to be "so bad they're good"—another label for plain bad taste, Sontag admitted that she was strongly drawn to Camp. "Camp taste is a kind of love, love for human nature," she wrote. "It relishes, rather than judges, the little triumphs and awkward intensities of 'character'...Camp taste identifies with what it is enjoying. People who share this sensibility are not laughing at the thing they label as 'a Camp.' They're enjoying it. Camp is a *tender* feeling."[14]

Thomas Meehan, writing in *The New York Times* in 1965, noted that New York intelligentsia had made a parlor game of labeling things "Camp" or "not Camp," and had divided Pure Camp into subdivisions—high Camp, middle Camp, low Camp, intentional Camp and unintentional Camp. As examples, Meehan listed Virginia Woolf's *Orlando* (high Camp), *Winnie the Pooh* (middle Camp), *Batman* comic books (low Camp), Barbra Streisand (intentional Camp) and Lana Turner in *Love Has Many Faces* (unintentional Camp).[15] Meehan noted that Eric Partridge's *Dictionary of Slang and Uncommon English* said that Camp, in the sense of meaning "pleasantly ostentatious," was part of London street argot as early as 1909.[16] Around 1925, Camp came to be a term for "homosexual" in England. Meehan writes, "This is hastily not to say, however, that all those with Camp tastes are homosexuals or that all homosexuals have Camp taste, but rather, as Miss Sontag put it, that 'homosexuals, by and large, constitute the vanguard—and most articulate audience—of Camp.'"[17] Meehan concludes, "Camp not only involves finding fun and delight in things that others find banal, boring, worthless or hopelessly out-of-date, but also involves a certain amount of parody (especially unconscious parody) and what is colloquially known around New York as 'the put on.' Anarchic, anti-Establishment and often infuriatingly perverse, Camp is frivolous about serious things and serious about frivolous things, celebrating, as Miss Sontag put it, 'the contrast between silly or extravagant content and rich form.'"[18]

While the influence of pop art could be seen in British films of the early 1960s, especially the Beatles' films *A Hard Day's Night* (1964) and *Help!* (1965), and while the James Bond films *Goldfinger* (1964) and *Thunderball* (1965) introduced a Camp sensibility to moviegoers worldwide, it took *Batman* to introduce American TV viewers to a potent concoction of comics, Camp, and pop art all in one.

ORIGIN OF THE SERIES

In the early days of television, there were those who believed it would become a great tool for educating the masses, bringing them cultural programs like operas and Shakespeare plays to which they might otherwise never be exposed. Then there were those who saw the proliferation of game shows, sitcoms, Westerns and violent dramas and pronounced TV a "vast wasteland." William Dozier, who had been involved with television since the early days of its development, saw things another way. Dozier knew that from a network's standpoint, television was all about the commercials, and the surest way to get the largest audience to view a commercial was to appeal to their basest instincts. "Maybe," Dozier told *Los Angeles Times* reporter Charles Champlin, "television is just not supposed to be what we think it ought to be. After all, you don't expect Woolworth's to carry Tiffany merchandise."[19]

A clear insight into Dozier's feelings about the television viewing audience can be gleaned from an editorial he wrote in the July 16, 1967 issue of *The Los Angeles Times*, in which he said, "It is fashionable these days to say television underestimates the taste of the American audience. Nonsense. Time and again it has been proven that the taste of the great majority is pretty low. Given two competing programs, they will invariably watch the bang-up Western or the broad comedy and tune out the show which attempts something better. During my several years tenure as head of production at Screen Gems, one of the series we produced was *Dennis the Menace*, hardly an intellectual milestone. Nor was it intended to be. It was on the air four seasons, and the night it achieved its highest Nielsen rating in four seasons was the night it was opposite the first half hour of *Macbeth*. That was George Schaefer's memorable production with Judith Anderson and Maurice Evans which deserved and won several Emmy Awards. Brilliant as it was, it drove millions of viewers to *Dennis the Menace*, for the first time, and possibly the last. So much for the public appetite for so-called quality television."[20] A few months later, when Dozier addressed the Publicity Club of Chicago, he said that television was "primarily a merchandising medium, not primarily an entertainment medium. It has been allowed to entertain only if it has sold merchandise. There are countless examples of this in operation. At the peak of its success in the ratings, the original *I Love Lucy* show was canceled by Philip Morris when its research demonstrated the show was not reaching cigarette buyers. On the other hand, *Lawrence Welk* has never been a particularly high-rated show, but for a long time has reached an audience which has purchased one hell of a pile of Geritol."[21]

It was this sophisticated man, with a supremely pragmatic approach to television production, who would guide the development of Batman on television. Born in the rolling hills of Omaha, Nebraska on February 13, 1908, Dozier attended Creighton University, then sold real estate in Buffalo, Toronto and Indianapolis before moving to Los Angeles in 1934. There, he joined a talent agency and represented such writers as *Lost Horizon* author James Hilton, *Perry Mason* creator Erle Stanley Gardner, F. Scott Fiztgerald, Dalton Trumbo, Sinclair Lewis, Ketti Frings, and Cornelia Otis Skinner. In February 1941, he became head of the story and writing department at Paramount Pictures, where he stayed for three years before joining RKO Radio

William Dozier at a 4th of July celebration in 1965 (© Deborah Dozier Potter).

Pictures as an assistant to the vice president in charge of production. When his boss fell ill with leukemia, Dozier took over his duties, supervising production of classic films like Alfred Hitchcock's *Notorious* (1946). In 1947, he moved to Universal-International as head of production. He had now married actress Joan Fontaine, and started a production company with her, Rampart Productions, through which he executive produced the films *Letter From an Unknown Woman, Kiss the Blood Off My Hands* and *You Gotta Stay Happy* (all 1948) while still at Universal. Unfortunately, Dozier and Fontaine did not stay happy; after the birth of their daughter, Deborah, the couple divorced in January 1951.

Relocating to New York, Dozier became head of dramatic programming for CBS and was involved in some of the most prestigious anthology series on television, including *Suspense, Danger* and *Studio One*. He also produced the innovative educational series *You Are There*. In 1953, he married actress Ann Rutherford, and two years later returned to Hollywood as west coast director of television programs for CBS. He briefly returned to RKO as vice president in charge of production in 1956, turning out 12 films in a 14 month period. Then he went back to CBS, supervising series such as *Perry Mason, Twilight Zone, Gunsmoke, Playhouse 90* and *Rawhide*.[22]

"My father was a very well-educated man," recalled Dozier's daughter, Deborah Potter. "He read constantly and he was a major debater in college. He wasn't the kind of person you usually find in the film business. In those days, you tended to find people who were more interested in literature than you do today. The medium that my father grew up in wasn't as commercial as it is today. The focus was on trying to recreate culture and put it on television. They put things like Shakespeare on television, and couldn't understand why the ratings were so low. They were opening up a new medium, and they were trying to transfer theater and other mediums they knew to television. It was in its infancy, really, when my father started out in it."[23]

When James Aubrey became president of CBS in 1959, Dozier moved to Screen Gems Inc., the TV subsidiary of Columbia Pictures.[24] "When he was at Screen Gems, the shows that he oversaw were *Hazel, Route 66* and some of the first generation of shows that were made just for television as a commercial medium, and were tailored just for that medium," said Potter. "Television went into another phase then, in the early '60s. *The Donna Reed Show* was one of the series he oversaw. Donna Reed and her husband Tony Owen were very close friends of the family. And then my father was approached by Fox to be head of television for Fox, and Screen Gems wouldn't let him do it. They wouldn't release him from his contract. Not too long after that, Abe Schneider brought in his son Bert Schneider to run Screen Gems and they phased my father out. It was really unkind. But then, you don't get into this business for kindness."[25]

In 1963, Dozier was running his own production company, Greenway Productions (named after the Beverly Hills street on which he lived), and developing TV shows to pitch to the networks. He worked frequently with a young, quick-witted writer named Lorenzo Semple Jr., a New York playwright who also worked in early television as a writer on *The Alcoa Hour* in the 1950s. According to Semple, Dozier "lived in Hollywood but was basically a New Yorker, a highly sophisticated man. He was almost like no other television producer, certainly very few television producers or movie producers. He was an exceptional guy, with a sense of humor, very funny."[26]

Semple had contributed short stories to *The Saturday Evening Post* and *Collier's Weekly* and had two plays staged on Broadway, *Tonight in Samarkand* (1955) and *The Golden Fleecing* (1959). When the latter was produced as the 1961 film *The Honeymoon Machine* by MGM, Semple went West and began writing for television. "Bill Dozier was a producer and I knew him socially," said Semple, "and we tried two or three half-hour comedy pilots that I wrote, and we were unable to sell any of them. So sometime after that, ABC proposed to Bill doing an hour series called *Number One Son* about Charlie Chan's son." The show, according to Semple, would have focused on the famous Chinese detective's son, now a private detective himself in San Francisco. "So I wrote a pilot, an hour script, and I don't think it was the greatest thing I've ever written, but it was adequate," said Semple. "We sent it to ABC, and they liked it. And so we were waiting around, and then about two weeks later, ABC called Bill, and said, 'We are horribly embarrassed, but orders have come down from on high that we don't want to do anything with an ethnic character.' And so that sort of put paid to Charlie Chan. And they said, 'This is very bad of us. And so, we owe you guys one.'"[27]

Semple returned to writing plays, eventually moving with his family to Torremolinos, Spain, far from the hullabaloo of the TV and film industries. Meanwhile, Jacob Liebowitz, president of National Periodical Publications, was looking for ways to gain exposure for the company's most popular comic book heroes to help increase comic book sales. He made deals to bring Superman to Broadway as a live show and to Saturday morning television as an animated character. And though the deal with Ed Graham to do a live action Batman for Saturday morning had fizzled, he was still pursuing the idea of launching a *Batman* TV series similar to *The Adventures of Superman* series of a decade earlier, which was still a moneymaker in continuous syndication.[28]

As early as 1963, ABC-TV vice-president of daytime programming Harve Bennett had been interested in doing a *Batman* TV series as "a kind of a show like Dick Tracy." Bennett proposed the idea to the network's director of program development, Doug Cramer. The idea kicked around for the next two and half years, with the network eventually buying the rights to the character from National Periodical Publications.[29]

Finally pushing forward with a *Batman* series, ABC decided now was the time to make good on an old debt. "I was in New York on a routine business trip, and the Vice-President in Charge of Program Development at ABC, a bright young man named Doug Cramer, asked me to have lunch with him," William Dozier told Canadian Broadcasting Corporation's Fletcher Markle in a TV interview, adding, "and he told me that ABC had recently bought the rights to *Batman*, not knowing exactly what to do with it or how to do it, just having a kind of seat-of-the-pants hunch that it might be a good television series. And he asked me if I would be interested in producing it in my company at 20th Century Fox, and I was little taken aback because I had never had a *Batman* comic book in my hands."[30] Dozier quickly rectified that situation; he bought about a dozen Batman comic books, and boarded a flight back to Hollywood. "And I was sitting in an aisle seat," said Dozier, "doing my homework with five or six copies in my lap, and reading one, not thinking how this would look to somebody, and sure enough a friend of mine who was in the ad agency business in New York who was on the same flight tapped me on the shoulder and he said, 'Well, I guess those scripts do get dull after a while.' And I couldn't tell him why I had a lapful of comic books, because it was a big secret, you know, this approaching series."[31]

"He worked all his life, he worked his way through everything, he didn't have time to read comic books as a kid," said Potter. "And he got on an airplane with this stack of Batman comic books—and my father's very dapper, he was probably very well-dressed, wearing hand-made London shoes and some sort of very expensive Alpaca sweater—anyway, there he is with this stack of comic books, and he was laughing out loud and the stewardess was giving him the strangest looks, and when he was reading the comic books, he had the idea to do the show just like the comic books. He was kind of almost the inventor of camp humor, because it was his idea to do them just like the comic books and not try to make it sexy or romantic or high-tech or anything."[32]

When Bob Kane heard that Dozier was producing Batman, he wrote him a letter: "It seems Batman has caught his second wind and is 'red hot' now," wrote Kane. "Judging from the many articles and unsolicited tributes being paid to us this year, I am sure that it will burn up the TV tubes when my 'cult' of Batman fans tune in. I really feel this is breaking at a most opportune time." He closed his letter, "Bats wishes."[33]

As Dozier thought about the idea, he knew who he wanted to write it—the man he called "the most bizarre thinker I knew."[34] Lorenzo Semple, Jr. recalled, "I'm living in the south of Spain with my family, working on a play, and no phone in the house or anything, and I got a cable from Bill, saying, 'Fly up and meet me at the Ritz in Madrid.' So I flew up to Madrid and met Bill in the garden of the Ritz, and he pulled something out of his pocket, and he actually was rather shame-faced about it. He said, 'This is what they have given us,' and it was a copy of a *Batman* comic. And I have to say, Bill was very chagrined. It seemed a great comedown to do a comic."[35]

Semple, although not a huge comic book fan, had read some *Batman* comics in his youth. Looking at the comic book Dozier plopped on the table in front of him, he began to see a way to go with Batman that would be fun. "I said, 'Terrific idea. I'll do it.' And Bill said, 'How? What are you gonna do?' And this is the truth, I said, 'Don't worry, I'll write it, you go back to L.A.' And Bill went back to L.A. There was no further discussion except that I would write a pilot using one of the four main villains, the Joker, Riddler, Penguin and Catwoman."

Semple wrote a pilot pitting Batman and Robin against the Riddler, who sues Batman in an effort to get him to reveal his true identity in court. With it's absurd leaps of logic and general loopiness, the script set the tone for the series to come. Semple's Batman/Bruce Wayne is an earnest, overgrown Boy Scout, motivated by the murder of his parents but certainly not tortured by the memory of it. He's also not quite as bright as Robin, the Boy Wonder, who is usually the first to decipher the wacky clues left by the various villains. The TV Robin's constant exclamations of "Holy (fill in the blank)" were a Semple addition to the character. "I made up that holy something stuff," said Semple. "That was never in the comic books. That was based on something from *Tom Swift* books I'd read when I was a child."[36]

When the pilot script was completed, Semple sent it off to William Dozier. "I have to emphasize, because it's amusing if you know anything about television, I sent it by mail," said Semple. "I mean, there was no other way of sending it, except by ordinary mail. I mailed the script from Torremolinos in the south of Spain to Bill, just Air Mailed it. And he got it, and he liked it a lot. He had no suggestions of any kind. He just said, 'This is great. I love it.' And he sent it to ABC. And they liked it also a great deal but they were kind of thrown by it. And so I flew to New York, Bill came from L.A., and we met with ABC, once. And Doug Cramer was the guy that was in charge of the project at that time, and the script was very much like the finished thing. I mean it had all those 'bams' and 'pows' and stuff all written into the script. And they said, 'Well, good.' And I went back to Spain, and there never was any notes given or anything, I never had another meeting, with Bill or anybody, but they decided to shoot the pilot. Almost unheard of. No notes from Fox or anybody."[37]

Semple's script showed a way to approach the material that appealed to the cultured, erudite Dozier, who already had one show on the air—a Western called *The Loner* created by Rod Serling and starring Lloyd Bridges—and four others in development: *Journey Into Fear*, an Eric Ambler espionage series; a comedy series for Broadway comedienne Tammy Grimes; *They Went Thataway*, a Western produced by Dozier's son; and now *Batman*.

"The fairly obvious idea," recalled Dozier, "was to make it so square and so serious and so cliché-ridden and so overdone, and yet do it with a certain elegance and style, that it would be funny, that it would be so corny and so bad that it would be funny."[38] Though ostensibly a kid's show, the intent was never to make *Batman* a program that would only appeal to children, since the purpose of TV programming is to put money in the sponsors' and networks' pockets, and children have no real buying power. As Dozier told Judy Stone of *The New York Times*, "This is a merchandising medium, not an entertainment medium."[39]

"From the very beginning," said Semple, "Bill Dozier and I had seen millionaire Bruce Wayne and his Bat regalia as classy comedy, hopefully appealing to kids as an absurdly jolly action piece and to grown-ups for its deadpan satire, entirely nonfraught with psychological issues."[40] Dozier was sold on Semple's take on the material. "That appealed to me," said Dozier, "and I then began to enjoy it, and I began to enjoy working on it."[41]

By August 25, 1965, *Daily Variety* was reporting that ABC and 20th Century Fox Television were developing *Batman* as an "hour-long action-adventure series" for television. The trade paper revealed that the pilot script had been written by Lorenzo Semple, who was due to arrive from Spain at the beginning of September for revisions. Filming was due to begin in October.[42]

When Bob Kane got wind of the script, he was baffled by the choice of villain. In another letter to Dozier, he lamented, "The Joker is by far the better known villain to my fans and is truly the arch-enemy of Batman, such as Dr. Moriarty is to Sherlock Holmes. In fact, the Joker was the one who created 'riddles' for Batman to solve. In a sense he was the original Riddler and to my thinking is the wildest and most bizarre-looking villain of them all. I can picture him in color, with his chalk white face, green hair and blood-red lips—a combination to chill the most ardent mystery lovers. I can only hope that you use him in future scripts."[43]

Dozier assured Kane that the Joker would appear in a future episode. But when Kane read the pilot script, he had a few more suggestions for the producer, writing, "I read the shooting script for the pilot and although it is not the mysterious and grim Batman that I have lived with all these years, I realize that your version is an updated 'camp style' that is in keeping with today's TV market a la James Bond and U.N.C.L.E. and that if I were to produce it today, I would do it very much the way you are handling the concept; tongue-in-cheek; along with the pop art feeling. The only suggestion I would like to make is perhaps a combination of a bit of the old, mysterious along with the new 'camp style.' This is to say, that when the opportunity in the script affords itself, have a giant shadow silhouette of the Batman cast up on a building or a room, preceding Batman's entrance. I have done this quite a bit in the comic strip and it is quite effective in establishing an eerie mood, especially with appropriate mysterious music for accompaniment. In keeping with a mysterious mood, Batman could bring his cape up around his face when lurking in dark shadows."[44]

While the TV series was in development, *Batman* also got a boost from Playboy. Chicago was then the headquarters of the Playboy empire, where publisher Hugh Hefner opened the first Playboy Club on 116 E. Walton Street in 1960. He also opened a movie house, the Playboy Theater, which began showing individual chapters of the

Made in '43.....Discovered in '65!

THE GREATEST SERIAL
EVER FILMED...NOW THE
IN-TERTAINMENT
SCOOP OF THE YEAR!

COLUMBIA PICTURES PRESENTS

AN EVENING WITH

BATMAN
AND ROBIN

ALL 15 EPISODES COMPLETE!
ALL LIVE-ACTION!

"TWO HIGH-CAMP FOLK HEROES
IN A MARATHON OF FIST-FIGHTS,
ZOMBIES & RAVENOUS ALLIGATORS!"
TIME Magazine, Nov. 26, 1965

© Detective Comics, Inc. 1943

The return of the 1943 Batman serial, which became a camp hit in 1965 (© Columbia Pictures).

1943 *Batman* serial daily beginning July 9, 1965.[45] The screenings became a Camp "happening," attracting people from all walks of life who came to laugh at the low-budget heroics. "The response was tremendous," Jerry Dukor, manger of the Playboy Theater, told Clifford Terry of *The Chicago Tribune.* "People actually walked away from the box office if the serial wasn't on that night. Woody Allen saw a chapter and he flipped. He came back three times in one week. The audiences were mostly college students or people in the 21-35 age bracket. Some came just to laugh—the film is bad—and some came for sentimental reasons and there was even a hard-core of serial buffs who viewed it as an art form. We showed all 15 chapters through twice and then went into the really good chapters again—the Best of Batman."[46]

On October 9, 1965, Dukor presented all the chapters back-to-back in a marathon that began at midnight and ended at 4:45 AM. By 12:15 AM, all 654 seats were sold out. The price of admission was $1.25, with each patron getting a bat symbol stamped on their hand that would allow them to exit and reenter as they pleased. *Daily Variety* reported that the screening set a new confectionary record for the venue; in the first three hours of the showing, the theater sold $200 worth of popcorn, along with an almost equal amount of candy bars, peanuts, mints and soda. One man arrived dressed in a Batman costume; at first, filmgoers thought it was Hugh Hefner, but it turned out to be the manager of a rival theater.

Approximately 400 patrons stayed till the end. *Variety* reported one man leaving the theater "flushed from excitement hoarse from shouting," mumbling, "Man, that was longer than *Gone With the Wind*." The screening grossed $850 for the theater.[47]

The surprise box-office success of the serial led Columbia to distribute it in other major cities, under the title *An Evening With Batman and Robin*. Riding the wave of Camp hysteria, it opened at Cleveland's Continental Theatre on November 24, where it was shown in one four-and-a-half hour marathon, with intermissions after chapters 5 and 10. Posters and newspaper ads for the serial said, "Come to Jeer! Stay to Cheer!—and Vice Versa!"[48] It was also booked into the Champaign Art Theatre in Champaign, Illinois where, as in Cleveland, it was held over due to popular demand. Based on the popularity of those tryouts, Columbia booked the serial into theaters in New Orleans, Kansas City, Louisville, Akron, Springfield, Tucson, Toledo, Fullerton, Denver, Dayton, Columbus, Santa Ana and other cities, where it played particularly well among college-age audiences.[49] In a Madison, Wisconsin theater, the film grossed $3,204 in one day.[50] It was set for a Christmas run at San Francisco's Presidio Theater.[51] On December 22, it opened at the Eighth Street Playhouse in Greenwich Village and the Liberty Theater on West 42nd Street in New York.[52]

Legend has it that an ABC executive saw some of the *Batman* chapters at the Playboy Theater, noticed the audience reaction, and began thinking about a *Batman* TV series as a mid-season replacement. Harve Bennett's statements that the show had been in development for two and a half years negate this, as does the fact that the films didn't begin screening in Chicago until about the time that Lorenzo Semple Jr. was beginning work on the pilot script for the series.

With the pilot budgeted at $400,000, Dozier set about assembling his cast. Although Alfred the butler had been killed off in the comics, he was resuscitated for the TV show (he was later also brought back to life in the comics). To play the faithful servant, Dozier immediately thought of Alan Napier. "Alan Napier to me has always been the absolute essence of the perfect English manservant or butler," said Dozier.[53] The English actor, a cousin of former British prime minister Neville Chamberlain, came to Hollywood in 1939, appearing in a host of films from *The Invisible Man Returns* (1940) to *Lassie Come Home* (1943) to *Tarzan's Magic Fountain* (1949).

For Aunt Harriet, Dozier selected another veteran, Madge Blake. The Kansas native entered films in 1949 playing Spencer Tracy's mother in *Adam's Rib*, though Tracy was less than a year younger than she. Her numerous TV appearances included recurring roles on *The Real McCoys* and *Leave It to Beaver*. Dozier said, "She had to be very carefully cast because she had to be not a stupid woman, and yet she had to be stupid enough so it never occurred to her that Bruce Wayne and Dick Grayson could possibly be doing something besides fishing when they say they're going out fishing."[54]

To represent the boys in blue of the Gotham police force, Semple created the character of Chief O'Hara. "He's the all-time bumbling Irish cop," said Dozier, "up from the beat who's now become chief, worked his way up in the ranks. He's so stupid he finally became chief."[55] The role was played by Stafford Repp, a San Francisco-born character actor who began as a sound effects man in live television. Repp, who made a career of playing Sheriffs and bartenders in Westerns and policemen and detectives in numerous TV sitcoms, adopted a thick Irish brogue as Chief O'Hara.

The role of the Gotham police commissioner went to an actor Dozier had worked with previously. "I never at any time saw anybody else in the role of Commissioner Gordon but Neil Hamilton," said Dozier. Hamilton was a true industry veteran, having begun his career as the star of D.W. Griffith's silent Revolutionary War epic, *America* (1924), though late-show viewers remembered him most for his role as Harry Holt opposite Johnny Weissmuller's Tarzan and Maureen O'Sullivan's Jane in *Tarzan the Ape Man* (1932) and *Tarzan and His Mate* (1934). "To me, he was the all-time square public servant, dedicated, un-swervable, honest, exemplary and monolithic almost in his dedication to his job," said Dozier.[56]

ENTER LAUGHING

Casting the pivotal role of Batman was a no-brainer. Dozier knew exactly whom he wanted for the part—Ty Hardin, a 6'2" New York-born actor who had won acclaim on television as the star of the 1958-62 series *Bronco*, a spin-off of the popular Western series *Cheyenne*. However, Hardin wasn't available; he had gone to Europe in search of better roles. "So his agent then very enterprisingly showed me some stills of another client he just happened to have," said William Dozier, "and I was impressed by this man's looks, whom I had only seen once in a commercial, and didn't know his work at all, really."[57] The commercial that Dozier had seen was one for Nestle's Quik, in which a young, handsome actor with a smooth voice named Adam West played Captain Quik, a spoof of James Bond. Almost a parody of an ad, it ended with the line, "Some people will do anything to get rich...Quik," which West delivered perfectly.

Long before he became Adam West, the actor was known as William West Anderson, or Bill to his friends. A product of the American northwest, he was born in Seattle, Washington on September 19, 1928. While attending Walla Walla High School and Lakeside School in Seattle, he spent his summers working on ranches or in canneries, saving money for college. After graduating high school, he went to Whitman College, where he earned a Bachelor of Arts degree in Literature with a minor in Psychology. During his final year of studies, he married for the first time, to 17-year-old Billie Lou Yeager. Now with a wife to support, he got his first taste of show business as a disc jockey at a local radio station, where he began to think about a career in acting.

He received an education in the new medium of television when he spent two years in the Army as part of a team assigned to set up military TV stations in San Luis Obispo, California and Fort Monmouth, New Jersey. Once out of the service, his childhood friend Carl Hebenstreit invited him to come to Hawaii, where Hebenstreit was co-hosting a comedy variety TV series called *The Kini Popo Show* with a chimpanzee named Peaches. During the run of the show, Bill Anderson's first marriage ended in divorce. He soon remarried, to Tahitian beauty Ngatokoruaimatauaia Frisbie Dawson, with whom he had a daughter in 1957 and a son in 1958.

Besides playing various characters on *The Kini Popo Show*, Anderson also appeared in small roles in films that shot in Hawaii, including the Boris Karloff thriller *Voodoo Island* (1957) and *Ghost of the China Sea* with Jon Hall (1958). When Hebenstreit left *The Kini Popo Show,* Anderson took over the hosting reins. He also continued acting in local theater productions, and was spotted by a Hollywood agent visiting the islands who thought the young man would be good in Westerns.[58]

Anderson left Hawaii when MGM invited him to come to Hollywood for a screen test. He also tested at Warner Brothers, and the studio immediately signed him to a seven-year contract, thinking he would be perfect for a series they were developing about gunslinger Doc Holliday, to be produced by Howie Horwitz, producer of the popular *77 Sunset Strip.* Warner Bros. also changed his name. Since there had already been a silent cowboy star named Bronco Billy Anderson, and since he was going to be appearing in a Western TV series, he adopted his middle name, West, as a surname, and coupled it with Adam because he liked the way the two names sounded together.[59] The *Doc Holliday* pilot, however, didn't sell. "I played a consumptive and an alcoholic," said West. "ABC was reluctant to go with it. I can understand—it wouldn't be good for merchandising, except for hospitals."[60] For the next seven years, West made guest appearances on numerous Western TV series such as *Maverick, Laramie, Sugarfoot* and *Gunsmoke,* and drama series like *Goodyear Theatre* and *Westinghouse Desilu Playhouse.*[61] He also starred in three other pilots: *Johnny Cinderella* for Desilu, playing a troubleshooter for a retired gambling czar; *Rio* for RonCom; and *Alexander the Great* for Selmur, a pilot that reportedly cost close to one million dollars to produce.[62]

He also picked up small roles in films, acting opposite Paul Newman in *The Young Philadelphians* (1959), Chuck Connors in *Geronimo* (1962) and Steve McQueen in *Soldier in the Rain* (1963). The pressures of launching a film and TV career took their toll on his second marriage; he and his wife divorced in 1962.

After a small role in the 1964 cult sci-fi classic *Robinson Crusoe on Mars,* West starred in two films in 1965, *The Outlaws is Coming,* the last feature film starring the Three Stooges, and *Mara of the Wilderness.* Though television offered the promise of steadier work, West was becoming discouraged. "I had done four TV pilots here in Hollywood and they all had been approached with a great deal of enthusiasm and money and gloss," said West. "But I'm not an 8x10 glossy photo. I've got to find something special. The pilots had all gone right up to the wire but they never got on the air so my mortality rate in that area was high. And I had no desire to keep doing guest spots on TV."[63] Then, like Ty Hardin, he went to Italy. "I decided to go to Europe and approach my work as if it were completely fresh and new," said the actor. In Italy, West starred in the spaghetti Western, *I quattro inesorabili,* released in the U.S. as *The Relentless Four.* "I did the one picture and had offers to do five more. If I had done them, they would have opened some prestigious doors. But I decided to come home because I wanted to see my kids."[64]

When he returned to Los Angeles, West received a call from his agent, Lew Sherrell, who told him about *Batman.* Asked a couple of years later what his first response was when he heard he was being sent to read for *Batman,* West said, "My reaction was *Ecch!*"[65] He changed his mind, however, once he stepped into Dozier's office and was handed the script, which he was invited to read in an adjoining room. Soon, the down-on-his-luck actor who saw so many opportunities for a starring role in a TV series come and go, who saw his marriage disintegrate while he chased film and TV roles, and who fled to Europe in search of more meaningful and fulfilling work, was laughing. West thought Lorenzo Semple, Jr.'s script was hilarious. Not only was it funny, but it was something new and fresh and exciting. He knew he'd been handed a winner.

William Dozier later recalled, "I had him come in and let him read the first script and we talked and he had an immediate and very intelligent insight into what we were trying to do. He grasped the duality of this thing immediately, that he would have to play it very straight and very square in order to have it come through as humor."[66] Dozier always appreciated that West "could resist the terrible temptation to be charming. All we wanted from him was eternal squareness, rigidity and purposefulness."[67] Deborah Dozier Potter recalled that her father "loved Adam. He thought Adam was just spot on and right for the character."[68] Just three days after West's 37th birthday, *Daily Variety* announced that he had been set for the title role in *Batman*.[69]

West later told *Los Angeles Times* reporter Sylvie Reice, "When I got the part, I tried to remember Batman as I knew him when I was a kid—with emotional recall. We're trying to create a folk hero...when you play a legend, you have to play it with a straight direct line, direct speech and movement. Now Bruce [Wayne], on the other hand, has to come across as the kindest, noblest, most charitable guy—again 'straight line'—not Cary Grant charming—know what I mean?"[70] To another *Los Angeles Times* reporter, Aleene MacMinn, he said, "All the money is fine. But more important is the freedom I get in my work. It's the freedom I went to Europe to find. So many people ask if I fear losing my identity—if Adam West the actor is lost in this costume. Well, the answer is strongly negative. At the moment, I'm very happy to be Batman."[71] He was also happy to have a regular paycheck; the first season of *Batman* would pay him a salary of roughly $45,000.[72]

William Dozier's daughter, Deborah, poses with Adam West on the set of Batman. Off-camera, West wore a bathrobe to protect the Bat-uniform—and to give him pockets (© Deborah Dozier Potter).

"Adam was a terribly nice guy, unlike many actors," said Lorenzo Semple Jr. "When the show was at its height, he was mobbed everywhere he went, but he was very modest and gave autographs to anybody, he never acted badly at all. I mean, he was excellent. And of course it ruined any career he might have had because he was always Batman. I always liked him enormously. He was a genuinely nice guy."[73]

With a potential Batman on board, Dozier continued looking for a young actor to play Robin, the Boy Wonder. His search ended when Bert John Gervis, Jr. entered his office. Gervis, whose mother nicknamed him "Sparky" because of his energetic nature, was the son of an ice skater who owned and operated a traveling ice show called "Rhapsody on Ice." At age two, Sparky Gervis began appearing in his parents' ice shows, billed as "the world's youngest professional ice skater." After making his showbiz debut at the Flamingo Hotel in Las Vegas, he was featured in Ernest Hix's *Strange as It Seems* newspaper strip (a *Ripley's Believe It or Not!* imitator). But as he got older, neither his mother, who had been Miss Fort Worth, Miss Texas, and a professional tap-dancer performing with the Freddy Martin Band, nor his father, who later sold the ice show and worked briefly for MCA and NBC, encouraged Sparky to go into show business.[74]

While attending Beverly Hills High School, he changed the spelling of his first name from "Bert" to "Burt" because he thought it looked cooler.[75] Always an exceptional athlete, he made the varsity teams in track and field, wrestling and golf. [76] At age fifteen, he began studying karate and earned a brown belt. He also enrolled in a speedreading class, eventually being tested at 30,000 words per minute with ninety percent comprehension, or so it was claimed. Whether true or not, the assertion brought him national newspaper attention and an appearance on the TV program *Read Right*.[77] "That's like reading *Macbeth* in 60 seconds, or *War and Peace* in an afternoon," he later told Linda Crawford of *The Chicago Tribune*.[78] Most competitive speedreaders manage 1,000 to 2,000 words per minute with 50% comprehension; world champions generally read less than 5,000 words per minute, which indicates Gervis's claim of 30,000 words per minute was likely a publicity stunt.

At seventeen, Gervis fell in love with Bonney Lindsey, the daughter of Mort Lindsey, musical conductor on *The Merv Griffin Show*. Mort Lindsey arranged for Burt and Bonney to spend the summer of 1963 as apprentices at the Bucks County Playhouse in New Hope, Pennsylvania, where they met another young hopeful named Rob Reiner. At summer's end, Gervis returned to California and attended the University of California at Santa Barbara for a semester before transferring to UCLA, where he was a motion picture and theater major.[79] To earn money for school, he followed his father into the real estate business. His father introduced him to a client, Saul David, who was a producer at 20th Century Fox. Gervis asked David if he could help him find work as a film extra. Instead, David sent him to an agent, who signed him up only as a favor to David.[80]

In defiance of their parents, Burt and Bonney, who had begun living together and were barely scraping by, got married. They were, in Gervis's words, "starving to death." He told Aleene MacMinn of *The Los Angeles Times*, "We had a little apartment on the beach and we'd take Coke bottles back to get money to pay for food. We also had a horse and it took most of our money to feed him. I really felt terrible. I had taken on the responsibility of a husband but I wasn't supporting my wife."[81] Soon after, Bonney got a raise at her telephone company job, and Burt got a call from his agent about a role for a new TV series. He went to meet William Dozier at Fox. Dozier took one look at the slender, 5'8" Gervis and said, "You're big." Gervis replied, "I promise you, sir, I won't grow any more."[82] Reflecting on it later, Dozier said, "The moment he walked into this office, I knew he was Robin, because he had that 'Gee whiz, Mr. Dozier,' y'know, approach right off the bat that couldn't be duplicated. And he'd never done anything. He'd never acted in any medium before for five minutes, but he was just one of those natural kids."[83]

Three weeks later, Gervis was called in to test with Adam West. To give the network a choice, Dozier also tested another pair of actors—Lyle Waggoner, a 30-year-old former encyclopedia salesman who was just beginning his TV and film career, and a young actor named Peter Deyell, who had been appearing in TV and film productions since 1958. The screen test consisted of two scenes from the first episode. First, the actors appeared as Bruce Wayne and Dick Grayson, with Dick reading a newspaper article about how the Riddler was suing Batman, which would cause him to reveal his identity in court. Realizing that there were other clues they'd overlooked, the two headed to the Batcave. In the next scene, they were seen in costume as Batman and Robin, though Batman didn't put on his cowl until the end of the scene, when he figured out the address hidden in a coded riddle was that of a nightclub and told Robin he's too young to come along. In the screen tests, it's interesting to note that the Batman uniform was different from what would be seen on television—the cowl had longer ears, and the bat symbol on the chest was larger, more jagged, and not encased in a yellow circle. The dialogue in the scenes hinted at the camp parody that would become a staple of the series; when Bruce Wayne said, "And when our good housekeeper, poor Mrs. Cooper, finds out what you've been doing on these supposed *fishing* trips of ours, I'm afraid the blow will kill her," it was the kind of line that, taken out of context, would give Dr. Frederick Wertham fits.

Waggoner, whose comedic talents would later land him a long-running gig as part of the ensemble of *The Carol Burnett Show*, certainly looked the part with his matinee-idol handsomeness, jet-black hair and square jaw. "My experience in television was in comedy," said Waggoner, "and I considered this pretty much a comedy part, and so I was excited about trying out for it, and hopefully getting it, because it looked like a lot of fun. Campy."[84] However, Waggoner's radio announcer voice and earnest delivery lacked the distinctive character of West's. As for Deyell, he was not as handsome as Gervis, and his voice sounded too much the conventional teenager, a bit too squeaky for a crime fighter. Both performances were lacking in the energy and conviction of the West/Gervis screen test. Though West, with his sandy brown hair and more rounded chin, looked less the traditional hero than Waggoner, he inhabited the role in a captivating way that Waggoner missed. But while Lyle Waggoner didn't end up winning the role, he had no lasting regrets about it. Asked if, considering the typecasting that befell Adam West, he felt he dodged a bullet by not playing Batman, Waggoner said, "If I had gotten that part, it probably would have changed the whole career that I've had, and resulting in the business that I formed, and in that case, yes, I would've dodged a bullet, because the business that I have is more successful than any television role that I could've had."[85] In 1979, Waggoner formed Star Waggons, a company that provides custom location trailers for TV and motion picture productions.

Along with the brief scenes from the pilot script, Dyell and Gervis did tests to show their stunt prowess. Dyell, in street clothes, performed a choreographed fight with two stunt men, and appeared to miss one of his cues. Gervis, wearing the Robin outfit sans mask and cape, did some falls and throws with a companion, then demonstrated karate, breaking a board with his hand.

Two months passed, during which Gervis wondered if he'd won the part or not. He didn't realize he'd bagged it until he was asked to come to Fox to sign his contract. "The studio thought my agents had told me, and my agents thought the studio had told me," he wrote in his biography, *Boy Wonder: My Life in Tights*. He had just been turned down for a $1.25 per hour job as a gas station attendant; now he would be making $350 a week in his first professional acting job.[86] Before the pilot began filming, he changed his name, adopting the surname of his grandparents to become Burt Ward. Ward's natural athleticism and eagerness served him well as Batman's crime-fighting partner. "Robin was strictly one-dimensional in the comic book, but I've given him another side," Ward told *The Chicago Tribune*'s Linda Crawford. "I've made him appealing to teen-agers. I do this by being suave sometimes, youthful other times, very cool at certain moments. Robin had enthusiasm, but I've given him style and an attitude toward life. That attitude is typical of the American teen-ager—life is full of excitement, full of color, completely uncorrupted. I gave myself to the part by my body actions, my voice, my enthusiasm, and my style of showing that enthusiasm."[87]

THE PILOT

With the main cast selected, Dozier turned his attention to other elements of the show. To begin with, he did a slight redesign of the Batman logo. Deborah Dozier Potter recalled, "I remember when they were designing the logo, he asked my opinion about it, and I remember telling him it should be a little longer, and he did that. If you notice, the logo for the television series is a little bit skinnier than the logo for today's Warner Bros. films."[88]

Next, Dozier ordered an animated title sequence that would echo both the comic books and the pop art of Roy Lichtenstein. Lee Mishkin, who had animated *Linus the Lionhearted* for Ed Graham, created the iconic title sequence,[89] while jazz musician Neal Hefti composed a title theme. "When Bill Dozier originally called me in, I saw some footage and read some scripts," said Hefti. "It was so fantastic—funny, yet so deadly straight-faced. What I had to write couldn't be tongue-in-cheek or cute. You had to make it sound like you weren't putting it down—and there's a very fine line between put-down and put-on."[90] Hefti spent weeks trying to come up with a tune that captured the right flavor, but felt he was missing it; he later commented that it was "the hardest piece I ever wrote."[91] Finally, he settled on a traditional 12-bar blues tune, composed of a repeated two-note phrase.[92] The music was performed with bass guitar, low brass, and percussion, plus an eight-voice chorus singing "Batman!" in perfect unison, not octaves apart, in harmony with the trumpets on the first, fourth and fifth notes of the scale.[93]

When Hefti finally presented the theme to Dozier, he went into the meeting "reluctantly, apologetically, shuffling my feet and looking like Tom Sawyer. I thought they would throw it back in my face."[94] He needn't have worried—Dozier loved it. "I wrote the lyrics, too, so I get double credit on it," said Hefti. "As you know, the lyrics consist of the title repeated six times. One of the choir members on the recording session wrote on his part 'Word and Music by Neal Hefti.' Sure, you may say I could have written the theme itself in two minutes—but it took two weeks to work out the arrangement, which is inseparable from the melody. It often takes time to write something that sounds like you just turned on a faucet and it flowed out. Uncluttering is as big a job as cluttering. That's what made the *Dragnet* and *Peter Gunn* themes so great."[95] After the show's premiere, the theme became such a hit that it won Hefti a Grammy Award for Best Instrumental Song of 1966.

When ABC rushed *Batman* onto the air, Hefti was unable to continue as composer, since he was already committed to provide scores for the films *Duel at Diablo* and *Barefoot in the Park*. Consequently, William Dozier turned to another jazz great to provide the incidental music—Nelson Riddle. Riddle arranged music for classic recordings by Frank Sinatra, Nat King Cole, Dean Martin and Judy Garland, as well as releasing his own instrumental albums. In the early 1960s, he began composing music for TV shows such as *Route 66, The Untouchables* and *Naked City*, and movies like *Robin and the 7 Hoods* and *Ocean's Eleven*. His son, bandleader Christopher Riddle, said his father regarded scoring Batman as a way to increase his BMI royalties by writing "a lot of stuffing music, music to be punched by."[96] For *Batman*, Riddle made liberal use of Hefti's tune for shots of the Batmobile in action, and also wrote distinct, individual themes for the villains, all in a brash, over-the-top style that was a far cry from the lush arrangements of his collaborations with Sinatra, but was perfectly in tune with the comic book style of the show.

Batman went into production at a time when networks were still making the switch to color, although most households still had only black-and-white TV sets. At the beginning of the 1965 TV season, NBC broadcast nearly all of its shows in color, while CBS and ABC had almost half their primetime shows in color; the following year, all primetime TV shows on all three networks would be in color. From the beginning, *Batman* would showcase the bright primary hues one would expect of a program based on a comic book. The sets—which included stately Wayne Manor, the high-tech Batcave, and various villains' lairs—were the work of a 51-year-old Yugoslav named Serge Krizman. As *Batman*'s art director, he was also responsible for developing all the Bat-gadgetry. "I'm really having a ball with *Batman*," said Krizman, a sports car enthusiast who was the former vice-president of the International Jaguar Owners Association.[97]

Dozier himself was enough of a car enthusiast to realize the value of creating a Batmobile that would be more memorable than the nondescript sedans of the serials. He spent $30,000 to create what would become one of the decade's most iconic automobiles. Custom car maker George Barris, who began designing cars for movies and TV after one of his hot rods was used in 1958's *High School Confidential*, knew just the right car for the job. In 1955, Ford's Lincoln division had developed an experimental concept car called the Futura that was hand-built in Italy at a cost of $250,000. However, although it had been prominently featured in the 1959 Glenn Ford film *It Started With a Kiss*, the car had never been put into production, so Barris obtained it for the TV series. After meeting with the show's producers and preparing sketches, Barris was given a contract to create the Batmobile on September 1, 1965. He had just over a month to make the modifications and deliver the vehicle to the studio, where the pilot would begin shooting in October. He delivered the finished vehicle, with its bucket seats and Plexiglas bubble windshields, on October 11. Two months later, on December 21, 1965, he made one of the best car deals in history when he officially purchased the Futura from Ford for $1. After the show premiered, the Batmobile was valued at $125,000; after four decades, it is now valued at $2 million.[98] A second Batmobile was created in July 1966 exclusively for touring the classic car circuit.[99]

Jan Kemp designed the Batman and Robin costumes, as well as outfits for the show's villains. Kemp turned to the comic books for inspiration. "I soon realized that the series would require a whole new approach to the question of color and I decided to introduce a new and brighter combination of colors than had heretofore been used on television, and by so doing give my actor characters the same vivacity that their comic strip counterparts had," said Kemp. "At that time this approach was somewhat radical since the TV medium had been keeping to a sober middle-of-the-range color scheme in most of the shows and productions."[100] Creating the outfits for Batman and Robin, Kemp had to find materials that would be reasonably comfortable for the actors to wear and also durable enough to last through filming of all the action scenes. "For the basic outfit on Batman I decided on Helenca tights and leotards of a good stretch fabric similar to those used in ballet dancing since I knew that these would take a lot of hard work," said Kemp.[101] Since the tights were only available in white or black, he got white ones and dyed them to the gray hue he wanted. He made a cape of blue polished satin and found a similar fabric in stretch satin for the trunks, gloves and boots. The cowl consisted of a plastic bowl-like helmet that fit tightly to Adam West's head, so that it wouldn't shift in fight scenes, which was covered in blue stretch satin, except for the upper face portion, which was black satin with white eyebrows painted on. The ears were deliberately made shorter than in the screen tests, so they wouldn't be out of frame when Batman was seen in close-ups—although it must be remembered that in the 1950s, the Batman of the comics also had short, cat-like ears on his cowl. Instead of the big black bat silhouette seen on the chest of the uniform in the screen test, the TV outfit reflected the "new look" of the then-current *Batman* comic books, with a smaller bat silhouette encased in a yellow oval. In the end, this was the most accurate live-action representation ever of the Batman outfit from the comics.

Robin's outfit was also spot-on. Kemp again used Helenca tights for Robin's legs, dyed in a flesh-tone color. The vest was made of gabardine. "I decided on a red fabric I had used some four years previously when I worked on a Fox film in Canada about the Canadian Mounted Police," said Kemp. "The fabric for the police uniforms was exactly right for Robin's vest. Finding a yellow satin for the cape and green wool

Burt Ward and Adam West ready to leap into action, in their "new look" costumes (Twentieth Century Fox Television/Photofest, © Twentieth Fox Television).

for the trunks was relatively easy, and a leather supply store in downtown Los Angeles had the right leather skins for his gloves and boots."[102]

Both Adam West and Burt Ward found their outfits itchy and uncomfortable under the studio lights. "That helmet echoes all my words, and the worst thing for an actor is to hear his own voice," said West. "And that suit—it's hot as hell under the lights, and it picks up all the cold at night."[103] West, who wore glasses off-screen, also had difficulty seeing while wearing his cowl, which limited his range of sight like a horse wearing blinders.

Ward found his flesh-tone tights fit so snugly that he referred to them as his "python pants." "The costume was uncomfortably hot," he told Steve Swires in a 1987 *Starlog* interview. "Man was not meant to wear tights! God forbid if I ever went outside in the sun—I would quickly get a layer of water between my legs and the tights. There is nothing worse than sweating in tights." Additionally, the tights had a tendency to wrinkle at the knees, so when Ward walked onto the set, he used a stiff-legged gait not unlike that of the Frankenstein monster. Like West, Ward also had issues with his mask. "The mask completely restricted my field of vision," he said. "Worse than that, my eyelashes touched the mask, which made me blink and irritated my eyes."[104]

On the strength of Lorenzo Semple, Jr.'s pilot script, ABC committed to make sixteen episodes of *Batman*, with the idea of putting the program on the air in the 1966-67 TV season. However, the network's current season was a ratings disaster. Their rock music showcase, *Shindig*, broadcast twice a week on Wednesdays and Saturdays, fizzled, and the venerable *The Adventures of Ozzie and Harriet*, which had been on television for thirteen seasons and occupied a Thursday night slot, was also dragging. To win back viewers, ABC settled on a novel idea—the "second season." They would drop their lowest-rated programs and premiere a handful of new series in January, mid-way through the current TV season. To make room for *Batman*, they decided to cancel *Shindig*, move *The Adventures of Ozzie and Harriet* into *Shindig*'s Saturday time slot, and put *Batman* on two nights a week, Wednesdays and Thursdays at 7:30 PM.[105] "*Batman*, the series, was scheduled for immediate production even without shooting the pilot script, which now would be simply the series opener," said Lorenzo Semple, Jr. "Only the most trivial production rewriting was requested, and I was to immediately begin writing the next three scripts, each featuring one of the remaining Big Four villains."[106]

Filming of the initial episode got underway on October 20, 1965,[107] with Fox leasing space from Desilu's Culver City studio, previously the Selznick Studio, where *Gone With the Wind* was filmed nearly three decades earlier.[108] The format of the show called for one-hour adventures to be shown in two parts, the first half-hour on Wednesdays, and the second half-hour on Thursdays. The Wednesday episodes would end with a cliffhanger, with either Batman, Robin or both in mortal peril, as in the serials. And, as in the serials, a narrator would introduce each episode, and provide an overheated closing narration designed to make the viewers tune in the next night, "Same Bat-time, same Bat-channel." When asked who did the narration, Dozier said, "We call him Desmond Doomsday, when we have to tell his name." Deborah Dozier Potter recalled, "As a kid they'd go to the movie theater and see all these serials, and he wanted a voice like that to be the narrator of the series. And he auditioned all these guys, and none of them could do it, they weren't old enough. They didn't know what sound he was looking for. So, he decided to do it himself."[109] When pressed, Dozier admitted, "I do the narration, and I kind of backed into this. We started to do a promotional reel for the network, so they could have something to show advertisers before the show went on the air, and we were putting together a few scenes from the first film, and we needed narration to plug the gaps in it, so I did it. Then when we ran that for the network officials, they quickly said, 'Who's that narrator? Have we got him signed for the series?' And I said, 'No, I don't think we can get him for the series.' I strung them along for a few minutes. But then I was stuck, so I had to do it. So I had to join the Guild then, too." Joining the Screen Actors Guild posed a conundrum for the producer. "I'm just waiting for the day the Screen Actor's strike," said Dozier, "and then I don't know what I'm gonna do."[110]

Semple claims that he didn't really discuss much with Dozier, except for the opening teasers, which concerned Dozier because—as executive producer—he received special perks. "As you may remember," said Semple, "each show started with sort of a teaser in which Bruce Wayne and Dick Grayson were playing with darts or electric trains or something, and we decided what the teaser would be because Bill wanted to have those toys for himself in his house."[111]

The first episode, called "Hey Diddle Riddle," co-starred Frank Gorshin as the Riddler. "He was my first notion for the Riddler and never anybody else," said Dozier.[112] "At first, I wanted to turn it down," Gorshin told Don Page of *The Los Angeles Times*. "It seemed like a joke—like that old *Superman* series. But once I saw the script, I flipped. I could see they were going all the way to make *Batman* good and the idea of bringing a cartoon character to life became appealing."[113]

Though he strove to be taken seriously as an actor, Gorshin was best known as an impressionist, a talent that won him many bookings on TV variety shows and in nightclubs. "I discovered early in my career that I had the ability to do impressions, or assume the attitudes of famous people," said Gorshin. "I needed money to survive in the business, so I did impressions professionally in small clubs. My first break came when Steve Allen saw me and signed me for his variety show. I did many shows after that and became characterized in TV as a variety performer. Naturally, I went into every producer's file as a comedian. You see, they haven't got time to find out if a performer can handle something else, something dramatic."[114] On February 9, 1964, Gorshin landed what he thought was a prime booking—an appearance on *The Ed Sullivan Show*. However, the next day, all anyone remembered was the name of the musical guests: the Beatles.[115]

Gorshin signed on to play the Riddler at the end of September 1965.[116] His contract with 20th Century Fox Television allowed him to walk away from the *Batman* role whenever he wished, while at the same time guaranteeing him the first chance at playing the role whenever the character was used.[117] When he took the role of the Riddler, he was also doing the lead in a pilot called *Mr. Z,* a spy spoof in the vein of *Get Smart!,* for Jackie Gleason Productions.[118]

Though Gorshin's high-pitched giggle as the Riddler was thought to be an impression of Richard Widmark's maniacal Tommy Udo in *Kiss of Death* (1947), Gorshin sometimes said that he developed it from listening to his own high-pitched giggle at Hollywood parties.[119] A more honest answer was the one he gave to Norma Lee Browning of *The Chicago Tribune*, saying he worried about the laugh a lot at first. "The Riddler is such a bizarre character and I was trying to figure out how to laugh in a way that would be in keeping with his character," said Gorshin. "I practiced different ways of laughing just to listen to the sound. Then I found I didn't need to concern myself with the way the laugh sounded. I just had to believe in what I was doing, throw myself into the role, be honest with it, that's all."[120]

After the first three days of shooting, Burt Ward wondered if he'd live through the initial sixteen episodes. On the very first day of filming, the first scene shot showed the Batmobile roaring out of the Batcave. The location, Bronson Canyon on the southern edge of Griffith Park, was an old rock quarry until the 1920s, and since then had been used in practically every movie or TV show that needed a cave entrance, including Frank Capra's *Lost Horizon* (1937), *The Adventures of Captain Marvel* (1941), John Ford's *The Searchers* (1956), and countless TV Westerns. Ward suspected something was amiss when he got into the Batmobile and realized that the man in the Batsuit behind the wheel was not Adam West but rather Hubie Kerns, West's stunt double. As Kerns raced the car out of the cave and made a sharp turn, Ward's door flew open. To keep from being flung out, he reached his left arm behind and snagged the gear shift with his pinkie—which dislocated. The following day, the back of his neck was burned when an incendiary device was ignited too soon. On the third day, when Robin was tied to a table and Batman was to blow a hole through the wall coming to his rescue, the three sticks of dynamite used to blow the wall out blew a two-by-four into Ward's face that left a gash on the bridge of his nose. On the fourth day, for a scene where the Riddler gasses Robin, who is in the passenger seat of the Batmobile, and tries to steal the vehicle, the fireworks that shot out of the missile launchers on the back of the car spewed red-hot ash that scorched Ward's forearms, singed his hair, and left a first-degree burn on his scrotum. In the first four days, he'd been to the hospital four times. Ward, who rode his motorcycle back and forth to the studio, wrote in his book *Boy Wonder: My Life in Tights* that "it was ironic that Greenway Productions made such a big deal about how dangerous they thought it was for me to ride my motorcycle to work and consequently took out a $3 million insurance policy to protect their interests. The truth is that I never suffered from the danger of riding to work. I suffered after I got to work! At one point, with all the 'accidents' on the set, I almost believed the producers were trying to collect on that policy."[121]

Deftly directed by Robert Butler, whose long list of TV directing credits included *The Many Loves of Dobie Gillis, The Untouchables, Hogan's Heroes*, and *The Fugitive*, the pilot set the offbeat tone of the show from the very beginning. When Batman, in his full costume, enters a nightclub called What a Way to Go-Go, one woman faints, and the coat-check girl asks if he'd like to check his cape. A maitre d' then approaches, and the following exchange ensues:

Maitre d': "Ringside table, Batman?"

Batman: "Just looking, thanks, I'll stand at the bar. I shouldn't wish to attract attention."

Batman goes to the bar and orders a glass of orange juice, which the bartender calls a "Batman special" when he hands it to him. Molly, the Riddler's moll, played by the voluptuous Jill St. John, then entices Batman into a dance, and Adam West launches into the weird maneuvers of what would come to be known as the Batusi. St. John had the distinction of playing the only female character in any *Batman* episode to die. When Molly falls into the Batcave's atomic reactor, Batman sadly sighs, "What a way to go...go."

Batman was innovative in two other ways. Whenever the villains were seen in their lairs, the shots were filmed with the camera tilted in what is known in the industry as a Dutch angle. This was a visual pun, a suggestion that the bad guys were "crooked." Another visual joke was the superimposing of words like BAM! and POW! to accentuate the fight scenes. Though inspired by the words used in comic book drawings, these superimpositions had a more practical use—it meant that the crew didn't have to film as many shots for each fight scene, and it didn't matter if the punches missed by a mile—they'd be covered by words, anyway. These visual gags, as well as the Bat-symbol wipes between scenes and the old-time serial-style cliffhanger endings, became part of the signature visual language of the *Batman* show, setting it apart from other series on TV.

"These are very funny, ridiculous things," said Lorenzo Semple Jr. "And that was the show. That was for grown-ups, in other words, but at the same time the kids, without getting that humor, could enjoy all the running around and the Batmobile and punching people, you know, all that silly stuff. So it's always had more appeal to grown-ups than kids."[122]

With his deadpan delivery, West made the humor work. "Playing Batman is an actor's challenge," he said. "You have to reach a multi-level audience. The kids take it straight, but for adults, we have to project it further...When *Batman* was a comic it wasn't camp, but the show is."[123] Although he found the role tremendous fun to play, West said, "You have to take it seriously. I want to do it well enough that Batman buffs will watch reruns in a few years and say, 'Watch the bit he does here, isn't that great?'" However, to Bob Smith of *The Los Angeles Times*, he said, "This whole thing is an insane, mad fantasy world, and my goal is to become America's biggest put-on. Everyone on the set is just a little demented."[124]

By December 1965, three weeks before its premiere, the commercial advertising slots on the *Batman* show were 90% sold. Kellogg's, which had previously sponsored the *Adventures of Superman* TV series in the 1950s, committed to two minutes of commercials every other week at a price of $31,000 per minute. The show's other sponsors included Procter & Gamble, Colgate, Dodge and Bristol-Meyers.[125]

Batman premiered on ABC on the evening of Wednesday, January 12, 1966. To help kick off the show, ABC invited a cross-section of Manhattan socialites to a *Batman* "cocktail and frug party" at Harlow's, a discothèque on East 79th Street. Afterwards, guests were bused to the York Theater on 1st Avenue at 64th Street to see a theatrical screening of the show timed to coincide with its TV broadcast. Val Adams of *The New York Times* reported, "The room was jam-packed. Andy Warhol, the pop artist, was there. So was Harold Prince, president of the League of New York Theaters. Burgess Meredith was there, too. He portrays one of the guest villains in a future *Batman* episode." Jacqueline Kennedy had been invited, but was a no-show. Broadway actress Tammy Grimes, who was soon to debut in her own William Dozier-produced TV series, did appear. One gate-crasher showed up in a Batman outfit, and was allowed to stay. Adams wrote, "Theater guests were served champagne and popcorn, a combination not to be found in most Broadway movie houses. There was no applause when the world premiere of *Batman* ended, which may or may not be significant. It was reported that one of the pop artists present commented that he thought his kids would love *Batman* but he didn't know if adults would get it. Walter Wanger, the motion-picture producer, said: 'I loved it. It's my type of art.'"[126]

The next day, everyone was talking about the show. Was it art? Was it camp? Was it simply a great kids show with a wink to intellectuals? *The New York Times* wrote, "Bob Kane's heroes of the comic strip came to television last night as real-life people, and it looks as if the American Broadcasting Company has something going for it. The show was amusing in spots, though the avant-campists might contend it really wasn't bad enough to be excellent...The true test for *Batman* won't be this week or next, but in a couple of months when the novelty of his cape and expertise begin to wear off."[127] On the opposite coast, Don Page of *The Los Angeles Times* proclaimed, "If the aim had been satire, *Batman* would be hanging by its feet as a critical flop. But producer William Dozier wisely brought *Batman* to television as a live comic book and ABC probably has its biggest hit in many seasons." Page said that Adam West and Burt Ward were "flattering reproductions of cartoonist Bob Kane's paper heroes... Gorshin's portrayal was classic. He is the first in a list of impressive guest star villains to come...Critically, *Batman* is kicks, even though the intellectuals will call it 'in' and 'camp' (a device which allows them to lower themselves to enjoy it) and the kids will love it like when you and I were young."[128]

In *The Lowell (Massachusetts) Sun*, William E. Sarmento wrote, "I have to confess many long hours in my youth were spent reading that scourge of the literary field, the comic book. Thus it was with a tinge of nostalgia coupled with a flicker of boyhood pride that I tuned in to catch the first installment of *Batman* last night. Wonder of wonders, there it was, all of it, just as I had remembered. The hooded champion, his young comrade, the Batmobile, the flashing bat signal in the sky, the sinister Riddler, yes, all there right before my eyes."[129] Jack Gould of *The New York Times* enthused, "Even with instant books, folk-rock sheet music, Andy Warhol and the design of the new CBS building on West 52nd Street, there was a glaring gap in the arts. Batman wasn't on television."[130]

In Hollywood, gossip columnist Hedda Hopper, after noting that she had been approached to appear on the show, wrote, "I haven't time, so suggested Zsa Zsa Gabor with her Hungarian accent and an amazing hat would be mighty funny...I'm happy that Bill Dozier has a hit. I don't understand what *Batman* is about but it makes me roar with laughter. It will make millions."[131] Actress Lana Turner told a reporter, "It's so hokey, I just love it. How can that Adam West say all those lines without breaking up?"[132] George Burns said, "I think it's funny. I think it's not only funny but I think it will last. You've gotta take your hat off to something different."[133]

Trendex, a ratings system based on telephone surveys that claimed to represent 70 percent of American homes, reported that out of the 27.3 percent of all television-equipped households that were watching when *Batman* first aired, nearly half (49.5 percent) sat glued to the premiere adventure of the Caped Crusader. The following night, *Batman*'s rating increased to 58.8 percent of the viewing audience. In New York, according to Trendex, one out of three viewers tuned in for both nights' episodes, giving *Batman* the highest rating since the Beatles appeared on *The Ed Sullivan Show*.

In the Nielsen overnight ratings, the Wednesday night *Batman* scored a 38 rating, compared to 11.5 for CBS's *Lost in Space* and 13 for NBC's *The Virginian*. The rating for Thursday's segment was 39, compared to 12 for CBS's *The Munsters* and 11 for NBC's *Daniel Boone*.[134]

While ABC reveled in the high ratings, skeptics at CBS and NBC conceded only that ABC had done a good job in promoting the series and getting viewers to tune in. However, they felt that the numbers would not last and that *Batman* would be a "hula hoop hit," or passing fad.[135]

Among the critics who weren't won over was UPI's Rick Du Brow, who saw the pop art/camp aspects of *Batman* as just a calculated attempt by the show's makers to cash in. "Video cares nothing, understands nothing, about original, genuine motivations but rather grabs the trend by the pocketbook, wrings it dry of all things natural and stuffs it into a hard and fast format," wrote Du Brow. "The format, in this case with *Batman*, is tied to a cold, impersonal and brittle wise-crack humor because everyone involved is so painfully aware that he is making fun of something, that he is spoofing, that he is satirizing, that he is just so 'in'—in brief, the genuineness is totally lost because there is no spontaneous wit but only a series of gags directed at a trend already once removed from its source by promoters."[136]

Milton Berle agreed, saying, "*Batman* is really just an audience show. Bill Dozier has pulled the wool, in a brilliant manner, over everybody's eyes. Don't use the word 'Camp' with Batman. Let's use the term 'hoodwinked.' The strange thing to me is that long before the word took on its present meaning—whatever that might be, it had homosexual connotations. Like 'In' and 'Out,' 'Camp' is not going to last."[137]

After *Batman* had been on the air for a month, Charles Champlin of *The Los Angeles Times* also voiced his displeasure, writing, "*Batman* is now firmly enshrined as the boffo, socko, geewhizerooney showbiz smash of our times, the greatest thing since the safety pin, the graham cracker and soft ice cream, but greater than any. It is high-piled in ratings, merchandised beyond the dreams of avarice, affecting our speech patterns, wreaking insomnia the length and breadth of Madison Avenue, shaping our televiewing for years to come. It is also a listless, tasteless, witless, styleless, humorless bore of staggering proportions. It was born of a devout and monumental cynicism toward the television audience that has probably not been equaled since *Hair-raising Tales* of pre-coaxial cable days, or since the last car commercial."[138]

Batman's producer, Howie Horwitz, took all the brickbats thrown at the show in stride. "I'm amused at all the psycho-analytical answers for the show's success—the definitions of 'high camp,' 'the current mood of the country,' and all the pseudo-intellectual approaches to the show," said Horwitz. "Basically, we are in show business, providing damned good entertainment the public likes, and it's that simple. The show clicked because it's different." Responding to TV producers who bemoaned that if *Batman* was the future of television, then maybe it was time for them to get out, Horwitz said, "If some producers fancy themselves as creative, talented and knowledgeable people in the medium, let me assure them that putting out an episode of *Batman* requires all these. We do not spit them out. I don't understand anyone saying 'this is not for me—what is TV coming to?' This requires as much talent as any other form of entertainment. It's very difficult to produce a show successfully on two levels—for kids and adults."[139]

Initially, the show's ratings held. Throughout its abbreviated first season (actually a half season), *Batman* continued to place in the top ten, while other ABC series that debuted during its "second season" bit the dust. In Nielsen's report for the week ending February 13, the Wednesday episode of *Batman* was in fifth place, while the Thursday episode shot all the way to number one.[140] "It's entertaining a lot of people, and we're in the entertainment business," said Dozier. "We don't pretend it will elevate anyone culturally. Adults may not necessarily like Batman, but they are amused by it. Young kids take it seriously and teenagers see the humor in it, but those around 12 and 13 have blind spots. They don't take it seriously and don't find it funny."[141]

The show soon went international. In mid-February of 1966, soon after its debut, it was sold for broadcast in England on London's ABC-TV Ltd. (Associated British Corporation) for the record fee of $4,000 per half-hour segment. ABC began airing the show on Thursdays and Fridays in London, and in the North and Midland areas on Saturdays at 6:35 PM and Sundays at 7:25 PM beginning May 21.[142] The London midweek station Rediffusion picked it up for the 6:07 PM slot on Tuesdays and Wednesdays, beginning July 5.[143] In July, the Tyne-Tees-TV network cut the shows in half, presenting them in 15-minute segments Monday through Friday at 6:45 PM. Southern TV went the other route, showing episodes back-to-back in a one-hour slot.[144] The show was also exported to Japan, where it was televised Sunday evenings at 6:30, and became one of the top 10 imported programs in Tokyo and Osaka.[145]

Among some U.S. TV stations, *Batman* became a symbol of corporate greed. Up to that point, it was customary for a half-hour broadcast to include three commercial breaks. *Batman* went out over the airwaves with four advertising slots. Baltimore station WJZ-TV was so angered by this that they refused to carry the program. WJZ general manager Kenneth T. MacDonald argued that since long-established commercial format standards held that there would be only six commercial breaks per one hour of programming in prime time, if ABC put four commercials in *Batman*, then they should only air two during the next half hour.[146] ABC disagreed, saying that the total time allocated for commercials was within the standards of the National Association of Broadcasters code, and that the amount of program material was the same; they made room for the extra commercial by dropping the announcement that the show was in color, dropping announcements of co-sponsors, and cutting the ads for other shows. Further, they had notified both the Federal Communications Commission and the National Association of Broadcasters of their intention to add the extra minute of commercials, with no complaints from either regulatory body.[147]

After weeks of commercials touting the *Batman* premiere, Baltimore viewers were surprised when they tuned in on Wednesday, January 12, 1966 and, instead of seeing the Caped Crusader, they saw a broadcast of a statement that said, "WJZ-TV regrets it is unable to present *Batman* as originally scheduled. Permission to telecast the program has been withheld by the ABC Television Network because of WJZ-TV's unwillingness to carry the program with increased commercial content. WJZ-TV considers such increase in commercial content to be a break with a long

standing precedent of commercial standards within prime evening broadcast time and therefore not in the public interest. Consequently, *Batman*, originally scheduled tonight and tomorrow night at 7:30 PM, will not be broadcast on this station." Reaction was swift—over 2,000 calls came in to the station's switchboard. While most were disappointed by the cancellation, about one in three callers congratulated WJZ-TV for taking a stand against "over-commercialization."[148]

When the brouhaha erupted, ABC warned WJZ general manager Kenneth T. MacDonald that if he didn't accept the extra commercial in *Batman*, they would sell the program to another Baltimore station—which they did. NBC affiliate WBAL-TV bought it, and sidestepped the potential minefield by broadcasting it on Saturday afternoons, when the three commercial limitation was not in effect.[149]

For ABC, the additional commercial was no small potatoes. If they could get away with it in *Batman*, then they could carry it over into their other programming. The result would be an additional six commercial minutes per evening, and with that airtime selling for between $25,000 and $55,000, depending on a program's viewership, it could mean an additional $150,000 to $330,000 in revenues per night. ABC president Thomas W. Moore said the extra commercial experiment with *Batman* was dictated by simple economics; a half hour of *Batman* cost $70,000 to produce, and with the program airing in the early evening, when the viewing audience was not yet at its peak, the network could not recoup its financial investment with just three commercials. Thus, a fourth commercial was necessary.[150]

Two months after *Batman*—with four commercials—debuted, ABC affiliates meeting in Chicago voted against the network's proposal to add a fourth commercial to all programs in the 7:30 PM time slot. ABC management told the affiliates they would consider the resolution in formulating their formal plans.[151] In protest of the extra commercial, Herbert B. Cahan, the chairman of the affiliates advisory committee, resigned. Not coincidentally, Cahan was the vice-president of WJZ-TV in Baltimore, the station that refused to carry *Batman*. "Most affiliates are opposed to four commercials in *Batman*," Cahan told *New York Times* reporter Val Adams. "Last November, in an Eastern regional meeting of affiliates, a resolution was passed in opposition to the extra one-minute commercial in the show. The affiliates' advisory board is unanimously opposed to extending the *Batman* policy to other shows." Donald H. McGannon, president of Westinghouse, which owned WJZ and many other TV stations, wrote a letter to ABC saying, "This concern finds its root in projecting what the industry may reasonably expect as a consequence of increasing the commercial content in prime time from three to four minutes. It is safe to assume that the next step will be the escalation of this pattern from two to five nights...on ABC (a speculation that is practically a certainty, I gather), the spread of the same pattern to the other two networks in this time period and, finally, the escalation of the pattern to the entire four hours of prime time on all three networks."[152] Of course, at the time these complaints were being lodged, the average commercial break lasted one minute. These days, it lasts three.

Controversies aside, CBS-TV noticed *Batman*'s immediate success and took quick steps to get a similar series on the air, acquiring TV rights to *The Shadow* and *The*

Phantom. Both went into development as potential half-hour series. NBC, also looking for a comic strip property, snapped up producer Sy Weintraub's *Tarzan* TV series.[153]

The success of the TV show energized National Periodical Publications, publishers of the *Batman* comic books. At their annual meeting on January 25, 1966— two weeks after *Batman*'s premiere—company president Jacob S. Liebowitz said a 20 percent increase in earnings over the previous year's $55.7 million was expected in 1966, primarily thanks to the success of *Batman* and the production of an animated *Superman* cartoon for Saturday morning TV. Along with those successes, they were also increasing the rates charged for re-runs of the old live-action *Adventures of Superman* TV series, and still had a Broadway production of Superman in the works.[154] In 1965, National's stock price plummeted to a low of 17-1/2. By March of 1966, it shot up to a new high of 45-1/4. National received $1,000 plus 20 percent of the profits each time a *Batman* episode aired, as well as 5 percent of the wholesale price of licensed items such as Batlamps, Batkites, games, phonograph records and sweatshirts.[155]

The success of the show had a significant impact on sales of Batman comics. In 1965, *Batman* was the #9 top-selling comic book, with 453,745 average paid circulation (copies sold through newsstands as well as subscriptions); *Detective Comics* was ranked # 19, with 304,414 average paid circulation. By contrast, *Archie* comic books were #7. The following year, after the series premiered, *Batman*, with 898,470 average paid circulation, knocked *Superman* out of the top slot. For a title that had been on the verge of cancellation, it was an impressive comeback. Meanwhile, *Detective Comics* jumped up to #11, with circulation of 404,339 copies, and *World's Finest Comics*, featuring Batman-Superman team-ups, jumped from the #8 position to #6.[156]

THE ROGUE'S GALLERY

With a commitment from ABC to air the initial episodes, and the decision to begin showing them in January of 1966, Dozier and company went immediately from filming the pilot into filming the remaining first season shows. The next pair of episodes to go before the cameras featured the Penguin as the villain. Dozier, wanting to go after world-class actors for the villains' roles, approached Mickey Rooney. "I'm glad we didn't get him," Dozier said in a Canadian Broadcasting Corporation interview, "because our second choice was Burgess Meredith and I think he's a classic in the role."[157]

From his beginnings with Eva La Gallienne's theater troupe, Meredith had become an acclaimed actor on the Broadway stage, in films and on television. As the Penguin, Meredith said he took "a deliberately overblown approach. It may have done me more harm than good, but it made an impact. I thought it had a Dickensian quality—or a spoof of one. It was fun to act...I had an elaborate makeup—a huge nose and a great, extended stomach. It was as complete a disguise as you could get— but people recognized me in it."[158] Speaking to Digby Diehl of *The Los Angeles Times* in 1967, Meredith mused, "If I spend all my time in a Shakespearean company and only do art movies like Olivier does now, my position would be more dignified and more serious. I might even be a better actor. But this is America, and I'm a man moved by the rhythms of his time, so I'll just take amusement at being a paradox...*Batman* is great fun and hammy, like having a slightly drunken night out—and getting paid for it. It's very heady for me, and a very satisfying change to have all the children know me."[159]

Meredith accentuated the avian aspects of the character with a distinctive waddling walk and a quacking laugh. "The famous quack came by accident," said Meredith. "I had given up smoking years before, and whenever I put the lighted cigarette in my mouth it would irritate my throat—so instead of spoiling the scene by coughing, I would make a quacking noise."[160] In a way, Meredith felt that in playing the Penguin, he had come full circle in his career. "When Eva Le Gallienne was presented with an award and I was one of the speakers," he recalled, "I told her the first part she had given me was that of the Duck in *Alice in Wonderland*, in which I had to strap roller skates on my knees, and I said I wanted to thank her because 'it defined my career: I went from a Duck to a Penguin.'"[161]

In his 1994 autobiography, *So Far, So Good: A Memoir*, Meredith paid tribute to his Penguin stunt double, Al Cavens, writing, "He was also a brilliant swordsman—a champion fencer. He choreographed a majority of the great duels seen in films. I was thankful for that; that's how we met. He did all my dirty work as the dastardly Penguin in the *Batman* series. I would make the vocal threats against Batman and Robin and then Al would do battle for me, leaping off buildings with an umbrella as a parachute, dueling the entire police force of Gotham City on my behalf. He lost splendidly for me, and he did it with a foot-long cigarette holder in his mouth. He accomplished my heroics and I got the credit for his daring...He was the one who took the risks and performed the impossible leaps. I just appeared when it was time to quack!"[162]

Just as Burgess Meredith made a memorable impression as the Penguin, so did Cesar Romero as the Joker. Romero said in an interview, "Why Dozier wanted me I'll never know because I asked his wife, Ann Rutherford, 'Why did Bill think of me for this part? She said, 'I don't know. He said he saw you in something, and he said, "He's the one I want to play the Joker."' I haven't the slightest idea what it was that he saw me in, because I had never done anything like it before."[163] The truth is that Romero, like Meredith, was not Dozier's first choice; José Ferrer, who won an Oscar for his starring role in the 1950 film *Cyrano de Bergerac*, was the first actor approached. He declined, so Dozier next went to Gig Young, an Oscar nominee for his supporting roles in *Come Fill the Cup* (1951) and *Teacher's Pet* (1958) (he would win the Supporting Actor Oscar for 1969's *They Shoot Horses, Don't They?*). When Young passed, Dozier went to Romero, whom he later proclaimed was "just magnificent."[164]

In a 1966 interview, Romero—an actor and dancer known in his Hollywood heyday as "the Latin from Manhattan"—said that he loved playing the Clown Prince of Crime. "It's a kooky, way-out character," he said, "the easiest I ever played. I can be as hammy as I like and do all the things we were told not to do: mug, over-act, accentuate. It's fun because you're not tied down, inhibited. And I don't have to worry about circles under the eyes or whether my hair is combed."[165] As the Joker, Romero's handsome visage was covered in white greasepaint, and he wore a green wig. He refused to shave his famous mustache, so makeup was applied over it; the mustache is clearly visible in close-ups. "The make-up took about an hour to put on, but the wig was a thing that bothered me more than anything else. The wig was green, of course, but it sometimes photographed red, yellow—everything but green. They would glue the wig to the front of my forehead, and after a while it would give me a headache."[166]

It has been long rumored that after Romero was cast, Frank Sinatra expressed an interest in playing the role. Sinatra may not have had the chance to play the part, but the show did co-opt the title of his 1957 film for the first Cesar Romero episode, "The Joker is Wild."

Recalling the fervor among actors to appear on the show, Deborah Dozier Potter said, "It was the chic 'in' show at the time in the television business. The only equivalent was *The Soupy Sales Show*, I remember people would love to guest star on that and be hit in the face with a pie. Everybody was calling my father wanting to be on the show and he loved that. He suddenly became very popular socially again, not that he hadn't been, but it was a whole different kind of popular. And he just loved it, he loved every minute of it."[167]

William Dozier made Lorenzo Semple, Jr. the show's executive story editor, and solicited other writers to help ease his workload. At first, it was hard to find writers who would write for the show, until it went on the air and was an instant hit. "I even drafted my son, Bob, who I discovered knew more about Batman than I did," said Dozier. "I guess he was reading comic books, fortunately, when he was a boy and I was trying to get him to read *Moby Dick*." Robert Dozier, who had been writing for television for a decade, wrote the first pair of episodes featuring the Joker. "But now he's gone back to his movie writing," said William Dozier, "and other writers are knocking down the door to write for *Batman*."[168]

Among the writers contributing scripts were relative newcomers Max Hodge and Fred De Gorter as well as veterans like Charles Hoffman, screenwriter of 1946's *Night and Day*, and Stephen Kandel, who wrote several episodes of the Lloyd Bridges series *Sea Hunt*. "They mailed their scripts to me, and I rewrote them and mailed them back," said Semple. "And that went on for maybe three weeks. And then they said, 'You've got to come back. You have no phone and no communication.' We were just doing this by ordinary mail. So I said okay, I'll come back. I said I won't come all the way to L.A., and I came back as far as Westport, Connecticut. I rented a house there. I did the executive story editing from there. And finally, toward the end of the first year, I moved to L.A. with the family, and was in L.A. for the rest of it."[169]

One of the problems Semple faced was finding writers who understood the show. "They either made it too silly, or they didn't get the humor of it properly," said Semple. "I wrote Bat-notes, as I called them, which I would give to the writers to give samples of the type of humor it was meant to be."[170] With a sign that read BAT-BARD on his desk, Semple drew up a list of commandments for the other writers, including a prohibition against killing. "This makes our plotting more difficult; there isn't much for the villains to do except steal things," Semple told John Skow of *The Saturday Evening Post*. With characters such as the Riddler, the Joker, the Penguin and Catwoman returning regularly, he added, "It would be immoral for them to commit murder and then come back on the air."[171] However, to Judy Stone of *The New York Times*, Semple said of the show, "Of course, on a very sophisticated level, it's *highly* immoral, because crime seems to be fun."[172]

One writer who did get the show's tone was Stanley Ralph Ross, who began his career in advertising before becoming a TV writer and actor. It was Ross who penned the classic words, "Spanning the globe to bring you the constant variety of sport… the thrill of victory… and the agony of defeat… the human drama of athletic competition… this is ABC's *Wide World of Sports!*" Remembering Ross, who stood 6'6" and weighed nearly 300 pounds, Semple said, "We called him the Jolly Jewish Giant. He was a big guy, and joked a lot, and he got the spirit of the thing."[173] Ross broke into Hollywood rewriting the dialogue of the Annette Funicello-Frankie Avalon beach films to make them sound more authentic and youthful. He then began writing comedy songs for Allen Sherman, of "Hello, Mudduh, Hello, Faddah" fame, and wrote an album for Chris Nelson, one of Sherman's singers. At a listening party at Nelson's home in November 1965, he met *Batman* line producer Howie Horwitz. Ross's agent had been trying to get Ross a meeting with Horwitz, so now the producer, listening to the songs, put two and two together and asked Ross if he was the one whose agent had been calling him. When Ross said he was, Horwitz said, "I'll call you." The next day, Ross was given the assignment of writing the initial Catwoman episode. In an interview with Pat Jankiewicz in *Filmfax* magazine, Ross recalled, "My agent said, 'Look, they won't give you the job by yourself, so you'll have to write it with Lee Orgel.' Lee was a producer, always busy out of town, so when the time came for the second draft, I wrote it by myself, at Howie's house, in front of Howie so he knew I was the writer! After that, he gave me the rest of the jobs by myself."[174] Ross eventually wrote 28 episodes over all three seasons of *Batman,* including all but two of the episodes featuring the Catwoman. "I was always fascinated with the Catwoman," said Ross. "I liked to write the Catwoman shows because I wrote this underlying sexual tension between Batman and Catwoman. At one point she almost convinced him to marry her, and they were going to go off and fight crime. She said, 'We'll make a marvelous pair, Batman. You know how to catch criminals. I know how the criminal mind works. We'll get married. We'll fight crime together. I'm totally reformed.' And Batman said, 'What about Robin?' And she replied, 'Robin? We'll kill him.' I liked that."[175]

The Catwoman debuted in the twentieth episode of the first season. The producers wanted Suzanne Pleshette, a 28-year-old actress from New York, for the role, but when negotiations broke down with the 5'4", husky-voiced actress, the part went to 5'11", 32-year-old Julie Newmar. Once a prima ballerina for the Los Angeles Opera, Newmar danced her way through numerous films in the early 1950s, including as one of the brides in *Seven Brides for Seven Brothers* (1954), but it was her role as Stupefyin' Jones in the Broadway adaptation of the popular comic strip *L'il Abner* that made her a star. She reprised the role for the 1959 film version. She continued on stage with a Tony-winning role opposite Claudette Colbert in 1961's *The Marriage Go-Round*, and in the early 1960s began appearing on television. After guest appearances on *The Defenders, Route 66* and *The Twilight Zone* (playing the devil), she co-starred with Robert Cummings in the short-lived 1964-65 series *My Living Doll*, as Rhoda the robot.

In a 1989 interview for *Amazing Heroes*, Andy Mangels asked Newmar how she won the Catwoman role. "Someone must have thought I'd make a good cat," she replied. "Some casting agent from Hollywood called me, but I had never seen the series. My brother, who was going to Harvard, had. 'You've got to do it. This is great!' I was going to turn it down because I was having a good time in New York. I didn't want to fly out on a weekend."[176]

At her brother's urging, Newmar made the trip to Hollywood, and was won over when she read the script. "I always felt that cats went to ballet school, and I started at age 5," said Newmar in a 1995 *Entertainment Weekly* interview. "Catwoman had to have an intelligent body—which I have—and express physically what's not in the script." In a skin-tight black costume that accentuated her voluptuous, narrow-waisted figure, Newmar's Catwoman entranced male viewers, and inspired young women. "The girls identify with how good it feels to have that kind of mastery over boys," said Newmar. "Catwoman is one of the great roles for women in theatrical history." In a 2008 interview with Greg Hernandez, she said, "It's just a delicious character to sink your body into. First of all, you're wearing black so it slims you down and you slink around and it's a very forthright kind of femaleness. It's just the right amount of aggression and seduction and sassiness."[177] As in the comics, Batman is shown as having a physical attraction to his evil female counterpart. "The Catwoman-Batman combination worked because she desired him and he desired her. But at the heart, they were just incompatible," Newmar told Brenda Rees of *The Los Angeles Times*. "She never wanted to destroy Batman; she played him how a cat plays with a mouse. She just wanted to ruin his day. She was naughty for naughtiness' sake. That's what made her such a delicious villain."[178] Newmar's first episode as the Catwoman was the one interrupted by the Gemini VIII newscasts; no wonder so many viewers complained.

One of the classic roster of Batman villains who did not appear in the series was Two-Face, though he was considered as a potential villain during the first season. Charles FitzSimons, the show's line producer—and real-life brother of actress Maureen O'Hara—told Donald Freeman of *The Chicago Tribune* that among the show's "guest villains" would be Two-Face, adding, "Two-Face is a television commentator, you see, who unfortunately has a TV tube blow up in his face. Henceforth, one side of his face becomes contorted and gruesome, while the other side remains even-featured. Although one half of him could have remained on TV, he decides instead to turn—naturally—to crime." Whether or not a script was commissioned, Two-Face did not make the cut, perhaps because he was considered too gruesome for the show's young viewers.[179]

In the first season, George Sanders, an actor best known for playing cads in films such as Joseph L. Mankiewicz's *All About Eve* (1950), appeared as Mr. Freeze, a villain who had first appeared in the *Batman* comic books in February 1959 as Mr. Zero. After the TV show changed his name to Mr. Freeze, the comic books followed suit.

Another first season villain who came straight from the comic books was Jervis Tetch, also known as the Mad Hatter, who first appeared in the comics in 1948 as a very short, auburn-haired thief patterned after the character from Lewis Carroll's *Alice in Wonderland*. He reappeared in the comics of the 1950s and 60s as a more average-sized man with red hair and a thick mustache who concealed all sorts of weaponry in his hat. Though this version of the Mad Hatter would later be revealed as an impostor in the comic books, it is the one that the TV show's Mad Hatter was based on. Tony Award-winning actor David Wayne played the role.

False Face also had his beginnings in the comics. Created by Bill Finger, the master of disguise and mimicry appeared in *Batman* #113 in February 1958, never to be seen again. It was the same with the TV show, where he became a one-off villain, played by character actor Malachi Throne, whose face was hidden under a plastic mask. This angered him so much that he asked for his name to be removed from the credits. The producers complied, and the opening credits read "Special Guest Villain ? as False Face."

The show also invented new villains, such as Zelda the Great, who was based on escape artist the Great Carnado from the comic books, but given a sex change by Lorenzo Semple Jr. because it was felt that women were underrepresented among the villains. Dozier originally wanted either Bette Davis or Zsa Zsa Gabor in the role, but it went to Anne Baxter, star of *All About Eve* (1950), who would return for three episodes in the third season as Olga, Queen of the Bessarovian Cossacks. The first wholly original villain created for the series was King Tut, a Yale professor of Egyptology who, after a bump on the head, believed he was the ancient King of the Nile. Though Charlton Heston and Yul Brynner expressed interest in the role,[180] it eventually went to 28-year-old Victor Buono, who had been nominated for a Best Supporting Actor Oscar for his role opposite Bette Davis in *Whatever Happened to Baby Jane?* At 6'3" and weighing nearly 400 pounds, Buono was a physically imposing presence who possessed a marvelous way with words. "Victor could say anything and make me laugh," said writer Stanley Ralph Ross. "He had this wonderful way of biting off a line. Even the simplest line would be funny in Victor Buono's mouth."[181] Buono would return as King Tut for four more episodes in the second season and two in season three.

The Bookworm, on the other hand, only made one appearance. Roddy McDowall, an actor who had been busy in film and television since age 10, played the villain, who—dressed in a brown leather coat and hat—was the living embodiment of a book (he was leather bound). Naturally, the Bookworm episodes premiered during National Library Week.

With the show not only a hit but a bona fide cultural phenomenon, Dozier became inundated with calls from people wanting to be *Batman* evil-doers. Among those who vied for villainy were Cyril Ritchard, Nanette Fabray, James Mason and Jonathan Winters. Winters was immediately disqualified. "We can't have any comedians on this show," said Dozier. "If any actor plays it for laughs, he goes. He's got to act as if he's deciding whether to drop a bomb on Hanoi."[182] Laying out his criteria, Dozier said, "They must be classic actors. John Barrymore would have been great, because the character must have a Machiavellian quality, a sense of humor, and above all be capable of murder." Those who won the coveted Guest Villain slots were paid between $3,500 and $4,500 to menace the Dynamic Duo.[183] This was considered quite high in a time when guests on Lucille Ball's *The Lucy Show* received no more than $2,500.[184]

William Dozier found a novel way of dealing with the overflow of celebrities who wanted to be seen on the show—the wall climb window cameo. The gag was initiated with the Bookworm episodes. While Batman and Robin are scaling a building (a shot achieved by turning the set and the camera sideways, so the actors are actually walking horizontally but—when the shot is projected normally—appear to be walking vertically), Jerry Lewis opens a window and says, "Are you Batman? Oh, you must be because that's Robin. Hi, Robin."

"Yes, citizen," says Batman, "but don't be alarmed. We're here on official business."

"Holy human flies!" exclaims Lewis, closing the window.

Other performers who made window cameos included Dick Clark, Ted Cassidy as Lurch from *The Addams Family*, Edward G. Robinson, Art Linkletter, Werner Klemperer as Col. Klink from *Hogan's Heroes*, Bill Dana as José Jimenez, Sammy Davis Jr., Don Ho, and—for the Christmas episode—Santa Claus, as played by veteran B-Western sidekick Andy Devine. "It was a huge fad for stars to play the cameo bit for a while," said Semple. "Everybody wanted to get in the show."[185] The lucky few who made the cut, according to *Daily Variety*, were paid $100 for their window-popping bits.[186]

Not all of the actors who were approached to appear on *Batman* leapt at the chance, however. Doris Day was asked in January 1966, and politely declined.[187] Venerable actor Spencer Tracy was also courted. "Just the other day Bill Dozier sent me a letter and asked me to do—what the devil do they call it?—a cameo," said Tracy. "Said didn't I have a grandchild who'd get a kick out of seeing Grandpa as a cameo on *Batman*. Wasn't even one of those villain things." Tracy said it reminded him of when Margaret Sullavan was asked to play a role in an Andy Hardy film. Said Tracy, "She wrote back and said she'd be delighted to appear in the one entitled *Death Comes to Andy Hardy*."[188] After the second season, the cameos were dropped.

BATMANIA

In the spring and summer of 1966, Batman fever exploded across the nation. At the end of January, when the show had been on the air for only three weeks, Chicago DJ Ron Riley announced on his program that he was beginning a *Batman* club. Riley ordered 25,000 *Batman* kits, which included bumper stickers, club cards, and buttons. Within 24 hours of announcing the club, he received 30,000 requests.[189] By the end of the week, the number had climbed to 90,000.[190] In Orange County, California, students at McPherson Junior High School circulated a petition to keep their teachers from assigning homework on the evenings that *Batman* was broadcast. *The Los Angeles Times* said parents and school officials cheered the show for providing teens with clean-cut role models instead of long-haired rebels.[191] At the University of Michigan, *Batman* became the theme of the winter wonderland. UCLA's Mardi Gras also adopted a *Batman* motif.

In New York, Upper East Side bars such as Geordie's, Friday's and the White Horse Inn posted signs notifying their customers that *Batman* was on the house TV every Wednesday and Thursday. "The customers come in here, sit around and have a few laughs watching *Batman*," said the owner of Geordie's. "They joke about the show and yell out when certain things happen. *Batman* is more enjoyable when you're

having a couple of beers."[192] A marquee over a bar on Chicago's Clark Street read "Protected by Batman." Across the street, a sign at a laundry said, "Help Batman and Robin Fight Grime."[193] In Albuquerque, New Mexico, the Peacock Lounge was renamed the Peacock Batroom, and featured a combo that billed itself as "The Batmen with Linda Robin."[194] A laundry service in the San Fernando Valley, just above Los Angeles, advertised on its trucks, "Batman capes cleaned free."[195]

San Francisco seemed to go particularly "batty," as reported by *Daily Variety* on February 7, 1966. KGO-TV, the local ABC outlet, had promoted *Batman* by using a spotlight to project a Batsignal on city landmarks like the Mark Hopkins Hotel, the Hall of Justice, and City Hall, as well as some low-lying clouds. Meanwhile, a North Beach cabaret called Big Al's began featuring a topless Batgirl costumed in hood, cape, utility belt and tights—effectively covering everything but her naked torso. She writhed to music provided by a combo called The BatMen. A Sunnyvale discotheque changed its name to "Wayne Manor" and redecorated itself as the Batcave, offering "Batinis" served by Batgirl cocktail waitresses. At bars like the Pierce Street Annex, a popular after-hours watering hole for advertising executives and young professionals, patrons began Batman Fan Clubs, gathering together on Wednesdays and Thursdays to cheer Batman and boo the villains while downing martinis. KGO-TV morning show host Jim Dunbar began offering "Batman for Governor" bumper stickers, and received more letters and mail requests than for any other promotional campaign in the station's history.[196]

In Los Angeles, elementary schools enticed children to buy school lunches by serving a special *Batman* lunch. Virginia Starr, director of school food services, said, "When the lunch prices were raised from 25 cents to 35 cents this year, the number of lunches served dropped about 300 a day. I had to do something so I dreamed up this way to make the lunches attractive to the children. After all, the food service has to be self-supporting. And if we can bring nutrition to the children by giving it a fancy name, this is good." The *Batman* lunch included a Bat Burger (hamburger and relish on a bun), Robin Succotash (lima beans and corn) and Commissioner's Salad (chopped fruit in raspberry Jell-O topped with marshmallows). Steven O'Connor, an 8-year-old at Santa Anita School, said, "This sure tastes different," as he bit into his Bat Burger, which—despite its fancy name—was regular school fare.[197]

The success of the show kept the 1943 Columbia Pictures *Batman* serial in the limelight. Already a hit in college towns, Columbia now rolled the serial out to other theaters nationwide as a two-part kiddie matinee attraction, showing eight chapters in one sitting and seven in the next.[198] When it was shown at the Cinema Theater in Los Angeles in January—after the premiere of the TV show—it broke house attendance records.

The serial became an international phenomenon when it played in London in February, where it was such a hit at the Columbia Theatre that it was moved to the Gala Royal Theatre to finish its run.[199] *The Daily Mail* said the London audience "almost steals the picture from the actors. Boos and hisses rend the air, cheers raise the rafters and laughter drowns the ballroom-fabric dialogue."[200]

On March 12, 1966, the chapter-play began a 16-day run at the prestigious DeMille Theatre in Times Square, which normally presented first-run features

Batman's Batmobile became as big a star as the superhero. It spawned miniature Corgi and Hot Wheels versions for kids, as well as an Aurora model kit. The original still tours on the classic car circuit (Courtesy Adam West, © Twentieth Century Fox Television).

with reserved seating.[201] On its first two-day weekend, it grossed a very respectable $11,800.[202] One of the reviewers who saw it in New York was Raymond Durgnat, who wrote in *Films and Filming* that the serial "raises abysmal awfulness to the heights of hilarity. It stirs the critical faculties, activating the mind on that strange level where boredom allies itself with total relaxation, so that utter irresponsibility comes bubbling exhilaratingly up, like champagne...one of its charms is that it's so ideal for amateur satirists that one can't help but surrender to its anti-aesthetic delights."[203]

Meanwhile, current Batman Adam West delighted in piles of fan mail. In one three week period in February, he received 4,000 fan letters. "I even get them from teachers, with little drawings from grade school kids," said West, who reflected on his own childhood by saying, "I was a maverick. I went to five different colleges looking for I don't know quite what…Teens are mavericks today. I like that. It keeps them from that terrible thing—the herd. I dig their individualness."[204] Two months later, the piles of mail became mountains; in April, West received 33,958 letters, 24,731 addressed simply to Batman and 9,587 addressed to him personally.[205]

Burt Ward also received "from 3,000 to 5,000 letters a week," he said, adding, "One girl was so far gone that she said, 'I watch you every night of the week.' We're only on two nights." Teenage girls wrote begging Ward to call them, and on occasion, he did. "That really drives them crazy," he said. Once, a young girl wrote asking Ward to call her collect. He complied, but the girl's mother answered the phone when he called. "Her mother said, 'She's a minor. She can't accept the call. I said, 'This is Burt Ward, I'm Robin, and your daughter asked me to call her.' 'Yeah,' her mother said, 'and I'm a monkey's uncle.'"[206]

Batman received more requests for press visits than any other program in 20th Century-Fox Television's history.[207] Its Batcave location at the Desilu Culver City lot also became one of the most-visited sets in film history; practically everyone working in the film industry who wanted to seem like a hero to their kid had to take their young ones to visit the *Batman* set; by the second season, it was common for as many as 200 guests to be watching the filming from the sidelines.[208]

In an era when practically every top TV star released a 45rpm novelty record—and some, like Sebastian Cabot of *Family Affair*, released whole albums— the *Batman* stars were corralled to record a trio of singles. Frank Gorshin fared best, recording vocals to "The Riddler Song," composed and arranged by jazz great Mel Tormé. Adam West, who had a pleasant enough voice, recorded "Miranda," an ode to a woman who wants to look under his mask. Burt Ward, on the other hand, should have called in sick to the studio. His 45 single contained two songs produced by Frank Zappa, featuring Ward backed by The Mothers of Invention. "Boy Wonder, I Love You" was a typical novelty song, which basically consisted of Ward reading a love letter from a fan. The flip side, "Orange Colored Sky," was Ward's take on a song recorded earlier by Nat King Cole. Instead of talking his way through it, Ward actually tried to sing. He claims that the recording company hired a voice coach to work with him, but the coach quickly gave up in frustration. The end result was one of the worst songs ever committed to acetate. Another Ward recording, "Teenage Bill of Rights," was never released. Four albums that included the *Batman* theme were released almost simultaneously in March, 1966—*The Ventures Play Themes From Batman, Get Smart and Other TV Shows* (Dolton LP), *Neal Hefti* (RCA LP), *The Marketts Interpret the Batman Show* (Warners LP), and *Sunday Morning With the Comics* (Reprise LP).[209] In the following months, Jan and Dean recorded the theme, and the British rock group The Who covered it on their album, *A Quick One*. Even Bob Kane got into the act, writing sketches for the comedy team of Marty Allen and Steve Rossi for their parody album, *The Adventures of Batman and Rubin* (Mercury).[210]

Adam West made his television singing debut when he was a guest on ABC's variety series *The Hollywood Palace* in early March. Milton Berle, handling the hosting chores that week, kicked off with a monologue in which he said Batman was on his way to the Hollywood Palace. After a cutaway to a stock shot of the Batmobile leaving the Batcave, West—in full Batman regalia—strode onto the stage to trade jokes with Berle (and this just weeks after Berle had publicly slammed the show). West sang "Miranda" and "Only You Can See Her" on the program. Later in the show, Berle appeared as Superman in a sketch that had Martha Raye trying to destroy the Man of Steel by seducing him, until Batman comes to the rescue. On October 8, West returned to host *The Hollywood Palace*, with guests Ray Charles, Roy Rogers, Dale Evans and Joey Heatherton. This time around, he sang "Orange Colored Sky"— the song Burt Ward had recorded—and "The Summer Wind." When Bing Crosby hosted the program's Christmas show, West was back, this time joining Louis Nye in a sketch where Bruce Wayne tries to return a Batman costume to a department store before sitting down with the Crosby children to sing "This Old Man."

The popularity of the *Batman* series also brought Bob Kane into the limelight. Sought out for newspaper and talk show interviews, Kane proudly touted himself as Batman's creator. Publicly, Kane championed the series, but privately he was less enthused, according to scriptwriter Stanley Ralph Ross. "He was pleasant, complimented me a few times, but he thought the show was 'too funny,'" said Ross. "He was very annoyed with what we were doing to Batman, didn't like it, and wanted it more serious. But the show went far beyond what Bob created originally. Bob's original stuff was sort of primitive."[211]

In April 1966, a 50¢ Signet paperback reprinting some of the early comic book adventures, *Batman: The Best of the Original Batman*, entered *The New York Times* paperback bestsellers top ten list upon publication.[212] The first printing was originally to have been 850,000 copies, but while the presses were still turning, it was upped to 1,150,000. Signet followed this with another paperback, *Batman vs. Three Villains of Doom*, by Winston Lyon, with an initial printing of 850,000 copies.[213] Winston Lyon was a pseudonym for William Woolfolk, a prolific writer of Golden Age comic books such as *Batman, Superman*, and *Captain Marvel* who was known in the industry as "the Shakespeare of the comics." He later moved into television, where he earned Emmy nominations for scripts he penned for the TV series *The Defenders*. Later, Woolfolk— again using the pen name Winston Lyon—wrote *Batman vs. The Fearsome Foursome*, a novelization of the *Batman* movie.[214]

Besides books, there were Batman costumes, soap, greeting cards, tee shirts, toy Batmobiles, jigsaw puzzles, model kits and board games. The first store to carry Batman tee shirts, Gimbels of Philadelphia, sold out of their entire stock of 360 in one day, and immediately ordered 2,400 more.[215] National Periodical Publications made so much money from these items that they purchased their sales agent, Licensing Corporation of America, on June 23, 1966.[216] Sales of Batman items were projected to bring in $3 million in profit for the year.[217] This was good news for William Dozier, whose production company, Greenway Productions, greatly benefited from the sale of Batman products. "In our first year of merchandising from *Batman* we expect gross sales up to 80 million dollars. We have toys, capes, masks, shirts, recordings—some

500 items—every title preceded with the distinguishing word, bat," said Dozier. "Greenway, in its corporate set-up, has substantial interest in the profits of all these enterprises."[218]

Even E. William Henry, the head of the Federal Communications Commission, was infected with Bat-fever. At a benefit dinner dance at New York's Shoreham Hotel on March 5, Henry played Batman and writer Philip Stern played Robin in a skit written by columnist Art Buchwald, in which Batman helped President Johnson solve the Vietnam War. Among those observing the shenanigans were Franklin D. Roosevelt Jr., who was the Master of Ceremonies, Senators Claiborne Pell of Rhode Island, Joseph D. Tydings of Maryland, Warren G. Magnuson of Washington, and Frank Church of Idaho, Presidential assistant Jack Valenti, Associate Justice Potter Stewart and ambassadors from Algeria, Belgium, Ireland, Kuwait, New Zealand, Spain, and Sweden.[219] A month later, when Henry resigned as FCC chairman, Mrs. Edmond Howar, fashion advisor to Lynda, Luci and Mrs. Lyndon B. Johnson, saluted him with a *Batman*-themed party at a Washington discothèque, featuring a huge statue with a Batman cape and napkins that said "Holy Resignation?" The guests were encouraged to come in costume, and *The New York Times* noted that Robert Vaughn, star of the TV spy series *The Man From U.N.C.L.E.*, came as the man from U.N.C.L.E.[220]

Pravda, the Soviet newspaper, commented on *Batman* in April, accusing the show of brainwashing Americans to become "willing murderers in the Vietnam jungle" and saying that Batman was "the representative of the broad mass of American billionaires" who "kills his enemies beautifully, effectively and with taste, so that shoulder blades crack loudly and scalps break like cantaloupes." The article said those responsible for *Batman*, besides becoming rich, were "striving to brainwash the ordinary American, to get him used to the idea that murder is beautiful, that it is a worthy occupation for a real man, a superman." An ABC spokesman countered, "*Pravda*, as usual, is a little mixed up. Batman doesn't kill anyone. He socks them— BIFF! POW! BAM!—but they always come back. The underlying theme of *Batman* is good triumphing over evil. Pravda seems to have difficulty understanding this or the humor of *Batman*."[221] Later in the year, a Russian satirical magazine, *Krokodil*, said that Batman and Robin were "like idealized representatives of the F.B.I." and accused them of "deepening the spiritual vacuum of the United States." The magazine went on to say that *Batman* had hardened American schoolchildren to violence so that they no longer flinched at cruelty and took the death of relatives in their stride. It also called the Dynamic Duo tools of capitalism, claiming that businessmen had made $75 million to $80 million from the "children, teen-agers and underdeveloped adults" who followed Batman's exploits.[222]

When tens of thousands of protesters marched through major cities across the country on May 26, 1966 in protest of America's involvement in Southeast Asia, marchers on Pennsylvania Avenue carried a sign saying, "Batman opposes the war in Viet Nam."[223] In fact, *Batman* was being seen in Vietnam by the summer, when ABC struck a deal with the Armed Forces Radio and Television Network to beam *Batman* to U.S. soldiers in the Asian country.[224] By August, the Caped Crusader had entered the war zone in another way. When a development group called the Army Combat Team in Vietnam equipped combat helicopters with a prototype night vision technology, the experiment was called Project Batman. After months of testing, five helicopters were equipped with television systems that amplified light cast by the moon or stars sufficiently to illuminate the landscape, allowing the soldiers to see enemy movement in the darkness. On the nose of each helicopter was a silhouette of a black bat inside a white circle. Each member of the team wore a shoulder patch that said "Batman" with a cartoon of the bat symbol on a TV screen. When the helicopter pilots spoke over their radios, they used the call sign "Batman."[225]

Not everyone was swept up in Bat-fever, however. In February, Compton Advertising, Inc. handled a promotion for Procter & Gamble that, on the surface, seemed innocuous enough. The plan called for an announcement during the *Batman* program telling kids that they could get an autographed photo of Batman and Robin by simply mailing an empty Gleem toothpaste carton to "Batman, Bat Cave, North Carolina." The agency had prepared 250,000 photos, with an option for another million.[226] The New York advertising agency wanted a memorable address for the offer, so they checked the post office for a Gotham City, but found none. However, looking under "B" for "Bat," they found Bat Cave, population 200. The agency also contacted the regional post office headquarters in Asheville, North Carolina, who said they would be willing to cooperate.

In advance of the promotion, news offices around the country were flooded with a press release that read: "The Batman cometh—into your home via an offer of a personal photo." The release predicted "one of the largest avalanches of photo requests in history." The news release prompted a mention of the gimmick in *The New York Times*, a newspaper read by Mrs. Walter Flinch. Mrs. Flinch, the granddaughter of the late Harley Procter, a founder of Procter & Gamble, lived in St. Louis, but also just happened to have a home in Bat Cave, North Carolina. In fact, she owned the cave that gave the community its name. She also owned a lot of stock in Procter & Gamble. Mrs. Flinch promptly phoned Procter & Gamble to voice her displeasure with the stunt, which was sure to overwhelm the tiny Bat Cave post office. William Donaldson, of Procter & Gamble's promotional staff, said Mrs. Flinch "expressed considerable displeasure—I might even say she made her protest in spades. We felt it worthwhile to listen to her." As a result, the TV commercials, which were already prepared, were hastily revised, so that viewers were now asked to send their empty toothpaste cartons to Maple Plain, Minnesota. "That's a town of 754 souls 20 miles from Minneapolis," said Donaldson. "It has nothing to do with bats, but it is a mailing address used by a large custom service firm which handles such premium offers for P&G and other companies. They are geared for this operation."[227]

Batman also came under attack from Dr. Benjamin Spock, the author of *Baby and Child Care*, which became one of the biggest best sellers of all time after its publication in 1946. When the show first appeared, Dr. Spock, a professor of child development at Western Reserve University in Cleveland, said he thought it would be fine viewing, although he hadn't watched it himself. By the summer, he had changed his mind. "I may have said casually that *Batman* was okay, I don't deny it," said Spock. "I've made mistakes before. But if I said it, I said it in ignorance. I was thinking about it in regards to teenagers and adults." After hearing from parents, psychologists, psychiatrists and students, he concluded, "*Batman* is bad for pre-school children. It encourages free expression for violence. All this smash, bang, it says to children that adults think this is all right...We are a country of people who indulge themselves in free expressions of aggressiveness. There's much too little restraint on aggressiveness. Television is one of the places where you see our appetite. We delight in Westerns, crime and brutality. Our treatment of Indians, Negroes and immigrants is unbelievable. We seem to glory in aggressiveness if we make believe or if we think the other guy is a bad guy. I make an earnest plea that we stop." Dr. Spock believed that *Batman* on TV was more harmful than the comic book version, because he was "a lot more vivid in motion. There are flesh and blood people. It's easier to recognize fantasy in books. But pre-school children have no way of telling what's make-believe. The fact that parents let them see this makes children consider it okay."[228]

Dr. Joyce Brothers also hopped on the Bat-bashing wagon. Addressing a meeting at the Iowa Floor Covering Club in Des Moines in June, 1966, Brothers said, "A child can point a toy gun at another child and say, 'bang, bang' and the other child plays dead...But little kids can punch each other and do a lot of damage...There's been a rash of nursery school incidents in which kids were kicking and hitting each other as a way of solving their conflicts."[229] Other newspaper columnists echoed Spock's and Brothers's concerns, noting that *Batman* seemed to provoke young children to fight in mimicry of their TV idols. William Dozier responded by saying, "As for the criticism that it incites youngsters to slug one another and yell 'pow' and 'wham,' I suspect they'd do it anyway but just not yell 'pow' and 'wham'."[230]

When *Variety*'s Army Archerd asked Adam West about rumors that the show had a "homosexual leaning," West quipped, "Can't understand that—how could anyone claim it when all we do is fly around in tights and boots, and shun any female entanglements?"[231] Archerd got a first-hand demonstration of Batman and Robin's sex appeal when he observed Adam West and Burt Ward, in costume, making an appearance at a 20th Century-Fox/Bristol Meyers party on the Fox lot to promote the local test of ten specials to be produced by Fox and sponsored by Bristol Meyers. Archerd wrote that the duo was attacked by a horde of adult female fans, adding, "the excitement equaled the squeals, yells exhibited by teen and sub-teenagers to the Beatles. Bill Self, Fox-TV production boss, seated at our table, observed, 'And to think I came close to turning down Bill Dozier's ideas for this series!'"[232]

A Congressman, Democratic Representative Andrew Jacobs Jr. of Indiana, decided to use the power of *Batman* to effect positive change. When one of his nephews refused to wear a seat belt because "Batman never uses seat belts," Jacobs said in a House of Representatives speech, "If Batman can get millions of American children to turn their coats into capes, I just have the suspicion that he could also get them to wear their seat belts. Holy belt buckle! Think of the lives that might be saved if Batman could influence more people to fasten their seat belts."[233] In that instance, Dozier listened, and in subsequent episodes of *Batman*, when the crime fighters leapt into the Batmobile, they were seen snapping their seat belts together before the vehicle roared out of the Batcave.

Besides being phenomenally popular, *Batman* also received industry recognition at the end of April 1966. When Emmy Award nominations were announced, Frank Gorshin was honored with a nomination in the category of Outstanding Performance by an Actor in a Comedy Supporting Role.[234] He lost to Don Knotts, who won for an episode of *The Andy Griffith Show* where Barney Fife returned to Mayberry.

As the first season of *Batman* ended, the show rode high in the ratings, was splashed across countless magazine covers, and moved millions of dollars in merchandise. Having conquered television, *Batman* was now poised to conquer movies.

BATMAN—THE MOVIE

William Dozier set the wheels in motion for a *Batman* feature film at the end of February 1966, just weeks after the show exploded on the airwaves.[235] "We'll have the Joker, the Riddler, the Catwoman and the Penguin get together to stamp out Batman," said Dozier, "and the humor comes in when they fight about what to do. It's an exploitation film."[236] With a budget of $1,600,000, the film was scheduled for 26 days of first-unit shooting and six days of second unit filming.[237]

Dozier hired Leslie H. Martinson, director of a couple of *Batman* episodes featuring the Penguin, to bring the show's peculiar brand of camp humor to the big screen. Martinson, who a few years earlier had directed *PT 109*, a film about the World War II experiences of John F. Kennedy starring Cliff Robertson, appreciated that the *Batman* script's ending made a wry comment about international relations. "I've waited all these years to make a picture with a great social comment," said Martinson, "but I never thought it would be on *Batman*."[238]

The same actors who made the roles famous on television played the villains in the *Batman* film, with the exception of the Catwoman. On March 31, 1966, *Daily Variety* announced that Julie Newmar would be reprising her role,[239] but on April 19 came the news that she would have to bow out of the feature because of a recurrence of a chronic back ailment[240] (not, as has often been reported, because she was filming *McKenna's Gold*, which didn't start rolling until late in 1967). With Newmar unavailable and less than a week to go before the commencement of filming, Dozier found a last-minute replacement in Lee Meriwether, a stunning 5'8-1/2" former Miss America who was about to start filming 20th Century-Fox's TV series *The Time Tunnel*.

Meriwether beat out hundreds of other actresses who were vying for the part by becoming a feline. In her audition with director Leslie H. Martinson, she curled up in a chair and licked her hand, imitating a cat. Martinson was sold, and Meriwether was measured for a catsuit. In a 1966 interview with Don Alpert of *The Los Angeles Times*, she said, "I'm very big in the neighborhood now with the kids. I took the costume home and worked in it to get the cat movements. My daughters insisted I parade up the street to show their friends. The looks I got from the mailman and the Helms man [bakery salesman] and the man up the street who was watering his lawn—he took a leap into the house. And I had to stop at Netta's house and Holly's house. It was double-take time."[241]

The production office at 20th Century Fox generally allowed ten weeks for the completion of a script. Dozier joked that the entire *Batman* film would be made in that time. "Lorenzo Semple Jr., our principal TV writer, wrote the feature treatment in one week, the script in 10 days and a revised one 72 hours later," said Dozier. "The whole picture should be finished within these 10 weeks."[242] Semple recalled, "They said they wanted to do a movie, and so I wrote a feature *Batman* movie. I just said I'll write one. The only requirement was that it have all the villains in it. So I wrote it. And they did it."

"I haven't made features in 10 years, the last at RKO," said Dozier. In fact, his last film, *Stage Struck*, a backstage drama directed by Sidney Lumet and starring Henry Fonda, had been made eight years earlier, but those years had seen a lot of changes in the industry. "All my friends are in pictures and I've heard many of them say that most of the fun has gone out of it," said Dozier. "I don't anticipate the fun going out of *Batman* because that's what it is—fun."[243]

Before the cameras rolled, however, there was a major detail that had to be worked out. 20th Century Fox prepared a contract offering Adam West $45,000 to play Batman in the film, roughly the same as for 10 weeks of the TV show. But with the explosive popularity of the series, West decided to take a gamble—he demanded $100,000. With filming imminent, the studio agreed to his terms.[244]

Filming began Monday, April 25, 1966 on Fox's Stage 10, less than a week after the first season episodes finished shooting. "It's a total amplification of the television show," said Dozier. "Big screen—plus color, which 30 to 40 million people who haven't got color at home will be seeing for the first time in theaters. Plus four of their favorite villains at once. Plus 1-1/2 hours of entertainment instead of 30 minutes. And a much more involved plot, a much broader-scope story."[245]

Adam West, who pronounced that the movie's script was "like *What's New Pussycat*—only funnier and wilder,"[246] pressed for more scenes as Bruce Wayne than the average TV episode allowed. Leslie Martinson, who directed West's failed *Doc Holliday* TV pilot, helped the actor find some new insights into the dual characters of Bruce Wayne and Batman. In *Back to the Batcave*, a book he wrote with Jeff Rovin, West said, "I found things in the characters that surprised me, for example some steel in Bruce. He didn't have to put on the Batsuit to stand up for himself or be sexy or confident. Conversely, I realized how much he needed the Batsuit for other things. In musicals, people sing things that would be ludicrous if expressed in dialogue. The costume is like that. When he's Batman, Bruce can express anger or sadness that his social standing and emotional walls won't let him show in his day-to-day life."[247]

Once on the set, Lee Meriwether's biggest challenge was keeping a straight face, especially in the love scenes with Adam West. "The kissing in films as an actress is ridiculous," she said. "I have trouble from getting giggly. You have thirty men staring at you. And at eight in the morning, to kiss Adam West! I mean, he's very nice, but I giggled. I was afraid he would take it personally."[248]

With a budget more befitting of a movie than a TV episode, production designer Serge Krizman was tasked with building some new vehicles. "We've done lots of new things for the movie which also will be used in the new TV episodes," said Krizman. "There's a Batboat—jet-powered, of course—a new Batcycle with sidecar, a Batcopter with bat-type wings—believe me, that wasn't easy to do—and Penguin will have a submarine."[249] The film also answered a question that schoolchildren had been debating all winter: After sliding down their Batpoles, how did Batman and Robin return to stately Wayne Manor? Krizman came up with the answer: jet-powered platforms.[250] The shot of Bruce Wayne being propelled up the pole would be recycled for later TV episodes.

As it turned out, the Batcycle had been seen once before. In a pair of Penguin episodes two-thirds of the way through the first season, Batman and Robin leapt on a Batcycle. Leased from a Hollywood company that rented vehicles for motion pictures and TV shows, the first Batcycle was a 1959 Harley Davidson and sidecar, painted black with red trim and with a scalloped Plexiglas windscreen added. While the series was in production, Dan Dempski, a mechanic who worked for car customizer and Batmobile creator George Barris, decided to create his own version of a Batcycle for possible use on the show. He contacted Yamaha, who agreed to provide a Yamaha Catalina 250 to be customized. Working with designs sketched by Tom Daniel, Dempski and a friend, Korki Korkes, began building the bike in Dempski's garage. When it was finished, Dempski contacted Charles FitzSimons, the line producer of Batman, to sell him on the bike. With the movie about to go into production, there was more money available for assorted Bat toys, so FitzSimons agreed to have a look at Dempski's Batcycle and sidecar. Impressed, he entered into an agreement with Dempski and Korkes, who formed their own company, Kustomotive, to market the bike. The agreement called for Kustomotive to deliver the Batcycle to the 20th Century Fox lot on April 18, 1966—in time for filming of the movie—at which time they would be paid $350. Kustomotive would also receive $50 per week for each week that the bike was used by the producers, up to a ceiling of $2500. Kustomotive got to keep all profits from car show exhibitions, and promptly made four duplicates to put on the car show circuit.[251]

Part of the idea behind the Batcycle was that the sidecar was actually a go-kart that could shoot off on its own course. Though a neat idea in theory, it was rather scary in practice. The four-wheeled go-kart, with a 50cc Yamaha engine, rested inside a wooden platform attached to the Batcycle. As the Batcycle slowed, the go-kart would shoot out and take off under its own steam. Stuntmen Hubie Kerns and Victor Paul—doubling for Adam West and Burt Ward—were less than impressed when they were initially shown the vehicle. "They brought it out at four o'clock at night and we gotta use it at eight o'clock the next morning," said Paul. "I said, 'Jesus, give me a break—this is ridiculous.' The guy who built this nightmare, as I call it, takes it around the parking lot and almost kills himself. He hits a parked car with it, gets up, and says that's the way it works. I said, 'That's the way it works? You almost killed yourself!' Sam Strangis, the production manager, just put his eyebrows up and walked away and left us standing in the parking lot, so Hubie and I stayed until six o' clock at night trying to work this out."[252]

Operating the go-kart while on his hands and knees was perilous for Paul. "Hubie wasn't that much of a bike man at that time," said the stuntman. "He drove a motorcycle but this weirdo thing was different. If Hubie was doing 35 miles an hour, I really had to rev it up and really gun it to shoot off this platform going the same direction, and that was hard to do. That was the nightmare of it. I used to yell, 'Would you slow down for crying out loud, before you kill me?' He used to laugh."[253]

The Batcopter was a Bell 47 helicopter—the same type seen years later in the opening credits of *M*A*S*H*—provided by National Helicopter, a company begun in 1957 and located at the Van Nuys Airport, northwest of Hollywood. National developed some of the first traffic helicopters used in the Los Angeles areas, and also ran aerial tours, conducted geological surveys, and dusted crops. They also provided helicopters for the 1957-1959 Desilu TV series, *Whirlybirds*. By the mid-1960s, National had a stable of over thirty Bell 47's, which they rented out to movies and TV programs. When they were asked to provide a helicopter for the *Batman* feature, they chose a G3B-1 model Bell 47 that was built in 1964, which had previously been used as a news helicopter by ABC. The helicopter was painted red and fitted with bat wings—actually, tubular frames covered with canvas, which unfortunately reduced the power of the helicopter by 50%. All of the shots involving the helicopter were filmed at the Van Nuys airport, except for shots of the helicopter at sea, which were shot at Marineland in Palos Verdes, and the shots of the helicopter after landing at the Foam Rubber Wholesalers Convention, which were filmed on the New York Street on the Fox backlot. National leased the helicopter to Fox for five days at a rate of $750 per day. Pilot Harry Hauss doubled for Adam West flying the helicopter, while Hubie Kerns doubled for West for the shot of Batman getting dunked in the ocean while holding onto the helicopter ladder.[254]

The Batboat was designed by Glastron, a company founded in Austin, Texas in 1956 by Robert Hammond, an aircraft designer who had seen what a new material called fiberglass had meant to aviation, and was eager to see what it would do for the family boat. The first year, Hammond and his designer, Mel Whitley, built 24 boats. Over the next two years, they built nearly 5,000. When it was decided to give Batman a boat, Dozier contacted Glastron with the specifications: it needed seating for Batman and Robin, glowing bat eyes, a red flashing bat beacon, hatches for the Batzooka, a glowing Batsignal in the tailfin, and it had to pass a Coast Guard inspection and be done in good taste. It also had to be ready in 31 days. Designer Mel Whitley took up the challenge. With contractors Tony Bell and Rob Robertson, he got a Glastron V-174 test hull and created a mock-up using ten rolls of masking tape and a hundred pounds of cardboard. Production designer Serge Krizman and producer William Dozier approved the design, and Whitley and his team set to work in earnest, building the boat in a garage. Working double shifts, they outfitted the craft with prop gadgets, twin windscreens, a center console, and an aft to deck cover with a bat fin that included the glowing bat signal. There was also a fake jet nozzle that squirted water and gave the illusion of a nuclear boat motor; in fact, the boat was powered by a MerCruiser Chevrolet V-6 engine. The finished boat had a top speed of 45mph. When it was tested, the bat fin in the back was too heavy, and wouldn't allow the boat to plane down. An adjustment to the drive and the addition of a new prop solved that problem, but then a new one arose—the water squirter in the rear wasn't seated properly, and was taking in too much water, threatening to sink the boat. After that was corrected, the boat was delivered.[255]

Adam West piloted the Batboat for several scenes, and wrote in his book *Back to the Batcave* that it was his "favorite show toy."[256] Burt Ward had somewhat different feelings about it, especially after a frightening accident. He arrived on location at the Santa Barbara pier one morning to see the boat moored at the dock, and learned that stuntman Hubie Kerns, dressed as Batman, would be driving the Batboat for a shot where, in pursuit of the villains, Robin stands up in the boat and shoots a Batzooka. Since the camera boat would be alongside and filming tight on Robin when he fired the weapon, it was felt that Ward's stunt double, Victor Paul, could not be used. Ward was apprehensive; he remembered the first day of filming the series, when Kerns was at the wheel of the Batmobile and Ward was almost flung from it as the car zoomed out of the Batcave. Now, faced with a similar set-up, Ward said to the stuntman, "Hubie, I swear I'll kill you if you drive this boat recklessly." Soon, they were on the water, bouncing along at 45 knots, one second airborne, the next second slamming into the waves. When the director on the camera boat, signaled "Action," Ward stood and pretended to fire the Batzooka. The camera boat, bouncing on the waves ahead of the Batboat, hadn't gotten a steady shot, so they swung around to get a close up. Unfortunately, this created a trough, which the Batboat fell into, flipping over on its side—the side where Ward was positioned. Forced underwater, he was dragged through the brine, holding his breath and holding on to the Batzooka until the boat righted itself.[257]

Since the four villains spent about half the movie aboard the Penguin's submarine, that craft also had to be fabricated. Production designer Serge Krizman knew of a submarine hull built for the Frank Sinatra film *Assault on a Queen*, which just finished shooting at Paramount. Krizman added a penguin to the conning tower of the hull and repainted it, then had a matching 6-foot model created for underwater shots. At the suggestion of line producer Charles FitzSimons, Krizman added penguin flippers to the back of the sub instead of propellers. Both the miniature and the full-size sub were filmed at 20th Century Fox's Malibu Ranch location, where they had a 4' deep lake and a giant blue sky backing. During filming of the climactic fight scene, the stuntmen had to dive into the water at an angle to keep from hitting the bottom. One stuntman, Ace Hudkins, still ended up in the hospital when he dove into the shallow water and struck his head.[258]

While filming on location on the Santa Barbara pier, 20,000 fans showed up to observe the proceedings. As the crowd became more and more restless and were threatening to break through a police barrier, Adam West grabbed a bullhorn and calmly walked over to them, explaining what the crew was doing and asking for cooperation. The crowd settled enough for filming to resume, but when they were finished, West and Burt Ward had to leave by boat.[259] Filming wrapped on May 31, 1966.

INTO THE SECOND SEASON

After completing the *Batman* movie, Adam West finally took a break, his only official time-off since he'd begun filming the series eight months earlier. With a grand total of three days to relax before filming of the second season commenced, West went sailing off Catalina. He returned to the set with the color of his hair lightened by the salt breezes, so he had to have it dyed "Bat-brown."[260] He told Clay Gowran of *The Chicago Tribune* that he felt *Batman* would be a long-running show. "This was a matter of concern at first," said West, "but now we definitely feel it's not a hula-hoop fad but real gold." He also confided that *Batman* would become "socially satirical" in the second season, saying, "We will start making comments, for instance, on social phenomena, like the poverty program and school dropouts."[261] Speaking to *Los Angeles*

Times critic Charles Champlin, West seemed optimistic about the upcoming season, saying, "When people who have talent and ideas get together and have a good time doing what they're doing, that's half the battle. I've always said that if we can keep the show fresh and fun, it could go on and on. We're not patronizing the audiences. We're not putting them on; we're giving them credit for understanding what we're doing." Reminded of all the pundits who said *Batman* wouldn't last, West simply responded, "Poor deluded journalists."[262]

With *Batman* a hit, William Dozier set about preparing other hero-themed TV shows. He hired Stan Hart and Larry Siegel to write a pilot for a *Wonder Woman* series, but unwisely discarded the comic book conception of the character. In Dozier's version, Diana Prince, played by Ellie Wood Walker, was an awkward woman with super powers who clearly had an idealized view of herself. When she changed into her Wonder Woman outfit, she preened in front of a mirror, seeing the reflection of a much more attractive woman, played by Linda Harrison. The five-minute pilot failed to generate a series. Dozier had better luck with an adaptation of the popular radio series *The Green Hornet*. Van Williams starred as Britt Reid, a newspaper publisher who fought crime in the guise of the Green Hornet with his trusty Asian manservant Kato, played by martial arts phenomenon Bruce Lee. Unlike *Batman*, *The Green Hornet* was played straight. "It would be foolhardy to try to copy *Batman*," said Dozier. "*Batman* is in a class by itself and any imposter would fall on its Batface."[263] As it happened, *The Green Hornet* fell on its face anyway, despite Dozier's effort to boost its ratings by having the Green Hornet and Kato make a window cameo on *Batman*, and joining the Caped Crusaders in a pair of episodes in *Batman*'s second season; ABC cancelled the show after one season. Dozier also produced a half-hour pilot for a *Dick Tracy* series, with Ray MacDonnell as Chester Gould's detective, which was supposed to have been a mid-season replacement for NBC in the 1966-67 season, but when *The Green Hornet* fell to the bottom of the ratings, NBC changed its mind.

For *Batman*'s second season, ABC-TV ordered 52 half-hours, with a $3,500,000 budget for the bunch.[264] The premiere episodes introduced the Archer, a villain who had originally appeared as a nemesis of Superman in *Superman* #13 (November/ December 1941). Famed actor Art Carney, immortal to many as Ed Norton from the *Honeymooners* shows and skits, played the villain, who dressed like Robin Hood and spoke in pseudo-Olde English. "It's an opportunity, basically, to overact and to have some fun," said Carney.[265] Stanley Ralph Ross, who wrote the Archer episodes, was less than thrilled with their execution. "The favorite *Batman* episode that I wrote was not the best one on the air," he said in an interview in James Van Hise's book, *Batmania*. "I really liked writing the Archer, but it didn't play well. I don't know if Art Carney was wrong for the part or if it was the director...It was very slow for me."[266]

Next up was a pair of episodes featuring the Catwoman, with Julie Newmar returning to the role she'd been unable to perform in the movie, and then another new villain was introduced, the Minstrel. Van Johnson, a top star of MGM dramas and musicals in the 1940s, was cast in the role. "I still have trouble with this baby-face of mine," said the actor, who was 50 years old at the time but looked younger. "You know I've never been able to play a villain? Until now. I'm going to play a character called Minstrel on *Batman*. My agent had a dickens of a time convincing them I could play a villain."[267] As with the Archer episode, the villain was poorly conceived, and Johnson's performance lacked the spark that Julie Newmar, Cesar Romero, Frank Gorshin and Burgess Meredith regularly brought to their recurring characters.

In-between filming new episodes, as the *Batman* movie was being edited and readied for theaters, Adam West and Burt Ward went on promotional tours around the country. West was scheduled to kick off the "Concerts at the Shea" series at Shea Stadium with a Batman-themed show on the afternoon and evening of June 25. Sharing the bill were Frank Gorshin, the Warren Covington Orchestra, musical acts including the Young Rascals, Junior Walker and the All-Stars, and the Chiffons, and 24 Batusi girls.[268] Within a month, 20,000 tickets were reportedly sold (the Beatles had played Shea Stadium the previous August, to a record crowd of 55,600).[269] However, events over the next few weeks threatened to derail the concert.

First, a newspaper exposé of the show's producer, Harry Bloomfield, revealed that the city had previously refused him a show license because in 1949 he had been sentenced to four months in jail for failing to give the Federal Government income tax and Social Security money from a production that failed.[270] Next came threatened defections by some of the scheduled rock groups, which led to rumors that the show might be canceled.[271] Then, just three days before the show, a thousand tickets were stolen from the offices of the publicist, Mal Braveman Associates. The tickets, valued at $6 each, had been set aside for the press. Braveman discovered the theft after arriving at work and finding the office doors unlocked.[272] As if that wasn't enough, the day before the show Parks Commissioner Thomas P.F. Hoving threatened to cancel the concert unless the sponsors, Concerts at the Shea, Inc., put up a $5,000 security against possible damage to the park. Hoving set a 9 PM deadline, and waited. As the hour grew later and later, he began to wonder what would happen if he followed through and pulled the plug on the show. "I was sweating it out," he said. "I had visions of real screams and teen-agers marching on City Hall." Finally, at exactly 9 PM, a representative from the sponsors arrived at Hoving's office with the cash.[273]

The next afternoon, on a blistering hot day, only 3,000 fans showed up. An hour before the 2 PM show time, carpenters and stagehands who feared they would not get paid began dismantling the stage platforms. Adam West had to personally assure them that, if necessary, he would pay their fees to keep them from sabotaging the show. When the show started, the hot-dog chomping kids, anxious to see their hero, had to endure two and a half hours of one rock group after another coming out and performing to little or no applause. But then, at 4:40 PM, Batman appeared from left field, circling the stadium in a Cadillac. *New York Times* reporter Robert Sherman wrote "shouts and cheers rolled down from the stands—the 3,000 sounded like 30,000." Frank Gorshin appeared as the Riddler, joining West for a routine that included the Riddler asking, "Why are the Mets like my mother-in-law's biscuits? Answer: they both need a better batter." Then, both West and Gorshin appeared dressed in normal attire to sing a few solo songs. "Gorshin's impersonations were, for the most part, lost in the wide open spaces," wrote Sherman, "but Adam West revealed a mellow, resonant, crooning voice that set the kids to cheering all over again." Then, after a performance by The Temptations, the show ended, to be repeated at 7:30 PM—again to a crowd of only approximately 3,000 fans.[274] Wrote

Herm Schoenfeld in *Weekly Variety*, "There is nothing more oppressive than the sight of enormous expanses of empty seats bearing down on a handful of people."[275] After the shows, West went to the post-show party, where Bob Kane handed him a script for a feature he hoped to produce called *Blind Man's Bluff*.[276]

But the saga was not quite over. In July, *The New York Times* reported that Licenses Commissioner Joel J. Tyler had opened an investigation of the Batman concert following complaints by creditors that they had not been paid. Three investigators were assigned to the case, and Tyler ordered Concerts at the Shea, Inc. to turn over their records from the event. The executive director of the Parks Department, Henry J. Stern, nonetheless reported that the city had received its $10,000 rental for the stadium and the $5,000 security against damage to the field.[277] Adam West had also been paid his $20,000 fee up front. Losses for the Batman concert ran to over $100,000, an amount that bankrupted Concerts at the Shea and ended plans for additional concerts, including one in August 1966 that was to have featured Bob Dylan.[278]

West returned to Los Angeles to continue filming new second-season episodes, and entertained an honored guest on the *Batman* set. His Highness Prince Surachatra Chatrachaya Purachatra of Thailand, visiting the United States in mid-July, made it a priority to meet Batman. The prince told Leonard Greenwood of *The Los Angeles Times*, "I'd like to buy *Batman*, but I'm not sure it would be hip in Thailand. Not yet, anyway. We'd have to educate the people to this sort of thing first, so I'm thinking of buying the full-length *Batman* film. This will prepare the ground and we might buy the television series later. The big difficulty is with the jargon. How do you translate 'Zap' and 'Zowie' into our language?"[279]

When the *Batman* film was completed, it had its first screening on a Saturday morning at the Carthay Circle theatre in Los Angeles on July 23 for a select audience that included director Leslie Martinson, Neil Hamilton, *Lost in Space* star Mark Goddard and his daughter, and a lot of kids. Before the film began, Adam West told the audience, "I can remember when my mother used to bring me to the Roxy early Saturday mornings—now, 20th-Fox is MY mother!"[280]

Filming of new episodes was again interrupted for the premiere of the *Batman* film, held in Austin, Texas, as a tribute to Glastron, builders of the Batboat.[281] On July 30, 1966, William Dozier, Adam West, Burgess Meredith, Cesar Romero, and Lee Meriwether flew to Austin, where the film had two premiere screenings to benefit the Austin Aqua Festival. After a press conference, the stars, wearing their costumes, were driven in open cars past 10,000 fans lining Congress Avenue to the theater, where the Batboat was on display. Burt Ward, whose wife was expecting, remained in Los Angeles.[282] The Batboat, but not the stars, then moved on to San Antonio, where local radio station KBAT sponsored two showings only of the film the following Friday at 11 PM and Saturday at 10 AM. Tickets for the special preview showing sold for $1 in advance, and $1.25 after 5 PM on the Friday.[283]

On August 6th, 20th Century Fox held a screening of the film at the studio to benefit the Los Angeles Orphanage Guild, followed by a luncheon[284] The following day, *Batman* received a public blessing from a clergyman. In a Sunday sermon at Manhattan's All Saints Episcopal Church, the Rev. Dr. Robert E. Terwilliger proclaimed that *Batman* was so successful not because it appealed to people's love of adventure and satire but because it provided a "much-needed emotional and almost religious" outlet for viewers. He qualified his statements, however, by saying it was a "second rate" emotional release, since it was grounded in a world of fantasy where total good triumphs completely over total evil. He went on to say that while he did not want to make too much of a "passing fad," Batman overcoming demonic characters like the Joker with Bat-gas and other "incredible devices" appealed to the public's attraction to "practical messiahs." "Batman is the savior who comes in from above to rescue the victims of malignant power with absolute goodness," said Dr. Terwilliger. "He is called into situations the police can't handle with a special cultic or prayer device called the Bat-phone. His miracles are the kind modern man likes most—not supernatural but scientific." Terwilliger said that Batman was "a savior figure," but added that he didn't like "this cultish worship of *Batman*," which he felt was unhealthy because "it is worship without commitment."[285]

The sermon, which was reported in *The New York Times*, earned Dr. Terwilliger a chance to meet Batman and Robin. Three weeks later, Adam West and Burt Ward came to Manhattan to promote the New York opening of the *Batman* movie. They were put on a bus and carted from theater to theater along with 20 bodyguards dressed as Gotham City police officers. Upon arrival at each venue, they charged out of the bus, ran through the mob, dashed into the theater and down the aisles, interacted with the filmgoers, and dashed back onto the bus before the screaming fans tore them to pieces. At one appearance, a teenager conked West over the head with a piece of pipe; luckily, his plastic cowl took the brunt of the blow, but still left him dazed. At another stop, the fans crowded around the bus and rocked it so violently it nearly overturned.[286]

The Rev. Dr. Terwilliger's encounter with the Caped Crusaders came at an event in Central Park, where 7,000 children turned out to see Batman and Robin at ceremonies honoring 43 children who had been selected as Junior Good Citizens. Parks Commissioner Thomas P.F. Hoving congratulated the Junior Citizens, but his remarks were drowned out by the army of youngsters screaming for their heroes. Hoving introduced Batman, and West, as loudly as he could, said, "Welcome on behalf of Robin the Wonder Boy and all those people in Gotham City." With Ward's assistance, he called off the names of the Junior Good Citizens—children selected from 25 youth groups who were ranked high in helping their youth centers—presenting each one with an award. Then, it was off in the Batbus to three parks in the Bronx—St. Mary's Recreation Center, James L. Lyons Square, and St. Mary's West playground. For safety's sake, they stuck close to the bus at each location, having become a little fearful of the cultish worship of savior figures.[287] "I had wanted to experience New York," wrote Adam West, "but all I got to experience was Batmania."[288]

During the few days that West and Ward were in Manhattan, *The New York Times* carried a story of an unfortunate accident resulting in the death of a child that was being blamed on *Batman*. While wearing a homemade Batman-style outfit, Charles Lee, a 12-year-old from Leicester in the English Midlands, had leapt from a cabinet in the garden shed and was hanged when he got his neck caught in a nylon loop hanging from the roof. After the inquest, at which the death was found to be the result of misadventure, the boy's father, 51-year-old engineer Reginald Lee, said that he hoped *Batman* would be taken off British television. "It is far too dramatic and hair-raising," said Lee. "It encourages children to attempt the impossible." A spokesman for England's ABC Television, Ltd., which broadcast the series to 20 million viewers, replied, "We regret that the death of Charles Lee should be attributed to his viewing of *Batman*. Young viewers are cautioned that they should make no attempt to imitate Batman's activities. Before each episode young viewers are reminded that Batman does not in fact fly and that all of his exploits are accomplished by means of his 'secret equipment.'"[289]

Despite the accident and the resultant outcry, Batman was still a hot commodity in the U.K. In mid-August, after the first five weeks of the series being shown by Scottish Television in Central Scotland, Batman dolls, shirts, candies, guns, planes, comics and cars had disappeared from store shelves. A buyer for Wylie Hill's, a legendary Glasgow department store with an elaborate toy department, told *Weekly Variety*, "We have been cleaned of our complete range of Batman toys over the past week, but Batman suits, and all the rest of the gear, should be available again by the end of August." Stores in Dundee and Aberdeen, where Grampian-TV carried the show, were also selling out.[290]

In America, the Batman merchandising boom continued with the introduction of new products, including food items like Batman bread, Batman cola, and Batman milk and ice-cream products. Licensing Corporation of America's Jay Emmett estimated that they had negotiated more than 1,000 Batman toy, game, doll and other official licenses for the Caped Crusader, including a new bumper sticker: "Send Batman to Vietnam."[291]

The *Batman* feature opened on 56 screens in New York City on Wednesday, August 24, 1966. With the excitement provided by West and Ward's personal appearances, the film grossed $250,000 in five days.[292] Howard Thompson, film critic of *The New York Times*, wrote, "Photographed in excellent color, with Adam West and Burt Ward repeating their key roles, along with other TV colleagues, the show is pretty good for half an hour, and there's the rub. The joke has been stretched out for nearly two hours. But those first 30 minutes—the exact length of a TV segment, minus the commercials, which were mercifully absent yesterday—are fun. The older home-screen fans who relish *Batman* for its 'high camp' calorie quota, and the legion of young viewers who take the comic-strip derring-do straight, shouldn't be disappointed. It's exactly the same thing, only longer. Infinitely. *Batman* addicts, be warned."[293]

When the film opened in Los Angeles the following Wednesday, *The Los Angeles Times* critic Philip K. Scheuer said, "Reviews of *Batman* on television have long since become superfluous and I doubt if there's any sensible reason for this one on *Batman*, the feature film. It is just more of the same, although stretched interminably. For myself, I became numb and came out numb."[294] By mid-September, it was playing in Chicago, where reviewer Clifford Terry of *The Chicago Tribune* took a somewhat kinder view, writing, "A wild, zany film filled with good, hoked-up fun, *Batman* was imaginatively written by Lorenzo Semple Jr. and directed by Leslie Martinson, who turned out a much more careful and elaborate production than its tube counterpart.

In addition to the Batomobile [sic], they have added a Batcopter (with Bat Ladder), a Batcycle, Batboat, and even Bat Repellent to subdue a terrifically phony-looking shark...If you dig the TV series, you'll love the movie. If not, Holy Dragsville!"[295]

Daily Variety's John Dooley wrote, "With a big, opulent color feature production *Batman* is now ready to take on the world. The *Mary Poppins* of high camp, pic is packed with action, clever sight gags, interesting complications and goes all out on a bat with batmania: batplane, batboat, batcycle, etc., etc. Deadpan humor is stretched to the limit, De Luxe color is comic strip sharp and script retrieves every trick from the popular teleseries batbag, adding a few more sophisticated touches. Pic should prove a big success although hour and 45 minutes length may prove too much of a dose for one sitting."[296]

Looking back on the film, screenwriter Lorenzo Semple, Jr. said, "It was not terribly well done, if I may say. The movie, they were trying to make on the cheap. At that time, studios were making so-called features of series, like there was one called *The Man From U.N.C.L.E.,* I remember. What they really did was take a few episodes and kind of patched them together with a little connective tissue and call that a feature. The *Batman* feature was entirely new, but nobody went to it particularly. They didn't realize it was something completely new. They thought it would probably be some recycled old junk."[297] Burt Ward blamed Semple, not the marketing or the budget, saying, "I wish they had put more effort into the script, so it wouldn't have been just a giant TV show. I would have loved to do a first-rate, top-notch *Batman* feature. But Dozier and Fox just hurried the picture, to knock out a movie. It was too rushed and didn't have the stature of a real film. It should have been much better."[298] In retrospect, the lackluster performance of the *Batman* film may have been the first indication that the Batboom was waning. As the second season began, there were also signs *Batman* was losing steam overseas. *Variety* reported that the series had been taken off the air in Switzerland and Holland, and that in a survey of Tokyo school children, it ranked second among least-liked programs, behind *Popeye.* Dozier remained optimistic, however, saying, "It's a big hit in Ireland. Different countries have different reactions, but generally the show is doing very well."[299]

Just as the film was opening, Ed Graham, the producer who had tried to do a live-action *Batman* for CBS's Saturday morning line-up, filed a lawsuit in New York State Supreme Court seeking $7,500,000 in damages. Graham alleged that his contract with National Periodical Publications had been an exclusive one, which the publisher breached by making a deal with ABC-TV to produce the *Batman* TV show.[300] This was not the only legal action the producers had to deal with; at the beginning of May, Shirley Louise Smith filed suit in Los Angeles's Superior Court asking for an injunction restraining the use of the title *Batman* on the TV series. Smith claimed ownership as successor-in-interest to a painting titled *The Batman,* and alleged that the painting had been submitted to Bob Kane by its previous owner prior to 1939, when he created the iconic comic book character. Kane, according to the suit, had agreed to pay the previous owner if he used the title.[301] Since there are no other mentions of these cases in newspapers, it is likely that they were dismissed.

DISQUIET ON THE SET

Adam West and Burt Ward returned to the 20th Century Fox soundstages to face another new villain—Ma Parker, played by stage and screen dynamo Shelly Winters. A Supporting Actress Oscar winner for 1959's *The Diary of Anne Frank* and 1965's *A Patch of Blue*, Winters took the role to placate her daughter. "I was on some kind of a panel show with Bill Dozier and some others and afterward he asked if I'd like to play a villainess for *Batman* sometime," she told *Los Angeles Times* reporter Hal Humphrey. "I said, 'Sure, when I'm in Hollywood and have the time.' The next thing I know he's mailed me a script. My 13-year-old daughter, Vittoria, opened it and pleaded with me to do it because she likes the show and does her higher calculus homework while she's watching—these kids! So the next thing I know I'm dressed up as Ma Perkins or Parker or somebody, wearing hand grenades in my hair and shooting a machine gun. We didn't even get to read the script or rehearse before shooting. No wonder that Adam West and Burt Ward look about dead. You hardly have time to eat lunch." Winters, known for being outspoken, said, "Somebody is going to get killed on that set. They don't even observe minimum safety regulations. I slipped in a puddle of water left over from some stunt and turned my ankle. You'd think that show was a flop the way they try to save 20 cents here and 20 cents there. I still don't get it. I thought this show was a big success. They wanted my stand-in to get in a jet-propelled wheelchair and crash through a wall, but offered her only $40. I told her she was nuts to do it for less than $100. They paid her the $100, but she had to crash three times. And everybody's so serious. I like to joke around, like one morning Batman and Robin were strapped in electric chairs. I went up and tickled them, just as a gag, and yelled, 'All right, this morning we'll play Batman, but this afternoon you've gotta play doctor.' You know what happened? Some guy, who'll remain nameless, said, quite seriously, 'No, Shelley, doctors are out now—that was last year.' I mean, really."[302]

The next second-season villain introduced was the Clock King, a character who had originally menaced the Green Arrow in comic books. During the two-parter, Batman and Robin were trapped inside giant hourglasses and left to be buried in the sand. Oversized props like the giant hourglasses were the hallmark of the Batman comic books written by Bill Finger, so it's no surprise that Finger was one of the writers of those episodes, along with his frequent scriptwriting collaborator Charles Sinclair. Finger was reportedly put off by having to do rewrites based on notes not only from producers William Dozier and Howie Horwitz but also from the story editors and the network.[303] The Clock King was played by Viennese actor Walter Slezak, an actor best remembered as the U-boat engineer in Alfred Hitchcock's *Lifeboat* (1944).

Egghead, another character created expressly for the series, made his first appearance in a pair of episodes written by Stanley Ralph Ross from a story by Ed Self. "That was based on a one-page story by the son of the studio boss," said Ross. "All it said was 'The world's smartest comedian.' There was no plot or anything, so I devised the plot and his manner of speech."[304] Identified by his bulbous bald head, white suit, egg-shaped gas bombs and penchant for using egg puns ("egg-zactly," "egg-cellent," etc.), Egghead was a great genius with an even greater ego. The role was played to perfection by horror icon Vincent Price, who was known as a connoisseur of art as well as an actor. "I was amazed at the dedicated attention to the production in every detail," said Price. "My make-up as Egghead was supervised by Dozier himself and created by a master make-up artist, Ben Nye. My costumes were a triumph of camp, done by Jan Kemp. But the real surprise came in the inventiveness of the sets as imagined by the art director, Serge Krizman."[305] Writer Stanley Ralph Ross said that of all the *Batman* episodes he wrote, these Egghead shows were the ones he wrote the fastest. "The Writers Guild was going on strike Monday at noon, and I got the assignment on Friday. They said, 'Stanley, we need a script by Monday.' So, I wrote the whole script over a weekend! I started out by going to a dictionary and looking up every word that began with 'Ecc-,' 'Eg-,' 'or 'Ex-,' and they became 'Egg-splosive,' 'Egg-centric,' or 'Egg-zactly.' I had 72 words and I must have used 68 of them."[306]

Piano impresario Liberace was up next, as ivory-tinkling villain Chandell, who unfortunately didn't make a very credible villain. As Adam West wrote, "Lee at his most dastardly had a friendly twinkle in his eye which gave away the sweetheart inside."[307] He was so nice, in fact, that during lunch breaks he would sit at the piano and entertain the cast and crew with impromptu concerts.

When Mr. Freeze returned to the show, the icy villain was no longer played by George Sanders but rather by famed producer-director Otto Preminger. When first approached, Preminger had declined. "Bill Dozier wrote me about being a villain on the show," Preminger said, "but I felt I was much too busy."[308] He changed his mind at the insistence of his 5-1/2-year-old twins, Mark and Victoria. "They're crazy about the program, and I like it too, strangely enough," said Preminger. "When Mr. William Dozier, who's now my boss, asked me if I would be interested in the part and I told the children, they wouldn't leave me alone until I accepted."[309] As a director, Preminger had a formidable reputation as a bullying taskmaster. When *New York Times* reporter George Gent asked him if he had seen the Mr. Freeze script, Preminger roared, "Do you think I would accept the role without first reading the script?"[310] Once on the set, Preminger showed director George Waggner—who had produced and directed the 1941 horror classic *The Wolf Man* and produced *The Ghost of Frankenstein* (1942) and *Frankenstein Meets the Wolf Man* (1943)—what a real monster was like. For once, Adam West and Burt Ward didn't have to act—the animosity they felt toward their guest villain was genuine. "I couldn't wait to get rid of our second Mr. Freeze," wrote West, adding, "the man insisted on enhancing his reputation as one of the meanest bastards who ever walked a soundstage."[311] When the episodes were in the can, Preminger was canned, as well. "Mr. Dozier did not offer me an option to return," said Preminger. "Come to think of it, I should be hurt."[312]

While filming those episodes, just a week after Shelley Winters' pronouncements about the unsafe conditions on the *Batman* set were published in *The Los Angeles Times*, Burt Ward was injured by an explosion that left him with severe powder burns. He was lucky it didn't do more damage. "I sensed that a particular charge was going to be highly dangerous," said Ward. "I closed my eyes just in time for the cue for the explosion. It's a good thing I did, because I was knocked down by the impact. Instead of going up, the explosion blew outwards. I had second and third degree burns on my face and arms."[313] He was treated at Culver City Medical Center and returned to work later in the day.[314] "The doctor said that if my eyes had been open, I would have been blind," said Ward.[315]

Mr. Freeze reappeared later in the season, and was played by yet another actor, Eli Wallach. "Eli Wallach phoned me up," said William Dozier. "He said he was a flop with his grandchildren because he'd never been on *Batman*."[316] An esteemed character actor, Wallach had just returned from Italy, where he co-starred with Clint Eastwood and Lee Van Cleef in *The Good, the Bad and the Ugly* (1966). In his autobiography *The Good, the Bad and Me: In My Anecdotage,* Wallach wrote, "The most fan mail I ever got for anything I've ever done was for an appearance as Mr. Freeze on the TV series *Batman*. I was the villain of the episode, and I spoke with a heavy German accent—'I *vill* freeze *zee* whole *vorld!* I *vill* conquer every country!' I felt like a haughty Hitler."[317]

Marsha, Queen of Diamonds, was one of the less memorable Batman villains. A jewel thief, she used love darts to make men become enamored of her. The role was originally intended for Zsa Zsa Gabor, but instead went to Carolyn Jones, a Texas-born actress who had won fame as Morticia on the 1964-1966 TV series *The Addams Family*. In 1964, Jones had ended her first marriage to another actor, whom she had encouraged to give up the profession and turn to writing and producing instead; his name was Aaron Spelling.

Another Stanley Ralph Ross creation was the dull-witted cowboy villain, Shame, portrayed by Cliff Robertson. Robertson was approached for a role on *Batman* before the character had been written. "I do remember the producers making several phone calls ahead of time, saying, 'What kind of character would you like to play?' I said it might be fun to play a very, very, very dumb cowboy, who took himself very, very seriously. Then they decided to do a takeoff of *Shane*. That is how they came up with the name Shame. I recall they kind of let me pick my own costume, and I did a lot of my own stunts."[318] Before scripting the Shame episode, writer Stanley Ralph Ross did some digging. "I bought a book of Western clichés from the University of Oklahoma," he said. "It gave me every Western cliché, and I put all of them into the script."[319]

A pair of Catwoman episodes that aired in December featured the pop singing duo Chad and Jeremy, whose voices were stolen by the Catwoman's Voice Eraser. Also appearing was celebrity hairstylist Jay Sebring as "Seymour Oceanbring," proprietor of Mr. Oceanbring's Salon for Men. Sebring's real-life celebrity clients included Frank Sinatra, Bobby Darin, Howie Horwitz and William Dozier. In a time when most men still wore a Brylcreamed pompadour, Sebring introduced a looser style, with the hair combed forward and what Sebring called a "casual part," meaning you couldn't see the scalp. With his signature style catching on and being copied all over television, Sebring decided to debut a new style on *Batman*. "You will see by mine that the hair will be longer and looser, a little more flamboyant or tossed," Sebring said. "It might be called a 'modified mod' style, similar to Bobby Kennedy's, except I would give him a much better haircut. His hair lengths aren't even."[320] Sadly, three years later, on the evening of August 9, 1969, Sebring was murdered along with Sharon Tate and two others by followers of Charles Manson.

The *Batman* juggernaut had a way of winning over the unlikeliest of converts. Shakespearean actor Maurice Evans, who remarked in the 1950s, "Our job is to lead public taste, not play to what is thought to be public taste," took the role of the Puzzler for a couple of second-season *Batman* episodes. At the time, Evans was making frequent appearances on another ABC series, *Bewitched*, as the father of suburban witch Samantha Stevens. "Although I have artistic pretensions," Evans told Hal Humphrey of *The Los Angeles Times*, "I also have no intention of winding up starving in an attic. Y'know, people forget that Shakespeare wrote some bad plays, too. At any rate, if you want to be remembered, you've got to be in movies or on TV. Only my family writes to me to say, 'How dare you!' but later I send them a fat Christmas present, and there is no more criticism."[321] These episodes were originally written with the Riddler as the villain, but with Frank Gorshin unavailable, they were re-tooled first with a new villain named Mr. Conundrum, and then changed to the Puzzler. The Puzzler first appeared as a Superman nemesis in *Action Comics* #49 in June 1942.

Michael Rennie, best known for playing spaceman Klaatu in the original *The Day the Earth Stood Still* (1951), was *Batman's* next guest villain, portraying the Sandman, a part originally scheduled for Robert Morley.[322] The Sandman turned out to be another weak second season villain, even though he was aided in the episodes by Julie Newmar's Catwoman.

After appearing in the first season episodes and *Batman* feature film, Frank Gorshin became more in-demand than ever on the nightclub circuit. "What this has done to my career is unbelievable," he told Norma Lee Browning of *The Chicago Tribune*. "My night club price has tripled. I'm getting all kinds of offers. Now that I'm the Riddler I'm 'in.' I'm no more talented than I was before. But the Riddler has given my name importance. It has been a fantastic boost to my career...For the first time in my life I'm on *The Dean Martin Show*. You can't knock that...*Batman* is becoming a way of life. It's new, bizarre, and successful. People watch it because the 'in' thing is to watch something that's very successful."[323]

Gorshin's success was not necessarily good for the show, however. After having one Riddler episode rewritten for another villain, when Gorshin's nightclub bookings kept him unavailable, the producers recast his role. John Astin, who had just finished two years as the star of *The Addams Family*, was offered the part, and accepted. Speaking to Paul Henniger of *The Los Angeles Times*, Astin said, "You know, people forget that I've done Shaw, Shakespeare and Eugene O'Neill. This is what I've been reveling in since the *Addams* series went off. After doing *Oliver* and *Rattle of a Simple Man* I was asked by writer friends, why not do some TV guestings? I've since done six covering a wide range of roles."[324] When he was offered the *Batman* script, Astin was intrigued by what would cause someone to become a villain strutting around in green tights. "I had very little knowledge of how Gorshin played the role," he said. "I figure the guy's got to be in love with himself—a narcissist. I play him this way. You know, striding around. Striking a few muscle poses. It was fun."[325] Fun for Astin, perhaps, but for the show's loyal fans, he was no Frank Gorshin.

Portly Brooklyn-born character actor Roger C. Carmel popped up as Colonel Gumm, who threatened to make life-size postage stamps out of Batman and Robin, in episodes that also pitted the Dynamic Duo against the Green Hornet and Kato. It was a blatant effort to juice up the ratings of *The Green Hornet* series, but the more serious style of *The Green Hornet* simply didn't mix well with the humor of *Batman*, and Colonel Gumm was yet another lackluster villain.

Before the season ended with episodes featuring the Joker and Mr. Freeze, legendary actress Tallulah Bankhead came aboard as the last of the second season's originally-created villains, the Black Widow. Bankhead appeared on *Batman* at the invitation of William Dozier. "We worked together when times were good," said Bankhead. "We did the *Lucille Ball Show, General Electric Theater* and *Schlitz Playhouse*." She told Walt Dutton of *The Los Angeles Times* that the reason she accepted the role was because, "It's camp—and I've been using that word since I was 15—that's why. I have a great friend, a fine artist who watches *Batman*, and he's 47 years old." Speaking to Norma Lee Browning of *The Chicago Tribune*, Bankhead said the *Batman* crew was "doing everything to make me comfortable, the dahlings, treating me like a baby. Joan Blondell's niece is doing my hair and I'm wearing this black Mod suit with pants and riding around in a motorcycle sidecar. I'm a black widow bank robber and it's all very high camp but you know how it is with these TV camera close-ups, making me look like Grandma Moses' grandma. Someone told me they had to shoot Shirley Temple through gauze so I told them in that case they had better shoot me through linoleum."[326] Her appearance as the Black Widow was her last on-screen role.

With so many lackluster villains, not to mention the formulaic nature of the plots, *Batman's* ratings began to falter in the second season. In the final two weeks of October, 1966, less than two months into the season, the Thursday night episodes of *Batman* were finishing in the bottom of the top 40 programs for the week—quite a drop from the show's debut ten months earlier, when it was in the top ten. The Wednesday night episodes fared even worse, finishing 60th during one rating period and 62nd during another. Part of the slide had to do with the shows *Batman* competed against. On Wednesdays, it was scheduled opposite *The Virginian* on NBC and *Lost in Space* on CBS, which began broadcasting in color that season. On Thursdays, it was up against *Daniel Boone* on NBC and the World War II espionage series *Jericho* on CBS.[327] But part of the problem, too, was that viewers figured out that the Wednesday night episodes were just the build-up to the Thursday night shows, and since the action of the Wednesday night shows was recapped at the beginning of the next night's episode—the episode that had most of the action—why did anyone need to watch it on Wednesday?

With such a precipitous ratings slide, William Dozier took drastic action. "I think we've found the answer," he told Hal Humphrey of *The Los Angeles Times*. "We're breaking up the pattern to shake the kids' confidence." In mid-January 1967, Dozier aired the first three-part *Batman* episode, which featured the Joker and the Penguin teaming up against the Caped Crusaders. "We started a story on Wednesday, but instead of ending it on Thursday, we continued it into the following Wednesday," said Dozier. It wasn't immediately clear, however, if the strategy worked. "We couldn't really tell," said Dozier, "because CBS on that particular Wednesday pre-empted *Lost In Space* with a rerun of its *Cinderella* special, which made it an unfair test for us." The three-parter was followed by a two-part Catwoman adventure, with the first part airing on a Thursday and the concluding part airing the following Wednesday. Then, another three-parter kicked off, featuring the Penguin and Marsha, Queen of Diamonds. It began the same Thursday that CBS unveiled a new variety series, *Coliseum*, which replaced the poorly-performing *Jericho*. "You see what that means?"

Batman (Adam West) on the Batphone, a hot line to Commissioner Gordon's office. (Courtesy Adam West, © Twentieth Century Fox Television).

asked Dozier, speaking the day the second part was scheduled to air. "They'll have to tune in tonight to see what they think will be the conclusion of last Thursday's show, and we'll get 'em away from *Lost in Space*, but still hang on to them for Thursday of this week because that's the concluding episode."[328] The executives at ABC-TV had a different idea for revamping *Batman*. They briefly contemplated converting the show into a one-hour series.[329]

As *Batman*'s ratings hit the skids, so did Burt Ward's marriage. Ward's 19-year-old wife Bonney sued for divorce in Santa Monica Superior Court in mid-November, and sought custody of the couple's three-month-old daughter, Lisa Ann.[330] When the divorce was granted in February, Bonney was awarded the couple's home, plus $800 monthly alimony and $400 a month in child support—nearly all of Ward's monthly *Batman* salary.[331]

The expectations of toy manufacturers were also dropping. Jerome M. Fryer, president of the Toy Manufacturers of America, said in mid-December, "At the beginning of the year it looked as if *Batman* toys of all types would be the biggest sellers this year, but this trend seems to have leveled off for Christmas."[332] The ratings leveled off, as well. The show never shot back up to the Top Ten levels it had held during its first weeks, but it was still performing respectably enough that when ABC president Thomas W. Moore announced preliminary plans for the fall season at the end of February, sixteen of the network's current programs were renewed, including *Batman*.[333] By April, however, the show was dropped by two British television companies. Britain's ABC-TV, serving viewers in the Midlands and north of England, replaced it with a spy series. Rediffusion, which broadcast the show in the London area on weekdays, dropped the series by the summer of 1967, while plans were underway to revamp the show for its third season.[334]

According to Adam West, the show's producers intended to make a series of Batman films, one every year, like the James Bond series. A second film was to have gone into production during the hiatus between the second and third seasons. One idea involved pairing a regular series villain with a new jetpack-outfitted villain called Disastronaut, who flew around with his Meteorettes causing mayhem. A horror plot was also discussed, but dropped when, according to West, "it began sounding too much like *Abbott & Costello Meet Frankenstein*."[335] By the time the second season hiatus arrived, the Batboom was waning, so plans for further *Batman* movies were scrapped.

Consequently, Adam West planned to spend his hiatus making a Western film called *King Gun*, for which he was to be paid $150,000 plus a percentage for three weeks' work. Unfortunately, weather and union problems in Mexico kept it from going before the cameras before his hiatus was over.[336] He did have time for personal appearances, however. When Alexander Dobritch brought his International Circus to the Los Angeles Sports Arena in March of 1967, he enticed celebrities to appear as ringmasters. On the evening of Thursday, March 16, West did the honors, appearing in his Batman costume in the Batmobile.[337]

Burt Ward, meanwhile, also received a film offer. According to his biography, he was approached by producer Lawrence Turman to play the lead role in a little film Turman was doing for Embassy Pictures, but—says Ward—he wasn't allowed to do the film because 20th Century Fox didn't want their Robin appearing in a motion picture while *Batman* was still on the air. The name of the movie? *The Graduate*.

ENTER BATGIRL

Midway through the second season, William Dozier began pondering ways that *Batman* could be revamped to bring in more viewers. Changing the pattern of how the shows were aired to include three-part adventures helped level off *Batman's* ratings, but Dozier still felt he was missing out on half of his potential audience, saying that market research had shown that the show had a strong following among young boys but not among young girls.[338] The answer seemed obvious—if the boys tuned in for Batman, maybe young girls would tune in for a Batgirl. And by injecting a healthy dose of sex appeal, maybe he would win back some of the older boys, too.

Dozier contacted the editor of DC Comics, Julius "Julie" Schwartz. As *Batman* artist Carmine Infantino recalled, "The *Batman* TV producer called Julie and said Catwoman was a hit, could we come up with more female characters? Julie called me and asked me to do that. I came up with Batgirl, Poison Ivy and one I called the Grey Fox, which Julie didn't like as much. Bob Kane had had a Bat-Girl for about three stories in the '50s but she had nothing to do with a bat. She was like a pesky girl version of Robin. I knew we could do a lot better, so Julie and I came up with the real Batgirl."[339]

With input from writer Gardner Fox, DC determined that Barbara Gordon, the daughter of Commissioner Gordon, would become Batgirl. Barbara, an independent young woman with a Ph.D. in library science, was the head of the Gotham City Public Library when not in her crime-fighting guise. Unlike Batman and Robin, who were motivated by the deaths of their parents, Batgirl fought crime out of a sense of civic responsibility and a desire to help others. Though she didn't have the resources of millionaire Bruce Wayne, she still had an array of gadgets, which she carried in a utility purse instead of a utility belt, and she rode a nifty motorcycle. She made her comic book debut in *Detective Comics* #359 (January 1967) in a story titled "The Million Dollar Debut of Batgirl."

An article by Jerry Buck in *The Chicago Tribune* of November 10, 1967 suggested another version of Batgirl's genesis. In Buck's article, Jay Emmett, the chairman of the board of Licensing Corporation of America, was quoted as saying that the company's president, Allan Stone, suggested adding Batgirl to "rejuvenate the show and to give the girls something to buy." By that point, merchandising of *Batman* products in the two years that the show had been on the air accounted for an estimated $150 million in revenue.[340]

Whether Dozier originated the idea of Batgirl or not, he certainly regarded it as a prudent move. As he said to Robert Windeler of *The New York Times*, "Anybody with a series which has been on for a couple of years or more is making a serious mistake if they are complacent and don't keep adding sensible new ingredients to a show."[341]

The first actress considered for the role of Batgirl was Mary Ann Mobley, a former Miss America, but producer Howie Horwitz remembered an actress he'd worked with on the series *77 Sunset Strip*, Yvonne Craig. Craig told Norma Lee Browning of *The Chicago Tribune*, "People in show business know me because I've played in lots of movies and on TV. They also know I've been trained as a ballet dancer. I was one of the swanniest swans who ever danced in *Swan Lake*."[342]

Though she was born in Taylorville, Illinois on May 16, 1937, Yvonne Joyce Craig grew up in Columbus, Ohio, where she began studying ballet at age ten. When the family relocated again, this time to Dallas, Texas, Yvonne went to Sunset High

School, and continued her ballet training at the esteemed Edith James School. She never graduated from Sunset High, because she flunked physical education three years in a row. "I refused to get dressed for gym classes," said Craig. "I didn't like wearing bloomers—they're so droopy in the seat."[343] Craig never dated in high school, saying, "I was very shy. The only thing I wanted to do was to get away from school to practice dancing. I thought of men only as a means of being carried from one part of a stage to another."[344]

During a performance at a Christmas show at the Edith James School, Craig caught the attention of renowned prima ballerina Alexandra Danilova, who arranged a scholarship for Craig to study with George Balanchine at the School of American Ballet in New York. After six months there, she auditioned for Fergei J. Denham of the Ballet Russe de Monte Carlo and was accepted, joining the company in 1954, when she was just 16. When the Ballet Russe arrived for a show at the Greek Theater in Los Angeles, a film producer approached Craig and asked if she'd like to be in movies. She said, "No, I wouldn't. I'd like to be a ballet dancer."[345]

On a later trip to California with the ballet company, Craig turned down an opportunity to make a screen test for producer Joe Pasternak. After three more years with the Ballet Russe, she returned to Los Angeles, studying dance at the Eugene Loring School, where she was spotted by Howard Hughes. Again offered a contract, this time, Craig accepted, and soon after won a role in *The Young Land*, opposite Dennis Hopper and Patrick Wayne (John Wayne's son).[346]

After making her TV debut in an episode of *Schlitz Playhouse of Stars* on April 4, 1958, she found more work in television than in movies. She married singer Jimmy Boyd, best known for a recording he made as a child, "I Saw Mommy Kissing Santa Claus," but the union lasted only two years. Afterwards, she dated Elvis Presley, with whom she starred in two films, *It Happened at the World's Fair* (1963) and *Kissin' Cousins* (1964). Next, she turned up in spy movies, including *In Like Flint* (1967), in which she played Natasha, a Russian ballerina opposite James Coburn's super-cool spy. She wasn't happy, however, with how her ballet number in the latter film ended up. "I worked and sweated and bruised myself for that," said Craig, "but it was shot so far back nobody could see me or the steps. I guess this is one of the reasons I took the Batgirl part. I've decided they'll never remake *Red Shoes* so I may as well forget it."[347]

Despite her film roles and numerous guest-starring spots on TV, fame seemed to be eluding Craig. "I've done lots of guest shots—everything from playing 15-year-old Goody-Two-Shoes to sexpots," she told Norma Lee Browning of *The Chicago Tribune* in 1967. "But people didn't remember my name. I've never had any real identity."[348] Then, she received a call from William Dozier, for whom she had appeared in an unsold TV pilot. "He called to ask if I would come in for an interview," said Craig. "When I got there, he said, 'We're thinking of adding a new character to the *Batman* series—Batgirl. Would you be interested in doing it?' I said, 'Very!'"[349] Dozier asked if she had seen *Batman*, and she admitted that she hadn't, but said that she would watch the reruns over the summer to get up to speed. "I had never seen anything like it," said Craig. "I didn't quite know what to think then, but now I love the show; there are so many fun things about it. It's wild and bizarre. While thrilling the kids with its action and costumes, its humor gets through to the adults who are watching with them. In fact, a politician recently told me he thinks *Batman* has produced some of the best political satire he has ever seen."[350]

By accepting the role of Batgirl, Craig hoped that TV viewers would finally get to know her name. "An actress likes to be noticed," she said, "and in purple tights, a gold and purple cape, and a masked hood—who could miss me?"[351] The 5'4", 109 pound actress wore a skin-tight costume that, although not an exact replica of the comic book Batgirl's black-and-yellow outfit, was still eye-catching, with it's cowl over a red shoulder-length wig. "The outfit is like a second skin," she said. "A masseur comes to my house twice a week to break down muscles it has taken me years to build as a dancer."[352]

To get the approval of the ABC execs, Dozier and Howie Horwitz produced a seven-and-a-half minute promo reel to introduce the character, and show how she would interact with the Dynamic Duo. At that point, the character hadn't been entirely fine-tuned. "Batgirl was more flippant than she was in the TV series," said Craig, "a little more Lauren Bacall." In the promo, her mask was made to resemble bat wings, with sharp points over her cheeks. "They changed my whole mask after we shot the promo, because my first Batgirl mask made little dents on my face," said Craig. "Basically, when I took it off, it looked like I had been crying for weeks! So they changed that and opened up the eyes so I could see better."[353] They also rounded the points, so she could speak and smile without being jabbed by the mask. The short promo reel, filmed January 26, 1967, featured Tim Herbert as Killer Moth, a villain who otherwise never appeared in the TV series.

Craig's ballet training came in handy for the fight scenes. Craig determined that her character would be "adroit, but not violent. I think the reason *Honey West* didn't stay on TV was because she was always going around clobbering somebody, and you can't look feminine when you're doing that."[354] Instead, Craig's Batgirl dispatched villains with high kicks.

One idea Craig had for how her character made her quick costume changes didn't fly. Instead of a Batpole, she said, "I've already suggested to producer Howie Horowitz that I slide down the banister in my split-level apartment. I don't think he's going to go for it though."[355] He didn't. She was, however, given a pet—a parrot named Charlie. "That bird was dreadful," she said. "They didn't want me looking like a lunatic talking to myself to advance the plot, so instead of me walking around the room muttering, they said, 'We'll give you a bird to talk to!' That would have been fine, except any time you approached his rotten little cage, Charlie would hop to the bottom and you would be talking to an empty perch! After that scene, he would then make horrible squawking noises and ruin all the takes!"[356]

SEASON THREE

The fate of *Batman* had been hanging in the balance in February 1967, with Quaker Oats, Colgate and Bristol Myers—advertisers in *The Flying Nun*, which was scheduled to follow *Batman* on Thursday evenings in the 1967-68 TV season— dissatisfied with the prospects of a weak lead-in. The network had even penciled in a possible replacement series, *Tay-Gar, King of the Jungle*, a Tarzan spoof for which

Screen Gems filmed a pilot starring Mike Henry, who was once set for the Batman role in Ed Graham's proposed Saturday morning series and whose Tarzan features were still playing in theaters.[357] But on March 1, *Daily Variety* announced that *Batman* had been renewed for a third season.[358] The anticipated addition of Batgirl helped win the series at least one more season on the air.

Besides the inclusion of Batgirl, there were other changes afoot. Chief among them was scheduling; in its third season, *Batman* was shown only once a week, the network having decided to give its Wednesday time slot to a new Western series, *Custer*, starring Wayne Maunder as the doomed Lieutenant Colonel of the Seventh Cavalry (as it turns out, the series was also doomed, ending after 17 episodes—before Custer got to the battle of the Little Big Horn). Since *Batman* was now airing only once a week, the network ordered only 26 half-hour episodes.[359] *Batman* also underwent some cosmetic changes. The title sequence was altered to feature an animated Batgirl and Yvonne Craig's credit, and—with severe budget cuts—Serge Krizman's sets for the villain's lairs became more expressionistic, generally featuring garishly-colored props set on a bare, cavernous black soundstage, the result looking like a sort of comic book *Our Town*. The budget cuts also dictated simpler stories with less special effects.

Filming of the third season got underway on July 5, 1967.[360] "We had a really tight schedule," said Yvonne Craig. "We would start on Monday, end on Wednesday, start a new episode on Thursday, end on Tuesday, start a new episode on Wednesday, and end it on Friday. I was so tired that sometimes I felt like an automaton. When the network would want to send me out on weekends for personal appearances, I would ask: 'Is this a Nielsen city?' 'Cause if it isn't, I would really like to sleep late.'"[361]

The third season of *Batman* debuted on September 14, 1967, beginning with an episode featuring the Penguin, in which the fowl fiend kidnaps Barbara Gordon with the intention of forcing her to marry him; with Commissioner Gordon as his father-in-law, he believes he'll be immune from prosecution. With all of the action crammed into a single episode, it had a brisker pace than many second-season entries.

For her debut episode, Batgirl roared into action with her own unique Batcycle—a modified Yamaha YDS-5E with a specially-made purple scalloped batwing faring, oval windscreen, lace ruffles, and a yellow bow on the seat. Behind a revolving wall in her apartment's bedroom was a hidden freight elevator that lowered the Batgirlcycle to the alley below, where a secret door opened allowing her to ride out into the street. According to Craig, when she first went to meet with William Dozier and Howie Horwitz, they asked if she had ever ridden a motorcycle, "which indeed I had and owned one at the time," she said. "The motorcycle ride out of the secret exit was an interesting episode. It was the first day of shooting, and I knew the special effects man from somewhere else in Warner Brothers. I had been practicing riding out because I was supposed to ride through a brick wall. It was set up like a long tunnel, and he said, 'Look, if you hit this mark and you at that point absolutely stand on it and give it all you got, it will look like you are riding the wall down. It will be real exciting.' I said 'Terrific!' So, I did exactly as he said, but a little voice in my head said, hand close to the brakes because, if something goes wrong, you would like to be able to hit the brakes. Sure enough, the first shot of the day, I went tearing out, and the wall didn't come down. It was made of plywood and I wouldn't have liked to have gone through it. I hit the brakes, and I went skidding sideways, missing the wall by about an inch. Nobody on the other side knew what was going on. They figured somewhere along the line I had chickened out and decided not to do it at all. Anyway, it worked the second time around."[362] The cycle wasn't the most comfortable ride, however. "They had taken off the shock absorbers to put on the bat wings, so whenever I went over a bump, it was like jumping off a table stiff-legged," said Craig. "It would really jar my teeth!"[363] Talking to Walt Dutton of *The Los Angeles Times* in July of 1967, she said, "I can ride it all right. I just have trouble when it's stopped; it's so heavy I can't hold it up. It fell over the other day and I decided to try talking to it. 'Come on,' I said nicely, 'you can get up, can't you?' It didn't, so I kicked it."[364] Filming an episode with guest villain Vincent Price as Egghead, she almost ran over the veteran bogeyman and art connoisseur. "In the scene I race in on the Batgirlcycle and make a panic stop at the curb, where Vincent is standing," recalled Craig. "Well, it stopped; but then— voom! voom!—it started again. He dodged it, but—voom! voom!—it went after him a second time. He ended up straight-arming it and cut his hand on the bat wing. It ran over his foot, too. I thought I was going to kill him; that would have been the end of art in Los Angeles."[365]

The next episode saw the return of Frank Gorshin as the Riddler, aided in his villainy by the Siren, a character created for the show. The next episode telecast featured a solo turn by the sultry Siren, aka chanteuse Lorelei Circe, portrayed by British actress Joan Collins. The episode ended with a shot of Batgirl on her Batgirlcycle, while "The Batgirl Theme," composed by Billy May and Willy Mack, was heard on the soundtrack:

> *Where do you come from? Where do you go?*
> *What is your scene? Baby, we just gotta know!*
> *Are you a chick who fell in from outer space,*
> *or are you real with a tender warm embrace?*
> *Yeah, whose baby are you? Batgirl, Batgirl!*

Unlike the *Batman* theme, Batgirl's theme was never released on a record.

By the third season, the writers and producers had entirely stopped relying on the comic books for fresh villains, instead falling into a pattern of casting the guest villain and then creating a criminal persona specifically for them. The result was villains who lacked the spark of the Joker, the Riddler, the Penguin and Catwoman. When the Penguin returned for the season's fourth and fifth episodes (the season's first two-parter), he was joined by Ethel Merman as Lola Lasagne. Merman, a Tony Award-winning Broadway legend famed for playing Mother Rose in *Gypsy*, was an outsized personality playing a minor scale villain—a childhood friend of the Penguin's.

After a King Tut episode, Milton Berle turned up as Louie the Lilac, who sought to control Gotham City's flower children by cornering the flower market. Berle had previously made a cameo in a second season episode, as Lefty, a prison inmate, popping up during a Batclimb. As Louie the Lilac, Berle toned down his manic comic persona so much that he seemed practically comatose, turning in a performance that had a soporific effect on viewers.

In a time when many TV series tried to boost their ratings by filming episodes in London, Batman did a three part adventure set in Londinium, a low-budget backlot London filmed on the 20th Century Fox stages. Rudy Vallee, the megaphone-wielding singing sensation of the 1920s, played Lord Fogg, who could conjure up man-made fog to aid in his criminal activities. Apparently, none of the main cast enjoyed working with the legendary crooner. "Crabby old Rudy Vallee was an absolute curmudgeon!" said Yvonne Craig. "What made it worse was that it was a three-episode shoot, so we had him around for a long time. He was so cranky, especially when you compare him to a wonderful guest like Vincent Price!"[366]

When Catwoman reappeared, she was no longer played by Julie Newmar, who was busy co-starring with Gregory Peck in *Mackenna's Gold* (1969), but rather by sultry songstress Eartha Kitt, whom no less an authority than Orson Welles once called, "the most exciting woman in the world."[367] With her pixie-ish singing style, the cabaret vocalist scored a hit in 1953 with the song "Santa Baby." While Kitt had a more smoldering sensuality as Catwoman than Newmar, the playful, sexually teasing banter between Catwoman and Batman that had been a hallmark of Newmar's appearances was absent. Though it was innovative and groundbreaking in 1967 to cast a black actress in a leading role on television, it was still taboo to suggest the possibility of any sexual liaison between a black character and a white character. Nonetheless, Kitt seemed to have fun in the skin-tight spandex, and Yvonne Craig appreciated that she was less statuesque than her predecessor. "Eartha Kitt was a marvelous Catwoman," said Craig. "Julie would have been too tall for me."[368] Even Julie Newmar approved of the casting, saying, "I think Eartha had absolutely the best voice of all. When she said 'Purrrrfect,' it was wonderful."[369]

As the season wound down, Barbara Rush turned up as Nora Clavicle, who convinces Mayor Linseed (a spoof of New York mayor John Lindsay) to make her police commissioner and turns the Gotham police force into an all-female organization. She then robs the Gotham City National Bank, after disposing of Batman, Robin and Batgirl in a rather kinky way by tying them into a Siamese human knot.

After episodes featuring returning villains the Penguin, Shame, King Tut and the Joker, the acting duo of Ida Lupino and Howard Duff popped up as Dr. Cassandra Spellcraft and her accomplice, Cabala. Writer Stanley Ralph Ross's initial script for the episode called the villains' weapon, a ray gun that removed the third dimension from people and turned them into cardboard cutouts, a "Ronald Ray-gun." Since Ronald Reagan was then the governor of California, Ross was pressured to come up with a different name. He settled on the Alvino Ray-gun; Alvino Rey was a 1940's swing-era bandleader.[370]

Zsa Zsa Gabor, who had been considered for the roles of Olga, the Queen of the Bessarovian Cossacks and Marsha, Queen of Diamonds, finally got her chance at *Batman* villainy in the series' final episode. As Minerva, who ran a mineral spa catering to millionaires, she hoped to use her Deepest Secret Extractor—which looked like an ordinary, everyday hair dryer—to get the combination to the Wayne Foundation vault. In *Back to the Batcave,* Adam West wrote of Gabor, "I understood how Zsa Zsa had managed to dazzle so many men over the years. It wasn't just her face and figure, which were impressive. When she talked to you, she had a way of making you feel like Adam, the first and only man and the one who was most important to her."[371] Producers William Dozier and Howie Horwitz appeared as themselves at the beginning of the final episode. As clients of Minerva, Dozier reveals that he keeps securities in a grandfather clock, while "millionaire producer" Horwitz claims to keep his cash in a TV set.[372]

At the beginning of 1968, Adam West traveled to London at the behest of Margaret Thatcher, then a Minister of Parliament representing Finchley. She asked West to appear in a traffic safety film for schoolchildren. West obliged, in full Batman garb. After shooting the safety film, he had dinner with producer Albert R. "Cubby" Broccoli and Broccoli's wife, Dana. When the subject of the 1943 *Batman* serial came up, West said, "That's the one we call the baggy pants Batman." Dana Broccoli replied, "Well, that was my first husband."[373] Despite putting his foot in his mouth, West made a good impression on the Broccolis; before dinner was over, Cubby, who was the co-producer of the James Bond films, asked West if he would like to take over the role of 007, which Sean Connery had just vacated. Though flattered, West said he felt that Bond should be played by an Englishman, and thus declined the opportunity to be seriously considered to star in *On Her Majesty's Secret Service.*[374]

West returned to the U.S. amid talks of extending *Batman* to a fourth season, but only if the budgets could be cut, which would entail losing cast members. The network suggested losing Robin and making Batgirl Batman's partner in crime-solving, but West felt that would be unfair to Burt Ward; he suggested alternating Robin and Batgirl as a compromise. In the end, Dozier apparently decided that he didn't want to do a bare-bones version of the show, and threw in the towel. "Batman Axed," read the headline in the January 18, 1968 *Daily Variety*; it was such a non-story that the trade paper printed it not on page 1 but rather on page 14.[375]

A week later, Dozier received a call from a reporter from *The New York Times* who was checking to see if the *Variety* story was true. The reporter had just spoken to a representative from ABC, who said no decision had yet been made on the series. Speaking afterward to *Daily Variety*, Dozier said, "ABC didn't order repeats of our show starting March 21, which means it automatically lost its position on the show, which is tantamount to cancellation. Why ABC chose to play this cozy game—especially with the *Times*—undoubtedly means the left hand doesn't know what the right hand is doing, or it is to lull thousands of youngsters into believing the show will remain on, knowing they will be disappointed. More so than this youngster." Dozier said he had called Adam West's agent to notify him of ABC's actions.[376]

Meanwhile, Howie Horwitz was giving a rather conflicting story to *The Los Angeles Times,* saying, "My own boss, Bill Dozier, has signed a deal with Warners-Seven Arts to make pictures. We will have nothing on TV next season unless *Batman* is picked up again, and that we won't know until April."[377] In fact, the very next day, *The New York Times* ran the headline, "Curses!!! 'Batman' Meets His Master: Television's Ratings." In the accompanying article, Dozier said that the network had notified him that *Batman* would not be back the following season. "They ordered 26 shows for this season and that should take them through the end of March," he said. "Repeats and preemptions should carry them through June. But there will be no *Batman* next season, whatever the network tells you." Leonard Goldberg, the vice-president of programming at ABC, said that in fact the network had reached no decision on the program, saying, "Mr. Dozier had not been told the program would not be renewed," but adding that Dozier "probably came to that conclusion after looking at the ratings." By that point, the series had dropped from the top ten of the Nielsen ratings down to the 48th position.[378]

By the end of February, after a couple of episodes featuring Cliff Robertson as Shame had aired, it had dropped to 75th place.[379] Lorenzo Semple, who called the show "a one-trick pony at heart,"[380] felt that ultimately, "It got too silly. They tried Batgirl, Batcycle, all those things, but it just wasn't right. It was a very delicate mix of things, I think, the original series."[381] Howie Horwitz told *The Los Angeles Times* he had no regrets, saying, "I make no apologies for the show—I'm proud of it."[382]

According to Adam West, NBC expressed interest in picking up the show, but by the time they came forward with an offer, the Batcave set had been destroyed and the other standing sets dismantled. Unwilling to spend the money to rebuild them, NBC withdrew their offer, and the series was over. "There were definitely bittersweet feelings about leaving the show behind," wrote Adam West. "I felt like the Thief of Baghdad rolling away the magic carpet that had taken me to so many interesting places, creatively as well as physically." A month after the series ended, there was a cast and crew farewell party at the Sand and Sea Beach Club, and then everyone went their separate ways.[383]

After *Batman* ended, Vanessa Brown of *The Los Angeles Times* asked William Dozier what was meaningful about the program. "I didn't feel there was anything meaningful about *Batman*," answered Dozier (with vehemence, according to Brown), adding, "*Batman* wasn't intended to be meaningful." So why, she asked, did he do it? "I'm in business, too," he responded, "the same as the networks. I don't feel that every television show has to be meaningful. They couldn't possibly be. There must be a variety. *Batman* was designed primarily and totally to entertain, and it did. It didn't demean its audience. Children didn't learn anything bad from *Batman*. They learned a few very high moral principles."[384]

AFTER BATMAN

The three seasons of *Batman* yielded plenty enough episodes for syndication, with a total of 120 half-hour shows completed. During the middle of the third season, it was sold into syndication, quickly racking up $2 million in gross bookings in 18 markets, including stations in Los Angeles, New York, Seattle, Salt Lake City and Philadelphia. The stations planned to start running the show the following September, at the beginning of a new TV season.[385]

Dozier set about working on film projects, leaving television behind. He told *Daily Variety's* Dave Kaufman, "I got very lucky with *Batman*, which financially was a jackpot. You don't do that very often—most people don't do it once. Also, I suddenly found myself referred to everywhere I went as 'the producer of *Batman*.' I said should I be hit by a truck the *New York Times* would say, '*Batman* producer killed;' the *New York News* would say 'Joan Fontaine's ex killed.' I would just not like to wind up having those labels my only recognition. So I figured if I don't do any TV, good or bad, I can at least insulate myself from the *Batman* image. I'm proud of what we did on *Batman*, but I don't want it to be my only memorable contribution."[386]

For the next four decades, *Batman* would remain an almost constant presence on TV, from after-school airings in the 1970s to cable's TVLand in the 1990s. "I really didn't think we were making *Gone With the Wind*—just an episodic TV series that would be over when it was over and then it would never rerun again," said Yvonne Craig. "I've been told that *Batman* has apparently never stopped rerunning somewhere in the world. That blows my mind!"[387]

In 1974, the U.S. Department of Labor called on Batman, Robin and Batgirl to do a public service announcement for equal pay for women. Yvonne Craig and Burt Ward agreed—as did William Dozier, who provided the voice-over—but West declined. "Adam wanted nothing to do with Batman at that time," said Craig, "and so he wouldn't do it. I teased him that it had nothing to do with Batman—he just didn't want equal pay for women! Burt came back as Robin, though, and they got Dick Gautier to do Batman—and he imitated Adam's cadences perfectly." Gautier, a comic actor, was best-known for his role as Hymie the robot on the TV series *Get Smart* (1966-68).

Madge Blake (Aunt Harriet) died a year after the show ended, on February 19, 1969, after suffering a heart attack at her home in Pasadena.[388] Stafford Repp (Chief O'Hara), who had become wealthy after investing in car washes, continued acting in guest roles on numerous TV series until passing away on November 5, 1974 after suffering a fatal heart attack at the Hollywood Park racetrack. On June 25, 1976, producer Howie Horwitz, who had gone on to produce episodes of the TV series *Banacek* (1972-1974) and *Baretta* (1975-76), was on vacation with his family at June Lake, California. Climbing up on a rock to admire the view, he lost his balance and died from injuries sustained in the fall. Neil Hamilton (Commissioner Gordon) retired from acting in the early 1970s, and passed away at age 85 in Escondido, California on September 24, 1984 from complications from asthma. Alan Napier (Alfred) remained busy in television until retiring in 1981. He died at the age of 85 on August 8, 1988 after suffering a stroke in Santa Monica, California.

After *Batman* ended, William Dozier produced the 1969 film *The Big Bounce*, starring Ryan O'Neal, then turned from producing to acting with bit parts in several TV and film productions. In 1972, he appeared with his wife Ann Rutherford in a segment of *Love, American Style* titled "Love and the Impossible Gift," which was directed by Sam Strangis, who had been unit production chief on *Batman*, and produced by Charles FitzSimons, one of *Batman*'s producers.[389] Later, he had a high-profile film role playing the lawyer of Lauren Hutton's character in *American Gigolo* (1980). "I was his agent for a while," said Deborah Dozier Potter, "and he did a few acting jobs, and he was wonderful." Dozier also became a book reviewer contributing to *The Los Angeles Times*. "You know, the series didn't make any money for him until right before he died," said Potter. "Fox didn't show any profit on the books until literally the month before he died, they sent him a check. He thought it was completely worthless and it was only after he died that it had any residual value at all, which is very sad. I'm so sorry he didn't live to see that. It's not like it's making a fortune, but to see its continued popularity, to see it in black and white like that." William Dozier died in

***William Dozier and his daughter, Deborah** (© Deborah Dozier Potter).*

Santa Monica at age 83 on April 23, 1991. "All I can say is most memories of my father are wonderful," said Potter. "My father loved me very much and I always felt that. Even though he was a very busy man, his actions always showed to me that he loved me and cared about me and that my opinion was important to him."[390]

Among the guest villains, Cesar Romero remained busy with film and TV work, including a role as Peter Stavros in the popular nighttime soap *Falcon Crest* from 1985 to 1988. He died peacefully on January 1, 1994 in Santa Monica. Frank Gorshin also kept busy with numerous TV guest-starring roles up until 2005, including reuniting with Adam West in a 1995 episode of *Lois & Clark: The New Adventures of Superman*, in which Gorshin played a lawyer and West a newscaster. In 2002, he opened on Broadway in the one-man show *Say Goodnight, Gracie*, playing George Burns. He toured with the show until May 16, 2005, when after a performance in Memphis, he boarded a plane for Los Angeles. Immediately upon landing, he was rushed to the hospital, where he died three weeks later from complications from lung cancer, emphysema and pneumonia. He was 72. Eartha Kitt remained active as a cabaret performer and TV and film actress, including giving a sexy, manic performance that managed to upstage even Grace Jones in the 1992 Eddie Murphy film *Boomerang*. She died on Christmas Day, 2008, at her home in Weston, Connecticut from colon cancer.

The original Catwoman, Julie Newmar, also remained busy with TV work in the 1960s and 70s, and made a cameo at the end of a film which paid tribute to her enduring influence as a feminist icon, *To Wong Foo Thanks for Everything, Julie Newmar* (1995), which featured Wesley Snipes, Patrick Swayze and John Leguizamo as a trio of drag queens. She became a real estate agent in the 1980s, holds two U.S. patents— one for pantyhose and one for a brassiere—and has a rose, a day lily and an orchid named in her honor. She has also become a writer, penning the ebook *The Conscious Catwoman Explains Life on Earth*, available at www.julienewmar.com, and a blog, *Julie Newmar Writes*, at www.julienewmarwrites.com.

After creating the TV *Batman*, Lorenzo Semple Jr. capitalized on his success by moving into screenwriting for motion pictures. "At that time the idea of everybody was to get out of television as soon as they could and get into real movies. And so, I never looked back," said Semple, who recalled that on *Batman* he had "a horrible deal. I mean, I got no 'created for television' credit, and I just got a small royalty for the first 20 shows, and the only money I got from it was ordinary Writer's Guild residuals on the first four shows that I wrote, but aside from that, nothing. If I'd made some deal that I wanted $25 for every time an episode was shown everywhere, I'd be really rich. But I never thought about that kind of stuff. My agent at that time didn't know anything about television. Nobody did. I mean, they didn't ask for any special credit, and I am not at all bitter about that. I figure I did better than Bob Kane and those people did."[391]

Leaving the Caped Crusader behind, Semple became an in-demand scriptwriter, beginning with *Fathom*, a spy story that was filmed in 1967 with Raquel Welch as a sort of female James Bond. In 1971, he wrote *The Marriage of a Young Stockbroker*, based on the novel by Charles Webb, who had previously written *The Graduate*. The film featured Richard Benjamin as a voyeur; his best friend, Chester, was played by Adam West. Semple next adapted Henri Charriére's *Papillon* (eventually sharing the writing credit with Dalton Trumbo), creating a classic that gave Steve McQueen one of his best roles. In 1974, Semple adapted L.H. Whittmore's book *The Super Cops*, a true story based on the exploits of New York City detectives David Greenberg and Robert Hantz, who were known on the streets as "Batman and Robin"—so who better to write the script? Next, Semple shared a writing credit with David Giler on *The Parallax View* (1974), a political thriller starring Warren Beatty and produced by Dino De Laurentiis. In 1975, Semple worked on *The Drowning Pool*, in which Paul Newman reprised the role of detective Lew Harper first introduced in 1966's *Harper*, then he adapted James Grady's novel *Six Days of the Condor* into the Robert Redford thriller *Three Days of the Condor* (1975). A trio of films written for De Laurentiis followed, beginning with 1976's *King Kong* and continuing with *Hurricane* (1979) and *Flash Gordon* (1980). Three years later, Semple wrote the script for Sean Connery's return to the role of 007, *Never Say Never Again*. But as he looks back on his career, it's the Caped Crusader who looms largest. "I'm very proud of *Batman*," said Semple. "People say, oh, you wrote *Three Days of the Condor, Parallax View*, and things like that, and I say I don't like them nearly as much as *Batman*."[392]

Terminally identified with their roles, both Adam West and Burt Ward found themselves too typecast to get other acting parts in the remainder of the 1960s and early 1970s, except for the occasional guest-starring spot in a TV show. "After I was the hottest thing in the country for two-three years I had a 'black period' for five years," West told Army Archerd of *Variety*. "But when they threw enough money at me, I put on the costume again and toured the world. I developed an enormous new younger audience. I did regional theater as well—anything to just get away."[393]

"Burt and Adam kept their costumes, and they'd go out and do all these trade shows and car shows and things as Batman and Robin, wearing the costumes, and my father didn't care," said Deborah Dozier Potter. "He said, 'You know what, if they want to do that, that's fine.' Most producers would have said 'how dare you' and issued restraining orders and all that. He was happy for them. And frankly, we owed them a great debt because they kept the fan base alive."[394]

Besides making personal appearances as Batman and Robin, West and Ward lent their voices to Filmation Studios' Saturday morning animated series *The New Adventures of Batman* in 1977 and '78. According to an upcoming book about Filmation founder Lou Scheimer by Andy Mangels, the cartoon studio planned to follow up the animated series with a live-action Batman revival for NBC, with West and Ward reprising their roles. That never happened, but in 1979 NBC did join with another producer of Saturday morning fare, Hanna-Barbera, to produce a pair of ill-conceived TV specials, *Legends of the Superheroes*, which was broadcast in two parts on NBC on January 18 and January 25, 1979. The first part, "The Challenge," pitted DC superheroes Batman, Robin, Hawkman (Bill Nuckols), The Flash (Rod Haase), Captain Marvel (Garrett Craig), Green Lantern (Howard Murphy), The Huntress (Barbara Joyce), and Black Canary (Danuta Rylko Soderman) against the supervillains Mordru (Gabe Dell), Sinestro (Charlie Callas), Dr. Sivanna (Howard Morris), The Riddler (Frank Gorshin), Solomon Grundy (Mickey Morton), the Weather Wizard (Jeff Altman), and Giganta (A'leisha Brevard). The second part, "The Roast," hosted by Ed McMahon, was a superhero version of the popular *Dean Martin Celebrity Roasts*, but without the laughs. Produced by Hanna-Barbera, the company behind the animated *Super Friends* cartoon series, the two programs qualify as the *Plan 9 From Outer Space* of superhero television. West appeared in a near-replica of his former costume, except that it was black and gray instead of blue and gray, and the cowl was not tucked under the cape. Also, the bat insignia rode higher on his chest. Ward's costume was a replica of his earlier outfit, but one felt embarrassed for the then 33-year-old actor, still playing a teenager. And though it was certainly nostalgic to see West back in the Batman outfit and looking amazingly fit and youthful for a 50-year-old man, it's a shame that he wasn't given better material. The writing and production values of the shows were nothing short of atrocious. Nonetheless, West and Ward—and Frank Gorshin, reprising his role as The Riddler—played the lame script for all it was worth, which wasn't much; really, who wanted to see Robin using charades to explain to Batman that he'd totaled the Batmobile?

West was back in the spotlight when production of Tim Burton's *Batman* feature ramped up in 1988. West, who had long hoped that he would be able to play Batman one more time in a feature film, told *The Wall Street Journal*, "It's disappointing not to have the chance to do the definitive, big-screen Batman." West also wasn't sold on the new film's dark approach, saying, *"Batman* isn't *RoboCop* or *Dirty Harry*. Batman is a fun character."[395] When Peter Guber, producer of the *Batman* feature, was asked if there would be a place for Adam West in the film, he responded, "Sure. We'll invite him to the premiere."[396] Upset that he wasn't asked to be a part of the new film, West told reporter Ray Richmond, "It really disappointed me; I was really angry...I guess we'll see if people prefer the Classic Coke or the new stuff."[397]

Adam West and Burt Ward did make a return, of sorts, to their signature roles with the 2003 CBS TV-movie *Return to the Batcave: The Misadventures of Adam and Burt,* based partly on West's book *Back to the Batcave,* as well as some anecdotes from Ward's book, *Boy Wonder: My Life in Tights.* Produced with a tongue-in-cheek tone, it featured Adam West and Burt Ward playing themselves trying to solve the mystery behind the theft of the Batmobile. To find the answer, they had to relive moments from the making of the *Batman* TV series, which were shown in flashbacks with actors Jack Brewer and Jason Marsden playing the late 1960's versions of West and Ward. Former Catwomen Julie Newmar and Lee Meriwether appeared in cameo roles, and the culprit was ultimately revealed to be Frank Gorshin. Lyle Waggoner provided voice-over narration, and made a cameo appearance at the end, saying, "If they'd have chosen me, we'd still be on the air."

"It was fun to be on-set again," recalled Waggoner, "and to make fun of the fact that I didn't get the part and Adam did. And it was good to see him. I knew Adam before that, and I always thought he was very good in anything he did and I thought he played that part extremely well. So it was fun to be on-set and do *Return to the Batcave.* Whoever thought of that particular script, I found it very interesting."[398]

One who didn't find the script interesting, and chose not to participate, was Yvonne Craig, who—after *Batman* ended—continued acting until the mid-1970s, then began producing industrial shows and went into real estate. "I was sent the script and declined," she said of *Return to the Batcave.* "This decision was based purely on my evaluation of the script and had nothing to do, as rumor now has it, with the size of my part. I'm inclined to agree completely with the old adage, 'There are no small parts, only small actors.' I would infinitely rather be remembered for my role in a well-written, inventive series as opposed to taking part in a project that, as best I can tell, was contrived simply because the *Gilligan's Island* TV movie did so well in the ratings."[399] Indeed, Return to the Batcave was co-executive produced by Dawn Wells, who played "Mary Ann" on TV's *Gilligan's Island* series.

Anita Gates of *The New York Times,* in her review of the TV movie, agreed with Craig's assessment, writing, "Someone should be held accountable for taking a popular, fun-loving, deliberately camp 60's series—and its stars, who are graciously willing to make fun of themselves—and turning it into one of the most painfully boring pieces of television this season...Mr. West and Mr. Ward still have likable screen presences; they're much too good for this material. The filmmakers are trying to be nostalgic about camp, and that may not be possible."[400]

In the decades after *Batman* went off the air, Burt Ward, a born entrepreneur, launched several successful business ventures. One was Entertainment Management Corporation, which ran fan clubs for actors such as Henry Winkler and Paul Michael

Glaser and singers such as Pat Benatar.[401] Later, when appearances as Robin at schools led him to become an advocate for children's' issues, Ward created the Early Bird Learning Program, an early education program for children ages 3 to 8.[402] In 1990, Ward married Tracy Posner, daughter of billionaire business mogul Victor Posner. Besides various business interests, the couple is involved in Great Dane rescues, and Ward manages a visual effects company, Boy Wonder Visual Effects, which did work on the films *Bulletproof Monk*, *Out of Time* and *Pirates of the Caribbean: The Curse of the Black Pearl* (all 2003).[403] He looks back on his time in tights without regret. "I learned a great deal from *Batman*," he told Steve Swires of *Starlog* magazine. "It was an experience I will treasure forever. It gave me a fantastic opportunity. It has enabled me to meet and be welcomed by people throughout the world."[404]

By the time Adam West made *Return to the Batcave*, he had finally become an in-demand actor once again. "A big meteor has hit Hollywood, and the dinosaurs are dying," he told *Entertainment Weekly* in 1994, after he'd won the role of Peter Weller's father in *The New Age*. "The guys and ladies in power are the ones who appreciated me." After a couple of decades where he had trouble getting roles, he now found that the kids who had grown up watching him on TV were writing and directing movies, and they not only remembered him but wanted to work with him. He remained busy doing cartoon voices, including playing Mayor Adam West on *Family Guy* and a cat-obsessed version of himself on the Nickelodeon series *The Fairly Oddparents,* as well as providing voices for feature films such as *Chicken Little* (2005) and *Meet the Robinsons* (2007). He also made guest appearances on TV shows like *The Simpsons, The Drew Carey Show* and *30 Rock*. He regrets, however, that he was never asked to appear in any of the modern Batman movies. "I look at it this way: they've got *The Dark Knight*, and I was the bright knight," he told Geoff Boucher of *The Los Angeles Times*. "Or maybe I was even the neon knight."[405] He did, however, provide the voice of Batman for *Batman: New Times*, an animated short featuring a Lego version of the Caped Crusader, and was the voice of Mayor Grange in six episodes of the animated series *The Batman* (2004-2006). "I'm like Madonna: I keep reinventing myself," West told Boucher. "I get called 'Mayor West' a lot in airports. I've been very fortunate to have a fan base that keeps growing, and the work gets such a warm response and humor from people."[406]

In 2009, West appeared in the film *Super Capers*, which put him back behind the wheel of the Batmobile, though not in his bat costume. "It's a very bright comedy adventure," he said. "In it, I'm a cabdriver who's gotten hold of the Batmobile and converted it to a taxi cab—with air conditioning. I meet up with a young guy who's trying to be a superhero, played by an actor named Justin Whalin, who is quite good, and I'm able to drive him around on some of his misadventures."[407]

Though he once tried to distance himself from *Batman*, West now embraces his association with the character. In 2009, he created a DVD which he sells through his website, www.AdamWest.com, called *Adam West Naked*. Despite its provocative title, it's basically West sitting in his basement, attic and home gym, reminiscing about anecdotes from the filming of each episode of the series. For die-hard fans, it's captivating, like listening to a favorite uncle talk about the good old days.

For the time being, *Adam West Naked* and the *Batman* feature film may be as close as fans can get to owning the series on home video. For four decades it has been held in limbo by foes too overpowering for even Batman to overcome—corporate lawyers. When the series was originally produced in the late 1960s, there was no such thing as home video; consequently, contracts between DC Comics, who owned the characters of Batman and Robin, and 20th Century Fox Television, who, along with Greenway Productions, produced the program, made no provisions for anything other than television airings. The contracts for the *Batman* movie, on the other hand, included provisions for ancillary non-theatrical markets (like, for instance, airlines) that, broadly interpreted, did allow for it to be released on home video. In order for the TV series to be released, rights will have to be settled between not only DC Comics, 20th Century Fox and Greenway Productions, but also with all of the directors, writers, actors, and musicians who worked on the show, or their estates. The show basically presents a Gordian knot of licensing tangles that, thus far, the studios have been unable to untie.[408]

Unlike other shows of the period, *Batman*, when seen today, retains much of its humor and freshness; because the series created its own warped universe, it doesn't feel dated. "If you look at the shows today, they're just as timely as they were then because it takes place in a fantasy land," said writer Stanley Ralph Ross. "Gotham City was not a real place. There was nothing anachronistic about the show. Occasionally we would do a joke about someone of the period. For example, the mayor of the town was Mayor Linseed, which was a play off of Mayor Lindsay of New York. But other than that, very seldom would you find a joke that would date the show."[409]

Even Bob Kane, who wasn't thrilled with the show's approach initially, came to appreciate it more as the years passed. In a 1988 interview with Jeff Gelb of *Comics Interview* magazine, he said, "I loved the show! You see, I love it on two levels—I love the mysterioso, but I also love the camp of the show. I thought *Batman* was the most unique show ever put on, because it was actually a transition from the strip to the screen, with the POWs and the SOCKs. Adam was great, and all the guest stars, the cameos, it was all great!"[410]

For the TV generation who grew up with the series, *Batman* proved inspirational. "The thing is, *Batman* is very, very sophisticated humor," said Lorenzo Semple, Jr. "Some of the biggest comedy writers today on *David Letterman* and even *The Simpsons* have said to me that they cut their teeth on *Batman* and that was really what inspired them, in many ways."[411] Looking back on the show in 2004, Adam West told Brenda Rees of *The Los Angeles Times*, "We were making overstated morality plays for children that adults could watch and enjoy. People from three generations still respond to the warmth and humor."[412] In an interview with the same paper five years later, West told Geoff Boucher, "I would hate to be a bitter, aging actor. I've been so fortunate to have this opportunity to bring Batman alive on the screen. There's a lot of talent, money and expertise with the new films. They're beautifully crafted, but there's something about our *Batman* that still strikes a chord. And as for me, I'm too young and pretty to retire, as somebody once said."[413]

Over four decades after its first broadcast, *Batman* is still finding fresh audiences, just as William Dozier predicted in the 1960s when he said, "It will go on forever. There's always a new crop of children growing up."[414]

1　Gowran, Clay, "Can We Stand More Batmen?" *The Chicago Tribune*, Feb. 20, 1966, p. IND_A10

2　Miles, Marvin, Gemini Pair Safe, *The Los Angeles Times*, Mar 17, 1966, p. 1

3　—, "TV Fans Protest Canceling of Shows For Gemini Report," *The New York Times*, Mar. 17, 1966, p. 21

4　—, "Batman Fans Blast Gemini Interruptions," *The Chicago Tribune*, March 17, 1966, p. 10

5　Skow, John, "Has TV Gasp! Gone Batty??" *The Saturday Evening Post*, May 2, 1966

6　—, "Batman Fans Blast Gemini Interruptions," *The Chicago Tribune*, March 17, 1966, p. 10

7　Buchwald, Art, "Red Alert and Redder Necks," *The Los Angeles Times*, Mar. 22, 1966, p. A5

8　—, "Marvel and DC Sales Figures," EnterTheStory.com, http://enterthestory.com/comic_sales.html, accessed Nov. 6, 2011

9　Bart, Peter, "Advertising: Superman Faces New Hurdles," *The New York Times*, Sep 23, 1962, p. 166

10　Archerd, Army, "Just For Variety," Daily Variety, Jan. 23, 1964, p. 2

11　Lopes, Paul, *Demanding Respect: The Evolution of the American Comic Book*, © 2009, Temple University Press, p. 94

12　Sloane, Leonard, "Shazam! Vintage Comics Prices Up, Up and Away," *The New York Times*, Jan. 30, 1965, p. 31

13　*Ibid.*

14　Sontag, Susan, *Against Interpretation and Other Essays*, © 2001, Picador, p. 291-292

15　Meehan, Thomas, "Not Good Taste, Not Bad Taste—It's 'Camp,'" *The New York Times*, March 21, 1965, p. SM30

16　*Ibid.*, p. SM30 & 113

17　*Ibid.*, p. 113

18　*Ibid.*

19　Champlin, Charles, "Batman's Boss Bats the Tube," *The Los Angeles Times*, May 18, 1966, p. D10

20　Dozier, William, "Television and the Creativity Gap," *The Los Angeles Times*, Jul 16, 1967, p. A13

21　—, "Series Shows Inferior, Says TV Executive," *The Chicago Tribune*, Oct. 12, 1967, p. B22

22　—, "William Dozier," *Daily Variety*, April 26 1991, p. 28

23　Deborah Dozier Potter Interview, conducted March 29, 2010

24　—, "William Dozier," *Daily Variety*, April 26 1991, p. 28

25　Deborah Dozier Potter Interview, conducted March 29, 2010

26　Lorenzo Semple, Jr. Interview, conducted July 29, 2009

27　*Ibid.*

28　Carlson, Walter, "Advertising: TV Getting Superman in Color," *The New York Times*, Sept. 16, 1965, p. 77

29　Hellman, Jack, "Light and Airy," *Daily Variety*, April 11, 1966, p. 7

30　William Dozier Interview, "Telescope," Canadian Broadcasting Company, http://www.1966batfan.com/dozierinterview3.wmv, accessed Aug 26, 2009

31　*Ibid.*

32　Deborah Dozier Potter Interview, conducted March 29, 2010

33　Arnott, Duane S., "Batman Revisited: A Look Behind the Scenes of the Creation of the TV Show," *Amazing Heroes* # 203, July 1992, p. 34

34　Johnson, Pat, "Krunch! There Goes Batman," *The Toronto Telegram*, 1968, http://www.1966batfan.com/dozier.htm, accessed Aug 26, 2009

35　Lorenzo Semple, Jr. Interview, conducted July 29, 2009

36　*Ibid.*

37　*Ibid.*

38　William Dozier Interview, "Telescope," Canadian Broadcasting Company, http://www.1966batfan.com/dozierinterview3.wmv, accessed Aug 26, 2009

39　Stone, Judy, "Caped Crusader of Camp," *The New York Times*, Jan. 9, 1966, p. 75

40　Semple, Jr., Lorenzo, "Requiem for a cheeky 'Batman': TV series creator speaks up for irreverent take," *Variety.com*, http://www.variety.com/article/VR1117988712.html?categoryId=3184&cs=1, accessed July 29, 2009

41　William Dozier Interview, "Telescope," Canadian Broadcasting Company, http://www.1966batfan.com/dozierinterview3.wmv, accessed Aug 26, 2009

42　—, "Greenway's 'Batman' To Air Over ABC-TV," *Daily Variety*, Aug. 25, 1965, p. 11

43　Arnott, Duane S., "Batman Revisited: A Look Behind the Scenes of the Creation of the TV Show," *Amazing Heroes* # 203, July 1992, p. 34

44　*Ibid.*, p. 35

45 —, "Batman & Wonder Serial a Constant Chicago Encore," *Variety*, October 6, 1965

46 Terry, Clifford, "Batcave, Mon Amour," *The Chicago Tribune*, Oct. 3, 1965, p. I21

47 —, "'Batman' Stirs Action In Candy & Popcorn," *Weekly Variety*, Oct. 20, 1965, p. 11

48 Krim, Seymour, "Batman New Camp Leader," *The Los Angeles Times*, Dec. 24, 1965, p. A12

49 —, "'Batman and Robin' Socko-Cum-Campo," *Weekly Variety*, Dec. 8, 1965, p. 4

50 —, "New York Sound Track," *Weekly Variety*, Dec. 22, 1965, p. 15

51 —, "'Batman and Robin' Socko-Cum-Campo," *Weekly Variety*, Dec. 8, 1965, p. 4

52 Krim, Seymour, "Batman New Camp Leader," *The Los Angeles Times*, Dec. 24, 1965, p. A12

53 William Dozier Interview, "Telescope," Canadian Broadcasting Company, http://www.1966batfan.com/dozierinterview3.wmv, accessed Aug 26, 2009

54 *Ibid.*

55 *Ibid.*

56 *Ibid.*

57 *Ibid.*

58 West, Adam with Jeff Rovin, *Back to the Batcave*, ©1994, Berkley Books, p. 13-26

59 *Ibid.*p. 33

60 Kaufman, Dave, "On All Channels: At First, Adam West Didn't Think Much Of 'Batman' Either," *Daily Variety*, March 1, 1966, p. 8

61 MacMinn, Aleene, "Adam West: Flying High as Batman," *The Los Angeles Times*, May 29, 1966, p. J4

62 Kaufman, Dave, "On All Channels: At First, Adam West Didn't Think Much Of 'Batman' Either," *Daily Variety*, March 1, 1966, p. 8

63 MacMinn, Aleene, "Adam West: Flying High as Batman," *The Los Angeles Times*, May 29, 1966, p. J4

64 *Ibid.*

65 Skow, John, "Has TV Gasp! Gone Batty??" *The Saturday Evening Post*, May 2, 1966

66 William Dozier Interview, "Telescope," Canadian Broadcasting Company, http://www.1966batfan.com/dozierinterview3.wmv, accessed Aug 26, 2009

67 Stone, Judy, "Caped Crusader of Camp," *The New York Times*, Jan. 9, 1966, p. 75

68 Deborah Dozier Potter Interview, conducted March 29, 2010

69 —, "Adam West 'Batman,'" *Daily Variety*, Sept. 22, 1965, p. 15

70 Reice, Sylvie, "With Batman in His Beach Lair," *The Los Angeles Times*, Feb. 13, 1966, p. J13

71 MacMinn, Aleene, "Adam West: Flying High as Batman," *The Los Angeles Times*, May 29, 1966, p. J4

72 West, Adam with Jeff Rovin, *Back to the Batcave*, ©1994, Berkley Books, p. 161

73 Lorenzo Semple, Jr. Interview, conducted July 29, 2009

74 Ward, Burt, *Boy Wonder: My Life in Tights*, © 1995 Logical Figments Books, Los Angeles, p. 40

75 *Ibid.*p. 39

76 *Ibid.*p. 42

77 *Ibid.*, p. 43

78 Crawford, Linda, "Robin Quick to Say He Is Boy Wonder," *The Chicago Tribune*, May 8, 1966, p. T4

79 Ward, Burt, *Boy Wonder: My Life in Tights*, © 1995 Logical Figments Books, Los Angeles, p. 44-45

80 *Ibid.*, p. 46-47

81 MacMinn, Aleene, "He's Truly a Boy Wonder," *The Los Angeles Times*, Jul 31, 1966, p. A4

82 Ward, Burt, *Boy Wonder: My Life in Tights*, © 1995 Logical Figments Books, Los Angeles, p. 49-50

83 William Dozier Interview, "Telescope," Canadian Broadcasting Company, http://www.1966batfan.com/dozierinterview3.wmv, accessed Aug 26, 2009

84 Lyle Waggoner Interview, conducted Aug. 8, 2009

85 *Ibid.*

86 Ward, Burt, *Boy Wonder: My Life in Tights*, © 1995 Logical Figments Books, Los Angeles, p. 52

87 Crawford, Linda, "Robin Quick to Say He Is Boy Wonder," *The Chicago Tribune*, May 8, 1966, p. T4

88 Deborah Dozier Potter Interview, conducted March 29, 2010

89 —, "Forums," *Golden Age Cartoons.com*, http://forums.goldenagecartoons.com/showthread.php?t=2462, accessed Sept. 16, 2011

90 Feather, Leonard, "Neal Hefti Bats 1,000 With Batman Theme," *The Los Angeles Times*, Jun 26, 1966, p. B28

91 Shaogo, *Neal Hefti*, http://www.everything2.com/index.pl?node=Neal%20Hefti, accessed Sept. 6, 2009

92 Feather, Leonard, "Neal Hefti Bats 1,000 With Batman Theme," *The Los Angeles Times*, Jun 26, 1966, p. B28

93 Burlingame, Jon, *TV'S Greatest Hits*, © 1996 Schirmer Books, New York, p. 214-215

94 Shaogo, *Neal Hefti*, http://www.everything2.com/index.pl?node=Neal%20Hefti, accessed Sept. 6, 2009

95 Feather, Leonard, "Neal Hefti Bats 1,000 With Batman Theme," *The Los Angeles Times*, Jun 26, 1966, p. B28

96 Burlingame, Jon, *TV'S Greatest Hits*, © 1996 Schirmer Books, New York, p. 215

97 Humphrey, Hal, "More Gadgets for the Dynamic Duo," *The Los Angeles Times*, Jun 9, 1966, p. E16

98 —, *The 1966 Batmobile*, http://www.1966batmobile.com/spec.htm, accessed Sept. 6, 2009

99 Archerd, Army, "Just For Variety,'" *Daily Variety*, July 18, 1966, p. 2

100 Wingert, Wally, *Costume Designer Jan Kemp's Presentation from 1989*, http://www.wallyontheweb.com/kemp.htm, accessed Sept. 6, 2009

101 *Ibid.*

102 *Ibid.*

103 Gowran, Clay, "Pirates, Telegrams, and TV Press Agents," *The Chicago Tribune*, Feb. 27, 1966, p. Q9

104 Swires, Steve, "Holy Sidekick! Burt Ward," *Starlog*, Nov. 1987, p. 56

105 —, "Inside TV: Network Shuffles Shows to Fill Slattery Void," *The Los Angeles Times*, Oct. 20, 1965, p. D18

106 Semple, Jr., Lorenzo, "Requiem for a cheeky 'Batman': TV series creator speaks up for irreverent take," *Variety.com*, http://www.variety.com/article/VR1117988712.html?categoryId=3184&cs=1, accessed July 29, 2009

107 —, "'Batman' Poised As Mid-Season ABC Replacement," *Daily Variety*, Oct. 19, 1965, p. 11

108 —, "20th Leases Space At Desilu To Telense 'Batman' Series," *Daily Variety*, Nov. 17, 1965, p. 14

109 Deborah Dozier Potter Interview, conducted March 29, 2010

110 William Dozier Interview, "Telescope," Canadian Broadcasting Company, http://www.1966batfan.com/dozierinterview3.wmv, accessed Aug 26, 2009

111 Lorenzo Semple, Jr. Interview, conducted July 29, 2009

112 William Dozier Interview, "Telescope," Canadian Broadcasting Company, http://www.1966batfan.com/dozierinterview3.wmv, accessed Aug 26, 2009

113 Page, Don, "Gorshin Impressive Villain," *The Los Angeles Times*, Jun 3, 1966, p. D17

114 *Ibid.*

115 McLellan, Dennis, "Frank Gorshin, 71; Impressionist, Actor Famously Played Riddler, George Burns," *The Los Angeles Times*, May 19, 2005, pg. B.10

116 —, "Gorshin Will Essay 'Batman' Character," *Daily Variety*, Sept. 27, 1965, p. 4

117 —, "Gorshin May Be His Own Opposition," *Daily Variety*, Oct. 1, 1965, p. 13

118 Lyon, Herb, "Tower Ticker," *The Chicago Tribune*, Oct. 15, 1965, p. 18

119 McLellan, Dennis, "Frank Gorshin, 71; Impressionist, Actor Famously Played Riddler, George Burns," *The Los Angeles Times*, May 19, 2005, pg. B.10

120 Browning, Norma Lee, "Frank (The Riddler) Gorshin Laughs Way to Bank," *The Chicago Tribune*, Aug. 30, 1966, p. B1

121 Ward, Burt, *Boy Wonder: My Life in Tights*, © 1995 Logical Figment Books, Los Angeles, p. 131

122 Lorenzo Semple, Jr. Interview, conducted July 29, 2009

123 Reice, Sylvie, "With Batman in His Beach Lair," *The Los Angeles Times*, Feb. 13, 1966, p. J13

124 Smith, Bob, "Batman, Robin Bound Into Camp," *The Los Angeles Times*, Jan. 13, 1966, p. C12

125 —, "Kelloggs Signs Up: 'Batman's' Near SRO," *Weekly Variety*, Dec. 29, 1965, p. 23

126 Adams, Val, "Discotheque Frug Party Heralds Batman's Film and TV Premiere," *The New York Times*, Jan. 13, 1966, p. 79

127 —, "TV: Pow! Zap! It's Batman and Robin," *The New York Times*, Jan. 13, 1966, p. 79

128 Page, Don, "Batman, Robin: Two for the Hee-haw," *The Los Angeles Times*, Jan. 14, 1966, p. C16

129 Sarmento, William E., "Huzza for Batman and Robin," *The Lowell Sun*, Jan. 13, 1966, p. 35

130 Gould, Jack, "Too Good to Be Camp," *The New York Times*, Jan. 23, 1966, p. 109

131 Hopper, Hedda, "Jane Fonda, Robards in 'Wednesday,'" *The Los Angeles Times*, Jan. 24, 1966, p. C20

132 Terry, Clifford, "Shed a Tear for Lana, but Only in Film," *The Chicago Tribune*, Mar. 13, 1966, p. F17

133 Archerd, Army, "Just For Variety," *Daily Variety*, Feb. 9, 1966, p. 2

134 Pitman, Jack, "Webs' 'Second Season' a Premiere Week Click in Overnight Scores; 'Batman,' Et Al. Lift ABC Levels," *Weekly Variety*, Jan. 19, 1966, p. 35

135 Gent, George, "Campy 'Batman' Flying High on TV," *The New York Times*, Jan. 15, 1966, p. 54

136 Du Brow, Rick, "Batman is Not as Hip as Advertised," Tucson Daily Citizen, Jan. 13, 1966, p. 29

137 Archerd, Army, "Just For Variety," *Daily Variety*, Feb. 9, 1966, p. 2

138 Champlin, Charles, "Taking a Bat at Batman...Plonk!" *The Los Angeles Times*, Feb. 28, 1966, p. C17

139 Kaufman, Dave, "Horwitz Defends 'Batman'; Fine-Friedkin's CIAntic," *Daily Variety*, April 13, 1966, p. 9

140 Gent, George, "Wife Is Not a Wife in New NBC Show," *The New York Times*, Feb. 19, 1966, p. 55

141 Humphrey, Hal, "Public 'Bats' Over Caped Crusader," *The Los Angeles Times*, Feb. 9, 1966, p. C13

142 —, "London Will Get Batman TV Series," *The Los Angeles Times*, Feb. 15, 1966, p. C15

143 —, "Sat.-Sun. Slots For 'Batman' In Britain," *Weekly Variety*, April 6, 1966, p. 46

144 —, "'Batman' Playing Three Different Ways in Brit., Hour, ½ Hr. & 15 Mins.," *Weekly Variety*, July 6, 1966, p. 22

145 —, "Peter Falk to Co-star in Musical," *The Los Angeles Times*, Jun 8, 1966, p. D16

146 Page, Don, "Baltimore Station Won't Carry Batman," *The Los Angeles Times*, Jan. 14, 1966, p. C16

147 Gould, Jack, "When Is a Blessing Not a Blessing?" *The New York Times*, Feb. 6, 1966, p. X19

148 —, "WJZ-TV Thwarts 'Batman,'" *Weekly Variety*, Jan. 19, 1966, p. 39

149 Page, Don, "Baltimore Station Won't Carry Batman," *The Los Angeles Times*, Jan. 14, 1966, p. C16

150 Gould, Jack, "When Is a Blessing Not a Blessing?" *The New York Times*, Feb. 6, 1966, p. X19

151 Adams, Val, "Friendly Weighs Bids Outside TV," *The New York Times*, Mar 28, 1966, p. 67

152 Adam, Val, "'Batman's' 4th Ad Arouses Protests," The New York Times, Mar. 17, 1966, p. 79

153 —, "CBS Acquires TV Rights To 'Shadow' And 'The Phantom,'" *Daily Variety*, Jan. 25, 1966, p. 12

154 Carlson, Walter, "Advertising: Big Brewer Changing Caves," *The New York Times*, Jan. 26, 1966, p. 62

155 Vartan, Vartang G., "Spotlight: Batman Fad Aids Stock Rise," *The New York Times*, Mar. 20, 1966, p. I48

156 —, "1966 Comic Book Sales Figures," The Comic Chronicles, http://www.comichron. com/yearlycomicssales/1960s/1966.html, accessed Nov. 5, 2011

157 William Dozier Interview, "Telescope," Canadian Broadcasting Company, http:// www.1966batfan.com/dozierinterview3. wmv, accessed Aug 26, 2009

158 Meredith, Burgess, *So Far, So Good: A Memoir*, © 1994 Little, Brown and Company, New York, p. 260-261

159 Diehl, Digby, "Dual Existence for Burgess Meredith," *The Los Angeles Times*, Dec. 1, 1967, p. E20

160 Meredith, Burgess, *So Far, So Good: A Memoir*, © 1994 Little, Brown and Company, New York, p. 225

161 *Ibid.*, p. 261

162 *Ibid.*, pgs. 224-225

163 —, *The Joker—Cesar Romero*, http://www. geocities.com/Hollywood/Hills/7537/joker. htm, accessed 9/8/09

164 William Dozier Interview, "Telescope," Canadian Broadcasting Company, http:// www.1966batfan.com/dozierinterview3. wmv, accessed Aug 26, 2009

165 —, "Romero Enjoys 'Joker' Role," *Florence (South Carolina) Morning News*, July 30, 1966, p. 11

166 —, *The Joker—Cesar Romero*, http://www. geocities.com/Hollywood/Hills/7537/joker. htm, accessed 9/8/09

167 Deborah Dozier Potter Interview, conducted March 29, 2010

168 Humphrey, Hal, "Public 'Bats' Over Caped Crusader," *The Los Angeles Times*, Feb. 9, 1966, p. C13

169 Lorenzo Semple, Jr. Interview, conducted July 29, 2009

170 *Ibid.*

171 Skow, John, "Has TV Gasp! Gone Batty??", *The Saturday Evening Post*, May 2, 1966

172 Stone, Judy, "Caped Crusader of Camp," *The New York Times*, Jan. 9, 1966, p. 75

173 Lorenzo Semple, Jr. Interview, conducted July 29, 2009

174 Jankiewicz, Pat, "The Bard of 'Boff!' 'Boof!' and 'Bang!' Stanley 'Batwriter' Ross," *Filmfax* No. 16, August 1989, p. 48

175 Van Hise, James, *Batmania*, © 1989 Pioneer Books, Las Vegas, NV, p. 76

176 Mangels, Andy, "Andy Mangels Backstage With Julie Newmar," *Amazing Heroes* #167, June 15, 1989, p. 61-62

177 Hernandez, Greg, "Thanks for the Interview Julie Newmar," *Out in Hollywood,* http://www.insidesocal.com/outinhollywood/2008/04/thanks-for-the-interview-julie.html, accessed Sept. 18, 2009

178 Rees, Brenda, "With the Kids: Heroic Efforts; Caped Crusaders Keep Watch -- and Are Being Watched -- at the TV and Radio Museum," *The Los Angeles Times*, Jul 1, 2004, p. E 30

179 Freeman, Donald, "Villains Aplenty for TV's Batman," *The Chicago Tribune*, p. Q12

180 West, Adam with Jeff Rovin, *Back to the Batcave*, ©1994, Berkley Books, p. 142

181 Van Hise, James, *Batmania*, © 1989 Pioneer Books, Las Vegas, NV, p. 77

182 Stone, Judy, "Caped Crusader of Camp," *The New York Times*, Jan. 9, 1966, p. 75

183 Humphrey, Hal, "Public 'Bats' Over Caped Crusader," *The Los Angeles Times*, Feb. 9, 1966, p. C13

184 Lowry, Cynthia, "A Money Tree Grows in Hollywood for Stars," *The Los Angeles Times,* Sep. 9, 1966, p. C15

185 Lorenzo Semple, Jr. Interview, conducted July 29, 2009

186 Archerd, Army, "Just For Variety,'" *Daily Variety*, Aug. 10, 1966, p. 2

187 Lyon, Herb Tower Ticker, *The Chicago Tribune,* Jan. 26, 1966, p. 20

188 Champlin, Charles, "Tracy and Hepburn to Rekindle That Old Magic," *The Los Angeles Times*, Sep 26, 1966, p. C1

189 Lyon, Herb, "Tower Ticker," *The Chicago Tribune,* Jan. 31, 1966, p. 22

190 *Ibid.*p. 18

191 Ehinger, Vi, "Batman Transforms Image of Teen-Agers," *The Los Angeles Times,* Feb. 13, 1966, p. OC1

192 Adams, Val, "Stars Are Rivals Again," *The New York Times*, Mar. 6, 1966, p. X19

193 Rohan, Barry, "James Bond for Juniors," *The Chicago Tribune*, May 28, 1966, p. F13

194 —, *Daily Variety,* Feb. 14, 1966, p. 18

195 —, "Soap Operatics," *Daily Variety,* Feb. 24, 1966, p. 10

196 —," Batmania in Bay City," *Daily Variety*, Feb. 7, 1966, p. 24

197 —"School Meals Go Better With Batman Touch," *The Los Angeles Times*, Oct. 6, 1966, p. SG1

198 —, "Col Giving 'Batman' Reissue Wide Spread," *Daily Variety*, April 8, 1966, p. 3

199 —, "Col. 'Batman' Invades First-Run Theatres," *Box-Office*, March 21, 1966

200 —, "They Dig 'Batman and Robin' in London," *Film Daily*, Feb. 10, 1966

201 —, "'Batman' On B'Way," *Daily Variety*, March 11, 1966, p. 18

202 —, "Col. 'Batman' Invades First-Run Theatres," *Box-Office*, March 21, 1966

203 Durgnat, Raymond, "Batman: Raymond Durgnat Pleads for the New Hooliganism," *Films and Filming*, April 1966

204 Reice, Sylvie, "With Batman in His Beach Lair," *The Los Angeles Times*, Feb. 13, 1966, p. J13

205 Archerd, Army, "Just For Variety," *Daily Variety*, May 20, 1966, p. 2

206 Crawford, Linda, "Robin Quick to Say He Is Boy Wonder," *The Chicago Tribune*, May 8, 1966, p. T4

207 Archerd, Army, "Just For Variety," *Daily Variety*, Jan. 31, 1966, p. 2

208 Horowitz, Murray, "Batcave As Tourist Trap," *Weekly Variety*, July 27, 1966, p. 30

209 Beck, Roger, "Musical Fallout From Batman Fad," *The Los Angeles Times*, Mar. 6, 1966, p. M22

210 —, "Barbra, Sinatra, 'Singing Nun,' Elvis, Sonny-Cher, Allen-Rossi, Love, Rolling Stones Top New LPs," *Weekly Variety,* March 30, 1966, p. 74

211 Jankiewicz, Pat, "The Bard of 'Boff!' 'Boof!' and 'Bang!' Stanley 'Batwriter' Ross," *Filmfax* No. 16, August 1989, p. 88

212 —"Books Today," *The New York Times*, Apr. 21, 1966, p. 36

213 Nichols, Lewis, "In and Out of Books," *The New York Times*, May 1, 166, p. 319

214 Oliver, Myrna, "William Woolfolk, 86; Novelist Wrote for Television, Comics," *The Los Angeles Times*, Aug 10, 2003. pg. B.18

215 —, "The Batboom," *Time*, March 11, 1966, p. 100

216 —, "Stores Are Sued on Rights to Batman," *The New York Times,* Jun 23, 1966, p. 70

217 Nichols, Lewis, "In and Out of Books," *The New York Times*, May 1, 166, p. 319

218 Korman, Seymour, "Producer Eyes Public Offering of Batstock," *The Chicago Tribune*, May 15, 1966, p. D9

219 Lanahan, Frances, "F.C.C. Chief Plays Batman for Charity," *The New York Times*, Mar. 6, 1966, p. 91

220 MacPherson, Myra, "F.C.C.'s Caped Crusader is Honored," *The New York Times*, Apr. 27, 1966, p. 51

221 Gent, George, "Pravda Meets 'Batman' Head On," *The New York Times*, Apr. 30, 1966, p. 31

222 —, "Russians call Batman 'Idealized F.B.I. Agent'" *The New York Times*, Sep 12, 1966, p. 38

223 —, "Crowds Pelt Marchers in Viet Protest," *The Chicago Tribune*, Mar. 27, 1966, p. 3

224 —, "Peter Falk to Co-star in Musical," *The Los Angeles Times*, Jun 8, 1966, p. D16

225 Beecher, William, "Batman, Army Copter-TV System, Enlisted in War," *The New York Times*, Aug. 12, 1966, p. 3

226 Smith, William D., "Advertising: A Strategy for Sophistication," *The New York Times*, Feb. 18, 1966, p. 44

227 Winship, F.M., "Woman Pulls a Few Strings, Ties Up Batman Promotion," *The Los Angeles Times*, Mar. 11, 1966, p. C18

228 Gysel, Dean, "Batman Foe? The Dread Dr. Spock!" *The Los Angeles Times*, Jul 11, 1966, p. C19

229 —, "Bat Example," *Weekly Variety*, June 8, 1966, p. 27

230 Crawford, Linda, "Hornet Like Batman? Not at All!" *The Chicago Tribune*, Aug 14, 1966, p. IND A8

231 Archerd, Army, "Just For Variety," *Daily Variety*, Jan. 31, 1966, p. 2

232 Archerd, Army, "Just For Variety," *Daily Variety*, Feb. 4, 1966, p. 2

233 —"Congressman Asks Batman to Buckle Up," The Los Angeles Times, Apr. 25, 1966, p. C32

234 MacMinn, Arleene, "Television Nominees Set for Emmy Awards Chase," *The Los Angeles Times*, Apr. 27, 1966, p. D1

235 —, "20th And Dozier Mulling 'Batman' Theatrical Feature," *Daily Variety*, Feb. 24, 1966, p. 1

236 Skow, John, "Has TV Gasp! Gone Batty," *The Saturday Evening Post*, May 2, 1966

237 Archerd, Army, "Just For Variety," *Daily Variety*, May 2, 1966, p. 2

238 *Ibid.*

239 —, "4 Who Menaced 'Batman' On TV To Ditto In 20th's Feature," *Daily Variety*, March 31, 1966, \p. 10

240 —, "Short Cuts," *Daily Variety*, April 19, 1966, p. 11

241 Alpert, Don, "The Girl Who Kissed (Smack!) Batman," *The Los Angeles Times*, Aug. 7, 1966, p. B4

242 Scheuer, Philip K., "Batman to Face 'Old Gang' in Film," *The Los Angeles Times*, May 3, 1966, p. D14

243 *Ibid.*

244 West, Adam with Jeff Rovin, *Back to the Batcave*, ©1994, Berkley Books, p. 33

245 Scheuer, Philip K., "Batman to Face 'Old Gang' in Film," *The Los Angeles Times*, May 3, 1966, p. D14

246 Archerd, Army, "Just For Variety," *Daily Variety*, April 12, 1966, p. 2

247 West, Adam with Jeff Rovin, *Back to the Batcave*, ©1994, Berkley Books, p. 163

248 Alpert, Don, "The Girl Who Kissed (Smack!) Batman," *The Los Angeles Times*, Aug. 7, 1966, p. B4

249 Humphrey, Hal, "More Gadgets for the Dynamic Duo," *The Los Angeles Times*, Jun 9, 1966, p. E16

250 *Ibid.*

251 Sutton, David, "The 1966 Batcycle," *1966 Batfan.com*, http://www.1966batfan.com/66batcycle.htm, accessed Sept. 29, 2009

252 *Ibid.*

253 *Ibid.*

254 *Ibid.*

255 *Ibid.*

256 West, Adam with Jeff Rovin, *Back to the Batcave*, ©1994, Berkley Books, p. 165

257 Ward, Burt, *Boy Wonder: My Life in Tights*, © 1995 Logical Figments Books, Los Angeles, p. 132-133

258 Sutton, David, "The 1966 Batcycle," *1966 Batfan.com*, http://www.1966batfan.com/66batcycle.htm, accessed Sept. 29, 2009

259 Champlin, Charles, "Batman West Keeps His Balance," *The Los Angeles Times*, Jun 24, 1966, p. C9

260 *Ibid.*

261 Gowran, Clay, "Shelley Winters Falls Off Drama Wagon," *The Chicago Tribune*, Aug. 24, 1966, p. A8

262 Champlin, Charles, "Batman West Keeps His Balance," *The Los Angeles Times*, Jun 24, 1966, p. C9

263 MacMinn, Aleene, "Green Hornet Buzzing Into Batman Domain," *The Los Angeles Times*, Apr. 30, 1966, p. B3

264 —, "Anticlimax Note: 'Batman' Renewed," *Daily Variety*, March 11, 1966, p. 18

265 Gysel, Dean, "Art Carney Looking Forward to 'Honeymooners' Revival," *San Antonio Express and News,* July 31, 1966, p. B-1

266 Van Hise, James, *Batmania,* © 1989 Pioneer Books, Las Vegas, NV, p. 83

267 —, "Stars Debbie Reynolds, Van Johnson Type-Cast," *The Centralia, Washington Daily Chronicle,* July 30, 1966

268 —, "Five Jazz and Pop Shows To Rock Shea This Summer," *The New York Times,* May 21, 1966, p. 18

269 —"Holy Shea Stadium! The Batman's Saved," *The New York Times,* Jun 25, 1966, p. 25

270 —, "'Batman' Concert Facing an Inquiry," *The New York Times,* Jul 8, 1966, p. 29

271 Sherman, Robert, "Batman to the Rescue in Shea Caper," *The New York Times,* Jun 26, 1966, p. L72

272 —, "Batman Concert Tickets Are Stolen From Office," *The New York Times,* Jun. 22, 1966, p. 41

273 —"Holy Shea Stadium! The Batman's Saved," *The New York Times,* Jun 25, 1966, p. 25

274 Sherman, Robert, "Batman to the Rescue in Shea Caper," *The New York Times,* Jun 26, 1966, p. L72

275 Schoenfeld, Herm, "Batman Strikes Out At Shea: B.O. Fiasco In Big Ballpark," *Weekly Variety,* June 29, 1966, p. 41

276 Archerd, Army, "Just For Variety,'" *Daily Variety,* June 27, 1966, p. 2

277 —, "'Batman' Concert Facing an Inquiry," *The New York Times,* Jul 8, 1966, p. 2

278 —, "Harry Bloomfield's Concerts at Shea In Forced Foldo After Batman Fiasco," *Weekly Variety,* July 13, 1966, p. 40

279 Greenwood, Leonard, "Titanic Trio: Thailand Prince, Batman and Hollywood," *The Los Angeles Times,* Jul 15, 1966, p. A1

280 Archerd, Army, "Just For Variety,'" *Daily Variety,* July 25, 1966, p. 2

281 Sutton, David, "The 1966 Batcycle," *1966 Batfan.com,* http://www.1966batfan.com/66batcycle.htm, accessed Sept. 29, 2009

282 Barrileaux, Gladys, "'Batman' Premieres in Movie Version," *The Galveston News,* July 31, 1966, p. 6-A

283 —, "'Batman' To Be Premiered," *The San Antonio Light,* July 31, 1966, p. 16-E

284 Archerd, Army, "Just For Variety,'" *Daily Variety,* July 20, 1966, p. 2

285 Fiske, Edward B., "Clergyman Sees Batman's Appeal as Religious," *The New York Times,* Aug. 8, 1966, p. 30

286 West, Adam with Jeff Rovin, *Back to the Batcave,* ©1994, Berkley Books, p. 168-169

287 —, "Wow! Bam! Socko! 7,000 Children Greet Batman," *The New York Times,* Aug. 25, 1966, p. 42

288 West, Adam with Jeff Rovin, *Back to the Batcave,* ©1994, Berkley Books, p. 169-170

289 —, "Young Britons Told Not to Copy Batman," *The New York Times,* Aug. 24, 1966, p. 38

290 —, "'Batman' Merchandise In Hot Scot Demand," *Weekly Variety,* Aug. 17, 1966, p. 31

291 —, "'Batman' Invades Pantry," *Weekly Variety,* Dec. 14, 1966, p. 28

292 —, "'Batman' Grosses 250G First 5 N.Y. Days In Spread Of 56 Houses," *Daily Variety,* Sept. 2, 1966, p. 3

293 Thompson, Howard, "TV Heroes Stay Long," *The New York Times,* Aug 25, 1966, p. 42

294 Scheuer, Philip K., "Holy Numbness! Batman Film Stretches Imagination," *The Los Angeles Times,* \Sep 1, 1966, p. D16

295 Terry, Clifford, Batman Booms on Big Screen, *The Chicago Tribune,* Sept. 12, 1966, p. C17

296 Dooley, John, "Film Review,'" *Daily Variety,* July 18, 1966, p. 3

297 Lorenzo Semple, Jr. Interview, conducted July 29, 2009

298 Swires, Steve, "Holy Sidekick! Burt Ward," *Starlog,* Nov. 1987, p. 57

299 Browning, Norma Lee, "Look for Many-Faced Mike," *The Chicago Tribune,* Sep. 2, 1967, p. 11

300 —, "'Batman' Offered CBS, NBC Before ABC, Suit Claims," *Daily Variety,* Aug. 30, 1966, p. 1

301 —, "Zam—'Batman' Belted By Suit Over Title Use," *Weekly Variety,* May 18, 1966, p. 42

302 Humphrey, Hal, "Batman Role No Fun for Shelley," *The Los Angeles Times,* Aug 31, 1966, p. D14

303 Sutton, David, "Second Season Episodes," *The 1966 Batman TV Tribute Site,* http://www.1966batfan.com/episodes2.htm, accessed Oct. 3, 2009

304 Van Hise, James, *Batmania,* © 1989 Pioneer Books, Las Vegas, NV, p. 76

305 Price, Vincent, "Art and TV Meet—Pow! It's Batman," *The Chicago Tribune*, Sep. 3, 1967, p. E4

306 Jankiewicz, Pat, "The Bard of 'Boff!' 'Boof!' and 'Bang!' Stanley 'Batwriter' Ross," *Filmfax* No. 16, August 1989, p. 88

307 West, Adam with Jeff Rovin, *Back to the Batcave*, ©1994, Berkley Books, p. 147

308 Champlin, Charles, "Preminger's Film Premises," *The Los Angeles Times*, Nov. 11, 1966, p. D1

309 Gent, George, "Can Batman Melt Preminger's Ice?" *The New York Times*, May 28, 1966, p. 54

310 *Ibid.*

311 West, Adam with Jeff Rovin, *Back to the Batcave*, ©1994, Berkley Books, p. 144

312 Gent, George, "Can Batman Melt Preminger's Ice?" *The New York Times*, May 28, 1966, p. 54

313 Swires, Steve, "Holy Sidekick! Burt Ward," *Starlog*, Nov. 1987, p. 56

314 —, "Robin Burned in Blast on Batman Set," *The Los Angeles Times*, Sep 2, 1966 p. D13

315 Swires, Steve, "Holy Sidekick! Burt Ward," *Starlog*, Nov. 1987, p. 56

316 Johnson, Pat, "Krunch! There goes Batman," *The Toronto Telegram*, http://www.1966batfan.com/dozier.htm, accessed July 28, 2009

317 Wallach, Eli, *The Good, the Bad, and Me: In My Anecdotage*, © 2005 Harcourt, New York, p. 286

318 Sutton, David, "Second Season Episodes," *The 1966 Batman TV Tribute Site*, http://www.1966batfan.com/episodes2.htm, accessed Oct. 6, 2009

319 Van Hise, James, *Batmania*, © 1989 Pioneer Books, Las Vegas, NV, p. 83-84

320 Humphrey, Hal, "Hair Stylist Pans the Unkindest Cut," *The Los Angeles Times*, Dec. 13, 1966, p. E21

321 Humphrey, Hal, "Evans: Bard for a Bird in Hand," *The Los Angeles Times*, Oct. 30, 1967, p. C26

322 —, "Liberace, Morley, Slezak, Johnson Menace 'Batman,'" *Daily Variety*, June 16, 1966, p. 12

323 Browning, Norma Lee, "Frank (The Riddler) Gorshin Laughs Way to Bank," *The Chicago Tribune*, Aug. 30, 1966, p. B1

324 Henniger, Paul, "John Astin Solves Riddler Problem," *The Los Angeles Times*, Feb. 8, 1967, p. E16

325 *Ibid.*

326 Browning, Norma Lee, "Call Me Tallulah, Dahling..." *The Chicago Tribune*, Mar 14, 1967, p. B2

327 Du Brow, Rick, "Fad Faded? Batman Ratings Take a Nosedive," *The Los Angeles Times*, Nov. 3, 1966, p. D20

328 Humphrey, Hal, "New Strategy in the War of Ratings," *The Los Angeles Times*, Feb. 1, 1967

329 —, "ABC-TV May Flit 'Hornet' in Spring; Mulls '3rd Season,'" *Weekly Variety*, Jan. 11, 1967, p. 35

330 —, "Wife Divorcing Batman's Robin," *The Los Angeles Times*, Nov. 19, 1966, p. A8

331 —, "Wife Divorces Actor Burt Ward," *The Los Angeles Times*, Feb. 10, 1967, p. A3

332 —, "Toy Sales Expected to Pass $2.5 Billion," *The New York Times*, Dec. 13, 1966, p. 96

333 —, "Fall Season Shaping Up for ABC Network," *The Los Angeles Times*, Feb. 27, 1967, p. D27

334 —, "Holy Ratings! It's Bye, Bye Batman," *The Los Angeles Times*, Apr 15, 1967, p. B2

335 West, Adam with Jeff Rovin, *Back to the Batcave*, ©1994, Berkley Books, p. 171

336 Archerd, Army, "1967: Problems plague 'King Gun'—A look back at past issues on West film," *Variety*, Sept. 18, 1967

337 Scott, John L., "Dobritch's International Circus Opens at Arena," *The Los Angeles Times*, Mar 18, 1967. p. B1

338 Windeler, Robert, "TV's Top Series Add Ingredients," *The New York Times*, Jul 21, 1967, p. 31

339 Fitzgerald, Michael, "Carmine Infantino: Decades at DC and Beyond," quoted in "Barbara Gordon," *Wikipedia*, http://en.wikipedia.org/wiki/Barbara_Gordon#Powers_and_abilities, accessed Oct. 17, 2009.

340 Buck, Jerry, "TV Today: Toys, Gimmicks Pile Up Profits for Shows," *The Chicago Tribune*, Nov. 10, 1967, p. SCL A7

341 Windeler, Robert, "TV's Top Series Add Ingredients," *The New York Times*, Jul 21, 1967, p. 31

342 Browning, Norma Lee, "Enter Batgirl," *The Chicago Tribune*, Sep 10, 1967, p. I36

343 *Ibid.*

344 *Ibid.*

345 *Ibid.*

346 *Ibid.*

347 Humphrey, Hal, "Batgirl Swings Onto TV Scene," *The Los Angeles Times*, May 10, 1967, p. E22

348 Browning, Norma Lee, "Enter Batgirl," *The Chicago Tribune*, Sep 10, 1967, p. I36

349 Jankiewicz, Pat, "Recalling Batgirl," *www. YvonneCraig.com*, http://yvonnecraig.com/up_close_interview.html, accessed Oct. 19, 2009

350 Dutton, Walt, "Batgirl Jumps Into Crime Fight (Zowie!)" *The Los Angeles Times*, Aug 1, 1967, p. D1

351 Purcelli, Marion, "Yvonne Craig, TV's Bat Girl," *The Chicago Tribune*, Nov. 25, 1967, p. E3

352 Browning, Norma Lee, "Enter Batgirl," *The Chicago Tribune*, Sep 10, 1967, p. I36

353 Jankiewicz, Pat, "Recalling Batgirl," *www. YvonneCraig.com*, http://yvonnecraig.com/up_close_interview.html, accessed Oct. 19, 2009

354 Humphrey, Hal, "Batgirl Swings Onto TV Scene," *The Los Angeles Times*, May 10, 1967, p. E22

355 *Ibid.*

356 Jankiewicz, Pat, "Recalling Batgirl," *www. YvonneCraig.com*, http://yvonnecraig.com/up_close_interview.html, accessed Oct. 19, 2009

357 —, "'Batman' Shortly Could Have Wings Clipped By ABC-TV," *Daily Variety*, March 15, 1967, p. 17

358 —, "Zounds! More Batman," *Daily Variety*, March 1, 1967, p. 2

359 *Ibid.*

360 —, "'Batman' 3rd Season Production Begins,'" *Daily Variety*, July 5, 1967, p. 12

361 Counts, Kyle, "Some Call Her Batgirl: In Form-Fitting Costume, Yvonne Craig Fought Goons. In SF-TV, She Got Green & Gigantic," *Starlog* # 149, December 1989, p. 30

362 —, "Batgirl Cycle," *BatMania.co.uk*, http://www.bat-mania.co.uk/main/batgirl/batgirlcycle.php, accessed Oct. 19, 2009

363 Jankiewicz, Pat, "Recalling Batgirl," *www. YvonneCraig.com*, http://yvonnecraig.com/up_close_interview.html, accessed Oct. 19, 2009

364 Dutton, Walt, "Batgirl Jumps Into Crime Fight (Zowie!)" *The Los Angeles Times*, Aug 1, 1967, p. D1

365 *Ibid.*

366 Jankiewicz, Pat, "Recalling Batgirl," *www. YvonneCraig.com*, http://yvonnecraig.com/up_close_interview.html, accessed Oct. 19, 2009

367 —, "Eartha Kitt," *Wikipedia*, http://en.wikipedia.org/wiki/Eartha_Kitt, accessed Oct. 20, 2009

368 Jankiewicz, Pat, "Recalling Batgirl," *www. YvonneCraig.com*, http://yvonnecraig.com/up_close_interview.html, accessed Oct. 19, 2009

369 Mangels, Andy, "Andy Mangels Backstage With Julie Newmar," *Amazing Heroes* #167, June 15, 1989, p. 62

370 Sutton, David, "Third Season Episodes," *The 1966 Batman TV Tribute Site*, http://www.1966batfan.com/episodes2.htm, accessed Oct. 25, 2009

371 West, Adam with Jeff Rovin, *Back to the Batcave*, ©1994, Berkley Books, p. 183

372 Sutton, David, "Third Season Episodes," *The 1966 Batman TV Tribute Site*, http://www.1966batfan.com/episodes2.htm, accessed Oct. 25, 2009

373 Interview with Michael G. Wilson, conducted July 17, 2009

374 West, Adam with Jeff Rovin, *Back to the Batcave*, ©1994, Berkley Books, p. 186

375 —, "'Batman' Axed," *Daily Variety*, Jan. 18, 1968, p. 14

376 —, "Memo To ABC-TV: Ask Dozier, He Knows 'Batman' Was Axed," *Daily Variety*, Jan. 26, 1968, p. 36

377 Humphrey, Hal, "Viewers Getting Less and Less," *The Los Angeles Times*, Jan 25, 1968, p. C10

378 —, "Curses!!! 'Batman' Meets His Master: Television's Ratings," *The New York Times*, Jan. 26, 1968, p. 95

379 —, "CBS Dominates Top Spots on Nielsen Poll," *The Los Angeles Times*, Feb. 21, 1968, p. E23

380 Semple, Jr., Lorenzo, "Requiem for a cheeky 'Batman': TV series creator speaks up for irreverent take," *Variety.com*, http://www.variety.com/article/VR1117988712.html?categoryId=3184&cs=1, accessed July 29, 2009

381 *Ibid.*

382 Humphrey, Hal, "Batman: Putting You On In Style," *The Los Angeles Times*, Feb. 25, 1968, p. C2

383 West, Adam with Jeff Rovin, *Back to the Batcave*, ©1994, Berkley Books, p. 183

384 Brown, Vanessa, "One of Television's Takers Puts Some of It Back," *The Los Angeles Times*, May 19, 1968, p. D11

385 —, "'Batman' Syndication Billings Exceed $2 Mil in 1st Sales Week," *Daily Variety*, Feb. 2, 1968, p. 26

386 Kaufman, Dave, "On All Channels: Why Dozier Left TV For Pix; Ironside To Travel" *Daily Variety*, Sept. 10, 1968, p. 13

387 Jankiewicz, Pat, "Recalling Batgirl," *www. YvonneCraig.com*, http://yvonnecraig.com/ up_close_interview.html, accessed Oct. 19, 2009

388 —, "Miss Blake; TV Batman's Aunt Harriet," *The Los Angeles Times*, Feb. 20, 1969, p. D8

389 —, "'Batman' To Have 'Love' Reunion," *Daily Variety*, Sept. 21, 1972, p. 1

390 Deborah Dozier Potter Interview, conducted March 29, 2010

391 Semple, Jr., Lorenzo, "Requiem for a cheeky 'Batman': TV series creator speaks up for irreverent take," *Variety.com*, http:// www.variety.com/article/VR1117988712. html?categoryId=3184&cs=1, accessed July 29, 2009

392 *Ibid.*

393 Archerd, Army, "1967: Problems plague 'King Gun'", *Variety*, http://www.variety. com/article/VR1117979560.html?categoryi d=1237&cs=1&query=dozier, accessed Aug. 29, 2009

394 Deborah Dozier Potter Interview, conducted March 29, 2010

395 Hughes, Kathleen A., "Batman Fans Fear The Joke's on Them In Hollywood Epic— They Accuse Warner Bros. Of Plotting a Silly Spoof Of the Caped Crusader,' *Wall Street Journal*, Nov 29, 1988, p. 1

396 Boyer, Peter J., "Film Clips: As Batman, West is Out of Movie Lineup," *The Los Angeles Times*, Aug. 5, 1981, p. H1

397 Richmond, Ray, "20 Years Later, Adam West Just Can't Get Away From His TV Role," *The Hawk Eye*, Burlington, Iowa, June 22, 1989, p. 6A

398 Lyle Waggoner Interview, conducted Aug. 8, 2009

399 Jankiewicz, Pat, "Recalling Batgirl," *www. YvonneCraig.com*, http://yvonnecraig.com/ up_close_interview.html, accessed Oct. 19, 2009

400 Gates, Anita, "Vacuous Villainy, Batman! Is This How It Used to Be?," *The New York Times*, Mar 8, 2003, p. B.21

401 Swires, Steve, "Holy Sidekick! Burt Ward," *Starlog*, Nov. 1987, p. 79

402 Ward, Burt, *Boy Wonder: My Life in Tights*, © 1995 Logical Figments Books, Los Angeles, p. 247

403 *Ibid.*, p. 265

404 Swires, Steve, "Holy Sidekick! Burt Ward," *Starlog*, Nov. 1987, p. 79:

405 Boucher, Geoff, "The Hero Complex," *The Los Angeles Times*, Mar 21, 2009. pg. D.13

406 *Ibid.*

407 *Ibid.*

408 Lambert, David, "Batman - Who Watches the Batman (1966)? Sorry, Nobody Just Yet!" *TV Shows on DVD.com*, http://www. tvshowsondvd.com/news/Batman-Watchmen-Batman-Deal-Reported/10573, Posted Sept. 23, 2008, accessed July 22, 2009

409 Van Hise, James, *Batmania*, © 1989 Pioneer Books, Las Vegas, NV, p. 84

410 Gelb, Jeff, "Bob Kane: 'I Never Talk About Batman. Actually, I'm Bruce Wayne," *Comics Interview Super Special: Batman—Real Origins of the Dark Knight*, © 1989 Fictioneer Books Ltd., p. 115

411 Semple, Jr., Lorenzo, "Requiem for a cheeky 'Batman': TV series creator speaks up for irreverent take," *Variety.com*, http:// www.variety.com/article/VR1117988712. html?categoryId=3184&cs=1, accessed July 29, 2009

412 Rees, Brenda, "With the Kids: Heroic Efforts; Caped Crusaders Keep Watch -- and Are Being Watched -- at the TV and Radio Museum," *The Los Angeles Times*, Jul 1, 2004, p. E 30

413 Boucher, Geoff, "The Hero Complex," *The Los Angeles Times*, Mar 21, 2009. pg. D.13

414 Johnson, Pat, "Krunch! There goes Batman," *The Toronto Telegram*, http:// www.1966batfan.com/dozier.htm, accessed July 28, 2009

Chapter Six:
BURTON'S BATMAN

"I don't know if I would go so far as to say that Batman is my alter-ego, but I certainly do respond to his split personality and obsessions in wanting things done a certain way. He's just a weird guy who does strange things. I wonder what that makes me?"
- Tim Burton[1]

HOLLYWOOD EXECUTIVES ARE A COWARDLY, SUPERSTITIOUS LOT...

Bob Kane wasn't the only young Jewish kid whose rise to riches from the Jewish quarters of New York was effected through a name change and a ruthless attitude about business. In 1927, a dozen years after Kane's birth, Steven Jay Rechnitz was born to immigrant parents in Brooklyn. Over the next six decades, he would gain control of the largest media conglomerate on the planet, one of whose biggest assets was the Dark Knight.

A few years after the birth of his son, and after losing all his money in the Great Depression, Jewish immigrant Max Rechnitz changed the family name to Ross, thinking that it would be easier to find work with a name that wasn't so obviously Jewish. By the time his son, now christened Steve Ross, was 8, he was doing his bit to help earn the family's keep. He made money by carrying people's food home from the supermarkets or collecting their laundry for a nickel. He also learned that if he bought cigarettes by the carton, he could sell them to his father a pack at a time and make a profit.[2] At age 11, he sold magazines—including comic books like *Batman*—on the streets of Brooklyn.[3]

When Steve was a teenager, he was summoned to his father's deathbed. His father had no inheritance to give him, save for a sage piece of advice: There are those who work all day; those who dream all day, and those who spend an hour dreaming before setting to work to fulfill those dreams. "Go into the third category," his father said, "because there's virtually no competition."[4]

Ross attended Paul Smith's College and served for a while in the Army before landing his first job at an uncle's store in Manhattan's garment district. But his rise to prominence really began when, at age 26, he married Carol Rosenthal. Edward Rosenthal, his bride's father, owned the Riverside funeral home in Manhattan. His wife's uncle, who was a business partner of Edward Rosenthal's, provided limousines for funeral services. When Ross saw that the vehicles were only used during the day, he arranged for a limousine service to hire the cars in the evening. The arrangement was an immediate moneymaker. In the late 1950s, Ross took out a bank loan and started Abbey Rent-a-Car. He then merged his rental car company with a parking lot and garage company named Kinney. Kinney snapped up Rosenthal's funeral parlor, as well as an office-cleaning business owned by Rosenthal's cousin. In 1962, the hodge-podge of companies went public as Kinney National Services, Inc., with a market valuation of $12.5 million, and with Steve Ross in charge.[5]

In 1967, Ross ventured into entertainment, with Kinney National Services, Inc. purchasing Panavision (makers of movie cameras), the Hollywood talent agency Ashley-Famous, and National Periodical Publications, also known as DC Comics; the comic book company cost $60 million.[6]

Around that same time, Warner Bros.-Seven Arts expanded by buying Atlantic Records, a deal that left them cash-strapped. Ted Ashley, of Ashley-Famous, urged Ross to buy out the ailing film production company, which Elliot Hyman had purchased from founder Jack Warner. Now Hyman was ready to sell. However, a part owner of Warner-Reprise Records had veto power over any sale; Ross would have to convince him separately. That owner's name was Frank Sinatra. Ross made his pitch and the $400 million deal was signed over dinner with Sinatra at the home of the singer's mother.[7]

With Sinatra's signature, DC Comics became a part of Steve Ross's Warner conglomerate. The acquisition was finalized in 1969. Because federal anti-trust laws prohibited a movie studio from owning a talent agency, Ross sold Ashley-Famous, but he kept the agency's Ted Ashley, putting him in charge of Warner Bros.-Seven Arts. Though Warner Bros. had been faltering in the 1960s, soon after Ross and Ashley took over, the company scored an unexpected hit with the concert documentary *Woodstock* (1970). It was the beginning of a long string of box-office hits that reestablished Warner Bros. as a major player. Broadening his empire, Ross then bought Elektra Records and Nonesuch Records in 1970, putting them all together under the new Warner Communications banner.[8]

With DC's acquisition by Kinney National and later Warner Communications, a lot of the old guard who had presided over Batman's descent from noir-ish vigilante to space-age camp icon retired. Harry Donenfeld and Mort Weisinger left the company with lucrative golden parachutes. Sol Harrison became DC's publisher, with Julius Schwartz promoted to editor and artist Carmine Infantino raised to editorial director. Schwartz decided it was time to take Batman back to his roots as an avenging detective of the night. Working with writer Denny O'Neil and artist Neal Adams, Schwartz sent Dick Grayson off to college and moved Bruce Wayne out of his mansion and into a luxury apartment, with a Batmobile that was more sleek sports car than gaudy war wagon. The stories veered away from the bright, strictly-for-children tales of the 1960s, becoming darker and more adult. Batman's costume was also transformed—the ears on his cowl became longer, and his cape more flowing; in some of the comic book panels, when Batman perched on a rooftop, his cape billowed out on the night gales as though it were twelve feet long. The overall effect was to emphasize the vampiric, mysterious "creature of the night" aspect of Batman. The quipping punster Batman was no longer seen in the comics.

Fans responded positively to the changes, though sales of the comic book went into a predictable slump once the TV show went off of network TV and into syndication. This new take on the Caped Crusader seemed tailor-made for a film adaptation, but the overwhelming success of the *Batman* TV show had a lasting impact—no producer in Hollywood could envision making a movie based on a comic book, *any* comic book, and taking the material seriously. But while no producer in Hollywood could envision it, a producer in Europe did.

After co-producing a crowd-pleasing 1973 adaptation of Alexandre Dumas' *The Three Musketeers*, Ilya Salkind was in Paris preparing for a meeting with his father, film financier Alexander Salkind, to discuss ideas for their next project. Walking around the city, he saw a billboard for a French film production of *Zorro*, and it inspired him to think of making a film about the greatest hero of all—Superman. Salkind approached DC Comics, and found them surprisingly willing to give up the film rights to their flagship character. Having acquired the rights, he put together a mammoth production. With director Richard Donner and creative consultant Tom Mankiewicz, a screenwriter who had contributed scripts to the James Bond series, Salkind produced a movie that took a reverential approach to the Man of Steel. Upon its release in the winter of 1978, the film became a critical and financial hit.

After the success of *Superman*, one would have thought that producing a film based on the other superstar in the DC Comics line-up would be a slam-dunk, but a young comic book enthusiast who dreamed of doing just that found it instead to be a Sisyphean task. Michael Uslan began collecting comic books when he was a child, and had dreams of becoming a film producer. "The only way you can figure out how to make a transition like that," said Uslan, "is to stay goal-directed and take small steps all in one direction, and try to get your foot in the door wherever you can."[9] While he was a law student at Indiana University, Uslan proposed an idea for a class within the university's Experimental Curriculum program. The class, initially called *The Comic Book in Society*, was a fully accredited course on the history of comic books, and received attention both from the news media and the comics industry. "It was the publicity that came about from the comic book course I was teaching at IU that really made things happen for me," said Uslan. "I never taught a class at IU in comics that the classroom wasn't filled with TV cameras and reporters from all over. As a result of the massive amount of publicity, I was invited on radio and TV talk shows. And about three or so weeks into it, I got a call from [Marvel Comics publisher] Stan Lee, and just a couple hours later from [editor] Sol Harrison at DC Comics, and the calls were very similar. They said, 'Everywhere we look we're seeing you on TV, we're reading about you in the papers and magazines. What you're doing is great for the entire comic book industry; how can we help you?' And Sol Harrison went a step further. Sol said, 'I think someone who is this innovative and that knows comics so well and loves comics so much is the kind of person we'd like to be working with. And [DC publisher] Carmine Infantino and I would like to fly you into New York and discuss ways we might be able to work together.' And that's exactly what happened."[10]

"The next thing I knew, I was leaving Bloomington and heading into New York for my first grown-up meetings ever, and they offered me a job that would be a summer job. This was long before there was a word 'internship;' they called us 'junior woodchucks' they were assembling, fans who could become the next generation of execs and editors and creative people in the comic book industry for DC Comics. And he agreed they would put me on retainer when I went back to school in Indiana, which was a godsend because I was making really no money at that time. So when

I joined the woodchucks, there was a young kid who was there about six months before I started; Paul Levitz was his name. I don't know whatever happened to the kid, but there's a rumor that he grew up to become the president and publisher of DC Comics.[11]

"Working at DC led me to meet so many of the editors, the creators, the executives, people who had been working in the business since the 1930s—it was a real education. And that led to an opportunity for me to start writing comics for Denny O'Neil. I started writing *The Shadow*, and then after my Shadow script had come out, [editor] Julie Schwartz offered me an opportunity to write *Batman*, which was the dream I had since I was 8 years old. And Bob Rozakis was becoming at that point Julie's assistant, so it turned out Bob and I wrote *Batman* comics and *Detective Comics*. And that was just phenomenal.[12]

"So, you can see how the steps were beginning to fall into place. And finally, at one point, 'round about the time I was finishing college, I talked to Sol Harrison and said, 'Well, my dream since I was 8 was to write *Batman* comics, and I've managed to do that.' I said 'My dream now is to make the definitive dark, serious version of Batman as a movie.' My goal in life, which kind of crystallized in seventh grade, was to try to wipe those words *Pow, Zap* and *Wham* out of the collective consciousness of the world. And Sol was very fatherly towards me. He really was an amazing guy. He put his arm around me, he says, 'Michael, please, save your money. Since *Batman* went off the air on TV he's been as dead as a dodo. Nobody's been interested in Batman in the media. Don't do it.' And I said, 'Yeah, but I think if we do it in a dark and serious way, the way it was originally created, it's an opportunity to do something like nobody's ever seen before, a whole new type of movie, a whole new type of hero.' And he said, 'Look, go get credentials. Get some credentials in the business, then come back and see me about it. In the meantime, I'll let you know if anyone's interested in the rights to Batman, but I'm sure nobody's gonna be interested.'

"And that's what I did. I wound up going to law school, and taking every course I could take having anything to do with communication and entertainment. I got out of law school, went to work for United Artists, which at that time was one of the major motion picture studios, they had just done *One Flew Over the Cuckoo's Nest*. And I got there just in time for *Rocky* and *Annie Hall* and *Manhattan* and *The Spy Who Loved Me*. We had *Bound for Glory*, *Network*, and then *Apocalypse Now*, *The Black Stallion*, *Raging Bull*. It was an amazing, amazing time to be there.[13]

"And it was while working at UA for about three and a half years that I learned how you finance and produce movies. And I networked like mad and met so many people in the motion picture business. And finally after doing that for three and a half years, I said, 'Okay, I've done my thing, I've gotten my credentials.' I went back and talked to Sol, and he said, 'Okay. Come on in. If I can't talk you out of it, come on in.'"

To show DC what he had in mind, and to help Hollywood executives understand his vision of a Dark Knight detective, Uslan decided to write a screenplay. He registered the copyright for his treatment *Return of the Batman* on April 1, 1979; less than three weeks later, on April 20, he registered the screenplay. "Going into it, a friend of mine, Michael Bourne, and myself had written a script called *Return of the Batman* that we were using not to sell it as a basis for the movies, but I had almost an impossible time making execs in the industry understand what a dark and serious Batman could be," said Uslan. "They were so completely into the pot-bellied funny Batman from the TV show and could not even begin to grasp how Batman could work as a dark and serious project, so we wrote *Return of the Batman*."[14] The script featured an embittered, 50-ish Batman coming out of retirement for one last hurrah.

Uslan knew that DC was unlikely to take a gamble with an inexperienced producer. "I knew I couldn't come in by myself," said Uslan. "I needed a partner, someone who knew how to mount a production, somebody who knew how to negotiate a deal that I felt I was too emotionally involved in to successfully negotiate." Uslan set up a meeting with an industry veteran, Benjamin Melniker. "I met Ben's son Charles at UA and Charles introduced me to Ben," said Uslan. "Ben was a legend at MGM in its Tiffany days. Ben was executive vice-president; all divisions reported to him. He was with MGM since 1940, until '72. And he put together *Ben-Hur, Doctor Zhivago, 2001*, all the musicals like *Gigi*, and was really truly a legend in the business."[15]

"And after a six month negotiation," said Uslan, "Ben Melniker and I acquired the rights to Batman on October 3, 1979." That same day, the duo officially formed a company, Batfilm Productions, Inc.[16] When Bob Kane got wind of Uslan's activities, he was pleased with the young producer's take on Batman. "Don't expect camp or Adam West in a reprise," Kane told *The Chicago Tribune's* Elaine Markoutsas. "It'll be more like James Bond, high adventure all over the world with lots of special effects like *Star Wars*. It will recapture the first year of mysterioso with fog-laden backgrounds, moors, the cape around Batman's face, none of the old villains and 'Holy this' and 'Holy that.' Robin will not clown it up with 'Holy frustrations.'"[17]

With the film rights to Batman secured, Michael Uslan was on top of the world—or so he thought. "I put it in my pocket and I quit and I thought Hollywood was going to line up at my door," he said, "and what then happened was I was turned down by every single studio in Hollywood. Everyone." Even United Artists, Uslan's former employer, rejected *Batman*, giving as their reason the fact that their aging Robin Hood drama, *Robin and Marian* (1976), had been a box office flop.[18]

"That began what ultimately would become a ten year journey to try to bring this dark and serious vision of Batman to the screen," said Uslan. "Part of the reason that we were turned down by every single studio when we pitched *Batman* as a dark movie initially was because they kept coming back to me and saying, 'You can't do this. The only Batman everyone will remember and love is the pot-bellied funny guy,' or they would say, 'Michael, you're crazy. You can't make a movie out of some old TV series. That's never been done.' And it was even a struggle to make them comprehend and accept the fact this was a comic book that had been around since 1939 as opposed to an attempt to make a movie based on an old TV series. But that gives you kind of the frames of mind that we were dealing with at that time. We'd been turned down by every studio in Hollywood, the clock was ticking, and Ben said, 'You know, when I was at MGM, there was this bright young man around 1968, '69 that I wanted to make president of production at MGM in a troika with Barry Beckerman and Jerry Tokofsky, and it was Peter Guber.'"[19]

Peter Guber, who started his career as a lawyer in New York, became head of film production at Columbia Pictures in 1969, when he was just 26 years old. In 1976, he left to join Neil Bogart, the guiding light behind Casablanca Records (a company best known for giving the world music acts such as KISS, Parliament, and Donna Summer) in the formation of Casablanca Filmworks. While there, Guber produced *The Deep* (1977) and *Midnight Express* (1978), both of which became box-office hits. With the company on a roll, Guber and Bogart were now attracting the attention of international investors; the entertainment conglomerate PolyGram bought a half interest in Casablanca Records and Filmworks in 1977.

Benjamin Melniker thought that Peter Guber, unlike the more entrenched Hollywood veterans, would see the promise in *Batman*. "Ben said Peter is younger and a lot more hip than the guys we've been talking to," recalled Uslan, "and he said he may have a different perspective on this. So Ben got Peter on the phone, put me on the phone with him, I pitched it, and Peter said, 'Wow! Okay, I see where you're going with this. I get this. This is good. You should get out here.' We were in New York, Peter was in L.A. He says, 'Get out here, like, tomorrow, and let's talk about this.' And we couldn't, of course, get out there in one day, but we were there maybe the second day or the third day and pitched it in person to Peter, and he said, 'Absolutely, I get this. We will finance the development of this project and we will bring in distribution.' And three days later we had the deal."[20] In November of 1979, Uslan and Melniker entered into an arrangement with Casablanca that promised them creative control, credit as producers, and forty percent of whatever profits Casablanca received.[21]

During the next year, Neil Bogart left the company, and Guber teamed with a new partner, Jon Peters. Peters, himself a highly motivated young entrepreneur, had graduated from being a reform school roughneck to becoming a hairdresser to the stars; the Warren Beatty character in *Shampoo* was reputedly based on him. After he began dating Barbra Streisand, he spearheaded a successful 1976 remake of *A Star is Born*, and suddenly became a producer.[22] He was also a pugnacious personality and a ceaseless self-promoter. Though he may have lacked Guber's polish, he shared with his new partner a burning desire to be a major Hollywood player. They soon became the chiefs of Polygram Pictures, with $100 million of Polygram's money backing them. Unfortunately, they got off to a rocky start when their first joint production, a film about street racing called *King of the Mountain*, earned only $2.1 million at the box office. However, their next film, a story of teen obsession starring Brooke Shields called *Endless Love*, brought in over $30 million domestically.[23]

Shortly after teaming with Guber, Jon Peters met with Uslan and Melniker at New York's Carlyle Hotel. In his hyperbolic way, Peters later intimated to an interviewer that *Batman* was a natural project for him. "I grew up on Batman," he told *Starlog*'s Adam Pirani. "I was a Batman fanatic. One of the reasons that we took on such a thing—when I was a kid, I always used to go to parties in a Batman outfit, and jump off second stories onto people. Batman has always been the kind of superhero that I loved."[24] At this early meeting, Peters asked if Uslan and Melniker could give him a memo outlining their vision for *Batman*. Uslan duly prepared one. Dated November 6, 1980, the single-spaced, 9-page document said, "No longer portrayed as a pot-bellied caped clown, Batman has again become a vigilante who stalks criminals in the shadow of night." Uslan went on to recommend that Robin should either not appear in the film or should only be a minor character, and that the villain should be the Joker—preferably played by Jack Nicholson.[25] "I have to say, from the very beginning, he was the only actor I thought could really play the Joker," said Uslan. "For me, the final straw on that happened in 1980. It was Memorial Day weekend, and *The Shining* and *The Empire Strikes Back* were both opening up, and I got on the bus in New York heading back to New Jersey and picked up *The New York Post*. And I open it up on the bus, and there I see for the first time the classic still from *The Shining*, the 'Here's Johnny' shot of Jack Nicholson, and I looked at it, and it hit me like a ton of bricks. I tore it out, I raced home, I sat down and I whited out Jack's face, I took a red pen and did his lips, I took a green magic marker and did his hair, and I used that from that moment on to show everybody that this is the only guy who can play the Joker."[26]

In February of 1981, at the annual Sho-West convention of 1,500 cinema exhibitors and distributors at the Las Vegas' MGM Grand hotel, PolyGram Pictures held a three-hour marathon of their coming attractions. Peter Guber announced that the company had "20 to 25" pictures planned, including *A Chorus Line, The Deep II,* Costa-Gavras' *Missing,* two Dudley Moore vehicles (*Dangerously* and *Six Weeks),* and *Batman.*[27] But by 1982, PolyGram had severed ties with Guber and Peters. Undeterred, the dynamic duo set up their own company, Guber-Peters Entertainment, at Warner Bros. Uslan and Melniker were not privy to the details of Guber and Peters' new deal, but they assumed their original agreement with Guber was part of the package.[28] It would prove to be a costly assumption.

Under Steve Ross's stewardship, Warner Communications had branched out into the new industries of cable television and video games, but at a considerable price, both personal and financial. In 1978, Ross and his wife, Carol, divorced. Two years later, he suffered a serious heart attack. Upon recovery, Ross married Amanda Burden, the daughter of CBS chairman William S. Paley. That marriage lasted only 16 months. During this time, Warner stock plummeted after the videogame company Atari collapsed, and Warner Communications seemed ripe for corporate raiders. In 1983, in order to stave off Rupert Murdoch's attempt to buy Warner Bros., Ross sold 20 percent of the company to Chris-Craft Industries. For the next five years, Ross would be partnered with Chris-Craft chairman Herbert J. Siegel. The two clashed often over which assets Warner Bros. should sell to extricate itself from the Atari meltdown.[29]

During this time, Uslan and Melniker, with their new partners Guber and Peters, set about coming up with a workable screenplay. The obvious template for a long-running film series was the 007 films, which had begun with 1962's *Dr. No* and by early 1981 had sustained ten sequels with the eleventh, *For Your Eyes Only,* due out that summer. Uslan had some preliminary talks with Richard Maibaum, who had scripted the majority of the 007 film adventures, but those discussions proved unfruitful. However, as it happened, Peter Guber knew a screenwriter who had written two James Bond movies—Tom Mankiewicz. "I'd known Peter Guber before, when he was head of production at Columbia," said Mankiewicz, "and I'd rewritten some pictures for him over there, and of course, the first picture he ever produced, which was *The Deep,* I rewrote down in the Caribbean. So I knew Peter very well."[30] Perhaps more importantly, Mankiewicz, a first-rate script doctor, had solid comic book credentials; he had been brought in by director Richard Donner to whip the scripts for *Superman* and *Superman II* into shape, eventually receiving a "creative consultant" credit.

"We were very comfortable with Tom," said Uslan. "He was just really, really great to work with. Tom's script came in with a bit of a Bond flair to it, in an attempt to do it a lot more seriously. You know, we wanted a real serious approach to The Batman as opposed to Batman."[31]

To help research the character, Mankiewicz returned to the source—the comic books. "I re-read some of them, and I had several long sessions with Bob Kane, who was a very gregarious guy and he was so desperate to get it on. As a matter of fact, Bob Kane made an original drawing for me of Batman in front of the moon, the original version of Batman, like he drew him in the 30's or the 40's, much more angular, and that's one of my proudest possessions. And he loved the script, but I think Bob Kane at that point was going to love just about any script because he really wanted to see it on screen."[32] Jon Peters said of Kane, "He has been helpful in going back to ideas, material and graphics from the beginning. He's the father of Batman, so it's like dealing with his child. We're trying to keep some of the integrity and yet be creative in making our own vision."[33]

Mankiewicz agreed with Uslan that the way to interpret that vision for the big screen was to avoid the campiness of the *Batman* TV series. "One thing they did know was they were not going to do a *Poof! Pow!* kind of thing," said Mankiewicz. "*Batman* had worked on television because they made fun of it. And a lot of it was hedging your bets, because nobody knew at that time what would happen with a comic strip character, and you had this strange desire as a writer, especially if you're a good one, to show the audience you're smarter than the material. And I think the trick to writing something like *Batman* or *Superman* is to not be smarter than the material, but to get inside it. "

When Mankiewicz was brought on to *Superman*, director Richard Donner asked him to pare down the combined script for the two movies, which was over five hundred pages long. "Dick and I on *Superman* had little signs on our doors at Pinewood; each one said 'Verisimilitude.' So Superman landing on Lois's balcony was like two kids on their first date, and when he takes her flying, it's just romantic. You get inside it. And *Batman* was hugely successful on television, but they stayed outside it. It was *Oof! Pow! Bing!*, you know."[34] Mankiewicz took the dark approach to *Batman* literally. "I always saw 90% of it as happening at night," he said, "and I thought that *Batman* was just based on revenge. I think my script starts with the murder of his parents. It's among the first couple of scenes. And again, that happens at night.[35]

"In my concept, there was such fury inside the guy at night, when he appeared, and a guy whose parents had been murdered, a guy who in my script, because I tried to throw the whole ball of wax in there, who adopts Robin, it's almost like he's the parent of a kid who had been deprived of his own parents. I saw him as a very complex fellow. And I remember saying, boy, if you ever let him go out and walk down 5th Avenue at twelve o'clock noon, he's a guy in a funny suit, but at night, he's terrifying."[36]

Mankiewicz finished his script in the summer of 1983. Structurally, it was much like the script for *Superman*, beginning with the murder of Bruce Wayne's parents, following him through his teenage years into young manhood as he trained his mind and body to perfection, then cutting to the present day story, where he assumes the black cowl and cape of The Batman. Once The Batman appears, there follows a *Superman*-esque montage of Batman performing good deeds for a night, while bewildered police commissioner David Gordon (not Jim Gordon) wonders about the identity of the caped avenger.

While not as campy as the TV series, the script was still laden with Mankiewicz's trademark witty one-liners, as when the Penguin, in his ice-cold lair, says to the Joker, "I'm heart-broken you haven't touched your food. I had that clown fish cooked especially for you. Do you prefer codfish balls?" The Joker responds, "I don't know. I never attended any."[37]

Mankiewicz's script is laden with an abundance of villains, from Rupert Thorne, who orders Joe Chill to murder Thomas Wayne, his rival for a City Council seat, to the Joker, who helps Thorne make Gotham City safe for criminals. The Penguin, in his brief appearance, uses a helicopter umbrella and has three goons with 007-style jetpacks. Near the end, in the third act, we get the murder of Dick Grayson's parents. In a nod to Bill Finger's penchant for using giant-sized props in the comic books, the finale takes place in a museum exhibit honoring the craft of writing, with giant-sized typewriters, pencil sharpeners, erasers and inkwells employed during the inevitable melee. Dick Grayson assists Batman in his ultimate battle with the Joker, and in the final shot, Grayson appears in uniform as Robin. There's also a romantic interest, Silver St. Cloud, who was a character created by comic book writer Steve Englehart and introduced in *Detective Comics* # 470 in June, 1977.

Mankiewicz had fun writing the Joker. "My model for the Joker was Henny Youngman, the old one-line comic of just bad jokes," said Mankiewicz. "Henny Youngman used to have an old joke saying, 'A bum came up to me and told me he hadn't had a bite in days, so I bit him.' And, in my script, there's a bum on the street, and people are walking by, and you just see the bottom half of them, and suddenly these big pair of clown shoes goes by, and he says, 'Please, mister, I haven't had a bite in days,' and the Joker leans down and bites him on the hand, viciously. That was my introduction of the Joker as I recall. But he was based more on a one-line comic, with the rapid-fire delivery."[38]

Though Uslan was enthused about Mankiewicz's work, the executives at Warner Bros. had some concerns. By that time, Steve Ross had appointed Robert Daly Chairman of the Board and Chief Executive Office of Warner Bros., and Daly chose Terry Semel to be the company's President and Chief Operating Office. Tom Mankiewicz recalled that Daly and Semel "were terrific people, and their big concern over my draft was that it was too dark. Why couldn't it be more fun and up like *Superman*, with Lex Luthor and so on? And I tried to explain to them the rules. I said, 'Guys, Batman is a dark figure. The rules about Batman are completely different than Superman. Superman comes from the planet Krypton. You can have jokes about Superman, you can have fun with Superman as well as the drama that was in that movie, but Bruce Wayne is a human being. And, in my opinion, we should never see Bruce Wayne, Batman, on the street during the day. He's got to work at night; otherwise he becomes a guy in a silly suit because he's a man. He's not, you know, an alien powerful creature.'"[39]

With a script completed, the filmmakers began considering possible directors. Still thinking of putting Batman in the James Bond mold, a former 007 director was approached. "We had some talks with Guy Hamilton," said Uslan. "The best of the best of the adventure-action franchises were the Bonds, and Guy Hamilton had done *Goldfinger*."[40] The script also went out to Richard Rush, director of the critically acclaimed *The Stunt Man* (1980), and then the execs at Warner Bros. sent it to a more unlikely choice. "They thought, well, we've got to get more fun in it, it's so dark," said Mankiewicz, "and they had me meet with Ivan Reitman, who had just done *Ghostbusters*, and Ivan and I got along fine. And Ivan agreed with me, he thought Batman should be dark. They, I guess, thought that Ivan would add some humor, and they knew I could write the humor."[41]

When Reitman eventually passed, the script went to Joe Dante. "He had done *Gremlins* for them," said Mankiewicz. "And I'd helped out on *Gremlins*, and then it was just clear, Jon and Peter were really anxious to get it going." Dante, however, was less anxious. He recalled, "After *Gremlins* started making money, they came to me and asked 'Would you like to do our *Batman*?' So I signed on. It was a good project, I grew up with *Batman*—but the problem was, I didn't really believe in *Batman*. I just couldn't swallow the idea of the guy living up on a hill, dressing up as a bat, Robin and all that. I didn't feel right about it so I went in and told them that I didn't think I was the right guy for the movie. They, of course, said 'You must be crazy!' But I seriously believed, and still do, that I wasn't the right choice for the movie."[42]

Warners also approached Richard Donner, director of *Superman*. "They talked to Dick Donner about it once," said Mankiewicz. "Dick did not want to follow *Superman* with *Batman*."[43] What Donner did want to do was *Ladyhawke*, a medieval romantic fantasy, and he took his favorite script doctor, Mankiewicz, with him. With that, Mankiewicz moved on from the *Batman* project. "I never wrote a second draft," he said.[44] "And frankly, while I was paid very handsomely for the first draft, *Ladyhawke* really intrigued me. It was nowhere near the hit that *Batman* was, but I sort of wanted to get away from comic strips. I thought I would be Mr. Comic Strip. *Superman*, and then *Batman*. In fact, I got offered a lot of comics at that time."[45]

Guber and Peters, meanwhile, also busied themselves with other projects. "We were making thirty other pictures," said Peters, "everything from *The Color Purple* to *Flashdance* to *Caddyshack* to *The Witches of Eastwick*. We paid Tom Mankiewicz $750,000...and still came up with something that was too derivative, too much like *Superman*."[46]

While the project went through development, the Hollywood rumor mill began to buzz with possible names to play the Caped Crusader. For a while, Guber and Peters entertained the idea of Bill Murray playing Batman to Eddie Murphy's Robin. "I wanted an action picture that was funny," said Peters.[47] Though he admitted Murray wasn't a conventional choice, he thought the former *Saturday Night Live* comedian would be "funny, offbeat and aggressive."[48] He also admitted, "Peter and I have done 67 movies, and a lot of them began, in concept, as party jokes."[49] Murray, who had ventured into more dramatic territory with the film *The Razor's Edge* (1984), later told MTV's Shawn Adler, "I would have been a fine Batman...It's obviously — it's a great role."[50]

For his part, Michael Uslan didn't have a definite actor in mind for the lead role. "I don't know that I ever particularly focused so much on an actor to play Batman as I did the Joker," he said. "You know, we had talked for years that we would probably get an unknown to play Batman the way that Christopher Reeve was chosen to play Superman."[51] Nonetheless, the producers prepared a list of probable Batmen. "It was the people who were doing anything action-wise at the time," said Uslan, "and it must have been a list about ten long."[52] Over the years, the list included such names as Alec Baldwin, Tom Cruise, Daniel Day-Lewis, Pierce Brosnan, Kevin Costner, Arnold Schwarzenegger, Mel Gibson, Robert Downey, Jr. and Tom Selleck.

As Christmas of 1984 approached, the *Batman* project seemed hopelessly stalled. However, events were about to unfold that would prepare the public to see the character in a new light.

THE DARK KNIGHT RETURNS

On the night of December 22, 1984, a self-employed New Yorker named Bernard Goetz got on the Seventh Avenue express subway in Manhattan. Fearing that four young black men on the train were going to mug him, Goetz pulled out an unlicensed revolver and shot five times, wounding all four men. When the train stopped, he jumped out onto the track, exiting at the next station. With his identity initially unknown, newspaper and TV reporters dubbed him "the subway vigilante." The shooter was lauded by some and lambasted by others, as the incident set off a nationwide debate on self-defense. Nine days after the shooting, Goetz surrendered to police. Charged with attempted murder, assault, reckless endangerment and firearms offenses, a Manhattan jury found him guilty only of possessing an illegal firearm; he served eight months of a one-year sentence.

One resident of New York City who took notice of the Goetz case was a comic book writer and artist named Frank Miller. Miller broke into the industry in 1978 when, at age 21, he illustrated a story for Gold Key's *The Twilight Zone* comic book. He was soon hired by both DC Comics and Marvel Comics. At Marvel, his work helped rejuvenate the *Daredevil* series. Miller had long hoped that comic books could attract a more adult readership, and after the subway vigilante shootings, he had an epiphany: "Think of the noise that came from what Bernie Goetz did, and imagine if there was a very powerful, huge, terrifying figure doing that on a regular basis."[53] Re-imagining Batman as "sort of like Zorro meets Clint Eastwood,"[54] Miller wrote about a 55-year-old Batman coming out of retirement and fighting crime in a violent modern world, where he not only encountered his old nemesis the Joker but also faced opposition from the Gotham police force, the U.S. government, and the government's chief enforcer, Superman.

Debuting in March 1986 and published in four issues stretching to June, *Batman: The Dark Knight* immediately sold out its first printing.[55] Adults who hadn't read a comic in decades snapped up the subsequent one-volume paperback edition. Re-titled *The Dark Knight Returns* and now called a "graphic novel" instead of a comic book, it sold over 110,000 copies.[56] With that one story, the comic book world, along with its readership, matured.

Among those praising Miller's interpretation was Batman creator Bob Kane, who said, "Frank Miller brought Batman back to his origins—back to that brooding, mysterioso quality."[57] At least, that's what he told *The Los Angeles Times'* Pat Broeske. In another interview, with Jeff Gelb of *Comics Interview* magazine, he said, "I've read the book, but I don't understand it. I'm certainly appreciative that it brought the Batman back to the dark, mysterioso roots that I created him in. However, Frank went to another extreme. Frank is very political, and there is a lot of symbolism in there I'm not sure I understand, like swastikas on a woman's breasts and buttocks."[58]

For Michael Uslan, it was a vindication that his vision of a darker Batman would resonate with the public at large. His friend and fellow former junior woodchuck, DC Comics writer Paul Levitz, saw a similarity between *The Dark Knight Returns* and *Return of the Batman,* the script Uslan and Michael Bourne had written to promote Uslan's film concept. As Uslan recalled, "Paul Levitz pointed out, 'Oh, my god, remember that script you guys wrote?' I said, 'Yeah.' He said, 'Really, it was *The Dark Knight Returns.* It was Batman in his 50s coming out of retirement really bitter for one last battle to the death.' So I said, 'Y'know, I never thought of it that way.'"[59]

A SURREAL, BRIGHT DEPRESSION

During the early years of *Batman*'s development, a young artist named Tim Burton was toiling away at Walt Disney Studios, creating concept sketches for their animated features *The Fox and the Hound* and *The Black Cauldron.* By his own admission, Burton was not Disney material. "I almost went insane," he said. "I really did...I could just not draw cute foxes for the life of me...And it took them five or six years to make a movie. There's that cold, hard fact: Do you want to spend six years of your life working on *The Fox and the Hound?* There's a soul-searching moment when the answer is pretty clear."[60]

Born in Burbank, California in 1958, Burton was of that generation of filmmakers who grew up with a steady diet of television and genre magazines like *Famous Monsters of Filmland.* He and his younger brother grew up in a typical suburban environment. His father worked for the Burbank Parks and Recreation Department, his mother ran a gift shop called Cats Plus where all the items were cat-themed. The whole family lived in a house directly under the flight path of the Burbank Airport.[61] Tim Burton, however, was not a typical youth. Speaking to David Breskin of *Rolling Stone* in 1992, he said, "I guess childhood was a kind of surreal, bright depression. I was never interested in what everybody else was interested in. I was very interiorized. I always felt kind of sad."[62] As a young boy, he enjoyed Edgar Allen Poe stories and horror movies starring Vincent Price, and dreamed of growing up to be an actor, though not just any actor—he wanted to be the guy inside the Godzilla costume, crushing miniature buildings under oversized rubber reptilian feet. "Since I couldn't be Godzilla," said Burton, "I decided to be an animator."[63]

After graduating from Burbank High School, Burton enrolled in CalArts, a university located north of Los Angeles that was begun by Walt Disney in the early 1960s to help train talent for the Disney Studios. Burton thrived in the collaborative atmosphere of CalArts, a school he felt was much less competitive and cutthroat than other film schools. There, he created his own characters, wrote his own scripts, and shot and edited short films. "I got a very solid education," said Burton.[64] After graduation, he went to work for Disney, and found himself being expected to draw cuddly animals.[65] He couldn't stomach it. Luckily, the studio recognized that he wasn't cut out for the assembly line, and funded Burton's short animated film, *Vincent* (1982), the tale of a 7-year-old boy named Vincent Malloy who dreams of being Vincent Price. The clever black-and-white film, which succeeded in being both a tribute to Price and to the horror tales of Edgar Allen Poe, featured puppet animation and narration read by Vincent Price himself. "I was so struck by Tim's amateur charm," said Price. "I mean amateur in the French sense of the word, in love with something. Tim was in love with the medium, and dedicated to it."[66] Two years later, Burton made his next film, a live-action half-hour short, *Frankenweenie*.[67] Also filmed in black-and-white, it starred Barrett Oliver as a young boy named Victor Frankenstein who reanimates his cherished dead dog—appropriately named Sparky—with electricity.

After seeing *Frankenweenie*, Warner Bros. president of worldwide production Mark Canton decided that Burton would be perfect to direct a movie the studio was developing with comedian Paul Reubens.[68] As part of the Los Angeles comedy troupe The Groundlings, Reubens had created a character named Pee-wee Herman, a grown man who acted like a young child and always dressed in a tight gray suit, white shirt, red clip-on bowtie and white patent leather shoes. With fellow Groundling Phil Hartman and screenwriter Michael Varhol, Reubens had concocted a script called *Pee-wee's Big Adventure*, and Canton felt Burton had just the right offbeat sensibility to bring it to the big screen. After showing *Frankenweenie* to Reubens, the comedian agreed. Entrusted with a $6 million budget, Burton and Reubens created the surprise hit of the summer of 1985; *Pee-wee's Big Adventure* grossed nearly $41 million at U.S. theaters.

After the unexpected success of *Pee-wee's Big Adventure*, Burton directed one episode each of TV's *Faerie Tale Theatre* and the revived *Alfred Hitchcock Presents*. Around this time, he was approached by Roger Birnbaum, who—after becoming president of Guber-Peters Entertainment in 1986—became interested in the company's languishing *Batman* project.[69] "One of the unsung heroes of the *Batman* story is Roger Birnbaum," said Michael Uslan. "Roger was instrumental in bringing Tim Burton onto the scene, and deserves a lot of credit for the success of that first *Batman* movie."[70] Birnbaum pressed Guber and Peters to see *Frankenweenie* and *Pee-wee's Big Adventure*. After the screenings, Peters said, "I felt that Tim was a very inventive director." Warner Bros. production chief Mark Canton arranged a meeting. "Mark Canton had worked with him before and introduced us," said Peters. "We really felt that he was very inventive and very creative and had a different approach to things."[71] Burton was asked if he would be interested in directing *Batman*. He was.

Eschewing Tom Mankiewicz's *Batman* script, Burton wrote a treatment with Julie Hickson, his then-girlfriend, who had produced *Frankenweenie*. The 43-page treatment, completed on October 21, 1985, was divided into three acts. In an article he wrote for *Wizard* magazine, Andy Mangels synopsized the treatment, writing that Act 1, "Loss," begins with a full-screen shot of the Joker laughing, then fades to a shot of Gotham City, described as "a little New York, a little Max Fleisher [producer of the 1940s *Superman* cartoons], a lot of Fritz Lang's *Metropolis*."[72] The scene then shifts to the Gotham Municipal Courthouse, where Thomas Wayne, counsel for the Subcommittee on Investigation into Racketeering, rails against mob boss Rupert Thorne. Next, Thomas Wayne is shown with his wife and child at their home, preparing to go to a costume party after a performance of *Der Fledermaus* at the Gotham Opera. Thomas wears a "majestic bat costume," Martha a "delicately shimmering fairy queen" and Bruce the outfit of a "small whirling harlequin." On their way home from the party, the Waynes are gunned down by a killer driving a Mr. Softee ice cream truck. Young Bruce catches a fleeting glimpse of the murderer—a green-haired, white-skinned 17-year-old boy with a red-lipped grin. The police show up, and so does the Wayne butler, Alfred Pennyworth, who tells Bruce, "as long as I live, you will never be alone." The act ends with Bruce at his parents' funeral, where he makes a vow to avenge their deaths and declares war on crime.

In Act Two, called "Preparation-Transformation," Bruce trains to become Batman. He befriends Commissioner Gordon and collects information about Rupert Thorne, whom he believes ordered his parents' death. Years later, Thorne becomes mayor of Gotham, and a newspaper headline announces "Joker Escapes Prison! Vows Revenge Against Mayor Rupert Thorne." The Joker begins causing mayhem in the city, releasing animals from the zoo, painting skyscraper windows black, and causing subways to run backwards. When he inserts himself into a TV broadcast of *The Love Boat*—described as featuring guest stars Tom Bosley, Cloris Leachman, and Andy Warhol—Bruce Wayne takes notice. Bruce dons his Batman outfit for the first time and goes out a window; at this point, the treatment says, "The Prince of Darkness is Born!"

Batman encounters the Joker in Gotham Square, where the clown prince of crime is about to launch the city's Christmas tree into space. They engage in a fight on the ice-skating rink, "punctuated by all the requisite silliness of pratfalls." The Joker escapes and causes even greater chaos, painting the entire city in candy-stripe colors and setting off bombs. He also sets off fireworks at a performance of *A Midsummer Night's Dream*, where Bruce intervenes and saves the life of the featured singer, Silver St. John. Bruce spends the night with Silver, while the Joker declares himself mayor and throws a parade with overhead balloons carrying his "grimacing gas." Commissioner Gordon summons Batman with the Batsignal. The Joker next appears at a charity circus attended by Bruce and Silver. The ringmaster turns out to be the Penguin in disguise. The Riddler is also there, disguised as a clown, and the Catwoman, as a trapeze artist. Catwoman kills aerial artists John and Mary Grayson by pouring acid onto their trapeze, but their son, Dick, survives. Bruce Wayne scoops up the sobbing lad and takes him to his car, where he tells him, "As long as I live, you will never be alone."

In the final act, "Retribution—Family," Bruce adopts Dick. Meanwhile, the Joker kills Rupert Thorne and throws a Christmas Eve parade, again with huge balloons filled with deadly grimacing gas. Batman attempts to stop the Joker, and both are carried aloft by the balloons, crashing through the skylight of the Gotham City Natural History Museum. There, Batman's life is saved by a new hero, Robin. Commissioner Gordon arrives to find Batman choking the Joker and holding a gun to the criminal's head. The treatment ends with Bruce, Silver, Dick and Alfred opening presents on Christmas Day. When he pulls the last present out from under the tree, Bruce is shocked to see that it's wrapped in purple and green paper, with a clown face on it. The screen fades to black as the laughing face of the Joker appears again.[73]

Warner Bros. was not sold on Burton's treatment. With the on-again, off-again project seemingly off again, Jenette Kahn, editor of DC Comics, decided to take some pro-active measures. She approached Steve Englehart, a writer of some of the darker-toned *Batman* comic books of the late 1970s, and asked him to write a treatment and to possibly act as a general consultant on the character for the movie. Englehart was told the treatment should include origin stories for Batman, Robin and the Joker, and a love interest. Since Englehart preferred to see Batman as a "creature of the night" rather than a father figure, his story began with Batman and Robin fighting thugs in an alley. Almost immediately, one of the thugs whips out a gun and "blows Robin's head off." Englehart felt this was the strongest way to differentiate the movie from the old TV series. Jenette Kahn wasn't pleased; she told Englehart that according to the studio, Robin had to be in the movie.[74]

After several stormy meetings, Englehart wrote a second treatment that seemed to make everyone happy. About a month after he turned the treatment in to Jenette Kahn, he learned that a new scriptwriter had been hired for *Batman*. Englehart wasn't surprised; he had been told at the outset that even if he wrote an outstanding treatment, he wouldn't be writing the screenplay.[75]

It was Bonnie Lee, Warner Bros. vice president of creative affairs, who suggested that a young screenwriter and comic book fanatic named Sam Hamm should write *Batman*, despite the fact that Hamm only had one produced credit so far, the 1983 fact-based drama *Never Cry Wolf*. Following that film, Hamm had written a spec script that ended up at Columbia Pictures after a bidding war, but it was the other bidder, Warner Bros., who offered Hamm a two-year term deal. At Warners, Hamm wrote a basketball comedy called *Hang Time*, and began looking into the status of the long-simmering Batman project. One of the people he approached was Bonnie Lee, who had championed both Hamm and Tim Burton within the company. Lee got the word around that Hamm was interested in writing the *Batman* script, and Hamm eventually secured a meeting with Tim Burton, who asked if he would be interested in taking a whack at *Batman*.[76] The two were soon collaborating on the screenplay. "We had a great time together," said Hamm. "I think Tim's the first director out there to be filtering junk culture through an art-school sensibility. He's also got a fairly strong morbid streak, but he's too much of an ironist to take his own morbidity seriously."

Hamm and Burton presented their ideas to Guber and Peters and then Warner Bros. "I essentially just wanted to play the story straight, and that sounded fine to Warner Bros.," said Hamm. "The only thing that they really told us was to include the Joker and include Robin."[77]

Michael Uslan and Benjamin Melniker provided research and ideas, and Hamm spent the next year working on the script with Burton and Birnbaum. "My instructions were to make it real," said Hamm. "I felt that gave me a license to treat the material seriously as opposed to getting the yocks out of it. Once you try to ground the characters in the real world, the plot basically generates itself."[78] In an interview with

Jeff Gelb in *Comics Interview* #70, Hamm said, "I've always conceived of this movie as sort of a really, really dark deadpan comedy. In other words, it's not anything that's going to play as comic, but the premise that we've got is that there is a millionaire who puts on a costume to go out and fight crime, you know. He discovers that not only is this very, very dangerous, but it starts to seriously screw up his love life. That, to me, is an inherently comic premise—but it's played out in very straight and serious terms."[79]

Hamm and Burton began delving into the psychology of Bruce Wayne, which brought up some interesting questions. "Is he nuts?" asked Hamm. "That's the big question in the bat-fan community. Is Batman the real identity, or is Bruce Wayne the real identity? I feel essentially that they are two characters. That Batman erupts out of Bruce Wayne and takes control. In a sense, Bruce Wayne is an addict: He's addicted to putting on the suit and changing himself into an entirely different persona."[80] Hamm saw Wayne as "somebody who's larger than life and a little frightening...a millionaire who can have anything he wants, and what he wants is to get dressed up and scare people."[81] Burton felt that Bruce Wayne was mentally deranged. "What compels a man to put on a bat suit?" asked Burton. "If you hate crime, why not just write a letter to *The New York Times*?...He is as maniacally good as the Joker is maniacally evil. They're two psychotics."[82] In a *Rolling Stone* interview, Burton said, "If Batman got therapy, he probably wouldn't be doing this, he wouldn't be putting on this bat suit, and we wouldn't have this weird guy running around in a cape."[83]

Mid-way through the first draft, Hamm began receiving notes from DC Comics editor Jenette Kahn and Batman creator Bob Kane. "Jenette had forwarded to me a sort of Batmanifesto—you know, various aspects of what they thought Batman should be—and I went through it going, 'Yeah, yeah, yeah, of course, how else would you do it!' And we also got a memo from Bob Kane detailing the same kind of stuff. But the fact is that what DC wanted us to do was pretty much what we were doing already, so there was never any real area of conflict."[84]

Hamm turned in his first draft script on October 20, 1986. Much to his surprise, everyone seemed to like it. "I'm one of those guys who is constantly being told that the main character is not sympathetic enough and that sort of thing, so I wrote a script with a lead character who to my mind is a flat-out psychotic, and it was the first thing I've ever written where nobody had any sympathy problems—which raises some disturbing questions."[85]

Jon Peters was one of the script's champions. "I never liked the *Batman* TV series," said Peters. "I wanted to do a real aggressive picture, and it wasn't until we got Sam Hamm's script that we found the rough, dark edge we wanted. There's lots of peril in this film and humor, but it's not *Raiders of the Lost Ark* or *Ghostbusters*."

In the opening scenes, Hamm's script is very much like the eventual movie, introducing Batman as an almost mythical figure and establishing that his costume is also his body armor, an idea borrowed from Frank Miller's *The Dark Knight Returns*.[86] However, in the script, newspaperman Alexander Knox and Vicki Vale have a prior history; in the film, they meet for the first time. Also, in the initial Gotham Globe newsroom scene, the artist who hands Knox a drawing of "the bat" is named Jerry (perhaps an allusion to Jerry Robinson?), and there's another reporter in the newsroom that wears spectacles and is named "Clark," seemingly a nod to Superman's Clark Kent.

After the scene where Jack Napier falls into the chemical vat, we cut to *The Gotham Globe* newsroom, where Knox has society editor Miranda Reitz tell Vicki about Bruce Wayne's playboy reputation—he's known as "Mister One-Nighter." We then cut to Vicki's first date with Bruce, which begins on Bruce's 40-foot cabin cruiser, *Die Fledermaus*. We get some insight into Vicki Vale's background before Bruce takes her to *La Donna e Mobile* at the Gotham City Opera House, and then back to Wayne Mansion where he sleeps with her.

Soon after, we see Jack Napier reborn as the Joker. When he passes by a couple of punk rock kids outside a club, a gust of wind blows his hat off, revealing his green locks and causing one of the punks to comment, "Nice hair, dude!" Following the Joker's killing of crime boss Grissom, we go back to Wayne Manor, where Vicki awakens and finds Bruce singing "Honeysuckle Rose" in the bathroom. She enters and he stops, embarrassed. She notices that his body is covered in bruises and abrasions. "Poor thing," she says, "You should stay off that horse."

There then follows a scene at *The Gotham Globe*, where Knox goes through morgue files on Bruce Wayne and finds a number of articles, but only two photos—one from 1973, and another, more recent one where he's blocking his face by waving at the camera, leading Knox to wonder, "Why don't you like your picture taken?"

When the Joker announces he's now leading Grissom's gang, and kills one gangster with his high-voltage joy buzzer, he then, on a whim, decides to kill all the other gang leaders. There follows three scenes of mob bosses being killed, the first after playing cards and drawing a hand with five Jokers, the second in the park by a clown selling balloons who roasts him with a flamethrower, and the last after an attack by machine-gun-toting mimes, a murder witnessed by Bruce Wayne and Vicki Vale. Interestingly, Bruce Wayne, in daylight, unable to find a place to change, is overwhelmed by the violence and has a momentary breakdown; this is a man who needs darkness to be in control. As Hamm puts it in his script, "Suddenly Bruce is running frantically, looking for a secluded spot, an alleyway, anything. No go. He's out in the open, with onlookers everywhere. In his civvies, he's just another citizen... TOTALLY IMPOTENT. He darts around a corner, backs against a wall. Women, children, grown men race past. No privacy. He's practically quaking now, in the throes of some terrible anxiety. He looks up at the sky overhead, terrified. A brilliant sun bears down on him as machine guns chatter."

At the midpoint, Dick Grayson is introduced. The Joker kills the Flying Graysons, who are performing an acrobatic act with trapezes suspended from helicopters. Bruce, of course, takes the youngster under his wing. As the script proceeds, the Vicki Vale-Bruce Wayne romance is explored more thoroughly; before the end of the script, Vicki figures out who Bruce is, and so does Alexander Knox, who dies in the confusion at the finale.

The third act ends with Batman, in the Batwing, pursing the Joker and his goons, who are in a tank. Batman fires a missile that opens up the street in front of the tank, but not before the Joker manages to shoot down the Batwing. The tank crashes into the crevice, and the Batwing crashes behind it. Batman's leg is broken, and he's trapped in the Batwing, but Dick Grayson arrives to pull him out of the burning wreckage. Grayson then pursues the Joker into Gotham Cathedral, until Batman appears and knocks Grayson out with a ninja star. Batman continues the pursuit, following the Joker up into a bell tower. By the time he reaches the top, Batman is so weak he's virtually powerless, collapsing helplessly. The Joker calls for a helicopter, and then approaches Batman. Wiping blood off Batman's face, he finally recognizes Batman as Bruce Wayne.

Batman then sets off a device that the Joker mistakes for a ticking bomb; instead, it's a sonar device that causes hundreds of bats to fly up through the belfry. The bats cause the Joker's helicopter to crash, killing the criminal. The end of the script finds Bruce Wayne recuperating in the indoor pool of his mansion, with Vicki by his side, while Dick Grayson goes through a gymnastics routine in the gymnasium. The final shot echoes the ending of Mankiewicz's script—the Batsignal lights up the night sky of Gotham, and Batman and Robin stand on a building ledge, ready to undertake new adventures.

Initially, producer Jon Peters was satisfied with the screenplay. Nevertheless, Hamm was requested to make revisions, eventually churning out five drafts of the script. "It was a great responsibility," said Hamm. "What you wind up doing when you're putting an existing character in a major Hollywood film is you're essentially defining that character for a whole generation of people; and most people have certainly heard of Batman, but they are probably not that familiar with it. So what you're doing becomes sort of *ipso facto* canonical. That was something that I was very, very conscious of. The thing that I decided early on was that I wanted really to do what would be a really, really cool Batman story that would be as good as the way you remember the comics being from when you were a kid."[87]

While the script was being hammered out, Tim Burton made his second feature, *Beetlejuice* (1988), the tale of ghosts haunting their former home who want to drive out the new owners and hire a "bio-exorcist" named Beetlejuice to do it. The Warner Bros. film featured a bravura performance by Michael Keaton as Beetlejuice, and proved to be an even bigger hit than *Pee-wee's Big Adventure*, earning over $73 million in the U.S. After just two films, Tim Burton had arrived, in spectacular fashion. Warner Bros. was now satisfied that he was just the man to shepherd *Batman* to the big screen; after the first weekend's grosses from *Beetlejuice* came in, they officially hired Burton. "It was kind of charming in a way," said Burton, "because Sam and I would meet on weekends to discuss the early writing stages, and we had a great script, but they kept saying there were other things involved. They were just waiting to see how *Beetlejuice* did. They didn't want to give me that movie unless *Beetlejuice* was going to be okay. They wouldn't say that, but that was really the way it was. So, after that first weekend, it got the magical green-light."[88] Filming was set to begin in October 1988 at London's Pinewood Studios.

It was around this time that Melniker and Uslan read in the industry trade papers that *Batman* was going before the cameras, with Guber and Peters named as the sole producers. They contacted Jim Miller, the head of business affairs at Warner Bros., protesting that the studio was breaching the contract they had originally signed with Casablanca. Miller matter-of-factly told them they could either sign an amended contract or be forced off the project. Uslan, the man who had first envisioned making a dark, moody Batman film in the first place, had worked too hard for too long to throw it all away. He and Melniker reluctantly signed the agreement, which gave them credit as executive producers but little else.[89]

PRE-PRODUCTION REVISIONS

With Burton firmly on board, Jon Peters took over the day-to-day production of *Batman*. The script, he felt, still needed work, but in March of 1988, the Writer's Guild went on strike, and Sam Hamm decided it was more proper to be loyal to his union than to his employers. "I had a little falling out with Warner Bros. and the production in particular when I refused to work during the writers strike, which struck those guys as the height of ingratitude," said Hamm.[90] With Hamm sidelined (he spent the strike period writing three 50th anniversary Batman stories for DC's *Detective Comics*), Jon Peters began looking for other writers. He eventually brought in Warren Skaaren. Skaaren, like Hamm, was a relative newcomer; his first script sale was *Fire With Fire*, in 1985.[91] Unlike Hamm, the Minnesota-born Skaaren, who founded the Texas Film Commission and became its first director in 1971,[92] wasn't much of a comic book fan. "I read them sort of moderately," said Skaaren. "I wasn't a complete fanatic. I liked them, but I was a country kid, so I was more likely trying to look at a muskrat somewhere than read a comic."[93] After doing rewrites of *Beverly Hills Cop II* (1987) and *Beetlejuice* (1988), Skaaren developed a reputation as a first-rate script doctor. He was also acquainted with *Batman*'s director. "Tim Burton and I had just done *Beetlejuice* together," said Skaaren. "Sam Hamm was writing *Batman*. He's a very good writer, and did a lot of excellent work on it, but somewhere along the way, they wanted another point-of-view, so Warners called me."[94] Skaaren was already doing research in preparation for writing the racecar film *Days of Thunder*. He later said that he "had no inclination to do *Batman*, but they called about three or four times. I finally read it, and saw some contributions I could make."[95]

One of Skaaren's first moves was to eliminate Robin (something previous writers had been all but forbidden to do), putting more of the focus on Batman and giving more time to develop Bruce Wayne and Vicki Vale's relationship.[96] Burton agreed with the move. "Ultimately it was too much psychology to throw into one movie," said Burton. "If there's another movie, Robin would have to be established at the beginning, not be crammed into the third act."[97] Besides that, Burton wasn't sure how to make Robin's outfit work without getting laughs. "We would lift our arms up and say, 'Let's have them both go to Frederick's of Hollywood to pick out that little green costume,'" said the director.[98] It was a problem that had also plagued the previous screenwriter, Sam Hamm. "I always wanted to have a scene," said Hamm, "where having established that the Batman wears his costume because 'criminals are a cowardly, superstitious lot,' we would then introduce Dick Grayson in his Robin costume, his little red vest and green trunks and bare legs and yellow cape, and Batman says, 'Yeah, that'll scare the hell out of them.'"[99]

With Robin jettisoned, Skaaren had room to add other scenes. It was Skaaren who decided that the murderer of Bruce Wayne's parents would be a young Jack Napier, later to become the Joker. "I did that because, psychologically, the Joker and Batman create each other," said Skaaren, interviewed by Pat Jankiewicz for *Comics Scene* magazine. "All good hero/villain matches have some deeply personal connection, and what more permanent violence could you do to someone than kill his parents? You've made an enemy for life. I like that. At the same time, I wanted to deal with the real history in the comic books, that his parents were murdered in front of him. Batman has many problems because he has to operate without being caught and the fact that he falls in love with Vicki Vale exposes him in a way that makes it harder for him to function. On top of that, he begins to sense that there's something special about this character, the Joker. He doesn't know what it is, but it starts to affect him because his unconscious knows before his conscious does that this guy killed his parents. Batman has a much more complicated life than the Joker, because he has many obstacles in his way, where all the Joker wants to do is blast through."[100] When Sam Hamm heard that Skaaren had made Napier the murderer of Bruce Wayne's parents, he was not pleased, to say the least, calling the change "grotesque and vulgar." In an interview with Jeff Gelb for *Comics Interview* magazine, Hamm said, "It turns the story into more of a sort of *Death Wish* thing, where a guy goes out and gets revenge for having been wronged...My feeling is once he nails the guy who ruined his life, he can hang up the suit happily."[101]

Among the scenes that didn't make it into the final film were some that helped provide some background for the Joker's deadly Smilex gas, clearly showing it as a CIA experiment from the 1970s that resulted in dead soldiers with lips drawn back in chemical-induced grimaces before it was discontinued.[102] Another scene had Vicki called to a photographer's studio, where she was told that the client who'd hired her was named Joseph Kerr. Just as she realizes who Joe Kerr is, the models die laughing, with frightful, chemical-warfare-type grins on their faces.[103]

Afterwards, when the Joker comes to Vicki's apartment, he shoots Bruce Wayne, who is saved by the bullet hitting a leather bag he's carrying with his utility belt inside (the bullet strikes the belt). The Joker and his goons leave with Vicki, and Bruce gives chase on a stolen police horse, wearing the utility belt and a black ski mask he takes from Vicki's closet. He hits a button on the utility belt that acts as a tracer, and soon Alfred arrives in a yellow VW, handing him his Batman outfit. The Joker goes to the town square, where the Mayor is about to unveil a new statue of city founder John T. Gotham. But when the mayor pulls a cord that causes the shroud covering the statue to drop, it reveals a polychrome statue of the Joker holding two Uzis like six-shooters. Batman arrives to stop the Joker from killing the Mayor. The Joker disappears down an open sewer, and Batman fires a line up to the top of a nearby building and zips away, with Vicki snapping photos with a camera that had been handed to her by one of the Joker's goons. Later, she learns that there was no film in the camera. The scene was one of Skaaren's personal favorites. "The best scene that's not in the film," said Skaaren, "that I miss the most, that hurts the most, was after Batman comes down on a wire with Vicki. Someone calls out, 'Look—Batman's fallen over here!' People run over, and the bat cape's down on the ground. Batman's under it, but you can't see his face. Vicki and Commissioner Gordon come over, pull the bat-cape off, we're gonna reveal who Batman is—when it turns out to be Alexander Knox! Batman has covered him up, and you see Batman escaping through the crowd, wearing Knox's coat. It works because one of the themes I inserted into the movie was that no one ever sees

Batman with his mask off. I guess they shot it, and there was something technically wrong with the scene in the film processing."[104]

Despite his contention that "no on would ever see Batman with his mask off," Skaaren wrote a scene that would raise the hackles of die-hard Batfans, with faithful butler Alfred allowing Vicki Vale into the Batcave to confront Bruce Wayne. Skaaren felt the scene was justifiable if one thought of Alfred as a surrogate father for Wayne. "He tries to talk Batman into engaging in this relationship with Vicki," said Skaaren. "He says at one point, 'I'm getting too old to mourn the loss of old friends... or their sons.' That line indicates Alfred is getting to be an older guy, and he's afraid that Batman—that Bruce Wayne is going to be hurt, so he wants Bruce to become more healthy. Part of that would be to accept this relationship with Vicki. So, Alfred's in cahoots with Vicki, as an unspoken conspirator. He brings her into the Batcave because he wants Bruce to be with her."[105]

With Dick Grayson no longer involved in the ending, Skaaren pared down the finale and put Vicki Vale in the belfry with the Joker. Unlike the previous draft, Batman is not as physically damaged as he closes in on the Joker, so that the end result was a fight that seemed perhaps too heavily weighted in the Caped Crusader's favor. "There's an inherent problem there," said Skaaren. "You're dealing with Batman and supposedly all this armor, but the way I wrote it, which didn't quite get shot, is that Joker deals him a couple of tough blows in the beginning. I also added that ledge, so that Batman's hanging off that, trying to save himself much of the time. The way I wrote it, the helicopter comes in earlier, so the Joker has the advantage of some men up there with guns and a helicopter, but the way they actually shoot something and the way it's cut is different. The key contribution I made there is the whole gambit where it looks like Batman has fallen off the tower. What I did was just sit down with a chalkboard. I drew the tower, and all the possibilities I could think of that would be dramatic. The best I could think of is that the audience thinks Batman has fallen with Vicki."[106]

Jon Peters was enthused with Skaaren's rewrite, saying that "ultimately, it worked out the story. It had a dark side and an aggressive, avant-garde quality that the others didn't. We cover how he began, and then we pick the story up when he's a grown-up, where he is in fact a man in search of his own identity, trying to deal with all of the crime and saving Gotham City. He's powered by his own pain, the loss of his parents, and dealing with that as an adult. The Joker is the king of Gotham, dedicated to crime and to the complete control of the city by intimidation and menace. And Batman is the only thing that stands in his way."[107]

As he was writing the script, Skaaren received unsolicited guidance from Batman's creator. "DC Comics never voiced any opinion while I was writing it, but I did get notes from Bob Kane a couple times," said the screenwriter. "He would read the script and send me notes, which was nice."[108]

While the script was being finalized, a production designer was hired to begin building the massive sets the film would require. Burton chose Anton Furst, having admired Furst's work on Stanley Kubrick's *Full Metal Jacket*. Born in England in May 1944, Furst studied theater design at the Royal College of Art in London. In the 1970s, he became one of the early designers of laser special effects and started the company Holoco. He entered films doing laser effects for *Star Wars* (1977), *Superman* (1978), *Moonraker* (1979) and *Alien* (1979). His first production design credit came with the British TV movie *It's a Lovely Day Tomorrow* (1975), but it was his fifth film, 1984's *The Company of Wolves*, that really made people stand up and take notice. The film brought him a BAFTA Award for Best Production Design, and led to him working with Kubrick. Impressed by how Furst had turned the derelict Beckton Gasworks in East London into a convincing facsimile of Vietnam, Burton felt Furst would be just the man to create Gotham City from the ground up.[109] "Anton is one of the best people in any country and I like him," said Burton. "I always have to feel like I'm friends with the production designer and the cameraman."[110]

Michael Uslan was also enthused about Furst's hiring. "I think you've got to give credit where credit is due, and I believe on that first film there were two geniuses involved—Tim Burton and Anton Furst," said Uslan. "I remember when Sam Hamm's script came in and it said that Gotham City is as if Hell had erupted from under the earth, and Anton said to Tim, 'What does that mean?' And Tim said, 'I think that means New York City had there never been planning and zoning.' And Anton said, 'I get it.' He goes off and studies all kinds of conflicting styles of architecture, a lot of Japanese, and he came back with blueprints for Gotham City and the Batmobile, the whole look of the picture. And it was genius work. It was really genius work, because Tim had said, 'If we are going to make the world's first dark, serious, comic book superhero movie, we have to make Gotham City the third most important character in the piece, because if the audience doesn't believe in Gotham City from the opening scenes, they'll never believe there could be a Batman fighting the Joker in this world.' And he was right about that."[111]

Furst found visual inspiration for Gotham City in Orson Welles' 1965 film *Chimes at Midnight*. "There's fascism and German Expressionism and a sort of general industrial mix to these buildings," said Furst. "The result is timelessness that runs from the 40's to the future. And the humor comes from taking the brutalism to the limit." The production was based at Pinewood Studios, located 20 miles west of London in Buckinghamshire. Five months before filming was due to begin, Furst went to work with an art department crew of 14, a construction crew of 200, and a budget of $5 million. "With a main street which is a quarter of a mile long, I am told it's the biggest set since *Cleopatra*," said Furst.[112] The interior sets for the film filled nine soundstages, and an exterior Gotham City set covered most of the studio's 95-acre backlot.[113]

With the sets taking shape, Burton and the producers turned their attention to casting. For the pivotal role of the Joker, Burton wanted an actor who had a kinetic, unpredictable screen persona, a real live wire. For him, that meant just one person— Robin Williams. An offer was made, and Williams, who was a comic book fan, was enthusiastic about taking the role.[114] However, from the very beginning, Michael Uslan had felt the only actor who could play the Joker was Jack Nicholson. Jon Peters and Warners Bros. executive vice president Mark Canton agreed with Uslan. Peters had already begun laying the groundwork for casting Nicholson in the summer of 1986 when he was in New England producing *The Witches of Eastwick*, in which Nicholson played the devil. "We were talking at 3 A.M. on the night before Jack had to do the church sequence in which he denounced women and threw up over everybody," said

Peters. "I said he should play the Joker, and he said, 'Are you crazy? Here I am playing the devil and making every woman mad at me. You want me to throw my career down the toilet?'"[115]

Nicholson's real life was filled with as much drama as his films. Shortly after Nicholson was born in Neptune, New Jersey on April 22, 1937, his father abandoned the family. In *Jack's Life: A Biography of Jack Nicholson*, biographer Patrick McGilligan writes that once when young Jack was sent to the neighborhood grocery store to buy bread and milk, he spent the money instead on comic books. When he returned home, he received a spanking and the comic books were taken away.[116] Another biographer, Peter Thompson, writes in *Jack Nicholson: The Life and Times of an Actor on the Edge* that when Nicholson was in fourth grade, he was punished by being sent to stand in the corner, next to a blackboard. Picking up an eraser, he powdered his face with white chalk, then turned and grinned—white faced—at the class.[117] If Nicholson's life were a screenplay, that would be called foreshadowing. So would the honor he received as graduation from Manasquan High School approached; the Class of 1954 voted him "Class Clown."

Upon graduation, he left New Jersey for California, where he went to work at MGM, becoming a messenger boy in the cartoon department. He also began taking acting classes, and by the early 1960s was appearing in low-budget films at American International Pictures, including director Roger Corman's *The Little Shop of Horrors* (1960), *The Raven* (1963) and *The Terror* (1963). He also worked frequently on television and began writing screenplays, making his first script sale in 1963 with *Thunder Island*, a low-budget quickie thriller co-written with Don Devlin and filmed in Puerto Rico. He went on to write scripts for Corman's *The Trip* (1967), starring Peter Fonda as a TV director experiencing LSD for the first time, and *Head* (1968), a feature film starring the TV singing sensations, The Monkees. Nicholson might have continued as a screenwriter if he hadn't been asked to play a small but pivotal role in a film being made by his friends Peter Fonda and Dennis Hopper. The film, *Easy Rider* (1969), became a cultural phenomenon, with Nicholson receiving critical praise for his role as George Hanson, an alcoholic lawyer who joins two hippie bikers on a cross-country journey. The part earned him his first Academy Award nomination.

Through the 1970s and 80s, Nicholson established his reputation as a powerful, unpredictable screen presence, and racked up more Academy Award nominations for his performances in *Five Easy Pieces* (1970), *The Last Detail* (1973), *Chinatown* (1974), *The Shining* (1980), *Reds* (1981), and *Prizzi's Honor* (1985). He won Oscars for Best Actor in a Leading Role for *One Flew Over the Cuckoo's Nest* (1975) and Supporting Actor in *Terms of Endearment* (1983). By the time he took the role of Daryl Van Horne in *The Witches of Eastwick* (1987), he'd also earned a reputation as a ruthless industry player and an unapologetic ladies man. He'd also learned, from a *Time* magazine reporter who was doing a feature on him in 1974, that the couple he thought were his parents were actually his grandparents, and the woman he regarded as his sister was actually his mother. By the time he learned the news, both his mother and grandmother were deceased.

With the projected costs of *Batman* climbing (they had doubled since the original estimate), Warners executives felt that Nicholson's name on the marquee would give them some much-needed box-office insurance. Peter Guber flew Tim Burton to Aspen to meet Nicholson and talk to him about the movie. Upon arrival, Nicholson said, "Let's go riding." Burton wasn't an equestrian, but he joined Guber and Nicholson for a horseback ride. "I was terrified," said Burton. "I didn't realize that horseback riding was part of my job description."[118]

Nicholson was impressed with Burton, so Jon Peters was told to cement the deal.[119] He contacted Nicholson and asked if the actor would like to fly to London on Warner Bros. Gulfstream 3 jet to see the sets under construction. The aircraft would be stocked with caviar, and there would be a personal trainer and a masseuse on board. Nicholson agreed.[120] "Convincing people to do things, or drawing pictures in one's mind, it takes a while," said Peters.[121] Arriving in England, Nicholson was taken to Pinewood Studios to see the massive Gotham City sets and production drawings. Peters told him he would only be needed for about three weeks of shooting, but as Nicholson boarded the jet back to Los Angeles, he was still non-committal.[122]

Upon arriving back in Los Angeles, Nicholson let it be known that he'd be interested in playing the Joker—for the right price. By the time the dust settled, Warner Bros. had agreed to pay the actor $6 million plus a portion of the film's gross earnings and a 17.5% royalty on merchandising products bearing his visage. It was a deal that would eventually bring Nicholson a reported $50 million;[123] some estimates put Nicholson's earnings as high as $60 million.[124] Producer Peter Guber said, "Jack is as difficult a deal to make as any talent deal in Hollywood. He has certain beliefs in his value that have been tested over time. [But then], you're buying somebody who has an audience from the Sixties, the Seventies, the Eighties, and the Nineties."[125] Nicholson felt he was worth whatever he could get. In an interview with Jean-Paul Chaillet of *The Vancouver Sun*, he said, "The minute someone signs a deal with me, they've made money, so what does it matter? The most expensive item in a film's cost that people complain about—the star's salary—is merely a guarantee against financial failure. I've made 40 or 50 movies. Only three haven't gotten more than they guaranteed me. This is an amazing record, if you don't mind my saying so. In other words, I am not out there destroying the movie business, I am making the movie business."[126]

When Nicholson agreed to the role, Michael Uslan was ecstatic. "The day he was hired was one of the greatest days of my career, maybe one of the great days of my life," said Uslan. "I was just thrilled beyond thrilled."[127]

Having agreed to take the role, Nicholson embraced it with his usual professionalism. He contacted Warren Skaaren and began working with him on the Joker's scenes. "He was like an encyclopedia of culture and history and art," said Skaaren. "I threw out a line from Nietzsche, and Jack threw out a line from Nietzsche."[128] Nicholson also consulted with Batman creator Bob Kane, and learned that the look of the Joker had been partly based on Conrad Veidt's make-up in the 1928 silent thriller *The Man Who Laughs*, in which Veidt portrayed a character whose face was disfigured when he was a child, resulting in him having a permanent, grotesque smile. Nicholson tracked down a copy of the film and watched it.[129] He also met with Batman's creator. "I stressed to him that the Joker is not the buffoon clown that Cesar Romero played on the TV series," recalled Bob Kane. "He is a psychotic killer, as ghastly as his smile."[130] Kane, who gave Nicholson a Joker lithograph, was immediately enthused about Nicholson's casting, saying, "He is going to blow this film away."[131]

With the hiring of Jack Nicholson, the casting of the central role of Batman/ Bruce Wayne took on much greater importance. Michael Uslan had thought they would go the *Superman* route, and hire an unknown for the title role since they had landed a superstar for the villain. Tim Burton, however, thinking about the eventual reaction of film critics, doubted whether that approach would work. Burton said, "In my mind I kept reading reviews that said, 'Jack's terrific, but the unknown as Batman is nothing special.'"[132] Burton shared his apprehensions with Michael Uslan. "Once Nicholson was hired," said Uslan, "Tim said, 'Do you agree with me that we can't get an unknown, because Nicholson would wipe the screen with the guy?' I said, 'Yeah, I get that.' And he says, in terms of that list of serious actors, he didn't know how to use them and have them getting into a Batsuit without getting unintentional laughs from an audience."[133]

Jon Peters had his own idea of who would make a good Caped Crusader, having just screened Tim Burton's latest movie for Warner Bros. executive Mark Canton and come away impressed with Michael Keaton's scene-stealing performance as the title character. "When Mark Canton, Peter Guber and I saw *Beetlejuice*, we went, 'Wow!'" said Peters. "Michael is so explosive in that character and almost dangerous. We already knew that he had the sweet side, the lovable side and the funny side, but I really didn't know he had that dangerous side. And that's when we decided to go for it. It was a big risk, but that's what makes a movie like this fun and exciting, taking those risks."[134] Having just worked with Keaton, Burton was enthused about the idea. "It's funny," said the director, "getting Michael wasn't my idea. One of the producers, Peter Guber, I think, said to me, 'What about Michael Keaton?' I said, 'Whooaaa.' I actually had to think about it. The more I did, the more it made sense. I met with some very good square-jawed actors, but I had real trouble seeing them put on the outfit. Physical presence didn't seem to be enough. I was looking for the unknown. Michael has an incredible temper, and I thought that was important for Batman. Plus, I'd had a very good experience with him on *Beetlejuice*. He comes up with a lot of ideas. We're going for a very shorthand psychology here. And Michael is very good at shorthand."[135]

Not everyone was immediately sold, however. After feeling euphoric about the hiring of Jack Nicholson, now just ten days later Michael Uslan was dumbfounded by the choice of Keaton. "I got the call from one of the execs, who said, 'What do you think about Tim's idea about hiring Michael Keaton to play Batman?' And I said, 'Oh, great, *Mr. Mom* as Batman. That's a great idea. That's how we'll do a serious Batman.' Took him about a half an hour to convince me that it wasn't just a gag that they were playing on me. And of course I was apoplectic. I had now spent about seven years of my life to bring a dark, serious Batman to the screen and it was like all my hopes and dreams were going up in smoke, and it was terrifying for a short period of time, until Tim really explained to me what his vision was. And I remember he started the conversation with me, he said, 'Michael, going from comic books to movies, a square jaw does not a Batman make.' And that was just part of his genius. He saw something that nobody else really clearly understood. When Tim came up with Michael Keaton, it just blew everybody away."[136] Since the actor playing Batman would spend much of the film with 2/3 of his head covered in a black rubber cowl, Burton knew it was important to get an actor with very expressive eyes. "Eyes are windows into the soul," he said. "You can see in Michael's eyes that the guy has something going on. And Bruce Wayne is somebody who's definitely got too much going on in his mind."[137]

Among those who thought Keaton was all wrong for the role was Keaton himself. "When Tim first came to me with the script, I read it out of politeness," said Keaton. "All the while, I'm thinking there's no way I'd do this. It just wasn't me. My name doesn't spring to my mind when somebody says, 'Batman.'"[138] Keaton was already feeling thoroughly exhausted. "I had just finished four films in a row," said the actor. "I was tired and not really looking to work for a while. All I was looking to do was take a break and read some scripts."[139] Then he cracked the cover of the *Batman* script. "I read it and thought, 'This guy's fascinating!' I saw him as essentially depressed. I told that to Tim, thinking he wouldn't agree, but he said, 'That's exactly what I see.' The choice was to play Batman honestly. So I started thinking, 'What kind of person would wear these clothes?' The answer seemed pretty disturbing. This guy is in pain."[140] Keaton's interest was definitely piqued. "There was a lot to like about this character from an acting standpoint and so, as tired as I was, I jumped at the offer."[141] The actor signed a contract that obligated him for only one picture. "I haven't signed for a sequel and I don't know if I will do another one," he said. "If the director and the script were good, I would consider it. But I didn't jump in with this one and say, 'Yeah, I'll do three of these suckers.'"[142]

Keaton looked no farther than the text of the script for clues about how to play the character. "I decided early on that I didn't want to start going through comic books and stuff," he said. "I didn't want to work that way; I wanted to make this man stand on his own."[143] Keaton had never really been a comic book reader, nor had he paid much attention to the 1960s TV show.[144] "Michael brought a freshness to the role," said Tim Burton. "In other words, he knew absolutely nothing about it."[145]

For Keaton, playing Batman was a chance to be in a big Hollywood blockbuster that would kick his career into overdrive...if it didn't kill it. "I looked at the script of *Batman*, considered who was involved, and my instincts told me that it was huge," said Keaton. "Now, huge means a lot to an actor. If *Batman* succeeded, it could be a huge success. But if it failed, it could be a huge failure. Not only it—but me! Maybe I never really stopped to consider what could have happened to my career if it had bombed...but I usually trust my instincts, and my instincts told me that I knew how to play this character, and I trusted Tim's vision."[146] Later, speaking to Bill Zehme of *The Chicago Daily Herald*, Keaton looked to his future as Batman with tongue-in-cheek self-deprecation. "This is what will happen," he said. "I'm gonna do four or five of these movies, and it's gonna become my career. I'll have to keep expanding the bat suit because I get fatter every year. I'll be bankrupt. I'll have a couple lawsuits going. I'll be out opening shopping malls, going from appearance to appearance in a cheesy van. I'll kind of turn into the King, into this bloated Elvis, smoking and drinking a lot. I'll invent a little metal attachment, like a stool, for my hip, where kids can sit because my back can't take their weight. I can hear myself already—'Just climb right up there, li'l pardner. Is that yer mom over there? Heh-heh-heh. Go tell her ol' Batman would like to have a drink with her a little bit later...'"[147]

Despite having taken a dramatic role as an alcohol and cocaine addict in the downbeat film *Clean and Sober* (1988), Keaton was known primarily as a comedic actor. The youngest of seven children of George and Leona Douglas, Michael was born on September 5, 1951 in Coraopolis, Pennsylvania. "Our whole family was funny," he told Lou Gaul of the Doylestown, Pennsylvania *Intelligencer*, "but my mom was the funniest...Once or twice a year, my mom would set up my brother, Paul, by saying, 'These mashed potatoes smell funny.' He would go to smell them, and she'd push his head right in the bowl. He'd fall for it every time, though no one else would. As soon as she would say, 'These mashed potatoes smell funny,' all of the rest of us would back up."[148]

After graduating from Montour High School, he spent two years at Kent State before dropping out and moving to Pittsburgh, where he ended up as a cameraman for a cable TV station and worked as a stagehand on *Mister Rogers' Neighborhood*. He then honed his comedy skills in Pittsburgh area nightclubs, before moving to Los Angeles in the early 1970s, where he began performing at The Comedy Store. "I never bought into any comedy 'rules,' such as that certain words are funny," he said. "I tried to find my own timing, rhythm and spin. Without sounding too pretentious, I tried to style myself like certain jazz musicians who find that real dissonant chord or that extra beat, which makes the music more interesting. Without being too esoteric, that's probably where it comes from."[149]

It was around this time that he changed his professional name from Douglas to Keaton, since there was already a Mike Douglas in broadcasting and a Michael Douglas who was doing quite well as an actor. He took his new last name in honor of actress Diane Keaton.[150] Performing in comedy clubs led Keaton to guest starring shots on TV shows like *Maude* (1977) and *The Tony Randall Show* (1978), and recurring roles in the shows *Working Stiffs* (1979) and *Report to Murphy* (1982). His big break came in 1982, when he co-starred with Henry Winkler in Ron Howard's comedy *Night Shift*, followed by the phenomenally successful *Mr. Mom* (1983). After *Clean and Sober*, he went to Canada to co-star with Christopher Lloyd and Peter Boyle in the comedy *The Dream Team*. It was while shooting that film in the summer of 1988 that the news broke that he had been cast as the Caped Crusader, creating a firestorm in the Batman fan community, who felt their beloved Batman was about to be lampooned on the big screen.

Warner Bros. went on the defensive. They began by enlisting the aid of Bob Kane, who said, "When I heard about Michael Keaton, I admit, I kind of panicked."[151] Speaking to Jeff Gelb of *Comics Interview* magazine, Kane said, "They asked me five years ago, I told them to go for a young Cary Grant, a young Robert Wagner, and they came up with a guy who's 5'10", kind of slight in a way, and the hair is kind of funny."[152] Warners arranged a screening of *Clean and Sober* to show Kane that Keaton was capable of doing a non-comedic role. He also got assurances from Tim Burton that the film would not be turned into a comedy. "I was confused, and then Tim and I discussed this," said Kane. "What Tim was looking for was a three-dimensional human being, not a cardboard cutout from the comic book, and not the TV show. He was looking for a Mr. Ordinary, and my concept, of course, was Mr. Extra-ordinary. In other words, how does an ordinary guy react when his parents are killed, and then when he puts on this awesome costume he becomes the idealized image of the ordinary person he is...in other words, if you're already idealized to begin with, then why put on a costume? Where's the connection? As Tim says, if he's 6'2" and strong and husky, he can just go out in a ski mask and beat the hell out of criminals. But just think, if you take an ordinary guy as Bruce Wayne, like anybody in the movie theater, and all of a sudden he becomes this superhero as Batman, then there's a reason for putting on this awesome costume."[153]

In August, Kane made an appearance at the San Diego Comic Con, where he very publicly lauded the casting of Keaton.[154] He told the fans that Keaton would look awesome in his Bat-costume, and asked them to "give the guy a chance."[155] But the fans remained skeptical. "Most people are dismissing Bob Kane, saying Warner is paying him to say nice things about the movie," said *Comics Buyer's Guide* co-editor Don Thompson. "No one seems to have taken him seriously."[156]

In addition to Kane, the studio sent specialty press publicist Jeff Walker to science fiction and comic book conventions to let the fans know that Warner Bros. was definitely not planning to make fun of the character. At the 46th annual World Science Fiction Fest in New Orleans, Walker's *Batman* presentation was met with boos and hisses. Maggie Thompson, co-editor of *The Comics Buyers Guide*, said, "It's the talk of the comic world. Some fans have even taken ads out, directing letter-writing campaigns to DC and Warner Bros. If you've followed the new *Batman* comics, you know that his is a dark and brooding tale, with hints that he may even be psychotic. So the question is, can Keaton do this?"[157] When fans complained that Keaton was too slight for the role, Walker revealed that Batman would wear a type of body armor underneath his outfit to add some musculature.[158] "Comic book people are very specific; they have a very strong image in their minds," said Tim Burton. "But it's a real source of argument because every comic book fan has a different opinion. When we went into (Batman) we decided to try to be true to it, but to do our own thing also."[159]

In October, Jim Waley, manager of the Dragon Lady comic shop in Toronto, Canada, got 1,200 of his customers to sign a petition denouncing Keaton, which he then sent to Warner Bros. He took a copy of the petition to the Chicago Comic Con, where he had it signed by "most of the people who work for DC Comics and the editor-in-chief of the Batman books," said Waley, "but they have little or no control over the film."[160]

News reports of the outrage over Keaton's casting continued into the fall of 1988, as the actor arrived in London for rehearsals. "I am shocked-slash-fascinated," said Keaton. "I'm telling you, man, these people must have the same lobbyists as the NRA. These guys have some clout; I can't believe it. I mean, how many are they? It's just funny to me."[161] It wasn't so funny to producer Jon Peters, who had millions riding on the public's acceptance of Keaton as Batman. "It was the same concern of Batfanatics all over the world, and there are millions of them," said Peters. "They felt that we were bastardizing the concept in the movie. I mean, these were very aggressive people."[162]

Peters and his co-producer Peter Guber were particularly concerned when the august *Wall Street Journal* printed a front-page story by Kathleen A. Hughes on November 29, 1988 headlined, "Batman Fans Fear The Joke's on Them In Hollywood Epic—They Accuse Warner Bros. of Plotting a Silly Spoof of the Caped Crusader."[163] The article quoted Batfans like Beau Smith of Ceredo, West Virginia, who said of Keaton, "If you saw him in an alley wearing a bat suit, you would laugh, not run in fear. Batman should be 6-2, 235 pounds, your classically handsome guy with an imposing, scary image."[164] J. Alan Bolic, a real-estate appraiser from Suwanee, Georgia, said that Warner Bros. was "after the money of all the people who only remember Batman as a buffoon with a twerp for a sidekick in the campy TV series from the '60s. Hollywood is just in it for the money, and Warner Bros. has been doing a bit of duplicity. I don't think Mr. Burton has any intention of making a serious Batman movie. But Batman has been part of everyone's childhood. He deserves a bit of respect."[165]

"A huge contingent rose up against this picture being made with Michael Keaton," said Peters. "Fifty thousand letters of protest arrived at Warner Bros. A lot of people in the company lobbied against it. One of the most powerful men in Hollywood went so far as to call (Warner chairman) Steve Ross and tell him casting Michael Keaton was such a horrible idea it would bring Warners to its knees. That the entire studio would crash and burn as a result. *Heaven's Gate* revisited. Whatever happens, I know one thing: This movie's going to make Michael Keaton a folk hero."[166] Ultimately, Keaton used the protests as a motivator. Before filming got underway, he began training with Dave Lea, a British martial arts and kickboxing champion, learning the swift moves that would make Batman a lethal combatant.[167] "There was something in that negative response that stirred in me what I'm going to call a healthy 'attitude,'" said Keaton. "I secretly liked the challenge, and was determined to prove that I could nail it."[168] But, ever the comedian, Keaton lampooned all the controversy by quipping to *Time* magazine, "After all, it's only a movie. I am a little nervous, though, about the scene where I fantasize making love to Mary Magdalene."[169]

SUPPORTING PLAYERS

Another casting choice was controversial for a different reason. For the role of Vicki Vale, the filmmakers chose Sean Young, who had gained international attention as Harrison Ford's love interest in the futuristic detective thriller *Blade Runner* (1982). She had a steamy coupling with Kevin Costner in the 1987 political thriller *No Way Out*, and a bit part in *Wall Street* (1987) as the wife of Gordon Gekko (Michael Douglas), but by 1989 she was making headlines not for her film roles but rather for allegedly harassing actor James Woods, with whom she co-starred in 1988's *The Boost*. Woods accused Young of terrorizing him and his then-fiancée, leaving a mutilated doll on Woods's doorstep and trampling the couple's flowerbed. Young has always adamantly denied the accusations. Woods sued the actress, and the case was settled out of court in 1988. Young hoped that a role in a blockbuster movie would put the lurid allegations behind her and steer her career back on track.

The cast was rounded out with an eclectic mix of relative newcomers and old pros. Former stand-up comic Robert Wuhl, coming off a pair of hits after roles in *Good Morning, Vietnam* (1987) and *Bull Durham* (1988), was given the role of Alexander

Knox. Wuhl said he was cast due to "Tim Burton's momentary loss of senses." To prepare for the role, he studied reporters who worked for the New York *Daily News*.[170]

Billy Dee Williams, best known to international audiences as Lando Calrissian in the *Star Wars* films *The Empire Strikes Back* (1980) and *Return of the Jedi* (1983), played District Attorney Harvey Dent. "The last thing I expected was to be a part of *Batman*," said Williams. "I was doing *Fences* on stage on Broadway and told a friend I was dying to play a supervillain in a movie. Two weeks later, he called to say they wanted me to play a good-guy role in *Batman*."[171]

For Commissioner Gordon, the producers chose veteran character actor Pat Hingle, an actor whose film debut came in 1954 as a bartender in *On the Waterfront*. He went on to be an almost constant presence in TV and movies from the 1960s through the 1980s, portraying policemen, judges, bankers, and salesmen. Hingle once said, "I played so many law enforcement officers that at Brooks Costumes in New York, they had 'the Hingle cop costume;' then all they had to change were insignia and cap badges!"[172]

When it came to casting the role of Bruce Wayne's faithful butler, Alfred Pennyworth, Tim Burton chose Michael Gough. Born in Kuala Lumpur, Malaysia in 1917, Gough made his film debut in the 1948 version of *Anna Karenina*, with Vivien Leigh in the title role. He played supporting parts in a wide array of British films, but is best known to horror fans for his roles in *Horror of Dracula* (1958), *Horrors of the Black Museum* (1959), *Konga* (1961), *The Phantom of the Opera* (1962), *Dr. Terror's House of Horrors* (1965), *The Skull* (1965) and *Trog* (1970). "I was in a play in New York," said Gough, in producer Constantine Nasr's *Batman Returns* special features DVD documentary. "It was called *Breaking the Code*, and I won an award for it, and as I was getting the award, apparently Tim saw this, and he said, 'I know that man! You'd believe anything he said! We'll have him.' Then he asked me to play Alfred. And he was sweet because he told me about what he felt about Alfred, but very much encouraged me to have ideas about Alfred. It's got to be your idea of a servant who is totally honorable, totally straight and totally square, you know." Gough based Alfred on an actual butler that he knew, and also observed the butler at Knebworth House, where the Wayne Mansion scenes were filmed.[173]

For crime boss Carl Grissom, the producers chose Jack Palance, who was born Volodymyr Palanyuk in Pennsylvania coal country in 1919. After winning a football scholarship to the University of North Carolina, the 6'4" athlete became a professional heavyweight boxer in the late 1930s, fighting under the name Jack Brazzo. He won 15 fights before enlisting at the outbreak of World War II. After being discharged in 1944, he worked a variety of jobs before landing on Broadway as the understudy of Marlon Brando in *A Streetcar Named Desire*, directed by Elia Kazan. He eventually replaced Brando for a performance, and his good notices for that and succeeding plays won him a contract with 20th Century Fox. He made his film debut in director Elia Kazan's *Panic in the Streets* (1950), and was nominated for back-to-back Best Supporting Actor Oscars for his third and fourth film roles, in *Sudden Fear* (1952) and *Shane* (1953). Over the next 35 years, he starred in numerous films and ventured into TV with guest-starring roles on a variety of series and title roles in TV productions of *The Strange Case of Dr. Jekyll and Mr. Hyde* (1968) and *Bram Stoker's Dracula*

(1973). "Because Jack Nicholson is such a strong, cinematic figure, there aren't many you can imagine as his boss," said Burton, "but Jack Palance fills out the role perfectly, and is, in fact, able to make Nicholson look like a kid at times."[174]

Grissom's moll, Alicia, was played by Texas-born fashion model Jerry Hall, who ventured into acting in 1980 with a role in *Urban Cowboy* but was known mostly as Mick Jagger's fiancée; they married in 1990. Hall was shooting a commercial at Pinewood Studios when she happened to meet *Batman's* set decorator, Peter Young. "I was on a 15-minute break and saw the sun filtering through a window in a corridor," said Hall. "I went to take a look. Peter ran into me and that's how I got the part."[175]

The cast gathered for rehearsals in London in September, along with screenwriter Warren Skaaren, who was continuing to hone the shooting script. "We had a week or two of rehearsals in London," said Skaaren, "where we would sit around a big table and read things through and read it through again. I would go write at night, make changes, and start again in the morning. The set was built all around us while we were doing that. We got to the point where we could actually rehearse on the set, block things out, and I would make more changes. It was exciting."[176]

At that time, the screenplay still contained a horse-riding scene with Vicki and Bruce Wayne. One day, Sean Young and Michael Keaton went to practice their horsemanship and Young ended up falling from her mount, seriously injuring her shoulder.[177] "Sean fell off a horse two days before we started shooting and we didn't get a chance to shoot with her," said Burton. "I'm only happy that she didn't get killed or that we weren't five weeks into it, because then we would have all been in trouble."[178] The director didn't want to lose the actress. "I kept saying, 'Are you sure you broke your arm, you can't do it? You can't?' At first, I couldn't believe it."[179] In the book *Hit and Run: How Jon Peters and Peter Guber Took Sony for a Ride in Hollywood,* authors Nancy Griffin and Kim Masters wrote that Jack Nicholson wasn't so sorry to see Sean Young depart; he had found her difficult in script readings and had supposedly expressed his doubts about the actress to Warner Bros., leading some to joke that she hadn't fallen from the horse—she was pushed.[180]

The producers and Burton knew they would have to replace Young. They briefly considered Michelle Pfeiffer, but Michael Keaton had just broken off a romance with the actress the year before and felt it might be awkward to work with her. Jon Peters called Mark Canton at Warner Bros., and the two eventually decided on Kim Basinger.[181] Born in Athens, Georgia in 1953, Basinger had been a model before moving to Hollywood and embarking on an acting career. A number of TV appearances in the late 1970s eventually led to a co-starring role in 1983's *Never Say Never Again*, Sean Connery's final 007 film. After that high-profile turn, she found herself much in demand, from period dramas like *The Natural* (1984) to the erotic thriller *Nine 1/2 Weeks* (1986) to the Blake Edwards comedy *Blind Date* (1987). Basinger recalled, "I got a call on Friday night in California that they wanted me Monday morning and I said, 'You're out of your mind. To fly to London and be there Sunday?' I said, 'You've lost it.' Ten minutes later, I was on a plane in my mind. I knew I would wind up doing it."[182]

Reading the script, Basinger saw parallels between *Batman* and *The Phantom of the Opera*. "That's a story and a theme that I've always loved and I always saw this as," said Basinger. "I love *Beauty and the Beast, Phantom of the Opera*—those themes, which I think this is in a way. It's a human being who dresses up like a bat. It has a very operatic feel, in the sense of the characters—a man in a bat suit and a guy turned into a clown. They're operatic in the sense of just good clear images, just strong, simple, classic images based in psychology. I love that about it. That's not the main thrust, but it's a feel which I think is nice. The Batcave is basically the underground of Paris. It's a guy hiding behind a mask, it's a guy who has internal scars as opposed to external, and it's all of those themes, very classic stuff."[183]

Basinger joined the cast and crew in the final week of October.[184] "I've got to hand it to Kim," said Burton. "It can't have been easy to join a movie which we'd already started shooting. Kim has added a lot to it. She has a positive, 'let's get going' attitude which is also very much part of the Vicki Vale character. In short, she has been great for the movie."[185]

Comic book fans had become used to seeing Batman in a blue and gray costume that was a slight variation of the union-suit-with-a-cape model initiated by Superman. For the movie, the filmmakers took a different approach. Having cast an actor who didn't have the bodybuilder physique of the Bruce Wayne of the comics, they decided to incorporate "muscles" into the costume, explaining them as "body armor." And, in Tim Burton's vision, this Batman would truly be a creature of the shadows, in an outfit that was almost entirely black from head to toe, the only exceptions being the yellow utility belt and the oval surrounding the bat insignia on the chest. To make the costume a reality, Burton turned to Bob Ringwood. Like Jerry Hall, Ringwood got the job by being in the right place at the right time. He had come to Pinewood Studios to see about joining the crew of the James Bond film *Licence to Kill*. While there, he ran into *Batman's* British co-producer, Chris Kenny, with whom he had worked previously on director Steven Spielberg's *Empire of the Sun* (1987), for which Ringwood was nominated for an Academy Award for Costume Design. Kenny recommended that Ringwood meet with Burton.[186] "I had spent about ten minutes meeting with Tim Burton when he hired me to design the costumes for *Batman*," said Ringwood. "I think he'd never met anyone who talks as much as I do."[187]

Born in London, Ringwood had set out to be a painter, but was disillusioned by the abstract art that was popular at the time. Instead, he studied theater design and costume design at Central Saint Martin's School of Art and Design in London.[188] From there, Ringwood spent ten years as a set designer and costumer in the theater before he was asked to join the crew of the film *The Corn is Green* (1979), starring Katharine Hepburn. His work on that film led to his hiring on director John Boorman's King Arthur film *Excalibur* (1981). "From there," said Ringwood, "my theater career stopped abruptly and almost overnight, I became a costume designer in movies."[189]

In an interview for Deborah Nadoolman Landis's superb book *Costume Design*, Ringwood said, "The *Batman* films were an extraordinary experience...I have to confess I'd never seen a *Batman* comic. I read about six of the early comics before I designed the movie. For me, the goal was to get the essence in my head and go for it. I expected a big, superhero-type of actor to play Batman, but they cast Michael Keaton. Michael is not overly muscular, so we had to turn him into a superhero, hence the rubber muscle suit. I was aiming to make his costume a 'super-costume' so that it was almost unbelievable. I wanted Batman to be bigger than reality on the screen."[190]

Ringwood began by dispatching an aide to Canada while Keaton was wrapping *The Dream Team*. The assistant returned with head and body casts of the actor, from which a full-size fiberglass model of Keaton's body was made. "It was like having Michael here in the studio," said Ringwood, "only in fiberglass. I spent a week with Lynne Burman, who is a wonderful sculptress, building up this fiberglass body with clay, trying to get a dynamic shape out of the body. We rejected several of them—some got far too big and looked almost like *The Incredible Hulk*—but finally we came down to a streamlined, aerodynamic version of the muscular body."[191]

Burton had instructed Ringwood to make the costume all black, rather than blue and gray. Ringwood complied, redesigning the Batsuit so that it expressed Bruce Wayne's psychology. "One of the things I tried to do is that when he was in the costume, he and it were one," said Ringwood. "I wanted it to be Batman, not to be a man dressed up in a costume—although, of course, you know full well that it's Bruce Wayne in a costume. It's as though the costume's surface was him and that was his body and that was his head, and if you don't make that believable, it doesn't work. In the Adam West show, he was definitely in a costume. This, in a way, is meant to be him. When Bruce Wayne's dressed up, it's as though he becomes another animal."[192]

The Batsuit was made of tight-fitting Lycra, with specially cast foam rubber muscle pieces glued on top.[193] "So even though it looked like it was one piece," said Ringwood, "it was actually made up of many separate parts—a chest piece, upper arm, lower arm, a crotch and side piece, kneecaps and the lower leg. It had a zipper in the back so that Michael could just step into it. All I really did with the costume was streamline Michael's body—instead of having him go to a gym for two years. And I think we ended up with a more interesting costume than we would have had if there had been a muscular guy underneath. We were able to exaggerate muscles and stylize them, whereas on a muscular body we would have had just real muscles."[194]

"It was at first difficult for Michael Keaton to move convincingly," said Ringwood. "For example, the muscles on the suit moved in a different direction from Michael's own muscles. We actually made four prototypes before we got it right. The result is a very light outfit, though you might find Michael disagreeing!"[195]

The headpiece proved a challenge for Ringwood. "We had to fit the seams in such a way that they didn't show on camera," said the costume designer. "Since the outfit has to look as though it's part of his body, the magical impact would be lost forever if you could see the seams."[196] Ringwood used the headpiece the same way he used the muscle suit—to pad Michael Keaton out to heroic proportions. "Michael has a rather round face, yet the image of Batman is this very sculptured, chiseled creature," said Ringwood. "So we had to 'chisel' Michael's features with the shape of the headpiece. We did that by putting aluminum cheek plates inside his mask every time he put it on." The next challenge for the costumer was getting the ears correct. "Making them look sexy was extremely hard," said Ringwood. "We had to make ten prototypes just to get them the perfect shape and size. The ears really have no function at all, when you think about it. He doesn't hear through them and he doesn't fly with them—they are purely visual. So I figured they were a bit like the 'go-faster' fins on 1950s American cars—just nonsense, really, to make him look mean and fast… They had to look tall and elegant, as if they were aerodynamic. Otherwise, they were just ludicrous things with no function—like in the TV program, where Batman wore those silly little mouse ears."[197] As a final touch, the actor's eyes were ringed with black make-up to make the cowl blend more seamlessly with Keaton's face.

Ringwood also made half a dozen different Batman capes in varying weights, lengths and textures. A stiff cape with a membrane appearance was used for Batman swooping down into the museum, shorter capes for easy access jumping into and out of the Batmobile, and heavier capes for standing ominously.[198] They first tried making the capes out of rubber, but found that rubber capes tended to ripple rather than swing when Batman was in motion. Other fabrics were tested before the costumer decided on an expensive Venetian wool that was rubberized on one side. The wool was cut into segments and, instead of being sewn together, was bonded together with a thin sheet of wet rubber embedded with gauze. "Michael wore a body harness underneath the costume," said Ringwood, "which had two bolts at the shoulders, and the cape was literally screwed into these bolts on each side. The hardware was covered by the bat symbol, which was bolted onto the chest. So there was a lot of understructure holding the cape in place. If there had not been, the weight of it when he swung around would have torn the entire costume right off his body."[199]

Once the latex Batsuit was perfected, Ringwood made twenty-eight of them for Keaton and his stunt doubles, along with twenty-five capes and six headpieces. The total cost was $250,000.[200] "I just saw this thing, and I thought, Yes!" said Keaton about first seeing the Batsuit. However, once he tried on the outfit, he found that it was extremely hot and cumbersome. An assistant with special tools was needed to bolt it together at the shoulders, which meant, among other things, that the actor had limited bathroom breaks.[201] At first, it took the actor two and a half hours to get into the suit. Eventually, the costume team was able to get Keaton suited up in twenty minutes.[202] "I'm a little masochistic, I guess," said Keaton. "The hardest part was learning how to move in the suit. I don't necessarily mean run and jump and fight. I mean move to get the optimum effect. Turn your head so the light hits it right, because it's very dramatic and operatic."[203]

Like any good costume designer's creation, the Batsuit helped Keaton hone his characterization. "When you're in the suit, you feel and act differently," said Keaton. "Also, you're very isolated in the Batman suit, which is great. On the first *Batman*, I really used that isolation to help create the character, who feels cut off from the mainstream."[204] "The point of the Batman costume and cape is to interpret the cartoon character and turn him into the Dark Knight of the movie," said Ringwood. "Our process has been to take something which is easy in two dimensions on the page, and turn it into a three dimensional moving thing that actually has some sort of animal quality."[205]

The Batman outfit was revolutionary. Not only did it strike fear into the hearts of criminals, but it also struck fear into the heart of action hero Sylvester Stallone. "The action movies changed radically when it became possible to Velcro your muscles on," said Stallone. "It was the beginning of a new era. The visual took over. The special effects became more important than the single person. That was the beginning of the end...I wish I had thought of Velcro muscles myself. I didn't have to go to the gym for all those years."[206]

Besides Batman's costume, Ringwood also clothed the other characters. For Carl Grissom and his gangsters, Ringwood went for "a soft sell retro Forties" or "timeless modern" look. The suit worn by Jack Palance was one of two hundred unused outfits from the 1940s that were found in a warehouse in New York.[207]

The Joker's outfits were custom-made with input from Savile Row couturier Tommy "the Tailor" Nutter, who had previously created flashy, colorful outfits for the Beatles and Mick Jagger.[208] In the comics, the Joker was tall and thin and wore lots of coats with tails. "Jack is stocky and more bulldog-like, so we focused more on hats and neckwear," said Ringwood. He put together a mix-and-match wardrobe of 25 shirts, six suits, six coats and 12 hats. "You have to be brave to wear orange, purple, green and turquoise together," said Ringwood. The fabrics for the suits were woven in Scotland from yarns specially dyed because Ringwood couldn't find enough purple fabric elsewhere, bringing the cost of making the Clown Prince's wardrobe to $40,000. When filming was finished, Nicholson kept all of it.[209]

While Ringwood was busy crafting the Batsuit and other costumes, production designer Anton Furst, art director Terry Ackland-Snow and special effects supervisor John Evans were working to produce two fully functional Batmobiles. "Three of us worked on it and looked at every car ever made, I think," said Furst. "We ended up with something that has brute force and forbidding power coupled with form, shape and sculpture. Something that is, frankly, quite rude."[210] The idea, said Furst, was "to get menace, violence and all the intimidation that comes out of (Batman's) character into the car."[211] Furst said the Batmobile was partly influenced by Bonneville Salt Flats racers and partly by Corvette Stingrays of the 1950s, but added "we just went into pure expressionism in the end."[212]

To fabricate the car, John Evans and his crew spent less than $11,000 for a couple of aged Chevy Impalas, whose chassis were lengthened by 30 inches, and drive shafts extended by 18 inches. Spacers were used to increase the rear track to 97 inches, and the engine was dropped a foot to allow for a low hoodline. Large intakes in front of the rear wheels supplied cool air to enlarged radiators.[213] The final vehicle was 20 feet long with an 8-foot wheelbase, weighed 1-1/2 tons and featured a front, back and intake taken from jet aircraft and incorporated into a fiberglass shell. The car was fitted out with Browning machine guns hidden in the wheel housings, afterburners and an explosive grappling hook.[214] The car was supported by twenty-four inch drag racing wheels imported from the U.S.[215] It took a team of twelve technicians racing against the clock twelve weeks to build the Batmobile, though they were very enthusiastic about their work. Special effects supervisor John Evans said, "This was the only time I can remember my boys coming in early!"[216]

BATMAN BEGINS

In October of 1988, cameras finally began rolling on *Batman*.[217] The first day got off to a rocky start. Burton was on the set of crime boss Carl Grissom's office, filming a shot of Jack Palance as Grissom entering from a bathroom. The director called action, but Palance didn't come out. Burton went to ask Palance why he didn't enter on cue, and there was an immediate disconnect between the Young

Turk director and the old pro Method actor. Palance's temper flared, and he hissed at Burton, "I've made over a hundred movies. How many have you made?" On the audio commentary to the DVD of the film, Burton says that he had an "out of body" experience at that moment, intimidated by the physically imposing actor.[218] This was just a small taste of the nerve-wracking pressures Burton would face. It was only his third film, and at a projected cost of $30 million, it had a budget five times that of *Pee-wee's Big Adventure* and twice that of *Beetlejuice*.[219] As filming progressed, the budget climbed even higher, eventually ballooning to a reported $48 million. It was a huge sum for the studio to gamble on a director who hadn't had any experience directing an epic-sized action film. To keep Burton from being completely overwhelmed, the studio packed the crew with experienced technicians, such as first assistant director Derek Cracknell, who had served in the same capacity on *2001: A Space Odyssey* (1968), *Battle of Britain* (1969), *A Clockwork Orange* (1971), the James Bond films *Diamonds Are Forever* (1971), *Live and Let Die* (1973) and *The Man With the Golden Gun* (1974), and *Aliens* (1986). Second unit director Peter MacDonald had worked on the *Star Wars* film *The Empire Strikes Back* (1980), *Excalibur* (1981), *Dragonslayer* (1981) and *Rambo: First Blood Part II* (1985) and had just directed his first feature, *Rambo III* (1988). Handling model effects was Derek Meddings, who began as a model maker with Gerry Anderson's TV series such as *Thunderbirds* and *UFO* before graduating to films like the 007 adventures *Live and Let Die, The Spy Who Loved Me* (1977), *Moonraker* (1979), and *For Your Eyes Only* (1981), as well as the first three *Superman* movies. Special effects supervisor John Evans had worked with Meddings on *The Spy Who Loved Me, Moonraker, Superman II* (1980) and *For Your Eyes Only. Batman* kept him busy not only with big explosions but also designing an array of bat gadgets.

Shooting the film was cinematographer Roger Pratt, who had photographed Terry Gilliam's ambitious fantasy *Brazil* (1985). Pratt decided to give the film a vibrant look through his use of lighting. "We're going with tonal separation, lighting it as if it were black and white but shooting in color," he said. "And we're using a Kodak film stock that enables us to shoot in very low light while retaining bright effects. But the key is using sets of a single tone against which the Joker just pops out."'

"You have to rely on your people," said Burton. "Luckily, I had Anton [Furst, production designer], Bob Ringwood [costume designer], Roger Pratt [lighting cameraman] and Peter [MacDonald] to rely on—basically everybody. But I found myself relying on people a little bit more than I usually do, which scared me and made me more anxious, and that had a lot to do with my mental state during the picture. I've never had a second unit—I've usually done it all—so it's just hard to let go. But again, I couldn't have had better help."[220]

Warren Skaaren continued rewriting the script even as shooting began. With continuing input from Jack Nicholson as well as from producer Jon Peters, he kept expanding the Joker's role. "I think I had the most effect on that character," said Skaaren. "Jack, as an actor, was the most available to me, as opposed to Michael, during shooting. Jack and I spent a fair amount of time on it."[221] It was Nicholson who came up with Jack Napier's line, "Ever dance with the devil in the pale moonlight?" As Patrick McGilligan points out in his Nicholson biography *Jack's Life*, the line is reminiscent of one Nicholson spoke as George Hanson in *Easy Rider*, "Did ya ever talk to bullfrogs in the middle of the night?"[222] The more involved Nicholson became, the more the Joker's role grew. What was originally supposed to have been a three-week filming commitment eventually became more than three months.[223]

The veteran actor supported the young director's vision, which gave the rest of the crew assurance in Burton's abilities. "Jack gave the entire cast the confidence and courage—that's not an overstatement—to make this film," said Burton. "He was terrific. I had heard people talk about him before, but to watch him work was a pure education in the true art of filmmaking. In an instant, he could amend his performance at a particular time to give more menace, or less, as directed. He could alter his facial expression at a stroke, without having to reconstitute himself."[224] Nicholson had chosen to play the Joker "short-wired," as he put it, saying, "I'd do anything that came into my mind."[225] And he did it while sometimes wearing make-up that took two hours to apply and one hour to remove.[226]

To differentiate between the flamboyance of the Joker and the somberness of Batman, Michael Keaton gave a much more controlled performance. "With the way (Nicholson) played the role so high dramatically," said Skaaren, "we decided that Michael Keaton should take the quiet, more thoughtful road, because you can't have two people that big shouting and chasing each other around."[227] Said Keaton, "I discussed the role with Tim as well as Jack. The character was clearly more powerful if he was more internal. As Jack said to me in makeup one day, 'Just let the wardrobe act, kid.' There was great wisdom in that statement. The real power came from within. My natural tendency is to do more because you sometimes fear you're not doing enough. The longer I'm an actor, the more I discover that less is more."[228]

Batman (Michael Keaton) has the Joker (Jack Nicholson) in his clutches (Warner Bros./Photofest, © Warner Bros.).

Keaton enjoyed a good working relationship with his on-screen nemesis. "Working with Nicholson was a definite incentive for me as an actor," Keaton told *Comics Scene* magazine's Marc Shapiro. "With Nicholson, you get much more than his talent. You get his knowledge and his point-of-view about movies. You get an actor who comes to life right in front of your eyes." The on-set camaraderie evolved into an off-set friendship as well. "Jack and I are basically the same kind of people, which is why we got along so great," said Keaton. "We would sit around between shots and talk about all sorts of things. We would eat dinner together, hit the art museum. It was a great experience."[229]

Even though Tim Burton had directed Michael Keaton in *Beetlejuice*, the working relationship between the two was different on *Batman*. "It was more difficult," said Burton. "This was a tough one for Michael because much of what he had to do, especially at the beginning, was, he would come in at the day's end, put on his Batsuit, which was a very uncomfortable suit, and do two shots. For Michael, the kind of actor he is, that's very difficult."[230] It was especially difficult for an actor who had to sometimes work through physical pain. "Occasionally, I have back problems," said Keaton. "I hurt my back a little bit on *Batman*, but I hurt my back much worse on *Mr. Mom*. That's the great irony."[231] According to second unit director Peter MacDonald, Keaton had wanted to do all of his own stunts, "but it's harder than normal to do that when you've got this almost immovable suit on. You have to be a kind of superman to be able to move. So we had the normal stunt guy and we had a martial arts guy, and we had a ballet dancer. The ballet dancer was the one that did the walk in, because this guy could swish his cape and look great, you know—and then two quite tough guys to do the fighting."[232] Keaton spent a lot of time exploring how to move in ways that would make the angular cowl and cape catch the light dramatically, but the Batsuit reacted differently with each lighting set-up. "It's a can of worms," said Burton. "We truly were learning things as we went on this. Mike and I would try to figure out how he should move. We'd come up with a movement that was great. Then we'd try it again, and it would look ridiculous in another shot."[233]

Batman's creator, Bob Kane, traveled to London with his wife, Elizabeth Sanders, to keep an eye on the proceedings. He appeared in a short featurette, walking around the thirty-foot high sets of Gotham City and talking about how they reminded him of the New York of his youth, and he was scheduled to do some other work in front of the cameras. "I was supposed to be in the film," said Kane, "in a newsroom as Bob the cartoonist, drawing a bat in a suit. When I first read the scene, it said Jerry the cartoonist, and I told Tim they'd spelled Jerry wrong, 'It's not J-E-R-R-Y, it's B-O-B.' So I was in it; I went to London in November, but they had to put my scene back to the middle of January. I had an engagement in New York so we flew back across."[234] Kane and his wife returned to New York in mid-December, just a week before Pan Am Flight 103, bound from London to New York, was destroyed by a bomb in mid-air over Lockerbie, Scotland. "We left on that same plane a week earlier," said Kane. "So I was a little apprehensive, obviously...So, I wouldn't fly back in the winter just to do my scene."[235]

As filming progressed on the massive sets, the biggest problem Burton encountered was not his actors but his producer, Jon Peters, whose quest to improve the film threatened to make it implode. Besides constantly firing and hiring crewmembers, Peters was forever pushing Skaaren to rewrite scenes, and eventually brought in Charles McKeown, scriptwriter of *Brazil* (1985) and *The Adventures of Baron Munchausen* (1988), to make yet more revisions. The tension of dealing with the mammoth production and ever-changing script began to get to Burton. "I was probably as sick as I've ever been on a movie, all the time," said the director. "I was out of it. I was sick. See, the problem is, it was my first big movie. There's all these people around. There's a different energy. There's no way to prepare. No way to prepare. More money. More tension. More fear. Everything: more, more, more. More. And I just let something happen, which I'll try to never let happen again, which is to let the script unravel...Here we started out with a script that everybody said...'Oh, it's a great script, it's a great script.' But at the end of the day, they basically shred it. So it went from being the greatest script in the world to basically unraveling. And once it unravels, it unravels...And a lot of it had to do with dealing with the energies of the studio and the producers and everybody just being there and doing it—there was no one thing; it was a big animal."[236]

Burton was also worn down by the long hours. On his previous, smaller-budgeted films, he'd had a five-day work week. On *Batman*, it was a six-day week. "Usually, if you have the weekend, you can regroup a little bit. There was absolutely no time to regroup," said Burton.[237] "I'll never do six days a week again. It's counter-productive. It looks good on paper, but when people are working that hard on this kind of movie, myself included, Saturday rolls around and you're working in negative space. You're so scatterbrained, and then the problems just build up. You don't have a second to think about it and resolve it, and step back and say, 'Well, see, let's cut this out,' because you are blindly going through it. Plus, we had a full second unit which I had never had or dealt with before, so I felt like there was no time to think on this film. By the end, I was taking it almost a day at a time. It got to be very frightening. It just stems from the problems on the script. Things change anyway, but usually, you have Saturday."[238]

There was drama off the set as well as on. After Kim Basinger arrived in London with her husband, Ron Snyder, Jon Peters took them to dinner. Before the meal ended, Snyder and Peters were at each other's throats. Snyder returned to America soon after, and Peters, whose own marriage had ended, began romancing Basinger. Before long, they had begun an affair which lasted throughout filming; Basinger called Peters her "sweetheart hoodlum."[239] Burton, meanwhile, embarked on a romance of his own, with a German artist he met at a party named Lena Gieseke.[240]

Burton later admitted that while Peters' micro-managing could be maddening, it was sometimes beneficial. "Before I met Jon, people said, 'Watch out—Jon's this, Jon's that, he's not creative,'" said Burton. "And I definitely argue that point. He is creative, and he did have some good ideas...I was not seduced by Jon. What I responded to in Jon was just the insanity, the nuts quality. I loved that somebody just said whatever they thought. You don't hear people doing that."[241]

When it came time to film a scene where the Joker and his goons interrupt Bruce Wayne in Vicki Vale's apartment just as he's about to reveal his identity to her, the producer felt the script as written didn't show enough of Wayne's attraction for Vale. He also felt that Wayne's face-off with the Joker lacked drama. "We ran into troubles because, by the shoot's end, there were sequences that weren't quite solidified," said Burton. "I figure if I ever had it to do over again, I would want to make the script better. But there's no point in freaking out. You must stick by what you're doing, and I think it got a little bit out of hand."[242]

One day after filming had ended, Peters asked Burton to come to his hotel suite, where the producer and director improvised dialogue for the scene, with Peters playing Bruce Wayne and Burton as Vicki Vale. The following morning, they continued working out the scene on the apartment set at Pinewood, along with Warren Skaaren. Burton then brought in the actors, who had their own ideas.[243] "Especially near the end of the shooting, between the actors and myself, we sort of wrote the movie," Burton said. "Part of the rationale for the creation of new dialogue was to bring cinematic reality to a previously two-dimensional world. You're taking something which is very absurd and you want to make it as real as possible, and then it has to do with the actors, too. Some actors can say lines fine, other actors will come in and say, 'This is shit, I can't do this,' and I listen to them. If I feel that they're right, then I let them—with me—tune it to their individual selves, because otherwise, you shouldn't have had that person in the role."[244] The apartment scene was filmed the next day, and although Burton found the process unsettling, he later admitted, "It's one of my favorite scenes."[245]

One of Anton Furst's most impressive sets was the mammoth Batcave set. "I transformed it into the foundation of Gotham City, a bit like *Phantom of the Opera*," said Furst. "There's something amorphous and boring to me about cave structure, but if you start having piles of the bottoms of skyscrapers coming down through this great chasm in the ground, you can end up with an extraordinarily interesting set."[246] While filming on the set, however, Michael Keaton noticed there were sexual shenanigans going on as the cameras rolled. In the fake stalactites up above him, the live fruit bats brought in to lend a creepy atmosphere were gettin' busy. Between takes, Keaton would look up at them and yell, "Hey, you two! Don't make me have to come up there and separate you!" The set began to seem even more authentic as the days rolled by and it took on the heady aroma of fruit bat urine.[247]

Thanks to the last-minute rewrites, there was one scene filmed on the Batcave set that eventually offended die-hard Batfans. As Bruce Wayne sits pensively at the Batcomputer, Alfred enters, with Vicki Vale. Bruce looks up but doesn't question what she's doing there. "Obviously, that was the one thing I got killed for," Burton later told David Breskin of *Rolling Stone*. "It was rough...My impulse was, I said to myself, 'Fuck this bullshit!' This is comic-book material. I thought, you know, who really cares? But it was a mistake. It went too far...This is the trouble that I have. This is where sometimes there will be big gaps in something that I do. I try very hard to create my own environment. And so far it's worked out. But sometimes there will be a leap that people don't buy, they don't buy, they don't buy. They go, 'Whoa!' and it takes them out of it. I don't want to take people out of something. I spend a large time trying to not have that happen."[248]

Not all of the filming was done within the confines of Pinewood. For exteriors of Wayne Manor, as well as the dining scene between Vicki Vale and Bruce Wayne, the crew trekked out to Knebworth House in Hertfordshire, thirty miles outside London. Once the home of Victorian author Edward Bulwer-Lytton (author of the infamous line, "It was a dark and stormy night..."), the Tudor Gothic manor house had once hosted such esteemed visitors as Charles Dickens and Winston Churchill. "I see places like these," said Keaton, "and I get the urge to run down to Pier 1 Exports to pick out some wicker chairs and throw pillows. Kinda makes you appreciate a nice studio apartment, you know?" [249]

More location filming occurred at the Acton Lane Power Station in West London. Commissioned in 1899, the station generated electricity until October 31, 1983, when it was closed down. The 75,000 square foot space had been used as a film set in *Aliens* (1986) before the *Batman* crew came and dressed it as Axis Chemical, the site of Jack Napier's transformation into the Joker. At the end of the scene, stunt double Gerry Crampton took over for Jack Nicholson for Napier's fall into the vat of toxic chemicals. [250]

After filming the scene where Batman first confronts Napier and escapes from the Gotham police, the crew returned to film shots of the Batmobile speeding through the facility as explosions erupt around it. Though the shots would only last a minute on screen, they took two and a half weeks to prepare. [251] "Tim Burton wanted to go for full-size, 100-feet flames," said special effects supervisor John Evans. "You couldn't get within 50 feet of them. We wired up thousands of sandbags, pumped gas through galvanized piping and safely set the explosives in steel cases. The trick was to drive the car through all this before it melted!" [252] Michael Keaton's double for the scene was stuntman Sean McCabe, who drove the Batmobile through the flames wearing a safety helmet and fire suit. Even with the precautions, the stunt posed a risk. "When working in corridors of fire, an engine can die due to lack of oxygen," said stunt coordinator Eddie Stacey. "You see, fire burns up oxygen, so timing is crucial. Motorbike riders who weren't aware of this have perished in tunnel-of-fire stunts." [253] Forty-five tons of liquid gas was used for the shot, an amount that, according to Evans, "would heat a 20-30 house village for a whole year!" [254]

The exterior shots of the plant exploding were filmed at Little Barford Power Station in Bedfordshire, a coal-fired power station that had shut down on October 26, 1981. For the shot of the Batmobile barreling out of the factory as it explodes, visual effects supervisor Derek Meddings resorted to the kind of seamless model work he had employed on several James Bond films and *Superman*. After filming the car exiting the building, Meddings then built a model back at Pinewood that matched the top of the power station. The two shots were then combined, the lower half being the live-action shot of the Batmobile, and the upper half being the shot of the model exploding. Filming the model, Meddings said, "We were shooting at high speed, 120 frames per second. Because it is quite hard to make a building collapse in just the way you want, it was necessary to have breakaway plaster sections so that the right chunks of the building exploded."

Meddings also employed his considerable skill for scenes of the Batwing in flight and crashing onto the steps of Gotham Cathedral. The crash was filmed at a speed of 120 frames per second on a miniature set that was an exact replica of the Gotham main street set, built in 1/12 scale. "They had positioned a large section of the wrecked Batwing on the Cathedral steps," said Meddings. "We had to place our model in precisely the same position. To ensure it broke up, we made it out of pewter which is a nice, soft metal...You only really know what you've got when you see the rushes the following day. A mixture of clever cutting and spot-on camera angles means that you really can't see the joins."[255]

To capture a shot of Batman's point-of-view as the Dark Knight pilots the Batwing between Gotham City skyscrapers, catching the Joker's poison gas balloons as he goes, Meddings also had to construct a miniature of the city center. The buildings on the miniature set were only 18 feet high and the street 10 inches wide, so a special overhead motion-control camera had to be built that could duck and dive through the clutter of buildings and over the miniature trucks, cars, floats and searchlights.[256] "When we first shot the city center, it just didn't look right and I couldn't work out why," said Meddings. "I soon realized that even though they were varnished, the streets looked dull. The answer was to spray them with oil, which we also used to highlight sections of the vehicles."[257]

As the Christmas holidays approached, reports were still filtering in from American newspapers about the wrath of Batfans incensed over the casting of Michael Keaton. But by now, Warner Bros. had something more powerful than a public relations expert and Bob Kane to mollify the doubters—they had dailies. Cobbling together footage fresh from Pinewood, they put together a trailer that gave a tantalizing glimpse of the Batwing, the Batmobile, Nicholson's Joker, and—most importantly—Keaton as Batman.[258] And not just Keaton as Batman, but Keaton as Batman punching bad guys and kicking ass. The trailer was not artfully done, but it served its purpose. The protests died down almost overnight.

In December, the crew began a week of night shoots on the Gotham City main street set at Pinewood, filming the Joker's parade.[259] It was now the height of the British winter, and the actors and extras could see their breath hang in the chill air. After a three-week Christmas break—during which time producer Jon Peters angered the British crew by refusing to give them holiday pay[260]—the cast and crew reassembled to film the movie's climax.

The ending of the film had always been problematic, despite rewrite after rewrite. Peters decided to fix it by making it grander. The ending wouldn't simply occur in a cathedral bell tower, it would be in the highest bell tower imaginable. By the time Batman reached the top, he would have gone through a gauntlet of the Joker's goons, leaving him tired and barely able to fight (much as it had been in Hamm's original script, where Batman emerged from the Batwing with broken bones). "Towards the end of the film Jon realized you couldn't just have Batman beating up the fifty-year-old Joker," said production designer Anton Furst.[261] Furst listened to Peters's idea, then told him that the miniature effects involved would require a 38-foot high model of the cathedral. "Just the model alone cost $100,000. Jon said, 'Fine.' He observed that it was worth it," said Furst. "I think Jon has a pretty good sense of the broad stroke, whereas other producers would say '$100,000?'" Though the film was already well over budget, Warner Bros. liked the footage they had seen and quickly approved the overage.[262]

Once again working without a script, Burton largely improvised the ending. It was as confusing for the director as it was for his actors. Burton said, "Here were Jack

Nicholson and Kim Basinger walking up this cathedral, and halfway up Jack turns round and says, 'Why am I walking up all these stairs? Where am I going?' And I had to tell him that I didn't know. The most frightening experience of my life. I knew they had to go up to the bell tower and they better do something up there. That was always a given. But what? Help me! Help me!"[263]

When it came to filming the final showdown between the Joker and Batman, there was a moment of levity as Keaton and Nicholson, both in full costume and make-up, suddenly became aware that they looked like a couple of overage trick-or-treaters. Said Keaton, "We were just about to do a take and I leaned over and said to him, 'We're both grown men.' He died at that."[264]

In the end, Burton pulled it off, despite producer Jon Peters's meddling. "There was just no time for me to work on it. I was basically reacting to other people's ideas and then trying to come up with stuff of my own," said Burton. "Hollywood is a very control-oriented place, and if people want to feel in control, a very easy way to bring control back to yourself is to create chaos. Because if you're the one creating chaos, then you're the one who has to fix it. And on some level, that may be true with Jon."[265]

Michael Keaton wound up his work on the film at the end of January 1989.[266] He had spent four months in the Batsuit, and was now ready for a break. "I'm still not totally sure I know exactly what I did in this movie," he said. "It all happened real fast. This thing was bigger than me."[267] Speaking to Marc Shapiro of *Comics Scene* magazine, Keaton said, "I'm usually a lot of fun to work with, but I've got to be totally honest—I was not a lot of fun to work with on this movie. I was exhausted, tired and pretty burned out going into *Batman,* and I was a real pain in the ass during a good part of filming. But, it never got to the point where it got personal or I told Jack Nicholson or Tim to [screw] off. I would get angry for a while, then I would calm down and we would go ahead and get the next shot."[268]

Tim Burton summed up his own experience on the film saying, "Torture. The worst period of my life."[269] After celebrating the end of filming, he had something happier to celebrate a month later—his marriage to Lena Gieseke.[270]

SOUNDS OF SUCCESS

When it came time to think about scoring the film, Tim Burton knew exactly whom he wanted. His previous two films had been scored by Danny Elfman, a young composer who first gained attention as a member of the rock group Oingo Boingo, which was formed to create the music for his brother Richard's film debut, *The Forbidden Zone* (1982). "I always wanted to work on films," Elfman said in an interview for the TV program *Movie Time*, speaking about film scoring, "but I never thought I had any musical talent, so this is the area that I would've guessed that I had the least amount of chances of being involved in, if I'd have listed all the different areas of filmmaking...In many ways, I completely owe it to Tim, the fact that I have a film composing career. He took a major gamble on me when we did *Pee-wee's Big Adventure.* I had no orchestral experience at all, and I think at that point he probably had more faith in me than I did. So I owe him quite a lot. I owe him the fact that I have a career at all. I can't see that anybody else would've taken a chance on me in the orchestral sense. And I really wasn't interested in getting involved doing a synthesizer or contemporary score at that point."[271]

In his youth, Elfman had listened to the film scores of Bernard Herrmann and Erich Wolfgang Korngold, but for *Batman,* said Elfman, "they wanted a Wagnerian vibe." At Burton's invitation, Elfman went to London to visit the locations. "I've done that in all the films I've worked with him—spend a little time and see what it was like on the set," said Elfman. "I actually wrote the *Batman* theme walking through Gotham City with Tim and seeing just a little bit of footage, so it was enough to get a real flavor and feel."[272] Elfman's *Batman* theme begins with a note of mystery reminiscent of the music under the titles of the 1943 serial, but then builds into an energetic march. "In *Batman,* I wanted to approach it like an old-style film, almost like a 40s action movie would be," said Elfman. "And I went for a single, very simple theme that I could play in a big way, in a small way, in a romantic way or in a dark way. And so I just found that and played it for everybody and they seemed to like it, and I just carried that throughout the movie. So it's your old-fashioned style of composition in that respect."[273]

Elfman knew before he began composing that there were a couple of scenes that would be scored with music from Prince, so he simply skipped those scenes. Before shooting began, the filmmakers had toyed with the idea of having the score composed by not one but two pop music giants, Prince and Michael Jackson. As Prince related to Joachim Hentschel, who interviewed him for the German edition of *Rolling Stone,* "Did you know that the album was supposed to be a duet between Michael Jackson and me? He as Batman, me as Joker?"[274] Though those plans never went anywhere, Jack Nicholson—a Prince fan—was fervent about having the performer's music in the film. So was Prince's label, Warner Bros. Music.

Burton was also an enthusiastic Prince fan, but was less sure about how Prince's music would fit with his dark vision. "This is what happened," said Burton. "You learn something new every day. Now, here is a guy, Prince, who was one of my favorites. I had just gone to see two of his concerts in London, and I felt they were like the best concerts I'd ever seen. Okay. So. They're saying to me, these record guys, it needs this and that, and they give you this whole thing about it's an expensive movie so you need it. And what happens is, you get engaged in this world, and then there's no way out. There's too much money. There's this guy you respect and is good and has got this thing going. It got to a point where there was no turning back. And I don't want to get into that situation again."[275] Besides clashing with Elfman's score, Burton felt the music might date the film. "It completely lost me," said Burton. "And it tainted something that I don't want to taint."[276]

Prince, as it happened, was a Batman fan. Years later, when he was interviewed by Oprah Winfrey, the talk show hostess asked him, "What was the first song you taught yourself to play on the piano?" He played the theme to the 1960s *Batman* TV series.[277] "I brought Prince over to London and you could just tell his kind of genius was in touch with the movie," said Mark Canton. "By the time we had dinner that night, he had three songs in his head. Three weeks later he had nine songs. He did a few more that we felt would be better for the film and ended up creating an album up there with *Purple Rain*."[278] In the end, two of Prince's compositions, "Partyman" (heard cranking from the Joker's boom box in the museum scene) and "Trust"(heard during the parade near the finale) were prominently featured in the film, with three others being used incidentally: "The Future" at the beginning when the family is walking down the alley, "Electric Chair" during the party at Wayne Manor, and "Vicki Waiting," at the beginning of the party scene. Another song, "Scandalous," was used in the end credits. But Prince, in his enthusiasm to be involved, had written nine songs, enough for an entire album. Warner Bros. released Prince's "soundtrack" of *Batman*, including all the songs he had written for the film, on June 20, 1989, three days before the film opened. The album had pre-orders of 800,000 copies, eventually selling 4.3 million disks and spending six weeks at the #1 position on the Billboard 200 chart. On the U.S. charts, the "Batdance" single also went to #1, "Scandalous" went to #5, "Partyman" rose to #18, and "The Arms of Orion," a duet with Sheena Easton, climbed to #36. Regarding "Batdance," Warner Bros. VIP of A&R Michael Ostin said, "Prince was adamant about it being the first single, and he was right. It's a tremendous teaser for the film and the album. He's taken so many pieces of the dialog from the film and other music that's in it that it's like a collage."[279]

Tim Burton kept working on the edit of the film right up until four weeks before it was due to open. Once the final cut was locked, Danny Elfman set to scoring and recording with the London Symphony Orchestra, finishing two weeks later. The delay in getting the final edit meant that Elfman's soundtrack was delivered to Warner Bros. record division much later than Prince's; Prince delivered his soundtrack on April 22, while Elfman didn't get his in until June 6. As a result, Prince's soundtrack was released concurrently with the film, while Elfman's didn't come out until seven weeks later.[280]

Even as the film was in production, producer Jon Peters turned his attention to promoting it. He looked at the artwork that was supplied by Warner Bros. marketing department and hated it. Having spent nearly a decade bringing the movie to the big screen, he didn't want to blow it now with an inferior press campaign. He summoned production designer Anton Furst to his office. "Jon was there with the artwork in front of him," recalled Furst. "He said, 'Look at these.' One was sort of like *Conan,* or *RoboCop*—the word 'Batman' spelled in *Conan the Barbarian* type. Nothing original, nothing you hadn't seen before many times."[281] Peters told Furst to drop everything and design a logo that would tie all the merchandising together.

Furst created a logo that looked as though it was stamped out of Batman's body armor. "It became a sort of trompe l'oeil, it became ambiguous, so you had to look twice," said Furst. "But it was very definitely the Batsymbol, so there was no problem in people identifying it." Peters loved the design, and decided that the posters advertising the film would consist solely of the logo on a black background. The only lettering would be the opening date of the film: June 23. The studio wanted the names of the stars on the poster. Peters felt the star was Batman. The producer later told Furst that he had fought enormous battles with Warner Bros. over the poster, to the point of pinning executives against the wall.

The Batsymbol became ubiquitous in the months leading up to the film's release. "You couldn't walk across Times Square," said Michael Uslan, "it's like every fifth person either had a *Batman* hat or a tee-shirt on. People were breaking into the bus stops to get the posters. People were finding out what movies were showing the trailer, they would pay, go in and see the trailer and then leave, wouldn't even stay for the movie. Bootleg copies of the initial trailer were being sold at Comic Cons for twenty-five bucks back then. It was absolutely insane. How many movies are advertised without even putting the name of the movie on the poster? The symbol was so iconic, it was just the symbol and a date, and it became like a mania. It was unbelievable. People now who've only known in their consciousness what happened with *The Dark Knight*, have no idea how equally crazed it was with that first *Batman* movie. I think it might've been the best-marketed film up to that time."[282]

Even before *Batman* hit movie screens, Warner Bros., anticipating how to thwart pirated videotape copies from diminishing their box-office receipts, employed a technological solution worthy of Batman. The studio revealed that all 4,000 prints of the film shipped worldwide carried an electronic marking code not visible on the projected film that could be detected in all pirated film-to-video transfers. In addition, Warner Bros. offered rewards of $200 for the first 15 prated copies of the film received by the studio, as well as up to $15,000 for information leading to the conviction of anyone distributing pirated *Batman* cassettes.[283]

With anticipation for the film reaching a fever pitch, Warner Bros. booked not one but two theaters to host the premiere, the 1,500-seat Village Theatre and the adjacent 850-seat Bruin Theater in Westwood, a Los Angeles suburb adjoining the campus of UCLA. For the night of the premiere, the studio had originally planned to host a huge Batbash, turning Westwood into Gotham City at a projected cost of $100,000. But as they considered the idea, they began to get cold feet, worried that someone would get hurt. "When you make plans for these events, you have to think on all levels," said Rob Friedman, Warners' advertising chief. "From a security point of view, we got really afraid." When the studio canceled plans for the event, they decided to donate $100,000 to the Zahn Memorial Center for Social Services, an organization allied with the Salvation Army that earmarked the funds to help the homeless in Los Angeles. "We decided to think in the spirit of Batman—who works to better Gotham, if you will," said Friedman.[284]

The *Batman* premiere was set for 8 PM on the evening of June 19, 1989. With the studio announcing that seats would be set aside in both theaters for the general public, hundreds of fans began congregating on the sidewalks around the theaters in the early afternoon, segregated from the red carpet by police barricades. Though mostly young males, the fans were all ages, and many were in costume. There were Batmen in the all-black outfit of the movie, and there were Batmen in the Adam West costume from the 1960s. There were a few Robins, and more than a few white-faced, green-haired Jokers. Rising above the two theaters were brightly colored and rather silly-looking helium parade balloons, props from the movie's finale. As 8 PM approached, the crowds cheered the arrival of the movie stars. A thunderous roar went up for Jack Nicholson, and Michael Keaton emerged from his limousine and rushed to the fans, high-fiving several of them before whirling around to enter the theater. Celebrities in attendance included Eddie Murphy, Sylvester Stallone, Don Johnson with Melanie Griffith, Winona Ryder, Vanna White, Tom Selleck, Valerie

Bertinelli and Eddie Van Halen, Randy Quaid, Kirk Cameron, Chevy Chase and Glenn Close, who said, "It feels like the Academy Awards."[285] Kim Basinger, who turned heads in a black party dress that had a sheer skirt that revealed her sheer black stockings and lace panties underneath, said, "It's amazing. This isn't a film, it's an event."[286]

When the theaters were filled to capacity, the fans outside remained, hopeful that there would be a second showing and they would be among the first to see the summer's most highly-anticipated film. They weren't disappointed. To help set the mood, the theaters shined a Batsignal onto the theater curtains until the lights dimmed completely and the film began. The Warner executives in the back rows must have breathed a deep sigh of relief when the audience let out a collective astonished "Ooooooh!" when Batman was seen in the opening scenes, gliding down into the background of a mist-filled shot of two petty crooks. In the packed house, the film played like gangbusters.

Screenwriter Warren Skaaren, who had never encountered Bob Kane on the set, got a chance to meet him at the premiere. "I wouldn't have missed that for the world!" said Skaaren.[287] Michael Uslan echoed Skaaren's sentiments, saying, "As a fanboy, at the premiere of the first movie, to me the greatest thing was not the stars that were there and hanging out with them, it was hanging out with Stan Lee and Bob Kane at the premiere of my first *Batman* movie. That was as good as it gets for me."[288]

After the Los Angeles premiere, a private Washington, D.C. screening was held on June 22, with an audience of politicians including Vice President Dan Quayle and his family.[289] Then, on June 23, *Batman* opened at 2,193 U.S. and Canadian theaters.[290] There were reports that at some theaters, moviegoers had begun camping out the day before.[291] In its first weekend, *Batman* took in a record-shattering $42.7 million. Over the next ten days, it earned $100 million, the first movie in history to earn such a phenomenal amount so quickly.[292] By the time it ended its run, it had grossed over $400 million.[293]

TV reviewers Gene Siskel and Roger Ebert split on the film. They both admired the art direction, and Siskel called it "the first summer spectacular that I've really enjoyed...there's some true originality in the film's art design, sound and performances." Ebert also praised the art design, but felt the characters were not ones he could care about. The reaction of the TV critics mirrored the split among the nation's newspapers. In *The New York Times*, Vincent Canby wrote that "The wit is all pictorial. The film meanders mindlessly from one image to the next, as does a comic book. It doesn't help that the title character remains such a wimp even when played by Michael Keaton. Nobody could do anything with this ridiculous conceit, but asking Mr. Keaton, one of our most volatile actors, to play Bruce Wayne/Batman is like asking him to put on an ape suit and play the title role in *King Kong...Batman* is a movie without any dominant tone or style other than that provided by Mr. Furst. It's neither funny nor solemn. It has the personality not of a particular movie but of a product, of something arrived at by corporate decision."[294]

Richard Corliss, in *Time* magazine, concurred, writing, "*Batman*'s style is both daunting and lurching; it has trouble deciding which of its antagonists should set the tone. It can be as manic as the Joker, straining to hear the applause of outrage; it can be as implosive as Batman-Bruce, who seems crushed by the burden of his schizoid eminence. This tension nearly exhausts the viewer and the film."[295]

In *The Omaha World-Herald,* Jeff Bahr wrote, "Yes, the Joker is definitely wild in *Batman.* Nicholson's role is so large, in fact, that this film should almost be called *The Joker...*Considering all of the buildup this film has received, many moviegoers will find it a letdown. If Robin were around, he probably would say, 'Holy Disappointment, Batman!'"[296] Jeff Strickler in *The Minneapolis Star Tribune* echoed Bahr's sentiments, writing, "Bad news, batfans. In *Batman,* the Joker finally gets the better of the hero. He pulls off the crime of the century right below the Caped Crusader's nose: He steals his movie."[297]

In *The Wall Street Journal,* which had bashed Keaton's casting months before, Julie Salamon wrote, "*Batman,* as directed by Tim Burton, may be descended from the cartoon original, but it is no action comic, nor does it have either the camp jokiness of the '60s television show or the slick cut-and-shoot of the *Superman* pictures. Though there's plenty of high-powered gimcrackery, especially the Batmobile, *Batman* is least compelling during its action sequences. The big confrontation between Batman and his nemesis, the Joker, seems almost like an afterthought. Mr. Burton and his associates had something more complex and fascinating in mind—and they almost pull it off."[298]

Variety, on the other hand, said, "Director Tim Burton effectively echoes the visual style of the original Bob Kane comics while conjuring up a nightmarish world of his own... What keeps the film arresting is the visual stylization. It was a shrewd choice for Burton to emulate the jarring angles and creepy lighting of film noir."[299]

In *USA Today,* talk-show host Larry King raved, "I finally got around to seeing *Batman.* Wow! This is easily one of the best movies I've ever seen in my life. There was not one minute where I was bored. The lighting was right on the mark, the direction superb and the performances flawless. If you don't enjoy this flick you are comatose, my friend."[300]

Many parents thought the film was too dark for small children, but they were only too happy to introduce their kids to reruns of the old Adam West *Batman* series on television. A San Diego station doubled its 6 P.M. ratings when it began running the classic TV show, and the WWOR superstation in Secaucus, New Jersey beat all the New York network affiliates in the ratings when it broadcast the 1966 *Batman* feature. Cable's Family Channel had been about to drop the series, until the ratings shot up after the release of the new *Batman* film.[301]

In the Bronx, a desire to see *Batman* cost one young man his life. Before the 12:30 AM screening began on July 3 at the Whitestone Cinemas complex, two men got into a dispute in the concessions line over the last remaining bag of popcorn. One of them said he was going out to his car to get his gun. The other said, "Go ahead." Minutes later, the men encountered each other again inside the theater. Both pulled guns and fired. One fell dead; the other, a black man about 19 years old, ran. Police recovered the victim's gun, a .38-caliber revolver, which had been reported stolen in Pennsylvania. Luckily, no other patrons in the theater were injured.[302]

Some European countries found the film too dark and violent for children. In Britain, the film became one of the first to carry the new "12" rating, which meant that children under 12 were barred from seeing the film regardless of their parents' supervision, while in Belgium, filmgoers under 16 were banned.[303]

In Canada, Montreal psychiatrist Dr. Yves Lamontagne, speaking for The Association of Quebec Psychiatrists, said, "The film, despite its undeniable cinematic qualities, is too intense and contains scenes of violence that are much too frightening for children under 10 years."[304] A Montreal father, Xavier Lefebvre, after taking his son to see *Batman*, responded, "If anyone is going to have nightmares about this, it's parents. They have to pay for the admission, for the comics, for the lunch pails, for all that Batman junk they are selling."[305]

With the release of the film, the merchandising campaign went into overdrive. *Batman* board games, bubble gum cards, books, bedspreads, toy Batmobiles, dolls, key chains, hats, raincoats, towels and hundreds of other items flooded store shelves— and quickly disappeared. J.C. Penny stores set up special "Batman shops" in 1,100 outlets.[306] By September, Licensing Corporation of America was reporting more than $300 million in retail sales, with Christmas season yet to come.[307] Retail sales ultimately outgrossed the film's worldwide box-office, hitting the $1.5 billion mark.[308] Black T-shirts with the yellow *Batman* logo brought in over $75 million;[309] the 30 million shirts sold caused a global shortage of black material.[310]

To celebrate both the release of the film and Batman's 50th anniversary, Chicagoland Processing Corp. released a set of three individually matched and numbered Batman medallions of 1-troy ounce pure silver with a retail price of $105. On one side of all three coins was the Batman logo and the words "50th anniversary." The other sides showed Batman, the Batmobile and the Joker. The sets were packaged in a box that opened like a book and featured information on the character and letters of authenticity. Only 5,000 of the sets were sold, but an additional 20,000 of each of the three designs were made available for individual purchase, with a price tag of $29.95 per coin.[311]

Taco Bell, which had a tie-in with *Batman*, did especially well. Over a period of four weeks, the chain gave away 21 million 32-oz. *Batman* cups, more than twice the amount initially planned. Tim Ryan, senior vice president of marketing for the food chain, said, "We had 50,000 employees wearing *Batman* T-shirts, and we had employees who came to work for us to get a shirt. We had pre-screenings in 64 of our 180 markets for our employees, just so they could give their opinion of the movie when they handed out the cups on the first day." Eight foot tall cardboard standees of Batman, *Batman* banners and counter displays used to advertise the promotion were stolen from dozens of Taco Bells nationwide.[312]

By November, *Batman,* having taken in $250 million in theatrical grosses, had become the sixth most successful film of all time. On the 15th of that month, while the film was still playing in theaters, Warner Bros. Home Video released it on videotape. In an era when videotapes were generally released six months or more after a film's release, it was a precedent-setting move. Also precedent-setting was the price. At that time, newly released videotapes were meant to be rented more than sold, and carried average price tags of $89.95. *Batman* retailed for $24.95, a price meant to generate sales, not rentals.[313] Retailers expected to sell from 9 million to 11 million videocassettes, resulting in $150 million in sales. The videotape came with an extra bonus. At the beginning of the tape was a commercial for Diet Coke, shot while the film was in production, featuring Michael Gough as Alfred calling a Gotham store to order the soda while Batman sped to pick it up in the Batmobile.[314]

The success of Batman came at an opportune time for Steve Ross. Warner Communications was now poised for a merger with Time Inc., a union that would produce the world's largest entertainment conglomerate. Time Inc. was part owner of the cable station HBO, as well as the publisher of 24 magazines, including *People, Sports Illustrated,* and *Time.* Warners had DC Comics, the world's largest record business, Warner Bros. studios, and the TV production company Lorimar. The success of *Batman* helped boost Warner Bros.' finances. In the second quarter of 1989, the company made $83 million, or 46 cents a share, compared with $69.9 million or 38 cents a share in the previous year's second quarter. Revenue rose from $1.13 billion to $1.3 billion.[315] During the merger negotiations, Warner CEO Steve Ross and Time Inc. CEO Richard Munro code-named themselves "Batman" and "Robin." The deal was placed in jeopardy when Paramount Communications Inc. tried a hostile run at Time, offering $200 a share. Ross and Munro nicknamed Paramount "The Joker."[316] To keep the offer from being put to a shareholder vote, Ross and Munro revised their deal; now, instead of Warner Communications making a debt-free purchase of Time Inc., Time would buy Warners for $14 billion, taking on $11 billion in debt. Upon completion of the deal, the new Time-Warners stock plummeted. Time's shareholders were furious that they had been denied the chance to vote on the Paramount offer. Tensions between Time Inc. and Warner Bros. increased when, shortly after the merger, Munro stepped down and Nicholas J. Nicholas Jr. became head of Time Inc. He often clashed with Ross, whose free-wheeling style offended his button-down sensibilities.[317]

With the sudden financial downturn that resulted from the Time-Warner merger, Warner Bros. needed another overwhelming success. They needed another *Batman.* A sequel, however, would be a long time coming.

1   Shapiro, Marc, "Dark Knight Director," *Starlog* #180, July 1992, p. 75

2   Cohen, Roger, "The Creator of Time Warner, Steven J. Ross, Is Dead at 65," *The New York Times*, Dec. 21, 1992, http://www.nytimes.com/1992/12/21/obituaries/the-creator-of-time-warner-steven-j-ross-is-dead-at-65.html?scp=2&sq=steve%20ross%20dead&st=cse, accessed Oct. 14, 2011

3   Jones, Gerard, *Men of Tomorrow: Geeks, Gangsters and the Birth of the Comic Book,* © 2004, Basic Books, New York, pg. 311

4   Cohen, Roger, "The Creator of Time Warner, Steven J. Ross, Is Dead at 65," *The New York Times*, Dec. 21, 1992, http://www.nytimes.com/1992/12/21/obituaries/the-creator-of-time-warner-steven-j-ross-is-dead-at-65.html?scp=2&sq=steve%20ross%20dead&st=cse, accessed Oct. 14, 2011

5   *Ibid.*

6   Jones, Gerard, *Men of Tomorrow: Geeks, Gangsters and the Birth of the Comic Book,* © 2004, Basic Books, New York, pg. 312

7   *Ibid.*, pg. 313

8   Cohen, Roger, "The Creator of Time Warner, Steven J. Ross, Is Dead at 65," *The New York Times*, Dec. 21, 1992, http://www.nytimes.com/1992/12/21/obituaries/the-creator-of-time-warner-steven-j-ross-is-dead-at-65.html?scp=2&sq=steve%20ross%20dead&st=cse, accessed Oct. 14, 2011

9   Interview with Michael Uslan, conducted Sept. 1, 2009

10   *Ibid.*

11   *Ibid.*

12   *Ibid.*

13   *Ibid.*

14   *Ibid.*

15   *Ibid.*

16   "Jett," "An Interview with Michael Uslan," *Batman-on-Film.com*, http://www.batman-on-film.com/interview_muslan_2.html, accessed July 5, 2010

17 Markoutsas, Elaine, "For 40 years, Kane has gone to bat for justice," *The Chicago Tribune*, November 8, 1979, p. A1

18 "Jett," "An Interview with Michael Uslan," *Batman-on-Film.com*, http://www.batman-on-film.com/interview_muslan_2.html, accessed July 5, 2010

19 Interview with Michael Uslan, conducted Sept. 1, 2009

20 *Ibid.*

21 Griffin, Nancy and Kim Masters, *Hit and Run: How Jon Peters and Peter Guber Took Sony for a Ride in Hollywood*, © 1996 Simon & Schuster, New York, p. 165

22 Pollock, Dale, "Producers Guber and Peters: An Endless Honeymoon?" *The Los Angeles Times*, July 26, 1981, p. M1

23 *Ibid.*, p. M30

24 Pirani, Adam, "A Dark Night in Gotham City," *Starlog* # 142, May 1989, p. 72

25 Griffin, Nancy and Kim Masters, *Hit and Run: How Jon Peters and Peter Guber Took Sony for a Ride in Hollywood*, © 1996 Simon & Schuster, New York, p. 165

26 Interview with Michael Uslan, conducted Sept. 1, 2009

27 Grant, Lee, "Sho-West: New Films Unveiled," *The Los Angeles Times*, Feb. 12, 1981, p. J1

28 Griffin, Nancy and Kim Masters, *Hit and Run: How Jon Peters and Peter Guber Took Sony for a Ride in Hollywood*, © 1996 Simon & Schuster, New York, p. 165

29 Cohen, Roger, "The Creator of Time Warner, Steven J. Ross, Is Dead at 65," *The New York Times*, Dec. 21, 1992, http://www.nytimes.com/1992/12/21/obituaries/the-creator-of-time-warner-steven-j-ross-is-dead-at-65.html?scp=2&sq=steve%20ross%20dead&st=cse, accessed Oct. 14, 2011

30 Interview with Tom Mankiewicz, conducted July 26, 2009

31 Interview with Michael Uslan, conducted Sept. 1, 2009

32 Interview with Tom Mankiewicz, conducted July 26, 2009

33 Pirani, Adam, "A Dark Night in Gotham City," *Starlog* # 142, May 1989, p. 72

34 Interview with Tom Mankiewicz, conducted July 26, 2009

35 *Ibid.*

36 *Ibid.*

37 Mankiewicz, Tom, *The Batman*, revised first draft screenplay, June 20, 1983

38 Interview with Tom Mankiewicz, conducted July 26, 2009

39 *Ibid.*

40 Interview with Michael Uslan, conducted Sept. 1, 2009

41 Interview with Tom Mankiewicz, conducted July 26, 2009

42 —, "Director Dante Has No Regrets About Batman Snub," *WENN*, http://www.imdb.com/name/nm0000474/news#ni3153117, accessed July 4, 2010

43 Interview with Tom Mankiewicz, conducted July 26, 2009

44 *Ibid.*

45 *Ibid.*

46 —, "'Batman' Premieres Tomorrow," *The Hawk Eye*, Burlington, Iowa, June 22, 1989, p. 6A

47 *Ibid.*

48 Pirani, Adam, "A Dark Night in Gotham City," *Starlog* # 142, May 1989, p. 40

49 Strauss, Bob, "Producers Try to Make Batman for All Seasons," *New Mexican*, Santa Fe, NM, June 23, 1989, p. C1

50 Adler, Shawn, with reporting by Josh Horowitz, "Bill Murray Longs For a More Heated Presidential Race...and a Girl Ghostbuster," *MTV.com*, http://www.mtv.com/news articles/1596656/20081008/story.jhtml, accessed July 7, 2010

51 Interview with Michael Uslan, conducted Sept. 1, 2009

52 *Ibid.*

53 Pond, Steve, "The Darker Side of Batman Emerges," *The Los Angeles Times*, Mar 15, 1986, p. H8

54 *Ibid.*

55 *Ibid.*

56 Broeske, Pat H., "Bat Guy's Back on Film With Some Advice From `Dad'—Bob Kane, Who Created the Caped Crusader in 1939, Is a Consultant on Warners' Big-Budget Batfeature," *The Los Angeles Times*, Oct 16, 1988, p. 27

57 *Ibid.*

58 Gelb, Jeff, "Bob Kane: 'I Never Talk About Batman. Actually, I'm Bruce Wayne," *Comics Interview   Super Special: Batman—Real Origins of the Dark Knight*, © 1989 Fictioneer Books Ltd., p. 120

59 Interview with Michael Uslan, conducted Sept. 1, 2009

60 Breskin, David, "Yaaarrrgghh!! The Tim Burton Interview," *Rolling Stone*, July 9th–23rd, 1992, p. 41

61 Salisbury, Mark, editor, *Burton on Burton*, © 1995 Faber & Faber Ltd., United Kingdom, p. 1

62 Breskin, David, "Yaaarrrgghh!! The Tim Burton Interview," *Rolling Stone*, July 9th-23rd, 1992, p. 41

63 Gerani, Gary, editor-in-chief, *The Batman Official Souvenir Magazine*, 1989 The Topps Company, Inc., New York, p. 60

64 Breskin, David, "Yaaarrrgghh!! The Tim Burton Interview," *Rolling Stone*, July 9th-23rd, 1992, p. 41

65 *Ibid.*, p. 40

66 Morgenstern, Joe, "Tim Burton, Batman and the Joker," *The New York Times*, Apr 9, 1989, p. A.45

67 Breskin, David, "Yaaarrrgghh!! The Tim Burton Interview," *Rolling Stone*, July 9th-23rd, 1992, p. 40

68 Morgenstern, Joe, "Tim Burton, Batman and the Joker," *The New York Times*, April 9, 1989, p. A.45

69 Griffin, Nancy and Kim Masters, *Hit and Run: How Jon Peters and Peter Guber Took Sony for a Ride in Hollywood*, © 1996 Simon & Schuster, New York, p. 165

70 Interview with Michael Uslan, conducted Sept. 1, 2009

71 Pirani, Adam, "A Dark Night in Gotham City," *Starlog* # 142, May 1989, p. 40

72 Mangels, Andy, "Burton-Hickson Batman Treatment Summary." *Wizard* # 11, July 1992, http://www.batmanmovieonline.com/articles.php?showarticle=49, accessed Aug. 8, 2010

73 *Ibid.*

74 Mougin, Lou, "Steve Englehart," *Comics Interview* #70, © 1989 Fictioneer Books Limited, New York, p. 32

75 *Ibid.*, p. 35

76 Gelb, Jeff, "Sam Hamm," *Comics Interview* #70, © 1989 Fictioneer Books Limited, New York, p. 9

77 *Ibid.*, p. 11

78 Gerani, Gary, editor-in-chief, *The Batman Official Souvenir Magazine*, 1989 The Topps Company, Inc., New York, p. 47

79 Gelb, Jeff, "Sam Hamm," *Comics Interview* #70, © 1989 Fictioneer Books Limited, New York, p. 15

80 Zehme, Bill, "No Joking: Keaton's Batman is Dead Serious," *The Daily Herald*, Chicago, IL, June 28, 1989, p. 3

81 Gerani, Gary, editor-in-chief, *The Batman Official Souvenir Magazine*, 1989 The Topps Company, Inc., New York, p. 15

82 Zehme, Bill, "No Joking: Keaton's Batman is Dead Serious," *The Daily Herald*, Chicago, IL, June 28, 1989, p. 3

83 Breskin, David, "Yaaarrrgghh!! The Tim Burton Interview," *Rolling Stone*, July 9th-23rd, 1992, p. 115

84 Gelb, Jeff, "Sam Hamm," *Comics Interview* #70, © 1989 Fictioneer Books Limited, New York, p. 23

85 *Ibid.*, p. 17

86 *Ibid.*, p. 21

87 *Ibid.*, p. 17

88 Salisbury, Mark (editor), *Burton on Burton*, © 1995 Faber and Faber, Ltd., London, p. 70

89 Griffin, Nancy and Kim Masters, *Hit and Run: How Jon Peters and Peter Guber Took Sony for a Ride in Hollywood*, © 1996 Simon & Schuster, New York, p. 166

90 Gelb, Jeff, "Sam Hamm," *Comics Interview* #70, © 1989 Fictioneer Books Limited, New York, p. 15

91 Jankiewicz, Pat, "The Dark Knight Revised," *Comics Scene* # 14, August 1990, Starlog Publications, p. 48

92 — ,"Warren Skaaren, 44; Fixed Movie Scripts," *The New York Times*, Dec 31, 1990, p. 1.24

93 Jankiewicz, Pat, "The Dark Knight Revised," *Comics Scene* # 14, August 1990, Starlog Publications, p. 49

94 *Ibid.*, p. 48

95 *Ibid.*

96 *Ibid.*

97 Zehme, Bill, "Batman: As the Classic Comic Becomes a Movie, Its Star Contemplates Life in the Bat Lane," *Rolling Stone*, June 29, 1989, p. 43

98 Pirani, Adam, "The Lord of Gotham City," *Starlog* # 145, Aug 1989, p. 37

99 Gelb, Jeff, "Sam Hamm," *Comics Interview* #70, © 1989 Fictioneer Books Limited, New York, p. 22

100 Jankiewicz, Pat, "The Dark Knight Revised," *Comics Scene* # 14, August 1990, Starlog Publications, p. 48-49

101 Gelb, Jeff, "Sam Hamm," *Comics Interview* #70, © 1989 Fictioneer Books, New York, p. 16

102 Hamm, Sam and Warren Skaaren, *Batman*, Fifth Draft Screenplay, Oct. 5, 1988

103 *Ibid.*

104 Jankiewicz, Pat, "The Dark Knight Revised," *Comics Scene* # 14, August 1990, Starlog Publications, p. 50

105 *Ibid.*, p. 48

106 *Ibid.*, p. 50

107 Pirani, Adam, "A Dark Night in Gotham City," *Starlog* # 142, May 1989, p. 40

108 Jankiewicz, Pat, "The Dark Knight Revised," *Comics Scene* # 14, August 1990, Starlog Publications, p. 49

109 Griffin, Nancy and Kim Masters, *Hit and Run: How Jon Peters and Peter Guber Took Sony for a Ride in Hollywood*, © 1996 Simon & Schuster, New York, p. 167

110 Pirani, Adam, "The Lord of Gotham City," *Starlog* # 145, Aug 1989, p. 40

111 Interview with Michael Uslan, conducted Sept. 1, 2009

112 Marriott, John, *Batman: The Official Book of the Movie*, © 1989 Mallard Press, New York & London, p. 88

113 Morgenstern, Joe, "Tim Burton, Batman and the Joker," *The New York Times*, April 9, 1989, p. A.45

114 —, "Robin Williams: 'I Would Do 'Batman' in a Second,'" *www.StarPulse.com*, posted June 30, 2010, http://www.starpulse.com/news/index.php/2010/06/30/robin_williamsi_would_do_batman_in_a_s, accessed August 16, 2010

115 —, "'Batman' Premieres Tomorrow," *The Hawk Eye*, Burlington, Iowa, June 22, 1989, p. 6A

116 McGilligan, Patrick, *Jack's Life: A Biography of Jack Nicholson*, © 1994 W.W. Norton and Co., New York, NY, p. 52

117 Thompson, Peter, *Jack Nicholson: The Life and Times of an Actor on the Edge*, © 1997 Birch Lane Press, p. 63

118 —, Interview with Tim Burton, "Shadows of the Bat: The Cinematic Saga of the Dark Knight Pt. 2: The Gathering Storm," *Batman* DVD Special Features, © 2005 Warner Bros. Entertainment Inc.

119 Thompson, Peter, *Jack Nicholson: The Life and Times of an Actor on the Edge*, © 1997 Birch Lane Press, p. 212

120 Griffin, Nancy and Kim Masters, *Hit and Run: How Jon Peters and Peter Guber Took Sony for a Ride in Hollywood*, © 1996 Simon & Schuster, New York, p. 167

121 Pirani, Adam, "A Dark Night in Gotham City," *Starlog* # 142, May 1989, p. 40

122 Thompson, Peter, *Jack Nicholson: The Life and Times of an Actor on the Edge*, © 1997 Birch Lane Press, p. 212

123 Griffin, Nancy and Kim Masters, *Hit and Run: How Jon Peters and Peter Guber Took Sony for a Ride in Hollywood*, © 1996 Simon & Schuster, New York, p. 168

124 Busch, Anita M., "Arnold's Hot Deal for Mr. Freeze," *Daily Variety*, June 18, 1996, p. 7

125 McGilligan, Patrick, *Jack's Life: A Biography of Jack Nicholson*, © 1994 W.W. Norton and Co., New York, NY, p. 360

126 Chaillet, Jean-Paul, "Joker of the Pack: Jack Nicholson at 54 Has Exalted Celebrity, Fabulous Wealth and His Feet Planted Firmly Atop the Hollywood Pile," *The Vancouver Sun*, Dec 17, 1991, p. C.1

127 Interview with Michael Uslan, conducted Sept. 1, 2009

128 Thompson, Peter, *Jack Nicholson: The Life and Times of an Actor on the Edge*, © 1997 Birch Lane Press, p. 213

129 McGilligan, Patrick, *Jack's Life: A Biography of Jack Nicholson*, © 1994 W.W. Norton and Co., New York, NY, p. 361

130 Broeske, Pat H., "Bat Guy's Back on Film With Some Advice From `Dad'—Bob Kane, Who Created the Caped Crusader in 1939, Is a Consultant on Warners' Big-Budget Batfeature," *The Los Angeles Times*, Oct 16, 1988, p. 27

131 *Ibid.*

132 Salisbury, Mark, editor, *Burton on Burton*, © 1995 Faber & Faber Ltd., United Kingdom, p. 80

133 Interview with Michael Uslan, conducted Sept. 1, 2009

134 Pirani, Adam, "A Dark Night in Gotham City," *Starlog* # 142, May 1989, p. 40

135 Zehme, Bill, "No Joking: Keaton's Batman is Dead Serious," *The Daily Herald*, Chicago, IL, June 28, 1989, p. 3

136 Interview with Michael Uslan, conducted Sept. 1, 2009

137 Zehme, Bill, "No Joking: Keaton's Batman is Dead Serious," *The Daily Herald*, Chicago, IL, June 28, 1989, p. 3

138 *Ibid.*

139 Shapiro, Marc, "Detective Comic," *Comics Scene* # 9, 1989, p. 34

140 Zehme, Bill, "No Joking: Keaton's Batman is Dead Serious," *The Daily Herald*, Chicago, IL, June 28, 1989, p. 3

141 Shapiro, Marc, "Detective Comic," *Comics Scene* # 9, 1989, p. 34

142 *Ibid.*, p. 35

143 Strauss, Bob, "Producers Try to Make Batman for All Seasons," *New Mexican*, Santa Fe, NM, June 23, 1989, p. C1

144 *Ibid.*

145 *Ibid.*

146 Singer, Michael, *Batman Returns: The Official Movie Book*, © 1992, Bantam Books, New York, p. 18

147 Zehme, Bill, "No Joking: Keaton's Batman is Dead Serious," *The Daily Herald*, Chicago, IL, June 28, 1989, p. 1

148 Gaul, Lou, "Michael Keaton Has His Own Timing, Rhythm and Spin," *The Intelligencer*, Doylestown, PA, p. C-4

149 *Ibid.*

150 *Ibid.*

151 Broeske, Pat H., "Bat Guy's Back on Film With Some Advice From 'Dad'—Bob Kane, Who Created the Caped Crusader in 1939, Is a Consultant on Warners' Big-Budget Batfeature," *The Los Angeles Times*, Oct 16, 1988, p. 27

152 Gelb, Jeff, "Bob Kane," *Comics Interview* #70, © 1989 Fictioneer Books Limited, New York, p. 50-51

153 *Ibid.*, p. 51

154 Martin, Sue and Pat H. Broeske, "Keaton Rattles Batman Buffs," *San Francisco Chronicle*, Sept. 14, 1988. p. E1

155 Broeske, Pat H., "Those Mean Guys From the Comics—A Slew of Characters Invade the Big Screen...and Most are as Bad as the Bad Guy'" *The Los Angeles Times*, Dec 11, 1988, p. 32

156 Hughes, Kathleen A., "Batman Fans Fear The Joke's on Them In Hollywood Epic— They Accuse Warner Bros. Of Plotting a Silly Spoof Of the Caped Crusader,' *Wall Street Journal*, Nov 29, 1988, p. 1

157 Martin, Sue and Pat H. Broeske, "Keaton Rattles Batman Buffs," *San Francisco Chronicle*, Sept. 14, 1988. p. E1

158 *Ibid.*

159 —, "'Batman' Premieres Tomorrow," *The Hawk Eye*, Burlington, Iowa, June 22, 1989, p. 6A

160 Zekas, Rita, "Batman Keaton Wards Off Enemies," *Toronto Star*, Oct 25, 1988, p. B.1

161 —, "'Batman' Premieres Tomorrow," *The Hawk Eye*, Burlington, Iowa, June 22, 1989, p. 6A

162 Strauss, Bob, "Producers Try to Make Batman for All Seasons," *New Mexican*, Santa Fe, NM, June 23, 1989, p. C1

163 Hughes, Kathleen A., "Batman Fans Fear The Joke's on Them In Hollywood Epic— They Accuse Warner Bros. Of Plotting a Silly Spoof Of the Caped Crusader,' *Wall Street Journal*, Nov 29, 1988, p. 1

164 *Ibid.*

165 *Ibid.*

166 Zehme, Bill, "No Joking: Keaton's Batman is Dead Serious," *The Daily Herald*, Chicago, IL, June 28, 1989, p. 3

167 Singer, Michael, *Batman Returns: The Official Movie Book*, © 1992, Bantam Books, New York, p. 21

168 *Ibid.*, p. 20

169 Corliss, Richard and Elaine Dutka, "Show Business: The Caped Crusader Flies Again," *Time* Magazine, Monday, Jun 19, 1989, http://www.time.com/time/magazine/article/0,9171,957980,00.html, accessed Oct. 1, 2010

170 Marriott, John, *Batman: The Official Book of the Movie*, © 1989 Mallard Press, New York & London, p. 47

171 Scott, Vernon, "Billy Dee Williams Masters Art," *Pacific Stars and Stripes*, June 10, 1989, p. 13

172 Gerani, Gary, editor-in-chief, *The Batman Official Souvenir Magazine*, 1989 The Topps Company, Inc., New York, p. 14

173 Nasr, Constantine, producer, "Batman Returns: Heroes: Alfred," *Batman Returns* DVD, New Wave Entertainment, © 2005 Warner Bros. Entertainment Inc.

174 Marriott, John, *Batman: The Official Book of the Movie*, © 1989 Mallard Press, New York & London, p. 56

175 *Ibid.*, p. 58

176 Jankiewicz, Pat, "The Dark Knight Revised," *Comics Scene* # 14, August 1990, Starlog Publications, p. 50

177 Beck, Marilyn, "Redford Plans Low-Budget Movie for His Next Project as Director," *St. Petersburg (Fl.) Times*. Oct 18, 1988. p. 3D

178 Pirani, Adam, "The Lord of Gotham City," *Starlog* # 145, Aug 1989, p. 38

179 *Ibid.*, p. 39

180 Griffin, Nancy and Kim Masters, *Hit and Run: How Jon Peters and Peter Guber Took Sony for a Ride in Hollywood*, © 1996 Simon & Schuster, New York, p. 169

181 *Ibid.*

182 —, "'Batman' Premieres Tomorrow," *The Hawk Eye*, Burlington, Iowa, June 22, 1989, p. 6A

183 Pirani, Adam, "The Lord of Gotham City," *Starlog* # 145, Aug 1989, p. 40

184 Beck, Marilyn, "Leonard Nimoy Recovers From Directing Emotional 'Good Mother,'" *Orange County Register*, Oct 28, 1988, p. 20

185 Marriott, John, *Batman: The Official Book of the Movie*, © 1989 Mallard Press, New York & London, p. 42

186 *Ibid.*, p. 93

187 Landis, Deborah Nadoolman, *Costume Design*, © 2003 Rotovision, East Sussex, England, p. 121

188 *Ibid.*p. 117

189 *Ibid.*, p. 118

190 *Ibid.*, p. 121

191 —, "Reinventing the Batsuit for the Modern Era," *AMCTV.com*, http://blogs.amctv.com/movie-blog/2007/06/reinventing-the.php, posted June 29, 2007, accessed August 29, 2010

192 Pirani, Adam, "Gotham's Gothic Glamour," *Comics Scene # 7*, 1989, p. 48

193 Marriott, John, *Batman: The Official Book of the Movie*, © 1989 Mallard Press, New York & London, p. 93

194 —, "Reinventing the Batsuit for the Modern Era," *AMCTV.com*, http://blogs.amctv.com/movie-blog/2007/06/reinventing-the.php, posted June 29, 2007, accessed August 29, 2010

195 Marriott, John, *Batman: The Official Book of the Movie*, © 1989 Mallard Press, New York & London, p. 93

196 *Ibid.*

197 —, "Reinventing the Batsuit for the Modern Era," *AMCTV.com*, http://blogs.amctv.com/movie-blog/2007/06/reinventing-the.php, posted June 29, 2007, accessed August 29, 2010

198 Gerani, Gary, editor-in-chief, *The Batman Official Souvenir Magazine*, 1989 The Topps Company, Inc., New York, p. 57

199 —, "Reinventing the Batsuit for the Modern Era," *AMCTV.com*, http://blogs.amctv.com/movie-blog/2007/06/reinventing-the.php, posted June 29, 2007, accessed August 29, 2010

200 *Ibid.*

201 Strauss, Bob, "Producers Try to Make Batman for All Seasons," *New Mexican*, Santa Fe, NM, June 23, 1989, p. C1

202 —, "Reinventing the Batsuit for the Modern Era," *AMCTV.com*, http://blogs.amctv.com/movie-blog/2007/06/reinventing-the.php, posted June 29, 2007, accessed August 29, 2010

203 Strauss, Bob, "Producers Try to Make Batman for All Seasons," *New Mexican*, Santa Fe, NM, June 23, 1989, p. C1

204 Singer, Michael, *Batman Returns: The Official Movie Book*, © 1992, Bantam Books, New York, p. 20

205 Gerani, Gary, editor-in-chief, *The Batman Official Souvenir Magazine*, 1989 The Topps Company, Inc., New York, p. 56

206 Boucher, Geoff, "Comic-Con 2010: Stallone Says 'Velcro Muscles' Made Old-School Stars Expendable," *The Los Angeles Times*, July 18, 2010, http://latimesblogs.latimes.com/herocomplex/2010/07/comiccon-2010-expendables-stallone-willis-schwarzenegger.html, accessed Aug. 8, 2010

207 Marriott, John, *Batman: The Official Book of the Movie*, © 1989 Mallard Press, New York & London, p. 94

208 Thompson, Peter, *Jack Nicholson: The Life and Times of an Actor on the Edge*, © 1997 Birch Lane Press, p. 215

209 Spillman, Susan, "Clothes Fit for a Joker," *USA Today*, Jun 29, 1989, p. 5.D

210 Gerani, Gary, editor-in-chief, *The Batman Official Souvenir Magazine*, 1989 The Topps Company, Inc., New York, p. 32

211 *Ibid.*

212 Bingham, Phillip, "The Batmobile: Making a Big Flap Over the World's Newest Supercar," *Motor Trend*, July 1989, p.58

213 *Ibid.*

214 Gerani, Gary, editor-in-chief, *The Batman Official Souvenir Magazine*, 1989 The Topps Company, Inc., New York, p. 32

215 Marriott, John, *Batman: The Official Book of the Movie*, © 1989 Mallard Press, New York & London, p. 72

216 *Ibid.*, p. 71

217 Zehme, Bill, "Batman: As the Classic Comic Becomes a Movie, Its Star Contemplates Life in the Bat Lane," *Rolling Stone*, June 29, 1989, p. 41

218 Burton, Tim, *Batman* DVD Audio Commentary, © 2009 Warner Home Video

219 Zehme, Bill, "Batman: As the Classic Comic Becomes a Movie, Its Star Contemplates Life in the Bat Lane," *Rolling Stone*, June 29, 1989, p. 39

220 Pirani, Adam, "The Lord of Gotham City," *Starlog # 145*, Aug 1989, p. 40

221 Jankiewicz, Pat, "The Dark Knight Revised," *Comics Scene # 14*, August 1990, Starlog Publications, p. 49

222 McGilligan, Patrick, *Jack's Life: A Biography of Jack Nicholson*, © 1994 W.W. Norton and Co., New York, NY, p. 361

223 Thompson, Peter, *Jack Nicholson: The Life and Times of an Actor on the Edge*, © 1997 Birch Lane Press, p. 213

224 *Ibid.*, p. 215

225 McGilligan, Patrick, *Jack's Life: A Biography of Jack Nicholson*, © 1994 W.W. Norton and Co., New York, NY, p. 361

226 Marriott, John, *Batman: The Official Book of the Movie*, © 1989 Mallard Press, New York & London, p. 52

227 Jankiewicz, Pat, "The Dark Knight Revised," *Comics Scene # 14*, August 1990, Starlog Publications, p. 49

228 —, "'Batman' Premieres Tomorrow," *The Hawk Eye*, Burlington, Iowa, June 22, 1989, p. 6A

229 Shapiro, Marc, "Detective Comic," *Comics Scene # 9*, 1989, p. 35

230 Pirani, Adam, "The Lord of Gotham City," *Starlog # 145*, Aug 1989, p. 40

231 Gaul, Lou, "Michael Keaton Has His Own Timing, Rhythm and Spin," *The Intelligencer*, Doylestown, PA, p. C-4

232 —, "Reinventing the Batsuit for the Modern Era," *AMCTV.com*, http://blogs.amctv.com/movie-blog/2007/06/reinventing-the.php, posted June 29, 2007, accessed August 29, 2010

233 Strauss, Bob, "Producers Try to Make Batman for All Seasons," *New Mexican*, Santa Fe, NM, June 23, 1989, p. C1

234 Gelb, Jeff, "Bob Kane," *Comics Interview #70*, © 1989 Fictioneer Books Limited, New York, p. 54

235 *Ibid.*

236 Breskin, David, "Yaaarrrgghh!! The Tim Burton Interview," *Rolling Stone*, July 9th-23rd, 1992, p. 116

237 Pirani, Adam, "The Lord of Gotham City," *Starlog # 145*, Aug 1989, p. 37

238 *Ibid.*, p. 38

239 Griffin, Nancy and Kim Masters, *Hit and Run: How Jon Peters and Peter Guber Took Sony for a Ride in Hollywood*, © 1996 Simon & Schuster, New York, p. 169

240 Breskin, David, "Yaaarrrgghh!! The Tim Burton Interview," *Rolling Stone*, July 9th-23rd, 1992, p. 40

241 Griffin, Nancy and Kim Masters, *Hit and Run: How Jon Peters and Peter Guber Took Sony for a Ride in Hollywood*, © 1996 Simon & Schuster, New York, p. 168

242 Pirani, Adam, "The Lord of Gotham City," *Starlog # 145*, Aug 1989, p. 38

243 Griffin, Nancy and Kim Masters, *Hit and Run: How Jon Peters and Peter Guber Took Sony for a Ride in Hollywood*, © 1996 Simon & Schuster, New York, p. 170

244 Pirani, Adam, "The Lord of Gotham City," *Starlog # 145*, Aug 1989, p. 38

245 Griffin, Nancy and Kim Masters, *Hit and Run: How Jon Peters and Peter Guber Took Sony for a Ride in Hollywood*, © 1996 Simon & Schuster, New York, p. 170

246 Gerani, Gary, editor-in-chief, *The Batman Official Souvenir Magazine*, 1989 The Topps Company, Inc., New York, p. 41

247 Zehme, Bill, "Batman: As the Classic Comic Becomes a Movie, Its Star Contemplates Life in the Bat Lane," *Rolling Stone*, June 29, 1989, p. 39

248 Breskin, David, "Yaaarrrgghh!! The Tim Burton Interview," *Rolling Stone*, July 9th-23rd, 1992, p. 116

249 Zehme, Bill, "Batman: As the Classic Comic Becomes a Movie, Its Star Contemplates Life in the Bat Lane," *Rolling Stone*, June 29, 1989, p. 41-42

250 Marriott, John, *Batman: The Official Book of the Movie*, © 1989 Mallard Press, New York & London, p. 83

251 *Ibid.*, p. 75

252 *Ibid.*, p. 74

253 *Ibid.*, p. 83

254 *Ibid.*, p. 74

255 *Ibid.*, p. 63

256 *Ibid.*, p. 66

257 *Ibid.*, p. 69

258 Strauss, Bob, "Producers Try to Make Batman for All Seasons," *New Mexican*, Santa Fe, NM, June 23, 1989, p. C1

259 Pirani, Adam, "A Dark Night in Gotham City," *Starlog # 142*, May 1989, p. 37

260 Griffin, Nancy and Kim Masters, *Hit and Run: How Jon Peters and Peter Guber Took Sony for a Ride in Hollywood*, © 1996 Simon & Schuster, New York, p. 172

261 *Ibid.*, p. 171

262 *Ibid.*, p. 171

263 *Ibid.*, p. 171-172

264 Zehme, Bill, "Batman: As the Classic Comic Becomes a Movie, Its Star Contemplates Life in the Bat Lane," *Rolling Stone*, June 29, 1989, p. 63

265 Griffin, Nancy and Kim Masters, *Hit and Run: How Jon Peters and Peter Guber Took Sony for a Ride in Hollywood*, © 1996 Simon & Schuster, New York, p. 172

266 Zehme, Bill, "Batman: As the Classic Comic Becomes a Movie, Its Star Contemplates Life in the Bat Lane," *Rolling Stone*, June 29, 1989, p. 41

267 *Ibid.*, p. 3

268 Shapiro, Marc, "Detective Comic," *Comics Scene # 9*, 1989, p. 35

269 Griffin, Nancy and Kim Masters, *Hit and Run: How Jon Peters and Peter Guber Took Sony for a Ride in Hollywood*, © 1996 Simon & Schuster, New York, p. 168

270 Breskin, David, "Yaaarrrgghh!! The Tim Burton Interview," *Rolling Stone*, July 9th-23rd, 1992, p. 40

271 Interview with Danny Elfman, *MovieTime*, 1990, http://www.songdad.com/down-load/-7w1LkMHsUw/Danny_Elfman_interview_on_Movie.html

272 Garcia, Jr., René S., "Interview Danny Elfman: Composing Alice in Wonderland," *Buzzine*, http://www.buzzine.com/2010/03/interview-with-danny-elfman/, accessed Sept. 5, 2010

273 Interview with Danny Elfman, *MovieTime*, 1990, http://www.songdad.com/down-load/-7w1LkMHsUw/Danny_Elfman_interview_on_Movie.html

274 Hentschel, Joachim, "At home with Prince; No tape recorder, no phones, no camera—when Joachim Hentschel was granted a rare interview with Prince at Paisley Park he was told all he could bring with him was 'vibes' At home with Prince," *The Times. London*, July 24, 2010, pg. 1

275 Breskin, David, "Yaaarrrgghh!! The Tin Burton Interview," *Rolling Stone*, July 9th-23rd, 1992, p. 116

276 *Ibid.*

277 —, "Batman Theme," *Wikipedia*, http://en.wikipedia.org/wiki/Batman_Theme, accessed Sept. 5, 2010

278 Newman, Melinda, "Holy Soundtracks, Batman! There's Two!" *Billboard # 101*, June 24, 1989, p. 4

279 *Ibid.*

280 Grein, Paul, "With Prince or Elfman, It's a Case for `Batman,'" *The Los Angeles Times*, July 16, 1989, p. 76

281 Griffin, Nancy and Kim Masters, *Hit and Run: How Jon Peters and Peter Guber Took Sony for a Ride in Hollywood*, © 1996 Simon & Schuster, New York, p. 170

282 Interview with Michael Uslan, conducted Sept. 1, 2009

283 Stewart, Al, "'Batman' Pirates Beware: Warner Is On Your Case" *Billboard # 101*, June 24, 1989, p. 4

284 Broeske, Pat H. and Jack Mathews, "Troubles in Gotham Village Warners Eschews Batbash," *The Los Angeles Times*, June 8, 1989, http://articles.latimes.com/1989-06-08/entertainment/ca-1890_1_caped-crusader-gotham-batman-howard, accessed Sept. 12, 2010

285 Jeannie Williams, Jeannie, "That Jack, Ever a Joker," *USA Today*, June 21, 1989, p. 2.D

286 Spillman, Susan, "Will Batman Fly? Get Ready for Summer's Most-Hyped Movie," *USA Today*, June 19, 1989, p. 1.A

287 Jankiewicz, Pat, "The Dark Knight Revised," *Comics Scene # 14*, August 1990, Starlog Publications, p. 49

288 Interview with Michael Uslan, conducted Sept. 1, 2009

289 El Nasser, Haya, "No Joker! Batbash lures Time, Warner," USA Today, June 23, 1989, pg. 2.B

290 —, "'Batman' Premieres Tomorrow," *The Hawk Eye*, Burlington, Iowa, June 22, 1989, p. 6A

291 Griffin, Nancy and Kim Masters, *Hit and Run: How Jon Peters and Peter Guber Took Sony for a Ride in   Hollywood*, © 1996 Simon & Schuster, New York, p. 172

292 *Ibid.*, p. 173

293 Gaul, Lou, "Michael Keaton Has His Own Timing, Rhythm and Spin," *The Intelligencer*, Doylestown, PA, p. C-4

294 Canby, Vincent, "Nicholson and Keaton Do Battle in 'Batman,'" *The New York Times*, June 23, 1989, http://movies.nytimes.com/movie/review?res=950DE7D9133BF930A15755C0A96F948260, accessed Sept. 12, 2010

295 Corliss, Richard, "Show Business: Murk in the Myth," *Time* Magazine, June 19, 1989, http://www.time.com/time/magazine/article/0,9171,957972,00.html, accessed Oct. 1, 2010

296 Bahr, Jeff, "Batman Review," *Omaha World-Herald*, June 23, 1989, p. 33

297 Strickler, Jeff, "'BATMAN': The Joke's on the Caped Crusader, and Nicholson is Great," *Minneapolis Star Tribune*, June 23, 1989, p. 1.E

298 Salamon, Julie, "Film: All-New 'Batman' Is Sinister, Not Silly," *The Wall Street Journal*, June 22, 1989, p. 1

299 Variety Staff, "Batman," *Variety*, Dec. 31, 1988, http://www.variety.com/review/VE1117788899.html?categoryid=31&cs=1, accessed Sept. 12, 2010

300 King, Larry, "Povich Puts His `Affair' in Order," *USA Today*, July 24, 1989. p. 2.D

301 Stein, Joe, "TV Stations Have Jumped on the Batwagon," *The San Diego Tribune*, Sept. 7, 1989, p. D.1

302 James, George, "Movie Fan Is Killed In Theater Argument Over a Popcorn Line," *The New York Times*, July 4, 1989, http://www.nytimes.com/1989/07/04/nyregion/movie-fan-is-killed-in-theater-argument-over-a-popcorn-line..html?scp=631&sq=batman&st=nyt, accessed June 8, 2011

303 Snow, Shauna and Aleene MacMinn, "First Off..." *The Los Angeles Times*, Sept. 11, 1989, p. 2

304 —, "Batman Movie Too Frightening for Young Children: Psychiatrist," *The Ottawa Citizen*, July 13, 1989, p. D.14

305 —, "Bat Fatigue," *The Globe and Mail*, July 15, 1989, p. D.6

306 Liles-Morris, Shelley, "'Batman' Rules Tie-In Roost," *USA Today*, Sept. 6, 1989, p. 1.A

307 Elias, Thomas, "The Batman T-shirt Toll: $75 Million," *The Ottawa Citizen*, Sep 14, 1989, p. D.15

308 —, "Licensees Strut Stuff," *Daily Variety*, June 19, 1995, p. 33

309 Elias, Thomas, "The Batman T-shirt Toll: $75 Million," *The Ottawa Citizen*, Sep 14, 1989, p. D.15

310 James, Alison, "'Star Wars' Brand Stays Hot," *Daily Variety*, Oct. 19, 2005, p. 8

311 —, "Batman Silver Coins are Issued Series," *St. Petersburg Times*, July 23, 1989 p. 9.H

312 Takahashi, Dean, "Taco Bell Link to `Batman' Proves a Flying Success," *The Orange County Register*, Aug. 13, 1989, p. M.4

313 —, "'Batman' Video Sets Precedent With Early Release, Low Price," *Austin American Statesman*, Sep 22, 1989, p. E.5

314 Atkinson, Terry, "Video...What's New: `Batman' Buyers to Get a Diet Coke Ad Too," *The Los Angeles Times*, Sept. 8, 1989, p. 18

315 —, "Batman Helps Send Warner Profit Flying," *The Globe and Mail*, July 19, 1989, p. B.7

316 El Nasser, Haya, "No Joker! Batbash lures Time, Warner," *USA Today*, June 23, 1989, pg. 2.B

317 Cohen, Roger, "The Creator of Time Warner, Steven J. Ross, Is Dead at 65," *The New York Times*, Dec. 21, 1992, http://www.nytimes.com/1992/12/21/obituaries/the-creator-of-time-warner-steven-j-ross-is-dead-at-65.html?scp=2&sq=steve%20ross%20dead&st=cse, accessed Oct. 14, 2011

Chapter Seven:
BATMAN RETURNS

"In retrospect I don't think Warners were very happy with the movie. That's my feeling."
—Tim Burton[1]

BACK IN THE BATCAVE

As soon as it became apparent that *Batman* was a monster hit, producer Jon Peters began talking sequel, sort of. "We conceptualized this film as a trilogy," said Peters. "We wouldn't make a sequel, but we may well make a second episode." Peters noted that neither director Tim Burton nor any of the film's stars had signed for any more Batman films. "It's not in their contracts and we really haven't talked about it to anyone," he said. Asked if the Joker would return, Peters said coyly, "He could come back. He's the Joker."[2] A month later, Peters hinted that a sequel might be in theaters as early as the summer of 1990, with a third film in release by 1991. If Keaton and Nicholson were unable or unwilling to reprise their roles, said Peters, new actors might be used. A Warner Bros. executive said, "The sets are taking up an entire movie studio outside London. We obviously can't leave them there forever, so it's reasonable to expect action pretty soon." Even Jack Nicholson was playing it close to the vest, telling *Daily Variety*, "They'd be fools not to do another," though when asked if he would return, he said, "I would not discuss (the possibilities) with anybody. There is too much money involved."[3]

The talk of a potential sequel to *Batman* had Hollywood A-listers lining up for the anticipated blockbuster. In mid-August 1989, gossip columnist Liz Smith reported that Madonna, who had just completed work on *Dick Tracy*, had her agents negotiating for a role for her in *Batman II*.[4] Guber and Peters were also said to be negotiating with Danny DeVito to play a villain, which *The Toronto Globe and Mail* identified as the Riddler.[5]

As eager as Peters was to proceed, Tim Burton was reticent, having found the *Batman* experience a rather stressful one, and not one he was very eager to repeat. Although audiences made *Batman* the sixth highest-grossing film of all time, the more distance Burton had from it, the more he felt that it hadn't lived up to his own personal expectations. "The studio wanted to make a sequel the moment they knew the first film was successful, which was right after the opening weekend," Burton said in an interview with *Starlog* magazine's Marc Shapiro. "I was in no way, shape or form to do it at that point...I would just keep looking at it and think it could have been better. I saw the first movie as being flawed. I didn't like the tone—what I did with the elements of darkness and mood, and the character relationships. I felt like I hadn't done 100 percent of what I wanted to do with that picture, and part of me felt that I wanted another chance at it."[6]

Instead of immediately leaping into a *Batman* sequel, Burton sought to return to a more personal story, one that originated in his own brain and not in a decades-old comic book. His next film, *Edward Scissorhands,* had an almost comic-book look, and a storyline with a theme that could just as easily have applied to *Batman*—an emotionally wounded protagonist with unique talents becomes viewed as a threat by the community at large, even though his intentions are honorable. A much smaller and more personal film than *Batman, Edward Scissorhands* connected with audiences on a more emotional level, cementing Burton's reputation as a filmmaker with a special affinity for dark, twisted fantasy tales. Released just before Christmas of 1990, the film—which was budgeted at $20 million—made over $83 million worldwide.

Tempering Burton's joy over the warm critical reception of *Edward Scissorhands* was the sobering news that Warren Skaaren, who helped bring the script of *Batman* into focus, had died at his home in Austin, Texas. The 44-year-old screenwriter had only learned the previous summer, after he had completed the script for *Beetlejuice II*, that he had cancer. Three days after Christmas, on December 28, 1990, Skaaren lost his battle with the disease. "I think it was some weird sort of bone cancer," said Burton, "something strange. It was horrible."[7]

With Skaaren's death, Burton felt even less like tackling a *Batman* sequel. Warner Bros., feeling that the director was an essential ingredient in the success of *Batman*, decided to wait him out. As for producer Michael Uslan, he viewed a years-long gap between the original film and the sequel as nothing unusual. "You've got to go back to the context of the times," said Uslan. "Everyone was pretty tied in to the James Bond formula. And, if memory serves me, the Bond films were coming out at a pace of every three years. And I think that was just accepted as the standard for those few movies and sequels."[8] Uslan had little time to worry; he kept busy as executive producer of three TV series, *Swamp Thing, Fish Police* and *Where in the World is Carmen Sandiego?,* and was already laying plans for a prime-time *Batman* animated series.

After a year had passed, Warner Bros. execs finally began to lose patience. They eventually contacted Burton and asked, was he going to do the sequel or not? "I felt, for the longest time, I didn't want to do it," said the director. "Then one day, I realized I liked this world and it's a good canvas for different ideas and themes: politics, sexism, relationships, weird family issues."[9] It helped that Jon Peters, who had been a meddlesome presence during the making of the first *Batman*, was no longer actively involved in production of the sequel. A few months after the release of *Batman*, the Guber-Peters Entertainment Company was acquired by Japan's Sony Corporation, which had also swallowed up Columbia Pictures. Guber and Peters accepted a deal to take charge of Columbia. As part of their deal with Sony, the pair had to give up any profit participation they might have realized from any *Batman* sequels.[10] With Guber and Peters out, this meant that *Batman Returns* would be Burton's baby. Unlike *Batman*, for which he served only as the director, he was also a producer on *Batman Returns*. As scriptwriter Sam Hamm recalled, "Finally, the way that they kind of got Tim was to say, 'What if the second movie is really just a Tim Burton movie?' And that kind of got his attention and got him thinking about what he could do with it again."[11]

It also helped that Burton had gotten past thinking that the next Batman film had to outperform the original. "Part of me will always think *Batman* was a big hit because it was a wonderful movie," said Burton. "But the reality is that *Batman* was a success because it was a cultural phenomenon, which had less to do with the movie than with something else that I can't begin to put a finger on. I didn't see a second Batman movie falling victim to the same thing that happened with the first, so I felt free to just go in and make the best Batman movie I could."[12]

Burton now had his own production company, Tim Burton Productions, which he had formed after the release of *Batman* in 1989 with former journalist-turned-producer Denise Di Novi. The same year of *Batman's* release, Di Novi produced a black comedy about teen suicide, *Heathers*. She then made another film, *Meet the Applegates* (1991), before joining with Burton to produce *Edward Scissorhands*. "Tim is unique in that he's a commercially successful director who doesn't make mainstream movies," said Di Novi. "There's a simplicity and underlying sweetness to his work that embraces the outcast and differences in people. I think that's why his films are so accessible to moviegoers, and that certainly attracted me to working with him."[13] Di Novi shared Burton's assessment that the new film would never match the success of the previous *Batman*. "There's no way we can repeat *Batman's* success," said Di Novi. "The pressure's really off and we can relax. Nobody in their wildest dreams thinks we're going to catch lightning in a bottle a second time. But, having said that, we can just make the best movie we can—maybe even a better movie."[14]

Daily Variety announced that Tim Burton had agreed to direct the sequel to *Batman* on August 6, 1990.[15] Now that Burton had finally agreed to do the film, the first order of business was to come up with a workable screenplay. With Warren Skaaren deceased, Burton reunited with his original *Batman* scribe, Sam Hamm. "Tim and I had several kind of loose conversations about where the movie would go with input from the studio," said Hamm. "They really wanted the Penguin, because they sort of saw the Penguin as the number two Batman villain."[16] Burton wasn't thrilled about the Penguin, a character that he felt lacked the backstory and psychological complexity of the Joker.[17] "We wanted to do Catwoman," said Hamm, "so we wound up doing Penguin and Catwoman."[18]

In Burton's mind, pitting Batman against two adversaries would help differentiate the second film from the first. "I didn't feel having two villains was absolutely necessary," he said, "but it added some variety by helping us avoid doing the same kind of explanation things we did with the one villain in the first film."[19]

Burton felt he had a pretty good handle on the psychology of Batman and Catwoman, but the Penguin proved more elusive. "The Penguin was just this guy with the cigarette and the top hat, you know," said Burton. "So, we then started thinking about the Catwoman, Batman, sort of these animal people, the Penguin, and started thinking about him, trying to define a profile for him. So it was fun to kind of come up with a sort of bad freak, again that duality of somebody who's been sort of wronged and you know has that sort of split not like dark but sort of human animal, you know, and sort of using the animal motif as a strong image for the film. And then I started getting excited about it."[20]

Hamm set about writing the screenplay, with ideas from his producers and the studio, who felt that Robin—since he had been absent from the first film—had to somehow be included. Hamm obliged, but in a way that veered considerably from the way the character was presented in the comic books, making Dick Grayson a feral wild child who lived in a drainage tunnel.

Hamm also toyed with Bruce Wayne's family history, radically altering the origin of Batman that had been accepted by comic book fans for decades. In Hamm's story, Bruce Wayne's grandfather was one of a gang of five wealthy men who robbed the Gotham Treasury in the 1800s. After stealing the city's money, the city fathers needed help to rescue the bankrupt city. The same five men came forward, offering to help in return for all the service contracts and public lands, which they divided among themselves. Within five years, they were wealthy beyond imagining. These "five families" of Gotham never needed to use the money they raided from the Treasury. They had five ravens made that, when placed together, revealed the secret of where the stolen money was hidden. Since they never needed to use it, they passed the secret down from father to son through the generations. When Bruce's father, Thomas Wayne, heard the tale, he was going to expose the crime, but descendants from the other families arranged to have him murdered. Bruce then grew up in wealth without knowing the secret of its source.

Hamm's script also introduced an idea that was eventually dropped. When Bruce Wayne, at a society party at the Flugelheim Museum, goes to kiss Selina Kyle, he sneezes in her face. He tells her that he's allergic to cats; her cat Hecate has, coincidentally, just rubbed against his leg.

The script ended with Catwoman and Penguin invading Bruce Wayne's mansion. Catwoman immobilizes Bruce Wayne by kissing him while wearing paralysis-inducing lipstick. He's tied up and Alfred and Vicki Vale are taken hostage. Dick Grayson, meanwhile, having been taken in by Bruce, attempts to flee the mansion, but when he sees the intruders, he has a change of heart. He helps Bruce escape, leading to a final showdown between Batman and Catwoman in which Catwoman is killed. Batman then goes to the Batcave, where the Penguin has discovered that Bruce and Batman are one and the same, and also discovered the hidden gold from the Gotham Treasury in a stalactite. Before he can extract it, however, Batman uses a sonic device that causes bats to swarm around the Penguin, and he goes plummeting into the abyss of the cave.

Neither the studio nor Burton felt that Hamm's script quite hit the mark. In an interview for the documentary *Shadows of the Bat—The Cinematic Saga of the Dark Knight—Dark Side of the Knight*, produced by Constantine Nasr for the DVD release of *Batman Returns*, Hamm admitted, "Most of the stuff that I had done for that movie wound up being scrapped. And the decision that came out of that was just to basically go with pretty much a whole new direction for the story."[21]

It was clear that a fresh take was needed, and Burton and his co-producer, Denise Di Novi, knew just the man for the job. They put in a call to Daniel Waters, whose script for 1989's *Heathers*, which Di Novi produced, had catapulted the former video store employee to the A-list rank of writers. Waters and Burton knew each other from when the director was looking for a writer to do a *Beetlejuice* sequel. They clicked creatively, but no script came out of it. Now, Waters was in Italy, where his *Hudson Hawk* script was being rewritten on a daily basis. "I was definitely in a get-me-off-this-picture kind of mood," said Waters.[22]

At Burton's urging, Waters returned to the U.S. in mid-1990 and read Hamm's script. "Tim had the attitude of, 'I dare you to make me want to make this movie.' He had some ideas, but he did not have a story. He would have been very happy with five years, 20 different screenwriters and still not being satisfied. He definitely had the desire, but not the urge, to climb back up and do another Batman movie."[23]

Waters read Hamm's script and began brainstorming with the director. "Dan's a very interesting writer with a funny point-of-view, and he proved to be just the person I needed," said Burton. "The ideas were flying back and forth. We were attempting to piece together a story based on characters and a world that had no basis in reality...it was a matter of going through ideas to try and get a perspective, and to figure out what the hell this *Batman Returns* thing was all about."[24] In an interview with *Starlog*'s Marc Shapiro, Burton said, "Unlike Superman, Batman isn't simply a good-vs.-evil thing. You get a lot of gray areas with Batman, and that was a major consideration in the script's development. I wanted the villains to be these weird but interesting characters who could fill in those gray areas in Batman's life."[25]

Before writing began, Burton took the writer on several field trips. "On our first meeting, we went down to Sea World and looked at penguins, to get some idea of how the Penguin should look," said Waters. "The story meetings themselves were kind of minimalist in nature. The only thing Tim knew was that he wanted the Penguin and Catwoman in the film. So we would sit around and just throw ideas at each other. He would be sitting on his black leather couch, and if he responded to an idea of mine favorably, I would know it immediately, because he would sort of rise out of the couch and his eyes would light up."[26]

Taking Burton's ideas into account, Waters discarded the backstory about the founding fathers of Gotham and fashioned a new plot that involved millionaire department store owner Max Shreck conspiring to take control of Gotham City by unseating the mayor with a candidate of his own choosing, Oswald Cobblepot, a/k/a the Penguin. Selina Kyle is introduced as Shreck's secretary, who becomes Catwoman after Shreck pushes her out of a high window and she is revived by alley cats. Shreck, a character who had no antecedent in the Batman comic books, was named after Max Schreck, the actor who portrayed the Dracula-inspired Count Orlock in director F.W. Murnau's classic 1922 horror film, *Nosferatu*.

Waters' script was very close to the eventual film, though the initial draft he turned in on May 20, 1991 had some significant differences. In the prologue, which establishes how the Penguin came into being, the deformed infant has an "angelic" looking older brother, who peers into his cage in horror. The script's finale reveals that Max Shreck is the Penguin's brother. Waters had a difficult time getting a handle on the Penguin's character. In the first draft, he made the villain "a rude gangster type," said Waters. "But, as Tim and I discussed it, we agreed that for the Penguin to work he had to come across as more animalistic."[27]

As in Hamm's script, the Penguin and Catwoman join forces, committing crimes and framing Batman for them. Waters dropped Vicki Vale from the story, only having her mentioned in a scene where Alfred is trimming a Christmas tree while Bruce Wayne watches a newscast. "Oh look," says the butler, holding an ornament in his hand that says "Vicki," "do you remember...It's from the Christmas just before

Ms. Vale decided to leave Gotham City and..." "I remember," says Bruce. "Merry Christmas, Vicki Vale, wherever the hell you are." Bruce then "sadly throws the ornament past an alarmed Alfred, into a raging fireplace. A popping noise booms out."

Unlike the film, where Shreck's son Chip meets his demise in the climax, the script does away with him in a bizarre scene about a third of the way through, when Chip goes to Selina's apartment after she's become Catwoman. He opens her door to see that she's dressed in a strategically placed long black scarf—and nothing else. But as he enters the apartment, he finds that the pink carpet beneath him is really pink quicksand, and he disappears out of sight.

A constant in every iteration of the script was the underlying sexual attraction between Batman and Catwoman. "I felt that Catwoman, because of her circumstances in life, would allow me to explore some of the relevant themes of female rage in modern society," said Waters. "She is having to deal with the drive to fall in love while, at the same time, also fighting an id with the urge to kick the shit out of somebody. Catwoman gave me the opportunity to take some of those themes to the farthest possible point."[28]

It's in Waters's script that, during the fight scene between Batman and Catwoman, the feline villainess straddles the Dark Knight and licks him. Waters tapped into another aspect of Batman's personality—his disappointment that people see him more as a celebrity than a symbol. In Waters's script, after Catwoman destroys Shreck's department store, Batman pursues her up onto the rooftops, where he says to her, "People hurt each other, they lie to each other, they're more interested in what I drive, than what I stand for. I need their intelligence, they give me their lunch boxes." Waters also retains another idea from Hamm's script. When Bruce Wayne meets Selina Kyle on the street, they talk and become cozier with each other, until he goes in to kiss her and sneezes. He tells her he's allergic to cats; it turns out there's a tomcat nearby.

At this relatively late stage, the studio was still urging the filmmakers to include Robin in the plot. Waters discarded the feral wild-child teenager of Hamm's draft, but came up with a take on the character that was still far removed from his comic book origin. Late in the second act of the script, Batman is looking for a way to deactivate the Penguin's remote-control device from his Batmobile. He wrests control of the car long enough to crash it into a garage, where a "kid" mechanic who is a Batman fanatic helps him un-booby-trap the car. The kid also fights off some of the Penguin's goons with deft martial arts moves. As they continue to come under attack, Batman and the kid leap into the Batmobile—with the kid in the driver's seat. As he maneuvers the car past the Penguin's men, it jettisons its sides and becomes a streamlined missile-type vehicle. When Batman finally stops to let the kid out and peels away, the kid wipes some muck off his uniform, revealing a round patch with an "R" on it. The mechanic reappears at the end, using a descrambler he took off the Batmobile to help Batman neutralize the Penguin's bomb-toting penguin army. Recalling his and Burton's efforts to work Robin into the story, Waters recalled, "I could tell he was not enthusiastic about it from the get-go. But we went in more of a thing like it was something that would be hinted at, and then developed in a later movie."[29]

Waters was pleased with his final script, though he realized it was overly ambitious. "That first draft was hilarious," he said. "I wound up with 160 pages that would have cost $400 million and taken three years to film. We all had a good laugh at it, and then set about making things a little saner."[30] According to Di Novi, Burton was excited by Waters' script. "He said, 'Whether or not this is a Batman movie, I would make this movie,'" said Di Novi. "He felt that it was true enough to the real spirit of Batman, that it had a great story and that the Penguin and Catwoman characters excited him as much as Batman did."[31]

Waters was asked to write a second draft, then a third, and then a fourth. "It wasn't a bad experience," said Waters, "but it was definitely a brutal one. I was writing something that everybody had an opinion about. Everybody from the studio executives on down had read Batman comics and seen the first movie. Three times a day, I would hear things like, 'Batman wouldn't do that,' or 'Bruce Wayne wouldn't use toothpaste.' There was a constant battering involved in the writing of the script, and it got to be a bit much after a while."[32]

Although he had managed to flesh out the villains, Waters and Burton clashed over the writer's depiction of Batman. "Most of my drafts painted Batman as a very burned-out, cynical person," said Waters. "He kept asking himself why he always comes to the rescue of Gotham City, whose citizens are so gullible that they will always be taken in by criminals. In my drafts, when the Penguin begins his rise to power. Batman's response was that Gotham City was getting exactly what it deserved. Tim and Michael [Keaton] both had a problem with the fact that I had made him too aware and openly reflective. They still saw him as a wounded soul and so, in the succeeding drafts, a lot of the cynicism disappeared."[33]

"I was taking a much more operatic approach to the material than Tim was after. Tim wanted changes made, and I was not doing them. After the fifth draft, I was burned out and very angry that certain changes were being asked for. So Tim finally felt it was easier to get another writer than to keep fighting with me about changes he wanted."[34]

With Waters exhausted of ideas, Burton reached out to Wesley Strick. The New York-born writer made his debut with the script for the legal thriller *True Believers* (1989), followed by a rewrite of Don Jakoby's *Arachnophobia* (1990). In 1991, he was given the task of updating the classic 1962 thriller *Cape Fear* for director Martin Scorsese. By the time Strick turned in his August 1, 1991 draft of *Batman Returns*, the script was substantially what would end up on-screen. "Strick was basically brought in as the Terminator," said Waters. "His was more a matter of maintenance—to throw out most of my wild dialogue and make things a little less severe. He basically lightened things up and brought the script out of the shadows. The changes were minor and it's still essentially my script, so I guess I can't complain too much."[35] Strick's script introduced the political angle, with Shreck forcing a recall of the Mayor and an election. All thoughts of Shreck and the Penguin being related had been dropped, as had any mention of Robin.

"At some point, there was a discussion of Robin," said Burton, "and again, the only way I could see it was to try and find a profile that worked." In their attempts to make the character modern and relevant, Burton, his writers and the studio had contemplated making Robin black; before the character was dropped from the script,

Jim Lawson

What ended up happening was again, I
had too many characters," said Burton,
en without Robin, they complained that
there was always the idea that the third
it as a potentially ongoing thing, maybe,
do it in this one, we'll do it in the next
ee the sidekick go. He told a newspaper
Batman where he is this lone figure, and

the *Batman* films as a potentially never-
nxious to wring every cent out of every
dising arrangements as possible. From the
, this focus on maximizing the marketing
ho found that if toy manufacturers and
ducts coming out concurrently with the
nd production deadlines into account.

Burton recalled, "Unlike the first one, before I started the second one, toy companies and t-shirt makers are asking, 'Well, what's this character going to look like?' And I was having these meetings where it was like, 'We haven't designed the character yet.'"[39]

STARTING FROM SCRATCH

Once Burton had a script ready, the next task was convincing Michael Keaton to reprise the title role. When the actor made the first *Batman*, there was no clause in his contract requiring him to appear in a sequel.[40] One plus for the actor was the realization that he had already proven himself with the first film; this time around, he wouldn't have to face the maelstrom of negative publicity that erupted over his casting in *Batman*. "Any problems I had with the fans on the first film are over," said Keaton. "I don't think there's any doubt that I can play this guy. I'm so convinced of that fact that I have to admit that it would be pretty strange to see someone else playing Batman. I would be curious to see if somebody else could pull it off, and if he was really good. I would probably be very upset. It could happen, but I'm not going to worry about it... Playing Batman has definitely turned up the volume on my career four or five notches. Nobody could be more appreciative of the opportunities this role has given me. It's nice to walk down the street and have kids get excited. I don't have the anonymity that I had before *Batman*, but that came as no surprise. I knew I would lose that when I agreed to do these films."[41]

Tim Burton felt the lure for Keaton was much the same as it was for him, the chance to revisit the character with other actors in other situations. "I don't think it was the joy of climbing back into the suit," said Burton. By the spring of 1991, Keaton had agreed to come aboard, saying, "I like the story idea. I liked the idea of the two villains, and I loved the idea that Tim was going to do it again."[42] Keaton went into a rigorous training program to get into shape. As with the first film, he began working with British martial arts and kickboxing champion Dave Lea, who said, "Michael was an incredibly fast learner on the first *Batman*, and by now there isn't much more I can teach him."[43]

Among those happy to see Keaton reprising the role was Bob Kane, who said, "Michael Keaton was good in the first one, and I'm sure he'll be fine in this one, too. He fell into the role, and molded it to himself. As Tim Burton said, he wanted a guy who wasn't a super-hunk; a guy who *becomes* a superhero. A super-hunk wouldn't even have to wear the costume, but in it, Mr. Ordinary becomes Mr. Extraordinary. Burton thought the layman would recognize himself in the role—and it worked. Michael was cool as Bruce Wayne."[44]

With two villains in the piece, not to mention Max Shreck, the filmmakers had three major roles to fill. Burton and Di Novi immediately decided that there was only one choice to play the Penguin—Danny DeVito. "Danny was the first and only choice for that," said Burton. "There was no question about it."[45]

DeVito, a native of Neptune, New Jersey, went from the American Academy of Dramatic Art to winning a role in an off-Broadway production of *One Flew Over the Cuckoo's Nest* in 1971. Four years later, after appearing in a handful of small films, he reprised his role in the movie version of the play, produced by Michael Douglas and starring Jack Nicholson. However, it was his role as Louie DePalma, the volcanic taxi dispatcher in the TV sitcom *Taxi* (1978-1983) that made DeVito a household name. When the series ended, he embarked once again on a film career, with roles in two of the biggest hits of 1983, *Romancing the Stone*, with Michael Douglas and Kathleen Turner, and *Terms of Endearment*, with Shirley Maclaine and Jack Nicholson. After co-starring with Bette Midler in 1986's *Ruthless People*, he made his feature directing debut with *Throw Momma From the Train*, in which he starred with Billy Crystal. Two years later, he reunited with Michael Douglas and Kathleen Turner for *The War of the Roses*, which he both appeared in and directed. With a penchant for dark comedy, the short-statured actor seemed not only the perfect choice but practically the only choice to play the Penguin. "I think everybody just automatically said Danny DeVito's the Penguin," said Denise Di Novi. "Who else is going to be the Penguin?"[46]

Everyone was enthused about DeVito playing the Penguin except DeVito. Tim Burton went to meet with the actor/director to pitch him the role. "The last thing I wanted to hear from Tim," said DeVito, "was that we were going to do the Penguin like the comic book or the TV show. We talked about the origins of the characters and what Tim had in mind visually and psychologically. It turned the corner for me within an hour." Burton described his vision of the character to DeVito, saying "Imagine one night at the Cobblepot mansion. Mrs. Cobblepot is in labor. Two eyes, the nose, ears and mouth appear. Suddenly, this globular, unformed mass emerges. The Cobblepots are shocked and horrified. They hate it and they hate themselves. They take the infant in a stroller to the park and throw it into an icy stream." This bleak vision of the classic character struck a chord with DeVito. He told Burton, "I'm in. I feel like I can start there. We can create the opera from that." DeVito later told reporter Hal Lipper that he agreed to do the role before looking at the screenplay. "I came on this movie with Tim's enthusiasm and his vision," said DeVito.[47] DeVito's casting, along with Michael Keaton's, was officially announced on the front page of *Daily Variety* on Monday, February 25, 1991.[48]

Casting Catwoman proved more problematic. On April 19, 1991, *Daily Variety* reported that Burton and Di Novi had chosen Annette Bening, an actress who in the late 1980s had made the transition from TV to film roles.[49] She gained critical acclaim for her performance as Merteuil in *Valmont* (1989), followed by showy roles in the films *Postcards From the Edge* (1990), *The Grifters* (1990), *Guilty By Suspicion* (1991) and *Regarding Henry* (1991). However, it was her romance with legendary Hollywood Lothario Warren Beatty during the filming of 1991's *Bugsy* that made her ubiquitous in the tabloid press. The two had met when Bening auditioned for a role in a Beatty film years earlier and again when she auditioned for the part of Tess Trueheart in *Dick Tracy* (1990). After *Bugsy*, they were inseparable.

Late in pre-production, after Bening had already been measured for her Catwoman suit, Burton received a phone call from the actress. "There was sort of this long pause on the phone and she said she was pregnant," recalled Burton, "and I've never had such a split mixed feeling in my life. I was like very extremely happy for her and then was like dropping down a dark abyss at the same time."[50] With a six-month filming schedule looming, and considering the unforgiving tightness of the Catwoman suit, there was no way to shoot around Bening's condition. She was let go.

Overnight, a feeding frenzy erupted in Hollywood casting offices. Among the actresses contending for the role were Raquel Welch, Jennifer Jason Leigh, Ellen Barkin, Bridget Fonda, Cher, Lena Olin and Susan Sarandon.[51] "It was kind of a crazy period," said Denise Di Novi, "because I would say every single actress from 20 to 45 on the planet wanted to be Catwoman, and we were kind of barraged."[52] There was one actress in particular who felt she deserved the part—Sean Young. Young, after all, would have been in the first *Batman*, had it not been for a skittish horse; hell, they owed it to her to give her a second chance. And who better than she to play a beautiful but dangerous neurotic?

After missing out on *Batman*, Young had costarred with Ted Danson in director Joel Schumacher's *Cousins* (1989, a remake of a French sex comedy, *Cousin Cousine*), and with Matt Dillon in *A Kiss Before Dying* (1991). She had been cast as Tess Trueheart in *Dick Tracy*, but was replaced after seven days by Glenne Headley, reportedly because Young wasn't "maternal" enough (she claimed it was because she spurned the advances of the film's star, Warren Beatty). Now, to secure the role of Catwoman, the one-time ballet dancer was prepared to take extreme measures. "I thought that it would work to be sort of like aggressive in the sense that that's what Catwoman would have done," said Young. "She would've just gone Rrrrr and she would've gone in there and that's just what I did. I did like a major kind of Catwoman adventure."[53]

Young fashioned her own Catwoman costume with black leather pants, black leather bustier, a short black cape and a black half-mask that covered her face but not her auburn hair. She then went to Warner Brothers' Burbank lot.[54] "She came to the studio and into my office," said Burton. "I wasn't there, but she had somebody out in the parking lot, a bodyguard or assistant, and when she saw somebody who looked like me she said, 'There he is, grab him!' I guess it was the publicist of the movie and it freaked him out. Then the people in my office told her it wasn't me, and she stormed over to Mark Canton's office, where Michael Keaton was."[55] Canton, then the executive vice-president of the Worldwide Motion Picture Production unit at Warner Bros., vividly recalled Sean Young's assault on his office in an interview for the *Batman Returns* special edition DVD. "The next thing I knew, my office door flew open," said Canton, "and Michael Keaton and I saw Sean Young dressed as Catwoman leap over my sofa and say, 'I AM Catwoman!' We looked at each other and went, 'Whoa.'"[56]

Young next made an appearance on the syndicated *Joan Rivers Show*, arriving onstage in full Catwoman outfit and making yet another public appeal for Burton, whom she called "Timmy," to hire her. Ultimately, Young's aggressive tactics backfired. Frightened rather than impressed with her performance, the producers determined that she definitely would NOT be playing Catwoman. On Friday, July 26—the day after Young's *Joan Rivers Show* appearance—Warner Bros. issued a statement saying, "We had a particular vision in mind for the role of Catwoman, and we didn't feel Sean Young was right for the part...We continue to have great respect for Sean Young's talents as an actress."[57]

Nearly a year after the release of *Batman Returns*, *Playboy* magazine asked Young how she would spend one day if she knew she would be utterly and completely free of any personal consequences. "I'd fly directly to Tim Burton's house and completely demolish it," said Young. "Then I would rush over to Mark Canton's office and hold him at gunpoint until (he) hid under the desk and begged for forgiveness. And then I would probably leave him tied up, hanging from the ceiling. Then I'd visit (Michael Keaton) and make him apologize for causing my horse accident on the first Batman. Then I'd take Burton, Canton and (Keaton) and lock them up in a room and let them argue to figure out whose fault it was that they didn't make the right decision regarding me in *Batman Returns*. Then I'd visit Warren Beatty. I'd strip him down, tie him spread-eagle to the bed and walk away. I would also visit Barbra Streisand, Meryl Streep, Whoopi Goldberg, Geena Davis, Julia Roberts and Madonna, because I really like them. It would be to say hi and to show them I'm not a monster. Everybody's convinced I'm a monster."[58] In May of 1992, Jay Carr reported in *The Boston Globe* that Young and writer/director John Paragon were making the rounds of the Hollywood studios seeking backing for a film based on the 1940s comic book character the Black Cat. Conceived as a Hollywood star who fought crime in a cat costume, the character bore more than a passing resemblance to Catwoman.[59]

With the start of production looming, Michael Keaton suggested to Burton that perhaps Michelle Pfeiffer would be a good choice to play his feline nemesis.[60] The willowy blonde beauty from Santa Ana, California began her career in TV in 1979 with a continuing role as "the Bombshell" in *Delta House*, a TV spin-off of the raunchy fraternity comedy film, *Animal House* (1978). The following year, she played Samantha "Sunshine" Jensen in the series *B.A.D. Cats*, about a team of cops who investigated car thefts. Small roles in films and TV movie appearances followed, until she garnered good notices for her role in 1982's *Grease 2*. Her career then went into overdrive, with Pfeiffer earning critical acclaim for her performances in *Scarface* (1983), *Ladyhawke* (1985), *The Witches of Eastwick* (1987), *Married to the Mob* (1988), *The Fabulous Baker Boys* (1989), *The Russia House* (1990) and *Frankie and Johnny* (1991). Along the way, she'd been nominated for two Academy Awards and won a Golden Globe for *The Fabulous Baker*

Boys. Luckily for Burton, Pfeiffer was available, and curious to hear more about the Catwoman role. "When Michelle Pfeiffer expressed an interest, something just clicked where we thought, you know, she's perfect," said Denise Di Novi.[61]

"I met with Tim and I found him very unusual and interesting," said Pfeiffer, "and he explained the part to me and I thought it would be a couple of scenes and probably not a fully-developed character. Then, to my surprise, I read the script and I found she was just very actually more complicated than I could have even imagined, sort of psychologically."[62] Mark Canton said the role was a "creative turn-on" for Pfeiffer. "Michelle's a chameleon," he said. "Just as Batman has two personalities, so does Catwoman."

Pfeiffer was dating actor Fisher Stevens when she won the role of Catwoman. Stevens noted her enthusiasm, as Pfeiffer recalled to reporter Larry Hackett. "My boyfriend said at the time, 'I've never seen you so excited,'" said Pfeiffer. "I was sort of giddy, like a kid." Pfeiffer remembered the Catwoman character from the 1960s *Batman* TV series, which she watched when she was a young girl. "I was a fan of Catwoman as a child because I think she broke a lot of social taboos," said Pfeiffer. "I think I was about eight when I started watching the television series and I think in those days little girls were brought up to be good and behave and certainly not act in a physically aggressive way. And here was this character, this woman dressed as a black cat, and you were never sure whether she was good or bad. I think I had a fascination with the fact that she was bad but that you were allowed to love her at the same time."[63] Speaking to reporter Jamie Portman, Michael Keaton said, "I'm sure Michelle was salivating when she got this role."[64] Pfeiffer signed her contract at the end of July 1991.[65]

Having remained one of the few people on the planet who hadn't seen the original *Batman* movie, Pfeiffer made a point of watching it once she was cast. "I thought I'd better see what I got myself into," she said.[66] Speaking later to newspaper reporter Joe Pollack, Pfeiffer said that Catwoman was "a positive role model if you see it metaphorically," and said that in the mutual attraction between Batman and Catwoman, "there were elements of sexuality, but I don't see it as dealing with S&M."[67] Instead, her Catwoman role, she said, was "a statement about women and their empowerment. There's been a change in the character from its kittenish, voluptuous quality of the 1950s to something leaner and meaner today. Catwoman has beauty, elegance and grace but can explode into violence and sexuality at any moment."[68]

Like Michael Keaton, Pfeiffer began a fitness regimen to get her in shape for the physical demands of her role. She began kickboxing at trainer Stephanie Steele's Venice, California gym,[69] and started working with whip trainer and choreographer Anthony DeLongis, whom she called her "whip master."[70] "I never realized how difficult it was, or how much power the whip has," said Pfeiffer. "I took some skin off DeLongis' hand one day, and the blood scared me."[71]

To play evil department store magnate Max Shreck, Burton chose Christopher Walken, an actor who had spent his whole life in show business, first as a child dancer, then as an actor. After small parts in several movies, he won acclaim as the suicidal brother of Diane Keaton's character in *Annie Hall* (1977), soon followed by an Academy Award-winning performance in *The Deer Hunter* (1978). But in most of his film roles, the tall, gaunt actor played icy bad men, as he had in the 1985 James Bond adventure *A View to a Kill*. "I tend to play mostly villains and twisted people," said Walken. "Unsavory guys. I think it's my face, the way I look. If you do something effective, producers want you to do it again and again...I mean I don't play lovers. I wish I did. At least once I'd like to have a crack at one of those guys. A heartbreaker. Some people are born to it. I'm not."[72] Walken's casting was announced in *Daily Variety* on September 3, 1991.

Aside from Michael Keaton, only two actors from the previous film reprised their roles in *Batman Returns*, Pat Hingle as Commissioner Gordon and Michael Gough as Alfred. Michael Murphy, who had played a Congressional candidate for president in the 1988 HBO series *Tanner '88*, signed on as the mayor of Gotham City. Murphy told *Daily Variety* columnist Army Archerd that his mayor of Gotham City was "Kennedy inspired. Maybe more of a John Lindsay. But I remind myself of Mayor Dinkins—someone in slightly over his head. But, I'm not a buffoon-type mayor."[73]

A more surprising casting choice was announced in the October 2, 1991 issue of *Daily Variety*, when it was revealed that Paul Reubens, a/k/a Pee-wee Herman, would appear in the film as the father of the Penguin.[74] Since starring in Burton's first film, *Pee-wee's Big Adventure*, Reubens had starred in the 1988 sequel *Big Top Pee-wee* and taken his signature character to television as the star of the CBS kiddie program *Pee-wee's Playhouse*. After a five-year run that garnered 15 Emmy Awards, Reubens was feeling burned out, and decided to take a sabbatical. While visiting relatives in Sarasota, Florida in July 1991, he was arrested for indecent exposure after being caught masturbating in an adult theater. Though he was ridiculed in the press, his close friends and fans rallied around him; besides the small role in *Batman Returns*, he was also seen as a vampire in 1992's *Buffy the Vampire Slayer*.

Burton said casting, aside from re-casting Annette Bening with Michelle Pfeiffer, "went pretty easy. It wasn't the typical casting situation; everybody knew they would be spending much of their time in costumes and make-up. In that sense, the whole casting process came down to choice. We knew who we wanted and hoped they would be interested. We were very lucky in that we got exactly who we went after."[75]

Early on, it was decided that *Batman Returns* would not, like its predecessor, be filmed at London's Pinewood Studios. "We never considered shooting this movie in London," said Denise Di Novi. "The studio had that on their minds because some of the sets from the first film were there and it seemed so logical. What we discovered was that the only sets left in London were parts of Wayne Manor and the Batcave. We knew we were going to use a small part of Wayne Manor and that we were going to expand our use of the Batcave beyond the existing sets, so it didn't make sense to go all the way to England to use bits of two sets. Mexico was considered for a very short time, but the logistics—trucking in equipment long distances—ruled that out. Once we realized we were making a completely new movie requiring all-new sets, we figured we might as well shoot it in L.A."[76]

Production designer Bo Welch, who had worked with Tim Burton on *Beetlejuice* and *Edward Scissorhands*, set to work building sets for Gotham City at Warner Bros.

Burbank studio. The challenge for Welch was to give the new film a unique look while at the same time retaining enough of the flavor of the first film to keep its fans from being alienated. "In a way, I would like to think I tweaked a lot of what appeared in the first movie, but in the process I think the designs have given Gotham City a whole new personality," said Welch. "The feeling is of a city that's huge, dehumanizing and falling in on itself. That always felt appropriate for me; the idea of immense corruption and decay. I tried to give the impression, whenever possible, of a city and a world in a very tenuous position, a city whose world is falling apart and which is in dire need of Batman to save them."[77]

Warner's biggest soundstage was used for Gotham Plaza, which was meant to evoke what Welch called a "demented caricature" of Rockefeller Center, decorated with giant-sized statuary inspired by Fascist art. The sets were built in forced perspective to give them added depth, and augmented with clever model work to evoke a sense of immense size. "There were hundreds of carpenters scurrying all over," said Welch. "At quitting time, they'd pour out like guys from some '40s aircraft plant."

To keep the sets secure from prying eyes, crewmembers were required to wear photo ID badges to gain access. The badges were issued with a bogus movie title, Dictel, a name Burton and Welch made up when they worked together on *Edward Scissorhands*. "It's Dictel as in dictatorial," said Welch. "It was our word to represent a kind of faithless, huge corporation that makes some useless little product and bullies people." Getting into the spirit, the crew christened one particularly fascist-looking skyscraper on the set the Dictel Building.[78]

One special guest who was granted access to the set was Bob Kane, who was impressed by the massive sets. "Some of the sets are like Cecil B. DeMille or D.W. Griffith," said Kane. "Wayne Manor has what must be 500-foot-high ceilings—it's like a set that Griffith would have built for Babylon in *Intolerance*. They must have spent an awful lot of money on this one."[79]

After filling up seven soundstages and two backlot exterior spaces, Welch looked for a space on the Warner Bros. lot to construct the Penguin's lair, but felt the standard 35-foot-high stages remaining were inadequate for what he envisioned. "The space just lacked majesty," said Welch. "It didn't contrast enough with this evil, filthy little bug of a man." The solution was to go a short distance away to Universal Studios, where the *Batman Returns* production rented Stage 12, a 50-foot-high soundstage with a water tank. Welch added a vaulted ceiling, saying "The ceiling really sells it. It gives you a sense of enclosure that says, 'Not a set.'" The set was chilled to 38 degrees for the sake of the real penguins that would be used in the scenes.

Welch was also tasked with developing some new Bat-gadgets, including a new and improved Batarang and a Bat-ski boat. "One of the things I like about Batman's technology is that the more specific you make things, the stranger they seem. The real excitement has been in designing things that do one odd little task. Everything is consistent with the bat motif—webby, wingy and always in motion. And, because the time frame isn't specific, we're able to go all over the place in terms of the design. Some things are hi tech, others are low tech and some things are a combination of the two. There's a lot of the machine-age industrial revolution in what we're doing here. Gotham City is a great playground for us."[80]

Bob Ringwood returned to design the costumes, this time aided by Mary Vogt, who had worked with him on *Dune* (1984). The costumers had input from Tim Burton, who said, "Sometimes I do little weird sketches that could not be really applied to anything real. But when you work with artists and people you know, they can take what you do and get the idea of it."[81] Ringwood and Vogt began with the Batsuit, which was redesigned. "The first Batsuit was more muscular," said Vogt. "This takes it further with a rounded, sculpted, streamlined design. We looked at the Zephyr train, Rockefeller Center, the Electrolux vacuum cleaner and cars from the 1930s for visual cues." Batman's black bodysuit was made of Lycra, with body armor sections attached that were created from surgical-grade latex. Worsted wool was used for Batman's cape, with ten identical segments stitched together; as columnist Hal Lipper noted, twelve would have made a perfect circle. To create Batman's mask, the costumers began by taking laser images of Michael Keaton's head, since the claustrophobic actor wouldn't allow them to take a plaster cast. In the end, forty-six masks were created. Formed on collapsible molds, the masks were seamless, but so fragile that each one would only last a few days before it would stretch or tear.[82] Keaton's specially-designed boots were created by Nike, modeled after Air Jordans. Altogether, the outfit—including mask, cape, belt, Lycra bodysuit with foam rubber armor, gloves and boots—weighed 25 pounds.[83] Keaton later joked that he returned to the role because "they promised me the costume would be lighter, and it was. About four ounces lighter."[84]

Keaton felt that despite how stifling hot and uncomfortable it was, wearing the form-fitting Batman costume heightened his performance. "The Batman suit is so powerful as an image," said Keaton. "I enjoy being powerful like that. I like the idea of being on a big Hollywood movie like this, which doesn't necessarily have anything to do with reality, and being this guy wearing black rubber and kicking ass. At moments, it's tremendous fun. I wanted to lighten up Batman a little more this time. I didn't want to fall back into that contemplative, morose, really deep character."[85]

As heavy as Batman's costume was, the Penguin's outfit weighed twice as much. Burton sketched a conception of the character that looked more like a Charles Dickens character than Bob Kane's original idea, which Burton dismissed as "just some fat guy in a top hat and a tuxedo—it didn't make sense."[86] As Danny DeVito recalled, "Tim did a painting that he gave me. It was very colorful kind of circus tents, and there was a boy sitting in front of it that was Oswald as a toddler. He didn't have hands, he had flippers, and he was kind of rotund and small and he had kind of weird, pointed features, and the caption read, 'My name is Jimmy, but they call me the hideous penguin boy.' And it was a great image to start from."[87]

Turning Burton's Penguin sketch into reality required a three-hour make-up session.[88] Stan Winston Studios, creators of the creatures for *Alien* and *Predator* and the androids of *The Terminator*, not to mention *Edward Scissorhands*, was hired to bring Burton's vision of the Penguin to life. Said Winston, "For me, the Penguin was something that had to work for Danny DeVito and ultimately work for Tim Burton and his vision of the character. Tim Burton has a very specific look, a very cartoony, over-the-edge feeling. On the first makeup test at our studio, we went over the top, with Tim Burton-esque dark eyes and white skin. For the second test, our makeup artist, Ve Neill, did a beautiful job that looked extremely real. The problem was that it was so real, it was no longer Tim Burton-esque. I told Ve to go back to the more extreme look. It was good that as a makeup artist she had initially put that element of reality to it, but we had to fit into the color, texture and feeling of a Tim Burton movie."[89]

An initial design was sketched by Winston illustrator Mark "Crash" McCreery, and makeup artists Shane Mahan and John Rosengrant were tasked with creating the prosthetics. Prototypes were sculpted onto plastic shells of DeVito's face made from a life cast of the actor. "The initial concept was a pointy nose," said Winston, "but I wasn't really happy with that. The pointy nose just reminded me of a witch. So I got my hands back in the clay, which I love, and started playing with one myself. I felt the nose should have a beaklike quality. Yeas ago, for the Michael Jackson film *The Wiz*, I did some makeup for these crow characters that had enormous beak faces. I just loved that design, which involved the whole forehead and brow that went into this beak. Of course, that had nothing to do with penguins; but I felt I could use that concept with Danny and that turned out to be the look that was ultimately selected."[90] The makeup also included dental appliances to give the Penguin pointed teeth that looked decayed and neglected.

The makeup was accentuated by the Penguin's costume, designed by Bob Ringwood and Mary Vogt and executed by Vin Burnham. In a discussion with Danny DeVito, Ringwood learned that the actor dreamed of one day playing Shakespeare's *Richard III*. That influenced Ringwood's design for the Penguin. "If you look at it, the costume is a version of *Richard III* with a Dickensian twist, like Scrooge meets *Richard III*," said Ringwood.[91] The costume filled out DeVito's form with an air bag, a zip-on silicone tummy, and a skin-colored foam upper torso. The make-up and costume accessories added a hefty 50 pounds to the actor. It was so heavy that in the beginning of the shoot, an orthopedic doctor was brought in to make a brace so DeVito could wear it, but the actor refused to use it. "Danny didn't want it," said Vogt. "He said the Penguin was a mean, miserable character, so the costume had to add to that."[92]

Though it veered from the traditional depiction, Bob Kane gave his blessing to the new-look Penguin. "Danny DeVito has a big following, and he is a very fine actor, and he looks horrendous in his makeup as the Penguin—you would never know who's under that makeup," said Kane. "And he plays it straight and angry: he's not the clown that Burgess Meredith played on the TV show. He'll be well-accepted, because it's a different kind of Penguin."[93] In DeVito's Penguin, Kane saw echoes of a mystery thriller film he'd seen as a child. "There was a movie many years ago, a silent movie, *London After Midnight*, with Lon Chaney," said Kane. "He looked somewhat like the Penguin does in *Batman Returns*, a white face with dark circles around his eyes. His hair was straggly, with craggy teeth, and he wore a high hat."[94]

Catwoman's outfit posed its own particular challenges, since it had to be skin-tight and look like it was hand-made by Selina Kyle. "Tim Burton had a great deal of influence on the way that Catwoman's costume looked," said costume designer Bob Ringwood. "He wanted it to be unexpected, strange and offbeat. I showed Tim a photograph of a sculpture of a woman's head that looked like she'd had her skin sewn on. It was a strong image, and Tim, costumer designer Mary Vogt and I decided her costume would be black with white stitching, and it would look homemade. Tim invented a scene where Catwoman makes her costume from her patent leather slicker-style raincoat to justify the costume."[95]

In reality, the catsuit was sculpted by Andy Wilkes, who owned a Los Angeles latex clothing boutique that specialized in fetish wear.[96] "We wanted it to be tight to the body and sexy and that's an obvious area to go into," said Ringwood. "I mean, especially with someone like Michelle Pfeiffer who's got legs for days. You know, you want to expose all those wonderful limbs and everything."[97] Wilkes began by making a body cast of Michelle Pfeiffer to ensure that her costume would fit like a layer of skin, or as Vogt put it, as though "she had been dipped in black glass."[98] The stitches were sculpted into the design; in the end, the black paper-thin latex sections of the outfit were glued together, then waxed with silicone to produce a glossy sheen. Sixty-four form-fitting Catwoman costumes were created for Pfeiffer and her stunt doubles, in three different stages of deterioration.[99] In the beginning, Pfeiffer found the costume very restricting. "The first time I put the outfit on, I thought, I can't walk, I can't breathe, I can't hear, I can't act like this," said Pfeiffer. "And that's how I felt. It took me a long time to get used to all of the elements."[100]

The costumes and props for the film were deposited in Building 152, a two-storey aluminum-sided temperature-controlled warehouse with a reinforced steel door, at Warner Bros. In its cavernous, windowless interior, every costume for Batman, the Penguin and Catwoman was stored and protected by uniformed guards. Along with the costumes were back issues of the *Gotham Globe*, Gotham City phone books, stuffed penguins, blocks of fake ice and hundreds of wrapped presents.[101]

LIGHTS, CAMERA...ACTION!

Batman Returns began filming at Warner Bros. on September 3, 1991,[102] with a budget estimated at $55 million.[103] "That first day, I had what I would consider my normal case of nerves," said Burton. "I'm always kind of nervous and hyper. The first day is never a breeze. But I do remember that it was great, after all the preparation, to finally get to that point. Once the actual filmmaking process began, Batman became the normal thing; everything outside of that movie became frightening and ridiculous."[104]

Since she had never worked with the director before, Pfeiffer wasn't quite sure what to expect from Burton. "I thought Tim was going to be stranger than he was," she said. "He's really pretty normal. The images he creates are mind-boggling, and he brings the most unusual fantasy elements to his films...Tim's movies have an innocent darkness; that's what most people respond to...He's too provocative, too insightful to be adolescent. It's profound the way 6-year-olds are profound—and honest, too. And he's also that way as a person."[105]

After two years away from the role, Michael Keaton arrived on set ready to explore new facets of both Batman's and Bruce Wayne's characters. "It's Batman, but it's also a completely different movie," said Keaton. "I had to be careful that I wasn't doing an imitation of Michael Keaton playing Batman and Bruce Wayne...I had to become those characters once again, without anything else getting in the way. Why am I playing Batman a second time? Well, I've never played the same character twice, which is a challenge, and it's real interesting to take it further along. Also, Tim takes everyone on a fantastic voyage...and I'm totally with him on this quest."[106]

"Batman has always been a tricky character because, by his nature, he wants to remain in the shadows," said Tim Burton. "He's a tough character because he's so internalized. I got ragged on the first movie because Jack was so out there and Michael was laid back, but I didn't see any other way of doing it and keeping true to the character. Character-wise, we're not trying to up the ante with this film. We're not trying to make Batman too cynical or too dark. We didn't want to make him too dangerous or too aware, and Michael has been very clear on that. It took him a while to find that in his character in the first film, but he came in with it right away on *Batman Returns*. He's just this character dealing with other characters, so he's pretty close to where he was in *Batman*."[107]

"In *Batman Returns*, I tried to be real distinct and sharpen some of the character's edges," said Keaton. "I was more comfortable being Batman this time, but a hair less comfortable being Bruce Wayne, just because I felt some scenes weren't written as well as they should be. To be honest, I think the role is underwritten in the sequel, and I was partly responsible for that, by the way I was always taking lines and getting rid of them, especially in the Batman scenes, because I like the more Spartan approach to the character. I never wanted more to do in *Batman Returns*. I just wanted the film to be richer."[108]

The first scene Keaton shot in his full Bat-regalia was a confrontation between Batman and one of the Red Triangle Gang. "I liked the first Batman scene we filmed, where Batman pops the bad guy, spins him around and does the thing with the bomb," said Keaton. "Then, I turn and face the Penguin. It was a tough scene to choreograph because there was so much going on, and the timing and camera angles didn't help things. But what I worked real hard on in that scene was presenting Batman as somebody with a real attitude and presence. I did it with the way he stood, the way he set his jaw and things like that."[109]

Still, with his ex-girlfriend suited up as Catwoman and Danny DeVito in his Penguin make-up and outfit, it was sometimes an effort for Keaton to stay within the reality—or surreality—of the scene. "About every fifteenth day," said Keaton, "that's usually where it rolls around with me that I'm just kind of standing there waiting and I kind of look at what everybody's wearing, and I look at myself, and it gets really tremendously absurd, you know, where you kind of step outside yourself and you realize, this is really nuts, what we're doing. You just kind of laugh and say, well, here we go."[110]

Christopher Walken, outfitted with an array of stylish suits and coats and a wig that gave him a thick shock of eccentric white hair, employed a New York accent that caused some to see his portrayal of Shreck as a comment on a real-life New York tycoon, Donald Trump.[111] "I've heard that," said Walken. "Other people say that I speak like him. Well, we both come from Queens. It's true in most movies I don't use my own voice. I'm always from somewhere. Gotham City is really New York. I was born there. So I used my own voice.[112] But Walken maintained that when he was preparing for the role, Donald Trump was not the person on whom he based Shreck. "I thought about the big show business moguls I read about," said Walken.

Michael Keaton's Dark Knight returns (Warner Bros./Photofest, © Warner Bros.).

"Sol Hurok. Sam Goldwyn. Those guys who fought their way to the top. And then I thought of a lawyer I know. An older guy. Real tough. Real New York. Real smart. You wouldn't want to cross this guy. I thought about him a lot in this part. He's one of those guys—too mean to die.'"

Whatever trepidation former lovers Keaton and Pfeiffer may have had about working together was quickly dispelled when filming began. "I think it really helped because we both feel really comfortable with each other," said Pfeiffer. "I trust him."[113] As reporter Hal Lipper wrote, "Keaton and Pfeiffer say they were close enough to play their roles intimately, though not intimate enough to interfere with their performances."[114]

Pfeiffer's scenes were scheduled in such a way that she often had breaks of more than a week between her scenes, which made it difficult for her to stay in the groove and develop her character. Whenever she felt she was losing her way, she would turn to Keaton. "I had him on this one to go to to say, 'Listen, I feel like I don't know what I'm doing, I'm not having fun here,'" said Pfeiffer.[115] Keaton was happy to assist. "She's so talented," he said, "there was never any question in my mind that not only was she going to be really terrific in this but that she was going to figure out how to do this."[116]

The scene where Selina Kyle is revived was one of the most memorable for Pfeiffer, who told reporter Joe Pollack, "The cat stuff probably was the worst. I have a cat named Tracy...I used to have another one named Spencer, but he died." After completing the scene, Pfeiffer recalled, "I took a shower before I left the set, and I took a long bath when I got home, and Tracy still had a fit over all those strange cat odors."[117]

"She was very impressive," said Burton. "Two things that impressed me extremely was when the cats were kind of bringing her back to life, her sort of eye flutter and her eyes opening up. I still find that really chilling and amazing. And then that moment where she put a live bird in her mouth and held it there for several seconds and let it fly out. I mean, I don't know too many people that would do that, and she did it several times. And no bird or person was injured."[118]

Some of the most physically challenging scenes for the actress were the ones that involved Catwoman simultaneously trying to seduce Batman and destroy him on the rooftops of Gotham City. "Tim and I discussed the element of Selina Kyle coming into her own sexuality—the newness of that and the playfulness of that—and when it was manipulation and when it was sexuality," said Pfeiffer.[119] "The reason the fights between Batman and Catwoman work OK is due to this make-believe world," said Keaton. "It's such another world that the issue of a man fighting a woman isn't really much of a problem. It's well rationalized, because Batman at first feels uncomfortable fighting her and she sucks him right in and sets him up and pops him. That's a perfectly smart cat-like thing to do. Also, she's drawn as a classic villain. She just happens to be a female. The interesting thing that comes out of the fighting is the obvious sexual tension between them. It's compounded by this physical fighting element, which makes it hotter in a bad way. Some kind of sexual feeling, which isn't affectionate, comes out of this direct physical contact. Batman is confused by it, but he sees elements in her personality that he understands. When you enter that area, it probably gets into some primal questions. I wouldn't say the relationship is out-and-out S&M, but you are watching two people dressed up in black fighting each other and then making love."[120]

Though the scene plays beautifully, capturing it on film was a chore for Tim Burton, who said, "The action scenes were like several trips to the dentist. We were faking everything, so it wasn't like everything could happen quickly. The action process was very specific, so it went a little slower than I would have liked. Trying to create big action on a limited soundstage can be a drag...In that scene, we were dealing with complete fabrication. There was a lot going on and we were shooting things real tight. If we had moved the camera 1/16th of an inch up, you would have seen the studio ceiling. If we had moved it 1/16th of an inch down, you would have seen the floor. That was just the surface stuff."[121]

"Now, imagine Catwoman in four-inch high heels trying to kick the shit out of Batman while fighting on an upward-curving roof. But, I've got to hand it to Michelle. She took it upon herself to do all the weird stuff I had her do. In terms of selling the action scenes, she was so good, she was better than the stunt people."[122]

Pushed by Burton to look at Catwoman as an external representation of mousy little Selina Kyle's repressed sexuality, Pfeiffer found Catwoman to be ultimately a redeeming character. "It's somehow a positive role model for women," said Pfeiffer "I don't think that women are gonna go out and start whipping people, but it's an empowering character, and women need to be empowered."[123]

The most fun scene for Pfeiffer was the one where Catwoman destroyed Shreck's department store with her whip. "I guess I did feel powerful wielding that whip," said Pfeiffer. "In fact it's many things. It's kind of sensual, and at times it's very dance-like and at times it's lethal...I can't imagine Catwoman without a whip...It's very—actually, I don't know, it's hard to explain. It's empowering, and at the same time it's very graceful."[124] At the film's press junket, Burton admitted that the whip added an overt kinkiness to Catwoman's character. "She's wearing black and she's got a whip," said Burton. "Beyond that it's up to your filthy imaginations."[125] Filming the scene's finale was not so much fun, however, for four stuntmen who were injured by a special effects explosion. In his *Daily Variety* column of October 10, 1991, Army Archerd wrote, "We were assured the injuries were minor."[126]

Doubling for Pfeiffer in the more physically demanding scenes was stuntwoman Tricia Peters. Peters, who had spent seven years as a gymnastics teacher at the YMCA and worked out with circus acrobats on Santa Monica's Muscle Beach on weekends, performed Selina Kyle's fall from the high-rise window and Catwoman's fall into the truck full of kitty litter. "I love high falls, but that was the first time I fell onto a moving target," said Peters. "It made me a little nervous. We got to work it from lower points. By the time we filmed it, we went to a high point I had not fallen from. I'm not a real daredevil. I'm not a person who will try anything. I like to check everything out first. To make sure it's going to be as safe as possible. But I do like the rush. It keeps you safe. A slight fear, the nervous jitters. It makes you much more alert and in tune with everything going on around you. You need that as well."[127]

Once Danny DeVito had gone through his three-hour makeup transformation to become the Penguin, he remained in character on the set, much to the consternation of the cast and crew. "No one would talk to Danny on the set because he scared everybody," said Burton. "I don't know if that was his usual way of working, but there was a point where he just clicked into it and was completely this character who was totally antisocial, that had been out of the loop a little too long. Danny was one hundred percent into the transformation."[128] DeVito reveled in the part, saying, "I've never played anything like this before. This is from the bowels of I don't know where. I've never explored this in my life."[129] The actor's commitment to the role was so total that he even agreed to eat raw fish in one scene. "I always liked sushi, but this was really spectacular, raw and cold," said DeVito.[130]

To keep an air of mystery about the character, a special conveyance was made to hide DeVito's visage for his travels from the makeup department to the set. "We tried to keep it so that Oswald was not just exposed to everybody on the lot so they had this little thing," said DeVito. "Tim made a canopy with the art department, that I'd travel to the set in this little kind of circus canopy. It was good because you could stay in character, you could just be Oswald. And everybody respected Oswald, they kept their distance, but they, the crew and the other members of the cast and everybody was really into it and they were really respectful."[131]

DeVito had another special conveyance on-screen, when the Penguin uses one of his umbrellas as a personal helicopter to make a hasty exit. The flying effect was achieved without wires, using the same technique employed in the 1950s for the *Adventures of Superman* TV show. Chuck Gaspar, the film's mechanical effects supervisor, first had to rig an umbrella so that the cloth would fly off in pieces—pulled off by wires—leaving the spokes of the frame to spin like a rotor, which required a hidden motor. DeVito stood on the umbrella's handle, which was made of steel and affixed to a concealed harness connected to a bar that ran from his waist back through the barely-open doors of a church in the background of the set. As the actor was lifted aloft, his body hid the bar from view. "It was a levitation unit using counterweights for more control," said Gaspar. "We just picked him up and the camera stayed with him so you never saw the bar."[132]

Bob Kane occasionally stopped by the set. "Often in Hollywood, the creator is the last guy they want to see on the set," he said. "They want to feel it's theirs now, so they'll do it their way. But by being a nice guy, not criticizing anyone, offering my services without being too combustible, I find you can join the team, and they will use your help when they need it. But if you go down and try to tell them what to do, they don't like it at all. I don't go out to the set every day, maybe once a month, so they're glad to see me because I don't overstay my welcome."[133] His wife, actress Elizabeth Sanders, was offered a small role. Originally, she was to play the woman who is rescued by Catwoman, then roughed up by the villainess. When it was felt that it would be better to have a stuntwoman in that role for insurance purposes, Sanders was put into another scene. "Now she's in a scene in a mall," said Kane. "The camera comes in for a close-up, and it's very nice. She's in a crowd of Gothamites, all talking about the Penguin, who's now made out like he's a benign humanitarian. There are a few comments before Elizabeth, and then she says, ' Oh, he's just a frog, but he turns into a prince.'" After the scene was shot, Kane regretted that he hadn't played the man who has the next line, "Nahh, he's just a penguin." Kane remarked, "I could have said that and been up there with my wife, but Tim said I didn't ask him."[134]

Filming mostly went off without a hitch. "At one point during filming, Tim was starting to look pretty damn healthy and focused and mature; like he had his finger on exactly what we were doing," said Keaton. "That made me real nervous. I like him when he's pale, thin and gaunt, hair all over the place and in need of washing, shirttails flying, and he's pacing and looking lost. That's the kind of Tim I want to work with."[135]

For Denise Di Novi, the reason Burton seemed more inspired directing the second Batman film as compared to the first was obvious. "This is much more *his* movie," said Di Novi. "*Batman* was pretty much a Peter Guber-Jon Peters film, and although Tim was very much the creative person behind that film, there was always the matter of their input and his ultimately having to answer to them. *Batman Returns* is definitely a Tim Burton movie...With this one, he's much more able to do his thing."[136]

Though the shoot was going well, Burton still had to deal with some sobering news about halfway through the schedule, when he learned that his close collaborator from the first *Batman* film, production designer Anton Furst, had committed suicide. The 47-year-old, who had been living in Los Angeles while trying to line up a film to direct, had been undergoing treatment for drug and alcohol abuse, and had just ended a romance with actress Beverly d'Angelo. At 4 PM on Sunday, November 24, just four days before Thanksgiving, Furst leapt from the eighth floor of a parking structure, and died from his injuries.

BATMAN RETURN$

In January of 1992, Warner Bros. unveiled their new Batman logo to publicize the upcoming release of *Batman Returns*. Instead of a winged bat, it was a silhouette of Batman's head. Bob Kane saw the logo while driving past the studio, and he was decidedly unhappy with it. "Batman doesn't have a flat head," said Kane. "I was driving down the street, saw it, and went upstairs and told them it left a lot to be desired, and they agreed and said, 'How can we improve it?'"[137] In the end, it was decided to go back to the original Batman logo, now seen under drifting snow.

The trailer and one-sheet of *Batman Returns* were revealed on February 19 at a Warner Bros. luncheon at the ShoWest convention in Las Vegas, one day before the film completed principal photography.[138] By the time filming ended, the budget had ballooned, with some estimates putting the revised cost at $80 million, nearly double the budget of the first film.[139] Denise Di Novi felt the expenditures were justified. "I don't think anybody dares to dream of producing a movie like this," she said. "What was exciting to me about this movie was not only that it's such an extravaganza—which is a once-in-a-lifetime opportunity—but it's not merely big for big's sake. It's marrying artistic genius with scope, which is a rare thing."[140] On February 21, the trailer and one-sheet were released to more than 5,000 theaters.[141]

While fans were getting their first look at the new Batman, special effects supervisor Michael Fink set to work coordinating the film's 115 effects shots, half of which were computer-generated. Video Images created the digital bats that swoop through Gotham City, while Boss Film added digital penguins to the Penguin's underground lair. There were, in fact, only thirty-six actual penguins used in the film;

the others seen on-screen were either computer generated or were radio-controlled puppets built by Stan Winston's creature shop.[142]

Danny Elfman returned to do the film's score, which this time featured only one pop song, heard when Bruce Wayne and Selina Kyle are dancing in a ballroom scene and also during the end credits. The song, "Face to Face" was composed by English rock band Siouxsie and the Banshees in collaboration with Elfman, and featured lyrics that alluded to the attraction Wayne and Kyle felt for each other. Released as a single on July 13, 1992, the song peaked at number 21 on the UK singles chart, and number 7 on the U.S. Modern Rock Tracks chart. An album of Elfman's score was released on June 23, four days after the film hit theaters.

Elfman's score and the bangs and booms of the soundtrack would be heard by moviegoers in a revolutionary way. *Batman Returns* was the first film released in Dolby Laboratories' Dolby Digital technology. Originally known as Dolby Surround Digital, the crystal-clear sound system began the digital theatrical playback revolution.[143] During the next five years, the Dolby Digital system would be installed in over 9,000 auditoriums worldwide.[144]

As *Batman Returns* neared release, deals were signed with 130 licensees, 100 fewer than for *Batman*. Still, a $45 million promotional blitz was anticipated. Most of the tie-in toys were produced by Kenner Products, whose representative Krickett Neumann said, "It will be impossible not to know we're around."[145] Among the Bat items flooding the market were Batman, Penguin and Catwoman action figures, radio-controlled Batmobiles, and a Batcave Command Center playset.[146] There were Batman boxer shorts, snowboards, cookie cutters, cologne, rub-on tattoos, sweatshirts, swimsuits, sunglasses and sleeping bags.[147] Wilton Industries of Woodridge, Illinois made *Batman Returns* cake pans and cookie cutters. Norca Industries produced Batman cross-country skis. Street Kids Corporation of Los Angeles made Batman tortilla chips. Avon produced Batman shampoo, liquid soap, bubble bath and a gift set with a nailbrush, face scrub and sponge. Six Flags theme parks opened Batman attractions, including a Batman rollercoaster ride.[148] The inclusion of Catwoman allowed manufacturers to target teenage girls and young women with a girls' sleepwear line and women's dresses.[149] Los Angeles apparel company Chorus Line introduced a "sexy, club-dressing" line of Catwoman clothing, based on the form-fitting outfits worn by Michelle Pfeiffer in the film; Macy's, Bullock's and Robinson's displayed the fashions in boutiques decorated as Bat Caves.[150] For the woman who had everything, there were even Cat Woman chaise lounges complete with whip holders.[151] Karine Joret, director of marketing and public relations for Warner Bros. Consumer Products, called *Batman Returns* "our big bazooka this summer."[152]

Adding to the Batman blitz, GoodTimes Home Video released the 1943 *Batman* serial in a two-VHS tape set, with each tape retailing for $9.95. In a concession to the politically correct tenor of the times, the narrator's anti-Japanese slurs were edited out of the home video. The company also released the 1949 *Batman and Robin* serial on two VHS tapes, again for $9.95 each. Warner Home Video got into the game with their release of 1968's *Batman-Superman Hour*, retailing for $14.98, and Tim Burton's 1989 *Batman* for $24.98. For fans of the 1960s TV series, Playhouse Video released the 1966 *Batman* movie on VHS for $19.98.[153] As videotape had proliferated, the price for individual cassettes had dropped dramatically from a few years previously.

To make sure the market wasn't flooded with counterfeit merchandise, Warner Bros. and DC Comics contracted United States Banknote Corporation's subsidiary, American Bank Note Holographic Inc., to supply holographic stickers and hangtags to denote official *Batman Returns* merchandise. Paul Levitz, executive vice president and publisher of DC Comics, said, "This is the first time that a full-scale merchandising program has used full 3-D holograms either attached or applied to licensed products across every category. This program offers two distinct benefits: it assures retailers and consumers that they are buying an authentic licensed product; and it adds an enticing value to the product, since these high-visual-impact holograms are sure to become collectibles."[154] The licensees were ordered not to make the Bat items available until June 1, about three weeks before the film's June 19 opening, to avoid early consumer burnout.[155] Since Michael Keaton, Danny DeVito, and Michelle Pfeiffer had authorized their likenesses to be used in the merchandising, they were all poised to have Jack Nicholson-type paydays. A Warner Bros. spokesman said, "We funneled everything through them. We wanted to keep everyone happy." Nonetheless, Michael Keaton found the promotional barrage a little unsettling, saying in a press junket interview, "It's so huge that you don't relate to it. When you look at them, you get these moments where you go, 'Geez, that's me. I did that. I was in this. I am this guy,' and you get these little flashes of, 'This is pretty strange.'"[156]

While the studio was being generous with the stars, not everyone was feeling included in the fiscal bonanza generated by the Batman films. On March 26, 1992, three months before the release of *Batman Returns*, executive producers Benjamin Melniker and Michael Uslan sued Warner Bros. for breach of contract, claiming the studio was cheating them out of millions of dollars by refusing to pay them the thirteen percent of the profits they were entitled to from the first *Batman* movie.[157] According to Warners' bookkeeping, *Batman*, despite worldwide earnings of over $285 million, was $20 million in the red. Melniker and Uslan said Warner Bros. owed them at least $8 million combined, but had only paid them a total of $400,000 over three years. When settlement talks between Pierce O'Donnell, the attorney for Melniker and Uslan, and Warner Bros. chairman Robert Daly and general counsel John Schulman broke down after seven months, the producers filed their suit. Melniker and Uslan also sued Jon Peters and Peter Guber, who collectively had received $20 million in profits from *Batman*, in a separate breach-of-contract action.[158] Warners immediately released a statement saying that Melniker and Uslan had "no claim whatsoever," adding, "Warner Bros. stands firmly behind its position that the monies were paid strictly in accordance with the signed contracts between the various parties." In their suit against the studio, Melniker and Uslan contended that they were forced to sign a modified contract that stripped them of artistic and financial rights just before *Batman* went into production. Had they not signed the contract, according to the suit, they would not have received their executive producer credits on *Batman*. In exchange for the credit, they surrendered their portion of the film's "gross profits," receiving "net profits" instead.[159] The producers asserted the contract was invalid because they had been forced to sign it under "economic duress." For attorney Pierce O'Donnell, this was a continuation of the fight he'd begun waging against the studios and their questionable accounting practices. Shortly before the *Batman* lawsuit was filed, O'Donnell had concluded a case against Paramount Pictures, in which he represented columnist Art Buchwald and producer Alain Bernheim, who had come up with the idea for the 1988 Eddie Murphy comedy *Coming to America* only to have the concept stolen. Buchwald and Bernheim were awarded $900,000 after the judge in the case found language in their contract to be "unconscionable." Similar language was in the Warner Bros. contract with Melniker and Uslan. O'Donnell said, "This picks up where Buchwald left off. It shows people are still willing to battle over these unconscionable contracts."

According to Warner Bros. net profit statement of the *Batman* earnings, out of the more than $285 million *Batman* had brought in by the end of 1991, $88.9 million was deducted as a distribution fee, $60 million for advertising, publicity, prints, freight and taxes, $120.9 million for production costs, and $14.1 million for interest, leaving the film $20.2 million in the red. O'Donnell disputed the studio's figures, saying the film's real earnings were nearer to $425 million if all the video revenues were included.[160] It would be another two years before the case would come to trial.

Out of deference to Danny DeVito, the *Batman Returns* press junket was held in Chicago. By that time, DeVito had moved on to directing the biopic *Hoffa*, with Jack Nicholson playing the union leader whose demise remains an unsolved mystery. The press junket afforded Michael Keaton his first opportunity to see the completed film, with all of the opticals and special effects finished. Impressed, he said "Tim's handprints are all over this movie."[161] Burton himself admitted that he liked *Batman Returns* better than *Batman*, which "came out a little harsh."[162] Following the Chicago press junket, Keaton returned to Los Angeles, where on June 15, 1992, he left his foot- and handprints in the forecourt of Mann's Chinese Theater[163]

Audiences were bowled over by the film as well, and by Pfeiffer's turn as Catwoman. During one preview screening, European journalists were startled when a man in the front row cried out, "She's hot! She's really hot! Aooooow! Man, that chick is hot!"[164]

Prior to the film's opening, Warner Bros. spent about $12 million to promote it, with around $8 million going to network and spot TV, $3 million to print and $1 million to outdoor billboards and bus shelters.[165]

Batman Returns premiered June 16, 1992 in Los Angeles. On Thursday the 18th, 1,256 theaters previewed the film in late-night screenings.[166] The screenings brought in $2 million, just behind the $2.2 million *Batman* earned the night before its opening. Jack Holland, AMC marketing VP, commented on the chain's computerized ticket presales, saying, "This is the best response we've ever had. On *Basic Instinct* and *Lethal Weapon 3* we had a lot of activity—and this is doing three to four times what they did."[167] When the film opened on 2,600 screens nationwide the next day, it played to sell-out crowds.[168] Its opening weekend, the film set a new record, earning $45,687,771.[169] In its first 11 days or release, it grossed $100 million, making it only the second movie in history to reach that point so quickly, *Batman* being the first.[170] "We had so much riding on *Batman Returns* because it's not just a movie, it's an industry," said Robert A. Daly, chairman and chief executive of Warner Bros. Inc. "Once we saw the movie play before an audience, we became confident."[171]

As with the first Batman, the critical reviews were mixed. In his *Daily Variety* review, Todd McCarthy wrote, "On all counts, *Batman Returns* is a monster. Follow-up to the sixth-highest-grossing film of all time has the same dark allure that drew audiences in three years ago. But many non-fans of the initial outing will find this sequel superior in several respects, meaning that Tim Burton's latest exercise in fabulist dementia should receive even stronger across-the-board acceptance than the original...Batman's new adversaries—Penguin and Catwoman—are both fascinating creations, wonderfully played. And much of the film, particularly the first half, is massively inventive and spiked with fresh, perverse humor...Like its predecessor, *Batman Returns* is one big glob story wise, without a strong dramatic arc and propelled by weak narrative muscles."[172]

Janet Maslin, in *The New York Times*, wrote, "Mr. Burton's new *Batman Returns* is as sprightly as its predecessor was sluggish, and it succeeds in banishing much of the dourness and tedium that made the first film such an ordeal. Indeed, allowing for a ceiling on viewers' interest as to just what can transpire between cartoon characters like Batman and the Penguin, *Batman Returns* is often an unexpectedly droll creation. It stands as evidence that movie properties, like this story's enchantingly mixed-up Catwoman, really can have multiple lives... the upright hero Bruce Wayne, a.k.a. Batman (Michael Keaton), is easily overlooked amid all the toys and troublemakers that surround him. This Batman, with motives and magical powers that are never made interesting, is at best a cipher and at worst a black hole."[173]

In California, Kenneth Turan of *The Los Angeles Times* wrote, "Burton's Toys 'R' Us style of filmmaking leaves us hungry for something, anything more," while *The Orange County Register's* Jim Emerson called the film "entertaining without being compelling or involving." David Schultz of Chicago's *Metro News* found the film "very moody, with more colorful characters," but noticed "it takes two villains to make one Jack Nicholson." In Washington, D.C., Gary Arnold of *The Washington Times*, called the film "a solemn, morbid, oppressive rattletrap of an adventure fantasy." Desson How of *The Washington Post* had a more positive view, however, writing, "To come out of the summer haze and enter the dark (and cool) wonder is a pleasure not to be denied."[174]

BRICKBATS

As *Batman Returns* raced toward a $100 million gross, protests began to escalate. Lured by the Batman toys in McDonald's Happy Meals, which were marketed to children ages 1 through 10, kids pressed their parents to take them to the PG-13-rated movie. They were horrified by the Penguin, his plot to kidnap children, and the electrocution of Max Shreck, among other disturbing images. Parents complained, writing letters to Warner Bros. and to newspapers. NBC reporter Faith Daniels refused to take her 5-year-old son, and devoted a segment of her talk show, *A Closer Look With Faith Daniels*, to "Parents Against *Batman Returns*." Said Daniels, "It's fine to make *Batman Returns* an adult film, but don't market it to kids. It's rated PG-13, but who's buying the action toys? Not 13-year-olds." A spokesman for a Michigan-based non-sectarian Christian organization, the Dove Foundation, said, "Parents trust McDonald's, so why is McDonald's promoting a movie to little kids that's filled with gratuitous graphic violence?"

Stung by the criticism, McDonald's spokeswoman Rebecca Caruso said, "The objective of the (Happy Meal) program was to allow young people to experience the fun of Batman the character. It was not designed to promote attendance at the movie. It was certainly not our intent to confuse parents or disappoint children." McDonald's failed to explain how they were promoting the character in general and not the movie specifically when their Happy Meal toys included play scenes featuring Penguin in his Arctic World and Catwoman at a masquerade ball, and when the chain was offering discount coupons on *Batman Returns* merchandise at J.C. Penney stores.[175] For their part, a Warner Bros. spokesman said the Happy Meal promotion was tied to the Batman character but not specifically to the movie, saying the Happy Meals did not "provide actual toys from the movie," adding, "Clearly Batman is not meant for 5-year-olds. As for whether it's appropriate to Happy Meals, that's up to McDonald's. We don't tell them their business." *Los Angeles Times* film critic Kenneth Turan wrote, "If I had small kids, I wouldn't want them to see the movie." Apparently, other parents agreed; in its first four weeks, *Batman Returns* earned $141 million, but exhibitors began to worry when grosses dropped between 44% and 46% in its second, third and fourth weeks.[176]

Despite the controversy, Tim Burton said, "I really like the film...I like it better than the first one. There was a big backlash that it was too dark, but I found this movie much less dark than the first one. It's just the cultural climate...I think the culture is much more disturbed and disturbing than this movie, a lot more. But they just fixate on things and they choose targets."[177]

By the time it ended its run, *Batman Returns* grossed $162.83 million in the U.S. and $104 million internationally, for a combined worldwide gross of $266.83 million. Although it was the third highest-grossing film released in the U.S. that year, Warner Bros. hoped for more. And with the negative publicity arising from the sharp critical reaction against the film's violent and disturbing images, they began to rethink how Batman should be presented, and by whom.

1   Salisbury, Mark, editor, *Burton on Burton*, © 1995 Faber & Faber Ltd., United Kingdom, p. 113

2   Spillman, Susan, "'Batman II' is in Wings," *USA Today*, June 28, 1989, p. 1.A

3   —, "Short Subject: 'Batman' Sequel May Fly as Early as Next Summer," *Providence (R.I.) Journal*, July 23, 1989, p. I-1

4   Smith, Liz, "Holy Bombshell! Madonna Wants a Part in 'Batman II'; *Orange County Register*, Aug. 16, 1989, p. L.04

5   Renaud, Linda, "LA Clips: Batman 2 Waits in the Wings, Along With a Flock of Villains," *The Toronto Globe and Mail*, July 21, 1989, p. C.3

6   Shapiro, Marc, "Dark Knight Director," *Starlog* #180, July 1992, p. 41

7   —, "Cursed Movie?" *Syracuse Herald-Journal*, Friday, June 19, 1992

8   Interview with Michael Uslan, conducted Sept. 1, 2009

9   Lipper, Hal, "A Cat, a Bat and a Diabolical, Dirty Bird." *St. Petersburg Times*, June 19, 1992, pg. 21

10 Fabrikant, Geraldine, "Sony and Warner Settle Suit Over Producers," *The New York Times*, Nov 17, 1989, p. D.1

11 Nasr, Constantine, producer, "Shadows of the Bat: The Cinematic Saga of the Dark Knight—   Dark Side of the Knight," *Batman Returns* DVD, New Wave Entertainment, © 2005 Warner Bros. Entertainment Inc.

12 Shapiro, Marc, "Dark Knight Director," *Starlog* #180, July 1992, p. 75

13 Singer, Michael, *Batman Returns: The Official Movie Book*, © 1992, Bantam Books, New York, p. 12

14 Shapiro, Marc, "Gotham Cinema: When 'Batman Returns' Denise Di Novi's Challenge is Producing the Big Picture," *Comics Scene* # 28, p. 21

15 Archerd, Army, "Just for Variety," *Daily Variety*, Aug. 6, 1990, p. 2

16 Nasr, Constantine, producer, "Shadows of the Bat: The Cinematic Saga of the Dark Knight—Dark Side of the Knight," *Batman Returns* DVD, New Wave Entertainment, © 2005 Warner Bros. Entertainment Inc.

17 Lipper, Hal, "A Cat, a Bat and a Diabolical, Dirty Bird." *St. Petersburg Times*, June 19, 1992, pg. 21

18 Nasr, Constantine, producer, "Shadows of the Bat: The Cinematic Saga of the Dark Knight—Dark Side of the Knight," *Batman Returns* DVD, New Wave Entertainment, © 2005 Warner Bros. Entertainment Inc.

19 Shapiro, Marc, "Dark Knight Director," *Starlog* #180, July 1992, p. 41

20 Nasr, Constantine, producer, "Shadows of the Bat: The Cinematic Saga of the Dark Knight—Dark Side of the Knight," *Batman Returns* DVD, New Wave Entertainment, © 2005 Warner Bros. Entertainment Inc.

21 *Ibid.*

22 Shapiro, Marc, "Darker Nights When Batman Returns," *Fangoria* # 114, p. 30

23 *Ibid.*, p. 31

24 Shapiro, Marc, "Dark Knight Director," *Starlog* #180, July 1992, p. 41

25 *Ibid.*

26 Shapiro, Marc, "Darker Nights When Batman Returns," *Fangoria* # 114, p. 31

27 *Ibid.*, p. 32

28 *Ibid.*

29 Nasr, Constantine, producer, "Shadows of the Bat: The Cinematic Saga of the Dark Knight—Dark Side of the Knight," *Batman Returns* DVD, New Wave Entertainment, © 2005 Warner Bros. Entertainment Inc.

30 Shapiro, Marc, "Darker Nights When Batman Returns," *Fangoria* # 114, p. 32

31 Shapiro, Marc, "Dark Knights in Gotham Again," *Starlog* #178, May 1992, p. 42

32 Shapiro, Marc, "Darker Nights When Batman Returns," *Fangoria* # 114, p. 30

33 *Ibid.* p. 32

34 *Ibid.* p. 62

35 *Ibid.*

36 —, "Short Takes," *Daily Variety*, Sept. 3, 1991, p. 8

37 Nasr, Constantine, producer, "Shadows of the Bat: The Cinematic Saga of the Dark Knight—Dark Side of the Knight," *Batman Returns* DVD, New Wave Entertainment, © 2005 Warner Bros. Entertainment Inc.

38 —, "Cursed Movie?" *Syracuse Herald-Journal*, Friday, June 19, 1992

39 Nasr, Constantine, producer, "Shadows of the Bat: The Cinematic Saga of the Dark Knight—Dark Side of the Knight," *Batman Returns* DVD, New Wave Entertainment, © 2005 Warner Bros. Entertainment Inc.

40 Zehme, Bill, "Batman: As the Classic Comic Becomes a Movie, Its Star Contemplates Life in the Bat Lane," *Rolling Stone*, June 29, 1989, p. 63

41 Shapiro, Marc, "Night Life," *Comics Scene* # 29, p. 60

42 *Ibid.*, p. 9

43 Singer, Michael, *Batman Returns: The Official Movie Book*, © 1992, Bantam Books, New York, p. 21

44 Warren, Bill, "Creator's View," *Comics Scene* # 27, June 1992, p. 35

45 Nasr, Constantine, producer, "Shadows of the Bat: The Cinematic Saga of the Dark Knight—Dark Side of the Knight," *Batman Returns* DVD, New Wave Entertainment, © 2005 Warner Bros. Entertainment Inc.

46 *Ibid.*

47 Lipper, Hal, "A Cat, a Bat and a Diabolical, Dirty Bird." *St. Petersburg Times*, June 19, 1992, pg. 21

48 —, "Keaton, DeVito Set For 'Batman' Sequel," *Daily Variety*, Feb. 25, 1991, pg. 1

49 —, "Short Takes," *Daily Variety*, April 19, 1991, pg. 3

50 Nasr, Constantine, producer, "Shadows of the Bat: The Cinematic Saga of the Dark Knight—Dark Side of the Knight," *Batman Returns* DVD, New Wave Entertainment, © 2005 Warner Bros. Entertainment Inc.

51 Broeske, Pat H. and Anne Thompson, "Big-Game Hunting: Clawing for Catwoman—Many Actresses, Including Sean Young, Lena Olin, and Cher, Showed Interest in the Role That Went to Michelle Pfeiffer," *Entertainment Weekly* #78, Aug. 9, 1991

52 Nasr, Constantine, producer, "Shadows of the Bat: The Cinematic Saga of the Dark Knight—Dark Side of the Knight," *Batman Returns* DVD, New Wave Entertainment, © 2005 Warner Bros. Entertainment Inc.

53 *Ibid.*

54 Broeske, Pat H. and Anne Thompson, "Big-Game Hunting: Clawing for Catwoman—Many Actresses, Including Sean Young, Lena Olin, and Cher, Showed Interest in the Role That Went to Michelle Pfeiffer," *Entertainment Weekly* #78, Aug. 9, 1991

55 Salisbury, Mark, editor, *Burton on Burton*, © 1995 Faber & Faber Ltd., United Kingdom, p. 104

56 Nasr, Constantine, producer, "Shadows of the Bat: The Cinematic Saga of the Dark Knight—Dark Side of the Knight," *Batman Returns* DVD, New Wave Entertainment, © 2005 Warner Bros. Entertainment Inc.

57 —, "Short Takes: Young Didn't Fit WB's Vision of Catwoman," Daily Variety, July 26, 1991, p. 3

58 Camilli, Doug, "Burton better run if Young ever gets her wish," The Montreal Gazette, Apr 10, 1993, pg. D2

59 Carr, Jay, "Pfeiffer, Young Seek Purrfection," *The Boston Globe*, May 17, 1992, pg. 99

60 Lipper, Hal, "A Cat, a Bat and a Diabolical, Dirty Bird." *St. Petersburg Times*, June 19, 1992, pg. 21

61 Nasr, Constantine, producer, "Shadows of the Bat: The Cinematic Saga of the Dark Knight—Dark Side of the Knight," *Batman Returns* DVD, New Wave Entertainment, © 2005 Warner Bros. Entertainment Inc.

62 *Ibid.*

63 Portman, Jamie, "Kinky Catwoman Purrfectly Delightful," Toronto Star, June 14, 1992, pg. A16

64 *Ibid.*

65 —, "Hollywood," *Weekly Variety*, July 29, 1991, p. 9

66 Pollack, Joe, "Bad Kitty! Michelle Pfeiffer Shows Her Claws as Catwoman in 'Batman Returns,'" *St. Louis Post-Dispatch*, June 19, 1992, pg. 1G

67 *Ibid.*

68 *Ibid.*

69 Goldberg, Harold "Flashes," *Entertainment Weekly* #122, Jun 12, 1992

70 Pollack, Joe, "Bad Kitty! Michelle Pfeiffer Shows Her Claws as Catwoman in 'Batman Returns,'" *St. Louis Post-Dispatch*, June 19, 1992, pg. 1G

71 *Ibid.*

72 Weinraub, Bernard, "'Batman' Villain Takes Stardom With Grain of Salt," *The Houston Chronicle*, June 27, 1992, pg. 1

73 Archerd, Army, "Just for Variety," *Daily Variety*, Sept. 27, 1991, p. 2

74 —, "Reubens Penguin's Dad in 'Batman Returns,'" *Daily Variety*, Oct. 2, 1991, p. 3

75 Shapiro, Marc, "Dark Knight Director," *Starlog* #180, July 1992, p. 42-43

76 Shapiro, Marc, "Gotham Cinema: When 'Batman Returns' Denise Di Novi's Challenge is Producing the Big Picture," *Comics Scene* # 28, p. 17-18

77 Shapiro, Marc, "Dark Knights in Gotham Again," *Starlog* #178, May 1992, p. 46

78 *Ibid.*

79 Warren, Bill, "Creator's View," *Comics Scene* # 27, June 1992, p. 33

80 Shapiro, Marc, "Dark Knights in Gotham Again," *Starlog* #178, May 1992, p. 46

81 Lipper, Hal, "A Cat, a Bat and a Diabolical, Dirty Bird." *St. Petersburg Times*, June 19, 1992, pg. 21

82 Lipper, Hal, "Batrobe: Costumes For Latest Movie Are Technological Marvels," *St. Louis Post-Dispatch*, Jun 25, 1992, pg. 4

83 *Ibid.*

84 Shapiro, Marc, "Night Life," *Comics Scene* # 29, p. 9

85 Gaul, Lou, "Michael Keaton Has His Own Timing, Rhythm and Spin," *The Intelligencer*, Doylestown, PA, p. C-4

86 Daly, Steve, "Caped Couture: Tim Burton and His Thoughts on Batman Returns—A Preview of What's to Come in the New Batman Sequel," *Entertainment Weekly* #115, Apr 24, 1992

87 Nasr, Constantine, producer, "Shadows of the Bat: The Cinematic Saga of the Dark Knight—Dark Side of the Knight," *Batman Returns* DVD, New Wave Entertainment, © 2005 Warner Bros. Entertainment Inc.

88 Lipper, Hal, "A Cat, a Bat and a Diabolical, Dirty Bird." *St. Petersburg Times*, June 19, 1992, pg. 21

89 Vaz, Mark Cotta, "A Knight at the Zoo," *Cinefex* # 51, August 1992, p. 37

90 *Ibid.*, p. 38

91 Lindstrom, Jan, "Dressing the Part: Designers Define Character Through Clothing," *Daily Variety*, Nov. 21, 1997, p. 34

92 Lipper, Hal, "Batrobe: Costumes For Latest Movie Are Technological Marvels," *St. Louis Post- Dispatch*, Jun 25, 1992, pg. 4

93 Warren, Bill, "Creator's View," *Comics Scene* # 27, June 1992, p. 34

94 *Ibid.*

95 Landis, Deborah Nadoolman, *Costume Design*, © 2003 Rotovision, East Sussex, England, p. 121

96 Lipper, Hal, "Batrobe: Costumes For Latest Movie Are Technological Marvels," *St. Louis Post- Dispatch*, Jun 25, 1992, pg. 4

97 Pattyson, John and Mike Meadows, producers, directors & writers, "The Bat, the Cat and the Penguin," *Batman Returns* DVD, Pattyson/Meadows Productions, © 1992 Warner Bros. Inc.

98 Lipper, Hal, "A Cat, a Bat and a Diabolical, Dirty Bird." *St. Petersburg Times*, June 19, 1992, pg. 21

99 Lipper, Hal, "Batrobe: Costumes For Latest Movie Are Technological Marvels," *St. Louis Post- Dispatch*, Jun 25, 1992, pg. 4

100 Pattyson, John and Mike Meadows, producers, directors & writers, "The Bat, the Cat and the Penguin," *Batman Returns* DVD, Pattyson/Meadows Productions, © 1992 Warner Bros. Inc.

101 Lipper, Hal, "Batrobe: Costumes For Latest Movie Are Technological Marvels," *St. Louis Post- Dispatch*, Jun 25, 1992, pg. 4

102 —, "'Batman' Wraps," *Daily Variety*, Feb. 21, 1992, pg. 42

103 Lipper, Hal, "Batrobe: Costumes For Latest Movie Are Technological Marvels," *St. Louis Post- Dispatch*, Jun 25, 1992, pg. 4

104 Shapiro, Marc, "Dark Knight Director," *Starlog* #180, July 1992, p. 44

105 Pollack, Joe, "Bad Kitty! Michelle Pfeiffer Shows Her Claws as Catwoman in 'Batman Returns,'" *St. Louis Post-Dispatch*, June 19, 1992, pg. 1G

106 Singer, Michael, *Batman Returns: The Official Movie Book*, © 1992, Bantam Books, New York, p. 21

107 Shapiro, Marc, "Dark Knight Director," *Starlog* #180, July 1992, p. 41-42

108 Gaul, Lou, "Michael Keaton Has His Own Timing, Rhythm and Spin," *The Intelligencer*, Doylestown, PA, p. C-4

109 Shapiro, Marc, "Night Life," *Comics Scene* # 29, p. 11

110 Pattyson, John and Mike Meadows, producers, directors & writers, "The Bat, the Cat and the Penguin," *Batman Returns* DVD, Pattyson/Meadows Productions, © 1992 Warner Bros. Inc.

111 Weinraub, Bernard, "'Batman' Villain Takes Stardom With Grain of Salt," *The Houston Chronicle*, June 27, 1992, pg. 1

112 *Ibid.*

113 Hackett, Larry, "For Pfeiffer as Catwoman, It's Keen to Be Mean; Actress Pauses to Reflect on Her Strong Character," *Austin American Statesman*, June 17, 1992, pg. D8

114 Lipper, Hal, "A Cat, a Bat and a Diabolical, Dirty Bird." *St. Petersburg Times*, June 19, 1992, pg. 21

115 Hackett, Larry, "For Pfeiffer as Catwoman, It's Keen to Be Mean; Actress Pauses to Reflect on Her Strong Character," *Austin American Statesman*, June 17, 1992, pg. D8

116 Pattyson, John and Mike Meadows, producers, directors & writers, "The Bat, the Cat and the Penguin," *Batman Returns* DVD, Pattyson/Meadows Productions, © 1992 Warner Bros. Inc.

117 Pollack, Joe, "Bad Kitty! Michelle Pfeiffer Shows Her Claws as Catwoman in 'Batman Returns,'" *St. Louis Post-Dispatch*, June 19, 1992, pg. 1G

118 Nasr, Constantine, producer, "Shadows of the Bat: The Cinematic Saga of the Dark Knight—Dark Side of the Knight," *Batman Returns* DVD, New Wave Entertainment, © 2005 Warner Bros. Entertainment Inc.

119 Lipper, Hal, "A Cat, a Bat and a Diabolical, Dirty Bird." *St. Petersburg Times*, June 19, 1992, pg. 21

120 Gaul, Lou, "Michael Keaton Has His Own Timing, Rhythm and Spin," *The Intelligencer*, Doylestown, PA, p. C-4

121 Shapiro, Marc, "Dark Knight Director," *Starlog* #180, July 1992, p. 44

122 *Ibid.*, p. 45

123 Hackett, Larry, "For Pfeiffer as Catwoman, It's Keen to Be Mean; Actress Pauses to Reflect on Her Strong Character," *Austin American Statesman*, June 17, 1992, pg. D8

124 Portman, Jamie, "Kinky Catwoman Purrfectly Delightful," Toronto Star, June 14, 1992, pg. A16

125 Hackett, Larry, "For Pfeiffer as Catwoman, It's Keen to Be Mean; Actress Pauses to Reflect on Her Strong Character," *Austin American Statesman*, June 17, 1992, pg. D8

126 Archerd, Army, "Just for Variety," *Daily Variety*, Oct. 10, 1991, p. 2

127 —, "In a League of Their Own," *Daily Variety*, July 28, 1992, p. 61

128 Vaz, Mark Cotta, "A Knight at the Zoo," Cinefex # 51, August 1992, p. 38

129 Pattyson, John and Mike Meadows, producers, directors & writers, "The Bat, the Cat and the Penguin," *Batman Returns* DVD, Pattyson/Meadows Productions, © 1992 Warner Bros. Inc.

130 Nasr, Constantine, producer, "Shadows of the Bat: The Cinematic Saga of the Dark Knight—Dark Side of the Knight," *Batman Returns* DVD, New Wave Entertainment, © 2005 Warner Bros. Entertainment Inc.

131 *Ibid.*

132 Bennett, Ray, "Special Effects: Hollywood's Still Playing for Effect: From WB's 'Batman' to 'Alien,' Everyone Loves to Turn a Trick," *Daily Variety*, Jan. 18, 1993, p. 34

133 Warren, Bill, "Creator's View," *Comics Scene* # 27, June 1992, p. 36

134 *Ibid.*, p. 35-36

135 Lipper, Hal, "A Cat, a Bat and a Diabolical, Dirty Bird." *St. Petersburg Times*, June 19, 1992, pg. 21

136 Shapiro, Marc, "Dark Knights in Gotham Again," *Starlog* #178, May 1992, p. 45

137 —, "Flatman Returns," *Weekly Variety*, Jan. 27, 1992, p. 74

138 —, "'Batman' Wraps," *Daily Variety*, Feb. 21, 1992, pg. 42

139 Lipper, Hal, "Batrobe: Costumes For Latest Movie Are Technological Marvels," *St. Louis Post- Dispatch*, Jun 25, 1992, pg. 4

140 Singer, Michael, *Batman Returns: The Official Movie Book*, © 1992, Bantam Books, New York, pg. 12

141 —, "'Batman' Wraps," *Daily Variety*, Feb. 21, 1992, pg. 42

142 Rothman, Matt, "F/X Blending Digital Tech With Tradition," *Weekly Variety*, March 1, 1993, p. 27

143 Varela, Alan, "A Brief Lexicon of Sound," *Daily Variety*, April 18, 1997, p. 38

144 Johnston, Sheila, "High Tech in Short Supply: Equipment Manufacturers 'Swamped,'" *Weekly Variety*, June 23, 1997, p. 35

145 Broeske, Pat H., "Bat Blizzard: Batman Returns Launches Promotional Blitz—The Film Will Spend $45 Million on Marketing," *Entertainment Weekly* #123, Jun 19, 1992

146 *Ibid.*

147 —, "Holy Marketing Mania," USA Today, May 12, 1992, pg. 09A

148 Broeske, Pat H., "Bat Blizzard: Batman Returns Launches Promotional Blitz—The Film Will Spend $45 Million on Marketing," *Entertainment Weekly* #123, Jun 19, 1992

149 Arar, Yardena, "When Batman Returns, So Will Thousands of Spinoff Consumer Goods," *The Gazette*, Montreal, Quebec May 9, 1992, pg. C.3

150 Pendleton, Jennifer, "WB's Hopes Ride on Bat Sequel," *Daily Variety*, April 16, 1992, p. 22

151 Fabrikant, Geraldine, "Why Studios Bet On the Summer Blockbuster; With Big Debts and Big Budgets, Hits are More Critical Than Ever," *The New York Times*, July 3, 1995, p. A.37

152 Arar, Yardena, "When Batman Returns, So Will Thousands of Spinoff Consumer Goods," *The Gazette*, Montreal, Quebec May 9, 1992, pg. C.3

153 —, "Lite Knights: The Big-Screen Batman Might Be Too Dark a Presence for Young Kids. But There's a Kinder, Gentler Caped Crusader in These Old Movies, TV Shows, and Cartoons on Video," *Entertainment Weekly* #127, Jul 17, 1992

154 Joret, Karine & Gregory W. Miller, "Warner Bros. and DC Comics Team Up for `Batman Returns' Anti-Piracy Campaign; Batman Licensed Product to Include Hologram Security Device." PR Newswire, New York, Apr 22, 1992, Sec. 1. pg. 1

155 Arar, Yardena, "When Batman Returns, So Will Thousands of Spinoff Consumer Goods," *The Gazette*, Montreal, Quebec May 9, 1992, pg. C.3

156 —, "'Batman Returns' Just In Time For Warner Bros.," *The Salt Lake Tribune*, June 20, 1992, pg. B5

157 Elias, Thomas D., "`Batman' producers sue Warner's," Scripps-Howard News Service, *St. Petersburg Times*, May 20, 1992. pg. 2D

158 Horn, John, "Producers of `Batman' Sue Warner Bros. Claiming Breach of Contract," *Las Vegas Review-Journal*, Mar 28, 1992, p. 5B

159 *Ibid.*

160 *Ibid.*

161 Lipper, Hal, "A Cat, a Bat and a Diabolical, Dirty Bird." *St. Petersburg Times*, June 19, 1992, pg. 21

162 *Ibid.*

163 —, "Soundtrack," *Weekly Variety*, June 15, 1992, p. 15

164 Wells, Dominic, "Dark Knight Marks New Chapter in Batman's Seven Decade Screen Career," *The (London) Sunday Times*, July 12, 2008

165 Busch, Anita M., "'Batman' Lightens Up," *Daily Variety*, May 5, 1995, p. 14

166 —, "'Batman Returns' Just In Time For Warner Bros.," *The Salt Lake Tribune*, June 20, 1992, pg. B5

167 Fleming, Charles, "'Batman' Advances to the Front," *Weekly Variety*, June 22, 1922, p. 3

168 —, "'Batman Returns' Just In Time For Warner Bros.," *The Salt Lake Tribune*, June 20, 1992, pg. B5

169 Frook, John Evan, "'Batman' Dips Worry Exhibs," *Weekly Variety*, July 20, 1992, p. 7

170 Weinraub, Bernard, "Two at the Wheel of the Batmobile," *The New York Times*, Jul. 5, 1992, p. A.5

171 *Ibid.*

172 McCarthy, Todd, "Batman Returns," *Daily Variety*, June 16, 1992, p. 4

173 Maslin, Janet, "Batman Returns; A Sincere Bat, a Sexy Cat and a Bad Bird," *The New York Times*, Jun 19, 1992, p. C.1

174 —, "'Crix' Picks: Critics Unmask Diverse Views of 'Batman,'" *Weekly Variety*, June 22, 1992, p. 10

175 Pendleton, Jennifer, "'Batman' Returns With Big Sales Push," *Daily Variety*, Nov. 7, 1991, p. 3

176 Frook, John Evan, "'Batman' Dips Worry Exhibs," *Weekly Variety*, July 20, 1992, p. 7

177 Salisbury, Mark, editor, *Burton on Burton*, © 1995 Faber & Faber Ltd., United Kingdom, p. 113

Chapter Eight:
BATMAN FOREVER

*"There was more newsprint on the nipples and codpieces
than anything I've ever seen! What's wrong with our culture?"*
—Director Joel Schumacher[1]

BAT TO THE DRAWING BOARD

When he came to meet with Warner Bros. executives to plan the next installment of the Batman film series, Tim Burton could sense that the studio was looking to go in a new direction—one that might not include him. In Constantin Nasr's documentary *Shadows of the Bat: The Cinematic Saga of the Dark Knight* (on the *Batman Forever* DVD), Burton recalled, "I'm going, 'We could do this, we could do that,' and they go like, 'Tim, don't you want to do like a smaller movie now?'...About a half hour into the meeting, I go, 'You don't want me to make another one, do you?'...And so we just stopped it right there."[2] *Entertainment Weekly* quoted "a source close to the project" as saying, "Warner Bros. didn't want Tim to direct. He's too dark and odd for them." Robert Daly, co-chairman (with Terry Semel) of Warner Bros. said, "Terry and I wanted this Batman to be a little more fun and brighter than the last one. The first Batman was wonderful. The second got terrific reviews, but some people felt it was too dark, especially for young kids."[3]

Burton's long-term contract with Warners ended with the release of *Batman Returns*. His co-producing partner, Denise Di Novi, had already left Tim Burton Productions on June 3, 1992, a little more than two weeks before the release of *Batman Returns*. Di Novi relocated to Columbia Pictures, and it was thought that Burton might join her there. The director decided to put off a decision until the film was released. "I'll wait until my movie comes out," he said. "If it's a big bomb, I'll have to go scratching to do *Police Academy 8*."[4] By September, it was announced that Di Novi and Burton had set up their next film, *Ed Wood,* at Touchstone Pictures.[5]

Christmas of 1992 found Warner Bros. a studio in mourning. Steve Ross, who had built the company into the world's largest entertainment conglomerate, died of prostate cancer on December 20, at age 65. Ross's co-chief executive, Gerald M. Levin, assumed his title and responsibilities.[6] Ross's death, however, had little direct impact on Warner Bros. film operations, which had long been under the stewardship of Terry Semel and Robert Daly, who were now concerned with turning *Batman* into a more family-friendly franchise.

With Burton off of *Batman III*, the studio needed a new director to oversee the next entry in the series. They decided to go with one they were already working with, Joel Schumacher. Schumacher's most recent film at Warner Bros., *Falling Down,* was a solid moneymaker, plus he had a reputation for dealing coolly with difficult actors while making films that had a definite visual flair.[7] "*Batman* requires an awful lot of style," said Daly. "We wanted a kind of hip sensibility that we knew Joel had."[8]

Schumacher was in New Orleans filming his adaptation of the John Grisham novel *The Client* when Warner Bros. studio heads Robert Daly and Terry Semel summoned him to come back to Los Angeles. Schumacher said "I thought, 'Uh-oh. This is it. They're firing me.'"[9] But when he sat down with the Warner Bros. co-chairmen, he got a surprise. "Bob or Terry, I can't remember which one, started the discussion by saying they wanted to offer me the corporation's largest asset," recalled the director. "They didn't say, 'Do you want to make a movie?' It was very corporate. There was a seriousness to it, and it was kind of naive on my part because I didn't quite realize I'd be involved in the licensing and marketing, the Kenner toys, the McDonald's, Wal-Mart, Sears, you name it."[10] Indeed, McDonald's officials, who had been irked when Warner Bros. reneged on their pledge to match media dollars for *Batman Returns* when the film received negative reactions from parents' groups,[11] would now be allowed to review the script before production began.[12]

Schumacher, who read Batman comics as a child, was interested, but told the execs that he wouldn't do it unless he had Tim Burton's blessing. "I saw Tim, who's a friend of mine, and he was very anxious for me to do it," Schumacher later related to journalist Ian Spelling. "He obviously didn't want to do it anymore."[13] Schumacher accepted the job during the week of June 14, 1993.[14] He normally received $3 million per film, but *Daily Variety* reported that he was expected to earn at least $5 million for *Batman III*.[15]

Schumacher was an intriguing choice to become the next *Batman* director. A self-described "American mongrel," Schumacher was born in Queens, New York in 1939. "My father was a Baptist from Knoxville, Tennessee," said Schumacher. "My mother was a Jew from Sweden." When Joel was only four years old, his father died. His mother sold dresses to bring in money for the family, while Joel delivered meat for butcher shops and worked as a volunteer store window dresser. Leaving home at 15, he lied about his age to get a job at Macy's doing window displays. He then went to Miami, where he began living a fast life and experimenting with drugs. Soon, he was addicted. "I'm lucky to be here," he said. "I should have been dead 50 times."[16]

Upon returning to New York, he worked as a window dresser at Bendel's while studying at Parsons The New School for Design and The Fashion Institute of Technology. In the mid-1960s he achieved success with unusual concepts such as a short dress made entirely of mirrors.[17] He began hanging out with Andy Warhol and Edie Sedgwick, and ran the trendy boutique Paraphernalia on the Upper East Side of Manhattan.[18] But he was still living recklessly, partying and doing drugs on Fire Island.[19]

When his mother, a diabetic, died suddenly in 1965, he was devastated. "I was in a maelstrom. I lived on speed," said Schumacher. "I can't remember the number of acid trips I took. This was a period when you thought if you took a lot of drugs and had a lot of sex you could change the world. Well, those who didn't die became hopeless addicts."[20] By the time he reached 30, years of drug abuse had ruined his career and his health. The 6'3" Schumacher had lost five teeth, weighed only 130 pounds and was $50,000 in debt, $30,000 of which was back taxes. "I wore the same

Speedo all summer," Schumacher told *Entertainment Weekly's* Jess Cagle. "Everybody thought it was really sexy, but I was just too stoned to put on clothes...If I had continued shooting up, I'm sure I would have died." When he "reached the abyss," Schumacher went out one January morning and buried his syringes in Central Park.[21] His friends, including Geraldine Stutz, the former president of Bendel's, helped him recover. He returned to Bendel's creating store window displays and rebuilt his life.[22] Eventually he went to work for an advertising agency, breaking into commercials by designing a set for a Cool Whip spot.[23]

Work on television commercials led to a two-week trial as a costume designer for the film *Play It as It Lays* (1971).[24] Wishing to enter filmmaking, he moved to Los Angeles and found work as a costumer for films like Woody Allen's sci-fi comedy *Sleeper* while earning an MFA from UCLA. He got his first directing assignment on television, with *The Virginia Hill Story* in 1974, covering the same territory that would be mined by Warren Beatty for his 1991 film *Bugsy*. After his script *Car Wash* became a film in 1976, he was hired to adapt the Broadway musical *The Wiz* (1978) into a screenplay. He followed that up with the TV movie *Amateur Night at the Dixie Bar and Grill* (1979), which he both wrote and directed, then made the leap into feature films as director of the 1981 comedy *The Incredible Shrinking Woman*, starring Lily Tomlin. Throughout the rest of the 1980s and early 1990s, Schumacher directed a diverse array of films, gaining a reputation for crafting hit films on modest budgets with *St. Elmo's Fire* (1985), *The Lost Boys* (1987), *Flatliners* (1990) and the critically acclaimed *Falling Down* (1993).

Schumacher said that when he began preparing for the *Batman* film, instead of going back and looking at the previous movies, "I called D.C. Comics and got as many comic books from 1939 to the present as I could and immersed myself. I didn't look at what Tim did and try to be different. I wanted to do my own thing. I wanted to make a living comic book."[25] Though he expected his film to be less bleak than Burton's, he said, "This isn't the *Care Bears*. *Batman* will always have an edge."[26] The Batman character, Schumacher said, always appealed to him. "He's not a superhero but a real man with real vulnerabilities. He's also sexier and cooler than Superman. I mean, let's face it—any guy who chooses to go out at night dressed like a bat as a vigilante is an interesting and isolating character."[27]

Even before the release of *Batman Returns*, rumors were circulatng about who would be in the third Batman film. It was a given that Michael Keaton would return as Batman. The actor was reportedly enthusiastic about the hiring of Schumacher. Harry Colomby, a partner in Keaton's production company, said, "Schumacher can make Batman sexier and more heroic. Burton is not the hero type. His heart beats for the outsider—look at *Edward Scissorhands*." Speaking to *Entertainment Weekly*, Keaton said, "In the second one I had less input. But we haven't even scratched the surface on what we can do with [Batman]."[28]

With the character of Robin being dropped from the first two installments, it seemed certain that the Boy Wonder would finally appear in *Batman III*. "I grew up on the Batman character," said Schumacher, "and there was always Batman and Robin, always."[29] Schumacher decided to make the Boy Wonder a revenge-seeking heartthrob with a punk music vibe. "Dick Grayson's story is much more interesting than I'd ever seen it portrayed," said Schumacher. "Because of the TV series, he was seen as this kind of asexual, cartoony, wholesome airhead. You know, 'Holy bat smoke!'"[29] *Daily Variety* speculated that Marlon Wayans, who had reportedly been signed for the previous film, would finally get a chance to play the role.[30]

As for the villain, since three of the Big Four villains most familiar from the TV series—the Joker, the Penguin and Catwoman—had already been used, it seemed the next logical choice for a Bat-menace was the Riddler, and the trades assumed that Robin Williams, having lost out on a chance to be the Joker, would be wearing the Riddler's green tights.[31] Williams told reporters that he looked forward to playing the role, saying, "I loved *Batman* when I was growing up because we didn't have *Barney* then. I am just waiting to see the script, and if it's right, then I'll sign on."

At the same time Warner Bros. was beginning development of *Batman III*, they were also developing a spin-off from *Batman Returns*—a *Catwoman* feature they hoped would launch a new action franchise for Michelle Pfeiffer.[32] Dan Waters, the *Batman Returns* scriptwriter, was commissioned to come up with a plotline. Tim Burton expressed an interest in directing, and Denise Di Novi considered taking on the producing chores.[33]

In July 1993, while Schumacher busied himself with *The Client*, the studio proceeded by hiring the husband and wife writing team of Lee and Janet Scott Batchler. The Batchlers initially made their mark in television, with teleplays for *The Equalizer* (1988) and *McGee and Me!* (1989). But it was their spec screenplay *Smoke and Mirrors*, about French magician Robert Houdin being sent to Algeria to expose a sorcerer provoking attacks on French colonials, that got Hollywood's attention. In March of 1993, the script was one of those lucky few that, sent out to producers for a weekend read, ended up in a bidding war between Paramount, Disney, Tri-Star, Cinergi and Steven Spielberg. Cinergi, in a co-production pact with Disney's Hollywood Pictures, eventually claimed the script for $500,000, with the writers due to earn an additional $500,000 if a film was produced. Frank Marshall, producer of several Steven Spielberg movies, signed on to direct, and Sean Connery agreed to star. However, after Connery demanded a series of rewrites, the production stalled. Connery eventually moved on, and when Marshall then left for a deal at Paramount to direct *Congo*, the project was put on the back burner. Still, the script proved that the duo were capable of writing big-budget action, which seemed to make them ideal choices to script *Batman III*, as Schumacher realized when the *Smoke & Mirrors* script crossed his desk. "Joel was looking for a tone, and he read our script and said, 'These are our writers," said Lee Batchler.[34]

In an interview with Ben Yip on the website *Brother-Eye.net*, Janet Scott Batchler recalled that Tim Burton was involved in the early stages of the script's development, insofar as he was there to approve his creative successors. The Batchlers met with Burton, telling him, as Janet Scott Batchler recalled, "the key element to Batman is his duality. And it's not just that Batman is Bruce Wayne. All the villains also have secret identities...And when we said that, Tim just kinda went, 'Yes!' And at that point, we pretty much had the job." Janet Scott Batchler had read *Batman* comics as a kid, since her local store didn't carry *Wonder Woman*. Now, she and her husband Lee read the early comics of Bob Kane and Bill Finger as well as some of the more current comics, including Frank Miller's *The Dark Knight Returns* saga. They also read academic papers that psychoanalyzed Batman, which began to give them the idea of creating an analyst character as a love interest, one who, as Janet Scott Batchler said, "might be able to help him walk that dangerous line and keep him on an even keel— hence the name 'Meridian.'"[35]

"We worked out the essentials of the story, and Tim signed off on it," said Lee Batchler. "Then we flew to New Orleans, where Joel was finishing up on *The Client.* He wanted us to see him at work and see his directing style. When he wasn't directing a scene, we were brainstorming Batman. It was a lot of fun. We started with a blank slate and a production start date—a very interesting situation. There was just a general idea—no story, no script. That's what we had to provide them in 11 weeks."[36]

The studio insisted that they follow the *Batman Returns* pattern and have two villains. Schumacher already wanted Tommy Lee Jones, whom he had just worked with on *The Client*, to play Two-Face. The Batchlers were free to use any other villain they chose, and they decided on the Riddler, because they felt "we need a villain that everybody knows." Since they felt one good villain was enough to drive a movie, the only way they could see accommodating two villains was to split them, with one nemesis for Batman and another for Bruce Wayne. They gave the Riddler a new origin; as Lyle Heckendorf, he's a WayneTech employee who, snubbed by Bruce Wayne, develops an intense hatred for Gotham's multi-millionaire industrialist.[37] The Batchlers wrote the script with Robin Williams in mind for the Riddler, and assumed that Michael Keaton would be continuing as Batman.

Joel Schumacher insisted that the Riddler's costume needed to be motivated, so he came up with the idea of having Lyle Heckendorf steal the costume of a leprechaun fortune-teller at a circus. "Joel started off as a costume designer," said Janet Scott Batchler. "So costumes matter to him. He pays attention to them, while other directors might not." Schumacher also wanted to finally introduce Robin into the series. The Batchlers already had an assistant who grew up in the circus, so they quizzed her about circus life and the trapeze.[38]

Schumacher had other requirements for the script. "Visuals are very important to him," said Lee Batchler. "Joel wanted to do a *Thunderball* moment. We wrote him some underwater shots. He was very excited by the visuals. At one point he said, 'All I want is this one shot of Batman coming through a wall of flame. You can do anything else you want, but get me that one shot.' So we wrote a whole sequence setting up and built around that one visual."[39]

The writers never worried about budget as they were developing the script. Lee Batchler said, "There wasn't one time when they said, 'Oh, this is too expensive. Forget that.' It was a case of, 'Have fun! Go wild! ' It was carte blanche as to what you could imagine. And then it was up to the designers to figure out how to do it."[40]

The Batchlers' script laid out the basic structure of the final film, with very few scenes that were altered or dropped later. To give the screenplay a "bookending" structure, it begins and ends with scenes set at Arkham Asylum. In the beginning, a guard goes to Harvey Dent/Two-Face's cell and sees that Two-Face has escaped; the end shows the Riddler straight-jacketed in a cell (in the Batchlers script, he's called

Lyle Heckendorf, not Edward Nygma, the name given to the character in the comic books and in the revised script). Bruce Wayne has dreams of when he was a child, chasing a rabbit and falling into a hole that led to his discovery of the cave underneath Wayne Mansion, and later in the script, after Two-Face and the Riddler raid Wayne Mansion and the Batcave and Bruce is shot, the millionaire temporarily loses all memory of being Batman.

One of the strangest scenes in the Batchler script comes after Bruce and Batman have had several encounters with Chase Meridian. One night, she awakens to find Batman on her balcony. She opens the French windows to her terrace and goes to him. Without speaking, they kiss, and she leads him into her bedroom. She goes to remove his mask, but he stops her. The next description reads, "Int. Chase's Bedroom, Later—Post coital. Chase stands at the window, pulling closed her robe. Batman is before her. She touches his mask." She asks if the mask ever comes off, and he says no. He then tells her about falling into the hole, confronting the fear of the bat. When she asks, "Who are you?" he says, "I don't know anymore," and disappears into the night.

In his quest to make a lighter-toned film, Schumacher worked with the Batchlers on script revisions. "They're called comic books, not tragic books," said Schumacher, "and what we set out to do...was to make a living comic book."[41] When the Batchlers had to return to their earlier commitment at Disney, Schumacher brought in Akiva Goldsman, with whom he was already collaborating on *The Client*, to continue streamlining the story and smooth it into shape,[42] "but the storyline stayed the same all the way through," said Schumacher."[43] Goldsman, another native New Yorker, was a latecomer to Hollywood. His parents were child psychologists Mira Rothenberg and Tev Goldsman; Goldsman told Geoff Boucher of *The Los Angeles Times*, "I grew up, essentially, in one of the very first group homes for what was then termed as 'emotionally disturbed children'—these were days when, unimaginably, childhood schizophrenia and autism were lumped together in the same population. My parents founded this home, and I grew up there in this brownstone in Brooklyn Heights and my peers were, um, crazy. My definition of sanity is very labile; it's flexible and open."

After graduating from Connecticut's Wesleyan University in 1983, Goldsman became a therapist specializing in autistic and schizophrenic children. Finding clinical work too restricting for his imaginative mind, he decided to try novel writing, and studied creative writing at New York University. He finally found his true calling in screenwriting, and had just sold his first script—eventually produced as *Silent Fall*—when a Warner Bros. executive introduced him to Schumacher. Schumacher hired him to adapt John Grisham's best-selling legal thriller *The Client*.[44] "*The Client* was a month and a half from shooting, and they felt the script wasn't what they wanted," said Goldsman. Goldsman was on the New Orleans location with Schumacher when the director was offered the Batman film. "When Joel had been offered *Batman Forever*," said Goldsman, "I had salivated loudly, because I had been a Batman fan since I was little."[45] Still, streamlining the script was no easy task. "There was a lot of pressure coming in on that third film," said Goldsman. "The franchise's future was in danger after the second movie. People found *Batman Returns* too dark and disturbing and, because of the realities of commercial filmmaking, the franchise was in real jeopardy.

But Joel was fearless in his determination to turn things around. I assisted him, but it was really Joel Schumacher who revived *Batman*."[46]

In March of 1993, as the script was taking shape, Warner Bros. chairman Terry Semel prepared to celebrate his 50th birthday. Semel's wife Jane and his friend Joel Silver, a producer of high-octane action films, banded together to make a 45-minute spoof of Oliver Stone's *JFK* for the occasion. Their film, called *TSS* (for Terry Steven Semel), followed the "conspiracy theory" of how Semel had become the most successful studio head in town. It featured cameos from Kevin Costner, reprising his role of D.A. Jim Garrison from *JFK*, and Warren Beatty as Dick Tracy. The film also featured Batman, as played by "super agent" Mike Ovitz of the Creative Artists Agency. Ovitz was known to have a pet peeve with his business associate Ron Meyer, who dressed more casually than the suit and tie preferred by Ovitz. In the video, Ovitz, in full Batman regalia and seated in the Batmobile, turned to Meyer, dressed in jeans and a sweater, and asked why he wasn't wearing his Robin uniform. Meyer replied, "This is my uniform. I thought this was Batman and Ronnie."[47]

With a script that finally introduced Robin to the series, the studio began searching in earnest for an actor to play the role in November of 1993. Warner Bros. notified talent agencies in Hollywood that they were looking for a young actor between the ages of 16 and 18, of any race, proficient in the martial arts.[48] The following month, an open casting call was held on a Sunday at Warner's Burbank studio. Their press release said no previous acting experience was necessary, though a knowledge of martial arts would be beneficial, but applicants needed to be "sexy, streetwise, aged 14 to 20," with a "great, athletic, tough body," no taller than 5 feet 9 inches.[49]

BATTENING THE HATCHES

With pre-production picking up momentum, the script taking shape and the cast falling into place, Warner Bros. went into full protect-the-franchise mode; Batman was worth billions of dollars in ancillary licensing around the world, and they couldn't chance the next film alienating the audience. The hiring of Schumacher was the first step in a carefully planned strategy to lighten up the character and bring the studio's promotional partners back to the fold. Warner Bros. worldwide consumer product president Dan Romanelli told *Daily Variety's* Anita M. Busch, "We knew we had a problem. We knew that people felt the last film was kind of dark. We really turned around the feeling about Batman as a movie franchise, and Joel was key to that strategy. There was an effort for the retailers and licensees to meet him to understand his vision. We set the high water mark on the first *Batman* and it was an amazing success. The second was a disappointment comparatively. It was a significant challenge to get the licensees and retailers on board for the third one, and I give a lot of credit to Joel."[50]

In January 1994, Schumacher, producer Peter MacGregor-Scott and Warner Bros. marketing executives held an event on the Warner Bros. backlot for 200 licensees, during which they unveiled the characters for the new *Batman* film and promised the new film wouldn't be as dark as *Batman Returns*. One of the licensees in attendance said, "Warner Bros. knew they had to change the whole positioning of the film. And they did that. That meeting set the stage early on that it was going to be more fun. It was lighthearted, particularly with Schumacher joking around. He said—and we could tell because he's very flamboyant—that it was going to be a more adventurous, entertaining *Batman*." Schumacher didn't stop there; he also appeared at Toy Fair and the Magic Apparel Show, a men's fashion preview in Las Vegas, that summer.[51] Schumacher admitted there was a deliberate intent to keep the violence in the new film on a comic book level so that kids would not be terrified. "There was a conscious effort, but it wasn't dictated," he told *Variety*.

At the same time Warner Bros. was assuring their licensing partners that the new Batman film would be family friendly, the lawsuit filed by Benjamin Melniker and Michael Uslan against the studio over the profits from 1989's *Batman* finally came before L.A. Superior Court judge David Yaffe on Monday, January 10, 1994. The heart of the proceeding was a deal made between Warner Bros. and PolyGram Pictures that the plaintiffs maintained was a "secret" deal that cut them out of gross profits from the mega-hit film.[52]

Operating as Batfilms Inc., Melniker and Uslan optioned the rights to Batman in 1979. Although the 1989 film grossed over $300 million (according to court documents, that is; *Variety* estimated the gross at $411 million worldwide), the duo received only $400,000 for their producing interest. Claiming they were treated unfairly, especially considering that producers Jon Peters and Peter Guber were paid a portion of gross receipts, they sued Warner Bros. and PolyGram for $8 million.[53]

Melniker and Uslan originally struck a deal with Casablanca Filmworks, which later became PolyGram, to attach Peter Guber as producer. On the second day of the trial, Melniker testified that he only learned through the trade papers in 1988 that Guber, along with Jon Peters, had made a separate deal with Warner Bros. to produce the film. Warner Bros. then tried to push Melniker and Uslan into executive producer roles with a deal that would give them 40% of the net profits, whereas Guber and Peters were given a deal allowing them a percentage of the film's gross receipts. Continuing his testimony on Wednesday, Melniker said that he and Uslan agreed to accept the contract only because they were threatened with being thrown off the film's production team altogether. Melniker claimed that he and Uslan were only made aware of the terms of the deal in 1988. However, under cross-examination, when presented with notes he had made during a 1981 meeting with a PolyGram exec in which the Warner Bros. deal was discussed, Melniker had to admit that he may, in fact, have been advised of the deal earlier than 1988.[54]

On Thursday, a contract between Batfilms and Casablanca was introduced in court that said that if Universal, the original producer of the film, bowed out and Casablanca took over the financing, then Batfilms would, after costs of the film's negative were paid and Casablanca had received $5 million, receive 15% of the gross receipts thereafter. Melniker and Uslan's attorney introduced the document to show that their was intent in the original agreement to pay gross receipts, but lawyers for the defendants argued that the point became moot once Warner Bros. took over the film.[55]

On Monday the 24th, two weeks after the proceedings began, Judge Yaffe tossed out the Batfilms suit on the grounds that Melniker and Uslan hadn't provided enough evidence to warrant a jury verdict. Yaffe also ruled that it was disingenuous for Melniker, a trained lawyer, to complain that he was misled about profit participation when he knew the ramifications of the deal he signed. An attorney for Warner Bros., Robert Schwartz, said the ruling "says if you negotiate a deal with a studio with your eyes open and you're well represented, you don't come back two years later and say they treated me unfairly... This says the studios are not always bastards. You can't just file against a studio and expect a judge and jury to give you money." Schwartz expected the ruling would deter others from filing "net profits" lawsuits.[56]

As the lawsuit concluded, casting and script revisions were continuing for the next Batman movie. In February 1994, Tommy Lee Jones signed on to play Two-Face.[57] For Jones, one of the deciding factors in taking the role was his 11-year-old son, Austin. Schumacher recalled that when he went to meet with Jones to encourage him to do the role, "I got there and Austin had a pile of *Batman* comics with Two-Face on top. Tommy told me he's doing the character because it's Austin's favorite."

The following month, Chris O'Donnell was being courted for the role of Robin.[58] *Variety* reported that O'Donnell had competition for the role; Leonardo DiCaprio, who'd won an Oscar nomination for his role in *What's Eating Gilbert Grape?* (1993), was also vying for it.[59] Schumacher, meanwhile, carried the search for Robin across the pond, traveling to London with casting director Mali Finn. "The day I was in London," recalled Schumacher, "I met Ewan McGregor, Jude Law, Alan Cumming, Toby Stephens and a whole bunch more that have all become stars now."[60] In the end, the role went to O'Donnell, who had been a *Batman* fan almost since birth. "When I was a kid I always watched the TV show and had the toys, including the Batmobile," said the actor, "although they were different than what they have now."[61] An unnamed head of a Hollywood agency told *Entertainment Weekly*, "Batman's not exactly a thinking man's movie. It's a great career move, but it is a departure from the smaller, more interesting stuff he did earlier. It either shows he's reaching as an actor or that he's reaching as a capitalist."

O'Donnell grew up in the Chicago suburb of Winnetka, Illinois, the youngest of seven children in an Irish Catholic family. His father owned radio stations in Wisconsin, while his mother sold real estate. At 13, he decided to become a model, and was soon posing in pajamas for Sears and Montgomery Ward's, using his earnings to play the stock market. In 1987, while still in high school, he played a cashier who waited on basketball star Michael Jordan in a McDonald's ad.[62] As high school graduation neared, O'Donnell wasn't particularly planning on a career in acting, but when a casting director came to Chicago looking for a young actor to play a rebellious teenager in *Men Don't Leave*, one of O'Donnell's teachers recommended him. He landed the role, and ended up playing Jessica Lange's son in the 1990 film. Hollywood took notice, and after a cameo in *Fried Green Tomatoes* (1991), O'Donnell took a starring role in *School Ties* (1991). But it was his next role that made him a star. In *Scent of a Woman* (1992), O'Donnell held his own against powerhouse performer Al Pacino. The acclaimed film won O'Donnell a Golden Globe nomination. After completing his marketing degree at Boston College, he learned fencing and riding to star with Kiefer Sutherland and Charlie Sheen in *The Three Musketeers* (1993), then went to Ireland to star in the film adaptation of the best-selling novel *Circle of Friends* (1995). Now, the

24-year-old O'Donnell told *The Toronto Star's* Mal Vincent, "Everyone says the *Batman* movie is going to change my life. Maybe so, but I don't plan to be Robin for the rest of my life. My life has already changed a lot since *Scent Of A Woman*, but I think I'm keeping my feet on the ground."[63]

O'Donnell seemed to have cornered the market on playing "nice boys," and hoped that playing the rebellious Robin would show another side of his abilities.[64] He changed his persona with a close-cropped haircut with sideburns and a buff body. Schumacher took credit for O'Donnell's transformation. After casting him as Robin, he suggested that the actor bulk up, though "he had a good body to begin with."[65] Schumacher also suggested that O'Donnell's Dick Grayson should wear an earring. O'Donnell's Midwestern sensibilities balked at that. He called his Irish Catholic parents to ask them about it. His mother hung up on him. Schumacher joked, "The terrible scandal about Chris O'Donnell is that there's no terrible scandal."[66]

Robin Williams still had concerns about Akiva Goldsman's rewrite of the script, whose title had now changed from *Batman III* to *Batman Forever*, and so was still indecisive about taking on the Riddler role.[67] He finally passed in the final weeks of May, reportedly concerned that the character as written was "too intellectual" and not as comedic as the Riddler played by Frank Gorshin in the TV series.[68] With Williams gone, the studio immediately hired Hollywood's new golden boy, Jim Carrey, a rubber-faced comedian who first made a name for himself as part of the ensemble of the Fox-TV comedy revue series *In Living Color* before starring in the film *Ace Ventura: Pet Detective*, which was produced for a modest $12 million and earned a very impressive $72.2 million. That same year, he struck gold twice, first with *The Mask*, an adaptation of a comic book that was produced for $23.1 million and earned $351.3 million worldwide, then with co-star Jeff Daniels in *Dumb and Dumber*, which was produced for $16 million and earned $246.2 million worldwide. When Fox cancelled *In Living Color*, it freed up Carrey's fall schedule, making him available for what was expected to be the start of production of *Batman Forever* in September.[69] "It was a great surprise when I got the call that they wanted me to do it," said Carrey. "It's just amazing."[70] From Warner Bros. point-of-view, it wasn't just good casting, it was insurance—they expected Carrey's fans to make *Batman Forever* an instant hit.

The final major part to be cast was that of criminologist Chase Meridian. The role was initially offered to Robin Wright, who had been in high demand since industry buzz began to spread about her work in *Forrest Gump*, which wasn't due to be released for another two months.[71] Other contenders for the role, according to *Entertainment Weekly*, were Jeanne Tripplehorn, who made her film debut in *Basic Instinct* (1992) and had more recently co-starred with Tom Cruise in *The Firm* (1993), and Linda Hamilton, the take-no-prisoners heroine of *The Terminator* (1984) and *Terminator II: Judgment Day* (1991).[72] When Wright finally decided not to take the role, Hamilton was screen tested, and so was Rene Russo, who had just co-starred with Clint Eastwood in *In the Line of Fire* (1993).[73] Rene Russo was said to be Schumacher's top choice.[74]

By the end of June, relations between Michael Keaton and Joel Schumacher, which had begun amicably, had deteriorated. According to *The Los Angeles Times*, Keaton and Schumacher clashed over the amount and quality of screen time Bruce

Wayne and Batman were getting in the sequel.[75] This was, no doubt, a sensitive issue for the actor after some reviewers complained that Batman seemed like a guest star in *Batman Returns*, with most of the film's focus going to the Penguin and Catwoman. Keaton hoped that in the next film, unlike the first two, Batman wouldn't be overshadowed by the villains. As a production insider said, "Let's face it, the *Batman* movies are about who's playing the villains—and there's Michael stuck in a rubber suit."[76]

According to the actor's friends, Keaton was also angry that the filmmakers were forging ahead without seeking his input, since he had been promised more involvement in the development of the story. He requested a meeting with Warner Bros. executives to express his ideas, but the meeting never happened. He did later meet with Schumacher, but felt it went nowhere. According to *Entertainment Weekly*, a "Keaton source" said that after one meeting with Schumacher, "Michael was not feeling confident. Creatively, it wasn't happening. He was worried that the character he'd lived with for two films wasn't going to be developed the way he wanted it to be developed." The source said that as the script was being rewritten, "no one ever called [Keaton] to say, 'Wait! You've got to see this!' Or, 'Wait 'til you see what we've got for Batman!'" Another "Keaton source" was quoted by *The Los Angeles Times* as saying, "Michael wanted to breathe more life into the Batman character. This wasn't a matter of ego. It was a matter of making the story better and the character more interesting."[77]

Another concern of Keaton's was the salary he would receive for donning the claustrophobic Batsuit for a third time. When Robin Williams dropped out and exhibitor favorite Jim Carrey was pushed as his replacement, it was rumored that Keaton was unhappy that his costar might out-earn him as well as upstage him. Having earned $5 million for *Batman* and $10 million for the sequel, Keaton now reportedly wanted $15 million plus a percentage of gross receipts, a demand Warner Bros. was unwilling to grant.[78] Carrey, as it happened, earned between $5 million[79] and $7 million[80] to play the Riddler (depending on whether one believed *Entertainment Weekly* or *Daily Variety*).

With his frustrations mounting, Keaton finally decided it was time to hang up his cowl. He made the decision on Thursday, June 30, 1994, making his wishes known late in the day and surprising the film's principals. In a statement to the press, Keaton said, "I look forward to having the opportunity to play a wide variety of roles of many genres. I hope that several of them will be at Warner Bros. where I've had terrific experiences, both with the *Batman* movies and with such other projects as *Beetlejuice* and *Clean and Sober.*" The studio also released a statement, thanking Keaton for his work on the *Batman* films.[81]

Promoting his film *Speechless* in December 1994, Keaton spoke to reporter Mal Vincent about his reasons for leaving the *Batman* franchise. "It's just that I never felt really at home with the *Batman* thing, " said Keaton. "I had on this heavy suit, and I kept wondering if I was doing the right thing, if it was working. I wanted all this intensity to come through, and I was seldom sure if it was working...It is a huge corporate machine. That's not a bad thing. I liked being a part of it, but the new *Batman* script didn't seem that rewarding. For me, I'm always trying to get away from the last role. I like to try something different every time out. A woman came up to me the other day and asked if I still did comedy. She said, 'You're primarily a dramatic actor now, aren't you?' At one time, I couldn't get anything but comedy roles. Times change."[82]

In his statement to the press, Joel Schumacher took the diplomatic high road, saying, "Michael had contractual and financial lifestyle considerations as well as some artistic considerations that Warner Bros. and I had to consider. We also had the time to consider other possibilities. Hopefully this will be a fresh start for Michael and for Batman."[83] In *Entertainment Weekly*, Schumacher was quoted as saying, "Some people don't want to play superheroes the rest of their life. Even Sean Connery left James Bond." But to *Knight-Ridder News Service* reporter Frank Bruni, when Schumacher was asked why Keaton left the role, he joked, "The inside story? I had Tanya Harding break Michael's leg."[84]

When Michael Keaton walked away from *Batman Forever*, producer Tim Burton had his own idea about who the next Batman should be—his *Edward Scissorhands* star, Johnny Depp. In an interview with Robert Genola of *ComicBookMovie.com*, Depp said, "What happened was Tim was producing it and he was trying to talk Joel Schumacher and the movie bosses to give me a shot at the role but it just never really worked out."[85]

Warner Bros. drew up a short list of other viable candidates to play the Dark Knight: Val Kilmer, Kurt Russell and Billy Baldwin, younger brother of Alec, who had been considered for the role in the first *Batman* opus. Ultimately, it was felt that Baldwin was too young to play mentor to a teenage or early-20s Robin. Russell was a long shot favorite and a bona-fide action star, with tough-guy roles in *Escape From New York* (1981), *Tequila Sunrise* (1988), and *Tombstone* (1993), where he played Wyatt Earp to Kilmer's Doc Holliday. But it was Kilmer who stole the show in *Tombstone*, and it was Kilmer whom director Joel Schumacher championed for the Batman role. "Val was my first and only choice," said Schumacher.[86] "I've been a fan of Val's since *Top Secret*. When I saw *Tombstone*, I thought he'd make a great Batman/Bruce Wayne, not knowing we were ever going to change from Michael."[87]

However, finding Kilmer proved to be a challenge. He was finally tracked down in the African veldt, where he was researching a screenplay.[88] "It turned out that while they were discussing me as the next candidate for the role, I was researching a film about an African adventure," said Kilmer. "On the day that Warner Bros. called my agent and said, 'Yeah, he's who we want,' I was in a cave full of bats in South Africa."[89] Kilmer accepted the Batman role without even reading the script. "I said, 'Sure, why not?'" recalled Kilmer. "How many different variations [of Batman] can there be?...I knew I wasn't going to read anything that would make me gravely concerned about playing the part." With a new lead actor, Schumacher now felt more than ever that he could leave his own stamp on the series. "When Val came on board, that further made it a new franchise because we had a different Batman," said Schumacher. "So even though this was Warner's third *Batman*, it was our first."[90]

The new Batman was born in Los Angeles on New Year's Eve, 1959, to Eugene and Gladys Kilmer.[91] "My father was raised in the mountains of New Mexico, and he picked cotton for a dollar a day," said Kilmer. "He was working for the family from the time he was 7." Eugene Kilmer eventually became a real estate developer in the San

Fernando Valley, where Val Kilmer grew up with his brothers on a ranch once owned by Roy Rogers.[92] At the young age of 12, Kilmer appeared in an ad for a fast food company. He continued acting at Chatsworth High School, along with classmates Kevin Spacey and Mare Winningham, then attended the Hollywood Professional School.[93] At age 17, he became the youngest student ever admitted to the drama

Val Kilmer becomes Batman in Batman Forever. In a 2011 interview, Joel Schumacher remarked that he felt Kilmer was the best Batman of all (Warner Bros./Photofest, © Warner Bros.).

department of New York's Juilliard School.[94] He perfected his craft on stage in New York, appearing in *How It All Began*, a play he co-wrote with Juilliard classmates, and *The Slab Boys*, co-starring then-unknowns Sean Penn and Kevin Bacon. In 1984, he landed his first feature film role, playing an Elvis Presley-type singer who gets involved with spy intrigue in *Top Secret!* More feature films and TV roles followed, including a high-profile turn as Tom Cruise's nemesis in *Top Gun* (1986), and the starring role in the 1988 fantasy adventure *Willow*. But it was Kilmer's channeling of Jim Morrison for *The Doors* (1991) and his scene-stealing performance as Doc Holliday in *Tombstone* (1993) that put him solidly on Hollywood's A-list.[95]

Kilmer's hiring was announced the same day as Keaton's departure. But once the 42-year-old Keaton was replaced with the 33-year-old Kilmer, the studio decided that 40-year-old Rene Russo might be too old to play Batman's love interest.[96] Sandra Bullock, co-star of the surprise hit *Speed*, which had opened a couple of weeks earlier, was in the running to replace her. Bullock also had another offer, for the romantic comedy *While You Were Sleeping*, which was due to begin shooting at the same time as *Batman Forever*. Ultimately, she chose to go with the romantic dramedy, which gave the actress her first leading role and kept her from becoming typecast in action-adventure films.[97]

The next actress approached for the role was Nicole Kidman, who had most recently appeared opposite Michael Keaton in the drama *My Life* (1993).[98] Born in Hawaii to Australian parents in 1967, Kidman spent the first few years of her life growing up in Washington, D.C. before the family returned to their native Sydney. Her love of performing began early; she studied ballet at age 3 and mime at age 8, and later became a regular at Sydney's Philip Street Theatre. At 16, she was cast in *Bush Christmas* (1983), a TV movie that became a regular holiday attraction in Australia. Two years later, she received international acclaim in director Philip Noyce's *Dead Calm*, as a woman terrorized by a psycho on a yacht. This led to her first role in Hollywood, playing a neurologist who falls in love with a race car driver, played by Tom Cruise, in *Days of Thunder* (1990). Cruise was smitten with her, and the two wed on Christmas Eve of 1990 in a secret ceremony in Telluride, Colorado. Joel Schumacher had long been a fan of the actress, and was delighted when she accepted the role of Dr. Chase Meridian. "I've had my eye on her since *Dead Calm*," he said. "You meet a lot of beautiful people in this business, but there's something almost luminous about her. I wish I had a clause in my contract that said Nicole Kidman had to be in every one of my movies."[99]

Only two actors were retained from Tim Burton's ensemble. Michael Gough returned as Alfred, Bruce Wayne's faithful butler and aide-de-camp, and Pat Hingle reprised his role of Police Commissioner Gordon. In a *Starlog* interview with Tom Weaver, Hingle said, "When I went to do the new one...I said, 'Listen, are you guys gonna hire Michael Gough, the British actor, to play Alfred again? ' And they told me, 'Oh, yeah. You and Michael are the bookends—one on one end and one on the other, and we just put in other actors!"[100] Gough was happy to be back in the black suit and white collar, saying, "Luckily, I was blessed to have worked with Val in *Top Secret!*, so he was already a friend and we already had a working and personal relationship, which made acting with a new Batman and Bruce much easier."[101]

For the role of Edward Nygma's boss, Fred Stickley, Schumacher turned to an actor he'd worked with previously, Ed Begley, Jr. "Joel Schumacher had been a friend of mine for years," said Begley. "I had met him in 1978 when he directed a thing called *Amateur Night at the Dixie Bar and Grill*, with a very early in his career Dennis Quaid, Tanya Tucker, Candy Clark and myself...I suppose because of that I got a call to be in *Batman Forever*, and play Jim Carrey's boss at Wayne Industries."[102]

With the major roles cast, Bob Ringwood was engaged to once again work on costumes for the film, this time joined by Ingrid Ferrin, who had just worked with Schumacher on *The Client*. A new Batsuit was constructed out of a special foam rubber. It weighed about 30 pounds, and under the hot studio lights, temperatures inside it reached as much as 140 degrees. The Batsuit was designed so that it could be put on or taken off in 10 minutes, with zippers hidden beneath the sculpted muscles.[103] "By the time we filmed the third one with Val Kilmer," said Bob Ringwood, "we had perfected the Batsuit. It couldn't get sleeker."[104] To keep it looking fresh during filming, more than 130 Batsuits were made during the production.[105]

Despite Ringwood's enthusiasm, Val Kilmer found the Batsuit less than perfect. "It hurts," he said. "It shrinks all the time, whether it's on me or not. It's like being wrapped up. Fortunately, most of the time when [Bruce] Wayne puts it on, there's something he wants to hit or punch." Kilmer also said that the Batsuit "was like being old. You feel young, you don't stop feeling or reacting in your mind, but your body just can't do things at the same speed. Plus, you can't see. Or breathe. You can't find things. Your joints ache for no reason. And you can't hear anymore." A lot of his acting, he said, was done with his lips.[106] When *Movieline* magazine asked Val Kilmer what he wore underneath his Batsuit, the star responded, "Buff, man. He's dedicated, Batman."

Ringwood was also obliged to come up with an outfit for Robin. Although the Boy Wonder was shown with an updated version of the familiar red-vested, yellow-caped outfit during the circus performance, once he becomes a superhero, he's in a muscle-enhancing rubber suit similar to Batman's. "The tights were kind of tough to step into," said O'Donnell. The mask also had its downside; it had to be stuck to his face with adhesive.[107]

Schumacher was inspired by classic Greek statuary to add a design element to the Batman and Robin costumes for which he would be forever vilified: nipples. "The suits are very sexy because they're very body conscious," said Schumacher. "They're idealized, almost Greek, with a little steroid in it. It's playful sexy, of course. We're not talking *Basic Instinct* here."[108]

Flamboyant costumes were also created for both Two-Face and The Riddler. Jim Carrey helped design what was called the Riddler's "Vegas suit," adorned with 2,500 computer-controlled blinking lights. Despite all the electronics, the coat weighed no more than the average blazer.[109]

Besides over-the-top costumes, Tommy Lee Jones and Jim Carrey were subjected to grueling make-up sessions. It took two-and-a-half hours to transform Jones into Two-Face. The Jekyll and Hyde-inspired make-up was created by Rick Baker, who was on his way to collecting his third Academy Award for transforming actor Martin Landau into Bela Lugosi for Tim Burton's *Ed Wood*. Baker's Two-Face concept used just five prosthetic foam pieces. The two make-up artists who applied it to Jones eventually got the routine streamlined so that by the shoot's end the application only took 90 minutes.[110] Jim Carrey's Riddler make-up, including the day-glo red flat-top he wore for some scenes, and the green rubber domino-style mask affixed to his face, took up to three hours to apply.[111] Debi Mazar, who played Two-Face's paramour Spice, spent about two hours in the make-up chair, thanks to the five-piece wig that had to be weaved onto her head.[112]

Schumacher turned to another recent collaborator to be the film's production designer. Barbara Ling, a Los Angeles native who received a political science degree from UCLA before becoming a set designer for theatrical productions and films, had worked with Schumacher on *Falling Down*. Ling and Schumacher decided not to try and recreate the Gotham City of Anton Furst or Bo Welch, but to take a fresh spin. "When I first approached the design of Gotham City, my mind always went to the World's Fair idea of buildings and statues being so over-scaled that man is stunted," said Ling. "Gotham City is designed to be three times the height of New York, with everything on a monumental level. We examined lots of photos and films of the great World's Fairs of the '20s, '30s and '40s, which were filled with tiny people staring in awe at tremendous buildings."[113]

Ling designed more than 60 sets. The largest stage at Warner Bros., Stage 16, contained the Second Bank of Gotham vault, the Gotham Hippodrome Circus and the gigantic domed lair of the Riddler. Other soundstages held Chase Meridian's apartment, the Gotham Police Headquarters rooftop (complete with Batsignal), the abandoned Gotham Plaza subway station, and the Arkham Asylum exterior.[114] When the production overran the available stages at Warner Bros., Universal Studio's Stage 12 was rented for the interior of Arkham Asylum and the 50-foot-tall cylinder that led to the Riddler's lair.[115]

Still, the production needed more studio space, so the massive 140,000 square foot Long Beach Dome, which had once housed Howard Hughes' experimental Spruce Goose airplane, was taken over. Four sets were constructed there: the 60-foot tall Batcave, the 150-foot long Wayne Enterprises research laboratory, the interior of Wayne Manor, and Two-Face's lair.[116] An old Hughes Aircraft hangar in Playa del Rey became the headquarters of John Dykstra's visual effects department. There, Dykstra and his crew created a miniature of Gotham City that stretched 100 feet long, up to 50 feet wide and nearly 50 feet tall.[117]

Production designer Barbara Ling also redesigned the Batmobile for the new film. She and art department illustrator Tim Flattery, who had automotive design experience, took inspiration for the design from a videotape of a bat flying in a wind tunnel to create a car that was more torpedo-shaped, with a big Batfin on the back reminiscent of the Batmobile seen in *Batman* comics of the 1940s. "The Batmobile was quite a challenge, and we actually went through many stages to get to the final vehicle," said Ling. "We went for a stylized, automotive version of a bat. I wanted the Batmobile to look like a living, breathing thing."[118]

Special effects supervisor Tommy Fisher, working with Allen Pike and Charley Zurian of TFX, a vehicle fabrication company, took the design from the drawing board and turned it into reality, using cutting-edge materials. The body was made from carbon fiber, the same material used in F-16 fighter planes and Formula One racing cars, along with a high-temperature epoxy resin with all of the air vacuumed out. "It makes it super lightweight and super strong," said Pike.[119] Under the hood, the car featured a Chevy 350 ZZ3 high-performance 345 horsepower motor. The Batman logo now appeared on the hubcaps, which were backlit and affixed with counter-rotating gears to keep the logo still when the car was in motion. Its maximum speed was 160mph.[120]

There were three Batmobiles made for the film. One was a stunt version, with modified suspension and front and rear brakes for scenes requiring the car to spin out. Another was a fully operational "hero" model for partial interior shots, and finally a "buck" model that didn't actually run, but provided a complete mock-up interior for shots inside the vehicle.[121]

Ling and Tim Flattery also developed three other vehicles for the movie, the Batwing, Batboat and Batsub. The Batwing was redesigned to make it appear swifter, sharper and more consistent with the look of the new Batmobile. The same approach was taken with the Batboat, which was created with input from a marine expert to make sure it was seaworthy. The Batsub was never actually fabricated; all shots of it were created entirely digitally by John Dykstra's visual effects department.[122]

Bob Kane once again acted as a consultant on the film, and voiced his approval of the new Batman, telling *Variety's* Army Archerd that Kilmer "is near to my comic book character. He's more Batmanesque."[123] He later told *USA Today* reporter Andy Seiler, "Michael Keaton was very good, but Val Kilmer is even closer to the image of Batman."[124] Kane's wife, actress Elizabeth Sanders, was given a showier cameo role this time, playing Gotham City gossip columnist Gossip Gertie. "She really pops out of the screen," said Kane.[125] When the reporters were off the set, however, Kane was less effusive. "He didn't like the idea of Dick Grayson wearing an earring," said Schumacher. "He didn't understand why it was necessary. He also wasn't thrilled with the fact that the new Batsuit has nipples on it. He would come up to me every once in a while and say, 'Joel, I just don't understand.'"[126]

Schumacher went into the film thinking that it was going to be great fun, but as the start date loomed, he began to worry. "I thought to myself, 'What have I done?' I had never directed anything of this size or this complexity before," said Schumacher. "It dawned on me that this was not going to be fun and that this would be the most arduous thing I had every done in my life."[127]

MIRACLE MAN

Schumacher's fears began to evaporate on the first day of production, when he arrived on set in New York for a week of location shooting in Lower Manhattan. Filming began with shots of the Batmobile at Exchange Place. "We closed down Wall Street for five blocks and after years of planning, we were all ready for the first shot," said Schumacher. "We were standing out in the middle of the street and suddenly, the Batmobile comes racing down the street at 100 miles an hour. It was like the beginning of a dream come true."[128] To keep the filming as top secret as possible, sheets of plywood closed the location off from public view. Later in the night, a shot was needed of the car several blocks away on Gold Street. Dawn was approaching, and there was no time to put the vehicle into its custom-built truck to transport it there. So, early-morning risers in New York were astounded to see the Batmobile driving to the next location, with an N.Y.P.D. escort.[129] For the location shots, the Batmobile was put through its paces by stunt driver Dick Hancock, whose resume included street racing in Austin, Texas.[130]

Filming continued with New York's Surrogate's Court Building serving as the interior and exterior of the Gotham Municipal Police Complex. For exterior shots of the Ritz Gotham Hotel, the production company used what had once been the U.S. Customs Building, just weeks before it reopened as the Smithsonian Museum of the American Indian. Then the crew was off to Glen Cove, Long Island, where the Webb Institute of Naval Architecture became the exterior of Wayne Manor.[131]

Once filming moved to the interior sets, the actors found Schumacher calm, cool and in control. "He's real sensitive to actors' needs," said Chris O'Donnell. "He wants to make sure you're in the right frame of mind, and he makes you want to talk to him on an acting as well as a personal level."[132] O'Donnell learned more than just his lines during the production; while making the film, he was also attending night school at UCLA to complete the last four courses required for his marketing degree from Boston College.[133]

Michael Gough sang Schumacher's praises, telling Michael Singer, author of *Batman Forever: The Official Movie Book*, "Joel is a miracle man, as far as directors go. He's entirely sympathetic, but won't let anything go that he doesn't like. He really wants you to be good, and he likes actors."[134]

Nicole Kidman responded to Schumacher's earnestness. "He tells you what he likes in an honest and blunt way. And he makes it comfortable for you to take risks. Besides that, he'll tell you anything about his life, anything. I admire him for that."[135] Kidman threw herself into the role of Batman-bewitched Chase Meridian. "She's constantly trying to seduce him," she told *Entertainment Weekly's* Benjamin Svetkey. "She wears black slinky dresses, has perfect hair, perfect red lips, and talks in a deep, husky voice. It's definitely a heightened reality. Really over-the-top." Schumacher joked, "I know, I know, she doesn't look anything like a criminal psychiatrist. But it's my Gotham City and I can do what I want."[136]

One of the things Schumacher wanted was to make his Gotham look like a living comic book. To achieve that, he worked closely with cinematographer Stephen Goldblatt, who had previous event-movie experience photographing Steven Spielberg's *Young Sherlock Holmes* (1985) and the first two *Lethal Weapon* films (1987 and 1989). Goldblatt said that *Batman Forever* "was very different from anything else I'd ever done before. It's an extravagant opera. It borders on excess, which inevitably causes problems...I scared myself to death on this film."[137]

Despite the discomfort he felt inside the Batman costume, Kilmer worked to give as believable a performance as one could while dressed in black rubber. "He's very courtly," said Schumacher,[138] who also said of his star, "I hate metaphysical mumbo jumbo, but you know when people say other people are old souls? There's just something about Val..."

Kilmer's equanimity was put to the test filming the scene where Batman and Two-Face struggle with each other inside a cramped helicopter. As cameras rolled, one of the carefully choreographed blows accidentally connected. "At one point we were on a gimbals that was swerving and dipping in the air, and I was supposed to kick him in the face," said Tommy Lee Jones. "I think on the third or fourth take, the helicopter zigged when it should have zagged, and I popped him on the nose. I was mortified, but he was a perfect gentleman." It helped that Kilmer and Jones had already bonded off-camera, talking about their ranches and trading tips on raising cattle.

Chris O'Donnell also had an embarrassing mishap when at the end of a day's filming, he decided to take the Batmobile out for a spin. When it went out of control, he crunched its fender on a curb.[139] Schumacher didn't seem to mind. The director kept a loose mood on the set by playing practical jokes, often at O'Donnell's expense. As he was about to begin one scene, O'Donnell got a shock when he discovered a photo that Schumacher had enhanced. "It was my head on a naked body with this enormous, you know, male part," says O'Donnell, "and Joel put it on the Bat-screen in the Batcave just before I entered for a scene. Of course, they got it all on film." Schumacher also enhanced O'Donnell's convertible, filling it to the rim with popcorn.[140]

Ed Begley, Jr. spent his first couple of days working with Val Kilmer, for the scenes early in the movie when Bruce Wayne visits his factory. "I'd known Val for a while," said Begley. "He was very happy to play Batman. It's a James Bond kind of a thing, you know. Who's the new Batman? Who's the new James Bond? To play that part is quite an honor."[141]

Playing his scenes opposite Jim Carrey, Ed Begley Jr. went big. "You know, this was not *Remains of the Day*," said Begley. "It was not a Merchant-Ivory movie, clearly. Everybody knew that. So in a bold gesture, certainly the first rehearsal, I don't know that Joel or anyone knew what I was going to do, and I came out of the gate with 'Mister Waaaaaaayne.' You know, playing one of those very large characters that you might see in a '40s movie. And Joel liked it a lot. And that is the challenge as an actor, to do things that, hopefully, have a resonance to something real but also spike out from that carpet of reality that you lay down and then have very large things that grab people that occur within those parameters. And Jim Carrey certainly is good at that."[142]

Kilmer, O'Donnell and the other actors feared that Carrey's manic energy, with which he infused every atom of the Riddler, might upstage them. Schumacher, however, was unconcerned, describing Carrey as "one of the most courageous, inventive humans in our business. In playing the Riddler, Jim had several difficult tasks—the biggest having to be wearing the green unitard that showed every little thing he ate."[143]

As the Riddler's plans—and his outfits—became more outrageous, Carrey looked to a surprising source for inspiration: Elvis Presley. "I wanted to go to Elvis," said Carrey. "Elvis in Vegas with the eagle on his back. In Vegas, the art wasn't coming from inside Elvis any more. It was on the outside. 'Look at my diamond rings. Look at my eagle and my glasses.' You start adorning the outside. That's what I wanted the Riddler to do. He needed that because he had no identity."[144]

As filming progressed, Schumacher and the rest of the crew bonded with Carrey, who was then at the height of his fame. "You certainly get to know someone when you work with him," said Schumacher, "and I have to tell you Jim is handling success beautifully. When he finished work and left to promote *The Mask* in Tokyo, everyone he worked with on *Batman* felt very sad."[145]

By the end of February, with filming nearing completion, Schumacher was feeling upbeat. "I thought shooting would be more arduous," he told columnist Marilyn Beck. "There are so many gimmicks, toys and special effects. It's much more complicated to do than *The Client*, where I had great actors doing six pages of dialogue at a time. Here it's jokes and gags and cars flying and special effects."[146] Despite the pressures, he remained upbeat, sometimes joking, "I hope all of you have your next jobs, because if they let me direct again after this, it's a miracle."[147]

While Schumacher worked with the actors, Pacific Data Images was toiling to marry live actions shots with models, miniatures and matte paintings. In the end, they completed over thirty computer animated effects sequences for the film, including shots of a computer-generated Batman for scenes such as the one where the Caped Crusader does a 600-foot plunge off a building.[148] Asked if he was worried that the visual effects and action would outweigh the actors, Schumacher replied, "If you know these actors, it's pretty hard for anything to steal a scene from any of them. I think the visuals are there only to support the story and the characters. We really tried to blend it all together, so that the film looks great without taking away from anything or anyone."[149]

Of more concern to the director was Warner Bros.' decision to move the release date from the end of June to June 16, effectively cutting two weeks out of the post-production schedule. The move put added pressure on Schumacher. When he was asked when the final print would be ready, he quipped, "June 15—at midnight."[150] *Starlog's* Marc Shapiro interviewed the director on the final day of filming, and found him feeling confident. Schumacher told Shapiro, "When I was driving over to have lunch with Tim Burton to do *Batman Forever*, I was wondering, 'Is anybody even interested in a new Batman movie?' And now here I am on the last day of shooting and there's already this rumor that I'll be doing the fourth one. I guess that means there is still interest."[151] Schumacher already had a title in mind for the next installment. Impressed with Chris O'Donnell's work, he said, "I suggested that when they do the next one, they call it *Batman and Robin*."

When filming came to a close, Schumacher said, "It was kind of like climbing Mount Everest, and when it was over I thought, 'Wow, I could have died,' There's a kind of reckless feeling to filmmaking anyway. It's like building a 747 while you're flying it. You have absolutely no idea if it's going to land safely."[152] Looking at the bottom-line numbers, the studio was ecstatic. Warner Bros. co-chairman Robert Daly said, "I've never seen a movie as big as this one that went so smoothly. It stayed on schedule and actually came in under budget. That's the way Joel operates."[153]

Elliot B. Goldenthal provided the score of *Batman Forever*, creating his own *Batman* theme rather than recycling the one created by Danny Elfman for the first two films. "I saw the first two *Batman* movies, liked the music, but never referred to them again," said Goldenthal. "I thought that Danny [Elfman] did fantastic work with

Burton, but for *Batman Forever*, I needed to create a brand-new theme and a different approach. The thing that's been established about this new Batman world, which was created for the last film, is that the music is large and orchestral. And because Batman wears a black cape, lives in a cave and has a double life, you take it for granted that the music has a bit of darkness to it too. Then you also have the hero versus the villain, and you have a certain genre that's built in right there. Large, orchestral, dark, heroic, good versus evil."[154]

The soundtrack was adorned with cuts from current pop performers, such as the Flaming Lips, whose "Bad Days" is heard while Jim Carrey's Riddler makes mischief. When Dick Grayson races off in the Batmobile, the Damned's "Smash It Up" is heard, and the end titles crawl over U2's "Hold Me, Thrill Me, Kiss Me, Kill Me" and Seal's "Kiss From a Rose." The soundtrack that was released for the film included even more pop cuts, including Nick Cave's "There Is a Light" and Method Man's "The Riddler." Those songs, commissioned for the film but ultimately dropped from the final cut, were retained on the CD soundtrack.[155] Soon after the soundtrack's release, the U2 song climbed to #33 on the Top 40 Singles Chart.[156]

When the soundtrack album was released, Seal was outspoken in his opinion of the video for his song "Kiss From a Rose," saying, "As far as I'm concerned, it's kind of like a promotional movie for the *Batman* movie and for Seal. But it's creatively nothing to do with what I want." But he couldn't deny that having his song in the film's end credits helped it to gain exposure. "It's not a hard decision to make when your album was out of the Top 200 and it's now 130 with a bullet," Seal said. "It's not a hard decision at all." In mid-September of 1995, the song broke all records for the number of times a song was played on the radio in a given week (those records, however, had only been kept since 1991). The single eventually made it to Number 1 on the charts. "You have to make concessions here and there," said Seal.[157]

Throughout shooting, Schumacher had been conscious of making a Batman film that was less violent than the previous one. "I have a 6-year-old godson who's the most important person in my life," said Schumacher. "If I could make a movie that he thought was cool and I thought was cool, then we could get some of the people in between. Then I screened the film for him on the Warners lot, and he wasn't frightened."[158] For Schumacher, this meant he had met his mark. "The juggling game was to make it dark enough to be Batman, but light enough to be a living comic book," said Schumacher. "I've achieved that for me, but I really hope that I achieved that for the people who come to see this."[159]

By the time filming concluded, *Batman Forever* cost nearly $80 million to make. Warner Bros. was now poised to spend another $20 million to promote it.[160] The first ads for the new film hit the streets on Presidents Day weekend in February 1995, when one-sheets began appearing showing the Batman logo encircled with a neon green Riddler question mark. The poster was created by Christopher Wagner and Maseeh Rafani at the Idea Place, an in-house advertising unit of Warner Bros. No teaser trailers were prepared. Instead, as filming was nearing completion, Warner Bros. created a 3-minute and 15-second trailer that showed audiences enough footage to demonstrate the new film's brighter tone. "We wanted to introduce the characters," said Warner Bros. president of worldwide advertising and publicity Rob Friedman.

"We wanted to show that the movie was different from *Batman Returns*, and that tone is consistent throughout all elements of the marketing campaign." Warners' executive VP of creative projects Joel Wayne added, "I thought that because this was the third one, people might be sitting with crossed arms feeling that they weren't going to be seduced. So I wanted to show more of the movie."[161]

The promotional partners were also pleased that the new film was more family-friendly. By the time the film was ready to be released, Warner Bros. had commitments of between $45 million and $50 million from Six Flags amusement parks (which they owned), Kenner Toys, Kellogg's, Acclaim Entertainment and, significantly, McDonald's.[162]

The publicity blitz got under way in April 1995, when posters of the film's main characters began appearing on bus stops and subways. Famed photographer Herb Ritts, a friend of Schumacher's, took the photos for the campaign, which featured colorful individual posters of Batman, Robin, The Riddler, Two-Face and Dr. Chase Meridian. It was reported that about 20% of the posters were stolen from their bus shelter display cases. A poster featuring a composite of all the characters hit the streets on Memorial Day.[163]

McDonald's began running their promotional spots on May 25.[164] The fast food retailer pushed *Batman Forever* with special "hero" sandwiches (on a hero bread bun), drink cups and packaging aimed at adults. They refrained, however, from promoting the film with Happy Meals. "This is an adult promotion," McDonald's spokesman Steve Bender told *St. Petersburg Times* reporter Steve Persall. "We think the adventure and excitement of *Batman Forever* will appeal to our older audience."[165] Predictably, shots from the film's opening scene—where Alfred says, "Can I persuade you to take a sandwich with you, Sir?" and Batman responds, "I'll get drive-through"— were used in a McDonald's commercial.[166]

Throughout May, just prior to the film's opening, magazine racks were filled with images of *Batman Forever's* stars. Chris O'Donnell graced the cover of *YM* magazine, and got an 8-page spread in the June issue of *GQ*. Val Kilmer was on the cover of *Movieline* and *Details* magazines, and was profiled in *Harper's Bazaar*, whose reporter wrote, "Val Kilmer is a gorgeous human being in a way that filmed representations only begin to indicate; he has beautiful hands, he has a beautiful mouth, he has a beautiful voice...not to put too fine a point on it, but he is a major, major fox..."[167] Kilmer shrugged off the attention, saying, "It's been easy to promote because [reporters] laugh if they have any serious questions. There's no angle on it. Sometimes it's harder if you really care about the project, because there's something you want to make sure gets across, but there isn't with this. It is what it is. It's done. It's big."[168]

Warner Bros. began airing spots for the film the first week of June.[169] They also turned to more innovative ways to promote *Batman Forever*, creating a website, www.batmanforever.com, where computer-savvy Batfans could view clips from the film, hear cuts from the soundtrack, and read promotional material. It was believed to be the first time a website had been devoted to a single film,[170] as well as the most expensive and elaborate home page a studio had ever devised. Don Buckley, a spokesman for Warner Brothers, said, "It's smart business to stay in touch with the technology." According to Warner Bros., the *Batman Forever* home page received 1.8 million "hits" weekly.[171]

As the film's release date neared, plans were made to hold the press junket not in Los Angeles but in Atlanta, nearer to North Carolina, where Jim Carrey was filming a sequel to *Ace Ventura, Pet Detective*.[172] Nicole Kidman, Tommy Lee Jones, Jim Carrey, Chris O'Donnell and Joel Schumacher were on hand to greet about 150 members of the foreign and domestic press at the Ritz-Carlton Hotel. Val Kilmer did not attend; he was in Santa Fe, New Mexico awaiting a more important event, the birth of his child. His wife, actress, Joanne Whalley-Kilmer, was expected to go into labor around the same time as the Atlanta screening.[173]

Batman Forever had its official world premiere in Los Angeles on Friday, June 9, 1995. The film screened at two theatres simultaneously, Mann's Village and the Mann Bruin. Westwood Village was blocked off, with bleachers situated around the theatres for hundreds of photo-snapping Batfans. Afterwards, Batsignals guided guests to the nearby Armand Hammer Museum and Cultural Center for a reception. Among the more than 1,000 guests were the film's Joel Schumacher, Val Kilmer, Nicole Kidman and husband Tom Cruise, Chris O'Donnell, Tommy Lee Jones, Jim Carrey, Drew Barrymore, and Debi Mazar, as well as celebrities like George Clooney, Cindy Crawford, Geena Davis, Anthony Edwards, David Hasselhoff, director John Singleton, Faye Dunaway, Lauren Holly, Rosie O'Donnell, Steven Seagal, Wesley Snipes and Aaron Spelling with wife Candy and daughter Tori. Dinner was a hors d'oeuvres buffet served by waiters dressed as multicolored henchmen.[174] When asked his opinion of Kilmer's Dark Knight, Dean Cain, the star of *Lois & Clark: The New Adventures of Superman* said, "I envy Val Kilmer all the way. I think he's got a better costume, better gadgets, better special effects and he makes a heck of a lot more money than I do."[175] Kilmer, asked about the secret of playing Batman, said, "I wish I had an interesting answer for you, but it was really show up and get dressed. When your foyer is 480 feet wide, it's kind of easy to make-believe."[176]

Less than a week later, on Wednesday, June 14, 1995, *Batman Forever* had a $100 per person benefit premiere at the Warner Theater in Washington D.C., benefiting the Children's Inn at the National Institutes of Health. Nearly 2,000 fans, including Speaker of the House Newt Gingrich, attended the screening and party; Gingrich's wife Marianne was chair of the Children's Inn, which provided a home away from home for children with critical illnesses. Among the approximately 400 children in attendance were many from the Children's Inn,[177] as well as politicians including Representative John Dingell of Michigan, Labor Secretary Robert Reich, and Health and Human Services Secretary Donna Shalala.[178]

The screening came just a couple of weeks after Republican presidential candidate Bob Dole had excoriated the entertainment industry for peddling "nightmares of depravity." Among the entertainment companies Dole blamed for the plague of violence and sex in the entertainment industry was Warner Bros. The chairman and chief executive officer of Time-Warner, Gerald Levin, took the opportunity at the Washington screening to defend his company to reporters, saying that Dole "was sadly misinformed because this is a great company that does things that are highly beneficial to this society." Dole did not attend the benefit screening, and neither did President Clinton, who had also been critical of the entertainment industry.[179]

Following the screening, audiences went down the street to the Old Post Office Pavilion for a post-screening party. Upon entering the Pavilion, guests found that the food court and atrium had been converted into a Batcave with black walls, faux rock formations, glowing bats and a glowing Batsignal. Gingrich, detained by a surprise party to celebrate his 52nd birthday, missed half the film, but told a reporter, "Luckily, I used to read *Batman* comic books so I figured it out."

Democratic Senator Patrick Leahy had more than a passing interest in the film. He had been a Batman fan since he was four years old, when one Sunday after Mass, his parents stopped at a Montpelier, Vermont drugstore and bought him a comic book for ten cents. "I can vaguely picture it," said Leahy. "One of the scenes had Bruce Wayne down in the Batcave to work on the Batmobile."[180] Through the years, Leahy had become a Batman expert as well as an expert on agricultural issues, defense and foreign affairs. He was even asked to appear in *Batman Forever*; Leahy can be spotted dancing with a former Miss Vermont in the scene where Two-Face interrupts Edward Nygma's lavish launch party.[181] "My part was very easy," Leahy said. "It required no talent, no great knowledge, nothing in the way of good looks or natural ability. It was almost the same qualifications as being a member of the U.S. Senate."[182]

BATMAN REVIVED

Despite the fun that Schumacher had making it, the film opened to mixed reviews. Brian Lowry in *Daily Variety* said, "An enormous fun-house ride, the second *Batman* sequel succeeds in some basic levels while coming up short in others. On the plus side, the tone has lightened up after criticism of the last outing, Val Kilmer seamlessly slides into the Dark Knight's cape and the film boasts considerable action and visual splendor. In the negative column, that action isn't as involving as it should be, and there are so many characters the movie can't adequately service them all."[183]

Entertainment Weekly's Owen Gleiberman summed up the film by saying, "Watching *Batman Forever* is a little like spending two hours inside a happy asylum. Just about every character in the movie is undergoing some sort of an identity crisis, yet rather than making the picture feel 'dark,' these various schizoid head-cases bounce off each other like brightly colored billiard balls...And the movie itself is a loony-tunes extravaganza in which having a split personality doesn't constitute a serious emotional trauma so much as it does a fashion statement."[184]

Quentin Curtis, writing in the London newspaper *The Independent*, said, "Schumacher is a better story-teller than Burton, whose narratives were weighed down by Stygian gloom. Schumacher allows his plots to simmer nicely for a while, before bringing them to the boil. But neither director has much mastery of action scenes...Schumacher has also hit on a more consistent house acting style, half-way between cartoon and realism. Kilmer, taking over from Michael Keaton, has more butch presence, but less neurosis."[185]

In *The New York Times*, Janet Maslin wrote, "*Batman Forever* is a viable installment in the *Batman* series, though Joel Schumacher's flashy direction is messier and less interestingly macabre than Tim Burton's darkly ingenious films in this genre... High on the list of innovations we didn't need to see this year: nipples on Batman's redesigned rubber suit." Commenting on the film's over-hyped commercialization, Maslin wrote, "*Batman Forever* brings on the very secular sensation that you are part of something larger than yourself. Toys, games, comics, videos: each has its place in the cosmos of this multimedia phenomenon, and the consumer's role is no less well-defined. As for the actual movie, it's the empty-calorie equivalent of a Happy Meal (another Batman tie-in), so clearly a product that the question of its cinematic merit is strictly an afterthought."[186]

Rolling Stone's Peter Travers said, "The third Batman epic, with Val Kilmer replacing Michael Keaton as the Caped Crusader and Jim Carrey out-mugging Jack Nicholson's Joker as the rascally Riddler, is a long way from the dark poetry of Tim Burton's 1989 original. This 1995 version has cleaned up its act...*Batman Forever*, with Joel Schumacher (*The Client*) in for Burton as director, goes easy on the mayhem and doesn't dwell on our hero's pesky depressive side. Instead, the new film catches the campy innocence of the *Batman* TV series of the '60s. Schumacher's method is to use a lighter touch, to stay closer to the cartoon that Bob Kane created for DC Comics in 1939 and to temper Burton's nightmare world with an accessible, brightly colored TV palette."[187]

Jay Carr in *The Boston Globe* said *Batman Forever* should have been called *Batman Lite*, writing, "From beginning to end, it's a marketing strategy, designed to purge the franchise of the darkness and weirdness that made the first two films interesting, and transform it into something more mainstream-friendly. Unfortunately, it succeeds... It's saturated with color, but not with daring. It's a ride, not a nightmare, moved from the realm of dream to the realm of pinball."[188]

Among other unfavorable reviews was one from Steve Murray of *The Atlanta Constitution*, who wrote, "Director Joel Schumacher gives us a candy-colored Gotham closer to Vegas—or *Dick Tracy*—than Burton's morgue-like metropolis...Carrey is the film's best special effect. In contrast, Tommy Lee Jones' Two-Face is a lost opportunity. Great makeup, but his performance is a long rant. Kilmer's is a long pause. A black-clad blank as both Batman and Bruce, he's part Ken doll, part Darth Vader. He speaks in such a monotone, you wonder whether his contract came with a no-inflections clause."[189] Philip French in *The Manchester Guardian* was more harsh, writing, "Joel Schumacher's *Batman Forever* is the lowest point yet in the hi-tech cycle that began with *Superman* in 1978. About as entertaining as watching a video game over someone's shoulder, it is devoid of fun, narrative drive and simple emotional involvement."[190]

Regardless of the reviews, moviegoers were primed to see Val Kilmer's take on Batman. In its first three days of release, *Batman Forever* brought in an astounding $52,784,433 at the box office—the biggest three-day opening ever.[191] Wall Street responded; the stellar box-office performance helped push Time-Warner's stock up 6% to a 15-month high of $43.125, adding $950 million to the company's $16 billion total market worth.[192] Ed Mintz, founder of Las Vegas-based audience survey firm CinemaScore, said *Batman Forever* was the "most wanted-to-see film" of summer

1995.[193] After two and a half weeks, the film had raked in $141.8 million, becoming the first film of 1995 to earn over $100 million, and ensuring that it would soon surpass the $162.8 million earned by *Batman Returns*.[194]

When the film opened in Australia, it had the biggest opening day ever for an American film, though in Japan the first-week receipts of $2.2 million represented an 80 percent drop from the revenues that *Batman Returns* collected three years earlier.[195] Nonetheless, the film went on to earn $152.5 million overseas, and $184 million domestically. In the U.S., it was the #2 film of the year, behind Disney's *Toy Story*.

Batman Forever's toy story was just beginning. By the time the film hit theaters, *Batman Forever* merchandise was ubiquitous. As with the previous film, Warner Bros. issued more than 130 licenses for *Batman Forever* toys and products.[196] Stores were offering posters, play sets, mugs, notebooks, Batcycles, Batmobiles, Batwings and Batarangs. At Southern California's Six Flags Magic Mountain, a "Batman Nights" special effects, laser and fireworks show was added to the existing Batman ride and Batman stunt show. The 115 Warner Bros. Studio Stores throughout the country heavily pushed the film for a month before it opened, with scenes from the film playing on the stores' video walls and clerks wearing *Batman Forever* tee shirts and buttons.[197] The stores were temporarily rechristened "Batman Headquarters." Clothing designer Todd Oldham created a 21-piece *Batman Forever*-inspired line called "Todd Oldham Forever" exclusively for Warner Bros. Studio Stores, with items such as bat-shaped belt buckles and hair barrettes, Two-Face-inspired jeans and backpacks (half red zebra stripes, half yellow leopard spots), and $244 velour slip dresses with "emerald" question-mark chains.[198] Traffic at the Warner Bros. Studio Stores doubled, with sales almost equaling those experienced during the Christmas holidays.[199] Additionally, Batman Boutiques were opened in Sears stores, and displays with *Batman Forever* merchandise showed up in Toys "R" Us and Kmart stores.[200] Time-Warner's Atlantic Records sold more than a million copies of the soundtrack CD, and Warner Bros. Home Entertainment expected to sell 10 million videos at the end of the year.[201] Meanwhile, Warner Books published a novel based on the film, and DC Comics produced a book about the making of the movie.[202]

Christopher Bord, a motion picture analyst for media research firm Paul Kagan Associates, saw the renewed Batman mania as a sign of the decline of filmmaking. "What the studios are all trying to do is create a franchise," said Bord. "They're not concerned anymore with the creative aspect. They're trying to sell product. The bottom line is caps and theme park rides."[203]

Bord was correct in his assumption. With the release of *Batman Forever*, Batman was becoming such a money-making enterprise that no less august a financial publication than *The Wall Street Journal* reported on its significance. The paper said the film was Time-Warner Inc.'s "biggest synergistic gold mine ever," expected to generate more than $1 billion in sales of costumes, shoes, toys and countless other licensed products—a figure that excluded merchandise sold in the studio's own stores. Time-Warner was set to make even more from *Batman Forever* because, unlike the first two movies, there were no "first dollar gross" participants in the film, meaning that no star received a take of Warner's own box office receipts. Also, none of the talent got a piece of any of the merchandising, as Jack Nicholson had done with *Batman*.

Time-Warner, according to the *Journal*, expected *Batman Forever* to bring in about $300 million in cash flow over a two year period.[204]

Batman Forever helped Warner Bros. break a record no other studio had matched. When it passed the $100 million mark overseas in August of 1995, it became the fifth Warners movie to do so that year, a phenomenal record for the studio. The other high-earners were *Disclosure, Interview With the Vampire, Outbreak* and *The Specialist*.[205]

The film also generated a lawsuit. Minneapolis artist Andrew Leicester brought action against Warner Bros. for copyright infringement over use of his downtown Los Angeles artwork "Zanja Madre" in the Gotham City scenes of *Batman Forever*. The 47-year-old Englishman, known for his environmental art and outdoor sculptures, said, "I dislike *Batman* and most of these comic book movies in general." *Batman Forever,* said Leicester, was a "continuous sequence of violent acts. It has a weak plot. It is a terrible movie and the affect it has on my artwork is indescribable. It is a nightmare."

Besides seeking millions of dollars in damages for the alleged copyright infringement, Leicester also sought an injunction against Warners to halt further distribution of the film. Leicester's suit claimed the movie had interfered with his artwork and future business opportunities. "Zanja Madre," the Spanish name for the main channel of the Los Angeles River, was a $2 million art complex in the courtyard spaces at the 24-story 801 Tower building in downtown Los Angeles. The environmental art project included a series of waterworks and miniature skyscrapers. Leicester had won four public art and urban design awards for "Zanja Madre" since finishing the work in 1992. The piece, according to Leicester's lawsuit, was an "allegorical garden of calm and tranquility," and the film besmirched it by portraying it as an integral part of an "openly lurid, frenetic and violent Gotham City."

Leicester said he first learned Warner Bros. had used his artwork when friends showed him magazine articles featuring color photographs and scale models of "Zanja Madre" used in the production of the film. "I faxed a letter to Warner Bros. on June 3 asking them where they received permission to use my artwork," said Leicester. "The answer came back: What artwork?" When the studio showed no interest in compensating him, Leicester filed suit in Los Angeles Superior Court.[206] Leicester sought to show that Warner Bros. did not have the right to take pictures of his work for distribution, and that they had no license to build copies of the structure. The court eventually decided that Leicester had no case, since the sculpture made up part of the building, and the Architectural Works Copyright Protection Act of 1990 said that representations of public buildings could be used without specific licenses being granted.[207] "Congress intended the American landscape to belong to everyone, including filmmakers producing commercial movies," said Robert Schwartz of O'Melveny & Myers, who represented Warner Bros. "This decision holds that cities and streets can be freely filmed without fear of being dragged into court."[208]

Val Kilmer became embroiled in legal issues of a more personal nature. Shortly after the film's release, and just two months after the birth of their second child, he and his wife Joanne Whalley-Kilmer filed for divorce on the grounds of "irreconcilable differences." The couple, married for seven years and with a three-year-old daughter, separated on July 13, 1995.[209]

When Academy Award nominations were announced on Valentine's Day, 1996, *Batman Forever* nabbed three nominations, for Cinematography, Sound and Sound Effects Editing. Cinematographer Stephen Goldblatt said, "The morning they announced I was nominated for *Batman Forever*, I was up and sitting at the kitchen table but I couldn't bear to listen to the broadcast. I was pretending to be calm, filling in a magazine subscription, when the producer, Peter MacGregor-Scott, called and said I'd gotten the nomination. I woke my wife with champagne, and we began to celebrate. At about 7, my son came into the room. He went to school that day and told everyone his mom and dad had been drinking first thing in the morning."[210]

With *Batman Forever* a bona fide hit, Joel Schumacher was riding high, even if he didn't feel the film was necessarily representative of his style. "I don't think *Batman Forever* is a Joel Schumacher film," he said. "I think it's a *Batman* film. What I did was go back to the source. An enormous variety of *Batman* comic books have been done between 1939 and now, with different, interesting artists and story lines. Tim's films were his versions of *Batman* comic books. This is ours."[211]

1　Mallory, Michael, "Holy Caped Caper, IV," *Daily Variety*, March 5, 1997, p. 50

2　Nasr, Constantine, producer, "Shadows of the Bat: The Cinematic Saga of the Dark Knight—Dark Side of the Knight," *Batman Returns* DVD, New Wave Entertainment, © 2005 Warner Bros. Entertainment Inc.

3　Weinraub, Bernard, "Director Has Personal Batman Fascination / Profile: Veteran Schumacher, Haunted by Traumatic Childhood, Brings $80 Million Project in on Schedule," *The New York Times*, Jun 16, 1995, p. L12

4　Eller, Claudia, "Burton Partner Di Novi Departs For Solo Career," *Daily Variety*, June 3, 1992, p. 8

5　—, "Pining for Wood," *Weekly Variety*, September 28, 1992, p. 99

6　Cohen, Roger, "The Creator of Time Warner, Steven J. Ross, Is Dead at 65," *The New York Times*, Dec. 21, 1992, http://www.nytimes.com/1992/12/21/obituaries/the-creator-of-time-warner-steven-j-ross-is-dead-at-65.html?scp=2&sq=steve%20ross%20dead&st=cse, accessed Oct. 14, 2011

7　Weinraub, Bernard, "Director Has Personal Batman Fascination / Profile: Veteran Schumacher, Haunted by Traumatic Childhood, Brings $80 Million Project in on Schedule," *The New York Times*, Jun 16, 1995, p. L12

8　*Ibid.*

9　Singer, Michael, *Batman & Robin: The Making of the Movie*, © 1997 Rutledge Hill Press, Nashville, TN, p. 11

10　Weinraub, Bernard, "Director Has Personal Batman Fascination / Profile: Veteran Schumacher, Haunted by Traumatic Childhood, Brings $80 Million Project in on Schedule," *The New York Times*, Jun 16, 1995, p. L12

11　Busch, Anita M., "'Batman' Lightens Up," *Daily Variety*, May 5, 1995, p. 14

12　Persall, Steve, "McDonald's throws a curve with 'Batman' promotions Series: On Screen," *St. Petersburg Times*, Jun. 9, 1995, p. 6

13　Spelling, Ian, "Bat to the Past: Director Hopes to Take 'Batman Forever' Back to the Source," *The Sacramento (CA) Bee*, Jun 11, 1995, p. EN 20

14　Fleming, Michael, "If Harlin Helms, Will Arnie Hang On?" *Weekly Variety*, June 28, 1993, p. 39

15　Fleming, Michael, "Dish: Clancy Leaves Par for Savoy 'Without Remorse,'" *Daily Variety*, June 17, 1993, p. 43

16　Weinraub, Bernard, "Director Has Personal Batman Fascination / Profile: Veteran Schumacher, Haunted by Traumatic Childhood, Brings $80 Million Project in on Schedule," *The New York Times*, Jun 16, 1995, p. L12

17 Cagle, Jess, "Gotham City's New Boss: Joel Schumacher Has Come a Long Way—The ''Batman Forever" Director Has Made a Name for Himself," *Entertainment Weekly*, July 21, 1995

18 Weinraub, Bernard, "Director Has Personal Batman Fascination / Profile: Veteran Schumacher, Haunted by Traumatic Childhood, Brings $80 Million Project in on Schedule," *The New York Times*, Jun 16, 1995, p. L12

19 Cagle, Jess, "Gotham City's New Boss: Joel Schumacher Has Come a Long Way—The ''Batman Forever" Director Has Made a Name for Himself," *Entertainment Weekly*, July 21, 1995

20 Weinraub, Bernard, "Director Has Personal Batman Fascination / Profile: Veteran Schumacher, Haunted by Traumatic Childhood, Brings $80 Million Project in on Schedule," *The New York Times*, Jun 16, 1995, p. L12

21 Cagle, Jess, "Gotham City's New Boss: Joel Schumacher Has Come a Long Way—The ''Batman Forever" Director Has Made a Name for Himself," *Entertainment Weekly*, July 21, 1995

22 Weinraub, Bernard, "Director Has Personal Batman Fascination / Profile: Veteran Schumacher, Haunted by Traumatic Childhood, Brings $80 Million Project in on Schedule," *The New York Times*, Jun 16, 1995, p. L12

23 Cagle, Jess, "Gotham City's New Boss: Joel Schumacher Has Come a Long Way—The ''Batman Forever" Director Has Made a Name for Himself," *Entertainment Weekly*, July 21, 1995

24 Weinraub, Bernard, "Director Has Personal Batman Fascination / Profile: Veteran Schumacher, Haunted by Traumatic Childhood, Brings $80 Million Project in on Schedule," *The New York Times*, Jun 16, 1995, p. L12

25 Busch, Anita M., "'Batman' Lightens Up," *Daily Variety*, May 5, 1995, p. 14

26 Ascher-Walsh, Rebecca, "Wholly Neophytes! An Exclusive Look at Batman Forever's New Batface Val, His Pal, the Gal, Two-Face, and That Freak From 'Ace'" *Entertainment Weekly*, Mar 10, 1995

27 Weinraub, Bernard, "Director Has Personal Batman Fascination / Profile: Veteran Schumacher, Haunted by Traumatic Childhood, Brings $80 Million Project in on Schedule," *The New York Times*, Jun 16, 1995, p. L12

28 Brennan, Judy, "Batman Battles New Bat Villains: Jim Carrey and Tommy Lee Jones Confirmed While Robin Wright Still in Talks for Roles in the Next Installment in the Superhero Franchise," *Entertainment Weekly*, Jun 3, 1994

29 Weinraub, Bernard, "Director Has Personal Batman Fascination / Profile: Veteran Schumacher, Haunted by Traumatic Childhood, Brings $80 Million Project in on Schedule," *The New York Times*, Jun 16, 1995, p. L12

30 Eller, Claudia, "Holy Batman!" *Daily Variety*, May 19, 1992, p. 19

31 *Ibid.*

32 —, "Movies—'Batman 3' Ready to Fly," *The Boston Herald*, Jun 18, 1993, p. S.12

33 Fleming, Michael, "Another Life at WB for Catwoman and Burton?" *Daily Variety*, July 22, 1993, p. 1

34 —, "The Write Kind of Director," *Daily Variety*, March 5, 1997, p. 42

35 Yip, Ben, "Brother-Eye Exclusive: An Interview With Batman Forever's Janet Scott Batchler," *Brother-Eye* website, http://www.brother-eye.net/forumviewtopicphp?f=16&p=382, accessed 3/30/11

36 —, "The Write Kind of Director," *Daily Variety*, March 5, 1997, p. 42, 44

37 Yip, Ben, "Brother-Eye Exclusive: An Interview With Batman Forever's Janet Scott Batchler," *Brother-Eye* website, http://www.brother-eye.net/forum/viewtopic.php?f=16&p=382, accessed 3/30/11

38 *Ibid.*

39 —, "The Write Kind of Director," *Daily Variety*, March 5, 1997, p. 44

40 *Ibid.*

41 Shapiro, Marc, "Knightmare Master" *Starlog* magazine # 216, July 1985, p. 43

42 Yip, Ben, "Brother-Eye Exclusive: An Interview With Batman Forever's Janet Scott Batchler," *Brother-Eye* website, http://www.brother-eye.net/forum/viewtopic.php?f=16&p=382, accessed 3/30/11

43 Shapiro, Marc, "Knightmare Master" *Starlog* magazine # 216, July 1985, p. 43

44 Boucher, Geoff, "Akiva Goldsman on 'Lobo,' 'Jonah Hex' and the new 'Swamp Thing,'" *The Los Angeles Times*, Oct. 19, 2009, http://herocomplex.latimes.com/2009/10/19/fringe-lobo-jonah-hex-and-the-new-swamp-thing/, accessed April 23, 2011

45 —, "The Write Kind of Director," *Daily Variety*, March 5, 1997, p. 42

46 Shapiro, Marc, "Knight Moves: Screenwriter Akiva Goldsman Gets Into a 'Batman & Robin' Frame of Mind," *Starlog Presents Batman & Other Comic Heroes*, 1997, p. 35

47 Eller, Claudia, "Who Was That Masked Man? CAA's Caped Crusader," *Daily Variety*, March 23, 1993, p. 19

48 Fleming, Michael, "Roth Reels in Jerky boys; ICM, CAA in Battle of Benefits," *Daily Variety*, Nov. 18, 1993, p. 15

49 Moerk, Christian, "Robin Tryouts Sunday," *Daily Variety*, December 16, 1993, p. 24

50 Busch, Anita M., "'Batman' Lightens Up," *Daily Variety*, May 5, 1995, p. 14

51 *Ibid.*

52 Cox, Dan, "Possible Contradiction in 'Batman' Trial Vs. WB," *Daily Variety*, Jan. 13, 1994, p. 7

53 *Ibid.*

54 *Ibid.*

55 Cox, Dan, "'Batman' Plaintiffs Say Contract Shows Intent," *Daily Variety*, Jan. 14, 1994, p. 4

56 Cox, Dan, "'Batman' Case May Sting Suits," *Daily Variety*, Jan. 26, 1994, p. 3

57 —, "Holy Bat Villains!," *Weekly Variety*, Feb. 21, 1994, p. 10

58 —, "Holy Boy Wonder," *Weekly Variety*, March 21-27, 1994, p. 8

59 —, "Bat Update," *Weekly Variety*, May 16, 1994, p. 2

60 Nasr, Constantine, producer, "Shadows of the Bat: The Cinematic Saga of the Dark Knight—Reinventing a Hero," *Batman Forever* DVD, New Wave Entertainment, © 2005 Warner Bros. Entertainment Inc.

61 Schaefer, Stephen, "Boy wonder: Straight-laced Chris O'Donnell Gets a Masked-Man Makeover," *Boston Herald*, Jun 11, 1995, p. 41

62 Smith, Russel, "Chris O'Donnell's Personal High," *Rolling Stone*, Dec. 8, 2000

63 Vincent, Mal, "Robin the Boy Wonder Keeping Feet Grounded Chris O'Donnell Savors the Scent of the Spring That's His Career," *Toronto Star*, Apr 18, 1995, p. C4

64 *Ibid.*

65 Wells, Jeffrey, "O'Donnell Unmasked: Chris O'Donnell Increases His Sex Appeal—A Haircut and a Hot Body Change the Star's Image as Robin in ''Batman Forever,''" *Entertainment Weekly*, June 16, 1995

66 Smith, Russel, "Chris O'Donnell's Personal High," *Rolling Stone*, Dec. 8, 2000

67 —, "Bat Update," *Weekly Variety*, May 16, 1994, p. 2

68 Brennan, Judy, "Batman Battles New Bat Villains: Jim Carrey and Tommy Lee Jones Confirmed While Robin Wright Still in Talks for Roles in the Next Installment in the Superhero Franchise," *Entertainment Weekly*, Jun 3, 1994

69 Greene, Jay, "'Batman' Nabs Carrey as Riddler," *Daily Variety*, May 24, 1994, p. 3

70 Murray, Will, "Riddler Forever?" *Starlog* magazine # 218, Sept. 1985, p. 27

71 Fleming, Michael, "Dish: More Bat-Developments," *Daily Variety*, May 26, 1994, p. 15

72 Brennan, Judy, "Batman Battles New Bat Villains: Jim Carrey and Tommy Lee Jones Confirmed While Robin Wright Still in Talks for Roles in the Next Installment in the Superhero Franchise," *Entertainment Weekly*, Jun 3, 1994

73 Fleming, Michael, "Banderas in 'Mariachi' Sequel; Whoopi Goes West," *Daily Variety*, June 14, 1994, p. 47

74 —, "It's Still a Riddle Why Keaton Didn't Stay 'Batman Forever'" *The Los Angeles Times*, Jul 8, 1994, p. 4

75 *Ibid.*

76 Gordinier, Jeff, "Next at Batman: Michael Keaton Dropping Out of the Comic Book Sequel Could Breathe New Life in the Franchise — or Maybe Not," *Entertainment Weekly*, Jul 15, 1994

77 —, "It's Still a Riddle Why Keaton Didn't Stay 'Batman Forever'" *The Los Angeles Times*, Jul 8, 1994, p. 4

78 *Ibid.*

79 Brennan, Judy, "Batman Battles New Bat Villains: Jim Carrey and Tommy Lee Jones Confirmed While Robin Wright Still in Talks for Roles in the Next Installment in the Superhero Franchise," *Entertainment Weekly*, Jun 3, 1994

80 Greene, Jay, "'Batman' Nabs Carrey as Riddler," *Daily Variety*, May 24, 1994, p. 3

81 Fleming, Michael, "'Batman' Not Forever for Keaton; Kilmer In," *Daily Variety*, July 1, 1994, p. 1

82 Vincent, Mal, "Keaton Takes A Flying Leap Into New Movie Role," Virginian-Pilot, Norfolk, VA, Dec. 18, 1994, p. E7

83 —, "It's Still a Riddle Why Keaton Didn't Stay 'Batman Forever'" *The Los Angeles Times*, Jul 8, 1994, p. 4

84 Bruni, Frank, "Conflicts with `Batman Forever' put director Schumacher in corner," Houston Chronicle, Jul 13, 1994, p. 6

85 Genola, Robert, "Johnny Depp Was Almost Batman In Batman Forever: Johnny Depp talks about how he almost played Batman in Batman Forever and that he is open to being The Riddler in 'Batman 3,'" *Comic-BookMovie.com*, http://www.comicbookmovie.com/fansites/CookiepussProduction/news/?a=12646, accessed 9/12/10

86 —, "It's Still a Riddle Why Keaton Didn't Stay 'Batman Forever'" *The Los Angeles Times*, Jul 8, 1994, p. 4

87 Spelling, Ian, "Bat to the Past: Director Hopes to Take 'Batman Forever' Back to the Source," *The Sacramento (CA) Bee*, Jun 11, 1995, p. EN 20

88 Gordinier, Jeff, "Next at Batman: Michael Keaton Dropping Out of the Comic Book Sequel Could Breathe New Life in the Franchise — or Maybe Not," *Entertainment Weekly*, Jul 15, 1994

89 Nasr, Constantine, producer, "Shadows of the Bat: The Cinematic Saga of the Dark Knight—Reinventing a Hero," *Batman Forever* DVD, New Wave Entertainment, © 2005 Warner Bros. Entertainment Inc.

90 Spelling, Ian, "Bat to the Past: Director Hopes to Take 'Batman Forever' Back to the Source," *The Sacramento (CA) Bee*, Jun 11, 1995, p. EN 20

91 —, "Biography," *Official Website, Val Kilmer, Actor/Composer*, http://www.valekilmer.com/bio.html, accessed April 29, 2011

92 Ascher-Walsh, Rebecca, "Cool Hero: Val Kilmer: Val Kilmer is the Latest Batman—Will This Role Finally Provide the Actor Star Power?" *Entertainment Weekly*, Jun 30, 1995

93 —, "Biography," *Official Website, Val Kilmer, Actor/Composer*, http://www.valekilmer.com/bio.html, accessed April 29, 2011

94 Ascher-Walsh, Rebecca, "Cool Hero: Val Kilmer: Val Kilmer is the Latest Batman—Will This Role Finally Provide the Actor Star Power?" *Entertainment Weekly*, Jun 30, 1995

95 —, "Biography," *Official Website, Val Kilmer, Actor/Composer*, http://www.valekilmer.com/bio.html, accessed April 29, 2011

96 Fleming, Michael, "'Batman' Not Forever for Keaton; Kilmer In," *Daily Variety*, July 1, 1994, p. 6

97 Laski, Beth, "Bullock Speeds to 'While,'" *Daily Variety*, July 8, 1994, p. 18

98 Greene, Jay, "Kidman Says Yes to 'Batman,'" *Daily Variety*, July 27, 1994, p. 21

99 Svetkey, Benjamin, "Seeing Red: Nicole Kidman is Ready to Take the Spotlight—Mrs. Cruise is Set to Make Her Mark With 'Batman Forever' and 'To Die For,'" *Entertainment Weekly*, Jun 9, 1995

100 Weaver, Tom, "Gotham's Finest" *Starlog* magazine # 216, July 1985, p. 40

101 Singer, Michael, *Batman Forever: The Official Movie Book*, © 1995 Modern Publishing, New York, p. 40

102 Interview with Ed Begley Jr., conducted September 23, 2010.

103 Popkin, Helen A.S., "Batman Unmasked Series: Xpress," *St. Petersburg Times*, Jun 26, 1995, p. 1.D

104 Landis, Deborah Nadoolman, *Costume Design*, © 2003 Rotovision, East Sussex, England, p. 121

105 Popkin, Helen A.S., "Batman Unmasked Series: Xpress," *St. Petersburg Times*, Jun 26, 1995, p. 1.D

106 Smith, Liz, "Val Kilmer Hotter Than You Think," *San Francisco Chronicle*, Jun 6, 1995, p. E3

107 Schaefer, Stephen, "Boy wonder: Straight-laced Chris O'Donnell Gets a Masked-Man Makeover," *Boston Herald*, Jun 11, 1995, p. 41

108 Weinraub, Bernard, "Director Has Personal Batman Fascination / Profile: Veteran Schumacher, Haunted by Traumatic Childhood, Brings $80 Million Project in on Schedule," *The New York Times*, Jun 16, 1995, p. L12

109 Popkin, Helen A.S., "Batman Unmasked Series: Xpress," *St. Petersburg Times*, Jun 26, 1995, p. 1.D

110 *Ibid.*

111 *Ibid.*

112 *Ibid.*

113 —, "Batman Forever Production Information," *Batman Forever Presskit*, © 1995 Warner Bros., p. 11

114 *Ibid.*, p. 14

115 *Ibid.*, p. 15

116 *Ibid.*, p. 14

117 *Ibid.*, p. 15

118 *Ibid.*, p. 15

119 *Ibid.*, p. 16

120 Popkin, Helen A.S., "Batman Unmasked Series: Xpress," *St. Petersburg Times*, Jun 26, 1995, p. 1.D

121 *Ibid.*, p. 1.D

122 —, "Batman Forever Production Information," *Batman Forever Presskit*, © 1995 Warner Bros., p. 16

123 Archerd, Army, "Just For Variety," *Daily Variety*, Jan. 26, 1995, p. 4

124 Seiler, Andy, "Batman: Forever Bob Kane's," *USA Today*, Jul 6, 1995, p. 8.D

125 *Ibid.*

126 Shapiro, Marc, "Knightmare Master" *Starlog* magazine # 216, July 1985, p. 45

127 *Ibid.*, p. 40

128 *Ibid.*, p. 44

129 —, "Batman Forever Production Information," *Batman Forever Presskit*, © 1995 Warner Bros., p. 13

130 Webster, Emma, "Top Speed Racers," *Daily Variety*, Jan. 21, 1995, p. 22

131 —, "Batman Forever Production Information," *Batman Forever Presskit*, © 1995 Warner Bros., p. 13

132 Weinraub, Bernard, "Director Has Personal Batman Fascination / Profile: Veteran Schumacher, Haunted by Traumatic Childhood, Brings $80 Million Project in on Schedule," *The New York Times*, Jun 16, 1995, p. L12

133 Lauerman, Connie, "Rockin' Robin: With three summer movies—including the hyped 'Batman Forever'—Chris O'Donnell is truly Hollywood's boy wonder," *Tulsa World*, Jun 16, 1995, p. 14

134 Singer, Michael, *Batman Forever: The Official Movie Book*, © 1995 Modern Publishing, New York, p. 40

135 Weinraub, Bernard, "Director Has Personal Batman Fascination / Profile: Veteran Schumacher, Haunted by Traumatic Childhood, Brings $80 Million Project in on Schedule," *The New York Times*, Jun 16, 1995, p. L12

136 Svetkey, Benjamin, "Seeing Red: Nicole Kidman is Ready to Take the Spotlight—Mrs. Cruise is Set to Make Her Mark With 'Batman Forever' and 'To Die For,'" *Entertainment Weekly*, Jun 9, 1995

137 Rasine, Birgitte, "Twenty Cameramen Whose Aim Is True," *Daily Variety*, Feb. 23, 1996, p. 38

138 Ascher-Walsh, Rebecca, "Cool Hero: Val Kilmer: Val Kilmer is the Latest Batman—Will This Role Finally Provide the Actor Star Power?" *Entertainment Weekly*, Jun 30, 1995

139 Popkin, Helen A.S., "Batman Unmasked Series: Xpress," *St. Petersburg Times*, Jun 26, 1995, p. 1.D

140 Smith, Russel, "Chris O'Donnell's Personal High," *Rolling Stone*, Dec. 8, 2000

141 Interview with Ed Begley Jr., conducted September 23, 2010

142 *Ibid.*

143 Spelling, Ian, "Bat to the Past: Director Hopes to Take 'Batman Forever' Back to the Source," *The Sacramento (CA) Bee*, Jun 11, 1995, p. EN 20

144 Murray, Will, "Riddler Forever?" *Starlog* magazine # 218, Sept. 1985, p. 28

145 Beck, Marilyn and Stacy Jenel Smith, "Holy Release Date! 'Batman Forever' Production Speeds Up," *Los Angeles Daily News*, Feb. 15, 1995, p. L2

146 *Ibid.*

147 Singer, Michael, *Batman & Robin: The Making of the Movie*, © 1997 Rutledge Hill Press, Nashville, TN, p. 11

148 Stalter, Katharine, "F/X Houses Promo Work," *Daily Variety*, May 31, 1995, p. 3

149 Spelling, Ian, "Bat to the Past: Director Hopes to Take 'Batman Forever' Back to the Source," *The Sacramento (CA) Bee*, Jun 11, 1995, p. EN 20

150 Beck, Marilyn and Stacy Jenel Smith, "Holy Release Date! 'Batman Forever' Production Speeds Up," *Los Angeles Daily News*, Feb. 15, 1995, p. L2

151 Shapiro, Marc, "Knightmare Master" *Starlog* magazine # 216, July 1985, p. 40-41

152 Weinraub, Bernard, "Director Has Personal Batman Fascination / Profile: Veteran Schumacher, Haunted by Traumatic Childhood, Brings $80 Million Project in on Schedule," *The New York Times*, Jun 16, 1995, p. L12

153 Weinraub, Bernard, "Visual Flair, A Hip Sensibility And a Past," *The New York Times*, Jun 11, 1995, p. 2.15

154 Singer, Michael, *Batman & Robin: The Making of the Movie*, © 1997 Rutledge Hill Press, Nashville, TN, p. 125

155 Sullivan, Jim, "'Batman' Flies Without Many Of Its Original Tunes," *Los Angeles Daily News*, Jun 19, 1995, p. L.17

156 Silberman, Jeff, "'Friends' Paints a Rosy Picture for Rembrandts," *Daily Variety*, June 26, 1995, p. 8

157 Brown, Mark, "Pop Life: Is this way of selling out?" *The Orange County Register*, Sep 22, 1995, p. 51

158 Young, Paul F., "Hollywood Helmers Opt for Soft Gore," *Weekly Variety*, Aug. 14-20, 1995, p. 1

159 Busch, Anita M., "'Batman' Lightens Up," *Daily Variety*, May 5, 1995, p. 14

160 Weinraub, Bernard, "Director Has Personal Batman Fascination / Profile: Veteran Schumacher, Haunted by Traumatic Childhood, Brings $80 Million Project in on Schedule," *The New York Times*, Jun 16, 1995, p. L12

161 Busch, Anita M., "'Batman' Lightens Up," *Daily Variety*, May 5, 1995, p. 14

162 *Ibid.*

163 *Ibid.*

164 *Ibid.*

165 Persall, Steve, "McDonald's throws a curve with 'Batman' promotions Series: On Screen," *St. Petersburg Times*, Jun. 9, 1995, p. 6

166 Travers, Peter, "Batman Forever: Review," *Rolling Stone*, June 16, 1995

167 Smith, Liz, "Did You Hear About Batman?" *The Los Angeles Times*, May 22, 1995, p. 2

168 Ascher-Walsh, Rebecca, "Cool Hero: Val Kilmer: Val Kilmer is the Latest Batman— Will This Role Finally Provide the Actor Star Power?" *Entertainment Weekly*, Jun 30, 1995

169 Busch, Anita M., "'Batman' Lightens Up," *Daily Variety*, May 5, 1995, p. 14

170 —, "An Internet Site For 'Batman,' *The New York Times*, May 19, 1995, p. D2

171 Barboza, David, "The Media Business: Advertising; The Frontier in Movie Promotion is—You Guessed It—the Internet. But Will it Help the Box Office?" *The New York Times*, Aug. 22, 1995, http://www.nytimes.com/1995/08/22/business/media-business-advertising-frontier-movie-promotion-you-guessed-it-internet-but.html?pagewanted=2&src=pm, accessed Sept. 20, 2011

172 Murray, Steve, Eleanor Ringel and Tom Sabulis, "Movie Buzz: 'Batman' junket is partial to TV," *The Atlanta Constitution*, May 7, 1995, p. M2

173 Smith, Liz, "Val Kilmer Hotter Than You Think," *San Francisco Chronicle*, Jun 6, 1995, p. E3

174 Ehrman, Mark, "There Was No Robbin' Fans of a Bat Time," *The Los Angeles Times*, Jun 12, 1995, p. 2

175 *Ibid.*

176 *Ibid.*

177 Miller, Abigail D. and Cesar G. Soriano, "Fans Wanted to See Batman," *Washington Times*, Jun 16, 1995, p. C14

178 Horn, John, "The Movie Pols a Bipartisan Turnout for 'Batman' Screening," *The Buffalo (NY) News*, Jun 23, 1995, p. G.23

179 *Ibid.*

180 Belluck, Pam, "A Bigger Stage for a Senator," *The New York Times*, Jul 12 2008, p. A.9

181 Miller, Abigail D. and Cesar G. Soriano, "Fans Wanted to See Batman," *Washington Times*, Jun 16, 1995, p. C14

182 Zuckman, Jill, "Washington Notebook: Leahy Savors Role in Batman's Shadow," *The Boston Globe*, Jun 17, 1995, p. 3

183 Lowry, Brian, "Film Review: Batman Forever," *Daily Variety*, June 14, 1995, p. 4

184 Gleiberman, Owen, "Movie Reviews: Batman Forever," *Entertainment Weekly*, Jun 23, 1995

185 Curtis, Quentin, "Cinema: Wholly boring, Batman!" *The (London) Independent*, Jul 16, 1995, p. 26

186 Maslin, Janet, "Film Review: Batman Forever: New Challenges for the Caped Crusader," *The New York Times*, June 16, 1995, http://www.nytimes.com/1995/06/16/movies/film-review-batman-forever-new-challenges-for-the-caped-crusader.html?scp=70&sq=batman&st=nyt, accessed May 22, 2011

187 Travers, Peter, "Batman Forever: Review," *Rolling Stone*, June 16, 1995

188 Carr, Jay, "Wholly Hollywood, Batman! Stepping Out of the Stylish Shadows, Caped Crusader Goes Commercial," *The Boston Globe*, Jun 16, 1995, p. 59

189 Murray, Steve, "Caped Crusader Gets a Facelift," *The Atlanta Constitution*, Nov. 2, 1995, p. G.9

190 French, Philip, "Cinema: Flash! Crash! Splash! Cash! 'Holy hi-tech cash-ins, Batman. They've made another sequel.' 'Fear not, Boy Wonder. I'll get Philip French to review it,'" *The Manchester (UK) Guardian*, Jul 16, 1995, p. 7

191 —, "'Batman' Busts B.O. Records," *Daily Variety*, June 20, 1995, p. 10

192 Peers, Martin, "TW Stock Gets Pic up: Street Digs 'Batman's' Big B.O.," *Daily Variety*, June 20, 1995, p. 1

193 Cling, Carol, "Holy merchandising, Batman!," *Las Vegas Review*, Jun 15, 1995, p. 1E

194 Cagle, Jess, "Gotham City's New Boss: Joel Schumacher Has Come a Long Way—The ' 'Batman Forever" Director Has Made a Name for Himself," *Entertainment Weekly*, July 21, 1995

195 Fabrikant, Geraldine, "Why Studios Bet On the Summer Blockbuster; With Big Debts and Big Budgets, Hits are More Critical Than Ever," *The New York Times*, July 3, 1995, p. A.37

196 Popkin, Helen A.S., "Batman Unmasked Series: Xpress," *St. Petersburg Times*, Jun 26, 1995, p. 1.D

197 Cling, Carol, "Holy merchandising, Batman!," *Las Vegas Review*, Jun 15, 1995, p. 1E

198 Popkin, Helen A.S., "Batman Unmasked Series: Xpress," *St. Petersburg Times*, Jun 26, 1995, p. 1.D

199 Lippman, John, "Movies: `Batman Forever' Is Seen as Cash Cow," *The Wall Street Journal*, Jun 27, 1995, p. 4

200 Popkin, Helen A.S., "Batman Unmasked Series: Xpress," *St. Petersburg Times*, Jun 26, 1995, p. 1.D

201 Lippman, John, "Movies: `Batman Forever' Is Seen as Cash Cow," *The Wall Street Journal*, Jun 27, 1995, p. 4

202 Popkin, Helen A.S., "Batman Unmasked Series: Xpress," *St. Petersburg Times*, Jun 26, 1995, p. 1.D

203 Cling, Carol, "Holy merchandising, Batman!," *Las Vegas Review*, Jun 15, 1995, p. 1E

204 Lippman, John, "Movies: `Batman Forever' Is Seen as Cash Cow," *The Wall Street Journal*, Jun 27, 1995, p. 4

205 Groves, Don, "U.S. Films Sizzling at O'Seas B.O.," *Daily Variety*, Aug. 14, 1995, p. 1

206 Carlson, Scott, "`Holy Copyright Infringement, Batman!'" The Salt Lake Tribune, Jul 14, 1995, p. Z.3

207 —, "Batman Forever and the Water Vampire," *KerrKellerMediaStudies*, http://kerrkellermediastudies.blogspot.com/2010/10/batman-forever-and-water-vampire.html, accessed April 30, 2011

208 Shprintz, Janet, "Judge Dismisses Case of 'Batman' Sculptures," *Daily Variety*, June 4, 1998, p. 35

209 Whittell, Giles, "Batman's Wife Seeks an Amicable Divorce; Joanne Whalley Kilmer and Val Kilmer," *The Times (London)*, Jul 25, 1995, p. 1

210 Silberg, Jon, "Lensers Bask in Spotlight," *Daily Variety*, Jan. 22, 1997, p. 34

211 Spelling, Ian, "Bat to the Past: Director Hopes to Take 'Batman Forever' Back to the Source," *The Sacramento (CA) Bee*, Jun 11, 1995, p. EN 20

Chapter Nine:
BATMAN & ARNOLD

"Batman is more than a movie—it's an industry."[1]
- Warner Bros. co-chairman Robert A. Daly

IVY LEAGUE

After completing *Batman Forever*, Joel Schumacher went to work on *A Time to Kill*, another adaptation of a best-selling John Grisham novel, for Warner Bros. and New Regency Pictures. While Schumacher was scouting locations in Mississippi with his screenwriter, Akiva Goldsman, *Batman Forever* had its first screenings for film critics. The advance press screening results, said Goldsman, "were very positive, and industry people were excited. Joel got this kind of elfin gleam in his eye and said, 'I think they're going to ask us for another one.' I was very flattered to be part of 'us' at that moment."

Knowing that Warner Bros. was pleased with his take on the Dark Knight in *Batman Forever* was a relief to Schumacher. "I was finding my way on that film and so did most of my colleagues, because it was the first *Batman* film we had worked on," he said. "I don't think any of us expected or even dreamed that *Batman Forever* would be so accepted. So when Bob Daly and Terry Semel asked me to direct another *Batman* film, I called Barbara Ling, our great production designer, and asked if she wanted to do another one. She said, 'Joel...we haven't even scratched the surface!' I think I had that feeling too, because I felt that what we were able to bring to *Batman Forever* was a lot of humor, color and action, and if audiences liked that, we could bring them even more fun and games."[2]

Schumacher immediately began thinking about which villains would menace Batman and Robin the next time out. "Whenever I start to prepare a *Batman* movie, I always go right to the source," he said. "I just get piles and piles of *Batman* comic books, and really get inspired."[3] By the time the director and writer boarded a plane back to Los Angeles, the ideas were already percolating. "Joel started throwing out some ideas," said Goldsman, "and I started throwing back some ideas, and by the end of the plane trip we had the skeleton of our story."[4]

For the new film, Schumacher and Goldsman decided to focus on one of the classic baddies from the 1960s TV series and one that had never been portrayed in live action before: Mr. Freeze and Poison Ivy. Created by Robert Kanigher and Sheldon Moldoff, Poison Ivy was a relatively new villainess in the *Batman* canon, having made her debut in *Batman* # 181 in June 1966. She was Pamela Isley, a botanist who became Poison Ivy after a lab accident. A female eco-terrorist who could control plants and cloud men's minds with pheromones, her kiss was lethal. "Poison Ivy started out with a comics influence, and then I resurrected her from the ground up," said Goldsman. But rather than look to the Adam West TV series for inspiration on Mr. Freeze, Goldsman said, "The model for Freeze was actually the *Batman* animated series."[5]

In August of 1995, while *Batman Forever* was still in theaters, *Variety* reported that Demi Moore was in the running to play Poison Ivy, with Patrick Stewart, star of the TV series *Star Trek: The Next Generation*, under consideration for Mr. Freeze.[6] "Maybe in the future, there will be a *Batman* movie that is just about Batman," said Goldsman. "But right now, *Batman* movies, to a large extent, are about the colorful villains that inhabit Gotham City."[7]

Another colorful villain from the comic books was also written into the script: Bane. Created by Chuck Dixon, Doug Moench and Graham Nolan, Bane first appeared in *Batman: Vengeance of Bane* # 1 in January 1993. Bane was an inmate of the Peña Dura prison in the Caribbean Republic of Santa Prisca who developed his mind and body while incarcerated. When a doctor at the prison pumped him full of a serum called Venom, he became unnaturally strong. In a later comic book series, he came to Gotham City, released all the criminals from Arkham Asylum, deduced Batman's secret identity, confronted Batman in the Batcave and broke the hero's back, leaving him a paraplegic (*Batman* # 497, July 1993). Treated correctly, he would have been a formidable screen nemesis for the Dark Knight; in Goldsman's script, he becomes merely Poison Ivy's super-strong but dimwitted henchman.

While production began on *A Time to Kill*, Akiva Goldsman started hammering out the next *Batman* script, which he expected to complete by January 1996.[8] "We talked about it all the way through the shooting of *A Time to Kill*, until together we came up with the rhythm of the piece, what was happening where, when, and to whom," said Goldsman.[9] "During the last month of shooting, I went back to L.A. and did a first draft of the *Batman & Robin* script."[10] Meanwhile, *Batman Forever* went into general release, and was soon on its way to raking in a worldwide box-office take of $300 million.[11] "I really didn't know that *Batman Forever* was going to be as successful as it turned out," said Schumacher. "I think sometimes it's easier to analyze failure, because you can look at the mistakes you made. But the kind of success at the box office and with audiences that we had with *Batman Forever* is like catching lightning in a bottle."[12]

"Joel and I felt that, by doing such a good job on *Batman Forever*, we had earned the right to do it again and had learned how to do it right," said Goldsman.[13] However, the writer did have to switch styles from the Grisham adaptation to *Batman*. "In a reality-based picture like *A Time to Kill*, you can end a scene on a poignant look, or someone walking through a door and closing it behind them," said Goldsman. "On a *Batman* movie, there'd better be the flapping of a cape as somebody leaps out a window, or a giant building exploding before the sequence is over. It's really fun to switch gears, although sometimes there's grinding as you hit the clutch!"[14]

As sole screenwriter on the new film, Goldsman was able to chart a new course for the Caped Crusader. "Essentially, *Batman* is about how we as individuals reckon with loss," said Goldsman. "I assume that was Bob Kane's conscious or unconscious intention when he developed the character's origins. And so, I think for the *Batman* stories to be rooted in any kind of emotional authenticity, they have to start there."[15]

In an interview with Marc Shapiro of *Starlog* magazine, Goldsman said, "The emotional engine of this story is Bruce's relationship with and potential loss of Alfred. So, when it came to creating the villains, we felt it was important to develop characters who resonated with love, devotion and obsession. You'll find that every character in this film has those qualities."[16]

Director Joel Schumacher hoped to add a character with which young girls could identify. "I didn't realize that there were so many young girls who were Batman fans, and as I looked around I noticed that there weren't any teenage super heroines in our culture," said Schumacher. "Fortunately, Batgirl did exist."[17]

As reimagined by Schumacher and Goldsman, Batgirl became not the thrill-seeking daughter of Commissioner Gordon but another character suffering loss. "We re-conceptualized Batgirl for a few reasons," said Goldsman. "When you have a lot of characters, you need to create relationships so that they can be brought together. We tied Barbara to Alfred as his niece rather than retain her as Commissioner Gordon's daughter, because Alfred is a more central character in our story. And by re-creating her as an orphan, we echo both Bruce and Dick's plight."[18]

Given that he remained the sole writer throughout the process, Goldsman's screenplay, not surprisingly, is almost identical to the finished film, with only a few scenes that either weren't filmed or were cut. One surprise is that although the script is called *Batman & Robin*, Robin initially calls himself Nightwing, apparently to the chagrin of Batman. In their first dialogue exchange, Batman says, "Nice suit. And today you are?"

"Nightwing," responds Robin. "Scourge of darkest evil."

"This is all about fashion for you, isn't it?" asks Batman.

"It's the gear," says Robin. "Chicks love the gear."

In the final film, that exchange would be changed to Robin's line, "I want a car. Chicks dig the car," and Batman's riposte, "This is why Superman works alone"—the first time any of the Warner Bros. *Batman* films made reference to another superhero's existence.

From it's first major set-piece scene—the fight in the Gotham Museum—the Goldsman script devolves into the kind of puns that sucked the fun out of the movie. In the script, Mr. Freeze turns his freezing ray on a museum guard, then says, "Cop-sicle." Later, when policemen rush him during the fight, he quickly dispatches them with deft blows, and says, "Cop-suey." Later, when Freeze goes to look at his deceased wife in her glacier-like sarcophagus, he says, "Nothing frustrates a man like a frigid wife."

In a scene not in the film, after we see Freeze in his lair, we cut to Batman and Robin again battling Mr. Freeze in the museum. But when it looks like Freeze is about to get the best of Robin and Batman intervenes, we discover that it's all a virtual reality simulation.

In another scene absent from the final film, after Barbara Wilson is introduced, we cut to Gotham Airport, where Pamela Isley, dressed as a grieving widow, disembarks from a vintage DC-3. Luggage handlers carry off an immense coffin. Pamela says to them, "Be gentle. He's always been touchy." As they walk away, Bane bursts out of the coffin, picks one of the handlers up like a baseball bat and swings him into the others, sending the handlers sprawling. Meanwhile, a businessman approaches a limousine at the edge of the tarmac. As he opens the door, he sees Pamela lying on the back seat, showing some leg. She grabs the businessman's face and kisses him passionately, and the man falls dead. A hand then reaches into the car, snaps the driver's neck, and pulls him out. Bane then climbs into the driver's seat, thus explaining how he becomes Ivy's chauffeur.

Yet another missing scene has Bruce at a function with Julie Madison when he sees Pamela Isley and is inextricably attracted to her. Next, he's in the Batcave, where he finds that Alfred's "brain algorithms" have been put into the Batcomputer to create a virtual Alfred, who helps him see that Pamela and Ivy are one and the same, prompting Bruce to remark, "Amazing what a good wig and contact lenses can do. And I thought Clark Kent got away with murder just wearing those glasses."

During the climax, Goldsman describes the Batblade, Batsled and Bathammer shooting up the wall of snow covering the Gotham Observatory as Batgirl sings "to the old 60's *Batman* theme, 'Batgirl, Baatgirl, Baatgirl.'" A further nod to the TV show comes a couple of pages later, when Robin and Batgirl are fighting Freeze's thugs. Batgirl kicks a thug, and says, "Pow!" She punches another, and says, "Whap!" Then she backhands a third, exclaiming, "Kazow!" Robin, while fighting, asks, "What exactly are you doing?" She responds, "I don't know. It just feels right." A final TV show reference comes near the end of the sequence, when Batman goes to the computer console of the telescope and begins working the keyboard, saying, "Who ever thought Aunt Harriet's typing lessons would lead to this?"[19]

In the end, Goldsman wrote three drafts of the script, though the changes from one draft to the next were minimal. "These things always start longer," said Goldsman. "There was a lot of condensing and streamlining. The individual characters' plot arcs pretty much stayed intact. In fact, I feel that Freeze's plot arc really improved over the three drafts, in terms of depth. By the third draft, we were taking more seriously the notion that everything was propelled by the loss of his wife. Generally, having already written one *Batman* script, I kind of wrote this one with a final shooting script in mind from the beginning. Going in, I had a better idea of what worked and what didn't."[20]

The allusions to the old TV series, even though they did not survive in the final film, underscore how Schumacher and Goldsman were, from the outset, trying to make a family-friendly *Batman* film, one that even small children could go see without having nightmares afterwards. "Some of the scenes between Freeze and Ivy are deliciously funny," said Schumacher. "It's hard to top Jim Carrey, but this is definitely a comic-book movie. If you don't have humor, then you have something deadly serious, and I can assure you that this is not the Dark Knight."[21] Akiva Goldsman claimed he was trying to present an evolution in the characters of Batman, with a "less damaged" Bruce Wayne. "I think that's appropriate for the character at this point," said Goldsman. "Yes, there's a profound trauma in his past that drives him, but he's also a very rich guy with a very successful life. We're steering away from the self-obsession, and Batman is less internal than he has been. But I think that you'll find that he's far from being carefree."[22]

THE TROUBLE WITH VAL

As the new *Batman* script was taking shape and *A Time to Kill* was winding down, Schumacher began to think about casting. He expected to have Val Kilmer and Chris O'Donnell back in the leads, telling *Daily Variety's* Michael Fleming, "Even though ours was the third *Batman* film, it was the first for myself, Val, Chris and Akiva, and we were excited about what we were making. On a personal level, not only did the studio take a big chance on me, but the cast did as well, since I'd never done that kind of movie before. Val and Chris especially took a big leap off the high diving board, because if the movie had not been successful, it could have hurt their careers. I'd hate to say to them, 'Thanks for helping me, but now you're on your own.'"[23]

By October of 1995, Demi Moore was out of the running for Poison Ivy, but another high-profile actress was rumored to be considering the role—Julia Roberts.[24] The script, however, was still unfinished and evolving. "I make it a rule to never write with actors in mind," Goldsman told *Starlog* magazine's Marc Shapiro. "I think you underestimate actors if you do that. I wrote this script with the idea that whoever was cast would find a way to effectively inhabit the character."[25]

While the script was coalescing, Schumacher brought back much of his *Batman Forever* crew, beginning with production designer Barbara Ling and producer Peter Macgregor-Scott, who described his response to the invitation as, "The first reaction is 'Oh, God.' The second reaction is 'Thank you, God.' And the third reaction is 'God Almighty!'"[26] Ling set to work just a mere five months after finishing *Batman Forever*.[27] In the end, about 60 percent of the *Batman Forever* crew returned to work on *Batman & Robin*,[28] including cinematographer Stephen Goldblatt and composer Elliot Goldenthal.

Val Kilmer had been busy since completing *Batman Forever*, having starred alongside Marlon Brando in *The Island of Dr. Moreau* (1996) and opposite Michael Douglas in *The Ghost and the Darkness* (1996).[29] By the middle of November, he had signed on to play the lead in a new film version of *The Saint*, a crusading avenger created by novelist Leslie Charteris in 1928 that had been played in films by George Sanders, and on TV by Roger Moore, among others.[30] *The Saint* had been in development at Paramount Pictures for six years. Kilmer became involved in 1994, before he was tapped to play Batman. Originally, it was thought that if *The Saint* became its own franchise, Kilmer would be able to headline both that and *Batman*, alternating from one series to the next.[31] "Not to take anything away from Bob Kane, but you have a choice between a comic book and, with *The Saint*, a literary figure that has inspired this whole espionage genre, this notion of the gentleman thief, surviving by his wits, not brawn," said Kilmer. "Another thing about taking on the role that was very appealing to act is that it's a real journey—he goes from sinner to saint. Those opportunities don't happen very often and they're very fun to do."[32]

Kilmer was expected to begin filming *The Saint* for director Phillip Noyce at Paramount on March 22, 1996. Schumacher wanted him available to begin pre-production on the *Batman* film in August for a September 1 start date.[33] Rick Nicita, the co-chairman of the Creative Artists Agency, handled Kilmer's negotiations, and got Paramount to agree to a $6 million dollar salary for the actor, three times what he had been paid for *Batman Forever* and $2 million more than he had been promised for *Batman & Robin*.

Kilmer was in negotiations for *The Saint* in mid-November, but by early December talks had broken down. Kilmer was said to be off the project, yet he and director Philip Noyce continued to meet, and it was understood that Kilmer would in fact do the film, once his divorce from Joanne Whalley-Kilmer was completed.[34] It was speculated that Kilmer dropped out of *The Saint* until his divorce was finalized, so his $6 million payday wouldn't be included in the financial settlement.[35] *The Saint's* director, Philip Noyce, told *Daily Variety's* Anita M. Busch that when it came to Kilmer cutting off negotiations to star in the film, "There were a number of factors involved: fatigue, his divorce and Batman." According to Noyce, Kilmer had called him in December, saying he was too exhausted to work on the film. Noyce began doing damage control, booking a flight to South Africa, where Kilmer was already working on *The Ghost and the Darkness*. "If I thought he was going to do it, I wouldn't have flown to Johannesburg," said Noyce. "I went down three times to lay out the production schedule and the workload for Val."[36] Noyce's talks with the actor would continue into the new year.

Meanwhile, in January, Goldsman completed his *Batman & Robin* script, and by the middle of the month *Daily Variety* was reporting that Alicia Silverstone would play Batgirl alongside Kilmer and O'Donnell's Batman and Robin.[37] *Daily Variety* reported her signing on February 1, 1996.[38] "Alicia Silverstone is an extraordinary young woman, and of course, beautiful and talented," said Schumacher. "She's very popular with young audiences, and I thought it would be nice to give them a young heroine who was as intelligent, strong-willed and dedicated to justice as the men."[39] The 19-year-old Silverstone, daughter of a San Francisco real estate investor and a flight attendant, had been acting in TV commercials since the age of six. She landed a TV role in 1992 on *The Wonder Years*, and then segued into films, playing a young woman obsessed with an older man in *The Crush* (1993). That led to her being cast in several music videos for the band Aerosmith, but it was her starring role in director Amy Heckerling's *Clueless* (1995)—a charming update of Jane Austen's *Emma*—that catapulted her into the cultural zeitgeist. "I was in Japan on a press tour for *Clueless* when Joel called me from Mississippi, where he was filming *A Time to Kill*," recalled Silverstone. "I could barely hear him, but I was thrilled."[40] The young actress admitted to being a fan of the *Batman* TV series, saying, "I watched them when I was a little girl and loved the characters, especially Catwoman and the Joker."[41]

By the end of January, another name had joined Julia Roberts and Demi Moore in the Poison Ivy sweepstakes: Uma Thurman.[42] Born in Boston in 1970, Thurman was the daughter of Buddhist scholar Robert Thurman and model Nena Thurman; she grew up in a household where the Dalai Lama was sometimes a houseguest. At age 15, she went to New York to attend high school and pursue modeling, eventually being featured in magazines such as *Glamour*. She made her first film appearance in 1987's *Kiss Daddy Goodnight*, but it was the powerful one-two combination of Terry Gilliam's *The Adventures of Baron Munchausen* and Stephen Frears' *Dangerous Liaisons*, both released in 1988, that turned her into a sought-after sex symbol. In 1990, she married actor Gary Oldman, but the union lasted less than two years. After a string of mediocre films, she was nominated for a Best Supporting Actress Oscar in 1995 for her co-starring role opposite John Travolta in Quentin Tarantino's *Pulp Fiction*. Thurman met director Joel Schumacher at a New York restaurant to discuss the role, and by the time they'd finished dessert she was at the top of the list.[43] She was signed soon after.[44] "I've always wanted to work with Uma Thurman," said Schumacher. "The first time I saw her in a film was in *The Adventures of Baron Munchausen* as Venus. When that shell opened revealing her in imitation of Botticelli's painting, I said, 'Who is this gorgeous girl?' I think to find someone that beautiful who's also such a wonderful actress is very rare."[45]

Meanwhile, Val Kilmer, having met with *The Saint's* director Philip Noyce in London in January, recommitted to star in Noyce's spy film. However, no one at the Creative Artist Agency bothered to inform Paramount that Kilmer was contractually obligated for first position on *Batman & Robin*, which had a pre-production start date of August 1, until early February. By the time Paramount was made aware of Kilmer's situation, they were already six weeks into pre-production of *The Saint* and had spent about $10 million. *The Saint* was set to begin principal photography on March 27 for a two to three month shoot. When Paramount executives were told by CAA co-chairman Rick Nicita that Kilmer had to get clearance for his schedule from Warner Bros., they were stunned; they thought they had an unencumbered deal with Kilmer, especially since the actor had been meeting with Noyce about the script, and rewrites had been made to suit the actor.[46]

Nicita then reportedly went to Warner Bros. chairman Bob Daly and told him that Kilmer didn't want to do *Batman & Robin* because of a problem with Joel Schumacher. Daly was furious, reminding Nicita that Kilmer was contractually bound to do the *Batman* film. Under its option agreement, Warner Bros.—which had yet to release Kilmer from his contract—could insist that Kilmer report for the September 1 principal photography start date of *Batman & Robin*. Neither Warner Bros. nor Paramount were happy with the situation, and both threatened to sue CAA.[47]

The fall-out over how negotiations with Kilmer were handled had other repercussions. After ten years as a client, Joel Schumacher—upset over how Rick Nicita had handled Val Kilmer's negotiations for *The Saint* and *Batman & Robin*—left the Creative Artists Agency, and for a time was represented by Jake Bloom, his attorney.[48] Schumacher, who was represented by Nicita's friend Jack Rapke, another co-chairman of CAA, told *Daily Variety* that Schumacher left the agency just because he wanted to "hang loose for awhile." But sources told the trade paper that the director became unhappy when Nicita negotiated a $6 million deal for Kilmer to star in *The Saint*.[49]

Warner Bros. and Paramount decided to work the problem out between themselves. Paramount agreed to a stop date for *The Saint* at the end of July, and also agreed not to release their film near the June 5, 1997 scheduled release date of *Batman & Robin*. But once Schumacher became aware of the situation with Kilmer, he decided to institute a Plan B, and opened up discussions with George Clooney.[50]

Clooney was famous as pediatrician Dr. Doug Ross on the TV series *ER*, a role he began playing when the series debuted in 1994. After the TV show made him a household name, he starred opposite Michelle Pfeiffer in *One Fine Day* (1996) and Salma Hayek in Robert Rodriguez's *From Dusk Till Dawn* (1996). "I saw George in *From Dusk Till Dawn* and recognized immediately that he not only had looks and talent, but real charisma," said Joel Schumacher. "When I actually drew Batman's cowl onto George's face in a newspaper ad for the film, he looked perfect."[51]

The affable actor, born May 6, 1961 in Lexington, Kentucky, was the son of Cincinnati TV newscaster and talk show host Nick Clooney, and the nephew of singer Rosemary Clooney. After studying at Northern Kentucky University, he first sought a career as a baseball player, trying out for a position with the Cincinnati Reds. When that didn't pan out, his cousin, actor Miguel Ferrer, helped him land a small role in a feature film. In 1982, Clooney moved to Los Angeles to pursue acting, making his TV debut in an episode of the TV series *Riptide* in 1984. More TV appearances followed, including recurring roles in the series *The Facts of Life, Roseanne, Bodies of Evidence* and *Sisters.* He'd also made forays into films, beginning with such forgettable fare as *Return to Horror High* (1987) and *Return of the Killer Tomatoes!* (1988), but his career seemed to be going nowhere until he landed the featured role on *ER.*

Clooney had been sought for a leading role in a superhero adventure before. In October of 1995, he was reportedly close to signing a $3 million deal with Universal Pictures to play the Green Hornet, a character originally created for radio by the same team responsible for the Lone Ranger. The character had appeared in two serials in the 1940s as well as the 1966-67 TV series produced by *Batman's* William Dozier and starring Van Williams as the Green Hornet and Bruce Lee as his sidekick, Kato. Jason Scott Lee, who had just starred as Bruce Lee in *Dragon* for Universal Pictures, was reportedly going to be Kato to Clooney's Green Hornet. It was thought that Clooney would begin filming the movie in March or April of 1996 during a hiatus from *ER*, but once Clooney was in consideration for Batman, the Green Hornet project evaporated.[52]

Warner Bros., meanwhile, sought to protect their number one franchise by arguing that Kilmer had an ironclad contract to reprise his role as Batman, and notified Paramount that Kilmer was contractually obligated to show up for work on August 1. *Daily Variety* reported that Kilmer didn't like the title of the new Batfilm, because he didn't want to share the spotlight with Chris O'Donnell. With *The Saint*, he would be earning three times his *Batman Forever* salary, and wouldn't have to share the screen with a sidekick or scene-stealing villains. He also reportedly wanted his good friend Robert Towne, the screenwriter of *Chinatown*, to take a crack at the script.[53]

Finally, Joel Schumacher had enough, saying in interviews that Kilmer was "the most psychologically troubled human being I've ever worked with." Kilmer was surprised and hurt by Schumacher's reaction, telling *Los Angeles Times* reporter Steve Hochman, "The thing that Joel Schumacher said was so extreme. He's accusing me of being a disturbed person. So why did he offer me the lead role in *A Time to Kill?* Why was he so upset? He can't deny that he wanted me to do that job. So this is a guy that I had a very pleasant time working with's form of grief about me not working with him any more."[54]

As the tension between the director and the star rose, industry insiders felt Warner Bros. would eventually drop the irritable Kilmer in favor of Clooney, who had the reputation of being an easy-going actor.[55] And indeed, on Valentine's Day, *Daily*

Variety announced that Kilmer would not be returning as Batman.[56] A week later, on February 21, while noting that Kilmer was "willing" to return for Batman, the trade paper reported that the actor was scheduled to leave for Moscow to begin filming *The Saint* in the first week in March.[57] Two days later, they reported that Clooney had signed a three-picture deal with Warner Bros. said to be worth between $26 million and $28 million. *Batman & Robin* was expected to be his first project under the deal.

THE HARDEST WORKING MAN
IN SHOW BUSINESS

Now officially out of the *Batman* film, Kilmer explained that one of the reasons he left is that the role no longer held any challenges for him. "With *Batman*, the reason it's so popular has nothing to do with me," he told Steve Hochman of *The Los Angeles Times*. "One of the reasons it wasn't such a lure to go back to do *Batman* is that they were so happy with the product. There was nothing stimulating to me in that in a personal way. There's nothing wrong with success, and it's hard to conceive that it wouldn't be again. It's just not stimulating."[58]

When asked by *Daily Variety's* Michael Mallory if he could confirm or deny rumors that Val Kilmer had been difficult during filming of *Batman Forever*, Schumacher gave a diplomatic answer, saying, "A lot of film time these days is unfortunately spent just waiting for stars. I have no patience with overpaid, over-privileged people who cannot have the dignity and courtesy to be professional. I don't tolerate that kind of behavior."[59]

Warner Bros. immediately began discussions with Clooney's William Morris agents and with Dreamworks, trying to work out scheduling conflicts between the *Batman* film and his commitment to do Dreamworks' action thriller *The Peacemaker*.[60] *The Peacemaker* was scheduled to finish filming in August, with Clooney due to begin *Batman & Robin* in September. In the event Clooney wasn't able to begin the *Batman* film on time, Val Kilmer—still contractually bound to the role—would be waiting in the wings.[61] Part of Clooney's contract was an option to do another *Batman* film, though he wasn't guaranteed a return engagement.[62]

Batman & Robin was due to begin shooting at the same time as a new season of *ER*. Since Warner Bros. owned the show and wanted to assure its continued success, they began working out a schedule that would allow Clooney to do both *ER* and *Batman & Robin* simultaneously. Luckily, the *Batman* film would be shooting on the same Warners backlot where *ER* also had its sets, so Clooney could easily move from one set to the next. The problem was that *ER* shot five days a week, from Monday through Friday, which only left two days a week for Clooney to be Batman.[63] For his part, Clooney was eager to take on the role; *Variety* quoted sources saying that he "desperately wants Batman."[64] On March 4, *Daily Variety's* Peter Bart reported that Clooney would get $10 million for playing the Caped Crusader.[65]

Warner Bros. was not only courting George Clooney, they were also in talks with Arnold Schwarzenegger to take on the role of the villain, Mr. Freeze.[66] It appears that Sylvester Stallone might also have been considered for the Mr. Freeze role, but ultimately no offer was made to his representatives.[67] Stallone who, like

Schwarzenegger, was represented by International Creative Management, reportedly left the agency partly because he was upset that Schwarzenegger, and not he, received the offer to play Mr. Freeze.[68] However, when asked about playing the role, Stallone would later tell *Daily Variety's* Greg Evans, "I had no intentions of doing that film. They're doing what they want to do, and I'm where I want to be."[69]

At the National Association of Theater Owners/ShoWest convention in March, Arnold Schwarzenegger announced that he was still trying to work out his schedule so that he could play Mr. Freeze. But, since he had already committed to appear in Paramount Pictures' *Wings of Eagles*, he wasn't sure that he'd be available. In the event that he wasn't, *Daily Variety* reported that Bruce Willis was waiting to step into the villain's cryo-suit.[70]

By March 12, 1996, all the stars had aligned. On that day, Warner Bros. announced Val Kilmer had been released from his contract options, and that George Clooney would be Batman and Arnold Schwarzenegger would be Mr. Freeze in *Batman & Robin*, both having worked out their schedules.[71] "It sounded great, and I really wanted to work with Joel," said Clooney. "I had also been over at Warner Bros. for a long time on *ER*, and there's really a nice sense of family that doesn't exist anywhere else in Hollywood. The idea of being able to work on the biggest franchise of all time thrilled me, and we made the deal."[72] Clooney admitted that he hadn't been a big comic book fan as a kid, but that he was familiar with *Batman*. "Where we grew up, television was everything, and *Batman* was our favorite show. My cousin Miguel Ferrer used to make plaster statues of Batman and give them to everybody as gifts."[73]

Schumacher acknowledged that the tone of *Batman & Robin* would be lighter than the previous film, and attributed that partly to the hiring of Clooney. "Bringing George on has changed the tone in that he is a more humane Batman and less of the dark, brooding, damaged Batman...This Batman is older and wiser. He's a man who has left most of his childhood traumas behind and is much more concerned with his life today. He has a fiancée, conflicts with Robin, a stranger in the house with Batgirl and a drama being played out with Alfred. He's giving away money all day and running around in a rubber suit at night. This Batman is obviously way too busy to still be tormented by the death of his parents."[74]

Clooney agreed with Schumacher's assessment, saying, "We have now seen three *Batman* films in which he talks about how his parents were murdered when he was a little boy, and the truth is that people now want this man to stop talking about it already. It's time for Batman to enjoy being Batman, and deal with the problems at hand rather than the problems of his past. But that doesn't mean that he's not frustrated by the criminals who roam around Gotham, or that he doesn't still have some issues of his own to deal with."[75]

Clooney accepted the role knowing that it was fraught with potential pitfalls. "First and foremost, I don't want to screw up what has already worked so well," he said. "It's the most successful movie franchise ever, so I'm not trying to make this thing 'right.' You try and do it differently, but you don't want to be different just to be different. There are certain things that you have to uphold when playing a character like Batman. The secret to Batman is that he's kind of the Johnny Carson of superheroes. The reason Carson was such a great host was not only that he was funny and warm and we really liked him, but he also always made sure that the guest was the star. The truth of the matter is that the star of this movie is not Batman. The criminals are always the star, because they're so much bigger than life. Batman is the constant, the steady in this. So my job is to be the foundation to hold all this together,

George Clooney strikes a pose in Batman & Robin. He was the first Batman actor since Robert Lowery to wear a Batman outfit that did not include a yellow and black bat insignia (Warner Bros./Photofest, © Warner Bros.).

because in a way the audience watches the movie through Batman's eyes. Hopefully, the stars are the wild characters, the sets, the costumes, the wonderful camerawork. It's an epic! My task is not to try and grab the attention all the time."[76]

Schwarzenegger's deal was his most lucrative yet. He was reported to have earned over $20 million; some sources said his upfront deal was for as much as $25 million for six weeks' work. His cut from merchandising would bring in even more. On products using his likeness, he would earn anywhere from 2.5% to 8% of Warner Bros.' net; together with his salary, it was thought he could make as much as $35 million for playing the role.[77] "With Arnold Schwarzenegger as Mr. Freeze, we have a real action side to this movie so that Batman and Robin could do what they do in the comics," said Schumacher."[78] Schwarzenegger attacked the role with gusto, saying, "Obviously, it was the last thing I ever thought of. But Joel and I had often talked about the possibility of working together, and it seemed to be an interesting opportunity. I studied the comic books that featured Mr. Freeze and also looked at the way he was played by Otto Preminger, George Sanders and Eli Wallach on the TV series. Then I had to figure out how to separate my Mr. Freeze from theirs, and how to make it memorable within the context of all the other terrific Batman villains. Because, you know, these movies are going to go on forever, and after people see *Batman X*, they'll look back and talk about their favorite villains."[79]

For the role of Bane, Schumacher chose 6'4", 405-lb. wrestler Robert "Jeep" Swenson. The San Antonio, Texas native wrestled on the independent circuit under the names Jeep the Mercenary and Jeep Swenson, and on a WCW pay-per-view event as The Ultimate Final Solution. He had previously appeared on-screen in *No Holds Barred*, a 1989 film starring fellow wrestler Hulk Hogan, and as James Caan's bodyguard in 1996's *Bulletproof*. Swenson drew upon a literary inspiration for playing Bane, saying that the character's relationship with Poison Ivy was "almost like the relationship between George and Lenny in *Of Mice and Men*, with the more diminutive person taking charge and telling the bigger one how to think."[80]

Dr. Jason Woodtrue, Bane's creator, was played by John Glover, an actor who had worked with Schumacher before on *The Incredible Shrinking Woman*. "Joel simply explained to me what Dr. Woodtrue was going to be in the film, and that he hoped I would consider doing it," said Glover. "And when he told me that I would get kissed to death by Uma Thurman in the end...I thought, 'Well, why not?'"[81]

Australian model Elle MacPherson, famous for appearing on the cover of *Sports Illustrated* magazine's annual swimsuit issue a record six times, was chosen to play Julie Madison, Bruce Wayne's fiancée. MacPherson made her film debut in Woody Allen's *Alice* (1990), and won good notices for her role in the 1994 film *Sirens*, in which she played an artist's model. Julie Madison, the character she played in *Batman & Robin*, first appeared in *Detective Comics* # 31 in December 1939, in the fifth Batman story published. Originally a socialite engaged to Bruce Wayne, she was shown to be an actress in *Detective Comics* #40, and made her last appearance nine issues later, after a studio head and a publicity agent changed her name to Portia Storme. Three decades later, she appeared in two issues of *World's Finest Comics* (#248, December 1977/January 1978 and #253, October/November 1978) as Princess Portia, having married the king of Moldacia.

The doomed wife of Victor Fries was played by another fashion model, Vendala Kirsebom, an international spokeswoman for the United Nations' Children's Fund.[82] Kirsebom, who was set to marry Norwegian businessman Olaf Thommessen in Stockholm on August 4, 1996, told *Variety*'s Army Archerd, "I'll spend my honeymoon on the set of *Batman & Robin* as Mrs. Arnold Schwarzenegger."[83]

Bob Kane's wife, Elizabeth Sanders, reprised the role of Gossip Gertie from *Batman Forever*. "Gossip Gertie is a fun throwback to powerful 1940s gossip columnists like Louella Parsons and Hedda Hopper," said Kane. "And Elizabeth is adorable. She has presence that just pops out on the screen."[84] Super Bat-fan Senator Patrick Leahy made a cameo in a party scene, and Pat Hingle and Michael Gough reprised their roles as Commissioner Gordon and Alfred Pennyworth. "I did not expect to get such a great cast," said Schumacher. "You know, that's very rare in the fourth of a film series. Things sometimes begin to wind down at this point, and I think having such an exciting group of actors stimulated us all."[85]

FEEDING THE MONSTER

In February 1996, seven months before the start of principal photography, the creation of Gotham City began, in miniature. Some 26 miniature buildings, built on 1:24 scale and reaching as high as 25 feet, were constructed for Gotham City, all of them moveable to create different cityscapes for different sequences.[86]

Meanwhile, production designer Barbara Ling began creating the full-scale sets, which went up on the soundstages of Warner Bros. and at the Long Beach Seaport Dome. Ling created a Gotham City that was even bigger than the one seen in the previous film, still inspired by the Russian constructivists, but with a healthy dollop of art nouveau thrown in for good measure. "Gotham has always been for me a combination of everything we know, creating a world that feels familiar, but not enough to put your finger on," said Ling. "It has a size proportion bigger than anything that actually exists, but within those proportions you recognize elements of other histories of architecture and other places. Gotham is a fusion of many cultures and periods of time, but it has no time element. It could be anywhere in time. It's not the future. We're not the past. It's Gotham-time."[87]

Ling's set for the Gotham Museum of Natural History was inspired by her memories of childhood visits to the Field Museum in Chicago. "I felt like an ant in there, so I wanted to make the Gotham Museum much bigger than a real museum and went after creating a fusion of cultures for the exhibit on display in the great hall," said Ling. "We invented something called 'The Lost World of Tufa,' which squishes together many world cultures from different eras of history—like 20-foot-tall statues of a sphinx body with a Tibetan head, or a Mayan head on top of a Mesopotamian body."[88] Ling worked closely with the stunt department, creating a space with enough expanse for the ice floes and ramps for the extreme skaters that would be employed in the sequence. "Being able to have Yarek Alfer and his sculpture department build the dinosaur statue was crucial," said Ling, "because in any set as large as the museum, you need something to give it a sense of scale when you put a human next to it."[89] Standing roughly 60 feet high, 200 feet long, and 150 feet wide, the museum set took five months for the construction crew to build.[90] Schumacher felt the expanse of the set was crucial to the action he intended to shoot there. "I really don't like to place characters against white walls, and instead, you'll see that I place them in the middle of large spaces, so they can move, and we can move with them," said Schumacher. "Theater and choreography are very important for me in this way, and in *Batman & Robin*, I urged my stunt coordinator to use every inch of our big, beautiful space. Too often in movies with action in big spaces, most of the shots are in tight close-ups and two-shots. I don't understand that."[91]

Inspired by the use of color in the Batman comic books, Ling wanted lots of splashes of bright color in the film's Gotham City. She faced a challenge, however, when it came to covering the sets in ice. "We wanted them to have some translucency, to take ice into a surreal place," said Ling. "We probably did five months of research playing with every kind of toxic and non-toxic material known to man to come up with the right materials for the ice, before discovering a combination fiber resin. It took half a year to make the amount of ice we needed for this movie. The idea was to keep this twinkle about it, ice which feels cold but at the same time could explode because of this inner lighting that is always undulating. We didn't want to just use white ice, and as far as I know, we're the first to come up with this technique."[92]

While the icy museum set was under construction, Ling tackled another big project: the Batcave. Since Batman's lair had been destroyed by the Riddler in the previous film, Ling was able to recreate the set from the ground up for *Batman & Robin*. She was disappointed in how small the Batcave set appeared in *Batman Forever*, though she had tried to make it look immense. "This time, I was determined not to repeat my mistake," said Ling. "The first element of the Batcave I designed was actually the turntable for the Batmobile and the Redbird, which I thought should reflect the Bat-Signal as an enhancement of that visual theme. Just as the Bat-Signal shines in the skies above Gotham, this would be the Bat-Signal deep beneath the surface. The Batmobile surfaces in the middle of this rising Bat-Signal. It became a perfect symbol to have the car positioned on the wings of the Batman emblem as it drives off. Then part of the emblem rises and creates a pod, which splits open and reveals a neon Robin emblem and the Redbird within. The Batmobile turntable in *Batman Forever* was about 20 feet, but to get the Bat Emblem formed on top of it for *Batman & Robin*, I needed to expand it to 50 feet."[93] Since Batman, Robin and Batgirl are seen in armored suits late in the film, Ling created an armored metal motif for the Batcave, creating arches in the cave that looked as though they were manufactured from metal. She also created a large Batman emblem that split apart to reveal a six-foot Bat Monitor behind Batman's computer console.[94] The set was built at the Long Beach Seaport Dome, utilizing a huge amount of steel and pipe superstructure. Once that was in place, thousands of plywood sheets were cut into ribs and cleats, assembled, and then shot with plaster. Rising fifty feet from the floor, the set required 100 laborers working on it for four months.[95]

The Long Beach Seaport Dome housed not only the Batcave set, but also two other massive sets: the Wayne Manor interior and Gotham Observatory[96] Unit production manager Barry Waldman remarked, "I remember thinking that we had six months until shooting started in September, which was more than enough time for prep. But in fact, we could have used another six months. There's nothing small about *Batman & Robin.* This movie is a monster that has to be fed."[97]

Besides the gargantuan sets, the new film gave Barbara Ling a second chance to design the Batmobile, as well as the other special vehicles required by the script. "Ultimately, I felt like the Batmobile in the last film looked just too small on camera," said Ling. "This time I wanted its shape to be a giant version of some of the early roadster sports cars, like the Jaguar D types or the Delahane 165. I was also influenced by all of the Moon Company's vehicles, including the Moon Spinner and the X Streamliner. I also wanted the Batmobile, this time, to be a convertible, which had always excited me about the early comic-book Batmobile."[98] Ling worked with Allen Pike and Charley Zurian's TFX Company in North Hollywood to create the new Batwheels.[99] Automotive illustrator Harald Belker, who once worked for Mercedes-Benz in Germany, aided with the design, which Ling wanted to reflect the shape of Batman's cape. Instead of one flame shooting out the back, she wanted three on each of the two scalloped rear fins, and she designed it to have a single open cockpit, saying, "I think it's much more handsome for the shots where you have Batman's head right between the winged fenders."[100] Built from the ground up, the final car was almost 29 feet long on a custom-built chassis with racecar components, including a Chevy 380 engine that could reach a speed of 140 miles per hour.[101] "I think it should always feel like half a block is coming at you when you see it approach," said Ling, "and the size of the vehicle has to take on unnatural proportions for that to really happen.[102]

Since there was no seat for Robin in the Batmobile, he was given his own mode of transportation, a motorcycle called the Redbird. Like the Batmobile, Ling wanted the vehicle to be very long, so she again consulted with Harald Becker on the design. After about a dozen trials, they finally came up with one that was functional.[103] Allen Pike built the Redbird with a single-cylinder, 650cc, four valves per head Rotax racing motor, which weighed 98 pounds and delivered 65 horsepower. Like the Batmobile, the bodywork was fabricated from fiberglass and carbon fiber, the same material used in airplanes. "We created a chassis developed out of components rather than a frame, with a side and front section," said Pike. "That way, if anything breaks during the stunts, we can quickly repair the bike."[104] TFX made one "hero" Redbird for close shots, a stunt vehicle for jumping and wheelie scenes, and two "slider" bikes for sliding stunts and wire rigging.[105]

Three other Batvehicles were created for the climactic scene—the Bathammer for Batman, Batsled for Robin and Batblade for Batgirl.[106] Based on the Batmobile, the Bathammer was a single-seat vehicle with a center pod, a turbine and a single wing off the back. The 20-foot-long vehicle was black underneath with a silver top outlined in neon.[107] The Batsled was a two-seater combination of a hovercraft and a fan-driven Everglades vehicle, equipped with ice torpedoes, while the Batblade was a low-slung bike with dual fins coming off the back sides and ice-spiked tires, including a huge flat back tire that rode very low to the ground.[108]

Mr. Freeze also had his own unique mode of transportation, called the Freezemobile. "I loved the idea that for Mr. Freeze's vehicle, you have to have something bigger than he is," said Ling. "And when he's in costume, Mr. Freeze is humongous." The Freezemobile was first designed and articulated on TFX's Alias computer, to see if it would work.[109] A scale model was then built and the design refined. The data was digitized, put back into the computer, refined further, and then the final vehicle was cut full-size.[110] Another custom fabrication built from the ground up, the Freezemobile was 26 feet long and nine feet high. It was constructed of plywood and foam, then covered with fiberglass. Foil and rivets were applied to give it a metal appearance.[111] "It also required huge wheels," said Ling, "so that it felt like a tractor or steam engine was coming right at you."[112]

Before Charley Zurian and Allen Pike formed TFX, Zurian worked at the General Motors Concept Center, where he was partially responsible for the creation of the EV1 electric car. Like the EV1, the Freezemobile was a fully electric vehicle, capable of traveling up to 50 miles per hour.[113] "One of the things that motivated us to use electric power is because torque is almost instantaneous," said Zurian. "We knew that the Freezemobile was going to be utilized a great deal on soundstages where there isn't a lot of room to get up speed. And because of its size, we knew that there was no way a gas-powered vehicle could handle that. In addition, there are so many safety concerns with heat and fuel that we elected to go with the electric motor."[114]

Along with updating the sets and vehicles, new Bat costumes were designed for the film. Ingrid Ferrin, who had worked with Bob Ringwood on *Batman Forever*, and a new member of the team, Robert Turturice, set to work on updating the outfits, with input from production designer Barbara Ling and director Joel Schumacher.[115] Batman's costume was changed from black to a subtle blue-black,[116] and made with a lighter foam so that it weighed only one-third of the 35-lb. *Batman Forever* Batsuit. "There's a lot more flexibility and lightness, but the pay-off is that the foams don't last as long," said costume supervisor Don Bronson. "Another issue is that in the past we used black latex, but this time we're actually painting all of the surfaces with the blue element, which has to hold up on a stretchable, movable surface. A lot of detail went into the prototyping and testing of the different paints to see how durable they would be."[117]

A second, more advanced Batsuit was made for the film's climax, with armored highlights on the torso, gauntlets, boots and cowl. Designed by Barbara Ling, it was sculpted by Jose Fernandez and Kent Jones. Complementary suits were made for Robin and Batgirl. At least 50 individual Batsuits of both the basic and armored versions were created, with many of them suffering significant wear and tear during the rigorous stunt scenes.[118] The Batsuit was still uncomfortable for the actor inside it; asked by a foreign reporter during an international press junket about the most difficult stunts he performed, Clooney quipped, "Yesterday I had to raise my arms over my head while wearing the Batsuit. That was a traumatic experience."[119]

Robin's outfit was redesigned in the same blue/black material as Batman's, with the Nightwing emblem stretching from his chest and down his arms. Continuing on in the tradition of *Batman Forever*, both Batman's outfits and Robin's costumes had nipples and codpieces (Clooney joked that his codpiece was larger than the one worn by Val Kilmer), but Robin's wardrobe, much to Chris O'Donnell's relief, no longer featured an earring.[120]

Batgirl's costume evolved in the early stages of the production. The first concepts featured a cowl; one design was a full cowl that covered her head and the upper half of her face, like Batman's. Another design was more like a helmet that covered the upper half of her head and face but allowed her blonde hair to flow out beneath.[121] Neither design was ultimately utilized, probably because they would have made Alicia Silverstone look too much like Catwoman in a cape.

To help differentiate Batgirl from Barbara Wilson, once the crime-fighter put on her mask, make-up artist Ve Neill added a beauty mark near her lips. Neill explained that the beauty mark was a tribute to a character played by Anne Francis in a 1960s TV series. "It kind of reminded me of *Honey West*, although there probably aren't many people who remember who she was," said Neill. "She was a favorite of mine as a little girl, and I just thought that a beauty mark was something really cute and sassy for Barbara to have that could set her apart from the rest of the girls."[122]

Illustrator Mariano Diaz created the basic concept for Mr. Freeze's armored suit, again with input from Ling, Schumacher and vehicle manufacturers TFX.[123] The four "hero suits" made to be worn by Arnold Schwarzenegger were hand-pounded completely out of aluminum by armor designer Terry English, who a few years later became the armourer to Her Majesty, Queen Elizabeth II. The full suit was comprised of over 20 separate pieces and weighed about 45 pounds. Using one of the originals as a pattern, TFX made an additional fifteen suits, molding the pieces with aluminum zinc oxide.[124] Still more suits were created from fiberglass and sprayed with metallic paint to match the originals. The Freeze Suit backpack served a practical purpose: it housed the batteries that powered the thousands of LEDs placed throughout the suit to give it its distinctive blue light; each of the suits contained 2,500 LEDs, with the complex electronics designed and maintained by TFX.[125] "The costume limits you because you can only move so much under the heavy armor," said Arnold Schwarzenegger. "You move differently, like a big truck moves differently than a Porsche. But a big truck can still move very fast."[126] Referring to an earlier Schwarzenegger role, Schumacher described Mr. Freeze as *"The Terminator* meets the refrigerator." Playing the role tested Schwarzenegger's physical endurance; the cryogenic suit he wore weighed fifty pounds.[127]

On April 10, 1996 *Daily Variety's* Anita M. Busch reported that McDonald's had signed an exclusive 10-year promotional deal with Disney.[128] The McDonald's deal would have negative implications for *Batman & Robin*; the fast food giant had been Warner Bros. promotional partner on *Batman Returns* and *Batman Forever*, bringing in $35 to $40 million in promotional money for those two films.[129] Now, Warner Bros. would have to find another partner. They hoped to join with the next biggest fast food giant, Burger King, but that franchise had already signed a pact with Universal Pictures and Amblin for Steven Spielberg's *The Lost World: Jurassic Park*.[130] In June, Warner Bros. announced that they were partnering with PepsiCo's Taco Bell, who had been their partner on the original *Batman* in 1989,[131] an arrangement that had brought in between $10 and $12 million in promotional money.[132] The Kellogg Company, the Amoco Corporation, and the Frito-Lays unit of Pepsico Inc. joined Taco Bell for a cumulative television advertising campaign for *Batman & Robin* worth $44 million.[133]

Merchandising now played an enormous part in the *Batman* films, to the extent that it began to seem that the tail was now wagging the dog. In 1995, the year of *Batman Forever's* release, Warner Bros. sold $1 billion worth of Batman merchandise, and they wanted to keep the gravy train rolling. George Jones, president of worldwide licensing at Warner Bros. Consumer Products, told *Daily Variety's* Gary Levin, "If you look at *Batman & Robin*, we were a major catalyst behind this picture being made."

The budget of *Batman & Robin* was said to be in the $80 million range, slightly higher than the final tally of $78 million the studio reportedly spent on *Batman Forever*.[134] By the time filming had concluded, there were rumors that the budget had swelled to more than $100 million. *Batman & Robin* was set to enter a summer marketplace crowded with other mega-budget movies, including *Starship Troopers, Men in Black, Face/Off, Speed 2: Cruise Control* and *Alien Resurrection*. After the success of the blockbuster films *Independence Day* and *Twister*, not to mention the stellar box-office returns of *Batman Forever*, the economics of the movie industry were forever altered, with studios feeling that the risky mega-budget movies represented the most sound investments; although they were a huge financial gamble, when they hit, the pay-offs were enormous. Peter Bart of *Daily Variety* quoted one agent as saying that Hollywood had become "like a casino where all the bettors have become delusional."[135]

"I won't give you the exact budget figure, but it's safe to say this one is costing a touch under five percent more than *Batman Forever*," said producer Peter Macgregor-Scott. "Obviously, everybody would be happy if we could make this for $3 million less than the last one. They would love it. But everybody realizes that to make a *Batman* movie, you must spend a little more each time out. From a purely business point-of-view, however, a *Batman* movie is about as safe a bet as you can make."[136]

CLIMBING EVEREST

Production of *Batman & Robin* officially got underway on Thursday, September 12, 1996, with a scene between Alfred and Barbara in Wayne Manor.[137] Once filming got underway, Clooney literally became the hardest working man in Hollywood. He continued acting in TV's number one rated show, *ER*, for 14 hours a day, Monday through Thursday, and shot *Batman & Robin* from Friday through Sunday. "The truth of the matter is that although I'm working seven days a week right now, which is very difficult, no one wants to hear me complain," said Clooney. "So I don't, and that's fair enough, because my life is also a very good one."[138]

When asked why he stayed with *ER*, with his film career beginning to take off, Clooney said, "Eighty percent of what you do is shit. Crap. Eight out of 10 plays I see suck. Eight out of 10 movies I see suck. Eight out of 10 TV series are awful. So if you get in that 20 percent, you take it, you bathe in it as long as you can. And I have a contract. I have a responsibility to that show. I have lawyers who say, 'Okay, we can walk away.' It would be easier, physically, to leave. But it's not right. That show is why I've gotten to this position."[139]

Filming soon moved to the Long Beach Seaport Dome, for scenes involving Batman and Mr. Freeze. When Schwarzenegger made his first on-set appearance, Schumacher exclaimed, "A Time to Freeze!"[140] George Clooney came to the production with short-cropped hair, a result of having just finished playing a military figure in Dreamworks' *The Peacemaker*. The filmmakers contemplated putting a wig on him, but ultimately decided to go with Clooney's short-haired look. Schumacher also decided to keep the distinguished flecks of gray in Clooney's hair, to show that this Bruce Wayne was a bit more mature than in the previous film.[141] Chris O'Donnell's hair was also somewhat different than it had been in *Batman Forever;* for *Batman & Robin*, it was slightly shorter and lighter-colored. It was decided to give Dick Grayson a little tattoo on the side of his neck, but during the first day of shooting, it looked like a dirty smudge, so the idea was dropped.[142]

While Clooney, as is his custom, wore no make-up at all, Arnold Schwarzenegger was subjected to a daily three-hour regimen in the make-up chair to become the bald, blue-skinned, frost-covered Mr. Freeze.[143] Jeff Dawn, who had worked with Schwarzenegger on 14 films starting with 1984's *Terminator*, helped develop the actor's Mr. Freeze make-up. During pre-production, Dawn began experimenting with a double, coloring him various shades of blue and silver and adding little sparkles for a frost effect, duplicating a look he had used for *Terminator II: Judgment Day* for a scene where the T-1000 was frozen with nitrogen before breaking into pieces. After four makeup tests, Dawn tried the makeup on Schwarzenegger, but wasn't satisfied with the results. Dawn thought perhaps it would be better to start off by painting the actor with a silver base foundation, then airbrushing white and blue dots on top of it for texture.[144]

Seeing how long it took to apply the makeup with a baldhead cap, Dawn urged Schwarzenegger to shave his head for the role, to save time in the makeup chair. "Had Arnold shaved his head, it would have taken an hour off the makeup process in the morning, and another 20 minutes off at night," said Dawn. In the months leading up to the start of production, Schwarzenegger seemed to agree that shaving his head would be the most practical way to go. At the end of the first day of shooting, Schwarzenegger said that putting on the baldhead cap was a pain. He asked for the behind-the-scenes video crew to be brought in the next morning to videotape him having his head shaved, but when the morning came, and with the video crew standing by, Arnold, looking at his hairstylist Peter Tothpal standing ready with a razor, suddenly seemed uncomfortable. Then he said cheerfully to Dawn, "Okay, Jeff, let's put the cap on." Dawn said, "But we're gonna shave your head today." Schwarzenegger replied, "Oh no, you're not! You touch that razor to my head, and I'll make your life miserable the rest of your life!"[145]

For the rest of his work on the picture, Schwarzenegger went through the extra time to put on the bald cap. Each day, the process began with Tothpal slicking down Schwarzenegger's hair with a water-based resin that hardened like plastic when dried with a hair dryer. During the half hour that Tothpal worked on Schwarzenegger's hair, Dawn and his assistant Jim Kail covered the actor's face with a product that protected the skin against chemicals and glues.[146]

"In lieu of a conventional bald cap, we opted for a foam-latex bald cap, custom made to fit Arnold's hairline and skull shape," said Dawn. "We then stipple a putty-like product over the edge to add more skin texture, so that you can't tell where his real skin leaves off and the bald cap begins." By that point, Dawn and Kail were an hour and a half into the process. Next, they glued his eyebrows flat to his head with a medical adhesive and used appliances to cover them up.[147]

Acrylic silver metallic paint was then stippled all over Schwarzenegger. His eyes, lips and the hollows of his face were painted a darker shade of blue. Schwarzenegger was then walked outside to a special tent, where his face was splattered with blue and white acrylic paints to give it more texture. Then it was back inside, where he was sprayed with various sealers, and contact lens specialist Laurie Smith inserted rigid corneal opalescent lenses into his eyes to make them glow. Following that, the actor was hustled off to the costume department to be bolted and screwed into his heavy Mr. Freeze armor, and finally he was ready to face the cameras for a 12-hour day.[148]

The bulky Mr. Freeze suit caused Schwarzenegger a little trouble in one of his early scenes in the Freezemobile. "I was supposed to break through the wall, stop, open up the top, come out holding my Freeze Cannon, and make a joke," said Schwarzenegger. "I'm opening this up, delivering this funny line and I can't get out because the shoulders are too wide for the opening of the Freezemobile!" The problem was solved by cutting away to a shot of Poison Ivy.[149]

Uma Thurman, who described the relationship between Poison Ivy and Mr. Freeze as "star-crossed lovers separated by temperature,"[150] was rather awed by the scale of the production, saying, "In the beginning it was very nerve-racking, but because of this difference, it's also been fascinating. The bottom line is that this is a comic-book world, so everybody keeps it light and fun, which is just as it should be."[151]

Clooney, known as a practical joker, seemed to be having a great time, hitting it off with Chris O'Donnell, who said "I thought that Val Kilmer did a great job, but as long as Joel had to cast a new Batman, I'm glad he chose George. He's great in the role, and we have a lot in common. He's also addicted to basketball and golf, and he's famous for kidding around on the set."[152] Alicia Silverstone concurred, saying, "George is very kind, and when he and Chris get together they're a comedy team that helps make wearing the Batgirl suit more comfortable."[153]

With filming finally underway, Schumacher was also pleased with his new Batman. "Michael Keaton and Val Kilmer were both wonderful as Batman, but I think George is the best of all," said Schumacher. "He's very much a man, a wonderful actor and of course, extremely handsome. He looks very much like Bruce Wayne in the comic books. George has also brought a real humanity and humor in the piece, an accessibility that I don't think anybody else has been able to. George is also dynamic with Chris O'Donnell, who has matured since the last film. Chris has really grown into his looks and as a performer. Since *Batman Forever*, Chris has carried movies on his own, which is a great responsibility. So when you see George and Chris together on-screen as Bruce Wayne and Dick Grayson, you totally believe that they would be friends."[154]

Bob Kane made his customary visit to the set, and, as usual, was effusive with his praise, saying, "I feel George is the best Batman of all. He's suave, elegant, has a great profile with a strong chin, like the features of Batman in the comic books. Arnold Schwarzenegger's Mr. Freeze is just incredible, and Uma Thurman is superlative as Poison Ivy, every man's desire with her flaming red hair and beautiful costumes. Chris O'Donnell is back, and he's a tremendous Robin. He's a great personality, and he really delivers the goods. And Alicia Silverstone is such a cute Batgirl...teenagers will love her!"[155]

Kane also praised Schumacher. "Joel has a great vision, and he's an ardent comic book fan from way back," said Kane. "Joel was kind enough to write the preface for the revised edition of my book *Batman & Me*, and there's a wonderful phrase he used that sticks in my mind: 'The reveries of childhood sometimes become

Chris O'Donnell as Robin and Alicia Silverstone as Batgirl in Batman & Robin (Warner Bros./Photofest, © Warner Bros.).

the vocation of adults.' Batman was Joel's favorite comic book character when he was a boy, and I'm thrilled that he's the one who's inherited the *Batman* movies."[156]

For his part, Arnold Schwarzenegger enjoyed having a role that allowed him to be both menacing and humorous, saying, "Villains are fun to play, because you can dig as deep as you can inside of yourself to find whatever evil is there, and then play with it. Joel Schumacher is a very talented director who can really get to you and pull out the best performance."[157] In a *USA Today* interview with Andy Seiler, the Austrian muscleman added, "Mr. Freeze's story is really a love story. On the other hand, he wants to freeze Gotham City and freeze the world and tear Batman's heart out. But because it's all for the wife and I have tears in my eyes, I think that people find it very endearing."

Schumacher was pleased with Schwarzenegger's performance, saying, "His acting is wonderful, especially with Uma. He is very funny, which audiences have seen before, and he's very, very menacing, which they also have seen, but I'm not sure they've seen them together in the same role. He was my only choice for the role, and I was thrilled he said yes. He's one of the most amazing people I've ever known."[158]

Thurman, prancing about in the tight togs of Poison Ivy, quickly became a scene-stealer, especially in a party scene in which she makes an entrance in a gorilla costume—made from 450 Santa wigs dyed magenta and dipped with black roots and tips[159]—and does a sinuous strip-tease, an homage to a similar entrance made by Marlene Dietrich in the "Hot Voodoo" number of the 1932 classic *Blonde Venus*. "I've never gotten to be so flamboyantly over the top," said Thurman. "I felt like I was on the ceiling somewhere, an incredible, dangerous feeling of doing everything that you're trained not to do as an actor."[160]

Playing Poison Ivy, said Thurman, required generous amounts of narcissism. During a fight scene with Alicia Silverstone, the actress had an idea. "Holding the knife, I said to Joel, 'Would you mind if I interrupted this fight?' My idea was that her own image in the knife catches her eye, and frankly, that's more interesting to her." Schumacher liked the idea, and gave her a key bit of advice: "The key to the Batman villain, the key to characters, is that they love themselves," said Thurman. "And that's the difference between them and the classic villains. They just think that they're wonderful. They love evil. They love it with a genuine passion."

In October, a month into the production of *Batman & Robin*, Val Kilmer told *Daily Variety's* Army Archerd that he wouldn't mind returning to the series. "I'd like to come back as a bad guy," said Kilmer. "George Clooney could even kill me! I think I'll mention it to Bob (Daly) and Terry (Semel)."[161]

While there was harmony on the set, off the set, at the end of October, Clooney began a very public feud with Paramount Domestic Television. The actor claimed that a story about he and his girlfriend that aired on Paramount's syndicated entertainment news program *Hard Copy* in September violated a written promise from Frank Kelly, president of Paramount TV Group, that *Hard Copy* would refrain from doing any stories on Clooney in return for *Entertainment Tonight*, another Paramount program, getting access to him. After Clooney had complained about the intrusive practices of videographers, Kelly had written to the actor in March, saying, "I see no reason why there should be any areas of conflict in the future. We agree that *Hard*

Copy will not be covering you in any future stories." Kelly said that he would "look into the practices you referred to regarding video 'paparazzi.' I don't think it makes any sense for any of our shows to be airing footage that is created under the circumstances you described. These people may still try to sell footage to other programs, but at least they will not have our shows as outlets." For six months, Kelly kept his promise, running no stories about Clooney on *Hard Copy*. Then in September came the report about Clooney and his girlfriend. "What is most amazing to me is that he offered this deal in the first place," said Clooney. "In a letter! He actually wrote it down. A so-called news format show will agree that they will not be covering me in any future stories, if I do his other show... What an idiot!"

In a letter to *Entertainment Tonight* producer Linda Bell Blue, Clooney wrote, "He broke our deal. A deal that he proposed... So now we begin. Officially. No interviews from this day on. Nothing from *ER*, nothing from *One Fine Day* [a film Clooney had just completed co-starring Michelle Pfeiffer], nothing from *Batman & Robin*, and nothing from DreamWorks' first film, *The Peacemaker*. These interviews will be reserved for all press but you. *Access Hollywood, E!* whoever...Maybe other actors will join me. Maybe not. That doesn't matter. It's about doing what's right."[162]

Hard Copy was not the only TV tabloid program causing the production grief. After *Inside Edition* ran footage surreptitiously videotaped on the closed *Batman & Robin* set, three people were arrested. Warner Bros. vowed to press charges against them.[163] With the growth in popularity of the tabloid shows, which vied with each other for exclusive footage and paid top dollar for "first look" images, the studios had been increasing security on their sets and cracking down on violators. The *Batman & Robin* set had the tightest security of any Warner Bros. production. Crewmembers were required to go through metal detectors and to wear identification badges embossed with bat-shaped holograms.[164]

Nonetheless, two men were arrested on October 19 on Warners' Burbank lot, after infiltrating the *Batman & Robin* set and taking photos of George Clooney clad in his Batman costume, which they then sold to *Inside Edition*. Arraigned in Burbank Municipal Court, one was charged with burglary, trespassing, receiving stolen property, forgery of government documents and forgery of a driver's license, while the other was charged with burglary and trespassing. After posting bail of $10,000 each, both men were released. A female accomplice was arraigned on November 8 on charges of burglary, trespassing, forgery of government documents and forgery of driver's licenses. Warner Bros. officials suspected that the photos taken by the trio were sold to *Inside Edition* by a man in New York.[165]

The studio became aware of the illegal shenanigans on October 15, when an *Inside Edition* telecast included secretly videotaped behind-the-scenes footage of Clooney, Elle Macpherson, Uma Thurman and Chris O'Donnell. When officials contacted the show to see how they'd obtained the footage, producers at *Inside Edition* refused to reveal the source.

What then followed was old-fashioned detective work and a sting operation that would have made the Dark Knight detective proud. Working with Warner Bros. security, director Joel Schumacher, producer Peter Macgregor-Scott and other *Batman* staff analyzed the footage shot on the days when the illegal videotaping occurred and crosschecked the faces of people who had appeared in both scenes. After also checking official behind-the-scenes photographs, they picked out one person whose activities on the set were suspect. They then set up the sting, with Arnold Schwarzenegger as bait. Knowing that the culprit would return for Schwarzenegger's first day on the set on October 19, they circulated a photo of the suspect and hired extra security, which posed as members of the crew. When the man was spotted, Macgregor-Scott and other crewmembers kept tabs on him, while the studio exits were sealed off. When he was apprehended, he was identified as having worked on the lot previously as a stand-in for Matt LeBlanc on *Friends.* In his pockets, the man had a note that read, "Batman only—$35,000" and a phone number. He had a 35mm still camera stashed in his sock with exposed prints inside, and he was wearing a hat that appeared to be wired for use with a video camera, though no camera was found. When his accomplice was nabbed, she had several 8mm cassette cases marked "Batman & Robin" and "George Clooney," and there were several rolls of film in her car, as well as a walkie-talkie and a power pack from the *Batman & Robin* set. She also had ID cards, including five driver's licenses with different names. Burbank Police arrived later to take the culprits into custody, and a preliminary hearing was set for December 16. The studio began preparing a civil case, and urged federal authorities to press charges of criminal copyright infringement and theft of trade secrets.[166] In a press conference held to announce the arrests, Schumacher said, "As long as people are willing to pay a lot of money for anything illegal, people are going to do it."[167]

As Thanksgiving approached, the cast and crew celebrated the 80th birthday of Michael Gough on the set on November 23rd.[168] With the season of gladness and good tidings approaching, Joel Schumacher decided it was time to bury the hatchet with CAA. He returned to his old agency during the first week of December.[169]

At the end of January, a few weeks before *Batman & Robin* wrapped up shooting, George Clooney took a lunch break from *ER* to play some basketball on the Warner Bros. lot.[170] The actor often played pick-up games with Chris O'Donnell, Dean Cain of TV's *Lois & Clark: The New Adventures of Superman*, *ER*'s Eriq La Salle, and hair stylist Waldo Sanchez. On this particular day, the over-worked actor took a spill, spraining his ankle and tearing some ligaments.[171] He was taken immediately to Northridge Hospital for treatment and released,[172] but worked in pain and on crutches during the last two weeks of shooting.[173]

At the end of February, even though Clooney was continuing his boycott of *Entertainment Tonight*, the TV newsmagazine won the exclusive first rights to air the full 2-1/2 minute trailer for *Batman & Robin*. Joel Schumacher, who was interviewed by the program, made the decision to let them debut the trailer.[174] When screenwriter Akiva Goldsman saw it, he was taken aback by its comedic tone. "Unless I've totally lost my perspective, this movie isn't funny," said Goldsman. "Oh, it has its lighter moments, but I don't think it's funnier than *Batman Forever*. If anything, I think this movie is more consistent tone-wise. We had a tendency on *Batman & Robin* to find an emotional pitch and stay with it."[175]

Marc Shapiro of *Starlog* magazine visited the set on the last day of filming at the Batcave set in the Long Beach Seaport Dome in early February 1997. He found a very relaxed set, although producer Peter Macgregor-Scott was exasperated by the rumors that were already swirling about *Batman 5*. "Howard Stern as the Scarecrow! Jeff Goldblum as the Scarecrow! Just give me a break!" said Macgregor-Scott.[176]

One of the last scenes filmed was Bruce Wayne's confrontation with Dick Grayson in the Batcave. George Clooney hobbled onto the set on crutches, which he handed off to an assistant before cameras rolled. After doing the master shots, Schumacher shot close-ups of Clooney and O'Donnell, then officially released them from the picture.[177] For Clooney, it meant the end of six months of working seven days a week. "Doing *Batman & Robin* was more fun than I ever thought," said Clooney. "The crew, better than I ever thought. The cast, nicer than I ever thought. I was a little bit intimidated by working with such a giant group of people on a production of this size. I recall standing on a tremendous set on one of my first days of shooting, and telling Joel Schumacher that I felt a little out of my league. And Joel said, 'So do we all. This is the biggest thing any of us will ever do, so just enjoy it.'"[178]

Clooney was already looking forward to the next *Batman* film. "Playing Batman is a high point in my career, so I'm very happy to do it because the older you get, the more you realize that it all comes down to just enjoying what you do. On this movie, I got to spend six months out of my life truly enjoying my life."[179]

While the crew turned to filming insert shots, Schumacher joked to *Starlog*'s Shapiro, "I think my influence on this film comes from my drug days. It's all those hallucinogens I took that have damaged my brain."[180]

The film had been budgeted for a 98-day shoot, but it wrapped principal photography more than a week ahead of schedule, on day 88, "which is why you don't see any studio executives down here wringing their hands," said Macgregor-Scott. "I'm sort of amazed by it myself," said Schumacher. "But we were very well prepared and had a lot of the same team, and I think once you've climbed Mt. Everest, when you go back again, you know what equipment to take and who to tie to the rope."[181] Warner Bros. co-chairman Robert A. Daly was effusive in his praise of Schumacher. Speaking to *Daily Variety*'s Daniel Moore about the director's work on *Batman & Robin*, Daly said, "It's not easy to do it on schedule, with no craziness going on. You go to the set...it's ahead of schedule, everybody's happy. All the costumes are contemporary and hip; he makes you feel like it's happening today. Joel stays on a movie from beginning to end. He's a member of our family. We hope he's with us forever."[182]

When post-production got underway, supervising sound editor John Leveque had to find some unusual sounds to help "sell" the movie's myriad effects. For the sound of Mr. Freeze icing an entire city with his freeze gun, Leveque tried recording the sound of flash-freezing objects in liquid nitrogen, but the sound was too small. He finally took it upon himself to go seventy miles east of Los Angeles to Big Bear. Finding a deserted lake with the help of a park ranger, Leveque camped out and waited for morning. At the crack of dawn, before the rising sun could melt the layer of virgin ice that had formed on the lake overnight, he stepped out onto the ice sheet and recorded the sound of the ice slowly cracking beneath him as he fell through, sinking to his waist each time. After repeating the process several times, Leveque was satisfied. "The squeegee sound ice makes as it's giving way is fantastic," said Leveque. The sound editor reversed the sound and fed it through a digital processor. After building up about one hundred layers of the sound, he had something that he felt approximated the sound of an entire city freezing.[183]

To get a big, exciting sound for the Batmobile, Leveque and Bruce Stambler visited the Rocket Dyne Space Shuttle facility in Canoga Park, California to record the intense blast of an Atlas rocket engine. "The core of the Batmobile sound is an 800-horsepower, street-legal 1987 Buick Grand National with a wonderful turbocharger whine," said Stambler. "All in all, we used 60 different, individual sounds to build the sound of the Batmobile."[184]

The sound of Batman's cape posed another challenge. "We needed a large swooshing sound for Batman's cape," said Stambler. "We had already secured a number of recordings of bat wings that were very good, but we lacked a big sound that would really give the feeling of Batman rising into the air and moving off at high speed." Stambler thought of the Warner Bros. Studios water tower, which had been covered by a massive tarpaulin. "During a windy rainstorm," said Stambler, "the tarp came loose and ended up streaming off into the air held only by a single tether. We snuck under the tower with our microphone and a portable DAT recorder. What you hear in the movie includes the sound of this enormous tarp flapping, whipping and snapping around in the gale-force wind. It had exactly the right power, 'crack' and 'whoosh' that we needed."[185]

Batman & Robin had 450 visual effects shots, over 150 more than *Batman Forever*.[186] As he had on the previous film, John Dykstra again supervised the shots, many of them accomplished with a combination of CGI, live action and miniatures.[187] Several effects houses contributed to the film: Warner Digital for the Gotham City computer-generated extensions, characters frozen by Mr. Freeze and the rays emanating from the Freeze Gun; France's BUF Compagnie for Poison Ivy's love dust and magically growing plants, as well as the giant telescope Freeze Ray; and Pacific Data Images for computer-generated characters.[188]

One of the final elements was the score, again composed by Elliot Goldenthal. "I've been seeing which themes from *Batman Forever* can carry over, because it's always nice to have a continuum if you can," said the composer. "It's obvious that Robin is a more major figure in this film, so I have to come up with a bigger and more heroic Robin theme. There also have to be new themes for Mr. Freeze and Poison Ivy."[189]

THE MOST FUN JOB IN THE WORLD

Just two weeks after wrapping *Batman & Robin*, Joel Schumacher announced to *Daily Variety's* Michael Fleming that he was preparing the next entry in the *Batman* saga.[190] Schumacher felt a sense of allegiance to his stars, George Clooney and Chris O'Donnell. "This is the most fun job in the world," said Schumacher. "You just have no idea how much fun it is doing a *Batman* movie. There's no reality police, you're just making up this comic book with villains who make it fun. But also, I asked these actors to be in these movies, and I wouldn't just say thanks a lot, I'm moving on. That would be unethical and not attractive."[191]

Mark Protosevich, who had just turned in his script for *I Am Legend*, hired on to write the script for the franchise's fifth installment, after Akiva Goldsman made the leap from writer to producer with *Lost in Space*.[192] Goldsman was philosophical about not being involved in *Batman 5*. "I have had the greatest time of my life doing *Batman*," said Goldsman. "My dream *Batman* experiences would be the ones I've already had. There's nothing unfulfilled in my life about *Batman*. There are other *Batman* movies I would like to see but, at this point, there are no other *Batmans* I would like to write."[193]

"A few months ago," said Schumacher, "there were 12 movies being shot on the Warner Bros. lot, and Bob Daly and Terry Semel asked to see a sample reel of each film. Each director put together dailies from the film. After Bob and Terry saw ours, they ordered another script for *Batman*."[194] Warner Bros. sought to get an early start on the next entry, which they hoped to have in theaters in the summer of 1999, when it would face competition from *Terminator 3* and the first of George Lucas's *Star Wars* prequels.[195] "There's a double purpose, to get ahead of the game, but also to budget it early on" said Schumacher. "We had a lot of luck this time because we started so early. We started a week before I shot *A Time to Kill*, and we had a lot of preparation time, which is the key to these movies."[196]

It was rumored that Schumacher might pull down a $10 million salary for the next Batfilm, but the director was cagey, saying he hadn't formalized his deal but wouldn't say, anyway. "I'm over-paid, over-stimulated, over-hyped and over-age," said Schumacher, "but I have the distinction of being the only person in our business who'll admit it."[197]

Schumacher wouldn't divulge who the villain of the next film would be, though it was thought that the main contenders were Egghead, the Mad Hatter, King Tut and the Scarecrow.[198] Internet bloggers latched onto the news that the Scarecrow could be the next *Batman* villain, and rumors swirled that radio shock jock Howard Stern, who had just made his first foray into movies with the film adaptation of his autobiography, *Private Parts*, would play the baddie. Warner Bros. called such rumors "100% false,"[199] and director Joel Schumacher also denied it, saying, "All of us in the *Batman* family wish those in the Howard Stern family great success with their film careers, but we do not plan to collaborate at this point."[200]

In mid-March 1997, *Variety*'s Michael Fleming reported that the villains for *Batman 5* had been set: Scarecrow, who could make people hallucinate their worst fears, and Harley Quinn, who was seeking revenge on the Caped Crusader for the Joker's death. "There's no word on casting yet, but it'll be an A-talent search as usual," wrote Fleming.[201]

That same month, Warner Bros. hosted a *Batman & Robin* luncheon at the annual ShoWest Convention, with the film's stars, Joel Schumacher and Peter Macgregor-Scott in attendance. During the festivities, Arnold Schwarzenegger, always an eager self-promoter, referred to the new film as "Batman and Arnold."[202]

In April of 1997, Schwarzenegger had heart surgery to replace a congenitally defective aortic valve. "I did not have a health problem when I was shooting the movie," he said. "I have always had a heart murmur, and it's one of those things that gets worse through time. But I had all the energy in the world to do the movie. I was never out of breath. I was skiing at 8,000 to 9,000 (foot) altitude." Schwarzenegger didn't tell Warner Bros.. about his condition before shooting because he feared it might have made it impossible for the studio to insure him for *Batman & Robin*.[203]

George Clooney's confidence in *Batman & Robin* began to falter after he attended a press screening of the film on the eve of a publicity tour. Sneaking up into the balcony of Westwood's Bruin theater, he saw all too clearly that the film wasn't going over with the audience. "You're not stupid," said Clooney. "You can feel the lull. I didn't get the sense it was terrible, just that it was not everything that I'd hoped. The story got confused along the way. To say the least. But it was a tough call; this is what *Batman* is. And I walked into it with my eyes open." Despite his disappointment, Clooney couldn't deny that playing *Batman* had made him more famous than ever. "There's something amazing about getting on a box of cereal," he said. "It's an experience everyone should have once."[204]

In June, Clooney, O'Donnell and Schwarzenegger appeared together on *The Oprah Winfrey Show*, where Schwarzenegger talked about his heart surgery and joked that when given a choice between an artificial heart valve and a pig valve, "I'm not going to say which valve I chose, but now every time I see bacon, I start crying." The film was also the subject of a one-hour special on E!, "*Batman & Robin* Live Premiere," broadcast from Los Angeles as well as being streamed on the entertainment channel's website. Each of the film's male stars also appeared on NBC's *Tonight Show With Jay Leno* the week prior to the film's opening, with Clooney on Tuesday, O'Donnell on Wednesday and Schwarzenegger on Thursday.[205]

Batman & Robin's Hollywood premiere occurred Thursday, June 12, with the film screening simultaneously at two theaters, Mann's Village and Mann's Westwood, as the Batsignal illuminated the clouds overhead. Celebrities attending included the film's Elle MacPherson and John Glover and producer Peter Macgregor-Scott, as well as Gillian Anderson, Salma Hayek, the Smashing Pumpkins' Billy Corgan, and Antonio Banderas with Melanie Griffith.[206]

When the film went into general release on June 20, selected theaters received prints that drew on decades-old technology: Technicolor. Using the same three-strip color process that had been used for *Gone With the Wind* in 1939, Technicolor created prints to be shown at Mann's Village theater in Westwood, Mann's Chinese Theater in Hollywood and the Loew's Astor Midtown Theater in New York. Technicolor had made a deal with producer Peter Macgregor-Scott to try the process as an experiment, hoping it would lead film studios to use it for wide release. The three-strip color process was noted for its vibrant hues, deep blacks and bright whites, and the psychedelic panoply of *Batman & Robin* seemed the perfect test case.[207]

New Bat-products were manufactured in tandem with the film, including a nearly impossible-to-find Batgirl action figure, complete with "battle blade blaster and strike scythe," priced at less than $10. Stores that stocked more of the Batman, Robin and Mr. Freeze action figures, which were projected to be big sellers, quickly sold out of the Batgirl figures. There was also a Poison Ivy action figure, also at less than $10, which came with an "evil entrapment" flower weapon. The Bane action figure came with a "double attack axe and colossal crusher gauntlet." To accompany the Mr. Freeze action figure, one could buy Mr. Freeze's frozen command center with "ice disk" launcher and missiles for about $15, the same price as his Cryo Freeze Chamber, a laboratory that featured a device called the "capture claw" as well as "power diamonds that change colors when dropped in water." For $30, collectors could get a "triple action" set that came with a Batwing, Batmobile and Batboat all in one box. A tricked-out $20 Batmobile came with ice-shattering missiles and attack blades to cut through Poison Ivy's jungle vines.[208] The studio expected royalties from sales of 250 licensed *Batman & Robin* products to equal the $1 billion consumers spent on *Batman Forever* merchandise.[209]

A cynic might say that all of those toys demonstrated why the studio pushed for three heroes and three villains instead of the usual two. When executive producer Michael Uslan was asked if Warner Bros. insisted on the abundance of characters and costume changes not for artistic reasons but for commercial ones, he prefaced his answer by saying that he was not speaking specifically about *Batman* or Warner Bros., but said that generally, "the movie studios became in transition from movie studios to international conglomerates. More and more studios over the years had been getting into other businesses and diversifying, whether it's theme parks, or owning parts of a toy company or a T-shirt company or whatever it might be. And, at various points in time over the years, some studios have gotten a little bit wrapped up in merchandising, more than other things. And in those moments when that happens, I believe the tail begins to wag the dog, and that when movies are being driven by merchandising and they want to see as many heroes and as many villains put into a movie, with the insistence that each one have two costume changes and two vehicles, the danger quickly arises that they are making two hour infomercials for toys rather than great films."[210]

In his *Daily Variety* review, Todd McCarthy noted that, as with the earlier films, the bad guys overshadowed the heroes. "The villains, Arnold Schwarzenegger and especially Uma Thurman in this instance, remain the highlights here, as the rest of the gargantuan production lacks the dash and excitement that would have given the franchise a boost in its eighth year," wrote McCarthy. "Unfortunately, the operative word is bland, as the newcomers don't add much to the formula, leaving it to their nemeses to enliven the proceedings...[211] Physically, Clooney is unquestionably the most ideal Batman to date, but none of the series' screenwriters has ever gotten a handle on how to make the character as interesting as those around him."[212]

In *The New York Times*, Janet Maslin was effusive about Uma Thurman's performance, writing, "As played by Uma Thurman, Poison Ivy is perfect, flaunting great looks, a mocking attitude and madly flamboyant disguises. Like Mae West, she mixes true femininity with the winking womanliness of a drag queen...Poison Ivy captures the essence of *Batman & Robin*, a wild, campy costume party of a movie and the first *Batman* to suggest that somewhere in Gotham City there might be a Studio 54...Aiming for comic book fans with a taste for heavy sarcasm and double-entendres, the lavish *Batman & Robin* cares only about delivering nonstop glitter...There's not much more to Batman, now played affably but blandly by George Clooney and given only second billing, than a heroic jaw line, understanding gaze and anatomically correct rubber suit. The mixed-up, melancholy Batman of Tim Burton's first two films looks like the brooding Prince of Denmark next to this."[213]

Overall, reviewers in major markets were not kind to the film. In *Variety's Crix' Picks* compilation of notices from major cities, *Batman & Robin* received only 3 positive reviews, and 40 that were negative or mixed. By contrast, the controversial *Batman Returns* had received 30 positive reviews, and 37 negative or mixed.[214]

Despite the chilly critical reception, in its opening weekend, *Batman & Robin* amassed the seventh-highest three-day opening ever, earning a respectable $43.6 million on 2,934 screens for a per-screen average of $14,860.[215] However, that was less than *Batman Forever*, which had debuted with $52.8 million two years earlier.[216] But the big surprise of the weekend was Sony's comedy *My Best Friend's Wedding*, starring Julia Roberts. Sony had gambled on counter-programming by releasing the film the same weekend as *Batman & Robin*, which was expected to be a box-office juggernaut. Apparently, women who wanted to see an entertainment that wasn't all chase scenes and explosions flocked to the Sony film, giving it the biggest opening ever for a romantic comedy, with a $21.5 million debut.[217] In *Daily Variety*, Andrew Hindes quoted Warner Bros. distribution president Barry Reardon as saying that the low grosses were because "*My Best Friend's Wedding* took some nice business from us."[218] Reardon predicted that *Batman & Robin* would eventually earn $150 million domestically and $200 million overseas. It would need to, if rumors that the actual production budget was between $150 million and $200 million, nearly twice what Warner Bros. initially reported, were correct.[219]

In its second weekend, *Batman & Robin* faced competition from Paramount's action film *Face/Off* and Disney's animated *Hercules*. *Face/Off* won the weekend with a gross of $22.7 million, while *Hercules* took in $21.5 million. Box-office receipts for *Batman & Robin*, meanwhile, plummeted a whopping 64%—the film took in only $15.4 million, putting it in third place.[220]

Warner Bros. blamed part of *Batman & Robin's* domestic box-office troubles in the U.S. on a source whose power to influence public opinion had grown substantially since the release of *Batman Forever*—the internet. More specifically, they were irked about 25-year-old Harry Knowles, proprietor of the web's *Ain't It Cool News*. Knowles' tell-it-like-it-is blog was deemed so powerful that Hollywood studios began passing around photos of Knowles to gatekeepers at sneak previews to keep him out. But Knowles was only one of many whose opinions were beginning to influence the all-important "buzz" studios relied on to make their films into hits. Chris Pula, Warner Bros. marketing chief, told *Weekly Variety's* Rex Weiner, "Buzz is no longer two people at a cocktail party. Now anybody with a computer is a newspaper...What's disturbing is that many times the legitimate press quotes the internet without checking sources. One guy on the internet could start enough of a stir that causes a reactionary shift in the whole marketing program."[221]

In the U.K., *Batman & Robin* had the second highest premiere weekend in history, behind *Independence Day*. With a weekend gross of $8.2 million from 593 prints playing on 720 screens, the widest release ever in Britain, the film took in 69% of the total weekend box-office. It also opened strong in Australia with $2.9 million in box-office, about 14% less than *Batman Forever's* opening weekend, and made $2.3 million in Germany, with a 31% market share, 32% below the premiere of the original *Batman* eight years earlier.[222] Its overall international box-office receipts, including Puerto Rico and Austria, were $15.2 million. Warner execs held their breath to see how it would play in its second weekend, fearing the same precipitous drop as had happened domestically. But when the figures for the second weekend came in, the film was still going strong. Its revenues dipped 49% in the U.K. and Spain, 32% in Australia, and 26% in Germany in the second week.[223]

To boost its overseas performance, a new advertising campaign was devised for Japan, where Arnold Schwarzenegger made promotional appearances when the film opened on August 2.[224] Schwarzenegger visited three cities in Japan, and appeared at photo ops with a Japanese baseball star and prime minister Ryutaro Hashimoto. The previous two Batman installments had not done well in the Japanese marketplace, but when *Batman & Robin* opened, it brought in $1.2 million in its first two days on 133 screens, 24% better than the premiere of *Batman Forever*, largely due to Schwarzenegger's popularity in the Asian country. After the first week of August, the film raised $93 million internationally, and seemed on its way to be the 11th film of 1997 to earn more than $100 million overseas.[225]

Before the film ended its run, Jeep Swenson, the hulking 6-foot, 400-pound ex-wrestler who played Bane, was dead of heart failure, attributed to years of steroid abuse. The 40-year-old former wrestler died August 18, 1997 at the UCLA Medical Center in Los Angeles. Actor James Caan and wrestler Hulk Hogan gave eulogies at his funeral at Forest Lawn.[226] Later, interviewed by Andy Lines of *The London Mirror*, Swenson's widow, Erin, said, "He was so proud and happy when he landed his biggest-ever role in *Batman & Robin*." She added that her husband, who had a 65-inch chest, began using steroids in his early 20s and could not stop. He injected them, drank them, ate them and even rubbed them into his drug-ravaged body. But when he went into the hospital and knew he was dying, he looked up at her from his hospital bed and sobbed, "Oh my God! What have I done to myself?" Erin Swenson said, "He really wanted to be a small man again...to be free of the weight and the muscle. He couldn't take a shower properly, put on a shirt, or easily walk up stairs...He hated steroids and what they had done to him." Ultimately, she said, "His lungs failed, his liver failed, his kidneys failed and then his heart failed and he was dead."[227]

After completing *Batman & Robin*, Joel Schumacher planned to do three lower-budgeted films, including *8 Millimeter*, a thriller scripted by Andrew Kevin Walker, before returning for *Batman 5*. The director told *Daily Variety's* Michael Fleming, "I never planned to be the summer blockbuster guy. I began small, and all of these things just started happening and before you knew it, I'm up to my neck in John Grisham and *Batman* films. I'm grateful for all of it, but felt, especially on *Batman & Robin*, that the box office had become more important than the movie. I wanted to return to filmmaking, not blockbuster-making...When you do one of those movies, there's no gray area. Either it's a hit or a flop. But you can be disappointed in the box office of a film like *L.A. Confidential* and still regard it as a superb movie. I was looking for something unique and risky. I had been a fan of Andy Kevin Walker's writing since *Seven*, and this was so original and dark. I feel I'm doing this for my sanity."[228]

Speaking of *Batman 5*, Schumacher said, "I'd like to do one more, but I think we need to wait." The director was obviously unhappy with the box-office performance of *Batman & Robin*. "I felt I disappointed a lot of older fans by being too conscious of the family aspect," said Schumacher. "I'd gotten tens of thousands of letters from parents asking for a film their children could go to. Now, I owe the hardcore fans the *Batman* movie they would love me to give them."[229]

Schumacher indicated to Fleming that he'd like to scrap the idea of making a by-the-numbers film with Scarecrow and Harley Quinn as the villains. "Bob (Daly) and Terry (Semel) would like me to make another, and I have an idea of a way to go that would be far less expensive," said Schumacher. "But this is my own idea, and they may kick me onto Barham Boulevard after they hear it."[230]

In February, just weeks before the Academy Awards telecast, *Batman & Robin* earned 11 Golden Raspberry "Razzie" Award nominations, more than any other film of 1997. Besides Worst Picture, it picked up two nods for Worst Supporting Actor (Chris O'Donnell and Arnold Schwarzenegger), two for Worst Supporting Actress (Alicia Silverstone and Uma Thurman), one for Worst Screen Couple (George Clooney and Chris O'Donnell), one in the new category of Worst Reckless Disregard for Human Life and Public Property, and nominations for Worst Director, Worst Song, Worst Screenplay, and Worst Remake or Sequel—and this in the same year that gave us *Speed 2: Cruise Control* and Warner Bros.' *The Postman*.[231]

On July 1, 1998, Judith I. Brennan of *The Los Angeles Times* reported that Joel Schumacher was in talks to do *Batman 5* for Warner Bros., though it was unlikely filming would begin that year. Brennan reported that Kurt Russell was being approached to play the Caped Crusader. Warner Bros. and Russell refused to comment, but Schumacher said, "I can tell you I have no plans to do a *Batman* right now.". "But I have received so many calls in the past few days about this, it's amazing...This whole *Batman* issue is insane. It doesn't stop." Commenting on *Batman & Robin*, Schumacher said, "You know, I'm still very proud of what we did with that one, even though I took a big hit from the critics. But parents had asked me to make a *Batman* that little kids could enjoy, that wasn't as dark as the others and I felt like we did. You can't win."[232]

Two years after the release of *Batman & Robin*, in October 1999, Keanu Reeves was quoted in the British magazine *TV Times* as saying that he had signed on to appear in *Batman 5*. Warner Bros., however, denied that the movie was in production.[233]

On April 2-4, 1999, *Comics 99*, a UK comic book festival, was held in Bristol, England. In February, prior to the show, the organizers asked 200 members of the Comic Creators Guild and readers of magazines produced by the companies Comics International and SFX magazines to name their top ten worst comic book movies. Topping the list was *Batman & Robin*, followed by *Howard the Duck* (1985), *Spawn* (1997), *Judge Dredd* (1995), *Superman IV* (1985), *Dick Tracy* (1990), *Prince Valiant* (1998), *The Fat Slags* (1993), *The Punisher* (1994) and *The Fantastic Four* (1993).[234]

The two films Chris O'Donnell made prior to *Batman & Robin*—*The Chamber* and *In Love and War*—were also box office disappointments. In an interview with *USA Today's* Stephen Schaefer, the actor said that three flops in a row "rattles you a bit." "It's a tough business," said O'Donnell. "As much as you don't want to pay attention to reviews, you hear about them. Everyone sees the box office results. It's followed as closely as the standings of Major League Baseball. There are not too many jobs in this world where you're critiqued so publicly. You've got to have a tough skin."

O'Donnell said he thought *Batman & Robin* was released "too early. There had been one (*Batman* movie) every three years, and this was after two. People weren't ready." He also added, "It just didn't work as well as the previous one." When asked if he would reprise his role of Robin, the then-29-year-old O'Donnell said, "It's very unlikely...I'm probably too old. If I were Warner Bros., I'd have a new cast and new look and reinvent it."[235]

As the star of *Batman & Robin*, George Clooney publicly took responsibility for the film, saying, "I may have buried that franchise. I look at it as a bit of a black eye. I'll take another look at it to see what I could have done. It's a disappointing movie in a lot of ways."[236] Joel Schumacher shared the blame with him. "I'd had such a string of successes," said the director. "You kind of think, like, wow, I'm hitting these balls out of the park every time. And I felt I was making quality films, and so I think I didn't have passion to do *Batman & Robin*. I think I was paid a lot of money, and we were supporting the Warner Brothers stores, and so I felt like my job was very corporate for the first time in my life. I think it still made a fortune and stuff sold and all of that, and I blame no one else but myself—a Joel Schumacher film. The buck stops right here." But, the director added, "There was a desire at Warner Brothers to make it more for kids. It is a satire. It is in many ways. But I think the joke's on me."[237]

1   Moore, Daniel, "A Sure Thing at the Box Office," *Daily Variety*, March 5, 1997, p. 68

2   Singer, Michael, *Batman & Robin: The Making of the Movie*, © 1997 Rutledge Hill Press, Nashville, TN, p. 14

3   *Ibid.*, p. 17

4   *Ibid.*, p. 15

5   Shapiro, Marc, "Knight Moves: Screenwriter Akiva Goldsman Gets Into a 'Batman & Robin' Frame of Mind," *Starlog Presents Batman & Other Comic Heroes*, 1997, p. 35

6   Fleming, Michael, "'Batman' Sequel Sets '96 Shoot," *Daily Variety*, Aug. 21, 1995, p. 12

7   Shapiro, Marc, "Knight Moves: Screenwriter Akiva Goldsman Gets Into a 'Batman & Robin' Frame of Mind," *Starlog Presents Batman & Other Comic Heroes*, 1997, p. 33

8   —, "The Write Kind of Director," *Daily Variety*, March 5, 1997, p. 42

9   *Ibid.*

10   Shapiro, Marc, "Knight Moves: Screenwriter Akiva Goldsman Gets Into a 'Batman & Robin' Frame of Mind," *Starlog Presents Batman & Other Comic Heroes*, 1997, p. 32-33

11   Fleming, Michael, "'Batman' Sequel Sets '96 Shoot," *Daily Variety*, Aug. 21, 1995, p. 1

12   Singer, Michael, *Batman & Robin: The Making of the Movie*, © 1997 Rutledge Hill Press, Nashville, TN, p. 11

13   Shapiro, Marc, "Knight Moves: Screenwriter Akiva Goldsman Gets Into a 'Batman & Robin' Frame of Mind," *Starlog Presents Batman & Other Comic Heroes*, 1997, p. 33

14   Singer, Michael, *Batman & Robin: The Making of the Movie*, © 1997 Rutledge Hill Press, Nashville, TN, p. 15

15   *Ibid.*, p. 15-16

16   Shapiro, Marc, "Batman & Robin: Is This the End of the Dynamic Duo? Of Course Not!" *Starlog Presents Batman & Other Comic Heroes*, 1997, p. 30

17   Singer, Michael, *Batman & Robin: The Making of the Movie*, © 1997 Rutledge Hill Press, Nashville, TN, p. 17

18   *Ibid.*

19   Goldsman, Akiva, "Batman & Robin Screenplay," © Warner Bros. 1986

20   Shapiro, Marc, "Knight Moves: Screenwriter Akiva Goldsman Gets Into a 'Batman & Robin' Frame of Mind," *Starlog Presents Batman & Other Comic Heroes*, 1997, p. 34

21   Shapiro, Marc, "Batman & Robin: Is This the End of the Dynamic Duo? Of Course Not!" *Starlog Presents Batman & Other Comic Heroes*, 1997, p. 29

22   Shapiro, Marc, "Knight Moves: Screenwriter Akiva Goldsman Gets Into a ' Batman & Robin' Frame of Mind," *Starlog Presents Batman & Other Comic Heroes*, 1997, p. 34

23   Fleming, Michael, "'Batman' Sequel Sets '96 Shoot," *Daily Variety*, Aug. 21, 1995, p. 12

24   Fleming, Michael, "In Earnest, Roberts Eyes Hemingway Romance Next," *Weekly Variety*, Oct. 16, 1995, p. 4

25   Shapiro, Marc, "Knight Moves: Screenwriter Akiva Goldsman Gets Into a 'Batman & Robin' Frame of Mind," *Starlog Presents Batman & Other Comic Heroes*, 1997, p. 34-35

26   Singer, Michael, *Batman & Robin: The Making of the Movie*, © 1997 Rutledge Hill Press, Nashville, TN, p. 18

27   *Ibid.*, p. 46

28   *Ibid.*, p. 19

29 Fleming, Michael and Anita M. Busch, "Clooney May Bat For Kilmer: Caped Vac-i llator Might Follow Keaton Out of 'Batman' Series," *Daily Variety*, Feb. 14, 1996, p. 34

30 —, "Kilmer Inks With Par for 'Saint,'" *Daily Variety*, Nov. 16, 1995, p. 33

31 Hochman, Steve, "Entering the Sainthood: Val Kilmer Takes Off the Mask of Batman and Reveals Seven Characters, Plus That of Simon Templar Himself, in the Movie 'The Saint.' It Was a Choice Between Security or Fun," *The Los Angeles Times Calendar*, Apr. 3, 1997, p. 6:1

32 *Ibid.*

33 Fleming, Michael and Anita M. Busch, "Clooney May Bat For Kilmer: Caped Vac-i llator Might Follow Keaton Out of 'Batman' Series," *Daily Variety*, Feb. 14, 1996, p. 34

34 Busch, Anita M., "Schumacher Departs CAA," *Daily Variety*, Feb. 29, 1996, p. 46

35 Busch, Anita M., "'Saint' Always Looked Like a Kilmer Pic," *Daily Variety*, March 13, 1996, p. 36

36 *Ibid.*

37 —, "Silverstone Eyes Batgirl," *Daily Variety*, Jan. 16, 1996, p. 5

38 —, "Silverstone Dons 'Bat' Cape," *Daily Variety*, Feb. 1, 1996, p. 14

39 Singer, Michael, *Batman & Robin: The Making of the Movie*, © 1997 Rutledge Hill Press, Nashville, TN, p. 25

40 *Ibid.*, p. 39

41 *Ibid.*, p. 39

42 Busch, Anita M., "Choose Your Poison:Uma is 'Bat' Girl," *Daily Variety*, Jan. 26, 1996, p. 1

43 *Ibid.*, p. 44

44 Fleming, Michael and Anita M. Busch, "Clooney May Bat For Kilmer: Caped Vac-i llator Might Follow Keaton Out of 'Batman' Series," *Daily Variety*, Feb. 14, 1996, p. 4

45 Singer, Michael, *Batman & Robin: The Making of the Movie*, © 1997 Rutledge Hill Press, Nashville, TN, p. 25

46 Busch, Anita M., "Schumacher Departs CAA," *Daily Variety*, Feb. 29, 1996, p. 46

47 *Ibid.*

48 *Ibid.*, p. 1

49 *Ibid.*, p. 46

50 *Ibid.*

51 Singer, Michael, *Batman & Robin: The Making of the Movie*, © 1997 Rutledge Hill Press, Nashville, TN, p. 24

52 Busch, Anita M., "Crusader Clooney: 'ER' Star Nears $3 Mil 'Hornet' Deal," *Daily Variety*, Oct. 24, 1995, p. 1

53 Fleming, Michael, "The Buzz Behind Kilmer's 'Batman' Spat," *Weekly Variety*, Feb. 19, 1996, p. 4

54 Hochman, Steve, "Entering the Sainthood: Val Kilmer Takes Off the Mask of Batman and Reveals Seven Characters, Plus That of Simon Templar Himself, in the Movie 'The Saint.' It Was a Choice Between Security or Fun," *The Los Angeles Times Calendar*, Apr. 3, 1997, p. 6:1

55 Fleming, Michael, "The Buzz Behind Kil-mer's 'Batman' Spat," *Weekly Variety*, Feb. 19, 1996, p. 4

56 Fleming, Michael and Anita M. Busch, "Clooney May Bat For Kilmer: Caped Vac-illator Might Follow Keaton Out of 'Batman' Series," *Daily Variety*, Feb. 14, 1996, p. 4

57 Archerd, Army, "Just For Variety," *Daily Variety*, Feb. 21, 1996, p. 4

58 Hochman, Steve, "Entering the Sainthood: Val Kilmer Takes Off the Mask of Batman and Reveals Seven Characters, Plus That of Simon Templar Himself, in the Movie 'The Saint.' It Was a Choice Between Security or Fun," *The Los Angeles Times Calendar*, Apr. 3, 1997, p. 6:1

59 Mallory, Michael, "Holy Caped Caper, IV," *Daily Variety*, March 5, 1997, p. 50

60 Busch, Anita M. and Adam Dawtrey, "Clooney Fitted for Batsuit," *Daily Variety*, Feb. 23, 1996, p.

61 *Ibid.*, p. 76

62 *Ibid.*, p. 1

63 Busch, Anita M., "Clooney in Tight Spot With 'Batman', 'ER,'" *Weekly Variety*, Feb. 26-March 3, 1996, p. 14

64 *Ibid.*, p. 16

65 Bart, Peter, "Backtalk: A Man of Action Also Can Make an Artful Gesture," *Daily Variety*, March 4, 1996, p. 66

66 Fleming, Michael, "DISH: Actors Turn On, Then Drop Out; Lane Gets Seberg," *Daily Variety*, Feb. 15, 1996, p. 27

67 Fleming, Michael, "Sly Quits ICM After 4 Months, Joins WMA," *Daily Variety*, Feb. 26, 1996, p. 30

68 Busch, Anita M., "Bat-Cast Firms George, Arnold," *Daily Variety*, March 13, 1996, p. 36

69 Evans, Greg, "Stallone Scales Back Payday," *Daily Variety*, March 14, 1996, p. 27

70 —, "Inside Moves: If Schwarzenegger Chills, Willis is in Bat Wings," *Daily Variety*, March 7, 1996, p. 98

71 Busch, Anita M., "Bat-Cast Firms George, Arnold," *Daily Variety*, March 13, 1996, p. 1

72   Singer, Michael, *Batman & Robin: The Making of the Movie*, © 1997 Rutledge Hill Press, Nashville, TN, p. 33

73   *Ibid.*

74   Shapiro, Marc, "Batman & Robin: Is This the End of the Dynamic Duo? Of Course Not!" *Starlog Presents Batman & Other Comic Heroes*, 1997, p. 28

75   Singer, Michael, *Batman & Robin: The Making of the Movie*, © 1997 Rutledge Hill Press, Nashville, TN, p. 31

76   *Ibid.*, p. 33

77   Busch, Anita M., "Arnold's Hot Deal for Mr. Freeze," *Daily Variety*, June 18, 1996, p. 7

78   Shapiro, Marc, "Batman & Robin: Is This the End of the Dynamic Duo? Of Course Not!" *Starlog Presents Batman & Other Comic Heroes*, 1997, p. 29

79   Singer, Michael, *Batman & Robin: The Making of the Movie*, © 1997 Rutledge Hill Press, Nashville, TN, p. 28

80   *Ibid.*, p. 44

81   *Ibid.*, p. 43

82   Archerd, Army, "Just For Variety," *Daily Variety*, May 8, 1996, p. 2

83   *Ibid.*

84   Singer, Michael, *Batman & Robin: The Making of the Movie*, © 1997 Rutledge Hill Press, Nashville, TN, p. 5-6

85   *Ibid.*, p. 24

86   *Ibid.*, p. 116

87   *Ibid.*, p. 47

88   *Ibid.*, p. 48

89   *Ibid.*

90   *Ibid.*, p. 49

91   Koehler, Robert, "Designing Man at the Helm," *Daily Variety*, March 5, 1997, p. 46

92   Singer, Michael, *Batman & Robin: The Making of the Movie*, © 1997 Rutledge Hill Press, Nashville, TN, p. 47

93   *Ibid.*, p. 50

94   *Ibid.*

95   *Ibid.*

96   Shapiro, Marc, "Batman & Robin: Is This the End of the Dynamic Duo? Of Course Not!" *Starlog Presents Batman & Other Comic Heroes*, 1997, p. 29

97   Singer, Michael, *Batman & Robin: The Making of the Movie*, © 1997 Rutledge Hill Press, Nashville, TN, p. 19

98   *Ibid.*, p. 61

99   *Ibid.*, p. 60

100 *Ibid.*, p. 61

101 *Ibid.*

102 *Ibid.*

103 *Ibid.*, p. 62

104 *Ibid.*

105 *Ibid.*

106 *Ibid.*, p. 63

107 *Ibid.*

108 *Ibid.*

109 *Ibid.*, p. 64

110 *Ibid.*

111 *Ibid.*

112 *Ibid.*

113 *Ibid.*, p. 65

114 *Ibid.*

115 *Ibid.*, p. 74

116 *Ibid.*, p. 76

117 *Ibid.*

118 *Ibid.*

119 *Ibid.*, p. 77

120 *Ibid.*, p. 81

121 *Ibid.*, p. 84

122 *Ibid.*, p. 97

123 *Ibid.*, p. 78

124 *Ibid.*

125 *Ibid.*, p. 79

126 *Ibid.*, p. 29

127 Mallory, Michael, "An Ice-Cold Arnold Sends Batman Back to His Cave," *Daily Variety*, March 5, 1997, p. 68

128 Busch, Anita M., "A Big Deal For McDonald Duck," *Daily Variety*, April 10, 1996, p. 1

129 Busch, Anita M., "'Batman' Rings Up Taco Bell," *Daily Variety*, June 11, 1996, p. 33

130 —, "WB Courts Burger King for Superman," *Daily Variety*, Jan. 14, 1997, p. 59

131 Busch, Anita M., "'Batman' Rings Up Taco Bell," *Daily Variety*, June 11, 1996, p. 1

132 *Ibid.* p. 33

133 Adelson, Andrea, "The Battle Of Summer Blockbusters Extends From Theaters To Fast-Food Chains To Grocery Aisles," *The New York Times*, Jun 9, 1997, p. D.25

134 Johnson, Ted, "Schumacher Sets Sail on Next 'Batman' Epic," *Daily Variety*, Sept. 12, 1996, p. 4

135 Bart, Peter, "H'Wood Megapix Beg $100 Mil Question," Daily Variety, May 27, 1997, p. 23

136 Shapiro, Marc, "Batman & Robin: Is This the End of the Dynamic Duo? Of Course Not!" *Starlog Presents Batman & Other Comic Heroes*, 1997, p. 31

137 Singer, Michael, *Batman & Robin: The Making of the Movie*, © 1997 Rutledge Hill Press, Nashville, TN, p. 8

138 *Ibid.*, p. 31

139 Waxman, Sharon, "George Clooney, Uncowled; He Was Disappointed but Undaunted by 'Batman and Robin' and 'One Fine Day'" *The Washington Post*, Sept. 28, 1997, p. G.04

302 *Billion Dollar Batman*

140 Singer, Michael, *Batman & Robin: The Making of the Movie*, © 1997 Rutledge Hill Press, Nashville, TN, p. 27

141 *Ibid.*, p. 95

142 *Ibid.*, p. 96

143 Archerd, Army, "Just For Variety," *Daily Variety*, Jan. 28, 1997, p. 2

144 Singer, Michael, *Batman & Robin: The Making of the Movie*, © 1997 Rutledge Hill Press, Nashville, TN, p. 102

14 *Ibid.*

146 *Ibid.*

147 *Ibid.*, p. 104

148 *Ibid.*

149 Seiler, Andy, "Villains Make Batman Soar: Arnold and Uma Relish Roles as Evil Mr. Freeze, Poison Ivy," *USA Today*, Jun. 20, 1997, p. D, 1:3

150 Singer, Michael, *Batman & Robin: The Making of the Movie*, © 1997 Rutledge Hill Press, Nashville, TN, p. 37

151 *Ibid.*

152 *Ibid.*, p. 35

153 *Ibid.*, p. 39

154 *Ibid.*, p. 24-25

155 *Ibid.*, p. 6

156 *Ibid.*, p. 7

157 *Ibid.*, p. 28

158 Mallory, Michael, "An Ice-Cold Arnold Sends Batman Back to His Cave," *Daily Variety*, March 5, 1997, p. 68

159 Singer, Michael, *Batman & Robin: The Making of the Movie*, © 1997 Rutledge Hill Press, Nashville, TN, p. 87

160 Seiler, Andy, "Villains Make Batman Soar: Arnold and Uma Relish Roles as Evil Mr. Freeze, Poison Ivy," *USA Today*, Jun. 20, 1997, p. D, 1:3

161 Archerd, Army, "Just for Variety," *Daily Variety*, Oct. 8, 1996, p. 2

162 Hontz, Jenny, "Par TV Irks Clooney," *Daily Variety*, Oct. 28, 1996, p. 21

163 Johnson, Ted, "More Charges for 'Batman' Trio?," *Daily Variety*, Nov. 4, 1996, p. 5

164 *Ibid.*, p. 17

165 *Ibid.*

166 *Ibid.*

167 *Ibid.*

168 Singer, Michael, *Batman & Robin: The Making of the Movie*, © 1997 Rutledge Hill Press, Nashville, TN, p. 40

169 Johnson, Ted, "Schumacher Back in CAA's Ranks," *Daily Variety*, Dec. 6, 1996, p. 1

170 Cox, Dan, "The New Batman Shoots...And Misses," *Weekly Variety*, Jan. 20-26, 1997, p. 4

171 Singer, Michael, *Batman & Robin: The Making of the Movie*, © 1997 Rutledge Hill Press, Nashville, TN, p. 32

172 Cox, Dan, "The New Batman Shoots...And Misses," *Weekly Variety*, Jan. 20-26, 1997, p. 4

173 Singer, Michael, *Batman & Robin: The Making of the Movie*, © 1997 Rutledge Hill Press, Nashville, TN, p. 32

174 Hontz, Jenny, ""Batman and Robin' Air on ' ET'", Feb. 20, 1997, p. 39

175 Shapiro, Marc, "Knight Moves: Screenwriter Akiva Goldsman Gets Into a 'Batman & Robin' Frame of Mind," *Starlog Presents Batman & Other Comic Heroes*, 1997, p. 34

176 Shapiro, Marc, "Batman & Robin: Is This the End of the Dynamic Duo? Of Course Not!" *Starlog Presents Batman & Other Comic Heroes*, 1997, p. 27

177 *Ibid.*, p. 27-28

178 Singer, Michael, *Batman & Robin: The Making of the Movie*, © 1997 Rutledge Hill Press, Nashville, TN, p. 31

179 *Ibid.*, p. 33

180 Shapiro, Marc, "Batman & Robin: Is This the End of the Dynamic Duo? Of Course Not!" *Starlog Presents Batman & Other Comic Heroes*, 1997, p. 28

181 Mallory, Michael, "Holy Caped Caper, IV," *Daily Variety*, March 5, 1997, p. 50

182 Moore, Daniel, "A Sure Thing at the Box Office," *Daily Variety*, March 5, 1997, p. 68

183 Grove, Chris, "The Roaring Season: This Summer's Big Pics Will Shake Auds With Crystal-Clear Digital Audio," *Daily Variety*, April 18, 1997, p. 24

184 Singer, Michael, *Batman & Robin: The Making of the Movie*, © 1997 Rutledge Hill Press, Nashville, TN, p. 124

185 *Ibid.*

186 *Ibid.*, p. 113

187 Shapiro, Marc, "Batman & Robin: Is This the End of the Dynamic Duo? Of Course Not!" *Starlog Presents Batman & Other Comic Heroes*, 1997, p. 30

188 Singer, Michael, *Batman & Robin: The Making of the Movie*, © 1997 Rutledge Hill Press, Nashville, TN, p. 113

189 *Ibid.*, p. 125

190 Fleming, Michael, "Helmer's 3rd at Bat: Schumacher Signals He's Up for 'Batman 5,'" *Daily Variety*, Feb. 21, 1997, p. 3

191 *Ibid.*, p. 66

192 *Ibid.*, p. 3

193 Shapiro, Marc, "Knight Moves: Screenwriter Akiva Goldsman Gets Into a 'Batman & Robin' Frame of Mind," *Starlog Presents Batman & Other Comic Heroes*, 1997, p. 35

194 Fleming, Michael, "Helmer's 3rd at Bat: Schumacher Signals He's Up for 'Batman 5,'" *Daily Variety*, Feb. 21, 1997, p. 3

195 *Ibid.*, p. 66

196 *Ibid.*, p. 3

197 Fleming, Michael, "Helmer's 3rd at Bat: Schumacher Signals He's Up for 'Batman 5,'" *Daily Variety*, Feb. 21, 1997, p. 66

198 *Ibid.*, p. 66

199 Fleming, Michael, "Hollywood is Taking Stern Look at Howard," *Daily Variety*, March 3, 1997, p. 66

200 Fleming, Michael, "Belushi in 'Total'; Howard's End of 'Batman,'" *Daily Variety*, March 4, 1997, p. 82

201 Fleming, Michael, "Weber to Wing It; Smart a Woman of 'Style,'" *Daily Variety*, March 18, 1997, p. 31

202 Cox, Dan, "WB Lunch Long—On Talent: Bucks and Yuks Mark Studio's Upcoming Features," *Daily Variety*, March 6, 1997, p. 83

203 Seiler, Andy, "Villains Make Batman Soar: Arnold and Uma Relish Roles as Evil Mr. Freeze, Poison Ivy," *USA Today*, Jun. 20, 1997, p. D, 1:3

204 Waxman, Sharon, "George Clooney, Uncowled; He Was Disappointed but Undaunted by `Batman and Robin' and `One Fine Day'" *The Washington Post*, Sept. 28, 1997, p. G.04

205 Littlefield, Kenny, "Channel Surfer: 'Batman & Robin' Cast Makes the Rounds," *The Atlanta Constitution*, June 9, 1997, p. D, 9:5

206 —, "Heavy Hitters at 'Bat' Preem," *Daily Variety*, June 16, 1997, p. 35

207 —, "'Batman' Brings Back Old Colors," *Daily Variety*, June 20, 1997, p. 10

208 Stack, Peter, "Direct From Movies, the Toys of Summer Set Their Sights on Mayhem," *San Francisco Chronicle*, Jun. 18, 1997, p. E, 1:1

209 Adelson, Andrea, "The Battle Of Summer Blockbusters Extends From Theaters To Fast-Food Chains To Grocery Aisles," *The New York Times*, Jun 9, 1997, p. D.25

210 Interview with Michael Uslan, conducted Sept. 1, 2009

211 McCarthy, Todd, "Film Reviews: Batman and Robin," *Daily Variety*, June 16, 1997, p. 2

212 *Ibid.*, p. 22

213 Maslin, Janet, "Movie Review: Holy Iceberg! Dynamic Duo Vs. Mr. Freeze," *The New York Times*, June 20, 1997, http://www.nytimes.com/1997/06/20/movies/holy-iceberg dynamic-duo-vs-mr-freeze.html?scp= 376&sq=batman&st=nyt, accessed July 3, 2011

214 Bart, Peter, "The Back Lot: Sequels Segue Into the Box Office Blahs," *Daily Variety*, July 14, 1997, p. 18

215 Hindes, Andrew, "'Wedding' Rattles Batcage: Summer B.O. Finally Takes Off," *Daily Variety*, June 23, 1997, p. 1

216 *Ibid.*, p. 32

217 *Ibid.*, p. 1

218 *Ibid.*, p. 32

219 *Ibid.*

220 *Ibid.*, p. 1

221 Weiner, Rex, "Cybergeek Leaks Freak Pic Biz," *Weekly Variety*, July 28-Aug. 3, 1997, p. 73

222 Groves, Don, "'Batman' Flying High in O'Seas Run," *Daily Variety*, July 1, 1997, p. 9

223 Groves, Don, "'Bat' Beats Up B.O.: WB Sequel Conquers 5 Markets; 'Men' Bows Big," *Daily Variety*, July 8, 1997, p. 12

224 Groves, Don, "'Bat' Beats Up B.O.: WB Sequel Conquers 5 Markets; 'Men' Bows Big," *Daily Variety*, July 8, 1997, p. 12

225 *Ibid.*, p. 17

226 —, "Obituary: Jeep Swenson," *Daily Variety*, Aug. 27, 1997, p. 14

227 Lines, Andy, "Batman Fat Man Killed By Steroids," *The London Mirror*, Aug. 28, 1997, p. 7

228 Fleming, Michael, "Schumacher Trims Sails," *Daily Variety*, Dec. 11, 1997, p. 42

229 *Ibid.*

230 *Ibid.*

231 —, "'Batman' Leads Bad-Movie Pack," *Los Angeles Daily News*, Feb. 10, 1998, p. L5

232 Brennan, Judith A., "Reports From the Batcave: Another Sequel in Works?" *The Los Angeles Times*, July 1, 1998, p. 2

233 Durgin, Vance, "People: Michael Jackson, Wife Divorcing, Keanu Reeves in Next 'Batman' Movie?" *The Orange County Register*, Oct. 9, 1999, p. A.02

234 Garner, Clare, "Why Batman is Really a Turkey," *The (London) Independent*, Feb. 23, 1999, p. 3

235 Schaefer, Stephen, "Holy Box Office! He Swings Again After Three Strikes," *USA Today*, Nov. 4, 1999, p. 04D

236 —, "News Lite: Clooney Taking It Easier After Series of Film Flops," *Los Angeles Daily News*, Sept. 19, 1997, p. N.2

237 —, "Film: Back to a Land Well Visited: Teenage Angst," *The New York Times*, July 25, 2010, p. AR8

Chapter Ten:
FALSE STARTS

BATMAN: THE MUSICAL, or
GUYS & DOLLS ON MESCALINE

Though *Batman & Robin* was definitely a disappointment, it wasn't the huge bomb that many believe it to be. The film did make money for Warner Bros., just not nearly as much as they'd hoped. And, perhaps because they'd had a good time making it, when it became clear that the film had become a Hollywood punch line, there wasn't the usual finger-pointing among the principals involved. In fact, it was quite the contrary. Director Joel Schumacher, actor George Clooney, and scriptwriter Akiva Goldsman all publicly shouldered responsibility for the film's perceived failure. "I think we just went off the rails with *Batman & Robin*," said Goldsman, "and nobody wants to make a movie that doesn't work and each and every one of us is like 'blame me, blame me.' It just was, sometimes that happens. It was reasonable after *Batman & Robin* for the franchise to take a rest."[1] Rumor has it that if you meet George Clooney and tell him you paid to see *Batman & Robin*, he'll personally refund your money. For a celebrity roast of the actor, Clooney's pal Matt Damon recorded a video that showed him outside a theater in Africa, where he was filming a movie, confronting a group of irate moviegoers who had just seen *Batman & Robin*. After placating the crowd, Damon says, "You can try and give people their money back, but with projects like that what they really want is their time."[2]

Warner Bros. began to regroup. While Joel Schumacher pondered a lower-budget *Batman*, the studio began thinking even farther outside the box. Andrew Lloyd Webber's stage musical *The Phantom of the Opera* had earned more than 2.6 billion worldwide in a little more than a decade. During that same period, Webber's previous musical, *Cats*, earned $2 billion through its various touring companies. The Walt Disney Company jumped on the bandwagon with a musical adaptation of their animated film *Beauty and the Beast*, which racked up an estimated $500 million in four years, not including merchandise sales.[3] Disney was now reaping the benefits of another Broadway hit, *The Lion King*, with more shows in preparation. Maybe, thought Warner Bros., the same treatment would work for the Caped Crusader...

Warner Bros. was tempted to take a gamble on Broadway because of the potential ripple effect of a hit show. Even a mediocre show could revive DVD sales of the original movie and create a lucrative revenue stream from touring road companies, toys, T-shirts and collectibles.[4] But unlike Disney, Warner Bros. did not have a division specifically dedicated to the production of musicals. However, one of their TV executives, Gregory Maday, had been a former theater director in Pittsburgh before moving on to CBS, where he oversaw shows like *Murphy Brown* as head of comedy and drama development. From there, he moved on to Warner Bros., where he toiled for two decades before he was tapped to head the new division, which would eventually become Warner Bros. Theatre Ventures. "I love the theater," said Maday, "and for me, getting to do this is a way to go back to something that I never got out of my blood."[5]

With veteran Broadway producer Emanuel Azenberg—producer of Neil Simon's plays as well as the hit *Sunday in the Park With George*—as an advisor, Maday began meeting with various playwrights about turning the most memorable films in the Warners' library into musicals.[6] "We've seen the Broadway explosion and we're trying to see if there's a way we can participate," said Maday.[7]

Of course, Warners subsidiary DC Comics already had some experience bringing one of their characters to the Great White Way. *It's a Bird...It's a Plane... It's Superman!* opened at the Alvin Theatre on March 29, 1966 to generally positive reviews, but closed on July 17 after 129 performances; its camp treatment of the man from Krypton quickly turned it from a legit tuner into kiddie matinee fare.

Warner Bros. now made plans to bring *Batman*, one of their most valuable assets, to the stage. The question was—who to write it? They first went to Larry Gelbart, who developed *M*A*S*H* for television and was the writer of both the 1982 film *Tootsie* and the 1990 Tony Award-winning musical *City of Angels*. However, Gelbart was not interested in exploring the dark streets of Gotham.[8]

To compose the music, the studio approached Elliot Goldenthal, who scored Joel Schumacher's *Batman* films. Goldenthal turned them down, saying he had a problem with the idea of putting Batman into a long-running musical, where the story would be the same every night. "*Batman* is disposable culture," he said. "It is mythic, but you throw it away and next week Batman is doing something else. The beauty is Batman's continued exploits."[9]

Looking for a musician with Broadway experience who would also have an affinity for the darkness of Batman's world, Maday and Azenberg next approached Jim Steinman. A composer, lyricist and record producer best known for his collaborations with Meat Loaf (their two *Bat Out of Hell* albums sold more than 50 million copies), Steinman had written lyrics for the Andrew Lloyd Webber musical *Whistle Down the Wind* and had just finished collaborating on a successful stage adaptation of the 1967 Roman Polanski film *The Fearless Vampire Killers*. Called *Tanz der Vampire (Dance of the Vampires)*, it opened in Vienna, Austria on October 4, 1997 and went on to win the International Musical Award Grammy in 1998. Steinman's rock and roll music, known for its majestic, operatic sweep, also seemed in keeping with the style of music that was then popular on Broadway. He had long wanted to do a musical based on *Peter Pan*, to be called *Neverland*, but plans for that were shelved when he began work on *Batman*.[10]

Warners' began negotiations with Steinman in 1998. When *Entertainment Weekly* asked the composer about his work habits, he said, "I'm nocturnal. My favorite thing is to go to sleep around noon, and work through the night...I listen to Wagner and the Beach Boys. And I watch Hitchcock. I once got kicked out of an apartment for playing the score from *Psycho* too loud." To get ready for *Batman*, he said, "I'm starting to sleep upside down in a tree."[11]

To write the book for the musical, Warners again went for a proven talent. By April of 1999, they were working out a deal with David Ives, best known for his plays *Ancient History, Mere Mortals* and *English Made Simple*. Ives began his stage career with *Encores!*, the "musicals in concert" series presented at the New York City Center, where he retooled the texts for almost a dozen vintage musicals.[12]

Around the same time that Ives came aboard, Warners approached Stephen Daldry, director of the London and Broadway productions of *An Inspector Calls*, to direct the show. Daldry passed. They next began courting Robin Phillips, director of the Broadway hit *Jekyll and Hyde*.[13]

The original plan was to have the musical ready for the Broadway stage by 2000 or 2001.[14] Steinman and Ives struggled to nail down a story, eventually seeking inspiration from Tim Burton's *Batman* films. "David and I floundered around for a year trying to figure out how to musicalize *Batman*," said Steinman. "Then we looked at Tim's original movie and thought, that's it."[15] The final storyline borrowed elements from both *Batman* and *Batman Returns*, pitting Batman against the Joker and Catwoman. "It's loosely based on the Tim Burton movies," Steinman told *Entertainment Weekly*. "There's a thrilling 20-minute opening spectacle of Gotham City. It's like *Guys and Dolls* on mescaline. In a good way."[16] He would later tell *The New York Post* that his *Batman* score was a mixture of "Brecht, Weill, Rodgers & Hammerstein and rock 'n' roll," and the overall design concept was "Gotham City as Berlin in the 1930s."[17]

Warners hoped to get a draft of the script and score from Steinman and Ives in early November 2000.[18] But that date came and went, and the musical dynamic duo were still hard at work in December. By that point, it looked like the play wouldn't reach Broadway until 2002 or 2003.[19]

The studio continued searching for a director for the musical, and in the summer of 2001, they signed a ringer. On July 27, *The New York Post* announced that Tim Burton, whom Warner Bros. had been courting for over a year, had finally agreed to make his Broadway directing debut with *Batman: The Musical*. The studio sealed the deal the previous week, after Burton had several positive meetings with Steinman and Ives. "We're thrilled he's going to do it," said Steinman, adding that Burton "has already got a list of 20 designers from all over the world he wants to talk to about the production."[20] Steinman told *Playbill On-Line*, "It was my dream that he do this."[21]

Reportedly, Burton was keen to direct the musical because he was unhappy with the lighter tone the *Batman* films took after he left the series. An unnamed source said the director wanted to "redeem the soul of the *Batman* series." Burton planned to begin work on the musical full-time in 2002, with the intention of opening it out of town in 2004 and on Broadway in 2005.[22]

During all the years that *Batman: The Musical* was in development, David Ives kept busy writing the book for other musicals. After Ives accompanied Steinman to Stuttgart to see a production of *Dance of the Vampires* in 2002, Steinman asked him to join that project, which had had a troubled history on its way to Broadway. The musical went through several producers and directors and, according to reports, as much as $14 million.[23] Ives was also toiling on Disney's stage version of *The Little Mermaid*.[24]

By November 2002, Ives had written a draft of the script for *Batman: The Musical* which Burton reportedly liked, and Steinman had completed half a dozen songs.[25] Steinman told *New York Newsday* that the musical was about 70 percent done. "But it's got a lot of work to do," said Steinman. "Tim Burton's directing it, and he'll change a lot." He added, "The musical is very similar to the first movie. Very dark and wild, with some very anarchic comedy."[26]

Just as it seemed the project was picking up steam, Maday put it on the back burner. In 2003, he began to concentrate on a Broadway version of *The Vampire Lestat,* with music by Elton John and Bernie Taupin and a book by Tim Rice. Warners was pushing the project despite the fact that Steinman's similar *Dance of the Vampires* also opened in 2003 and closed after only a month. Likewise, Lestat got scathing reviews in its previews, and Warner Bros. Theatre Ventures first official Broadway production closed after only 39 performances.[27]

Maday was now pushing other projects besides *Batman: The Musical,* including musicals based on *Harry Potter* and *Charlie and the Chocolate Factory.* He also developed an interpretive dance version of *Casablanca,* which debuted in China in 2005.[28]

Eventually, Steinman and Ives stopped work on the musical and moved on to other projects. Looking back on his own involvement, Tim Burton shrugged it off as something that never really interested him, telling a reporter that when he was first asked to do it, "I thought: 'Oh no—*Batman On Ice!*'"[29] Over the weekend of July 15 and 16, 2006, Steinman debuted demos of several of his songs for *Batman: The Musical* on his website.[30] They can still be downloaded from Jim Steinman.com (http://www. jimsteinman.com/dreampol.htm), though a more complete collection of the songs is at Ryan Letizia's website *The Dark Knight of the Soul: The Unofficial Memorial to Batman: The Musical* (http://www.freewebs.com/batman_themusical/home.htm).

Listening to the demos, one can begin to get a sense of what *Batman: The Musical* might have been like. The music has the typical Steinman sweep, from Batman's opening number, "The Graveyard Shift," where the Caped Crusader sings a dirge-like tune with the repeated phrase, "I work the graveyard shift," to Catwoman's plaintive "I Need All the Love I Can Get," to the Joker's frenetic "Wonderful Toys," whose main phrase is a line from the 1989 *Batman* film, "Where does he get those wonderful toys?" Two of the songs written for the musical were covered by Meat Loaf on his 2006 album *The Monster is Loose*: "In the Land of the Pig the Butcher is King," a song written from the point-of-view of corrupt Gotham City executives, and "Cry to Heaven," which is a beautiful but bleak lullaby. Steinman is currently working on a new stage production, *Bat Out of Hell: The Musical,* and it is believed that some of the songs originally written for *Batman* may appear in this new venture.

It's debatable whether *Batman: The Musical* would ever have worked. In recent films, Batman has become such a dark and brooding figure that it's difficult to picture him singing. But, before Andrew Lloyd Webber came along, the same could have been said for the Phantom of the Opera. And a few years ago, the same would have been said of Spider-Man. From the few snatches of music that have been made public, it at least seems possible that the show would have been much more than *Batman on Ice.* But unless Warner Theatre Ventures decides to resurrect it, on ice it shall remain.

Although the Steinman and Ives show bit the dust, Batman did arrive in the flesh for the *Batman Live* arena show. The £7.5 million extravaganza, featuring Batman, Robin, the Joker, the Riddler and Catwoman, kicked off at the Manchester Evening News Arena in Manchester, England on July 19, 2011; from there, it moved on to Paris and other European cities. The script for the show was provided by writers who had some history with the character, Stan Berkowitz and Alan Burnett. Both were comic book veterans and multiple Emmy-award winners for various *Batman* animated series. Sets were created by Es Devlin, designer of Take That's *Progress* tour, who had also worked with Lady Gaga and the English National Opera. Rolling Stones tour veteran Patrick Woodroffe supervised the lighting, and Formula One designer Gordon Murray created the Batmobile.[31]

Sam Heughan and Nick Court alternated performances playing Batman in the show. Heughan, 31, told Paul Croughton of *The Times of London*, "I've done a bit of TV, a few films and a lot of theatre, but this is totally different. Before we started rehearsals, I thought I was in pretty good shape. Then we had two weeks of Batcamp, where we'd spend the morning on different styles of fighting—capoeira, boxing, stick fighting, karate—and the afternoon on core conditioning. Which was hardcore. But it was really helpful with the flying."[32]

The *Batman Live* show played 87 shows in 10 major arenas around Britain and Ireland over a three-month period. In a review in which he gave it 3 out of 5 stars, *The Times of London's* Dominic Wells, who saw the show on opening night, wrote, "The production's simple plot tells how Robin came to live with the Caped Crusader; the son of circus performers killed by an extortionist, he, like Batman, was orphaned by crime. You wouldn't think it hard to wring sympathy from the violent deaths of two sets of parents while their only sons look helplessly on, but neither killing carries a shred of pathos...Yet as the show goes on, the positives more than outweigh the negatives... The Joker makes a spectacular entrance, springing 20ft into the air from a jack-in-the-box, gleefully inquiring: 'Tooooo subtle?' His adoring girlfriend, Harlequin, is his match in madness, with a voice like Cyndi Lauper channeling Marilyn Monroe...By the time the new-look Batmobile skids on to the stage, the audience is equally revved up and ready to roar. In short, it's a wildly ambitious show that more than fills an arena space."[33]

BATMAN: YEAR ONE & BEYOND

While the Broadway show was in development, Warner Bros. contemplated how to continue their *Batman* film series. In August of 2000, *Daily Variety* reported that Boaz Yakin, director of *Remember the Titans*, had been hired to co-write and direct a live action adaptation of *Batman Beyond*, the WB Kids Network animated series that took place in a future Gotham City, where Bruce Wayne was retired from crime fighting but aiding Tim McGinnis, a high schooler who became a new, younger Batman, battling the evil corporate forces that killed his father and now controlled Wayne's empire. The creators of the series, Paul Dini and Alan Burnett, would co-write the film's script with Yakin, and cyberpunk sci-fi novelist Neal Stephenson, author of *Cryptonomicon*, was negotiating to be a consultant.[34] Dini and Burnett had already written several Batman animated straight-to-video features, including *Batman Beyond: The Movie*, *The Batman/Superman Movie* and *Superman: The Last Son of Krypton*, as well as the 1993 Warner Bros. Animation theatrical feature *Batman: Mask of the Phantasm*. Burnett also wrote numerous episodes of *Batman: The Animated Series*, a celebrated show that ran for six seasons beginning on the Fox Network and continuing on the WB Network before spawning several successful spin-offs.[35]

For industry observers, Warner Bros.' inability to quickly re-launch *Batman* was a mystery, since the Burbank studio was Hollywood's most successful when it came to launching blockbuster franchises. Their *Lethal Weapon* series had been going for 11 years, and *Harry Potter* was off with a bang; the first film in that series took in a whopping $969 million at the worldwide box office, threatening to make *Batman* Warner Bros.' *second* biggest corporate asset.[36]

At the dawn of the 21st Century, every major studio pursued films based on comic book characters. 20th Century Fox had the *X-Men* and *Daredevil,* Universal was prepping *The Hulk,* Sony/Columbia had *Spider-Man,* and Warner Bros. had *Batman* and *Superman*—two series that each ran out of steam after less than a decade.[37] Movie studio executives looked for "tentpole" movies—the big megahit whose overwhelming success would cover the losses of lesser-performing films. They sought properties that would spin off two or more sequels and generate income from merchandising tie-ins. This was especially important for Warner Bros., whose parent company, Time-Warner, was plunged heavily into debt after merging with AOL in 2001.[38]

The studio's recent rocky ride with *Superman* began in 1993, when Warner Bros. president of theatrical production Lorenzo di Bonaventura visited Joel Silver's ranch in South Carolina. While there, he went on a five-mile jog with another guest, former *Batman* producer Jon Peters, who had begun work on developing a new *Superman* film. After di Bonaventura returned to California, Warner Bros. bought the film rights to *Superman* from Alexander Salkind, producer of the Superman movies starring Christopher Reeve. Working with Peters, the studio commissioned a script from Jonathan Lemkin, writer of the fourth *Lethal Weapon* film, in 1995. When the studio received Lemkin's script, they found it too dark, and hired another writer, Gregory Poirier, to take a crack at it. Still unsatisfied, they turned to Kevin Smith to write a third script. Smith clashed with Peters, and when Tim Burton was attached to direct and Nicholas Cage to star, yet another scriptwriter, Wesley Strick, was brought in. Strick's script looked promising, but when a budget for the film came in at over $100 million, the studio shelved it.[39]

Meanwhile, Warner Bros. took a two-pronged approach to reviving *Batman.* Besides developing the live-action *Batman Beyond* feature, on September 21, 2000, *Daily Variety's* Dana Harris reported that Darren Aronofsky, director of *Pi* (1998) and *Requiem for a Dream* (2000), had been tapped to direct *Batman: Year One.*[40] Bryan Singer, director of the 2000 movie *X-Men*, lobbied to be the director of *Batman: Year One*, but the job was given to Aronofsky because Lorenzo di Bonaventura had seen an advance print of *Requiem for a Dream* and was impressed with Aronofsky's style.[41]

Frank Miller's script for *Batman: Year One* was similar to his comic book of the same name, and included a couple of set piece scenes that were taken almost verbatim from the comic. Yet it deviated from the comic book in strange and interesting ways. The comic book tells the parallel stories of Jim Gordon, a police detective who has just arrived in Gotham City, and is immediately suspect because he's an honest cop who, unlike all the other cops around him, won't take graft, and 25-year-old millionaire Bruce Wayne, heir to the Wayne fortune, who returns to Gotham City after 12 years spent abroad. In the comic, after Bruce settles in at Wayne Manor, he soon begins making forays out among the criminal elements of the city, trying to clean up Gotham in his own vigilante way. His first encounters almost get him killed; he decides to adopt the persona of a bat to frighten his victims. Alfred is largely absent, but in the few panels where he does appear, he's obviously aiding "Master Bruce." Though suspicious of each other at first, Wayne and Gordon become allies by the end of the tale, two crusaders who both want the best for Gotham City.

As dark and cynical as the comic book was, it presented versions of Gordon and Bruce Wayne that fit within the established canon. The film script, on the other hand, seemed intent on totally re-inventing the characters, canon be damned. It presented a Jim Gordon with suicidal tendencies; the first time he's seen, he's in his boxers on the toilet in his apartment with a gun in his mouth, an image repeated later in the script. He's still a newly arrived cop, still untrusted by his associates because he's too honest, but this Gordon is much more of a brooding depressive, particularly in the beginning of the story. Bruce Wayne received a particularly drastic makeover. According to the script, after his parents were killed, Bruce ran away and ended up in a junkyard, where he was found by a black man named Big Al who, with his son, Little Al, ran a junkyard and garage. Bruce turned up on a scrap pile, hungry and wild. Big Al took him in and raised him. After Big Al died, Bruce stayed on at the garage, helping Little Al, who once had aspirations to go to Medical School, run the repair shop of the garage. In this script, Alfred Pennyworth is nonexistent; there is only Little Al to look after Bruce, and later become his ally-in-vigilantism, putting him back together when he comes back to his squalid apartment above the garage broken and bloody. This Bruce Wayne is also a depressive, constantly writing letters to his dead father (we hear them in voice-over) that he never mails, but keeps in a cardboard box. He's filled with rage, driven by revenge, and presented as being a grade-A delusional psychopath. Some of the big set piece scenes are preserved from the comic book, and the story still ends with Batman and Gordon becoming trusted partners in their war on crime, but it's an unrelentingly grim and ultra-violent ride.[42]

Warner Bros. didn't stop there. In August of 2001, the studio hired Andrew Kevin Walker to write an untitled script that would put Batman and Superman together in one film—as enemies. Wolfgang Petersen, director of the acclaimed *Das Boot* (1982) and Warner Bros.' 1993 hit *In the Line of Fire*, not to mention the studio's top-grossing film of 2000, *The Perfect Storm*, was immediately attached to direct and to produce the film with Diana Rathbun.[43]

The *Batman vs. Superman* script began with Superman capturing a terrorist who, with his confederates, attempts to destroy the Freedom Monument, a towering glass-domed structure, in Metropolis. When the lead terrorist is captured on a bridge by a group of citizens who are ready to beat him to death, Superman stops them, insisting that justice will be done, but not vigilante justice.

Back in his guise as Clark Kent, he returns to his apartment, which seems emptier now that Lois Lane has divorced him. When we next see Kent, he's best man at Bruce Wayne's wedding. We learn that Wayne has been retired from crime fighting for ten years, since the death of Robin. Wayne marries a woman named Elizabeth and takes her on a tropical honeymoon, where she's tragically killed by a poison dart, dying in his arms with her lips distorted in a grotesque, wide smile.

Crushed by his grief, Wayne once again assumes the guise of Batman, but he's more brutal than ever. Clark Kent, meanwhile, returns to Smallville, where he reconnects with Lana Lang, now a nurse, and has a brief, nostalgic romance with her.

As the story progresses, we learn that the Joker has returned from the dead, resurrected by Lex Luthor, who is using the clown prince of crime in a scheme to obliterate Superman. He knows that Batman will want to kill the Joker to exact revenge for his wife, and that Superman, ever the good boy scout, will try to stop Batman from doing so. He also knows that Batman is so driven and so resourceful that he won't let Superman stop him—he'll kill the Man of Steel, if he has to.

The film climaxes with two huge set-piece battles. The first is the fight between Superman and Batman, who nearly kills the Man of Steel by wearing a Kryptonite-infused Batsuit and shooting a Kryptonite arrow into Superman's shoulder. He breaks the arrow off so Superman can't pull it out.

As Superman lies apparently dying, Batman ascends Freedom Monument for a battle with the Joker and two of the Joker's zombie-like goons. When it seems the Joker will get the upper hand, Superman appears, having ascended the building despite his super-strength being nearly depleted. The Joker's goons take on Superman, who, in his weakened state, is barely able to detain them. Meanwhile, Batman gets the Joker on the deck, about to crush the life out of him by stepping on his windpipe. Superman pleads with him, saying if he's going to do it, to first remove his mask, so he won't pretend there's some other part of him doing it. Batman removes his mask, and it appears he's going to go through with it, but ultimately he can't.

Then Lex Luthor appears, disappointed in Batman for not killing the Joker, and for not completely killing Superman (the kryptonite was not in the point of the arrow, but in the shaft; by breaking it off, Batman had weakened but not killed Superman). Luthor pushes the Joker off the monument, then—wearing a suit designed by the U.S. military that gives him super-speed—begins fighting both Batman and Superman, moving so fast they can't see him. Batman eventually grabs Luthor and topples over the edge of the monument with him. Superman also goes over the edge, but as he falls down into the rays of the rising sun, enough of his superpowers return to allow him to rescue Batman. Luthor crashes into the concrete below, his super-suit exploding.

The script ends with Batman and Superman once again friends. Batman suggests they go get a beer. Superman says maybe a soda. Batman says, "Oh god, what is it with you?" and they walk off into the dawn.[44]

The tight, fast-paced script moved relentlessly to set up the big fight scenes at the end, but the overall tone was extremely bleak and mostly humorless, and the fights were long, extended, brutal punch-ups. In the end, one could imagine that the resulting film would have been rather like a movie version of a World Wrestling Federation bout, with the main attraction being a fight to the almost-death between two of the world's finest heroes.

Nonetheless, Warner executives saw *Batman vs. Superman* as a way to reinvigorate both the *Superman* and *Batman* franchises. Though the film was dark and pitted the heroes against each other in the third act, studio executives figured that after audiences were reintroduced to Batman and Superman through this film, then the studio could make separate films with the characters acting independently.[45] Overseeing *Batman vs. Superman* was di Bonaventura and Warner Bros. senior vice-president Bob Brassel.[46] "We are pleased that Wolfgang Petersen is bringing his considerable talents to this newest episode of two of our most import franchises," di Bonaventura said. "In his hands, *Batman vs. Superman* will carry forward the Warner Bros. superhero tradition; we look forward to starting this project as soon as possible."[47]

Petersen didn't yet know who he wanted for the title roles, but he told *Variety* that he sought actors who not only had good physiques but who also had the acting chops for the complex emotions required by the script. "Everything after September 11 is different," he said. "You want to change the image of these superheroes."[48]

Petersen hoped to begin filming in early 2003, expecting to shoot for five or six months. However, at the same time as he was developing *Batman vs. Superman*, he was also developing other projects for the studio, including *The Trojan War* and a pair of films to be based on novels by Orson Scott Card, *Ender's Game* and *Ender's Shadow*. But, he said, "It was just too exciting to me not to do *Batman vs. Superman* now. It's good to have a handful of projects cooking in your drawer. Let's see what happens after this."[49]

On July 9, 2002, *Daily Variety* reported that Petersen was definitely directing *Batman vs. Superman* for a 2004 release. "It is a clash of the titans," said Petersen. "They play off of each other so perfectly. (Superman) is clear, bright, all that is noble and good, and Batman represents the dark, obsessive and vengeful side. They are two sides of the same coin and this is material for great drama."[50]

Already, however, events were transpiring that would set di Bonaventura on a collision course with Warner Bros. president Alan Horn. On July 5, 2002, J.J. Abrams turned in to the studio the first 88 pages of a script for a new *Superman* movie, but not just any *Superman* movie—it was part one of a trilogy. After Bob Brassel read it, he immediately called producer Jon Peters and told him he had to read it, saying, "I did, and it was amazing. In a world of chaos, it's about hope and light." Lorenzo di Bonaventura also liked the script, feeling that it was more epic and ambitious than earlier *Superman* screenplays. He called both Alan Horn and Barry M. Meyer, the chief executive of Warner Bros., encouraging them to read it.

Abrams continued working on his *Superman* story, turning in the final 50 pages in mid-July, just as Warner Bros. announced plans to move ahead with *Batman vs. Superman*; the studio said Petersen would begin filming the superhero match-up in February 2003. Meanwhile, producer Jon Peters, writer J.J. Abrams and Brassel met in di Bonaventura's office to discuss the completed *Superman* script. Reportedly, di Bonaventura indicated that he liked the script and the studio wanted to make it, but they were going to proceed with both that film and *Batman vs. Superman*. However, they would release the Wolfgang Petersen film first. Abrams balked at that idea, suggesting it would be like making a movie called *When Harry Divorced Sally* before making *When Harry Met Sally*. Reportedly, di Bonaventura saw it another way. For one thing, McG, the director Warner Bros. still wanted to direct the *Superman* movie, wasn't yet available, but he might be if the picture were delayed. Secondly, a movie featuring a clash of Batman and Superman might attract fans of the older movies before the new individual series reinvented the characters.

As the producer of *Superman*, Jon Peters had an interest in seeing his film made first, and several executives at Warner Bros. agreed, worried that the darker tone of *Batman vs. Superman* might turn off audiences and kill both franchises. Warner Bros. president Alan Horn, who often clashed with di Bonaventura over which films the studio should make, read Abrams's script in mid-July. He liked it, but instead of championing it outright, he decided to give both scripts to ten Warner Bros. executives, including representatives from international and domestic theatrical marketing, consumer products and home video, to see if they would rally behind him.

The ten executives met in a second floor conference room on an early morning in August to decide which film to make first. Only two people in the room, production executive Jeff Robinov and senior vice president Bob Brassel, knew which script was favored by Horn and which by di Bonaventura, so as not to bias the proceedings. After the vote was taken, the more upbeat *Superman* script came out the unanimous winner. But di Bonaventura would not give in easily; he argued that *Batman vs. Superman* was filled with action, which would make it easier to market. The executives, however, felt that Abrams's story, as the first of a trilogy, would spin off two other movies, and thus it would potentially bring in three times the amount of money from DVDs and merchandising. And if it bombed, the studio could still go ahead with *Batman vs. Superman*.

According to *The New York Times*, di Bonaventura was so upset by the outcome that he flew to New York to meet with AOL Time-Warner's chief executive, Richard D. Parsons, and the new chairman of the company's entertainment and network group, Jeff Bewkes. For di Bonaventura, this was the last straw. He laid out his issues with Horn and argued for his removal, but Parsons and Bewkes were not about to knock the president of Warner Bros. out of his job.

At the end of August, after asking *Batman & Robin* screenwriter Akiva Goldsman to do a rewrite of *Batman vs. Superman*, Warner Bros. pulled the plug on the project. It was the end of the road for di Bonaventura. After twelve years at Warner Bros., he packed up his office and left the studio. Publicly, both he and the studio denied that he was leaving over the battle about which superhero film would be made first. Horn told *The New York Times* that while he respected creative differences, "I said I wanted to do *Superman*. At the end of the day it's my job to decide what movies we make."[51] Ultimately, neither of the films would ever make it into production.

Wolfgang Petersen moved on to another project he'd been developing, *Troy*. He had wanted to make that film first anyway, but had been coerced by Warner Bros. to set it aside in favor of *Batman vs. Superman*. Even though the superhero film had been cancelled, Petersen told Dana Harris of *Daily Variety*, "I'm looking forward to directing *Batman vs. Superman* in the future."[52] As late as 2004, while Petersen was preparing to film *Troy* and Christopher Nolan was deep into pre-production of a new Batman feature, Petersen told *Daily Variety's* Michael Fleming that he was still interested in doing *Batman vs. Superman*.[53]

After going through more rewrites, more directors, and millions of dollars, the *Superman* trilogy also was eventually scuttled. It took director Bryan Singer to bring the Man of Steel back to movie screens, in 2006's *Superman Returns*, a film that looked backward to the *Superman* films of the 1970s instead of to the future.

In July 2002, while Warner Bros. juggled opposing *Batman* and *Superman* film projects, Mattel scored a coup by winning a five-year contract to produce toys and games based on Batman, Superman and Looney Tunes characters from Warner Bros. The toy company won the rights, projected to be worth between $200 million and $500 million, after impressing Warners with their toys for *Harry Potter and the Sorcerer's*

Stone. They wouldn't get the *Batman* rights, however, until Warners' contract with Hasbro, Inc. ran out at the end of the year.[54]

The deal between Warners and Mattel came together almost by accident. Warners thought they could get a better deal for the licenses by packaging five properties together—*Batman, Superman, Looney Tunes, Baby Looney Tunes* and *Justice League*—than by selling them individually. Hasbro put in a bid on the package, but Mattel's offer was larger. Now that the deal was sealed, the toymaker was keen for Warner Bros. to get superhero films into production to help drive toy sales.[55]

As evidence of how much a hit superhero film could promote sales, one only had to look at Marvel Enterprises. In 2004, during a time when much of the toy industry saw flat sales, Marvel reported $4 billion in worldwide licensed retail sales, enough to give them a ranking in fourth place on *License!* magazine's list of top licensors. The previous year, the company had been ranked at number 69, with sales of $189 million. The reason for the huge increase in sales was the fact that films had been released featuring Marvel characters *Spider-Man, The Fantastic Four* and *X-Men.* Warner Bros. Consumer Products, meanwhile, even without any superhero films in theaters, took second place (behind Disney) with sales of $6 billion, mostly due to *Batman* and *Superman* licensed products.[56] This was despite the fact that in the summer of 2003, DC Comics, with a 26% share of the comic book market, was in second place to Marvel, which had 32%.[57]

Just two months after the Mattel deal was signed, a real-life detective case involving Batman was solved. In March of 1996, a Batman uniform and mannequin valued at $150,000 went missing from Warner Bros. In April 2001, four Spider-Man suits valued at $50,000 each were pilfered from the set of *Spider-Man* at Sony Pictures Entertainment. Police from Culver City, California investigated for 18 months before serving search warrants in Los Angeles and New York, where three of the Spider-Man suits were found. The remaining Spider-Man suit was located in Japan, while the Batman outfit and a mannequin were traced to a collector in New York. The suits were stolen by a security guard who worked first at Warner Bros. and then at Sony Pictures Entertainment. He was charged with two counts of receiving stolen property, while his confederate was charged with one count of receiving stolen property.[58]

By the time development of *Batman vs. Superman* was postponed, *Batman: Year One* was also running out of steam. Director Darren Aronofsky told Stuart Wood of *CinemaBlend.com,* "I never really wanted to make a *Batman* film, it was a kind of bait and switch strategy. I was working on *Requiem for a Dream* and I got a phone call that Warner Bros wanted to talk about *Batman.* At the time I had this idea for a film called *The Fountain* which I knew was gonna be this big movie and I was thinking, 'Is Warners really gonna give me $80 million to make a film about love and death after I come off a heroin movie?' So my theory was if I can write this *Batman* film and they could perceive me as a writer for it, then maybe they'd let me go ahead, which worked out great until Brad Pitt quit."[59] Besides Pitt's departure, Warner Bros. had balked at the $70 million dollar budget for *The Fountain;* Aronofsky eventually made it in 2006, with Hugh Jackman starring.[60]

Development of the live-action *Batman Beyond* also fizzled eventually. But one Batman-related project that had been bouncing around the studio since the release of *Batman Returns* in 1992 did make it to the screen...

CATWOMAN

From the moment *Batman Returns* opened in 1992, and the public responded so enthusiastically to Michelle Pfeiffer's take on Catwoman, Warner Bros. began thinking "new franchise." The studio immediately set about developing a Catwoman film for Pfeiffer.[61] A year later, Michael Fleming of *Daily Variety* reported that although no deals had been signed, some of the creative minds behind *Batman Returns* were hard at work on the *Catwoman* movie. Denise Di Novi had signed on as producer, Tim Burton was expected to direct it, and screenwriter Daniel Waters was banging out a storyline.[62]

A couple of years passed, and the project lost momentum. It ended up in development hell, with numerous writers taking a crack at the script, including *Cosby* show writer John Rogers. But then, in 2001, it began to take on a new life. By that time, both Tim Burton and Michelle Pfeiffer had moved on, but producer Denise Di Novi was still trying to make it happen. At the end of March 2001, Di Novi, Warner Bros. executive vice-president Kevin McCormick, and worldwide production president Lorenzo di Bonaventura met with an actress whose career was heating up, and whom they thought had the right grit and intensity to carry the lead in an action film—Ashley Judd.[63] Judd agreed to play Catwoman, but Warner Bros. president Alan Horn wanted to wait until the studio had the latest draft of Rogers's script before making the actress an offer.[64] Despite the studio's enthusiasm, the project again languished.

In the summer of 2003, the film finally began to come together. Ashley Judd was out, replaced by Academy Award-winning actress Halle Berry. Berry seemed an ideal choice. She had almost stolen the show from Pierce Brosnan in the 2002 James Bond adventure *Die Another Day* as a secret agent named Jinx, a character the 007 producers pondered spinning off into her own series. Plus, Berry had comic book credentials after playing Storm in two *X-Men* movies for director Bryan Singer. With *Catwoman*, she would finally be given the chance to move out of the ensemble and into the limelight, carrying an action/adventure film on her own slender shoulders.

Sharon Stone and Lambert Wilson—himself once a candidate for the role of James Bond—signed on to play the villains, while Benjamin Bratt was chosen to play Berry's love interest. Perhaps hoping to get a director with the same kind of vision as Tim Burton, the studio hired a Frenchman, Pitof, to direct. Pitof had made his reputation as a digital imaging innovator on quirky French films like *Delicatessen*, and had only recently graduated to the director's chair with *Vidocq*. With all the elements in place, *Catwoman* finally moved from the development-go-round to greenlight. Filming was scheduled to begin in Vancouver, Canada on September 29, 2003.[65] In June, well before filming started, Berry went to work getting in shape with trainer Harley Pasternak. Besides gymnastics and stunt and fight training, she learned Capoeira, a Brazilian martial art based on animal movements.[66]

Berry also worked with whip master Alex Green, learning the intricacies of a black whip. Green said that after one week of 90-minute sessions, Berry learned how to successfully crack the whip.[67] "You can't just get a whip and say, 'I'll just crack it.' It doesn't work that way," Berry told *Jet* magazine's Aldore D. Collier. "It's a piece of equipment where if you don't know how to work it very well, it can be deadly. And if you don't know how to do it well, you can injure yourself. It's something that I worked very hard on. And it's very sexy! When you get your first crack, you just want to keep on cracking. It's addictive. I loved it so much that I would have to be told, 'Halle, put the whip down. The class is over. Go away, you're done.' The whole time I shot the movie, on my downtime I was practicing the whip. Getting it to crack loud takes practice. I gave Oprah one on her show, and I think she's still trying to crack it."[68]

For producer Denise Di Novi, one of the most exciting challenges of the production was the creation of a new Catwoman catsuit. "We all wanted to create something that was a little more urban, a little more contemporary," said Di Novi. "It had to be tailor-made to reflect Halle's characterization, so she had a big hand in the design of the suit." Besides Berry, Pitof and the producers also had input into the suit, which was designed by Academy Award-winning costume designer Angus Strathie. "I'm very proud of the costume design," said Pitof. "Here again, it has elements of previous cat suits but it is so unique to Halle, to her shape and beauty. It shows a lot of skin but also has a warrior-like quality to it. When she wears it she looks like somebody who's ready for a fight." Berry appreciated how "you can see her spine, her ribs and the lean, sinewy musculature of the cat." For Strathie, one of the biggest design challenges was deciding on what type of material to use. "The costumes for the earlier television and film Catwomen were cutting-edge for their time," said Strathie. "Julie Newmar and Eartha Kitt wore lurex and Michelle Pfeiffer wore latex. Now, Halle is wearing a combination of leather and a brand new silicone fabric we created just for this costume." The outfit was capped off by claws created with nearly 800 individual crystals used to create the look of pavé diamonds on sterling silver settings.[69]

The project continued to churn through writers. Playwright Theresa Rebeck, who scripted *Harriet the Spy*, took a stab at it, as did John Brancato and Michael Ferris, writers of *Terminator 3*.[70] Others who reportedly toiled on it were Laeta Kalogridis, Kate Kondell, Jon Cowan, John O'Brien, David Reynolds, Harley Peyton, Valerie Breiman, Rita Hsiao and Andrew W. Marlowe.[71] When filming was completed, the script went to the Writer's Guild for arbitration; in all, twenty-eight writers had drafted *Catwoman* scripts during its decade of development.[72] By the time cameras rolled, the character of Selina Kyle/Catwoman from *Batman Returns* had been completely obliterated. The script now centered on a young, mousy woman named Patience Phillips, who worked for an evil cosmetics conglomerate. When she learns too much, the powers-that-be at the company attempt to kill her, but Patience survives, mysteriously revived by an Egyptian Mau cat. Once resurrected, she finds that she possesses new powers and abilities, which she uses to take down the cosmetics corporation. Although the script borrowed elements from *Batman Returns*, in the end the writers created a character who was more superhero than villain, and who had no connection whatsoever to Batman or the character of Catwoman as previously established in comic books, TV shows and films.

Berry told Noe Gold of *Daily Variety* that the role "wasn't just about getting the body in shape and putting on the costume. It turned out to be a really good acting job that needed to happen."[73]

"She's more the anti-hero," said Berry. "Unlike Superman, Spiderman or Batman, she won't save the world. She's kind of a heroic character, but she's also got kind of a naughty/nice quality to her, too. There's definitely something naughty

Halle Berry slinks into action as Catwoman (Photofest/Warner Bros. Photo: Doane Gregory. © Warner Bros. Entertainment Inc.).

about her. She's not villainous. That's our new take on her. She has an edge and she represents more of who people really are. She's a realistic heroine. Nobody's perfect and we all fall prey to our desires. And sometimes our desires aren't too admirable."[74]

The character of Patience, said Berry, "had a lot more depth by the time Pitof got involved...Pitof loves women and isn't afraid of a woman being strong and powerful; Benjamin Bratt is the same way. And with Denise, who is such a girl's girl and is for women's empowerment, everybody is all for this woman rising up. By the time we put our heads together, she became a character that was pretty significant and very complicated."[75]

"Catwoman isn't really an action hero, that's kind of what's really great about the movie," said producer Denise Di Novi. "Even in the comic she's not a superhero, she's an antihero. The part really is complex. Halle is playing three characters with three distinct looks, three sets of wigs and wardrobe. There is a lot going on about female identity and empowerment, wondering if someone will love you if they know you have a dark side."[76]

Berry, who separated from her husband, actor Eric Benét, shortly after filming began, said that for her, "it was a perfect time to play a character that was in search of and in need of feeling and finding her own sense of power and self and realizing that she really is OK in the world just the way she is."[77]

When filming got underway, much of it took place at Vancouver's Center for Performing Arts, formerly the Ford Theater, which was once part of the Livent chain before that company went bankrupt. Warner Bros. rented the theater for 27 days of filming.[78] The shoot was not without mishaps; at the end of January 2004, Halle Berry sustained minor injuries when she collided with a boom pole while filming a running scene.[79]

The climactic fight scene between Berry and Sharon Stone took nine days to film. Doubling for Berry in the action scenes was Nito Larioza, a 29-year-old male Hawaiian actor and martial artist.[80] For the final day of filming on February 20, 2004, many of the crew showed up in their pajamas. The official Warner Bros. presskit said, "The reason was two-fold: firstly, to prepare for a well-deserved and perhaps lengthy catnap; and secondly, to celebrate what was for them, the cast and the filmmakers, a truly extraordinary experience."[81]

To handle the visual effects, Warner Bros. chose San Francisco-based ESC Entertainment, a company founded by the studio and the Wachowski brothers in 2001 to create computer-generated effects for the sequels to *The Matrix*.[82] Over 600 visual effects shots were created, including fully digital shots of Halle Berry and Midnight the cat. "To create the digital replications of Halle, high resolution digital scans, photo references and plaster life-casts were taken," said visual effects designer/supervisor Ed Jones. "Additionally, we scanned her entire wardrobe to capture all the textural qualities so that we could replicate every detail. We filmed Halle doing a range of emotional facial performances that were then mapped on to her digital double to give us a synthetic character with real facial performances. The goal was to blend the digital characters with the real performers to create seamless, realistic and believable action. Several of the sequences also involved the same digital tools to create the environments virtually. Consequently, there are shots in the movie that are 100% digital."[83]

Before the film was released, it was being castigated by comic book fans on the internet, who claimed to have seen the script, the trailer and even rushes.[84] They were particularly strong in their dislike of Berry's Catwoman garb, after the first publicity shots of her in the outfit were released. Warner Bros. worried about all the negative buzz the internet chatter was generating, but there was little they could do to combat it. For her part, Berry shrugged it off, saying, "Well, I love the look…I think it's modern and edgy, but then again you can't please everybody!"[85]

As shooting wound down, the publicity machine began ramping up. In March, just a couple of months after filmed ended, Berry was honored as the Female Star of the Year at the 2004 ShoWest Convention in Las Vegas.[86] The theater owners who had gathered for the event were optimistic about the upcoming film. And while Warner Bros. didn't have nearly the same amount of merchandising partners on *Catwoman* as on their *Batman* features, there were still a couple of tie-ins. The upscale Manhattan department store Henri Bendel unveiled a line of *Catwoman* apparel in black leather.[87] And Mattel released a Barbie doll in a *Catwoman* outfit. Actually, they released two; the first, in 2003, had Barbie dressed more like the Catwoman of the comic books. The second, released in conjunction with the film, had Barbie in a replica of Halle Berry's *Catwoman* clothes.

When filming was completed, Berry adopted Playdough, an orange and white kitty that was one of the 43 cats specially trained for the film.[88] Having made the film during a difficult time in her personal life, Berry felt good about what she had accomplished. "I felt empowered and strong and sexy—connected with myself as a woman," Berry commented about the role. However, she added, "This is a popcorn-eatin', ass-whoopin' summer action adventure."[89]

Warner Bros. hoped they had an ass-kicking popcorn movie on their hands, but in preview screenings, it was *Catwoman* that took the ass-whoopin', testing poorly. The studio ordered reshoots just a month before its release date.[90]

The film premiered at the ArcLight Cinema in Hollywood on July 15, 2004. The after-party was held on the roof of the theater's garage, which had been converted into an all-black lounge setting with thousands of candles. Halle Berry and Sharon Stone were on hand, along with Warner Bros. executives Alan Horn, Barry Meyer and Jeff Robinov and Village Roadshow's Bruce Berman. Former Catwoman Lee Meriwether also mixed with a crowd that included the film's executive producer, Michael Uslan, producer, Ed McDonnell, and director, Pitof.[91]

Among the crowd that night was Richard Schenkman, a producer for MTV, who recalled, "When a buddy informed me that he'd scored tickets for the premiere, I was thrilled. It was to be a big, splashy Hollywood event, with the screening at the ArcLight Cinema, and the party on a rooftop nearby. And I wanted to like the movie, I really did, but it was clearly dead on arrival. Berry was fine as Patience Phillips and Catwoman, and certainly looked more than fine in the suit, but the movie itself…"

"Still, when the opportunity came to meet Berry at the party, I jumped at the chance. She was holed up in a corner of a sectional couch, not moving from the spot except to rise and greet people and then sit down again. She seemed a nervous wreck, as though she was carrying the weight of a stillborn franchise on her delicate shoulders. She seemed pleased to be talking to anybody who came along, even a complete stranger like me. Indeed I was surprised at just how friendly and outgoing she was. It only occurred to me later that perhaps the more important people had been avoiding her all night because of the film's obvious failings."

"Later that evening I also met Michael Uslan, executive producer of the film by virtue of the fact that he had cannily acquired the movie rights to Batman years earlier and had steadfastly held onto them. Interestingly, he seemed to feel the movie was a huge success, and would be a box office smash. He seemed blissfully unaware that the picture was a terrible flop."[92]

Schenkman was not alone in his judgment of the film. Reviewers were not kind, to say the least. In *Daily Variety*, David Rooney wrote, "After raising the bar for summer blockbusters with its lyrical and imaginative third Harry Potter, Warner Bros. plummets to the dimmest recesses of popcorn inanity with *Catwoman*, which, even by the standards of comic book adaptations, requires a suspension of disbelief beyond most audiences. Risible yarn about a mousy underachiever rendered superhuman by arcane pussy power plays like a *Lifetime* movie on estrogen overdose, barely held together by a script that should have been tossed out with the kitty litter."[93]

In *Rolling Stone*, Peter Travers also savaged the film by using feline metaphors, writing, "Not to be catty about it, but the stench of the litter pan is all over this big-screen $90 million disaster-in-waiting. It's not hard to see why Halle Berry would want to put on a cat suit and become the first woman of color to play the lead in a blockbuster. After all, Berry is the first African-American woman to win the Best Actress Oscar (for *Monster's Ball*). Sadly, *Catwoman*, allegedly a tale of female empowerment, declaws her ambitions."[94]

The negative internet buzz and scathing reviews put a damper on the film's box-office prospects. On its opening weekend, it generated a meager $17.2 million in ticket sales at 3,117 theaters.[95] The second weekend of its release, its earnings dropped 64%, to $6.1 million.[96] Overseas, the numbers were just as bad; the only country in which it performed well was France, Pitof's homeland. By the time it finished its run, the film had grossed $40,202,379 in the U.S., and $41,900,000 abroad, for a total worldwide box office of $82,102,379. For most films, those would be phenomenal earnings, but *Catwoman* had cost Warner Bros. and its producing partner Village Roadshow Ltd. $100 million to make.[97]

MTV producer Richard Schenkman encountered Pitof some time later at a Director's Guild of America event, and spoke to the director. "He'd been a highly respected special effects creator, and *Catwoman* was only his second feature," said Schenkman. "We chatted for a while until I finally felt comfortable enough to ask him about *Catwoman*, and what had gone wrong. He had plenty to say on the subject, and laid all the blame at the studio's feet. He said that the script was never completed, but they'd gone into production anyway. He said that he had not been given the resources he needed to shoot and complete the ending, and when it clearly didn't work and they demanded a new ending, he was given far too little time and money to do anything effective. In short, he was very disappointed that despite his vision for the movie and his affection for the material, he had simply not been allowed to make a good picture. And... he's paid the price for its failure, having directed only one feature film since 2004."[98]

Just three years after being honored with an Academy Award for Best Actress, Halle Berry now found herself nominated for a Razzie Award as "Worst Actress of

2004." No one was surprised when she won it, but they were astonished that she showed up at the 25th Annual Razzie Award ceremony on February 26, 2005 to collect it.[99] Said Berry, "I want to thank Warner Bros. for casting me in this piece-of-shit, god-awful movie."[100]

BRUCE WAYNE, DICK GRAYSON & BIRDS OF PREY

The first weekend of August 1999 saw the release of the animated film *The Iron Giant*. That same weekend, agents for the screenwriter of *The Iron Giant*, Tim McCanlies, contacted Tollins/Robbins Productions, producers of the TV series *All That*, *Keenan and Kel* and *The Amanda Show*, and told them that McCanlies had an idea to pitch to them. When McCanlies met with the producers, he spun a tale about a wealthy young man, an American icon in the mold of John F. Kennedy, Jr., who was about to inherit an empire. The young man was given moral direction by a butler who was also a father figure, and by a cop who was one of the only straight cops in a crooked city. As the pitch ended, McCanlies played his trump card, revealing that the young man was Bruce Wayne, and the series would be about his journey to becoming Batman. The producers pounced on the idea.[101]

McCanlies was commissioned to write a script for the pilot episode, which has since been synopsized by Craig Byrne of *KryptonSite.com*, a website which has several pages devoted to the proposed Bruce Wayne TV series.

The pilot begins in London, where Alfred bails Bruce Wayne, an international figure with the media profile of John Kennedy Jr., out of jail. Alfred takes Bruce to a plane, which he boards to return to Gotham City after having been away for 12 years. He's days away from his 18th birthday, and is anxious to sign the papers to give the Waynecorp trustees the authority to continue running his company. Back in Gotham, Alfred chauffeurs Bruce to Crime Alley, where he's set upon by some thugs. Bruce overpowers the thugs, and he and Alfred take them to the police station, where Bruce meets a 13-year-old redhead, Barbara, who is there to bring dinner to her father, Det. Jim Gordon. Bruce remembers Gordon from the fateful night in Crime Alley when his parents were murdered before his eyes; Gordon, then a policeman, had comforted young Bruce.

The next day, Bruce meets with Charles Palantine of Waynecorp. Bruce hesitates about signing the trustee papers, and before he leaves, he sees an old boyhood friend, Lucius Fox. Fox is now an intern at Waynecorp. Alfred now realizes that if Bruce dies or is killed before his 18th birthday, the trustee—Palantine—will fully control Waynecorp. Bruce wants a "trustworthy lawyer" to go over the papers with him, so he turns to another old friend, Harvey Dent. Dent, a laid back young man who likes to party, has just finished his first year of law school. Bruce and Alfred arrive at Harvey's place to find he's having a costume party. At the party, Bruce meets two young women: Harvey's beautiful younger sister, Susan, and Selina Kyle, who is dressed as a tiger, with long claws.

Bruce gets an urgent message to meet Gordon at Wayne Chemical. Alfred drives Bruce there. Bruce insists on going alone to meet Gordon inside the plant.

He finds the detective inside a room accessible by an access hatch. Gordon tells him, "I didn't send for you." Just then, the hatch slams shut, and Bruce and Gordon are trapped inside the room. They hear valves creaking open, and the sound of rushing water. Using his acrobatic skills, Bruce is able to escape and help Gordon to safety.

Bruce, Gordon and Alfred go to the home of Lucius Fox, where Lucius's mother, Billie, makes them breakfast. Billie and Lucius think that Lucius's father, a Waynecorp employee, was killed because he saw something incriminating at the company. Lucius says he'll try to get into the Wayne Chemical files.

Bruce next goes to see Harvey Dent, who tells him not to sign the papers to turn the company over to the trustees. If he can manage to stay alive until he turns 18, the trustees won't dare kill him; once he's 18, if he dies without a will, his estate will go into probate for years. Bruce asks Harvey where Susan works. Harvey tells him, and Bruce and Alfred take off in the Rolls. They're followed by two dark sedans. The men in the sedans shoot at them with machine guns. After a car chase, they escape the bad guys and end up at the Gotham City Youth Shelter, where Susan is employed.

After talking to Susan, Bruce returns to the mansion, where he learns that Palantine has left several messages. Bruce calls him, and says he's been so busy with supermodels he forgot to sign the papers. Gordon then calls, saying he heard about the car chase, and that Lucius has told him about the weekly shipment of hazardous waste going out that night. Bruce says he'll meet Gordon there; Gordon tells him to stay away.

Gordon arrives at Wayne Chemical with a couple of other officers. Bruce is also there, dressed in black. Alfred finds Bruce, and tells him to trust no one, insinuating that his father was killed because he trusted someone at Waynecorp. As Gordon and his men go through Wayne Chemical, Bruce does what he can to help, staying out of sight. Gordon rounds up the bad guys—and Bruce feels that he's finally found something he's really good at. Gordon takes the bad guys to the police station, where one drops hints that he wants to make a deal. While Gordon is out of the room, the prisoner commits suicide—or so it seems.

Bruce and Alfred return to the mansion, where all of Bruce's Gotham friends surprise him with a birthday party. Now that Bruce is 18, Dent says he doesn't need to worry about signing the Waynecorp contract, and tosses it into the fire. Just then, Palantine arrives. Seeing the contract going up in smoke, he gives Bruce a book, *Business for Beginners*, and offers to be his mentor. Bruce announces to everyone that he's decided to stay in Gotham City, to see if he can make a difference.[102]

Tim McCanlies prepared a "bible" for the series outlining where the show could go over a five-year period. Future shows would introduce psychology student Harleen Quinzel, consultant Selena Kyle, would-be comedian Jack Napier, TV gossip reporter Vicky Vale, and a teen from Smallville, Kansas named Clark Kent. As the seasons progressed, we would see Bruce restoring Wayne manor, taking martial arts lessons, applying to the Gotham City Police Department and deciding it wasn't for him, and finding a large cavern underneath the manor and bringing in workmen to set up what would eventually become the Batcave. He would also become more interested in Gotham's criminal element, going out in the night on a motorcycle dressed in black and wearing a helmet for anonymity. Once Bruce gained control of WayneCorp, he would use their R&D division to provide him with the tools he needed in his fight against crime. After five seasons, he would finally adopt a guise to strike terror into the hearts of criminals, and become Batman.[103]

The biggest hurdle was convincing the higher-ups at Warner Bros. that a TV series about a young Bruce Wayne could exist concurrently with an ongoing *Batman* film series. The WB Network loved the idea and wanted to move forward, but Warner Bros. film division said they were about to embark on a new *Batman* movie, and used that excuse to keep the TV show in limbo. According to Craig Byrne of *Kryptonsite.com*, when *X-Men* opened on July 14, 2000 and made over $54 million on its opening weekend, "suddenly all chances of Bruce Wayne on television were shot dead."[104]

According to Byrne, actors Trevor Fehrman and Shawn Ashmore were considered for the role of Bruce Wayne, and Michael Rosenbaum, who would later become Lex Luthor on *Smallville*, was mentioned as a possible Harvey Dent. David Krumholtz was thought of as a potential Jim Gordon.

Several years later, after *Smallville*, a TV series about a teenaged Clark Kent, became a hit on the WB Network, its creators Alfred Gough and Miles Millar again pitched the idea of doing a young Bruce Wayne series as a companion show. They were turned down. However, in February of 2002, Tollin/Robbins Productions and Warner Bros. Television began moving forward with a Batman-related TV series. *Birds of Prey*, inspired by the DC Comics series of the same name, was set in the future, in New Gotham, and centered on the crime-fighting efforts of Oracle, the former Batgirl, whose real identity was Barbara Gordon; Huntress, or Helena Kyle, the daughter of Bruce Wayne and Selena (Catwoman) Kyle; and Dinah Lance, who is revealed to be the daughter of Black Canary.[105]

Dina Meyer, cast as Oracle, filmed the pilot at the same time as she was shooting her role in Paramount's theatrical film, *Star Trek: Nemesis*. Ashley Scott, who played Huntress, also pulled double-duty; she was completing her season's work on the TV series *Dark Angel* while *Birds of Prey* got underway. Rounding out the cast was Rachel Skarsten as Dinah Lance, and Shemar Moore as Detective Reese, who became Huntress's love interest.[106] Ian Abercrombie, an actor best known for playing Elaine's boss, Justin Pitt, in the sixth season of *Seinfeld*, was Alfred Pennyworth, dutifully waiting on the crime fighting ladies just as he'd attended to Master Bruce for all those years.

Brian Robbins, a partner in Tollin/Robbins Productions, directed the pilot episode, which also featured Sherilynn Fenn as psychiatrist Dr. Harleen Quinzel, a/k/a Harley Quinn, the Joker's paramour. Filmed in March of 2002, the pilot was written by Laeta Kalogridis—one of the uncredited writers of *Catwoman*—who also served as co-executive producer on the series.[107] WB put the series on the fall schedule, but had to reshoot parts of the pilot when Sherilynn Fenn dropped out and the part of Dr. Quinzel was recast with Mia Sara.

The pilot began with a scene lifted from the comic book *The Killing Joke*, showing the Joker shooting and paralyzing Barbara Gordon. Enraged, Batman goes after the Joker, and has a final confrontation with him inside a burning building. We are told that Batman survived, but went into exile afterward. For the few glimpses viewers get of Batman, he's played by Bruce Thomas, who also played the Dark Knight in commercials for On Star. The Joker was played by stuntman Roger Stoneburner, though the criminal's voice was dubbed by Mark Hamill, the voice of the Joker in the popular *Batman* animated series.

In its October 9, 2002 premiere, *Birds of Prey*, following WB's hit *Dawson's Creek*, gave the network its strongest Wednesday audience ever in adults aged 18 to 34.[108] It also scored with critics. Laura Fried of *Daily Variety* began her review of the show saying, "As *Birds of Prey* would have it, Batman is a wimp—things go bad one day, and the Caped Crusader splits town. Isn't that just like a man? While die-hard fans may protest the slam to the hero's rep, the WB scores points for giving the Dark Knight mythology a complete feminine makeover with *Birds of Prey*, a fantasy-adventure tale of sisters doing it for themselves."[109]

Cary James, in *The New York Times*, also praised the show, writing, "Leaping from rooftop to rooftop above the dark streets of New Gotham, the crime fighter known as Huntress has everything a supermodern superheroine needs: smart-mouthed dialogue and a really great costume. The daughter of Batman and Catwoman, Helena Kyle transforms herself into Huntress with a black bustier, leather pants and a sheer, full-length black coat that Christian Lacroix might be proud of... She is the dominant character in a trio of heroines in *Birds of Prey*, the sleek, entertaining new series inspired by characters from DC Comics. The show may not please purists who have followed the comics, but the series is stylish fun calculated to please WB's young audience."[110]

However, though the show got off to a good start, by the time the third episode aired the ratings had dropped 60%.[111] They remained low for the rest of the season. By mid-November, the WB informed Tollins/Robbins Productions that they were not going to order any further shows past the original 13-episode commission.[112] After the final two episodes aired back-to-back on February 19, 2003, the series was cancelled.

In an interview with Gail Simone of the website *Comic Book Resources*, *Birds of Prey*'s co-executive producer Laeta Kalogridis said, "I will say that since I was pushed off the project shortly after the pilot was shot—and I was unhappy with elements of the pilot as well—I felt the direction the show took didn't come close to the potential it had. I had some great writers on staff—they have since gone on to write on *Heroes, Fringe, Lost, Dexter*—one of them is the screenwriter of the *Twilight* series, all the films...I think my team could have made something exceptional, and I'm sorry that *Birds of Prey* didn't live up to that for fans."[113]

The next Batman-related series proposed for television was announced on September 30, 2008, a few months after *The Dark Knight* began breaking box-office records, when *Variety* reported that the producers of *Smallville*, Kelly Souders and Brian Peterson, as well as McG, the executive producer of *Supernatural*, were planning a series based on Robin, the Boy Wonder, to be called *The Graysons*. The show would focus on the escapades of Dick "D.J." Grayson, before he took on the Robin persona and fought alongside Batman.[114]

The show was expected to be a one-hour drama set in modern times in which D.J. would deal with first loves and young rivals. It was thought that *The Graysons* would be a potential replacement for *Smallville*, should that series end its run after the 2008 season. Besides Souders, Peterson and McG, Peter Johnson would produce the series for Warner Bros. Television.[115]

But on November 7, 2008, after the concept of the series was greeted with much negative internet buzz, *Daily Variety* reported that the WB wouldn't be pursuing the show after all. Apparently, after initially giving his blessing, Warner Bros. production executive Jeff Robinov had a change of heart. In a prepared statement, the studio said they had "opted not to go forward with the development of *The Graysons* at this time as the concept doesn't fit the current strategy for the *Batman* franchise."[116] It was also said that Christopher Nolan was uncomfortable having a Batman-related series on television while his Batman films were ongoing.[117] *The Graysons* ended before the first script had even been written. But by then, the Bat was back with a vengeance.

---

1 Patches, Matt, "Akiva Goldsman Interview," http://www.ugo.com/ugo/html/article/?id= 18821, accessed June 29, 2011

2 —, "Matt Damon Mocks George Clooney at Tribute Roast," *Starpulse.com*, http://wwwstarpulse.com/news/index.php/2006/10/17/matt_damon_mocks_george_clooney_at_t ribu, Oct. 17, 2006, accessed Aug. 4, 2011

3 Gubernick, Lisa, "Hollywood Hopes the Neon Lights On Broadway Are Full of Riches," *The Wall Street Journal*, April 14, 1998, http://www.freewebs.com/batman_themusical/home.htm, accessed Jul. 27, 2011

4 Hass, Nancy, "'Lestat': Bringing Anne Rice's World to the Stage With Elton John's Help," *The New York Times*, April 23, 2006, http://www.freewebs.com/batman_themusical/home.htm, accessed Jul. 27, 2011

5 Hass, Nancy, "'Lestat': Bringing Anne Rice's World to the Stage With Elton John's Help," *The New York Times*, April 23, 2006, http://www.freewebs.com/batman_themusical/home.htm, accessed Jul. 27, 2011

6 Gubernick, Lisa, "Hollywood Hopes the Neon Lights On Broadway Are Full of Riches," *The Wall Street Journal*, April 14, 1998, http://www.freewebs.com/batman_themusical/home.htm, accessed Jul. 27, 2011

7 *Ibid.*

8 *Ibid.*

9 Hofler, Robert, "Tuners-to-Pic Trend Now in Reverse," *Weekly Variety*, Aug. 28, 2000, p. F30

10 —, "Jim Steinman on 'Batman' and 'Dance of the Vampires'," *NY Newsday*, Nov. 21, 2002, http://www.freewebs.com/batmanthemusical/home.htm, accessed Jul. 27, 2011

11 —, "It Broadway Rocker: Jim Steinman," *Entertainment Weekly*, June 20, 1999, http://www.freewebs.com/batman_themusical/home.htm, accessed Jul. 27, 2011

12 Hofler, Robert, "It's All About the Ives," *Variety*, Nov. 3, 2002, http://www.freewebs.com/batman_themusical/home.htm, accessed Jul. 27, 2011

13 Brodesser, Claude, "WB, Ives Set for 'Bat' Tuner," *Variety*, April. 22, 1999, http://www.freewebs.com/batman_themusical/home.htm, accessed Jul. 27, 2011

14 Furman, Phyllis, "Pow! Time Warner Eyes Batman for Broadway," *The New York Daily News*, Dec. 9, 1998, http://www.freewebs.com/batman_themusical/home.htm, accessed Jul. 27, 2011

15 —, "Bat-Song, *The New York Post*, Aug. 30, 2002, http://www.freewebs.com/batman_themusical/home.htm, accessed Jul. 27, 2011

16 Bernardo, Melissa Rose, "Great Adaptations: Broadway's Upcoming Film-to-Stage Adaptations,*Entertainment Weekly* # 597, May 25, 2001, http://www.ew.com/ew/article/0,,256552,00.html, accessed July 21, 2012

17 —, "Bat-Song, *The New York Post*, Aug. 30, 2002, http://www.freewebs.com/batman_themusical/home.htm, accessed Jul. 27, 2011

18 Letizia, Ryan, "Batman: The Musical Waiting in the Wings," *RainbowNetwork.com*, Oct. 17, 2000, http://www.freewebs.com/batman_themusical/home.htm, accessed Jul. 27, 2011

19 Lefkowitz, David & Sean McGrath, "Ives and Steinman Still Working on Warner Bros.' Bway Batman," *Playbill.com*, Dec. 26, 2000, http://www.freewebs.com/batman_themusical/home.htm, accessed Jul. 27, 2011

20 —, "Bat-Song, *The New York Post*, Aug. 30, 2002, http://www.freewebs.com/batman_themusical/home.htm, accessed Jul. 27, 2011

21 Hernandez, Ernio & Robert Simonson, "Steinman, Ives and Director Tim Burton in Pre-Production on Batman," *Playbill.com*, Sept. 19, 2002, http://www.freewebs.com/batman_themusical/home.htm, accessed Jul. 27, 2011

22 —, "Bat-Song, *The New York Post*, Aug. 30, 2002, http://www.freewebs.com/batman_themusical/home.htm, accessed Jul. 27, 2011

23 Hofler, Robert, "It's All About the Ives," *Variety*, Nov. 3, 2002, http://www.freewebs.com/bat-man_themusical/home.htm, accessed Jul. 27, 2011

24 *Ibid.*

25 *Ibid.*

26 —, "Jim Steinman on 'Batman' and 'Dance of the Vampires'," *NY Newsday*, Nov. 21, 2002, http://www.freewebs.com/batman_themusical/home.htm, accessed Jul. 27, 2011

27 Hass, Nancy, "'Lestat': Bringing Anne Rice's World to the Stage With Elton John's Help," *The New York Times*, April 23, 2006, http://www.freewebs.com/batman_themusical/home.htm, accessed Jul. 27, 2011

28 *Ibid.*

29 —, "Why Bloody Johnny Depp is a Cut Above," *The Daily Mail*, Nov. 16, 2007, http://www.freewebs.com/batman_themusical/home.htm, accessed Jul. 27, 2011

30 —, "Batman: The Musical by Jim Steinman?" *ContactMusic.com*, July 18, 2006, http://www.freewebs.com/batman_themusical/home.htm, accessed Jul. 27, 2011

31 Croughton, Paul, "The Kapow Factor: Spider-Man Belly-Flopped in America; Will Batman Fly Here as a Stage Show? What Does It Take to Put On the £7.5m Action Spectacle?" *The London Times*, July 10, 2011

32 *Ibid.*

33 Wells, Dominic, "Batman Live at the MEN Arena, Manchester," *The London Times*, July 21, 2011

34 Harris, Dana, "There's New 'Batman' in WB's Belfry," *Daily Variety*, Aug. 22, 2000, p. 1

35 *Ibid.*

36 Holson, Laura M., "In This 'Superman' Story, the Executives Do the Fighting," *The New York Times*, Sept. 15, 2002, p. 3.1

37 *Ibid.*

38 *Ibid.*

39 *Ibid.*

40 Harris, Dana, "WB Sends 'Pi' Guy Into the Bat Cave," *Daily Variety*, Sept. 21, 2000, p. 1

41 *Ibid.*, p. 21

42 Miller, Frank, *Batman: Year One* screenplay, © Warner Bros.

43 Harris, Dana & Fleming, Michael, "WB Powers Up Super Team," *Daily Variety*, August 8, 2001, p. 5

44 Walker, Andrew Kevin and Akiva Goldsman, *Asylum (Batman vs. Superman)* Screenplay, Radiant Productions, June 21, 2002 Draft

45 Holson, Laura M., "In This 'Superman' Story, the Executives Do the Fighting," *The New York Times*, Sept. 15, 2002, p. 3.1

46 Harris, Dana, "WB Finds a Referee For 'Batman vs. Superman,'" *Daily Variety*, July 9, 2002, p. 1

47 *Ibid.*, p. 1, 12

48 *Ibid.*, p. 12

49 *Ibid.*

50 *Ibid.*, p. 1

51 Holson, Laura M., "In This 'Superman' Story, the Executives Do the Fighting," *The New York Times*, Sept. 15, 2002, p. 3.1

52 Harris, Dana, "Petersen Marches Into 'Troy,'" *Daily Variety*, Aug. 13, 2002, p. 5

53 Fleming, Michael, "Scribe Pair's Ready to Play 'Ender' Game," *Daily Variety*, Feb. 10, 2004, p. 46

54 —, "Mattel Wins Right to Market Warner Characters," *The New York Times*, Jul. 9, 2002, p. C.6

55 Bloom, David, "Caped Commerce: Warners Superheroes Suit Up for Toy Wars," *Weekly Variety*, July 15-21, 2002, p. 7

56 Russo, Tom, "Up, Up and Away: Classic Superheroes Soar to New Profits Heights for Licensors," *Daily Variety*, June 21, 2005, p. A1

57 Amour, Meredith, "Warner Reassessed: Report: Studio Undervalued at AOL TW Share Price," *Daily Variety*, June 16, 2003, p. 7

58 Brodesser, Claude, "Caught in Crime Web: Police Nab Studio Costume Theft Suspects," *Daily Variety*, Sept. 13, 2002, p. 5

59 Wood, Stuart, "EIFF 09: Darren Aronofsky On Robocop & Batman Year One," June 23, 2009, *CinemaBlend.com*, http://www.cinemablend.com/new/EIFF-09-Darren-Aronofsky-On-Robocop-Batman-Year-One-13673.html, accessed July 16, 2011

60 Fleming, Michael, "Coen Brothers Do the Soft Shoe for Musical," *Daily Variety*, July 23, 2002, p. 22

61 Fleming, Michael, "Clancy Leaves Par for Savoy 'Without Remorse,'" *Daily Variety*, June 17, 1993, p. 43

62 Fleming, Michael, "Another Life at WB for Catwoman and Burton?" *Daily Variety*, July 22, 1993, p. 1

63 Fleming, Michael, "WB: Judd Purr-fect as 'Cat,'" *Daily Variety*, Apr. 2, 2001, p. 1

64 Harris, Dana, "WB: Fewer Pix, More Punch," *Weekly Variety*, July 1-14, 2002, p. 9

65 Dunkley, Cathy, "Making a Feline Bee-Line," *Daily Variety*, Sept. 18, 2003, p. 1

66 Gold, Noe, "Female Star of the Year: Halle Berry," *Daily Variety*, March 25, 2004, p. A4

67 —, "Catwoman (2004) Trivia," *The Internet Movie Database*, http://www.imdb.com/title/tt0327554/trivia, accessed Aug. 6, 2011

68 Collier, Aldore D., "Halle Berry is 'Purrrfect', as She Cracks the Whip in Movie Catwoman," *Jet*, July 26, 2004, p. 56

69 —, "A Suitable Fit," *Catwoman Production Notes*, © 2004 Warner Bros. Inc.

70 Christmas, Joe, "Catwoman: Super Hero # 4 of 5," *HuntingForIslaFisher.com*, http://huntingforislafisher.blogspot.com/2009/11/catwoman-super-hero-4-of-5.html, accessed Aug. 6, 2011

71 —, "Catwoman (2004) Trivia," *The Internet Movie Database*, http://www.imdb.com/title/tt0327554/trivia, accessed Aug. 6, 2011

72 Christmas, Joe, "Catwoman: Super Hero # 4 of 5," *HuntingForIslaFisher.com*, http://hunting forislafisher.blogspot.com/2009/11/catwoman -super-hero-4-of-5.html, accessed Aug. 6, 2011

73 Gold, Noe, "Female Star of the Year: Halle Berry," *Daily Variety*, March 25, 2004, p. A4

74 Collier, Aldore D., "Halle Berry is 'Purrrfect', as She Cracks the Whip in Movie Catwoman," *Jet*, July 26, 2004, p. 56

75 Gold, Noe, "Female Star of the Year: Halle Berry," *Daily Variety*, March 25, 2004, p. A4

76 *Ibid.*

77 *Ibid.*

78 Townson, Don, "Canuck Arts Center Fights to Stay Open," *Daily Variety*, Jan. 20, 2004, p. 18

79 McNary, Dave, "Tollin-Robbins Tackles Tale of Texas Drug Bust," *Daily Variety*, Jan. 29, 2004, p. 20

80 —, "Catwoman (2004) Trivia," *The Internet Movie Database*, http://www.imdb.com/title/ tt0327554/trivia, accessed Aug. 6, 2011

81 —, "The Cat's Pajamas," *Catwoman Production Notes*, © 2004 Warner Bros. Inc.

82 Graser, Marc, "For Pros Behind 'Matrix,' 'LOTR,' What's Next," *Daily Variety*, Jan. 8, 2004, p. A11

83 —, "Catwalks and Cat Scans," *Catwoman Production Notes*, © 2004 Warner Bros. Inc.

84 Bart, Peter, "Studios Try to Cope With the New 'Geek Chic,'" *Daily Variety*, Aug. 2, 2004, p. 2

85 —, "Taking a Break During Filming," *Talk Talk.co.uk*, http://www.talktalk.co.uk/entertain- ment/film/interviews/halle_berry2/2, accessed Aug. 6, 2011

86 DiOrio, Carl, "Halle of Fame for Berry," *Daily Variety*, March 5, 2004, p. 5

87 Goldsmith, Jill, "Batman Has His Eye On You: Warner Bros., Mattel Life VEIL on New Level of Interactivity," *Daily Variety*, June 14, 2004, p. 6

88 —, "Catwoman (2004) Trivia," *The Internet Movie Database*, http://www.imdb.com/title/ tt0327554/trivia, accessed Aug. 6, 2011

89 Collier, Aldore D., "Halle Berry is 'Purrrfect', as She Cracks the Whip in Movie Catwoman," *Jet*, July 26, 2004, p. 56

90 —, "Catwoman (2004) Trivia," *The Internet Movie Database*, http://www.imdb.com/title/ tt0327554/trivia, accessed Aug. 6, 2011

91 Higgins, Bill, "Purr-fectly Festive Fete," *Daily Variety*, July 22, 2004, p. 20

92 Interview with Richard Schenkman, conducted Aug. 6, 2011.

93 Rooney, David, "Film Review: Catwoman," *Daily Variety*, July 23, 2004, p. 10

94 Travers, Peter, "Catwoman," *Rolling Stone*, July 22, 2004

95 Bart, Peter, "Sleepers and Weepers: A Sum- mer's Tale," *Daily Variety*, July 26, 2004, p. 2

96 Groves, Don, "Night's Fright Ignites: Globe in Gear With 'Robot,'" *Daily Variety*, Aug. 2, 2004, p. 10

97 —, "Catwoman," *Box Office Mojo*, http://box- officemojo.com/movies/?id=catwoman.htm, accessed Aug. 6, 2011

98 Interview with Richard Schenkman, conducted Aug. 6, 2011.

99 —, "Catwoman (2004) Trivia," *The Internet Movie Database*, http://www.imdb.com/title/ tt0327554/trivia, accessed Aug. 6, 2011

100 Carroll, Larry, "Halle Berry Slams 'Catwoman' at Razzie Awards," MTV.com, http://www. mtv.com/news/articles/1497569/halle-berry- slams-catwoman-at-razzie-awards.jhtml, Feb. 28, 2005, accessed Aug. 6, 2011

101 Byrne, Craig, "Bruce Wayne—The Series That Never Was: What Happened?," *KryptonSite.com*, http://www.kryptonsite.com/brucewayne/ timeline.htm, 2005, accessed Aug. 6, 2011

102 *Ibid.*

103 *Ibid.*

104 *Ibid.*

105 Gregg, Melissa & Adalian, Josef, "NBC Votes for Brolin; Snow Lands in 'Pie,'" *Daily Variety*, Feb. 14, 2002, p. 34

106 *Ibid.*

107 *Ibid.*

108 Kissell, Rick, "'Birds' Fly High on WB," *Daily Variety*, Oct. 11, 2002, p. 4

109 Fries, Laura, "Television Review: Birds of Prey," *Daily Variety*, Oct. 8, 2002, p. 7

110 James, Caryn, "Superheroines vs. Crime in the Big City," *The New York Times*, Oct. 9, 2002, p. E.5

111 Kissell, Rick, "NBC, CBS Back Atop Nielsens," *Daily Variety*, Nov. 6, 2002, p. 26

112 Adalian, Josef and Michael Schneider, "'Birds' Down at WB, Fox's 'Firefly' Flies," *Daily Variety*, Nov. 19, 2002, p. 5

113 Simone, Gail, "Five Wonder Questions With Laeta Kalogridis," *Comic Book Resources Forum*, http://forums.comicbookresources.com/show thread.php?t=285311, accessed Aug. 6, 2011

114 Schneider, Michael, "CW's 'Graysons' Takes Flier on Robin," *Variety*, Sept. 30, 2008, http://www.variety.com/article/VR11179931 58?refCatId=14, accessed Aug. 10, 2011

115 *Ibid.*

116 Byrne, Craig, "The CW Scraps Plans for 'The Graysons,'" *GothamSite.com*, http://www.goth- amsite.com/,Nov. 6, 2008, accessed Aug. 10, 2011

117 Schneider, Michael, "'Graysons' Blackout:CW Tosses Plans for Boy Wonder Skein," *Daily Variety*, Nov. 7, 2008, p. 5

Chapter Eleven:
BATMAN BEGINS

"We tried to tell an enormous story, and we tried
to tell it on the grandest possible scale because that's
what Batman demands and what Batman deserves."

- Christopher Nolan[1]

BONDING BATMAN

On September 11, 2001, Americans were awakened to a scene so outlandish it could only have come from a comic book or a big-budget Hollywood movie—jets smashing into New York's World Trade Center, bringing the twin towers crashing down. But this wasn't a fantasy, and as the events of the day played out, there were no costumed heroes coming to the rescue, only flesh-and-blood heroes—firemen, policemen, EMTs. It was a day that changed America and the world, and one that had, at least temporarily, an effect on Hollywood, with films that featured lots of action and destruction of property being put on the back burner. When the superheroes returned, they returned darker, angrier, more cynical, more defensive, reflections of a world whose innocence was lost in the rubble of Ground Zero.

After Lorenzo di Bonaventura exited Warner Bros., Jeff Robinov was promoted to president of production. Unlike di Bonaventura, who often clashed with Warner Bros. president Alan Horn, Robinov shared Horn's sensibilities. Both men were anxious to revive the *Batman* franchise, and both sensed they needed to do something dramatic, totally different from the style of *Batman & Robin*. They just weren't sure what that would be, until they began to think about the idea of taking Batman back to his roots and doing an origin story. It was an approach that had proved successful for the TV series *Smallville*, which redefined Superman for a new audience of teenagers and young adults. And perhaps they were influenced in their decision by Tollin/Robbins Productions' idea of doing a Bruce Wayne TV series that would focus on the young Wayne's early years, before he became Batman.

As it happened, someone else had been thinking along those lines. Christopher Nolan, a young director who had scored critical successes with his low budget films *Following* (1998) and *Memento* (2002), had just directed a thriller for Warner Bros. called *Insomnia* (2002). Aware of the studio's troubles re-launching Batman, he began to think about how he might do it.

"First and foremost I know *Batman* from the TV show, from when I was four or five years old," said Nolan. "At that age, you don't realize how tongue-in-cheek and camp it all is. You take it seriously—and I loved the character. It says quite a lot about the elemental nature of the character that it can reach you through different interpretations, like the TV show—even though it was so kitsch and silly in a way. There's still something about that character, something about who he is and what he does, that comes through. It's part of everybody's upbringing—I was watching it ten years after it had gone off air."[2]

The second-born son of Brendan and Christine Nolan came into the world in London on July 30, 1970. Though his father, who worked in advertising, was British, Christopher and his brothers spent a great deal of their childhood in Chicago, home of their mother. Christopher grew up with a brother, Matthew, who was two years older, and another brother, Jonathan—known as Jonah—who was five years younger. The boys were privately educated and held dual American and British citizenships. Christopher was stiff and formal, unlike his older brother Matt, who was outgoing and charismatic and, like their father, a gifted storyteller, able to spin grand tales out of thin air, a talent that appeared not to have rubbed off not on Christopher. However, when the boys were very young, Brendan gave them an 8mm film camera, and 8-year-old Christopher found a means to express himself. He, his brothers and their friends began making little films together.[3] When he couldn't find actors, Christopher would use his *Star Wars* action figures.[4] As they grew older, Matt and Chris drifted apart; when Chris began to make a reputation for himself in Hollywood, it was his younger brother Jonah who became his collaborator rather than his older brother Matthew.[5]

During the 1980s, when Nolan entered his teens, he read a couple of graphic novels that left an indelible impression: Frank Miller's *The Dark Knight Returns* and *Batman: Year One*. "[It was] like the way you felt about the character when you were five years old," said Nolan. "Frank Miller was doing it for grown-ups, really. That was quite exciting, it put you back into that childlike appreciation of the magic of the character."[6]

Nolan was also a fan of the hugely popular James Bond films, and he felt there was a 007 influence in the *Batman* comics of his early youth. Those comics, edited by Denny O'Neil and illustrated by Neal Adams, said Nolan, "were influenced by the Roger Moore James Bond films of the time. It was really that period which excited me, because there was a tone of heightened reality."[7] And after Nolan saw Richard Donner's 1978 film *Superman*, he wondered why the other high-profile character of DC Comics didn't immediately follow the Man of Steel into the multiplexes. "I felt like there was a version of *Batman* that never got made in 1979—ten years before [Burton's film]. When Dick Donner made *Superman* in 1978, it seems odd that they didn't do *Batman* in that same way—with that same epic sensibility."[8]

Now, more than two decades later, Nolan had established himself as a young filmmaker with a spare, tension-charged style and a mastery of storytelling. He made his first film, 1998's *Following*, by scrounging up pieces of 16mm film stock and filming during a year's worth of weekends. The film was picked up for distribution and won the director enough attention that he was given a proper budget of $5 million for his next film, *Memento*. When that film became a critical success, he received his first studio assignment, with Warner Bros. entrusting him with $50 million to make *Insomnia* (2002), starring Al Pacino, Hilary Swank and Robin Williams.[9]

After finishing *Insomnia*, he began work on a script about reclusive billionaire Howard Hughes. But he really wanted to do the *Batman* film he felt should have been done in 1979, a film that would remake Batman in the 007 mold, with globe-hopping adventures, megalomaniacal villains, and gadgets dispensed by a wise Merlin figure.[10]

A meeting was arranged at Warner Bros., where president of production Jeff Robinov was looking for a Batman project to replace the now aborted *Batman: Year*

One, Batman Beyond and *Batman vs. Superman* films. "I've always been a fan of Batman," said Robinov. "I love the character, and Batman was always a piece of a puzzle that Alan Horn wanted solved. He always saw Batman as a very valuable property to the studio both in terms of liking the character and wanting the character out there."[11]

Nolan pitched the studio his take on the Caped Crusader. The director had no intention of making a film as outrageous as those of Tim Burton and Joel Schumacher, saying, "The world of Batman is that of grounded reality. Ours will be a recognizable, contemporary reality against which an extraordinary heroic figure arises."[12]

The studio liked Nolan's take on the character, and encouraged him to get started on a script. "I'd gone to the studio and said what I wanted to do with the film and the basic idea of the story, which was drawn from what I knew of the origin stories from the comics—and I was certainly no expert," said Nolan. "So I had the basic idea of dealing with the origin story and the seven years where Bruce goes around the world. I was looking for a writer to do a first draft, one who was very knowledgeable about comics, more than I was. I felt that the first draft needed to set us on the right track, in terms of the myth of Batman, the mythic quality and the iconography, and with all of the things we needed in there."[13]

The studio suggested that Nolan meet David Goyer, a former DC Comics staff writer who also scripted the successful *Blade* films, based on a Marvel Comics vampire character, for New Line Cinema. "I remember the very first discussion I had with Chris," said Goyer. "Very quickly over the course of 10-15 minutes we decided we had to tell an origin story. And I felt very strongly that we should use characters that hadn't been depicted in the films before." Goyer recommended using Ra's Al Ghul and the Scarecrow as the villains. "I just happen to think Ra's Al Ghul is unique as a *Batman* villain because his goals, you know, although they are certainly perverted somewhat, he's more realistic as a character. And the Scarecrow is unique because it allowed the opportunity, I think, to depict a villain that was truly scary and frightening. And because Chris and I wanted to tell a story about fear and overcoming your fear, it just seemed like a no-brainer."[14]

The Scarecrow, a/k/a Professor Jonathan Crane, was first introduced in *World's Finest Comics* # 3 in the Fall of 1941. From the outset, he was a character obsessed with uncovering the fears of his enemies and using those fears to destroy them. After one other comic book appearance in 1943, the character was resurrected in *The Brave and the Bold* # 197 in April 1983. In that story, he developed a hallucinogenic gas to instill fear in his victims. Ra's al Ghul was introduced in *Batman* #232 in June 1971. A terrorist who seeks to keep the earth in an ecological balance that, to his mind, means eradicating most of humanity, he has lived for several centuries thanks to his ability to rejuvenate himself in the Lazarus pits, reservoirs that can restore life to the dying.

"David Goyer had some great initial thoughts on who the villain would be, how the villain could relate to the origin story—so I got very excited about working with him," said Nolan.[15] "Ra's al Ghul was not a villain I was familiar with. As soon as he mentioned him, I went back and researched him and read a lot of the 1970s comics he appears in...Ra's al Ghul has a lot of similarities/affinities with the Bond villains of the 1970s, such as Hugo Drax from *Moonraker.*"[16]

Nolan was keenly aware that in previous *Batman* films, the villains were the real stars. He didn't want to repeat that with his film. "You're looking for a Bond villain in a sense because you're looking for a villain who is colorful and interesting, and has a degree of threat to him that relates to the real world," said Nolan. "So you're looking for a villain who can be threatening but doesn't overshadow the hero. And I think the best of the Bond movies have done that really well. They've given you these memorable villains, but Bond is always the center of the movie. That's never been in dispute."[17]

Goyer agreed with Nolan's take on Batman, and was glad to be charting a new course for the hero. "As the *Batman* films progressed, they became increasingly more cartoonish and more like the campy TV show," said Goyer. "We think the audience is tired of that, and it's at odds with the way Batman is depicted in the comic books over the last decade. Batman is a classic figure whose story is wrapped in tragedy."[18]

Goyer had as much respect for Nolan as the director did for him. "It's all filtered through Chris's vision and he is a very naturalistic director and that was what was very exciting to me," said Goyer. "Frankly, I don't know that I—as much as I love Batman—I don't know that I would have been interested in writing it for anyone else. I think Chris is such a great filmmaker, and that was the main appeal to me, that he was going to be telling the story in a way that it seems like that's the way the story always should have been told, but for some reason no one had ever approached Batman that way. It seemed like a no-brainer to me. But the fact that Chris was going to do it and that Warner Bros. was actually going to let him do it, it was an amazing experience."[19]

Unfortunately, it was an experience that would be short-lived for Goyer, who had just been given the opportunity to move up from screenwriter to director. "He was about to direct *Blade: Trinity*, so he had a very small window of time," said Nolan.[20] In the early days of the collaboration, Nolan and Goyer met with representatives of DC Comics, including DC president and publisher Paul Levitz. "Before they sat down with us, they had already done a tremendous amount of homework," said Levitz, who described working with Goyer and Nolan "a delight," adding, "We haven't been dealing with questions like, 'Is it Bruce Wayne or could it be Bob Wayne instead?' We started on the same emotional and intellectual level. We all want to make a movie that appeals to the most intense Batman fan as well as the person who's never seen a *Batman* movie or TV show before."[21]

DC Comics provided Nolan and Goyer with a set of guidelines that the comic book publishers felt should appear in every Batman story. Goyer referred to it as "the 10 Commandments."[22] "For us, it's not about what you have to do but about what you can't deny," said Levitz, who explained that DC had what it called a circle of "three rings" that made up Batman's universe.[23]

The first was the "aspirational experience," which consisted of how people reacted emotionally to Bruce Wayne, his traumatic childhood involving the death of his parents and how that led him to use his riches to fight crime. "It's all about making you feel that if you went through something traumatic, you'd rise to the challenge in the same way," said Levitz.[24]

For the second ring, Levitz said, "You go to a *Batman* movie expecting certain moments. You expect to see the Batmobile, the Batcave, the Bat Signal, his utility belt, Batman swinging across Gotham City. That's your wow." There was also the expectation of seeing something new, something that wasn't in the previous *Batman* stories. "There's always the question of how do you give the audience something they haven't seen before," said Levitz.[25]

The third ring was concerned with the creative interpretation that the director, writers and actors brought to the film. "They each want to bring things that are unique, but they can't fight the other rings of the circle," said Levitz. "It would be unique to have Batman tripping over himself, but that wouldn't be good."[26]

Despite their concerns, DC remained mostly hands-off during the making of the film. "When you're making a great movie, you need a great director who has a vision," said Levitz. "You can't stand behind a director's shoulders with correctional glasses. Our job is to help, whether it's to provide stories or to serve as a sounding board to talk about the creative issues."[27]

Levitz said that although DC was an adviser, they did not have script approval. "We're all part of the same company and trying to achieve the same goal: a wonderful *Batman* film that will delight old fans and make new fans. So there's no complicated contractual language ruling the creative process between us. We have the right to be consulted, the right to warn. We're happy to be part of the part of the process. It's just old-fashioned teamwork."[28]

In telling an origin story, Goyer said, "It was interesting when we were meeting with DC and Paul Levitz, when we were proposing to fill in some of these gaps, I was very curious as to how they were going to react. But they embraced everything that we were proposing because it seemed to fit in with everything that had been set before. It was exciting to do an origin story because we weren't beholden to any of the other films or to the TV series. In comic book terms, it was sort of a reboot in a way. The notion was that after our film finished, we could then go off and if Chris or Warner Bros. wanted to play with subsequent films, that they could sort of reintroduce the pantheon of villains and whatnot."[29]

In interviews, Nolan kept saying that he and Goyer were telling a story that had not previously been revealed. "There is no definitive account in the comics of the origin story," said Nolan. "What you get are these flashbacks and glimpses. Over the period of the history of the comics there have been some quite interesting things that have arisen. The studio sent me a *Batman* story early on called 'The Man Who Falls.' It's a DC Comics story from the 1970s. It's not even a whole comic. I think it appeared in an anthology. It was a very good jumping-off point. It suggested the idea of traveling around the world, meeting criminals and flirting with the criminal life and learning about them that way. Then, in the forest, he goes to a martial arts teacher. It had a great feel to it. It's very short, only a few pages. That was very important. So there are those kinds of influences. Then, looking at the middle act of *Batman Begins*, it draws a lot from *Batman: Year One*, with Bruce Wayne becoming Batman. But then, with all of the stuff in between, what we would call 'mileposts,' we were free to figure out what we wanted to do."[30]

Novelist James Dawson, author of *Wasted Talents*, disputed Nolan's claim to be telling "a story that hadn't been told before" in a letter to *The Los Angeles Times* published during the production of *Batman Begins*. Dawson pointed out that Batman's past was not a complete mystery. In fact, in 1989, Sam Hamm—one of the co-writers of Tim Burton's *Batman* movie—wrote a three-issue storyline called "Blind Justice" that appeared in *Detective Comics* issues 598-600. In the story, the government accuses Bruce Wayne of being a traitor, and asks him to account for his activities during the years he spent overseas. Wayne explains that he trained with a martial-arts master named Chu Chin Li before going to Korea, Thailand and the Philippines and training with a Yakuza named Tsunetomo. Afterwards, he went to Paris and spent six weeks as an apprentice detective to Henri Ducard, a troubleshooter affiliated with Interpol. We also learn in the story that Wayne had wanted to be a policeman at one point, and majored in criminology. Dawson questioned how no one at Time-Warner was aware of this backstory, since the company owned DC Comics.[31]

Aside from comic book influences, Nolan and Goyer found templates for Bruce Wayne's character in a couple of real-life millionaires. Having just been working on a script about eccentric industrialist Howard Hughes, Nolan infused some of Hughes's character into Bruce Wayne. "The thing about Howard Hughes as a young man that Bruce Wayne recalls is that Hughes was orphaned as a young man and given the keys to the kingdom and billions of dollars to play with," said Nolan. "Essentially, he was given complete freedom to do whatever he wanted to do, in practical terms. For me it was fascinating to see where that would lead. It's something we all think we want, but when you look at a story like Hughes's or, in fictional terms, Bruce Wayne's, you wouldn't want to be in their shoes.[32]

Besides Hughes, Nolan also saw a parallel between Bruce Wayne and America's 26th president, Theodore Roosevelt. Like Roosevelt, Bruce Wayne came from a wealthy, urban family active in philanthropy. Both had strong fathers whom they admired. Both suffered tragic losses; Roosevelt lost both his wife and mother on the same day. Both went into a period of self-exile; whereas Bruce Wayne went to foreign lands and trained in martial arts, Roosevelt lived in the North Dakota badlands for a few years. Both were inspired by grief to do good; Roosevelt fought the spoils system as a member of the United States Civil Service Commission and served as commissioner of the New York City Police which he then sought to reform.[33]

Most of all, Nolan wanted to present a more realistic take on Bruce Wayne's story than had ever been presented before. His would not be a movie filmed on stylized sets lit with an abundance of neon. "I wanted to treat it with a degree of gravity and with a sense of epic scope, but set in a world that is firmly grounded in reality," said Nolan.[34] While working on the script, rather than seeking inspiration from the previous *Batman* films, Nolan and Goyer kept returning to epics like *Lawrence of Arabia, The Man Who Would Be King, Blade Runner* and, most tellingly, the 1969 James Bond film *On Her Majesty's Secret Service*.[35]

The first 007 film to be made with an actor other than Sean Connery, *On Her Majesty's Secret Service* starred George Lazenby as James Bond in a film that set out to redefine the 007 character. After several films in which the gadgets had overtaken the storytelling, director Peter Hunt and scriptwriter Richard Maibaum decided to, in effect, start over. The result was a Bond film much more rooted in reality, with a more vulnerable Bond—by the end of the film, he's fallen in love and married, but his wife is tragically murdered by the villain, Ernst Stavro Blofeld. Although the film was a commercial disappointment, its reputation grew over the years, with die-hard 007 fans considering it one of the very best of the series. Now, Nolan and Goyer wanted to reestablish Batman in the same way that Hunt and Maibaum reestablished James Bond.

"One of Chris' mantras when we were working on the script was it has to be real, it has to be real," said Goyer.[36] "We applied that philosophy to every aspect of the story, even down to the most minute details—Why are the bat ears so tall? Why does the Batmobile look the way it does? We developed a logical explanation for everything that Bruce Wayne does and for every device he acquires in the film."[37]

"For me," said Nolan, "the most exciting aspect of telling this story is getting inside Bruce Wayne's head and going on that journey with him, so that we experience the process of becoming Batman through his eyes."[38]

"I remember Chris and I batting ideas around thinking there's no way they're going to let us do this," said Goyer. "Not that we were breaking any great rules, but it just seemed like we were doing the sort of story that I certainly had always wanted to see. And DC and Warner Bros. were great. They just embraced it. It's actually the best experience I've ever had working with a studio because they truly trusted us and just said, 'You guys know what you're doing. We're going to let you run with it.'"[39]

"We met for a couple of months and talked through the story and he came up with a story outline based on us thrashing around ideas and me saying what I wanted in the film," said Nolan. "Then, he—within seven or eight weeks—provided a first draft, gave that to me and then had to go off and do his thing. So I took it from that point and did another eight drafts."[40]

Nolan and Goyer decided on a title before handing the script in to the studio. "Internally with Warner Bros., we knew that that would kind of set the tone," said Goyer. "We were talking about how it would be promoted initially and we didn't want to have the same title as any of the previous films. I came up with *Batman Beginning*. And then Chris just said, 'Let's just say *Begins* because then when it's announced you can say I'm blah blah blah of *Batman Begins*.' I was like, 'Genius.' So from that point on, it was always that."[41]

Since Nolan was involved with the script from the very beginning, the initial script drafted by David Goyer and Nolan varies very little from the final film. In this seminal script, Rachel Dawes is named Rachel Dodson. The beginning scenes are almost exactly like the eventual film, except that after Bruce Wayne saves Ducard's life and leaves him with an old Sherpa, we get a scene of Wayne entering a smoky climber's bar in Bhutan filled with Sherpas and climbers. When he enters, filthy and ragged, all conversation stops, and everyone stares at him. He goes to the bar and uses the phone to dial Alfred, who answers with "Master Wayne. It's been some time." Bruce says he needs a ride, and that he thinks he's in Bhutan, without money or a passport. Alfred says, "I believe there's an airstrip at Khatmandu long enough for a G5. Make your way there, I'll have the jet down in fifteen hours." Bruce then asks Alfred to bring some painkillers.

After returning home, Bruce sees a bat flittering around the ceiling of the Wayne Mansion library. Alfred tells him they nest somewhere on the grounds. Later, Bruce arrives at Wayne Industries just as Earle is talking to Judge Phelan, convincing him that Bruce Wayne should be declared legally dead. This was dropped in the final film. In this early draft, Phelan was a public official in Falcone's control who appears in a few different scenes.

Phelan is mentioned in the very next scene of the script, in which we see Rachel hurrying down a marble staircase at the D.A.'s office to catch Finch. She tries to convince him that they should take the Falcone case to Harvey Dent. Finch tells her that Falcone has Judge Phelan bought and paid for. They continue their conversation out into the parking lot, where Bruce Wayne, sitting in the back of a Rolls Royce chauffeured by Alfred, watches her. When Alfred asks if he should park, Wayne says, "No, let's go," and Alfred registers disappointment. The scene then cuts to Wayne meeting Lucius Fox.

One of the plot threads given more prominence in the early script draft is Earle's machinations to drive Bruce Wayne out of his company. After Bruce, as Batman, has his first meeting with Gordon, the scene shifts to the Wayne Industries boardroom, where Earle and another board member have discovered that Bruce Wayne can't take control of the company until his 30th birthday, which is three months away. To prevent letting the "clown prince" take control of the company, Earle and the board member decide to have an initial public offering and take the company public, so that Bruce will be just another board member. Earle then notices his assistant and the receptionist gone. He finds them on the rooftop, where Bruce helps them improve their golf swings by knocking balls into the Gotham River. He tells Earle that he's going to have a "huge blowout" on his birthday and he expects everyone to be there.

In the next scene, Bruce is outside Falcone's nightclub, disguised as a homeless person. He surreptitiously takes a photo of Judge Phelan leaving the club with a young woman. He will later give this to Rachel as a way of blackmailing Phelan and keeping him in line.

Unlike the film, in which Dr. Crane is introduced early on, in the first script draft, he doesn't show up until a third of the way through. When Flass arrives at the dockside warehouse, he goes inside to find Falcone talking to Crane, who complains that they rendered his last shipment of drugs useless by cutting it with baby powder.

A recurring element in the film—the kid who witnesses Batman prowling outside a building, and is later helped by Rachel when the Narrows is under the influence of Crane's drug, is absent from the early draft. Also, in the early script, Earle fires Fox during Bruce Wayne's birthday party at Wayne Manor, not in Fox's underground warehouse.

The last major difference in the original script occurs in the climax. Instead of Gordon taking control of the Batmobile and blowing the tracks out from under the train, the script has Gordon driving an unmarked police car throughout the ending. The train jumps off the track and derails after Batman causes it to speed up.

Overall, one can see that 90 percent of the finished film is present in the draft script, written jointly by Goyer and Nolan. The changes made by Nolan after Goyer left the project helped to streamline sections of the story and made Gordon more of an integral player in the climactic scenes. But for both scriptwriters, the thing they most wanted to achieve with the script was to make Bruce Wayne a fully-rounded character, and not just that dull guy who takes up screen time while the audience is waiting to get to the next scene of Batman kicking ass. "If we're successful, the thing that will be talked about a lot and on what we worked on the hardest is that the audience will really care about Bruce Wayne and not just Batman," said Goyer. "It doesn't matter how much you spend on special effects—if it feels hollow, no one gives a damn."[42]

Even as he was working with Goyer on the script, Nolan began to assemble his production team. His wife, Emma Thomas, who produced Nolan's *Following* and was an associate producer on *Memento*, was on board from the beginning. Thomas and Nolan met when they both attended University College London; they were wed in 1997. Before becoming a producer, she worked as a script supervisor and as an assistant to director Stephen Frears on his film *High Fidelity* (2000).

Nolan also immediately hired a production designer, Nathan Crowley, with whom he had developed a good rapport while the two were working on their previous collaboration, *Insomnia*. While Nolan and Goyer worked on the script at Nolan's house in Los Angeles, Crowley began designing models of the Tumbler, which would become the new Batmobile, in Nolan's garage.[43] "I wanted to focus on the design of the new Batmobile during the scriptwriting stage because I felt that everything we were trying to do that defines our approach to telling this story, our emphasis on grounding the characters and the film in reality, would be evident in the look and feel of that vehicle," said Nolan.[44] Crowley's idea was to create a tank-like vehicle that was "a cross between a Hummer and a Lamborghini. We wanted a mid-engine sports tank, so I went to a model shop, got models of the two cars and then basically crushed them together."[45]

"I've never been on a project where I've gotten to do conceptual work so early on," said Crowley. "Chris would take a break from writing and come into the garage, where I'd be with my car concepts, covered in glue. We made about five or six versions of the Batmobile over a period of about eight weeks."[46]

"We were looking to present Batman as a very functional figure, somebody very concerned with utility, and so we wanted to create a vehicle that would actually perform in ways that are useful to the character," said Nolan.[47] The director was anxious to show Crowley's Batmobile concept to the studio, saying "I felt that would immediately explain to everybody the differences between approaches in the past and what we were doing."[48]

Instead of the curvilinear lines of past Batmobiles, Crowley seemed to take inspiration from the oversized tank used by Batman in Frank Miller's *The Dark Knight Returns*. "We figured the thing about Batman is he doesn't have any superpowers," said Crowley. "His only superpower is money. That gave us the opportunity to play realism as the logic to everything we did."[49]

Emma Thomas joked, "I think that from now on, any film that we make, we'll start in the garage. The synergy of having Chris, David and Nathan working simultaneously in the same creative space worked amazingly well and it advanced our development and production process considerably."[50]

A CHRISTIAN APPROACH

As the script took shape, Nolan began thinking about who would best embody his take on Bruce Wayne and Batman. Around the same time, a young actor named Christian Bale heard about the new Batman project in development. "Initially, I heard there was going to be a much lower-budget Batman," said Bale, "where they were going to go very dark with it, and I started calling my agents and asking, 'Can you find out about this?' And then I heard they were going with a big Batman, and I thought, 'Oh, that's probably not the one I would be interested in.' But hearing that Chris [Nolan] was helming it altered everything. I met with Chris, spoke with him and said to myself, 'Yeah, this is definitely the right one to do!'"[51]

Bale first met with Nolan and Emma Thomas in April 2003, just as he was about to begin shooting *The Machinist*, a film for which he was rapidly losing weight in order to play a delusional skin-and-bones insomniac; he'd already lost about 60 pounds. "I came to the meeting late," said Thomas, "and I didn't even recognize Christian. At that point, he probably weighed about 140 pounds—and still had further to go. We spoke with him, and clearly he's a special talent who takes things very seriously."[52] Bale was concerned about his gaunt appearance, so skin-and-bones that his spine was visible through his shirt, but Nolan took it in stride. "I remember Christian was worried because he was meeting to play a superhero," said Nolan. "But I came away from it feeling I'd never seen such focus and dedication from an actor."[53]

There were many actors who were interested in playing Batman, but Bale was the first one who met with Nolan. "We'd barely started writing the script when I met him," said Nolan. "I called the studio right away and said, 'You really should take a look at this guy because I think he's a very strong contender.' So I got in there early. It was very clear to me that he fitted the role."[54] Nonetheless, Nolan knew it would take some work to convince the studio that this was their new Batman. Nolan told Bale he'd have to make a screen test. Bale understood. "How the hell could I convince anybody, given the shape I was in?" he said.[55]

Thomas and Nolan expected to begin shooting in March of 2004. To give them adequate time for pre-production, they planned to start screen-testing actors in September 2003. Their biggest concern, said Thomas, was "How on earth were we going to put this skinny guy in the suit?"[56] As September approached, Thomas kept checking in with Bale's agent. She recalled, "I talked to his agent about it and asked him, 'How big is he?' 'He's tiny, but I'm sending him pizzas every day!'" Luckily, by September, Bale was back to looking like his old self.[57]

Nonetheless, during the first week of September, Nolan screen tested several actors for the role besides Bale, including Jake Gyllenhaal, Joshua Jackson, Cillian Murphy, and Eion Bailey.[58] Murphy recalled that the studio had a few different Batsuits for the actors. "I think if you ask any male if he wants to get into the real suit, I mean, that was a dream come true obviously." His, he believed, was "a Val Kilmer suit. I had to adjust it. It was very hot."[59]

Nolan felt nearly all of the actors he tested would make credible Batmen. "Other actors we would look at, it would be a question of different interpretations," said Nolan. "That is the very interesting thing about casting. It takes the character in a very different way if you cast it in a particular way. With Bruce Wayne, there are a lot of different ways he could've been played. But to me Christian was the way we were writing the character.[60]

On September 12, 2003, Cathy Dunkley and Jonathan Bing of *Daily Variety* made the announcement: Christian Bale had been chosen to play Batman. At that point, the film was untitled, and although *Variety* reported that Bale was only signed for the one picture,[61] the actor himself later said that he had signed for three.[62] Warner Bros. president of production Jeff Robinov proclaimed, "Now that we've found the best person to play Batman, we are really looking forward to moving ahead with the rest of our casting and are excited about the exceptional group we are assembling."[63]

Nolan was also happy to have gotten his first choice for Batman. "Christian Bale was the ideal choice to play a young Bruce Wayne, particularly a Bruce Wayne still struggling very much with the demons that drive him to become Batman. He is a very complex character who exists on the razor's edge between good and bad. Christian embodies that sense of danger and ambiguity that can be channeled into something very positive and very powerful. He has that kind of intensity, that fire burning inside. You look into his eyes and you believe that this man would go to those extremes."[64]

Although Bale, who was born in Wales on January 30, 1974, was just four years younger than Nolan, he had been in show business much longer. His mother, Jenny James, had once been a circus performer, and his father, a former RAF pilot and businessman named David Bale, was a stunt double for John Wayne on the 1962 film *Hatari!*[65] When Bale was just two years old, his family—including two older sisters, Sharon and Louise, and a half-sister, Erin, from his father's first marriage— left Wales. Bale spent his childhood moving about from Portugal to America to the English coastal resort town of Bournemouth.[66] His parents eventually divorced; in September 2000, his father married famed feminist Gloria Steinem.[67]

Bale began his acting career as a child, appearing with comedian Rowan Atkinson in the London stage show *The Nerd* in 1984. A couple of years later, he was chosen—over 4,000 other hopefuls—for the starring role in Steven Spielberg's World War II drama *Empire of the Sun* (1987). But movie stardom proved to be a mixed blessing at his English school. "Girls were all over me," said Bale. "Boys just wanted to fight me." His mother recalled, "The bullying was quite bad and it made him very sad. It really put him off the film and stardom thing. At the time he did not want to do any more acting."[68]

As he matured, he built up an impressive film résumé, with roles in Kenneth Branagh's adaptation of Shakespeare's *Henry V* (1989), the period musical *Newsies* (1992), and the historical drama *Swing Kids* (1993). While making *Little Women* (1994), he met and fell in love with Sandra "Sibi" Blazic, who was the assistant to the film's star, Winona Ryder. Bale and Blazic married the day before Bale's 26th birthday.[69] *Little Women* made Bale a heartthrob after an admirer in Canada began a fan website that spawned an army of "Baleheads."[70] As he entered his late 20s, Bale became known for playing dark, psychologically intense characters in films such as *Velvet Goldmine* (1998) and the film adaptation of Bret Easton Ellis' controversial novel *American Psycho* (2000), for which he won critical plaudits as serial killer Patrick Bateman.[71]

Interestingly, two years before Bale was cast as Batman, his older sister Louise Bale was the associate producer of a short fan-produced film called *The Death of Batman* (2003), an unrelentingly grim exercise in which Batman is captured by a thief and then drugged, shackled, beaten, raped and tortured to death. Written and directed by Donald Lawrence Flaherty and starring Christopher Stapleton as Batman, the film ends with the thief, an innocent man who had been wrongly sent to jail because of Batman's actions, committing suicide. Batman, wracked with guilt and now an addict himself after being injected with daily doses of heroin, takes the heroin syringe and overdoses; his badly beaten body is found floating in the Gotham River. Besides acting as associate producer, Louise Bale also played Mrs. Wayne, Bruce Wayne's mother, in a flashback showing young Bruce kneeling beside the body of his dead parents.

The announcement of Christian Bale's casting pleased the most vocal Batfanatics, the opinion-influencers who posted on websites such as *Superherohype. com* and *Joblo.com*.[72] "It's an awesome responsibility, because the fan base for Batman is extraordinary, and there's a lot of emotional investment in the character," said Nolan.[73] Warners hoped to avoid any negative buzz that might spread before the film was even released. But despite the secrecy surrounding the new film, daily updates and speculation about the plot, characters and production designs turned up on websites such as *Ain't It Cool News, Batman on Film, Dark Horizons, Chud* and *Superhero Hype*.[74]

Warner Bros. was now fully committed to the film. Their confidence in Nolan was evident in the astronomical budget they gave him: $180 million. "It's almost impossible to reinvent *Batman*," said Warner Bros. president of production Jeff Robinov. "Chris is reintroducing Batman, and it feels smart and cool and fresh. That's no disrespect to the other movies, but it's really Chris' vision of Batman, and that's what we're supporting."[75]

With generous financing behind him, Nolan felt free to pursue a dream cast for the film. "We looked back to the incredible cast of Richard Donner's 1978 film *Superman*," said Nolan. "He had Marlon Brando, Gene Hackman, Ned Beatty and so many other great actors in supporting roles. We cast our film in a similar fashion, with an ensemble of wonderful actors who bring a depth and complexity to the characters that make Bruce Wayne's world all the more real."[76]

By the end of November, Michael Caine was in negotiations to play Alfred the butler.[77] "We needed an actor who could bring humor and heart to the role, as well as a measure of gravitas," said Emma Thomas. "There was only one man for the job."[78] An icon of British cinema, Caine had gone from leading man parts in the 1960s to character roles later in his career. "I've always regarded myself as a movie actor as opposed to a movie star," said Caine. "When an actor gets a screenplay, he asks, 'How can I change myself to suit the script?' When a movie star gets a screenplay, they ask, 'How can I change the script to suit me?'"[79]

Caine was familiar with the earlier *Batman* movies. "I saw them all and liked most of them, I must say," he said. "But when I got this script, it was called *Batman Begins*, and I wondered about that. And then when I read the script, I realized it was true—Batman begins. It's a whole new thing in a whole new way—the way Christopher has done it. So it made me do it. There wouldn't be much point in just playing an ordinary butler in another *Batman*: you know, coming in saying 'Dinner is served' or something."[80] Caine was also drawn to the script because of the humanity with which Goyer and Nolan infused the characters. "I liked their vision of showing Batman coming from a natural man," said Caine. "If he's bulletproof, where's the suspense? If you have a real man, you have jeopardy and you have suspense. That's what interested me."[81]

Instead of being merely the Wayne butler, Nolan regarded Alfred's role as pivotal. "Alfred is a man given the responsibility to raise the most incredible child of a generation," said the director. "He helps him do incredibly important and frightening things that no parent would want their child to do."[82]

"Alfred is the one constant in Bruce's life, the one person who never gives up on him," said Caine. "He's also Bruce Wayne's moral compass. Batman walks a very fine line between himself and the criminals he pursues, so he must maintain a higher moral code. Alfred isn't afraid to give his opinion, especially when he thinks Bruce may have taken things too far."[83]

Prior to shooting, Caine came up with a backstory for his character. "I wanted to be the toughest butler you've ever seen—not the normal English suave butler," said Caine. "And so I made him an SAS sergeant, which is a very, very tough British army unit. And...he's wounded. He didn't want to leave the army, became the sergeant in charge of the sergeant's canteen—or the sergeant's mess, as it's called in the British army. And he got found by Bruce Wayne's father, who wanted the toughest butler he could find, and that's what he got. And I used the voice of my original sergeant when I joined the British army. That's his voice. That's the back-story, and I'm waiting for Christopher Nolan to do *Alfred: The Beginning*."[84]

In early December, Katie Holmes, a young actress who rose to fame as one of the stars of the WB's hit TV series *Dawson's Creek*, was offered the role of Rachel Dawes, subject to a screen test with Christian Bale. Although several actresses were considered, Holmes was the only one tested, in a scene directed by Christopher Nolan.[85] Rachel was an original creation of Goyer and Nolan; she was one of the few major characters in *Batman Begins* not based on a character from the comic books.[86] Nolan said he and Goyer created Rachel, the daughter of a Wayne house servant, to "represent the life Bruce Wayne might have if he weren't tied into his destiny of having to create a very dark alter ego through which he helps people."[87]

"One of the things about Rachel that I find so appealing is that she's so idealistic," said Holmes. "She's the type of person that wants to make the world a better place. She wants to help people, she wants to save her city and she doesn't have time for excuses."[88] Producer Emma Thomas said, "Rachel reminds Bruce of his father's legacy, his duty to carry on his family's philanthropic tradition, and she encourages him to do something meaningful with his life."[89]

The fourth actor cast was Cillian Murphy, who landed the plum role of Dr. Jonathan Crane/the Scarecrow in December. Murphy came to Christopher Nolan's attention after testing for the role of Batman a few months earlier.[90] Born in County Cork, Ireland in 1976, Murphy began his career as a rock musician before turning to acting. His appearance in 2003's *28 Days Later*, a post-apocalyptic zombie film directed by Danny Boyle, lead to meatier parts in *Breakfast on Pluto* (2005), in which he played a glam transgender orphan, and 2006's *The Wind That Shakes the Barley*, a film about the Irish War of Independence that captured the Palme d'Or at the Cannes Film Festival. Now, having landed the role of the Scarecrow, the actor read all the *Batman* comics in which the villain appeared.[91]

In mid-February 2004, Morgan Freeman joined the cast, in the role of Lucius Fox, a character originally created by Len Wein and John Calnan for *Batman # 307* in January 1979.[92] As reimagined by Nolan and Goyer, Fox served the same purpose as Q in the James Bond films—he's the gadget-master, the Merlin to Bruce Wayne's Arthur. And like Desmond Llewellyn, who played Q in most of the James Bond films, Freeman was absolutely clueless when it came to modern-day gadgetry. "Technology leaves me in the dark," said Freeman. "I've had a computer since the early days of the PC, but I still can't initialize a disk. That's Greek to me."[93]

Analyzing his character, Freeman said, "Fox and Earle are like sandpaper rubbing against each other. I don't think of Fox as being terribly ambitious or combative. He's just really smart and well-educated. Earle has a great need to get rid of Fox, but he can't just dump him; Fox knows too much. He has to keep him around so he can watch him. So he reduces him to being a warehouseman for all these wonderful toys."[94]

For the pivotal role of Henri Ducard, who later reveals himself to be Ra's al Ghul, Nolan cast Liam Neeson. The studio took pains to make sure the dual nature of the role remained secret. After the initial February 19, 2004 announcement that Neeson was playing "the villain, Ra's al Ghul,"[95] *Daily Variety* ran a correction the next day, saying Neeson would play "Ducard, mentor to Bruce Wayne."[96]

In describing his role, Neeson said, "Ducard had committed himself to an ideal of how he would love to see the world and he sees Bruce Wayne as someone who could make these ambitions tangible and real. Ducard reminds me of Ignatius of Loyola in the 15th Century, who formed the Jesuit Society. Ignatius was a very famous playboy and drunkard before he became an incredibly disciplined man and a saint. He's someone I have a lot of admiration for—an extraordinary disciplinarian on a quest to find a true, natural justice in this world that will help mankind...Ducard understands Bruce Wayne's pain because he lost someone in his life who was very dear to him, which led to his quest for a deeper sense of his destiny and spirituality. He believes you have to go into yourself to discover your dark side as well as your good side, and marry those forces in order to be able to achieve your full potential as a human being."[97]

Five days later, it was reported that Ken Watanabe would play Ra's al Ghul.[98] "Ra's al Ghul is a very mysterious, complicated character," said Watanabe. "He's very calm and quiet, but he's also extremely powerful. I think of him as a silent volcano."[99]

More casting news followed on March 4, when it was announced that Gary Oldman would be Lt. James Gordon.[100] It was an unusual choice; Oldman was known for playing psychologically troubled characters, from Sid Vicious in *Sid & Nancy* (1986) to Lee Harvey Oswald in *JFK* (1991), not to mention *Dracula* (1992). "Gary has never really played such a wholesome character," said Nolan, "but he is a chameleon, and he absolutely inhabits the role of Gordon. The essential goodness of the man is very apparent from his first scene."[101]

"I think Gordon's hair tuned gray at a pretty young age," said Oldman. "It's difficult in this day and age to retain any kind of integrity, whatever the line of work you're in, but trying to police Gotham City would turn anyone gray. What's nice about the role is that Gordon is so honest and true blue. I like playing the one good apple in the bunch."[102]

In make-up, Oldman looked the spitting image of his comic-book counterpart. "Chris wanted me to look as much like Gordon does in the comic as I realistically could, and not be identifiable as coming from any particular part of the country," said the actor. To project Gordon's world-weariness, Oldman said, "I just played the jet lag."[103] During the course of filming, Oldman ended up making 12 round-trip flights from his Los Angeles home to locations in Chicago and London. "I did twenty-four flights," he said. "I would fly in, go to the set—one day I flew in, I got out of a car and walked into a building, and I went then back, and I came back to L.A." Though the flights were wearying, Oldman took them because he did not want to spend long periods away from his family.[104]

At the end of March, the last two members of the principal cast were announced: Rutger Hauer as Earle, the corrupt head of Wayne Enterprises, and Tom Wilkinson, who took on the role of mob boss Falcone.[105] By the time he'd cast the main characters, Nolan had a two-time Oscar winner and two Oscar nominees in his cast. Michael Caine had been nominated for Best Actor Oscars for *Alfie* (1966), *Sleuth* (1972), *Educating Rita* (1983), and *The Quiet American* (2002); he won Supporting Actor Oscars for *Hannah and Her Sisters* (1986) and *The Cider House Rules* (1999). Morgan Freeman was a two-time Best Actor nominee, for *Street Smart* (1987) and *Driving Miss Daisy* (1989). Tom Wilkinson was a Best Actor nominee for *In The Bedroom* (2001).

While Nolan continued scriptwriting, casting, and assembling his crew—which included hiring Wally Pfister, his director of photography from *Insomnia*—production designer Nathan Crowley was busy with two tasks: designing the cityscape of Gotham City, and building a life-size working Batmobile. "Gotham will seem like this great city in a contemporary world and will be created through various cities," said Nolan. "We are trying to avoid a villagey feel for Gotham, as it starts to get claustrophobic."[106]

Instead of following the lead of the previous *Batman* films and going totally modernist or totally art deco, Nolan said that he and Crowley "wanted something that reflects the reality of a large modern city, which is a tremendous variety of architectures, a tremendous variety of periods in which things are built. We wanted to have a history to the place, as well as a contemporary feel."[107] Crowley sought to make Gotham City look like a place where audience members might actually live. "Gotham had to feel familiar," said Crowley. "I really wanted it to feel huge, like the biggest city in America." Not wanting Gotham City to be solely composed of computer-generated shots, Crowley built miniatures for many parts of the city. Digital effects were then used to extend the miniatures,[108] creating a vision of Gotham City than Nolan called "an exaggerated, contemporary New York, an overwhelming metropolis that completely immerses you to the point that you don't feel its boundaries."[109]

"Chris had clear ideas about realism and real cities like New York and its history," said Crowley. "He was trying to find 'a New York on steroids' as he put it, and that's what he asked me to come up with. I spent many hours wandering around New York, because there's that chaos you don't see in any other American city.

And if people can accept that more and more chaos is OK, they'll understand that Gotham City could possibly exist."[110] In the end, the Gotham City Crowley created was described by Nolan as "New York cubed."[111]

Recalling Tim Burton's *Batman,* Nolan said, "In Tim's film, Gotham itself is a very stylized place that Batman fits into. What I wanted to do was have Batman as an extraordinary figure in an ordinary world. So our Gotham is based more on a recognizable contemporary American city."[112]

The same quest for realism that infused the production design also carried over into Nolan's ideas about the Batmobile. "The creative mandate was really to do something fresh and original," said Nolan, "And that was coming straight from the studio, and it was the reason I wanted to get involved with the project—because it's pretty rare to have an iconic figure that's now owned and controlled by a studio that's asking you to do something different with it. But that really was the mandate. And for me, what that became was my desire to do something I hadn't seen before, which is a superhero story that is told in a realistic fashion and doesn't step outside itself and acknowledge the form or the medium that it's come from, but one in which the audience is hopefully just immersed in the reality of what's going on."[113]

Having designed a three-dimensional Batmobile model in Nolan's garage, Crowley now had the challenge of creating an actual, life-size working vehicle. He turned to Andy Smith and Chris Corbould, the special effects geniuses who modified Aston Martins and Jaguars to race across an Icelandic ice field for the 2002 James Bond film *Die Another Day.*[114] Smith was also part of the team that engineered the first Batmobile for Tim Burton's 1989 *Batman.*[115] The Batmobile, according to Crowley, "had dated itself sufficiently that we could start from scratch, and we had to start from scratch, because everyone was fed up with it."[116] Crowley showed his model to Corbould and Smith, and they set to work.

"Andy sourced everything: both the bodywork and the chassis have been made from scratch," said Corbould. "The only thing that was brought in were the engine components. The Batmobile has aerodynamic flaps, because the storyline requires it to jump reasonably sized distances, like 20-30 feet. It also has guns and a jet out the back. It isn't a killing machine as such; it doesn't fire guns at people to try and kill them. The guns are more of a way of getting out of tricky situations, like blowing a wall out of the way rather than shooting people."[117]

The new Batmobile had no front axel, which enabled the vehicle to make extremely tight turns. Nolan wanted the wheels to be held from the side, which at first was considered impossible. But Smith and special effects supervisor Chris Corbould devised a way to make it work.[118] "There's nothing holding the wheels in the conventional way that wheels are held on a normal car. We built one prototype and modified it and came up with a very good system—due to an increase in rear wheel diameter we turned the engine and gearbox around and went with a live axel. The design gives the vehicle an almost insect-like waist because it twists in the middle when being driven hard."[119] Equipped with a 5.7 liter, 350 cubic inch, 340-horsepower engine with approximately 400 pounds of torque, the Batmobile was 9 feet, 4 inches at its widest point, 15 feet long and weighed 2.5 tons. It accelerated from 0-60 in under 5 seconds and was capable of jumping 4 to 6 feet in height, up to a distance of 60 feet, and peel off as soon as it hit the ground.[120]

Depending on the driving performance the filmmakers were trying to capture, the treads of the tires were shaved off mechanically and their pressure was adjusted to give the driver varied levels of grip for performing sliding stunts. There were three basic sets of monster truck tires, with treads ranging from fully-skinned to semi-skinned to bald.[121]

A total of eight Batmobiles were created for the production, at a cost of $250,000 apiece.[122] In addition to the five fully operational, gas-powered models, there was an electric version that featured a sliding top to enable Batman and his passengers to easily enter and exit the car. The stunt driver was hidden behind the main seat and drove the vehicle from a sideways position. There were also two "cannon" vehicles, which were lightweight and contained no engines, which could be catapulted from a cannon for specific action sequences.[123]

"I never expected them to be able to build a version of the Batmobile that could actually do all the things that it's supposed to be able to do in the film, but they did it," said Nolan. "It's a monster, it's a beast, and it's beautifully designed."[124] In August of 2004, Warner Bros. took the new Batmobile from Chicago to New York to display it at the Licensing 2004 International trade show at the Jacob K. Javits Convention Center in Manhattan. The car's appearance underscored how important merchandising remained to the Batman franchise.[125]

The next challenge for Nolan and company was to design a new Batsuit, one that would look like the first prototype of an evolving design, and one that would hopefully be more flexible than the stiff Batsuits used previously. "I didn't think we could push the suit too far," said Crowley, "because you can't push the fans too far."[126] To oversee the creation of the new Batsuit, Nolan and Crowley turned to another veteran of the James Bond films, Lindy Hemming.

"A major consideration with the Batsuit was that Chris didn't want it designed just to look at, but to be very functional in execution," said Hemming. "He wanted the legs to be supple so that he could crouch down when necessary, and he very much wanted Christian to be able to move his head and not have to do the superhero movement of turning the shoulders and the head at once."[127]

Hemming set up her workshop at London's Shepperton Studios, where her costume department was given the nickname "Cape Town." The workshop was composed of portacabins that contained an administration office and canteen, as well as all the technical workshops, including the Sculpt Room, Dye and Laundry, Spray Room, Cutting and Sewing Room, Art Finishing Room, Mold Shop and Foam Lab.[128]

Hemming and her team designed a Batsuit comprised of a neoprene undersuit, much like a diver's wet suit, with seven separate molded latex sections glued to it: the knees, calves, legs, arms, torso, spine and cowl. "The suit is made of waterproof armor with components inside that maintain the body temperature and keep the muscles from freezing up, so it's multi-functional," said Hemming.[129]

Months before filming began, Christian Bale arrived at Cape Town to be molded for the Batsuit. The challenge for Hemming was that he had not yet begun training to build his body up for the role.[130] Nonetheless, a full body cast was taken, from which a plastic model of Bale was produced. Clay muscles were then sculpted onto the plastic model to approximate the shape they expected Bale would be by the time filming began. Plastiline was added to give the model a smoother surface, and then molds of Bale's body were made from the model. They were then taken to the foam lab to be injected with a latex foam mixture. Hours of research went into getting the mixture just right. It had to be light and flexible, but at the same time durable. It also needed to be as black as possible, but the more black pigment that was added, the weaker the foam. After finding just the right balance, the full body molds were injected with the foam, cooked in a large oven, and then the pieces were de-molded and trimmed with fine scissors to make it appear as if they had been cut by lasers.[131]

The cowl presented a special challenge. Previous cowls restricted the wearer's head movement. Hemming worked with Nolan and sculptor Julian Murray to devise a way to make the cowl thin enough to permit movement and supple enough to prevent it from wrinkling up when Bale turned his head. The result was a sleek, almost panther-like silhouette that was supposed to allow for more natural movement, though Bale later complained that he was still unable to turn his head freely.[132]

Nolan was especially keen to get the right look for Batman's cape. "There are wonderful illustrations of Batman striking iconic poses with his cape flowing, and we wanted to capture that element into our portrayal of the character," said Nolan.[133] "Chris didn't want that armored feeling," said Hemming. "He wanted to take the romanticism of the cloak from the comics, and he wanted him to be able to emerge from the darkness and fade into the darkness in places on the screen—it's almost like parts of him vanish."[134]

Hemming knew that to achieve this effect, Batman would need a matte black cape, not a shiny one. To attain that distinct look, the costumers invented their own fabric. They began by taking parachute nylon, which was very lightweight, and flocking it electro-statically with a process used in the making of London police force helmets. Hemming contacted police technicians to teach her team how to flock the nylon. It was achieved by brushing the material with glue and running a 60,000 volt static electric charge underneath it. Fine hairs were then dropped onto the fabric, and held in place by the electric charge.[135]

With the suit completed, it was now time to try it on Bale. After losing 63 pounds for *The Machinist*, the actor trained to build his body up to Batman proportions. "I finished *The Machinist* in July, and we had to start shooting this film at the end of February," Bale told *Starlog* magazine's Joe Nazzaro. "So, yes, I had a considerable amount of work to do. This part demands that you be in decent shape, and I also needed to be ready for being in that suit 12 hours a day. I was eating like crazy, trying to put on pounds and pounds, and I actually went way overboard. By the time I arrived in England, Chris stared at me in shock and said, 'My God, you look like some kind of grizzly bear!' because I arrived with long hair and a beard. I had put on exactly 100 pounds from the day of finishing *The Machinist* to arriving in England in January, and that wasn't a healthy way to go. I could lift a lot of weights, but if you had asked me to run across the room, I would have been exhausted. So when I got here, I started running and doing stuff like that, and I brought my weight back down again."[136]

Two months before arriving in England, Bale began learning the fighting method that director Christopher Nolan and fight arranger David Forman had chosen

Christian Bale, bulked up and suited up as Batman in Batman Begins (Warner Bros./Photofest, © Warner Bros. Photographer: David James).

for Batman.[137] They wanted one that was quick and lethal, marrying the intensity of street fighting with the discipline of martial arts.[138] "For Batman, everything is about function, it's about the most effective way of doing something, so we needed a style that is brutal, economical and real," said Nolan.[139] "We've gotten comfortable seeing fighting portrayed in this graceful, dance-like fashion to the point where the violence loses its threat. I wanted to take it back to a grittier place, where you feel the punches a bit more."[140]

Nolan and Forman decided on the Keysi Fighting Method, also known as KFM, a relatively new style developed in Spain in the 1950s by Justo Diéguez Serrano. Based on natural fighting instincts and tightly controlled, efficient movements, Keysi is an intuitive, low-grounded fighting method that requires superior leg and upper body strength, with a strong emphasis on mental focus and awareness. Unlike other martial arts developed for sport, KFM is ideal for combat in close quarters and can be applied to fighting in any environment, even against multiple attackers from all directions.[141] "A big part of the Batman persona is the aggressive, animalistic way he attacks his enemies," said Bale. "I wanted to show how devastating he is when he charges forward and attacks people, and his resilience in taking blows as well."[142] The Keysi Fighting Method, said Bale, "is a very intuitive kind of martial art, but also very, very brutal. It's all about going for the break straightaway. It's quite instinctive and it adapts to many different situations. So it truly looks as though this is Batman's own style that he's come up with."[143] Forman was impressed with Bale's ability, saying, "Christian is an excellent student. We were very surprised at how quickly he absorbed the information when we gave him his first lesson."[144]

Lindy Hemming was concerned when she saw the now-buff actor. "We always knew that when Christian came back from training, he would have developed into a different shape," said Hemming. "He did get enormously bigger, and when he first came back, we were like, 'Oh no. It's never going to fit!'" After his training slimmed him back down, the suit did fit Bale, but despite the efforts of Hemming's costume department to make it more wearer-friendly, it was still uncomfortable. It took three people to suit the actor up every day. Once he was inside the costume, overheating was a major concern. At times Bale wore a "cool suit" which had tiny plastic tubes running through the inside of it, similar to what high-altitude pilots and astronauts use as a cooling system.[145] "When you first put it on, you feel like you're scuba diving or something, and it feels kinda claustrophobic," said Bale. "I think that they made a lot of advances in the actual make-up of the suit...So I think I, by far, have had the easiest time of anybody, short of probably Adam West who I think was trotting around in some kind of cotton get-up or something. They really came up with some good stuff. And it's much more mobile than any of the other suits have been."[146]

Bale liked that the suit made him look like a dangerous jungle creature. "The suit gives you this huge neck, like a Mike Tyson neck, which you really rarely see amongst humans," said Bale. "It's more like a panther. It gives you this real feral look, as though you're going to pounce on somebody any moment."[147] Although Bale could do more in his suit than previous Batman actors, he still had difficulty raising his arms very high, and he needed help when it came time for toilet breaks.[148] Bale also found the cowl particularly uncomfortable. It fit so tightly that after about twenty minutes, it gave him a terrific headache. But when that happened, and the discomfort sent him into a foul mood, he refused to take the cowl off, preferring to use that anger in his performance. "I wasn't going to be some little acting ninny who says, 'I can't deal with it anymore. Take it off,'" said Bale. "I used the pain as fuel for the character's anger. Batman's meant to be fierce, and you become a beast in that suit, as Batman should be—not a man in a suit, but a different creature."[149]

"Christian had a very controlled and specific approach to how he wanted to portray the aggression and the animal-like quality of this character," said Nolan. "He spent a long time looking at graphic novels and illustrations of Batman, to form his own sense of how he should move and communicate with the other characters. I think that his portrayal is very striking in its intensity and its seriousness."[150]

Despite the discomfort, Bale said, "It's one hell of an honor to wear that Batsuit." And Christopher Nolan noticed that "everybody on set felt quite a charge when Christian would walk on in the Batsuit. It was quite shocking and quite striking. You felt it in your bones."[151]

INTIMIDATING CIRCUMSTANCES

For months, websites reported the new film's title as *The Intimidation Game*, but that was just a code name used by the studio while the film was in development, meant to throw Batman fans off the scent.[152] It didn't work; fans quickly deduced that *The Intimidation Game* was the new *Batman* film. To further throw fans off, once filming began, call sheets and marker signs carried the title *Flora's Wedding* to turn away gawkers; Flora is the name of Christopher Nolan and Emma Thomas's daughter.

On March 4, 2004, *Daily Variety* reported that the new *Batman* film had begun shooting in Iceland.[153] The first sequence filmed was Bruce Wayne's swordfight with Ducard, staged on a frozen lake atop the Vatnajokull Glacier in the South East of Iceland, the largest glacier in Europe.[154] The area was so remote that the film's construction crew had to build a road in order to access the icy location.[155]

Normally, this kind of sequence would have been handled by a second unit, with the stunt coordinator directing a couple of stunt doubles through the moves. Nolan, however, chose not to use a second unit director; when this *Batman* film was finished, every frame of film on the screen would bear his own personal stamp.[156]

In preparation for the sword duel, fight arranger David Forman and his team spent weeks rehearsing with Christian Bale and Liam Neeson at an ice rink. The actors were trained in the art of wielding Samurai swords, defending against blade attacks with forearm gauntlets, and—as Bale put it—"practicing how to fight while standing on ice without falling on your ass all the time."[157]

Filming on the ice was dangerous. The film's safety team only allowed six people at a time—including the two actors—to be on the frozen surface.[158] "Every so often between set-ups we'd see ice crumbling away at the head of this glacier and bits of rock and muck falling off, and we knew this thing was a big living force that was moving towards us," said Neeson.[159]

"We'd start hitting each other and smashing into the ice and then suddenly hear a big crack! right through the middle of the lake," recalled Bale. "We'd all stand dead still and look around. Then the safety guys would shout, 'Okay, get off! Get off!' Thankfully, we got the whole thing in that one day, because by the next, there was no ice whatsoever. It had melted into a lake again."[160]

The first day of shooting in the uncomfortable environment was grueling, but Nolan was pleased with the results, as was Forman, who said that fighting with Samurai swords "takes a lot of energy and Christian and Liam both put one hundred percent into their performances. They did very well, both with the Keysi and the sword fighting."[161]

Although they had gotten a difficult sequence out of the way right at the start, the crew still faced a tough time in Iceland. They still had to film Bruce Wayne's trek to the monastery, some of which was captured during a raging storm with 75-mile-per-hour winds that literally blew crewmembers off their feet.[162] The crew built a facade of the monastery gate to film Bruce Wayne's arrival at the compound. Wide shots of the monastery, including the shots of it exploding, were accomplished with a model.[163] After capturing shots of Bruce Wayne rescuing Ducard from falling over an icy cliff, the crew returned to the warmer climes of Shepperton Studios.

The bedrooms and an interior corridor of Wayne Manor were constructed on stages at Shepperton, as was the massive Batcave set.[164] As designed by Nathan Crowley, the hero's headquarters was approximately 250 feet long, 120 feet wide and 40 feet high, and housed 24 water pumps used to send 12,000 gallons of water through the set every minute, bringing to life the waterfall, a river and the dank, dripping cave walls.[165] "The Batcave has previously appeared to be a very elaborately and improbably constructed place," said Nolan. "In *Batman Begins*, we show the Batcave as a cavern that's damp and filthy and full of bats, and we see Bruce Wayne installing trestle tables, stringing lights and moving equipment in himself, building up the world of the Batcave that will eventually come to be."[166]

When Michael Caine first walked onto the enormous Batcave set, he had a déjà vu moment. It was the same stage where, nearly fifty years earlier, he'd acted in his first film, *A Hill in Korea* (1956). "I had eight lines in the picture," said Caine, "and I screwed up six of them. And it was on this stage that I said my very first line in a movie." Looking around the set now, Caine noticed the bats nestled up above. Turning to Christopher Nolan, he said, "Those are great false bats in the ceiling." Nolan replied, "They're not false, Michael. They're real. They're asleep." Caine said, "Well, don't wake 'em up, whatever you do."[167]

Christian Bale was soon filming his first scenes as Batman, wearing the Batsuit. "Inevitably, after six months of being in the suit, you get used to it, but that first day, I felt like a panther, like some kind of wild animal," said Bale. "I don't know if anybody else was looking at me that way, and I don't know if I appeared quite as ferocious as that, but it made me want to run and jump at people and beat the crap out of them!"[168] Bale created a voice for Batman that was more gruff than his refined and suave Bruce Wayne voice. "It makes sense in terms of identity," said Bale, "but I also saw it as a way for him to channel the clarity of mind that he must have had as a young boy when he first declared that he would get revenge. It's difficult to maintain that throughout your life. Things become memories, and it takes a great deal of energy to maintain that sharpness of emotion. So I figured everything about

Batman should be different—the look, the voice—so Bruce is able to have his own life. If he was just Bruce Wayne in a Batsuit, that would be a bit ridiculous—like any of us getting in a Batsuit and thinking we could go out on the town and intimidate people. You have to really go for it in every way, and for me that involved taking on a slightly beast-like voice."[169] Interestingly, Bale's Batman voice is similar to the raspy voice used by actor Christopher Stapleton in the final scenes of *The Death of Batman* (2003), the unauthorized fan film associate-produced two years earlier by his sister, Louise.

To help him stay in character, Bale had his own special character bibles. "I would refer to the different graphic novels," he said. "I had them on the set with me all the time just 'cause I loved the imagery of it so much."[170]

Batman Begins was the first feature film to utilize Cardington, a former airship hangar located approximately an hour north of London, as a production soundstage. The bulk of the film's Gotham City exterior sets were built inside Cardington's huge Hangar No. 2, a structure 812 feet long and 180 feet high at its apex, four times higher than the average soundstage.[171]

"Filming at Cardington gave the film a level of realism and scope that would not have been possible if we had been limited to using a normal soundstage," said Emma Thomas. "We also had more control over the environment, so we could do stunts involving fire and high falls without having to worry about winds and weather conditions. We were able to shoot a lot of what would have been night work in the day, because of this extraordinary facility."[172]

Cardington was home to Crowley's set for the Narrows, a decrepit and treacherous slum located on an island in the center of Gotham and connected to the city by a series of bridges. Inspired by New York's Roosevelt Island, the freeways of Tokyo and the old Kowloon city in Hong Kong, Crowley worked to create a design that felt claustrophobic, as if the Narrows is penned inside the city and "freeways are running down Fifth Avenue."[173]

As opposed to previous Batman films, where computer-generated images were used to show Batman soaring through the skies of Gotham, shots of Batman using his rigid high-tech cape to fly through the Gotham skies in *Batman Begins* were achieved without computer trickery. "We didn't do any green screen work at all," said director of photography Wally Pfister.[174] "The flying was done using real wires and real cameras. We put a camera on a wire and flew Batman 800 feet across the stage. That encapsulates Chris' philosophy of filmmaking: Let's do it for real."[175]

Likewise, the Gotham cityscape was achieved through the use of miniatures rather than CGI.[176] "The peak of visual effects is to produce shots that look real, and the best way you can do that is to shoot as much of it for real as possible," said visual effects supervisor Dan Glass.[177]

Miniatures were used for one other flying sequence, where the Batmobile jumps from one building to another and drives across several rooftops, smashing roof tiles as it goes. Although technically a miniature, the rooftop set was still huge. "We built the miniature rooftop set at one-third scale, so the span was approximately 100 by 150 feet," said Glass.[178] "Working at that kind of scale, things behave close to reality. So when the car drives across a roof made of tiles, they break and fall like they would in real life. This enabled us to shoot the sequence as if it were a full-size action sequence."[179]

Nolan wanted to set *Batman Begins* apart from the previous films in the franchise by filming on actual locations, grounding the film in reality as much as possible.[180] Consequently, dock scenes were filmed at Canary Wharf in mid-March, followed by filming of interiors and exteriors of Wayne Manor at Mentmore Towers, an estate built north of London by the Rothschilds in the 1850s.[181] At the end of April, exterior scenes of the courtroom were filmed at University College, London. Filming continued at Cardington and Shepperton through the end of July.

While shooting continued in England, Warner Bros. struck a sour note with Batfans at the July 2004 San Diego Comic Con. The company came to the annual convention to promote *Batman Begins* but offered no footage from the film. Suspicious fans thought the lack of a film reel meant there must be problems with the movie.[182] Fans had to be content with just a video postcard from director Christopher Nolan and star Christian Bale, and appearances by screenwriter David Goyer and actor Cillian Murphy, who by that point had wrapped up his scenes.[183]

The rest of the cast and crew were soon on their way to America; on July 31, location filming began in Chicago, Illinois. Having partly inspired Gotham City, Chicago proved an ideal place to shoot the film's exteriors. The Chicago Board of Trade on 171 West Jackson became the Wayne Corp. Building, parts of the climactic monorail scene were filmed on LaSalle Street, and the car chase through the streets of Gotham where the Batmobile outmaneuvers and crushes police cars was staged on Lower Wacker Drive, just south of the Chicago River, with 30 stunt drivers participating.[184] Amstutz highway, a two-mile stretch of highway that was never completed and does not flow into public traffic, was utilized for portions of the chase taking place on the Gotham freeway.[185]

"Chris really wanted the chase to have a loose, raw feel, something somewhere between a modern-day action-chase sequence with all the technology that we use today and something with the raw, gritty feeling of *The French Connection*," said director of photography Wally Pfister. "That's why I was determined not to use a digital Batmobile—Chicago has these amazing subterranean streets, and I really wanted to get it out there."[186]

Producer Larry Franco was amazed at how receptive Chicago was to the filming. "The cooperation we got in the city of Chicago was better than any film company has probably ever had in any city," said Franco. "We closed down city blocks and did some extraordinary work with helicopters filming the Batmobile and police cars rolling over vehicles in the middle of the street."[187]

To capture the action at ground level, Wally Pfister chased the Batmobile through the streets in an innovative new camera car, the AMG Mercedes ML camera car,[188] outfitted with the Ultimate Arm and Lev Head, a gyro-stabilized head on a robotically-controlled arm controlled from inside the camera car with joysticks. The Lev Head allowed the camera operator to shoot images of such clarity and stability that it was used for approximately eighty percent of the chase scene.[189] Nolan and Pfister rode inside the ML, watching the built-in monitors and communicating with the stunt drivers through an open microphone, allowing them to make real-time adjustments in the speed and handling of the cars.[190]

"The ML was the best tool we've ever had for a car chase," said stunt coordinator Paul Jennings. "It meant that we didn't have to pull back the speed of the

Batmobile, because it could keep up. It was invaluable in terms of getting shots that you couldn't dream of doing with a normal tracking vehicle. There are shots in the film that I'm sure people will think were sped up, but they're not—they were done for real."[191]

"You very rarely drive a car more than 50 or 60 miles an hour in a chase sequence," said Pfister. "We had the Batmobile up to 105 miles an hour. It was amazing to us, and it nearly outran a helicopter—particularly flying sideways, the helicopter couldn't even keep up with the Batmobile."[192]

"It really flies," said Bale. "They couldn't keep up with it, the camera cars... They were having to ask, 'Can you please slow down a little bit? 'Cause we just can't keep up with the thing.'"

Maneuvering the Batmobile was no easy feat. The vehicle doesn't provide the driver with much peripheral vision, so a video system was installed with cameras mounted on top of the vehicle facing backwards and just over the driver's eye-line to match his viewpoint, allowing the driver, if necessary, to pilot the car using just the monitors. "It's a handful," said the car's builder, Andy Smith. "It looks like it's very responsive but there's a lot of physical effort involved, a lot of wheel twirling in that cockpit to keep it under control."[193] Stunt driver George Cottle, who doubled for Christian Bale in most of the driving sequence, recalled, "I would spend all day driving the Batmobile and then get in my car to go home, and it would take me a while to adapt to driving a normal car. The whole body of the Batmobile rolls and flexes from side to side, making the vehicle up to six inches wider on either side because of the flexing movement."[194]

Other shots were captured using the Ultimate Arm and Lev Head attached to a motorcycle sidecar, and with an additional camera mounted to the front of a police car driven by one of the stunt men and kept as close as possible to the hard-charging action.[195]

The unusual-looking Batmobile elicited stunned looks from gawkers. Christian Bale recalled that there were a couple of times when, instead of loading the vehicle on the truck to go from one location to another a very short distance away, it was considered more efficient to just drive the Batmobile there, through city streets. "And you see that thing just going down the street, and everybody's stopping and looking," said Bale. "There was even this guy who crashed into it. This poor drunken guy who didn't have a license, who said he got so panicked when he saw the car, he thought aliens were landing. And he put the pedal to the metal. I wasn't in it; it was the stunt driver driving it at the time. Put the pedal to the metal and sideswiped the Batmobile. So, you know, it has this effect upon people."

Bale was allowed to get behind the wheel for a few shots. "It is a fantastic drive," he said. "Y'know, you get in it and—I've always been a fan of motorbikes and not so much of cars. You get in that and you can't help but love cars because also you see all of the inner workings inside of it. You can see the functionality of everything that's going on. And it screams, y'know?...It screams in your ear. And you've got the smell and everything inside of it. It's elating. My heart was pounding every time I'd step out of that thing."[196]

Katie Holmes, who also got to experience riding in the Batmobile, said "I finally understood men's fascinations with cars after I saw the Batmobile in action.

I thought, 'Okay, I get it. This is awesome!' I have the privilege of riding in it in the movie and it's even better on the inside."[197]

According to producer Emma Thomas, the amazing auto was, at one point, planned to meet its demise. "For a long time," said Thomas, "there was actually going to be a moment at the end of the movie where we were going to destroy the Batmobile. But in the end we just couldn't bring ourselves to do it —the Batmobile had become like a character to us."[198]

Director Christopher Nolan was thrilled with the work of his special effects and stunt teams. "The challenge was really to the stunt co-coordinator and the physical effects guys," he said. "And they rose to it admirably, and I think they actually— in a day and age where so much is done with computers—they really rose to the opportunity; they really enjoyed the opportunity of getting back to what they're best at, which is performing amazing feats and building amazing things that can actually work in the real world. For me, once I sort of set that all in motion, it was really just a question of filming it and trying to be disciplined about not listening to the little voice in your ear that says, 'Well, you could do this with visual effects, you can leave it for now, you can move on and not perfect it.'"[199]

The crew returned to England to capture final shots of Batman and Gordon from the film's climax. Nolan filmed a teaser ending that could set up a possible sequel, though he said, "It's also really just there, for me, to send the audience out of the theatre with a sense of possibility and a sense of excitement about where these characters could go. I certainly share that sense and have certainly talked and thought, in vague terms, about how you could follow on from this film...But at the same time, it's very important that this film stand on its own."[200] When the 128 days of shooting were all over, Nolan felt pleased with what he had accomplished. For a director used to making films on a much smaller scale and budget, he said, "The most challenging aspect of making this film was the sheer scope of it."[201]

As the film entered post-production, visual effects supervisors Dan Glass and Janek Sirrs and London-based special effects house Moving Picture Co. created computer-generated bats for the opening shot, where the massing of the bat colony momentarily suggests the Bat symbol, and created a colony to swirl around Christian Bale when Bruce Wayne faces his fear and accepts what he must become.[202] Christopher Nolan wanted to use the computer effects sparingly, to enhance but not overwhelm the realism he strove to create for the film. "I'd seen a huge proliferation of computer effects in films over the last 10 years," said Nolan. "I think the audience has become a little jaded. And in a weird way, this has started to make films seem smaller." The final film had 557 special effects shots; Nolan said that most of the work done by special effects supervisor Janek Sirrs was clean-up, removing visible wires from the rigs of flying stuntmen.[203]

Hans Zimmer was hired to compose the score, but when he realized that he had too many other projects on his plate and had overcommitted himself, he reached out to fellow composer James Newton Howard to work with him. Christopher Nolan agreed to the unusual arrangement, saying, "For two composers of such caliber to work together was very exciting. Hans was very honest with me. He said he didn't know what the nature of the collaboration would be. But they were clearly excited about working together."[204]

Nolan did ask, however, that they not simply divide the work in half. In the end, both composers had a hand in the music for every scene. They worked in two different rooms in a London studio with a corridor in between, but kept the doors open. "I would start playing on the piano and get an idea for a tune and his hand would slip in between my arms on the keys," said Zimmer.[205]

With different work habits, the composers had to adapt to each other. In the end, the very disciplined Howard conformed to Zimmer's more chaotic method of working long hours. Howard also had to get used to Zimmer's synthesizer-driven electronic music. "He's a much better player than I am, while I'm a better programmer," said Zimmer. "We didn't give up on our own styles, but we ended up coming up with something different." In the end, both men enjoyed the collaboration. "Our relationship is one of friends, of brothers in arms who know the weight of the unwritten tune, the desperation of not having found the great tune," said Zimmer. "We're passionate about music. We started off as good friends and ended up as great friends."[206]

Six months before the film's release, David Gritten in *The New York Times* noted that *Batman Begins,* even though it was set in America and had American characters, was largely a British film. The director was born in London, most of the crew were British, and eight of the ten leading roles were played by British actors. Christian Bale was Welsh, Liam Neeson and Cillian Murphy hailed from Ireland, and Michael Caine, Gary Oldman, Tom Wilkinson and Linus Roache (who played Thomas Wayne, Bruce's father) were all from Britain. Also, aside from some exteriors filmed in Chicago, Gotham City was largely recreated at Cardington in the English countryside.[207]

Ian Thomson of the U.K. Film Council noted that of all the American studios, Warner Bros. was the one that made the most use of British talent and facilities; its *Harry Potter* franchise was shot at another abandoned British air base, Leavesden, which had first been converted into a film studio for the 007 film *Tomorrow Never Dies.* The studio also shot *Charlie and the Chocolate Factory, Phantom of the Opera* and *Alexander* at British studios. "Studios know they get value for money here," said Thomson, noting that even though the dollar was weak against the pound, making filming in the U.K. expensive, there was world-class talent available in the British Isles.[208]

The studio was able to spend more on their movies thanks to the added influx of revenues from foreign home video. At a time when the Motion Picture Association of America was claiming losses of $3.5 billion a year due to the sale of illegally pirated films on videotape and DVDs, overseas the studios were seeing record profits from legitimate sales of home video in foreign markets. According to *The New York Times,* foreign home video sales were the fastest-growing revenue stream for the studios. British data firm Screen Digest calculated that the home video divisions of the studios brought in $11.4 billion in wholesale revenues from the $24.6 billion spent by overseas consumers buying and renting home videos in 2004.[209]

The increased cash flow from foreign home video sales had an impact on the business. Films with big international appeal, like the new *Batman* film, saw increased budgets. Top stars began negotiating a larger share of the profits, and the studios began spending millions more to fight piracy, particularly in developing markets in Asia and Russia. The labor guilds negotiated new contracts to give them a bigger slice of the DVD pie, which the studios vigorously fought against giving up. It became common practice for studios to underreport revenues from international home video and to misrepresent those revenues to talent who had back-end deals that guaranteed them a share of the profits. In filings with the Securities and Exchange Commission, studios did not specify which revenues came from international home video divisions; instead, those sums were lumped with theatrical revenues in a category called "filmed entertainment." In order for talent to get an accounting that would break the video numbers down between foreign and domestic gross revenues, they had to do an expensive audit.[210]

Part of the problem was that while domestic sales and rentals could be tracked through bar code information, no independent company or trade publication had the financial power to track international sales and rentals through bar codes. The most that the studios were willing to divulge was how many units had shipped. For instance, Warner Home Video reported that the third Harry Potter film, *Harry Potter and the Prisoner of Azkaban,* shipped 27 million units worldwide as of January 2005; Dreamworks *Shrek 2,* the top international seller of 2004, shipped 37 million units, with 13 million of those outside the U.S.[211]

For top stars, the audits were worthwhile. Unlike guild members who were locked into a royalty fee schedule, top film stars could negotiate their own portion of home video earnings, meaning they could pull in up to a 7% royalty of gross revenues, or about a dollar for every DVD sold. By contrast, the rest of the movie's cast normally earned a royalty share of 1.1%. But the studios had no intention of letting the guilds negotiate a larger share.[212]

Charles Roven, one of *Batman Begins'* producers, said, "For a long time, the film business was a single-digit business on investment return. Now, because of home video, it's a low double-digit business, and the studios want to make sure it doesn't go back into the single-digit business." With the expectation of high home video revenues, Roven was reportedly able to get a budget for *Batman Begins* of more than $180 million; it was expected that the film's worldwide marketing budget would be more than $100 million. Plunking down over a quarter of a billion dollars was a huge risk for Warner Bros., considering that their previous Batman movie, *Batman & Robin,* had brought in only $238 million in worldwide ticket sales. But, Roven said, "Warner Brothers would not be putting this kind of money into the film unless someone thought the investment would be retuned in home video."[213]

Warner Home Video was the leader among the studios, with a 20% share of international wholesale revenues; in 2004, the company grossed a reported $2.25 billion in international revenues, and the studio expected that that figure could hit as much as $6 billion in the next few years.[214]

The monster budget of *Batman Begins* was even less of a concern to the studio thanks to the intervention of Thomas Tull, the 35-year-old head of Legendary Pictures. Just as *Batman Begins* was set to open, Tull showed up on the Warner Bros. lot with a $500 million private equity fund. After meeting with Warners' execs, he put up half the funding of both *Batman Begins* and the upcoming *Superman Returns.*[215]

A self-described movie geek from Binghampton, New York, Tull made his first riches buying and selling a Laundromat chain. He then worked for the Atlanta-based

Convex Group, a company begun by WebMD founder Jeff Arnold that invested in new media networks such as LidRock, which Convex owned. LidRock put promotional CDs in the lids of soda cups. The company later got into the disposable DVD market when they bought Flex Play. He also made millions with hundreds of Jackson-Hewitt tax-preparation franchises. In 1996, Tull got his first taste of Hollywood when he helped create Red Storm Entertainment, a company that created games based on the novels of Tom Clancy.[216]

With his skills as a venture capitalist, Tull went to investors such as ABRY Partners, Banc of America Capital Investors and AGI Direct Investments and raised the capital to form Legendary Pictures. "We got a ticket to the ballgame," said Tull. "That's it. Now, we need to make things work."

In the fall of 2003, he attended a dinner party in the Hollywood Hills where he met MGM president Chris McGurk. The two men got into a conversation about the sometimes involved methods Hollywood uses to raise cash for film productions. Tull realized that the kinds of private equity and venture capital money he had access to were more concerned with manufacturing companies, technology and health care start-ups. Film production represented a new frontier for private equity investment.[217]

Joining together with several Hollywood veterans, including former TriStar Pictures production chief Chris Lee, marketing executive Scott Mednick and former Creative Artist Agency chief financial officer Larry Clark, Tull formed Legendary Pictures. The group raised $500 million in cash from investors.[218] Their deal with Warner Bros., in which they agreed to co-finance and co-produce films, made them equal partners with the studio. Besides bankrolling the *Batman* and *Superman* franchises, Legendary planned to develop their own projects in consultation with the studio. They would treat their slate of films as a portfolio, making films in different budget ranges and genres to insure against potential losses.[219]

At the end of April 2005, Warner Bros. moved the release date of *Batman Begins* from Friday July 17 to Wednesday July 15. The move was prompted by two factors—kids being out of school for summer, which would make for a bigger mid-week opening, and—more importantly—the plans to open the film internationally on the 15th. It was due to open not only in the U.S. but also France, Belgium, Mexico, the Philippines and Taiwan.[220] "Internationally, some territories historically prefer Wednesday openings," said Dan Fellman, Warners distribution president. "We felt we've had such great support from the fans that we did not want to have it open somewhere else before the U.S."[221] In its further efforts to promote the film, Warner Bros. hit right at a portion of its target audience on May 18, 2005, when the 90-minute season finale of *Smallville* ended with an 8-minute preview of *Batman Begins*.[222]

Batman Begins became the first film based on a DC Comics character to sport the new DC logo, created by Josh Bateman of Brainchild Studios. Previously, a DC logo had only appeared on comic books and graphic novels. Now, a newly-designed logo would brand not only the comic books but also the films, television programs, merchandising and games endorsed by DC. The new logo debuted on the May 25th cover of DC's comics; an animated version debuted at the beginning of *Batman Begins*.[223]

Instead of just relying on print and TV saturation, the marketing plan for *Batman Begins* began on the internet. Warner Bros. set up a website in March of 2004 to promote the film. When they posted a trailer on the website over the summer, it generated buzz on fan sites and blogs. Warner Bros. then invited the operators of some of the fan websites to the film's set.[224] An integrated marketing campaign drove website visitors to the 8-minute preview of the film that was presented during *Smallville*. Then there was a flurry of banner ads on websites until the film's release.[225]

Dawn Taubin, president of domestic marketing for Warner Bros., said, "We made a conscious decision to start and live in the on-line world for the movie. We felt we had a core audience, and that core fan showed slight disappointments [in the] direction the previous movies had taken. We wanted to go back to the original core material. We made a specific decision to release the new logo and the new art online—rather than give it to, say, *USA Today*."[226]

Advertising on the internet was a growing business. In 2004, the internet took in $86 million in advertising spending by movie companies. Though that was a pittance compared to the $1.8 billion spent on TV advertising and $1.2 billion spent on newspapers, it was 41% more than had been spent on internet advertising the year before. More importantly for the studios, internet ads targeted the coveted 12- to 24-year-old audience.[227]

On June 4, the 2005 MTV Movie Awards broadcast kicked off with host Jimmy Fallon being driven to the show by Batman in the Batmobile, thanks to some clever editing that mixed shots of Fallon with clips from *Batman Begins*. The piece ended with Batman revealing himself to be Napoleon Dynamite, played by Jon Heder.[228]

The movie had its Los Angeles premiere on Monday, June 6, 2005 at Graumann's Chinese Theatre in Hollywood. The film's Morgan Freeman, Liam Neeson, Michael Caine, and Gary Oldman were present, as was Katie Holmes with boyfriend Tom Cruise. Christian Bale arrived sporting a beard.[229] When asked about the TV concept of *Batman*, Bale said, "Only Adam West can fill those shoes. I've got a lot of respect for the way he chose to play Batman, but that was a spoof of what Batman is meant to be. I was looking to fill a whole different pair of boots."[230] Other stars present on the red carpet were Adam Brody, Chris Kattan, Dave Navarro and Brooke Burke.[231] An after-party was held at the Kodak Theatre next door, but Cruise and Holmes decided not to attend.[232]

When *Batman Begins* opened on Wednesday, June 15, 2005, it bowed in 3,718 theatres in the U.S.[233] The film also premiered in Imax theaters, digitally remastered in the Imax format and retitled *Batman Begins: The Imax Experience*.[234] On the following Friday, it added another 140 theatres, for a total of 3,858, the widest release in the studio's history. Internationally, the film opened in Belgium, France, Switzerland and the Philippines on Wednesday; Australia, Germany, Holland, Hong Kong and Singapore on Thursday; Italy, Spain and the U.K. on Friday; and Japan on Saturday.[235] Christopher Nolan, Christian Bale, Katie Holmes, Michael Caine and Morgan Freeman went on a worldwide tour to promote the film, with Warner Bros. staging five foreign premieres. The first was in Tokyo in late May, followed by London on June 12, Berlin on June 15, Paris on June 21 and Rome on June 23.[236]

Many observers expected the film would end up with an opening weekend tally around $70 million, provided it could widen its audience beyond the 18- to

34-year-old males who, according to studio tracking, were showing the most interest in seeing the film.[237] After 16 weekends in a row where revenues were down compared to 2004, Warners was hopeful that *Batman Begins* would reverse the trend. On its opening day, it brought in $15 million.[238]

Over the weekend, the film grossed $46.9 million, for a total Wednesday through Sunday box-office take of $71.1 million. Just looking at the grosses for the Friday through Sunday period, *Batman Begins* outperformed 1997's *Batman & Robin*, which made $42.9 million on its opening weekend, but earned less than 1995's *Batman Forever*, which took in $52.8 million. In reporting the figures, *Daily Variety* also noted that ticket prices had increased by more than 40% over the decade.[239] Although it was hoped that *Batman Begins* would bring the box-office out of its doldrums, the total weekend box-office of $133 million was down 2.6% from the previous weekend's $136.8 million take.[240] Overseas, the film grossed $41.7 million in its first five days.[241]

The film had its London premiere at the Odeon Leicester Square on June 12. Director Christopher Nolan spoke of a film "made in England...that only U.K. technicians could have made," drawing applause from the crowd, particularly after rumors had circulated in the press that both the James Bond and Harry Potter franchises might relocate to Eastern Europe because of fears that U.K. tax incentives would be cut. The premiere was followed by an after party at the Royal Courts of Justice on the Strand.[242]

REINVENTION

Todd McCarthy of *Daily Variety* gave the film a mediocre review, saying, "Ambitious, well made but not exactly rousing, lavishly produced Warner Bros. release will ride heavy promotion and want-see to big openings worldwide, but is too dark and talky to appeal to kids and won't inspire much repeat viewing, which casts sought-after blockbuster B.O. in some doubt...The filmmakers seem intent upon making Bruce/Batman and his actions as plausible (one resists saying realistic) as possible, emphasizing that he's a distinctly human hero with no super powers. All the same, guys, he was still born in a comic book, and it's doubtful Batman would have lived very long had the original DC comics been as drained of sheer childlike fun as this film is. There is talent and cleverness here, but not much excitement...With an ideal physique and bearing for the role, Bale makes for a committed, driven, urbane and intelligent do-gooder; only oddity is the somewhat electronic quality of his voice as Batman."[243]

The Wall Street Journal struck a similar note, with Joe Morgenstern writing, "A weaponized hallucinogen threatens to devastate Gotham City in *Batman Begins*, which stars Christian Bale as the latest, as well as the gravest, embodiment of the Dark Knight. For better and worse, Christopher Nolan's defiantly dark retelling of the pulp legend amounts to a theatricalized hallucinogen. This beautifully crafted film has the power to cloud our minds, even to bend them, with its visual splendors, sepulchral tone, vivid sense of place and elegant, if intermittent, action. But there may also come an awakening, at least for grown-ups—a realization that much is being made, at great length, of a ponderous story about a depressed hero who isn't much fun to be with."[244]

In *Rolling Stone*, Peter Travers wrote, "Director Christopher Nolan, who wrote the script with David Goyer, shows us a Batman caught in the act of inventing himself. Nolan is caught, too, in the act of deconstructing the Batman myth while still delivering the dazzle to justify a $150 million budget. It's schizo entertainment. But credit Nolan for trying to do the impossible in a summer epic: take us somewhere we haven't been before...Like any movie with a surfeit of villains, none of them stick. Cillian Murphy comes closest as Dr. Jonathan Crane, a skinny shrink they call Scarecrow when he puts a burlap bag on his head. Each person sees his own worst fears come to life when they gaze at the bag. The low-budget headgear is typical of a movie that succeeds best when it hews to the rule of less is more. Beginner's luck evaporates when Nolan ends with a tricked-out car chase and a doomsday plot about a poisoned water supply. Nolan's too good for Bat business as usual. His secret for making Batman fly is as basic as black: Keep it real."[245]

Most reviewers, however, were much more enthused about the film than McCarthy, Morgenstern and Travers. Kenneth Turan, film critic for *The Los Angeles Times*, wrote, "Batman has finally come home. Not just to a story that painstakingly details his origins but to an ominous style that suits it beautifully. Christopher Nolan's *Batman Begins* disdains the mindless camp and compulsive weirdness that mostly characterized its quartet of predecessors and unapologetically positions its hero at the dark end of the street...This Batman is a carefully thought out and consummately well-made piece of work, a serious comic-book adaptation that is driven by story, psychology and reality, not special effects."[246]

In *The New York Times*, Manohla Dargis wrote, "*Batman Begins* is the seventh live-action film to take on the comic-book legend and the first to usher it into the kingdom of movie myth. Conceived in the shadow of American pop rather than in its bright light, this tense, effective iteration of Bob Kane's original comic book owes its power and pleasures to a director who takes his material seriously and to a star who shoulders that seriousness with ease...As sleek as a panther, with cheekbones that look sharp enough to give even an ardent lover pause, Mr. Bale makes a superbly menacing avenger...It's amazing what an excellent cast, a solid screenplay and a regard for the source material can do for a comic book movie."[247] Dargis later put the film on her list of The Best Films of the Year.[248]

James Christopher, reviewer for *The Times of London*, wrote, "What might inspire a billionaire playboy to dress up in a bat suit in order to beat the stuffing out of shifty creeps at 2am? Is there anyone out there mad enough to take this challenge seriously? Step forward Christopher Nolan. I know you're mostly British but your days as an obscure and fashionable young auteur are over...I honestly thought we'd seen the last of *Batman* when Tim Burton and Joel Schumacher hammered wooden stakes through the hammy franchise in the 1990s. I never expected a guided tour of Bruce Wayne's brain ten years later, or a director crazy enough to conduct one. But Nolan bucks the lethal odds. *Batman Begins* is a clever surprise. It's an exhilarating medley of bruising action that begins in the dark corridors of the caped crusader's psyche."[249]

Warner Bros. pulled out all the stops in promoting the film, even going so far as to reach out to the Nascar audience. The studio spent $1 million to promote the film at the Michigan International Speedway on Saturday, June 19, 2005, for a race called the *Batman Begins* 400. An actor dressed as Batman gave the signal to start the race, and the new Batmobile acted as pace car.[250] Both Mark Martin's race car and Ricky Craven's Craftsman Truck Series truck sported the Batman logo. Neither, however, won the race; that honor went to Greg Biffle, though Martin managed to come in third.

As *Batman Begins* was poised for its theatrical release in China on June 29, the Hong Kong media group Tom Online was preparing to deliver Warner Bros. content into mainland China via internet. Warner Bros. Online's deal with Tom Online called for the web service to carry trailers, games, ringtones and mobile-formatted video. The Chinese market was expected to greatly expand the customer base of Warner Bros. Online, which already had 60 million registered subscribers.[251]

Though it had gotten off to a moderate start, *Batman Begins* picked up steam at the box-office and by mid-August became the third film of 2005 to gross over $200 million, along with George Lucas's *Star War: Episode III-Revenge of the Sith*—which could also have been called *Darth Vader Begins*—and Steven Spielberg's updating of *War of the Worlds*.[252] *Batman Begins* ended its theatrical run with grosses of $205 million domestically and $166 million overseas.[253]

In October of 2005, about the same time *Batman Begins* was set to make its debut on DVD, Warner Home Video released, for the first time, two-disc special editions of the four previous *Batman* films in a set called *Batman: The Motion Picture Anthology 1989-1997*. The DVDs included director commentaries, making-of-featurettes, deleted scenes, and music videos for each title.[254]

Batman Begins helped bring Batman back into the pop culture zeitgeist in the Fall of 2005. On Halloween, even NBC's *The Today Show* saluted Batman, with host Matt Lauer and weatherman Al Roker dressing up as Batman and Robin. Featured host Katie Couric, meanwhile, dressed as another icon, Marilyn Monroe.[255]

In the summer of 2006, a year after the release of *Batman Begins*, Warner Bros. finally released a new Superman film, *Superman Returns*. Unlike *Batman Begins,* which had won over the die-hard comic book fans and was well received by the public at large, *Superman Returns* was largely seen as a disappointment. This was made especially clear when *Batman Begins* was honored at the 2006 MTV Movie Awards, honoring films released the previous year. When Christian Bale won the Best Hero honor, beating out Jessica Alba of *Fantastic Four*, Kate Beckinsale of *Underworld: Evolution*, Ewan McGregor of *Star Wars: Episode III—Revenge of the Sith* and Daniel Radcliffe of *Harry Potter and the Goblet of Fire*, his award was presented to him by *Superman Returns* stars Brandon Routh, Kevin Spacey and Kate Bosworth. Bale began his acceptance speech by thanking director Christopher Nolan "for getting rid of those bloody nipples" before saying to Routh, "I'm sorry, Superman, but Batman is the badass!"[256]

In the end, by making a film that revolved around the theme of fear, with a villain who used fear as a weapon, Nolan created a movie that perfectly fit the tenor of the post-9/11 era, and its success ensured that there would be a sequel. "We were joking on *Batman Begins*, 'Hey, if we pull this one off we'll get to make a big film!'" said Nolan. "But at a certain point you have to acknowledge that this is it—there aren't any bigger films."[2]

1 —, *Batman Begins International Production Notes*, © 2005, Warner Bros. Entertainment, Inc., p. 43

2 Nolan, Christopher, and David S. Goyer, *Batman Begins, The Screenplay*, © 2005 Faber and Faber, London, p. xi

3 Goodwin, Christopher, "Batman, Robbin' and Murder: This is the True Story of the Three Nolan Siblings—Two Make Batman Movies That are the Toast of Hollywood, the Other is In Prison and a Murder Suspect," *The (London) Sunday Times*, June 27, 2010

4 Lawrence, Will, "Memories of the Joker: Heath Ledger," *The London Times*, July 16, 2008

5 Goodwin, Christopher, "Batman, Robbin' and Murder: This is the True Story of the Three Nolan Siblings—Two Make Batman Movies That are the Toast of Hollywood, the Other is In Prison and a Murder Suspect," *The (London) Sunday Times*, June 27, 2010

6 Nolan, Christopher, and David S. Goyer, *Batman Begins, The Screenplay*, © 2005 Faber and Faber, London, p. xi

7 Nazzaro, Joe, "Knight Haunts," *Starlog Magazine # 336*, July 2005, p. 64-65

8 Nolan, Christopher, and David S. Goyer, *Batman Begins, The Screenplay*, © 2005 Faber and Faber, London, p. xii

9 Halbfinger, David M., "Batman's Burden: A Director Confronts Darkness and Death," *The New York Times*, March 9, 2008, http://www.nytimes.com/2008/03/09/movies/09halb.html?ref=heathledger, accessed July 3, 2011

10 Graser, Marc & Cathy Dunkley, "The Bat and the Beautiful," *Weekly Variety*, Feb. 9-15, 2004, p. 1

11 *Ibid.*, p. 107

12 *Ibid.*, p. 1

13 Nolan, Christopher, and David S. Goyer, *Batman Begins, The Screenplay*, © 2005 Faber and Faber, London, p. xiv

14 Murray, Rebecca, "David Goyer and Cillian Murphy Discuss 'Batman Begins,'" *About.com*, http://movies.about.com/od/batman/a/batman072304_2.htm, accessed Aug. 7, 2011

15 Nolan, Christopher, and David S. Goyer, *Batman Begins, The Screenplay*, © 2005 Faber and Faber, London, p. xiv

16 *Ibid.*, p. xv

17 *Ibid.*, p. xv

18 Graser, Marc & Cathy Dunkley, "The Bat and the Beautiful," *Weekly Variety*, Feb. 9-15, 2004, p. 106

19 Murray, Rebecca, "David Goyer and Cillian Murphy Discuss 'Batman Begins,'" *About.com*, http://movies.about.com/od/batman/a/batman072304_2.htm, accessed Aug. 7, 2011

20 Nolan, Christopher, and David S. Goyer, *Batman Begins, The Screenplay*, © 2005 Faber and Faber, London, p. xiv

21 Graser, Marc & Cathy Dunkley, "The Bat and the Beautiful," *Weekly Variety*, Feb. 9-15, 2004, p. 107

22 *Ibid.*, p. 107

23 Graser, Marc, "The '3 Rings' of Batman," *Weekly Variety*, Feb. 9-15, 2004, p. 106

24 *Ibid.*

25 *Ibid.*

26 *Ibid.*

27 *Ibid.*

28 *Ibid.*

29 Murray, Rebecca, "David Goyer and Cillian Murphy Discuss 'Batman Begins,'" *About.com*, http://movies.about.com/od/batman/a/batman072304_2.htm, accessed Aug. 7, 2011

30 Nolan, Christopher, and David S. Goyer, *Batman Begins, The Screenplay*, © 2005 Faber and Faber, London, p. xvi

31 Dawson, James, "Counterpunch: 'Batman Begins': Is His Past Really Such a Mystery?" *The Los Angeles Times*, May 23, 2005, p. E.3

32 Nolan, Christopher, and David S. Goyer, *Batman Begins, The Screenplay*, © 2005 Faber and Faber, London, p. xix

33 Lorenzen, Dr. Michael, "Did Teddy Roosevelt Help to Inspire Batman?" *American Presidents.org*, http://www.american-presidents.org/2008/07/did-teddy-roosevelt-help-to-inspire.html, July 26, 2008, accessed Aug. 7, 2011

34 —, *Batman Begins International Production Notes*, © 2005, Warner Bros. Entertainment, Inc., p. 5

35 —, "Batman Begins International Production Notes," © 2005, Warner Bros.Entertainment, Inc., p. 6

36 —, *Batman Begins International Production Notes*, © 2005, Warner Bros. Entertainment, Inc., p. 5

37 *Ibid.*, p. 6

38 *Ibid.*

39 Murray, Rebecca, "David Goyer and Cillian Murphy Discuss 'Batman Begins,'" *About. com*, http://movies.about.com/od/batman /a/batman072304_2.htm, accessed Aug. 7, 2011

40 Nolan, Christopher, and David S. Goyer, *Batman Begins, The Screenplay*, © 2005 Faber and Faber, London, p. xiv

41 Murray, Rebecca, "David Goyer and Cillian Murphy Discuss 'Batman Begins,'" *About. com*, http://movies.about.com/od/batman /a/batman072304_2.htm, accessed Aug. 7, 2011

42 Graser, Marc & Cathy Dunkley, "The Bat and the Beautiful," *Weekly Variety*, Feb. 9-15, 2004, p. 106

43 —, *Batman Begins International Production Notes*, © 2005, Warner Bros. Entertainment, Inc., p. 6

44 *Ibid.*

45 White, Roland, "Zowie! Nice Wheels, Batman," *The (London) Sunday Times*, June 5 2005

46 —, *Batman Begins International Production Notes*, © 2005, Warner Bros. Entertainment, Inc., p. 21

47 *Ibid.*, p. 20

48 Nolan, Christopher, and David S. Goyer, *Batman Begins, The Screenplay*, © 2005 Faber and Faber, London, p. xii

49 Ventre, Michael, "Directors Drawn to Graphic Novels," *Daily Variety*, Jan. 11, 2006, p. A10

50 —, *Batman Begins International Production Notes*, © 2005, Warner Bros. Entertainment, Inc., p. 6

51 Nazzaro, Joe, "Knight Haunts," *Starlog Magazine # 336*, July 2005, p. 65

52 *Ibid.*, p. 63-64

53 Lim, Dennis, "Letting His Role Do the Talking," *The New York Times*, Dec. 3, 2010, http://www..nytimes.com/2010/12/05/ movies/05balehtml?scp=255&sq=batman&s t=nyt, accessed Aug. 17, 2011

54 Nolan, Christopher, and David S. Goyer, *Batman Begins, The Screenplay*, © 2005 Faber and Faber, London, p. xvii-xviii

55 Romanelli, Alex, "The Bat Flies Right," *Daily Variety*, June 9, 2005, p. 51

56 Nazzaro, Joe, "Knight Haunts," *Starlog Magazine # 336*, July 2005, p. 64

57 *Ibid.*

58 Dunkley, Cathy & Jonathan Bing, "New Dynamic for WB Duo: Are Franchise Heroes Ready to Fly Again?", *Weekly Variety*, Sept. 8-14, 2003, p. 5

59 Murray, Rebecca, "David Goyer and Cillian Murphy Discuss 'Batman Begins,'" *About. com*, http://movies.about.com/od/batman/ a/batman072304_2.htm, accessed Aug. 7, 2011

60 Nolan, Christopher, and David S. Goyer, *Batman Begins, The Screenplay*, © 2005 Faber and Faber, London, p. xvii-xviii

61 Dunkley, Cathy & Jonathan Bing, "...WB Casts Next Caped Crusader," *Daily Variety*, Sept. 12, 2003, p. 1

62 Canavese, Peter, "Christian Bale Wonder Con Batman Begins Panel Transcript," *Groucho Reviews*, http://www.grouchoreviews. com/interviews/47, May 3, 2005, accessed July 24, 2011

63 Dunkley, Cathy & Jonathan Bing, "...WB Casts Next Caped Crusader," *Daily Variety*, Sept. 12, 2003, p. 71

64 —, *Batman Begins International Production Notes*, © 2005, Warner Bros. Entertainment, Inc., p. 7

65 —, "'Knight's' Bale: Who is That Masked Man?" *CNN.com*, Jul. 28, 2008, accessed June 22, 2010

66 Brown, David, "Batman Star, Christian Bale, Arrested After 'Attacking His Mother and Sister in Hotel Suite'" *The London Times*, July 23 2008

67 —, "'Knight's' Bale: Who is That Masked Man?" *CNN.com*, Jul. 28, 2008, accessed June 22, 2010

68 Brown, David, "Batman Star, Christian Bale, Arrested After 'Attacking His Mother and Sister in Hotel Suite'" *The London Times*, July 23 2008

69 —, "'Knight's' Bale: Who is That Masked Man?" *CNN.com*, Jul. 28, 2008, accessed June 22, 2010

70 —, "Profile: Christian Bale—The Brooding Star of Batman Has Shades of His On-Screen Persona; But Last Week He Was Unable to Escape the Spotlight," *The London Times*, July 27, 2008

71 —, "'Knight's' Bale: Who is That Masked Man?" *CNN.com*, Jul. 28, 2008, accessed June 22, 2010

72 Dunkley, Cathy & Jonathan Bing, "...WB Casts Next Caped Crusader," *Daily Variety*, Sept. 12, 2003,   p. 71

73 Graser, Marc & Cathy Dunkley, "The Bat and the Beautiful," *Weekly Variety*, Feb. 9-15, 2004, p. 107

74 *Ibid.*

75 *Ibid.*, p. 106

76 —, *Batman Begins International Production Notes*, © 2005, Warner Bros. Entertainment, Inc., p. 10

77 Dunkley, Cathy and Carl DiOrio, "Next 'Batman' Raising Caine," *Daily Variety*, Nov. 25, 2003, p. 1

78 —, *Batman Begins International Production Notes*, © 2005, Warner Bros. Entertainment, Inc., p. 11

79 D'Alessandro, Anthony, "Prestigious and Prolific: For Seasoned Workhorses, Oscar is Merely Frosting on the Cake," *Daily Variety*, Oct. 27, 2005, p. A4

80 Canavese, Peter, "Sir Michael Caine & Katie Holmes —Batman Begins—05/03/05," *GrouchoReviews.com*, http://www.groucho reviews.com/interviews/94, accessed July 26, 2011

81 —, *Batman Begins International Production Notes*, © 2005, Warner Bros. Entertainment, Inc., p. 11

82 *Ibid.*, p. 10-11

83 *Ibid.*, p. 11

84 Canavese, Peter, "Sir Michael Caine & Katie Holmes —Batman Begins—05/03/05," *GrouchoReviews.com*, http://www.groucho reviews.com/interviews/94, accessed July 26, 2011

85 Fleming, Michael & Cathy Dunkley, "Helmer Nolan Has Eye on Femme for ' Batman,'" *Daily Variety*, Dec. 10, 2003, p. 7

86 —, *Batman Begins International Production Notes*, © 2005, Warner Bros. Entertainment, Inc., p. 15

87 *Ibid.*

88 *Ibid.*, p. 14

89 *Ibid.*, p. 13

90 Fleming, Michael & Cathy Dunkley, "Irish Thesp Gets the Call as 'Batman' Bags Baddie," *Daily Variety*, Dec. 11, 2003, p. 7

91 —, *Batman Begins International Production Notes*, © 2005, Warner Bros. Entertainment, Inc., p. 19

92 Dunkley, Cathy & Marc Graser, "Freeman to Boss 'Batman,'" *Daily Variety*, Feb. 19, 2004, p. 5

93 —, *Batman Begins International Production Notes*, © 2005, Warner Bros. Entertainment, Inc., p. 18

94 *Ibid.*, p. 17

95 Dunkley, Cathy & Marc Graser, "Freeman to Boss 'Batman,'" *Daily Variety*, Feb. 19, 2004, p. 5

96 —, "Corrections," *Daily Variety*, Feb. 20, 2004, p. 4

97 —, *Batman Begins International Production Notes*, © 2005, Warner Bros. Entertainment, Inc., p. 12-13

98 Dunkley, Cathy & Marc Graser, "Watanabe Becoming Villainous in 'Batman,'" *Daily Variety*, Feb. 24, 2004, p. 4

99 —, *Batman Begins International Production Notes*, © 2005, Warner Bros. Entertainment, Inc., p. 12

100 Dunkley, Cathy, "Oldman Joins 'Batman,'" *Daily Variety*, March 4, 2004, p. 4

101 —, *Batman Begins International Production Notes*, © 2005, Warner Bros. Entertainment, Inc., p. 16

102 *Ibid.*, p. 15-16

103 *Ibid.*, p. 16

104 Canavese, Peter, "Morgan Freeman & Gary Oldman—Batman Begins—05/03/05," *GrouchoReviews.com*, http://www.groucho reviews.com/interviews/94, accessed July 26, 2011

105 Fleming, Michael, "Hauer Powers Batpic," *Daily Variety*, March 25, 2004, p. 5

106 Graser, Marc & Cathy Dunkley, "The Bat and the Beautiful," *Weekly Variety*, Feb. 9-15, 2004, p. 106

107 Canavese, Peter, "Christopher Nolan & Emma Thomas—Batman Begins—05/03/05," *GrouchoReviews.com*, http://www.groucho reviews.com/interviews/94, accessed July 26, 2011

108 Wimberly, Rachel, "Fantasy Lands Rooted in Reality Checks," *Daily Variety*, Jan. 6, 2006, p. A2

109 —, *Batman Begins International Production Notes*, © 2005, Warner Bros. Entertainment, Inc., p. 39

110 Nazzaro, Joe, "Knight Haunts," *Starlog Magazine # 336*, July 2005, p. 62

111 —, *Batman Begins International Production Notes*, © 2005, Warner Bros. Entertainment, Inc., p. 39

112 Palmer, Martyn, "Christopher Nolan Brings the Bat Back," *The London Times*, June 11, 2005

113 Canavese, Peter, "Christopher Nolan & Emma Thomas—Batman Begins—05/03/05," *GrouchoReviews.com*, http://www.groucho reviews.com/interviews/94, accessed July 26, 2011

114 "Clarkson's Flunkey," "Hauer Speaks Again! Designer of 'The Tumbler' Revealed," *BatmanOnFilm.com*, http://www.batman-on-film.com/b5newsarchives28.html, accessed Aug. 7, 2011

115 *Ibid.*

116 Nazzaro, Joe, "Knight Haunts," *Starlog Magazine # 336*, July 2005, p. 58

117 *Ibid.*, p. 62

118 —, *Batman Begins International Production Notes*, © 2005, Warner Bros. Entertainment, Inc., p. 22

119 *Ibid.*, p. 22-23

120 *Ibid.*, p. 22

121 *Ibid.*, p. 23

122 Crowley, Nathan, "Not Your Father's Batmobile," *The Los Angeles Times*, Jun. 12, 2005, p. E.6

123 —, *Batman Begins International Production Notes*, © 2005, Warner Bros. Entertainment, Inc., p. 23

124 *Ibid.*, p. 22

125 Patton, Phil, "What Would Batman Drive? These Days, an Assault Vehicle," *The New York Times*, Aug 2, 2004, p. D.9

126 Nazzaro, Joe, "Knight Haunts," *Starlog Magazine # 336*, July 2005, p. 58

127 —, *Batman Begins International Production Notes*, © 2005, Warner Bros. Entertainment, Inc., p. 27

128 *Ibid.*

129 *Ibid.*

130 *Ibid.*, p. 27-28

131 *Ibid.*, p. 28

132 *Ibid.*, p. 29-30

133 *Ibid.*, p. 28-29

134 *Ibid.*, p. 29

135 *Ibid.*

136 Nazzaro, Joe, "Knight Haunts," *Starlog Magazine # 336*, July 2005, p. 65

137 —, *Batman Begins International Production Notes*, © 2005, Warner Bros. Entertainment, Inc., p. 34

138 *Ibid.*, p. 33

139 *Ibid.*

140 *Ibid.*

141 *Ibid.*, p. 33-34

142 *Ibid.*, p. 33

143 *Ibid.*, p. 34

144 *Ibid.*

145 *Ibid.*, p. 30

146 Canavese, Peter, "Christian Bale Interview," *Groucho Reviews*, http://www.grouchoreviews. com/interviews/47, Feb. 19, 2005, accessed July 24, 201

147 —, *Batman Begins International Production Notes*, © 2005, Warner Bros. Entertainment, Inc., p. 31

148 Canavese, Peter, "Christian Bale Interview," *Groucho Reviews*, http://www.grouchoreviews. com/interviews/47, June 3, 2005, accessed July 24, 2011

149 —, *Batman Begins International Production Notes*, © 2005, Warner Bros. Entertainment, Inc., p. 30-31

150 *Ibid.*, p. 31

151 *Ibid.*

152 Graser, Marc, "Fifth 'Batman' Gets a Title," *Daily Variety*, Feb. 27, 2004, p. 5

153 Dunkley, Cathy, "Oldman Joins 'Batman,'" *Daily Variety*, March 4, 2004, p. 4

154 —, *Batman Begins International Production Notes*, © 2005, Warner Bros. Entertainment, Inc., p. 35

155 *Ibid.*, p. 38

156 *Ibid.*, p. 36

157 *Ibid.*, p. 35

158 *Ibid.*

159 *Ibid.*

160 *Ibid.*

161 *Ibid.*, p. 36

162 *Ibid.*, p. 38

163 *Ibid.*

164 *Ibid.*, p. 41

165 *Ibid.*, p. 42

166 *Ibid.*

167 Canavese, Peter, "Sir Michael Caine & Katie Holmes —Batman Begins—05/03/05," *GrouchoReviews.com*, http://www.groucho reviews.com/interviews/94, accessed July 26, 2011

168 Nazzaro, Joe, "Knight Haunts," *Starlog Magazine # 336*, July 2005, p. 66

169 *Ibid.*, p. 66-67

170 Canavese, Peter, "Christian Bale Interview," *Groucho Reviews*, http://www.grouchoreviews. com/interviews/47, Feb. 19, 2005, accessed July 24, 201

171 —, *Batman Begins International Production Notes*, © 2005, Warner Bros. Entertainment, Inc., p. 40

172 *Ibid.*

173 *Ibid.*

174 *Ibid.*, p. 42

175 *Ibid.*, p. 43

176 *Ibid.*, p. 37

177 *Ibid.*

178 *Ibid.*, p. 39

179 *Ibid.*, p. 40

180 Boyd, Betsy, "How Much is Too Much?" *Daily Variety*, July 27, 2005, p. A4

181 —, *Batman Begins International Production Notes*, © 2005, Warner Bros. Entertainment, Inc., p. 42

182 Idelson, Karen, "Buzz Builders," *Daily Variety*, July 13, 2005, p. A2

183 Fritz, Ben, "Gaggle of Geeks Gabs at Confab," *Daily Variety*, July 14, 2005, p. 13

184 —, *Batman Begins International Production Notes*, © 2005, Warner Bros. Entertainment, Inc., p. 23-24

185 *Ibid.*, p. 39

186 *Ibid.*, p. 24

187 *Ibid.*, p. 39

188 —, "Cinematography the Analysis," *Daily Variety*, Feb. 13, 2006, p. A17

189 —, *Batman Begins International Production Notes*, © 2005, Warner Bros. Entertainment, Inc., p. 25

190 *Ibid.*

191 *Ibid.*

192 *Ibid.*

193 *Ibid.*, p. 24

194 *Ibid.*

195 *Ibid.*, p. 25

196 Canavese, Peter, "Christian Bale Interview," *Groucho Reviews*, http://www.grouchoreviews.com/interviews/47, Feb. 19, 2005, accessed July 24, 201

197 —, *Batman Begins International Production Notes*, © 2005, Warner Bros. Entertainment, Inc., p. 22

198 *Ibid.*, p. 26

199 Canavese, Peter, "Christopher Nolan & Emma Thomas—Batman Begins—05/03/05," *GrouchoReviews.com*, http://www.grouchoreviews.com/interviews/94, accessed July 26, 2011

200 *Ibid.*

201 —, "Batman Begins International Production Notes," © 2005, Warner Bros. Entertainment, Inc., p. 43

202 Cohen, David S. , "London's Calling: Charlie and the Chocolate Factory and Batman Begins" *Daily Variety*, July 27, 2005, p. A2

203 Boyd, Betsy, "How Much is Too Much?" *Daily Variety*, July 27, 2005, p. A1

204 Knolle, Sharon, "Tune Titans Team Up For 'Batman Begins,'" *Daily Variety*, July 17, 2006, p. A4

205 *Ibid.*

206 *Ibid.*

207 Gritten, David, "Batman Now Speaks With a British Accent," *The New York Times*, Dec. 19, 2004, p. 2.18

208 *Ibid.*

209 *Ibid.*, p. C.1

210 *Ibid.*

211 *Ibid.*

212 *Ibid.*

213 *Ibid.*

214 *Ibid.*

215 McClintock, Pamela, "A Tull Order To Fill," *Weekly Variety*, Nov. 21-27, 2005, p. 6

216 *Ibid.*

217 Gross, Daniel, "The New Deal," *Weekly Variety*, Jan. 9, 2006, VLife Oscar Portfolio 2006, p. 73

218 *Ibid.*

219 *Ibid.*

220 Snyder, Gabriel, "'Batman' Arrives Earlier Than Expected," *Daily Variety*, April 28, 2005, p. 2

221 Snyder, Gabriel, "Dark Knight Takes Flight..." *Daily Variety*, June 15, 2005, p. 47

222 Gustines, George Gene, "When Superman Meets Batman," *The New York Times*, Apr. 20, 2005, p. E.2

223 McClintock, Pamela, "WB Draws New DC Logo," *Daily Variety*, May 10, 2005, p. 6

224 Friedman, Wayne, "Dollars Go Digital: Emerging Platforms Like the Net Growing the Fastest," *Daily Variety*, May 19, 2005, p. A1

225 *Ibid.*

226 *Ibid.*

227 *Ibid.*

228 Burton, Natasha, "MTV Lights 'Dynamite,'" *Daily Variety*, June 7, 2005, p. 36

229 Robertson, Campbell, Joe Brescia, Fiona Byrne and Jordana Lewis, "Boldface," *The New York Times*, Jun. 8, 2005, p. B.2

230 Romanelli, Alex, "The Bat Flies Right," *Daily Variety*, June 9, 2005, p. 51

231 Robertson, Campbell, Joe Brescia, Fiona Byrne and Jordana Lewis, "Boldface," *The New York Times*, Jun. 8, 2005, p. B.2

232 Romanelli, Alex, "The Bat Flies Right," *Daily Variety*, June 9, 2005, p. 51

233 Snyder, Gabriel, "Dark Knight Takes Flight..." *Daily Variety*, June 15, 2005, p. 1

234 Morfoot, Addie, "It's Same 'Bat' Time for Imax," *Daily Variety*, March 3, 2005, p. 5

235 McMary, Dave, "...And WB Hopes O'seas Auds Go Batty," *Daily Variety*, June 15, 2005, p. 1

236 *Ibid.*, p. 47

237 Snyder, Gabriel, "Dark Knight Takes Flight..." *Daily Variety*, June 15, 2005, p. 47

238 Snyder, Gabriel & Dave McNary, "Crusade Begins: 'Batman' Tries to Reverse B.O. Trend," *Daily Variety*, June 17, 2005, p. 1

239 —, "The 'Bat' and the Beautiful: Comic Hero, Comely Couple Rule B.O.," *Daily Variety*, June 20, 2005, p. 1

240 *Ibid.*, p. 24

241 McNary, Dave, "...And Flex O'seas Muscle," *Daily Variety*, June 20, 2005, p. 1

242 Thomas, Archie, "Blighty Goes Batty," *Weekly Variety*, June 20-26, 2005, p. 47

243 McCarthy, Todd, "Batman Begins," *Daily Variety*, June 6, 2005, p. 7

244 Morgenstern, Joe, "Review/Film: Holy Melancholy, 'Batman'! Tale of Superhero's Origins Is Vivid, Stylish—and Dour; Solemnity May Fly With the Kids, Who'll Mistake It for Profundity; Bale Plays Bruce Wayne, Glumly," *The Wall Street Journal*, Jun. 17, 2005, p. W.1

245 Travers, Peter, "Batman Begins," *Rolling Stone*, June 15, 2005

246 Turan, Kenneth, "Wholly rebound; 'Batman Begins' Honors the Dark Knight and Filmmaking Itself," *The Los Angeles Times*, Jun. 14, 2005, pg. E.1

247 Dargis, Manohla, "Dark was the Young Knight," *The New York Times*, June 15, 2005, p. E.1.

248 Dargis, Manohla, "The Best Films of the Year," *The New York Times*, Dec 25, 2005, p. 2.7

249 Christopher, James, "Batman Begins," *The London Times*, June 16, 2005

250 Bernstein, Viv, "Nascar Knows Logos Make Wheels Go 'Round," *The New York Times*, Jun 19, 2005, p. 8.8

251 Frater, Patrick, "WB, Tom Click China Deal," *Daily Variety*, June 22, 2005, p. 12

252 Snyder, Gabriel, "Brotherly Love: Revenge Pic Lures Femmes, Bags $21 Mil," *Daily Variety*, Aug. 15, 2005, p. 40

253 "Ledger Joins Bat Pack," *Daily Variety*, Aug. 1, 2006, p. 16

254 —, "Disc Drive," *Daily Variety*, July 27, 2005, p. 5

255 —, "A Blonde Comes Between Batman and Robin," *The New York Times*, Nov. 1, 2005, p. E.2

256 Repstad, Laura, "MTV's Anything Goes Kudos," *Daily Variety*, June 6, 2006, p. 54

257 Leve, Ariel, "Britman: Gotham City's Been Invaded—By a Mostly British Film Crew and Cast. Can the Director Christopher Nolan Inject Batman With the Fresh Blood He Needs?," *The London Times*, May 29, 2005

Chapter Twelve:
A DARK DARK KNIGHT

"The psychopathic clown, that's an icon to stand with the guy with the ears and cape...it's just a wonderful visual relationship, and it's a terrifying image."
—Christopher Nolan[1]

BACK AT BAT

In 2002, Warner Bros. president Alan Horn promoted Jeff Robinov to president of production. After Lorenzo di Bonaventura's exit from the studio, it seemed clear that Horn was grooming Robinov to succeed him. Robinov began making subtle changes in the way Warner Bros. did business. The "Warner way" had been to produce star-driven movies that were efficiently and effectively marketed, while keeping stability in the executive offices. With that strategy, the studio—as of 2007—had sold over $1 billion in tickets at the domestic box-office annually for six years running, a remarkable achievement in Hollywood.[2]

But Robinov recognized that the industry's economics were changing, and the tastes of filmgoers were also evolving. He felt that the studio needed to make fewer films, but that more of those films needed to be big-budget blockbusters. And one way to achieve that was by making movies based on properties that already had brand recognition among the public, properties like the comic books of DC Comics. Consequently, Robinov pushed to integrate DC Comics into the movie division and produce more franchises based on DC characters.[3]

Toward that end, the studio made a good choice selecting Christopher Nolan to take over the ailing *Batman* franchise. After breathing life back into the Caped Crusader, Nolan moved on to another project, *The Prestige*, featuring Christian Bale, Hugh Jackman and Michael Caine. Based on a novel by Christopher Priest, the film was scripted by Jonathan "Jonah" Nolan, Christopher Nolan's younger brother, who began as a writer by penning the short story *Memento Mori*, which became the basis for his brother's film *Memento*.[4]

About three months after the release of *Batman Begins*, while filming of *The Prestige* was underway, Christopher Nolan met with David Goyer to toss around ideas for a *Batman* sequel.[5] "Chris called me up and said, 'Hey, let's have lunch,' and I thought maybe he wants to talk about the second one," said Goyer.[6] "It was not a foregone conclusion that we were going to do a second film, and even when we started talking about a second film, then it was a long process where we talked about whether or not this story that we were coming up with was worthy or better than the first one."[7]

Nolan and Goyer decided that the next film would pick up about six months after the conclusion of *Batman Begins*. "I thought we left the world of Batman at an interesting place in the first film, and the end suggested an intriguing direction in which the story could continue," said Nolan.[8]

"At the end of the first movie we've got that little grace note between Gordon and Batman where we talk about escalation, and once we started talking about doing another film, it became clear that that was what the theme was going to be," said Goyer. "The idea of the second movie, Batman is there, the public knows about him, so then it's like, where are all the repercussions of that? Good and bad. That was the starting place for the story. How are the villains of Gotham going to react and how are the people going to react? It's also the idea, which I really liked, of copycat Batmen. It just seemed like a natural thing that would come out of that."[9]

Since Batman's character arc was the subject of the first film, Nolan and Goyer began thinking about which character the new film would center on, and they chose Harvey Dent, the crusading district attorney who eventually becomes the villain, Two-Face. "It became apparent as we were talking fairly quickly on that Harvey was actually the protagonist of the movie, that The Joker doesn't change and Batman doesn't really change, but Harvey is the one that changes as a result of his interaction between the Joker and Batman," said Goyer. "And obviously he changes in a tragic way so that means the movie has to be a tragedy."[10]

Upon learning that the next film would feature the Joker and Two-Face, DC Comics sent the filmmakers every comic book story featuring the two characters.[11] Goyer, already well-versed in Batmania, was inspired by a few stories in particular. Although there were touches of Frank Miller's Batman, and some parts inspired by the comic book stories of Denny O'Neil, the biggest influence came from the graphic novel *The Long Halloween*, written by Jeph Loeb, a story that stretched over 13 comic books in 1996 and '97.[12] The story has Batman working with D.A. Harvey Dent and Lt. James Gordon to try and find Holiday, a killer who murders a victim each month around a holiday. During the course of the story, Dent becomes Two-Face when acid is thrown in his face. The Joker features in the story, as does gangster Sal Maroni, and in one scene Batman and Gordon burn a pile of Mafia cash, a scene mirrored in the film but with the Joker doing the honors.

Since Goyer was committed to direct *The Invisible* and produce *Ghost Rider*, and was also under contract to Warner Bros. to write and direct *The Flash*, it was apparent that all he would have time to do for the *Batman* sequel was help hash out the initial storyline. Christopher Nolan was not concerned; besides being a scriptwriter himself, his brother Jonathan had just proven his worth with *The Prestige*, so Nolan turned to him to work with Goyer in developing the story and then write the screenplay.[13] "David and Chris went off and butted heads for a while and came up with a story," said Jonathan Nolan, "and then they handed it over to me and let me take a crack at a first draft."[14]

Unlike Tim Burton's *Batman* (1989), the Nolans didn't see any reason to provide a backstory for the Joker. After all, when the villain made his first comic book appearance in 1940, he appeared fully formed, wreaking murderous havoc without any sort of explanatory origin. As Christopher Nolan pointed out, it's the same as the shark in *Jaws*: "You don't care where the shark came from, you don't care who the shark's parents were."[15] Jonathan Nolan agreed, saying, "My understanding of the character from the comic books, the aspect of him that appealed to me most, was the idea of the elemental bad guy. That opening shot of him standing on a corner—in my imagination he could have just appeared out of thin air."[16]

Christopher Nolan liked the idea of the Joker as a pure anarchist. "As the screenplay developed, we started to explore the effect one guy could have on an entire population—the ways in which he could upset the balance for people, the ways in which he could take their rules for living, their ethics, their beliefs, their humanity and turn them on themselves," said the director. "You could say we've seen echoes of that in our own world, which has led me to believe that anarchy and chaos—even the threat of anarchy and chaos—are among the most frightening things society faces, especially in this day and age."[17]

Christopher Nolan wrote the final draft of the screenplay, streamlining it into a script ready for shooting. "Chris is always going to take the last pass on these scripts going in, he's a writer as well as a director kind of 50/50," said Jonathan Nolan, "so he's always going to get in there and take that last crack at it."[18]

Nolan did some of the scriptwriting in Hong Kong, having traveled there in October of 2006 to get the right flavor of the Asian city for the scenes that were set there. As producer Charles Roven noted, "He likes to get out of town and be inspired."[19] The Hong Kong scenes added an international flavor to *The Dark Knight*, making it more like the James Bond films Nolan admired. The director included more 007 allusions in this script; besides Lucius Fox acting as a surrogate "Q" figure, providing Bruce Wayne with an array of gadgets (and even uttering a Q-like line, "Try reading the instruction manual first"), Batman uses a Skyhook to extract him and a Chinese businessman named Lau from a Hong Kong building. The Skyhook originally made its film debut at the clImax of the 1965 James Bond film *Thunderball*, lifting 007 and Domino out of a life raft before the closing credits. When Garth at the *Dark Horizons* website asked Nolan if he purposefully put 007 references into the film, Nolan responded, "We certainly did in both films. We started in *Batman Begins*, and I think the Bond films are a big influence tonally. In trying to explain to the studio, you know, if you look at the early Bond films you've got extraordinary things happening, but there's an overall tone you can buy into as a regular action movie. You're not completely stepping outside the bounds of reality." Indeed, Nolan has admitted in interviews that he would love to direct a James Bond movie.[20]

Not surprisingly, given the director's involvement in the writing, the final script was practically identical to the eventual film that was made from it; there are no scenes in the script that do not appear in the film, and almost every line of dialogue is exactly the same, save for a few instances of what may have been actor-inspired improvisation. For instance, when Batman appears on the Bat-Pod, in the script the Joker says, "Guess it was him," while in the final film, he says, "Now *there's* a Batman!"

There was no question of Warner Bros. greenlighting the film. The studio wanted a *Batman* sequel from the moment the first returns for *Batman Begins* came in. Having entrusted the franchise to Nolan, it was just a matter of waiting until he was ready to carry on. But while they were waiting, Robinov—anxious to exploit the DC Comics assets—set another Batman-related property into motion.

THE JUSTICE LEAGUE

Jeff Robinov had a vision. He was thinking bigger than a film that featured only Batman, bigger than a film that featured only Superman, bigger than a film that pitted Batman against Superman. What he envisioned was a film that teamed Batman and Superman with Wonder Woman, Aquaman, the Flash, Green Lantern and the Martian Manhunter—a Justice League of America film, based on the popular superhero team-up that first appeared in the comic book *The Brave and the Bold* #28 (February/March 1960). The Justice League of America later spawned the animated cartoons *Super Friends*, which ran from 1973 to 1986, and *Justice League Unlimited*, which ran from 2001 to 2006.

Daily Variety announced on February 23, 2007 that Warner Bros., searching for a new tentpole franchise, planned to bring *The Justice League of America* to the big screen, and had hired the husband-and-wife writing duo of Kieran and Michele Mulroney to write the script (Kieran Mulroney is the brother of actor Dermot Mulroney).[21]

Announcing the hiring of the Mulroneys, Robinov said, "The Justice League of America has been a perennial favorite for generations of fans, and we believe their appeal to film audiences will be as strong and diverse as the characters themselves."[22] The Mulroneys turned in their first draft script in mid-June. Warner Bros. was enthusiastic about it, but worried that if the Justice League movie went forward, it would delay, and perhaps derail, the planned *Superman Returns* sequel.[23] On the plus side, however, the studio thought a Justice League film might provide a launching pad for individual films of *Wonder Woman* and *The Flash*, the latter of which was already in development with David Goyer.

Released eight months earlier, the much-anticipated *Superman Returns*, which the studio expected to be a tremendous hit, had turned out to be something of a dud. The film grossed just barely more than $200 million in the U.S., less than its $209 million budget; worldwide, the total take was $391 million. Along with the mixed critical response, the disappointing box-office returns meant the chances for a Superman sequel were slim to none. But delaying the sequel meant the loss of a big tentpole feature for the summer of 2009, unless *Justice League* could fill the slot.

Both Christopher Nolan and Christian Bale expressed reservations about the *Justice League* film. To mitigate their concerns, Warner Bros. considered doing it as either an animated feature or with motion capture, but those notions were quickly dropped.[24] But getting the film launched was complicated by the number of roles to be filled and the large amount of special effects required by the script.[25]

In September 2007, the studio hired *Mad Max* director George Miller to shepherd *Justice League* to the screen. With the threat of a writer's strike looming, they needed to move quickly, so as the script took shape, they immediately began casting. Neither Christian Bale nor Brandon Routh were expected to be in the *Justice League* film, which meant the roles of Batman and Superman would be played by other actors.[26] On September 25, the studio released the first bit of casting news, with the announcement that Jessica Biel was in talks to play Wonder Woman.[27] She eventually dropped out, with Megan Gale signing for the role. Adam Brody was cast as the Flash, rapper Common as the Green Lantern, and 6'5" Armie Hammer Jr. signed to play Batman.[28]

The Writer's Guild went on strike on November 5, 2007. As the shutdown dragged into the new year, Warner Bros. decided to let the options lapse on all the cast members Miller had assembled for the film. The studio had set January 15 as the greenlight deadline for the film, but on the 16th, they announced that the production was on indefinite hold. The cast members were informed that their options would not be exercised, but they were assured that the studio intended to make the film with them, perhaps in the late summer or fall of 2008 at the earliest.[29] The studio said the film was sidelined because they had not received the official response they needed regarding tax breaks for filming in Australia, and also because they felt the script could use a little more work, which wasn't possible due to the writer's strike.[30]

When the strike was resolved on February 12, 2008, Warner Bros. again put *Justice League* on the production fast-track, hoping to have it ready for a 2009 premiere. Although they had let the options on the cast expire, the actors were advised to stay in training for their superhero roles. Writers Kieran and Michele Mulroney went back to work on the script, and director George Miller returned to pre-production in Australia.[31] But the project eventually ran out of steam, and the actors moved on. Armie Hammer, who was to have played Batman, took on another iconic role when he starred in *Billy: The Early Years* (2008), a biopic about the Rev. Billy Graham. Avoiding typecasting, he next appeared as the devil's son in the short-lived WB series *Reaper* before gaining accolades playing both Winklevoss twins in *The Social Network* (2010).[32]

In the summer of 2008, *Justice League of America* went back into development. This time, the studio worried not only what effect that film would have on its existing *Batman* and *Superman* franchises, but also whether the script was faithful to the way the characters were portrayed in the larger DC Comics universe. As Marc Graser in *Weekly Variety* succinctly put it, "The studio doesn't want to piss off the Comic-Con contingent."[33]

"These are big, iconic characters," said DC Comics senior vice president of creative affairs Gregory Noveck. "So when you make them into a movie, you'd better be shooting for a pretty high standard. You're not always going to reach it, but you have to be shooting for it. We're going to make a *Justice League* movie, whether it's now or 10 years from now. But we're not going to do it and Warners is not going to do it until we know it's right."[34]

BATMAN BEGINS, AGAIN

While Robinov put *Justice League, Wonder Woman, Green Lantern, The Flash* and a *Superman* sequel into development, Christopher Nolan gathered his creative team for the new *Batman* film, to be called *The Dark Knight*. He followed the same process that had worked so well with *Batman Begins*, working out of a garage that had been converted into an office at his Los Angeles home. Naturally, the team included his wife and producer Emma Thomas, as well as cinematographer Wally Pfister, a fellow Chicago native who had photographed all of Nolan's films beginning with *Memento*.[35] Production designer Nathan Crowley, a part of Nolan's team since 2002's *Insomnia*, was back, and so was Lindy Hemming, returning for her second film with Nolan, having taken time to outfit James Bond for *Casino Royale* after working on *Batman Begins*. The production team began brainstorming while Nolan and his brother Jonathan finalized the script.[36]

Very early on in the script's development came the first official casting notice. On February 7, 2006, *The New York Times* reported that Jake Gyllenhaal might "cop a role as the district attorney in the next *Batman* movie." The paper said that Gyllenhaal had once been in the running to play *The Green Hornet*, and had been set to replace Toby Maguire in *Spider-Man 3* until Maguire decided to return to the role.[37] Gyllenhaal ultimately moved on, but both his sister Maggie and his *Brokeback Mountain* co-star, Heath Ledger, ended up in *The Dark Knight.*

The moment Ledger found out that the Joker was going to be the next *Batman* villain, he had his agent contact Christopher Nolan to tell him that he had some ideas about how to play the part.[38] "I met Heath several times over the years," said Nolan, "and early on he told me that one of the things he was concerned about was not being thrust into the spotlight as a movie star before he'd shown what he could do as a serious actor. I've heard that from a lot of young actors but of all the people I'd heard it from, he was the only one I paid $10 to go and see deliver a crack performance. That was *Brokeback Mountain*. It's a performance of consummate skill. I think everyone recognizes the great acting in it but what I think is easy to miss is the boldness of what Heath does with that film, because he plays an introverted character, a lonely character. He plays it with no thought of vanity, and he takes risks doing that. He's really throwing the net away."[39] Nolan wasn't the only one who noticed Ledger's skill in *Brokeback Mountain*; the role won the actor an Academy Award nomination for Best Actor.

Nolan recalled that when he met Ledger to discuss playing the Joker, long before the script was finalized, "We talked about how we saw this character and we both had exactly the same concept—that the Joker was about the threat of anarchy and revels in creating chaos and fear on a grand scale. Heath seemed to instinctively understand how to make this character different from anything that had ever been done before."[40]

Named after a character in Emily Bronte's *Wuthering Heights*, Heathcliff Andrew Ledger was born April 4, 1979, in Perth, Australia.[41] After appearing in films and television in his native country, he gained notice in the United States as the star of the romantic comedy *10 Things I Hate About You* (1999). A year later, he played Mel Gibson's son in *The Patriot* (2000). In 2005, while playing gay cowboy Ennis Del Mar in *Brokeback Mountain*, he met Michelle Williams, who portrayed his on-screen wife. They later became engaged, and their daughter, Matilda, was born in October 2005. The couple never wed, and separated in September 2007.[42]

Ledger saw the Joker as a "psychopathic, mass murdering, schizophrenic clown with zero empathy." To prepare for the role, he spent a month alone in a hotel room working on the character, the voice and the hyena-like laugh. His inspirations included Alex, the violent delinquent played by Malcolm McDowell in director Stanley Kubrick's 1971 film *A Clockwork Orange,* and Pete Doherty, a British musician, writer and actor who was frontman of the band The Libertines and was as famous for his heroin addiction as for his music.[43]

Warner Bros. announced Ledger's casting on August 1, 2006.[44] In a statement released by the studio, Christopher Nolan said, "Our challenge in casting the Joker was to find an actor who is not just extraordinarily talented but fearless. Watching Heath Ledger's interpretation of this iconic character taking on Christian Bale's Batman is going to be incredible."[45]

Cast members from *Batman Begins* returned to reprise their roles in *The Dark Knight,* including Michael Caine as Alfred, Morgan Freeman as Lucius Fox and Gary Oldman as Lieutenant Jim Gordon. To play the crucial role of Harvey Dent, Nolan chose Aaron Eckhart. It was not Eckhart's first brush with Nolan or with Batman. Nolan had considered Eckhart some years earlier for the lead role in *Momento,* and Eckhart was reportedly Darren Aronofsky's choice to play James Gordon in the aborted *Batman: Year One* project.

"We were looking for somebody who could embody that all-American charm because you have to invest in him as a very attractive, heroic figure at the beginning of the movie," said Nolan. "But he also had to have an edge; he had to suggest this undercurrent of anger and darkness that Harvey Dent needed to have, so where he goes in the story is believable. You can't present a character like this as simply a heroic figure with no flaws, no dark side."[46]

"Harvey has charged himself with tackling organized crime and cleaning up the streets," said Eckhart. "He is the shining new hope of Gotham City, the 'White Knight,' as he is called. He starts out full of optimism and enthusiasm...where he ends up is somewhere completely different. It's a great role and I'm a big fan of Chris Nolan's, so when he approached me about doing the film, it was a no-brainer."[47]

Katie Holmes was expected to return as assistant district attorney Rachel Dawes, but on January 26, 2007, *Daily Variety* noted that the actress had dropped out of the film.[48] Six weeks later came the announcement that Maggie Gyllenhaal was in final talks to take over the role.[49] "When I was approached about this movie I wasn't looking to work at all," said Gyllenhaal. "I had a three month old. I wasn't reading scripts so I wasn't in the career-minded frame of mind at all. I was a fan of Chris [Nolan] and I knew who was in the movie, like Gary Oldman and Michael Caine and Morgan Freeman and Heath and Christian and Aaron Eckhart. It was a hard thing not to take seriously. But I think what made me do it at that time was really a couple of conversations I had with Chris where first of all he was so thoughtful and smart, honest and also he gave me the script to read after our first meeting and he said, 'She's not quite finished in this draft.' I read it and I had some ideas and most of them were about making sure that she would be a fully realized woman."[50]

"Maggie is just a fantastic actress," said Nolan. "I've always loved her work and had wanted an opportunity to work with her, and the role of Rachel in this film seemed like the perfect match. Maggie has great intelligence and maturity and she is also very warm and, of course, lovely. You really believe her in this role. I think she beautifully conveyed the conflict in Rachel standing between these two men in her life, and you can see why both men would naturally be drawn to her."[51]

Before accepting the role, however, Gyllenhaal contacted Katie Holmes. "First of all I wanted to make sure I had her blessing in terms of doing it," said Gyllenhaal. "When I found out I did I didn't think it would do anyone any good for me to try to imitate her. It would have been awful. I could never have done that so I thought, you know I have to make her a new woman. I think that was the best way to honor what Katie did as well to sort of really let [Rachel] really start anew. There are some plot points and some things in the narrative that happened in the first movie that had a big effect on our movie and I paid attention to those. Most importantly at the end of the previous movie she says to Bruce Wayne, 'I love you but I can't be with you as Batman and I understand why you need to be Batman, but let's see what happens.' And then of course that plays itself out all over the place in our movie so I did have to pay attention, but I started over in some ways."[52]

To fill the other major roles, Nolan chose Eric Roberts as Maroni, a Gotham City gangster, Chin Han as Asian business mogul Lau, Nestor Carbonell as the Mayor of Gotham City, and Anthony Michael Hall as a television news reporter. Cillian Murphy returned in a brief cameo appearance as the Scarecrow.[53]

Lindy Hemming looked forward to having another go at the Batsuit. Both Christopher Nolan and Christian Bale wanted a suit with more flexibility, so Hemming and her team did extensive research into the protective suits worn by motocross riders, as well as the protective armor plates used by the military.[54] "Chris Nolan and I were desperate to change things as much as we could," said Hemming. "But not just to change it. I looked at the way trainers are constructed, the mesh, the plastics and leathers. I also looked at the under-armor that people wear when they're motor biking or indulging in extreme sports."[55]

The base layer of the suit was made of a moisture-absorbing polyester mesh material, with individually molded pieces of flexible urethane attached to form the overall armor plating. For added protection, lightweight yet incredibly strong carbon fiber panels were placed inside a select group of the urethane pieces around the legs, chest and abdomen. When it was finished, the Batsuit was comprised of 110 separate pieces.[56]

"There were essentially three main components to the Batsuit in *Batman Begins*, and on this film there were more than 100, so it was a very complicated suit," said costume FX supervisor Graham Churchyard. "Add to that, all of those individual pieces had to be modeled and then molded and cast. Each piece also had to be replicated dozens of times for the multiple Batsuits needed for the overall production. It was an extraordinary amount of work."[57]

Hemming's main priority was to redesign Batman's cowl so that Bale could finally turn his head with ease. The solution was to make the headpiece separate from the neck, yet without compromising the costume's silhouette.[58] "I don't know about the other Batmans previously, but for Christian, because he's very physical, he does lots of his own fight scenes," said Hemming. "We removed the neck columns completely and changed the way it technically functioned so that he was able to compress his neck into his shoulders and move his head freely. Not completely freely, but much more freely!"[59] The new Batsuit featured other modifications to help the Caped Crusader in his crime fighting. The forearm gauntlets had razor sharp fins that could be extended and fired like ninja throwing blades, and the cowl had sonar-imaging lenses which flipped down over Batman's eyes, enabling him to see sonar images in 3D.[60] But one part of the suit remained unchanged: Batman's cape. "We spent a lot of time getting the cape right for the first film, and we didn't want to change it," said Hemming. However, the new outfit did have one cape modification—the cape could fold itself into a kind of backpack and then unfurl on command. That feature, however, was only able to be accomplished through digital effects.[61]

Christian Bale said the new Batsuit was much more comfortable than the one he had worn in *Batman Begins*. "It's a much more advanced suit than the original one," said Bale. "There had been some requests from myself and from Chris [Nolan] to be more maneuverable. At first I was fighting against the suit to do all of the fight sequences. This one was actually compatible with the Keysi fighting method. I could move my head. It was heavier than the original, but just so much more motion. I could breathe properly inside of it. It didn't squeeze my head like a vice throughout. So I had to act the rage and anger this time around."[62]

Besides costuming Batman, Hemming had to create clothes for his nemesis, the Joker. The task became easier once she decided that the Joker was basically Johnny Rotten.[63] "We had to make him appeal to a group of younger people and give them an understanding of what he does," said Hemming. "I was looking at all the anarchic younger people, from Pete Doherty to the Sex Pistols' Johnny Lydon. The idea of what he looked like came really easily to me and I managed to show Chris Nolan and Heath Ledger my drawings at the first meeting. I had all sorts of tear sheets of clowns and of fat ladies whose make-up was running. I decided the reason his hair was green is because he's bleached it out and something's gone on it and it's made it green, instead of painting it green in the first place."[64]

Hemming also found inspiration for the Joker in more contemporary fashion icons. "One of my nods is towards people like Vivienne Westwood and Alexander McQueen and the way they slightly extremize everything," said Hemming. "We tailored his jacket so it had the flow of a skirt and we made sure the lining was the burnt orange color. His cuffs are always open and pointed down."[65] Hemming kept to the Joker's traditional color palette, with a purple top coat worn over a green waistcoat, though in some scenes he wears a lighter jacket based on the Carnaby Street Mod look. His shirt was patterned after one that Hemming located at an antiques market. His shoes were from Milan, selected because they turned up at the front like a clown's shoes.[66] "His gloves actually came from Alexander McQueen, they were really expensive, then we made lots of stunt pairs. Just little things, that helped his body to have that slightly strange banana shape. It's subtly working on someone's silhouette to make them have more of the character they had already."[67]

The final touch was a custom tie, specially woven by Turnbull & Asser, the London-based clothier of British royalty. "Heath wanted it to be thin, so it's a '60s tie but in a Turnbull & Asser fabric," said Hemming. "I dare say it's the weirdest tie that Turnbull & Asser has ever made. When Heath came in and we showed him all the bits and pieces of the costume, he thought it was fantastically original and just went for it."[68] Hemming saw Ledger as "a real collaborator." "At his first fitting, he put on the prototypes of the clothes," recalled Hemming. "He became something immediately, he had an energy where he just made things work."[69]

For Maggie Gyllenhaal's Rachel Dawes, Hemming chose outfits that emphasized both her professionalism and her individuality. "Because she's so tall, and because we didn't think the character would have much money, but we thought she might be able to put things together in a slightly unusual way, I designed a wardrobe of clothes that picked details out of the Seventies and Thirties," said Hemming. "She had an *Annie Hall*-ish waistcoat and we made the pants flared at the bottom."[70]

Bruce Wayne's wardrobe was more upscale, in keeping with the style and image of a millionaire playboy. For his outfits, Hemming collaborated with legendary fashion designer Giorgio Armani, who suggested clothing Christian Bale in his newest line, Giorgio Armani Hand Made-to-Measure. Each suit carried Armani's traditional customized owner's label: Giorgio Armani for Bruce Wayne. "Chris Nolan and I wanted Bruce Wayne to have an elegantly tailored appearance," said Hemming. "We felt that the Giorgio Armani brand was emblematic of the contemporary classic look we were going for. We chose the fabrics and then worked directly with Mr. Armani and his people to tailor an entire wardrobe of suits, custom-made for the character."[71]

Harvey Dent's wardrobe was less expensive than Bruce Wayne's, but Hemming still wanted the character to have an air of authority and confidence. "We dressed him simply, but impeccably in suits by [Ermenegildo] Zegna," said Hemming.[72]

The next challenge the filmmakers faced in creating Batman's new villains was the make-up. The look of the Joker was far more creepy and sinister than previous incarnations. "Clearly, there was a perception in the audience's mind of what the Joker would look like," said make-up and hair designer Peter Robb-King, "but we wanted to get under the skin, so to speak, of what this character represents in this story. He is someone who has been damaged in every sense of the word, so it was important that we create a look that was not, forgive the pun, 'jokey.'"[73]

In *The Dark Knight*, the Joker's white pancake make-up is cracked, the black shadowing his eyes is runny, and the red grin is painted on sloppily over noticeable scars. His hair is still green, but it's longer, stringier and more unkempt. This is no funhouse Joker; it's a madhouse Joker.[74]

John Caglione, Jr., who applied the make-up to Heath Ledger, called the process "a dance," saying, "Heath would scrunch up his face in specific expressions, raising his forehead and squinting his eyes, and I would paint on the white over his facial contortions. This technique created textures and expressions that just painting the face a flat white would not. Then I used black make-up around Heath's eyes while he held them closed very tight, which created consistent facial textures. After the black was on, I sprayed water over his eyes, and he would squeeze his eyes and shake his head, and all that black drippy, smudgy stuff would happen."[75]

The Joker's scars were created with a newly-developed silicone-based prosthetic created and applied by prosthetic supervisor Conor O'Sullivan and prosthetic make-up artist Robert Trenton. "It took us about two years to develop the technology, but after a few glitches, we hit on it," said O'Sullivan. "We are now able to produce silicone pieces that are applied directly to the skin. And it blends with the skin perfectly; if you didn't know it was there, you would have a hard time seeing anything."[76] One of the greatest advantages of the new process was that whereas it might have taken three to four hours to apply traditional latex prosthetics, the silicone prosthetics went on in about 25 minutes.[77]

Two-Face's make-up was also achieved in a cutting-edge way. Instead of creating Harvey Dent's burnt visage entirely through prosthetics, actor Aaron Eckhart wore a skull cap and partial prosthetics, with motion capture markers on half of his face. The look of burnt skin and exposed bone and muscle was then created digitally by visual effects house Framestore. "It was interesting for me in that, because of the technology, I didn't have to spend hours in make-up every day," said Ekhart. "The whole process was effortless…at least for me."[78] As repulsive as Two-Face's visage was, Nolan admitted that some of the earlier concepts were even worse, but he pulled back from those because he didn't want people looking away from the screen so much that they missed the film.[79]

HOT WHEELS

Just as Christopher Nolan urged production designer Nathan Crowley to begin designing and building the Batmobile while *Batman Begins* was in pre-production, he now asked Crowley to design a new vehicle, the Bat-Pod, while the script for *The Dark Knight* was taking shape. Nolan conceived of a motorcycle-type transport that would eject from the front of the Batmobile, using the Batmobile's huge front tires. "Of course we were going to have the Batmobile back," states Nolan, "but we wanted to give Batman something new: a fresh means of transportation, something very exotic and very powerful looking. It's a two-wheeled vehicle, but it's definitely not a motorcycle. In essence, the Bat-Pod is to the world of motorcycles what the Tumbler is to the world of cars."[80]

To design the vehicle, Nolan and production designer Nathan Crowley once again set to work in Nolan's garage. "We figured, 'Let's just go for it; let's build it full-size,'" said Crowley. "So we did. We got some tools and put together a full-size model out of anything we could find that might fit."[81]

The two came up with an all-terrain vehicle that would be fast and maneuverable on the streets of Gotham City. It used the same 508 millimeter monster truck tires as the Batmobile. The tires were so wide that the Bat-Pod did not need a kickstand; it stood upright on its own. To ready it for battle against the city's criminals, the vehicle was equipped with weapons on both sides: 40mm blast cannons, 50-caliber machine guns, and grappling hook launchers.[82]

Once the appearance of the Bat-Pod was determined, the next problem was to actually make it work. Since neither Nolan nor Crowley were mechanically inclined, they turned to special effects wizard Chris Corbould. When he got the call, Corbould was skeptical. "First of all, I remember when Chris Nolan first showed me his idea for the Batmobile. I had no idea how we were going to make it work even though it ended up being very successful," said Corbould. "So when I got his call asking me to come have a look at something he called 'the Bat-Pod,' I thought, 'Uh-oh, what have you dreamt up this time?'"[83]

The effects man flew to Los Angeles, went to Nolan's garage, and took a hard look at the strange contraption. "I think he was almost in tears," said Crowley. "He looked horrified that he might have to actually mechanize that thing. We kept bringing him cups of tea, and he was just sitting there staring at it, looking like, 'Oh my God, what time is the next flight out?' It was the usual clash of design versus engineering."[84]

"I was flabbergasted," admitted Corbould. "I stood there silently, pretending I was mulling it over, but the thought going through my head was that they both had to be off their nut. Where was I going to put a power train? And with those massive wheels, would this thing actually steer? There were so many issues...The funny thing is, I don't think Chris or Nathan had ever ridden a motorcycle in their lives, so they were completely unaware of the mechanics needed to get that thing moving. In a way it was beneficial because they weren't steered towards a more orthodox bike, even subconsciously. The fact that they had no knowledge of the mechanics helped them create this weird, wonderful vehicle."[85]

After returning to London, Corbould and his special effects crew began brainstorming. After much trial and error, they finally came up with a working vehicle that was amazingly close to the original model constructed by Nolan and Crowley. "It really shouldn't work," said Nolan, "but somehow Chris and his team found a way to do it." Making it work was only the beginning of the challenge, however. Driving it was something else altogether. "The finished product that Chris and his team came up with was very striking, very effective and worked very well, but it's incredibly difficult to ride and to steer," said Nolan.[86]

Maneuvering the Bat-Pod required the driver to lean his upper body forward, almost horizontally, and steer from his elbows, rather than his wrists. Corbould could think of only one person who might be able to master it—French stunt rider Jean-Pierre Goy, with whom Corbould had worked on the 1997 James Bond film *Tomorrow Never Dies*. "He is one of the best bike riders in the world, if not the best," said Corbould. "Right away, he totally got in the mindset of learning that machine. He said, 'I'm not riding another bike until I finish this sequence,' because he had to concentrate on the Bat-Pod's unique handling qualities. I'd be lying if I said it was easy for even him to ride, but it looked spectacular when he did, so it was worth the effort."[87] Goy spent a few months practicing with the vehicle, and Corbould built five more, so there would be back-ups, if necessary, for shooting the film's chase scenes.[88]

After designing the Bat-Pod, Crowley turned his production designer's eye to the rest of Bruce Wayne's and Batman's world. Unlike *Batman Begins*, which showed a dark, shadowy city, the characters in *The Dark Knight* would inhabit brighter, sleeker, more modern environs. "It became clear that with our Joker character's chaos and anarchism we could delve deeper into realism," said Crowley, "and try to make the city feel really familiar for the audience—creating boundaries for Batman in the modern world."[89]

Crowley decided to focus on the modernist buildings erected in Chicago in the 1960s and '70s. "Wouldn't that give us a colder, sharper feel?" he asked. "Instead of sweeping Gothic halls, we wanted something raw: big, hard-hitting spaces." With Wayne Manor destroyed in the previous film, Bruce Wayne would now reside in a downtown penthouse. "If we put him into a big, powerful building and use modernism, how lonely would that feel?" said Crowley. "We realized that if he lived downtown we could play up the coldness of an unhappy man—a reluctant hero. It was very intentional to stick with clean lines and squares, empty spaces, blank walls and big, low ceilings."[90]

"At the end of *Batman Begins*, Bruce says he's going to rebuild Wayne Manor brick by brick," said Nolan. "That would take a long time, so it would be pretty unrealistic for him to be already moved back in. And there was also a period in the comic books where Bruce Wayne did live downtown in a penthouse, so we took that as a jumping-off point. We wanted to have him in the city because this is very much a story of a city and we felt it was important to put Bruce in the middle of that."[91]

With a new home downtown, Bruce Wayne also needed a new headquarters for all of his Batgear. "He can't go to his Batcave, so we came up with the idea of a bunker that ties back to the architectural theme of the penthouse in that it's vast but very plain," said Crowley. "It is essentially a large concrete box where everything comes out of the walls and then goes back. But it still had to be visually interesting. It was all about proportion and perspective, which was actually great fun to do."[92]

Contrasting with the cavernous spaces of official Gotham was the cramped underground world of the criminals, such as the institutional kitchen where the Joker confronts the city's crime bosses. "The film starts with the claustrophobia of the Joker—the way he stands under the low ceilings, hunched, all repression, about to explode," said Crowley.[93] A similarly cramped space was the police interrogation room where Batman attempted to extract information from the Joker. "You've got a messed-up Joker, with blood and makeup, purple and green, against a stark white wall—that's very powerful," said Crowley. "My big epiphany was to try to bring this huge simplicity into it."[94]

With filming scheduled to begin in March 2007, Christian Bale began getting back into shape for the role, including more training in the Keysi Fighting Method, or KFM. "It's a fascinating fighting method," said Bale, "because it uses the adrenaline that everyone feels entering into a threatening or violent situation. It really comes from the gut. Rather than the kind of Zen calm that some martial arts call on, KFM is based on animal instinct and honing those instincts to be lethal, so it's perfect for Batman."[95]

Every day, Bale spent two or three hours sparring with Keysi fight coordinators Andy Norman and Justo Diéguez Serrano. "In KFM, you learn to develop every part of your body as a weapon, and it's not easy," said Norman. "We worked Christian extremely hard, and it was fantastic how quickly he absorbed everything. There was a definite progression in his training since the first film. He understands KFM a lot better, so he was more powerful and his movement was incredible."[96]

KNIGHT, CAMERA, ACTION

Christopher Nolan decided to use *The Dark Knight* to realize a long-held desire: shooting in Imax. The 70mm format uses a film frame twice the size of a normal 35mm frame, and when projected on the larger Imax screens, it almost fills up a viewer's entire field of vision. "Chris has wanted to work in Imax for years," said Emma Thomas. "He's been waiting to find the right project that he could do it on. Right at the beginning when we first started developing this project, he came to us and said 'This is the way I want to do this. This is one of the ways I want to expand this movie and make it the biggest film-going experience it can be.'"

"I've always had an interest in shooting in Imax," said Nolan. "I've seen Imax presentations at museums and such and found the format to be completely overwhelming. The clarity and crispness of the images are unparalleled, so I thought if you could shoot a dramatic feature with Imax cameras—not just blow up a 35mm film to show on an Imax screen—it would really bring the audience into the action."[97]

To get used to filming with the heavier Imax cameras, Nolan and his director of photography, Wally Pfister, spent some time shooting tests with one of the large-format cameras in Los Angeles, on Sunset Boulevard and on Hollywood Boulevard.[98] Once he felt confident that he could do it, Nolan mapped out six scenes that he wanted to shoot in the Imax format, including the opening scene, showing a bank heist coordinated by the Joker. "In continuing Batman's story, the challenge was to make things bigger and better—to expand the world we established in the first film, both through the story and in the way we presented it," said Nolan. "I was thrilled with the way the Imax photography turned out. It throws the audience right into the action in a way no other film format could. It takes me back to when I was a kid going to the movies and experiencing the scope, the scale and the grandeur that great cinema can offer. As a filmmaker, I think you're always trying to get back to that, and expanding the canvas of our story with Imax seemed a great way to do it."[99]

The bank heist scene was filmed at the Old Post Office on Congress Parkway in Chicago in December 2006, a month before the crew was due to begin shooting in England.[100] In order to use the heavier Imax equipment, special camera mounts had to be made for Steadicam rigs and camera vehicles. During one shot, the weight of the camera collapsed one of the Steadicam rigs, but Nolan was undeterred. Recalling the hardships faced by David Lean in filming *Lawrence of Arabia* on location in Morocco, Nolan said, "If David Lean could carry a 65-millimeter camera through the desert, why shouldn't we be able to do this?"[101] Emma Thomas echoed Nolan's opinion, saying, "When you think about some of the Imax films we remember, they've taken these cameras up Mount Everest, they've taken them under the ocean, astronauts have had them in space… So if they can do that, then surely we can shoot on the streets of Chicago with an Imax camera."[102]

Cinematographer Wally Pfister assumed that the incredible size and weight of the Imax cameras would preclude him from doing any handheld shots, but the director had other ideas. "Early in pre-production, Chris said to me, 'You've got to try to handhold one of the Imax cameras at some point just to say you did it.' And I said, 'No way! I am not putting that thing on my shoulder.' But he kept nudging me and bugging me to try it, and finally I broke down and decided I had to give it a go. I actually did one handheld shot with the Imax camera, running in front of a S.W.A.T. team into a building. More than getting the shot, I think Chris was really proud of himself that he was able to get me to do that."[103]

Besides the cumbersomeness of the cameras, there were other factors the filmmakers had to take into account—the clarity of the Imax image, the amount of space the lenses take in, and the short focal lengths. "The composition of shots is entirely different because the frame is so much bigger, so you need to center things more to pull your attention to the action. And focus is much more critical because it is a shallower depth of field," said Pfister. "One of the most challenging things about filming in Imax is trying to hide the lights. With the expanded frame, you're seeing so much more from side to side and top to bottom so you can't place lights where you normally would. You have to put them behind objects and anywhere else you can hide them."[104]

The clarity of the Imax format also posed a challenge for production designer Nathan Crowley, who said, "Filming in Imax is a great bonus to a production designer because you notice things you ordinarily wouldn't even see. The perspective is huge. I mean, we purposely had a lot of low ceilings and beautiful shiny floors because they stay in frame. Then again, we also had to make sure the finishes were superb because you'll also see every speck of dust on the floor."[105]

"The cameras are enormous and much heavier than a 35mm camera," said Pfister. "It required an entirely different approach, but like any challenge in moviemaking, you can't be so intimidated that you shy away from it. You just bite off one piece at a time until you've tackled it...The week that we spent shooting the bank heist sequence was like Imax school for all of us."[106]

The Dark Knight marked the first time that a major narrative feature film was shot using the large-format cameras.[107] Besides the bank heist, Nolan used them for the Hong Kong scene, the Bat-Pod chase scene, the final fight in the skyscraper, the ending scene, and various helicopter shots of Gotham City. "Using Imax technology to shoot some of the action scenes gave us the greatest possible canvas on which to tell the story," said Nolan, "and the result is an incredibly immersive experience."[108]

By January, the cast and crew were congregating at the Cardington airship sheds, where many of them had worked on *Batman Begins* just a couple of years earlier. Filming officially began on January 11, 2007, with a budget of $180 million. Among the new sets constructed at Cardington was the Bat-Bunker, Bruce Wayne's temporary replacement for the Batcave. The ceiling of solid florescent lights made it appear "like a giant light box," said Pfister, "which obviously made it simple for me from a lighting standpoint."[109] There was also an interior skyscraper set, which would be the setting for the climactic showdown between Batman and the Joker.[110]

Once filming began, Christian Bale enjoyed working with Heath Ledger. The two actors were kindred spirits, both known for going to mental and physical extremes in the pursuit of perfection in playing a role. "I was almost kind of chuckling inside and I didn't want to let it show when we were doing our first scene," said Bale, "which was in the interrogation room and I saw what he was going to do with it, and I felt I recognized the satisfaction he seemed to be getting in the pleasure from the role to be similar to the satisfaction that I get from acting as well. I felt very comfortable working with him."[111]

Christopher Nolan also found Ledger to be a pleasure. "If there was anything surprising about him maybe it was how easy he was to work with. Because he was somebody who put so much into his performances I was a little worried that he might take himself very seriously and all the rest. Yet he didn't. He was very warm and fun to have around, a great collaborator."[112] When Michael Caine got his first glimpse of Ledger's performance, he was stunned. "I turn up every month or so and do a couple of bits then go back to London," said Caine. "I had to do this bit where Batman and I watch a video which The Joker sends to threaten us. So I'd never seen him, and then he came on the television in the first rehearsal and I completely forgot my lines. I flipped, because it was so stunning, it was quite amazing."[113]

Christian Bale as Batman looms over Heath Ledger, the scariest incarnation yet of the Joker, in The Dark Knight (Warner Bros./Photofest, © Warner Bros. Photographer: Stephen Vaughan).

The Dark Knight was Christian Bale's third film for Nolan, having just worked with him on *The Prestige*. "I think Chris has a great talent for satisfying the need for a rollercoaster ride, for just being purely entertained, without forgoing moments of great personal conflict and the duality within the characters," said Bale. "He manages to do both without compromising either."[114] Bale said that Nolan was clearly "a director who is very focused and knows what he wants but is open to the collaborative process and finding unexpected things in performances. He makes you feel very safe and prepares you for success."[115]

Nolan also had high praise for Bale, saying, "Working with Christian is a joy and just a lot of fun. He is a very engaging presence to have on the set. He also has an intensity about him; he is incredibly focused on tapping into the psychological reality of whatever character he's playing. He applies the same disciplined approach to finding the truth of that character and sticks to it. That is a great help to me as a filmmaker because I know he is prepared and has a handle on how his character is going to move through the story. In fact, he has a lot of the same qualities that Bruce Wayne brings to bear in changing himself from an ordinary man into this extraordinary crime-fighting figure."[116]

Nolan said that while Bale portrayed the same character in *The Dark Knight* and *Batman Begins*, the two films presented the actor with very different challenges. "On *Batman Begins*, it was a lot of physical effort—he had to get himself in terrific shape and learn all kinds of skills in terms of the way Batman fights, the way he moves," said Nolan. "On this film, I would say it required more of an internal process because Bruce is realizing the personal toll of living this double life and is questioning the choices he's made. Christian conveys that emotional struggle very convincingly, often without saying a word."[117]

Nolan was determined to expand Batman's world and do more location filming on *The Dark Knight* than he had on *Batman Begins*. "The real world is built on a scale you could never reproduce in the studio," said Nolan.[118] After months of filming in England, the cast and crew moved to Chicago for filming of exteriors and action sequences. "I spent some time growing up in Chicago, so it's a city I know and love. It is famous for its architecture and it is also a very film-friendly city. We shot there for weeks on *Batman Begins*...and the help and encouragement we got from the city was extraordinary."[119]

After shooting exteriors for the Joker's bank heist and school bus escape in the city from April 18 to the 24th, the unit returned to Chicago on June 9 for more than three months of filming. As with *Batman Begins*, Nolan shot every frame of the film himself, unlike other big-budget films that would delegate filming of action scenes to a second unit. Although Nolan storyboarded particular scenes, he nonetheless encouraged improvisation among both his cast and his crew. Speaking of his method, Nolan said, "It scares people a bit. We just go and shoot the stuff, and see what looks the best and what works. But on a big movie, you actually have more freedom. You can say, 'O.K., it's 3 in the morning—can we get the police to close down that street?'"[120]

The Dark Knight was the fourth film Nathan Crowley had worked on in the Windy City. "The Chicago architecture is phenomenal," said Crowley. "All of the great architects of the last century have worked there. And it's wonderfully cinematic."[121] Crowley chose the IBM Building and One Illinois Plaza, both designed by famed architect Mies van der Rohe, for use as a variety of sets. The IBM Building became the Wayne Enterprises Boardroom, Harvey Dent's office, the Mayor's office and the Police Commissioner's office, while the lobby of One Illinois Plaza became the main living area of Bruce Wayne's new penthouse.[122]

Using the lobby level of One Illinois Plaza for a penthouse meant employing a little movie magic to create top-floor views of Gotham City through the floor-to-ceiling windows. Bruce's bedroom was built separately on the 39th floor of Hotel 71 on East Wacker Drive.[123]

The penthouse was definitely more modern than the gothic corridors of Wayne Manor. "We were given access to these great modernist floors, and we felt that era of architecture was better suited for what we were trying to convey emotionally," said Crowley. "It's cold and it's vacant; there's no warmth to the environment."[124] Nolan agreed with Crowley's use of the sets to reflect Bruce Wayne's emotional state. "Bruce is living a very lonely existence in a way," said Nolan, "so the stark design of the penthouse was meant to reflect his state of mind."[125]

The party scene at Wayne's penthouse provided another opportunity for Vermont Senator Patrick J. Leahy, the Democratic chairman of the Judiciary Committee who had been seen in crowd scenes of *Batman Forever* and *Batman & Robin*, to return for another cameo appearance. This time, he was given dialogue. When the Joker bursts in, Leahy steps forward, proclaiming, "We're not intimidated by your thugs." The Joker says, "You remind me of my father. I hated my father." Then he grabs Leahy's head and thrusts a knife to his face.[126] Leahy said he spent all of one night filming the scene, in which Ledger would "punch or throw me halfway across the room."[127] It took a couple dozen takes for Leahy to nail his lines. "We tried it two different ways—one was authoritative, the other one was with a lot of fear in my voice," said Leahy. Nolan ultimately directed him to spout the line with a take-charge attitude reflective of the prosecutor Leahy once was.[128]

Other Chicago locations included the Convention Hall at McCormick Place West, which became the vast warehouse of Wayne Enterprises' Applied Science Division, and Navy Pier, where panicked citizens of Gotham City protested prisoners being loaded onto a ferry boat. In addition, the exterior of Chicago's Trump Tower, which was in the early construction stage at the time of production, was used for exteriors of the final confrontation between Batman and the Joker.[129]

The Sears Tower, the tallest building in the United States, became the location for a soaring exterior shot of Batman looking out over his city. When it came time to film it, Christian Bale decided he couldn't pass up such a rare opportunity. "I overheard my stunt double, Buster Reeves, saying he was heading up to the Sears Tower to do that, and I said, 'Sorry buddy, no way. I just have to do this one myself,'" said Bale. "I mean, how often do you get to be 110 stories up, looking out over all of Chicago? But it's a funny and probably quite dangerous thing, how quickly I felt very at home out there and how soon I was able to move around right on the edge, looking straight down."[130]

While most directors would have denied their star's willingness to put their neck at risk on insurance grounds alone, Christopher Nolan supported Bale's decision. "Christian likes to challenge himself and I knew we weren't putting him in any actual physical danger," said Nolan. "It was perfectly safe; it just required guts to stand there.

I certainly wouldn't want to do it, but he seemed to enjoy it and it made a beautiful shot for us. And after that, standing out on a ledge on a building in Hong Kong must have been easy."[131]

Nolan also made dramatic use of Chicago's multi-leveled streets, with parallel upper and lower roadways, for the climactic car chase between the Joker, the police and Batman. The fast-paced chase sent a variety of cars, armored trucks and an 18-wheeler hurtling down Upper and Lower Wacker Drive, Lower Randolph, Lower Columbus and LaSalle Street.

For one portion of the chase, the Bat-Pod took a detour through the newly-remodeled train station under Millennium Park.[132] Stunt driver Jean-Pierre Goy was astride the Bat-Pod for the entire chase scene, except for close-ups of Christian Bale, which were achieved with the Bat-Pod actually being towed behind a camera car. "There were world class bikers who were getting on this thing and coming straight off of it," said Bale. "I had to recognize at that point I wasn't going to manage it either. So whenever you see me on it, it's still an adrenaline rush, but I am getting dragged behind another vehicle. It's embarrassing to admit, but I have to give kudos to Jean-Pierre for being the only person in the world who was able to master it. He said so himself, it's not a motorbike, you have to actually ignore all of the skills you have learned as a biker in order to learn how to operate the Bat-Pod."[133] Bale did, however, get to ride an MV Agusta F4 motorbike in the film.[134] "I spent days just roaring up and down," said Bale. "All I had to do was pull up and get off it. I insisted it was absolutely necessary for my preparation."[135]

Bale also was not involved in any of the Batmobile scenes. For all of the chase scenes involving the Tumbler, stuntman George Cottle was at the wheel. "He's a wonderful driver," said Bale. "I mean, I did drive it, but I didn't drive it on film. I would just race up and down." Nonetheless, Bale managed to get behind the wheel of Bruce Wayne's Lamborghini. "Oh, I had to go practice on that for many hours," said the actor. "I would have to learn how to do the 180s on that, it was really essential."[136]

"The city of Chicago did extraordinary things," said producer Charles Roven. "They let us take over their financial district at night as long as we were safe and they made sure that we were. They were fantastic to us. We had one day where we had the Bat-Pod coming out of an alley and coming onto the street, and it created a huge sonic boom that bounced off the walls of the building and blew out a bunch of windows. That was not planned. But that was the only mishap. But because they were so great to us, we made sure that we honored that and we mobilized glaziers, the guys who put the windows in, and within 24 hours we had fixed every window."[137]

Even more incredible is that the city allowed Nolan and his film crew to flip a 40-foot tractor-trailer rig end-over-end in the heart of the financial district on LaSalle Street.[138] Chris Corbould, after reading the stunt in the script, was skeptical that it could even be done. He went to Nolan to discuss the problems. "I tried to make compromises with Chris—like maybe the whole truck doesn't go over or maybe we could use a smaller truck—but he wasn't having any of it,' said Corbould.[139] After listening to Corbould's misgivings, Nolan said that, "Finally I turned to him one day and said, 'Chris, it really ought to be an 18-wheeler. And I know you can find a way to do this because that's just who you are and that's what you do.'"[140] Corbould had previous experience working with tractor-trailers, having supervised special effects on the 1989 James Bond film *Licence to Kill,* which concluded with a chase scene involving big rigs.

With a direct challenge from Nolan, Corbould gave in. But now he had to find out if doing the stunt, which required using a nitrogen cannon to shoot a telegraph pole through a hole in the cab to bring the truck to an immediate stop, was even possible. "After about six weeks of calculations, we were ready to do an actual test," said Corbould. "We went out to an open space, got the truck up to speed and pressed the button, and it just sailed over. I had to go to Chris Nolan and tell him it worked perfectly."[141] Still, doing a test in the middle of nowhere was much different than doing the shot for real in the middle of a busy city street. Before they could film the scene, city engineers inspected the location to make sure that the tons of force necessary to send the truck end over end would not damage the infrastructure of LaSalle Street, including the various utility lines that run beneath it. Once safe parameters were determined, the production was given the green light.[142]

When the cameras rolled, Corbould hit the switch and the truck flipped exactly as expected. The cast and crew applauded. "It was an impressive thing to watch this truck fly over and land precisely where Chris said it was going to land," said Nolan. "At the top of its arc, it looked almost like a skyscraper standing there, and then it just continued going over very gracefully. I've never seen anything like it."[143]

A final spectacular shot came on August 28, when the crew destroyed a disused building that had once been the Brach's candy factory. Corbould and his crew teamed with Controlled Demolition, Inc., a company run by Doug Loizeaux, for the explosion. "Chris didn't want the building to go down like a deck of cards, like a conventional demolition," said Corbould. "I worked with Doug, who came up with a system to make the building go down more like a wave, in sequence. Then we added our special effects elements to make it more spectacular."[144]

Safety was a primary concern for the filmmakers, especially considering the surrounding street traffic and active rail lines that ran near the building. The railroad companies were contacted and the train schedules coordinated to make sure that no trains would be coming through at the time of the explosion. Nearby street traffic was blocked off to keep onlookers and passers-by from getting too close to the blast. The scene required a bus to be close to the explosion, so polycarbonate sheeting was placed on its windows to ensure that even if they broke, no glass would fly into the bus with cast members inside.[145] Again, when the time came, the effect went off without a hitch.

With these big stunts going so smoothly, it was a shock to Corbould when a relatively simple stunt went awry after the crew returned to England. On Monday, September 24, 2007, while the main unit was filming at Cardington, Corbould and his special effects crew went to the QinetiQ racetrack at Longcross near Chertsey, south of London, to do test runs involving a stunt vehicle.[146] Part of the test involved firing an old American police car off a ramp with a black powder cannon while pyrotechnic explosions were set off in its trunk. Upon landing, another cannon inside its trunk was supposed to fire and cause the car to flip over. The camera crew was to follow alongside the stunt car at about 20mph in a Nissan 4x4 driven by special effects technician Bruce Monroe-Armstrong.[147] Leaning out the window of the Nissan from the back seat was cinematographer Conway Wickliffe, operating the camera that was following the police car.[148] When it was time to do the test, the cannons in the police car went off as planned, but the Nissan failed to negotiate a 90-degree turn at the end of the run and collided with a tree.[149] Wickliffe suffered severe head injuries and was pronounced dead at the scene.

The cast and crew were stunned by the accident. A father of two, Wickliffe had previously worked on *Batman Begins* and *Casino Royale*.[150] Warner Bros. released a statement saying that the producers, cast and crew were "deeply saddened by this tragedy and their hearts and prayers go out to the family and loved ones of the deceased." Christian Bale and other film celebrities attended his funeral.[151]

Britain's Health and Safety Executive investigated the accident,[152] and the case went to the Crown Court in Guildford in March 2011. In court, prosecutors alleged that the accident was a result of a catalogue of safety blunders by special effects supervisor Chris Corbould.[153] Prosecutor Pascal Bates told jurors that Wickliffe's death was a tragedy waiting to happen, since Corbould had allowed Wickliffe to lean out of the car without wearing a safety belt while filming the practice scene. As Corbould sat grim-faced in the dock, Bates argued that the special effects supervisor was responsible for the "planning, conduct and supervision of the filmed special effects test. We say that there should have been a more thorough management of the risks."[154] After two hours of deliberation, the jury disagreed—unanimously. Corbould was found innocent of any negligence.[155]

Heath Ledger finished his work on the film in October. By the time shooting wrapped, the weeks of putting all his energy into the role had totally fatigued him. "He was exhausted, I mean he was really tired," said Michael Caine. "I remember saying to him, 'I'm too old to have the bloody energy to play that part.' And I thought to myself, I didn't have the energy when I *was* his age." Cinematographer Wally Pfister said that Ledger was so intense he seemed "like he was busting blood vessels in his head...It was like a séance, where the medium takes on another person and then is so completely drained."[156]

A few weeks later, Ledger told *The New York Times* that he was having trouble sleeping after finishing the shoot. "Last week I probably slept an average of two hours a night," said Ledger. "I couldn't stop thinking. My body was exhausted, and my mind was still going." The actor said he took two Ambien sleeping pills and fell into a stupor, then woke up an hour later.[157]

On November 6, a week of shooting began in Hong Kong. The city had been scouted nearly a year earlier, at the end of 2006. Once a decision was made to definitely film there, it took the producers nearly nine months to get all the necessary permits. The most prominent location in Hong Kong was the city's tallest building, the IFC2 Building. "I liked the idea of sending Batman someplace more exotic," said Nolan. "We had done that with Bruce Wayne in the first film, before he became Batman, but I really wanted to show the character of Batman outside the realm of Gotham City. I had been to Hong Kong many years ago at a film festival, and remembered it as a great location. It's an incredibly visual place, which makes it ideal in cinematic terms."[158] In fact, sending Batman to the Asian city marked the first time in the history of the Batman film franchise that the Caped Crusader was seen outside of Gotham City.

The crew arrived to find Hong Kong gripped in Bat-hysteria. "When we were up by the elevated train, we were shooting in one direction and behind us must have been 15-20,000 people watching us," said producer Chuck Roven. "They were in the windows, they were on the roofs, all looking. They treated every aspect of our being there like we were celebrities and they were hanging on everything. We finished shooting in one direction and I went up to the Chinese First A.D. and said, 'How the hell are you going to get the people behind us to move, because we've got to shoot in that direction now?' He said, 'It won't be a problem,' and he turned around, walked over, said a couple of words in Chinese and they were gone! It was amazing...It's like they didn't want to be intrusive. They wanted to watch but they were all very polite and everything."[159] The Hong Kong shoot wrapped on November 11, and the cast and crew returned to England.

Principal photography wound down in November, and by December Christopher Nolan was back in Los Angeles, overseeing post-production. "I loved making a film on a grand scale," said Nolan. "It took me back to being a kid and watching movies that were so much larger than life. That's particularly addictive. But I've always been driven by story, first and foremost. It has to fascinate me and make me feel something for a couple of years, because that's how long it's going to take to make a film."[160]

Paul Franklin and his company Double Negative Visual Effects began enhancing the footage shot live with computer generated imaging, which included augmenting shots of Gotham City, creating a digital Batman and Bat-Pod, and even creating a digital Batman for the hero's leap from a Hong Kong tower, where a real stuntman's jump was combined with a digitally-created Batman's glide.[161]

Richard King, the sound editor, went to work on the film's soundtrack, including enhancing the sound of the Batmobile's engines roaring to life by mixing recordings of big race boat engines and then adding in the roars and growls of large animals.[162] "The sound design of the film was extremely complicated," said Nolan. "There were an enormous number of elements encompassed in the sound mix and there are moments where it's hard to detect what is sound design and what is music... There are large segments of the film where we use little or no score. It was a major challenge for our sound designer, Richard King, and his team to create a range of sounds that would provoke the kind of emotional response that you would usually rely on music for. Then the end of the film is very heavily scored with music, but it develops as the action progresses."[163]

DARK DAYS

For the score of *The Dark Knight*, composers Hans Zimmer and James Newton Howard reunited, having had a successful collaboration on *Batman Begins*. "I like the score of the film to be an evolution that runs parallel to the editing of the film, and Hans and James have been amazing in accommodating that," said Nolan. "Usually without even seeing final footage, they give me pieces of music that my editor, Lee Smith, and I take into the edit suite. It's a very organic process that puts a lot of unusual demands on the composers, but they did a fantastic job with it."[164]

Building on the collaborative relationship they'd developed previously, Zimmer and Howard split duties on *The Dark Knight*. Zimmer composed the theme for the Joker, while Howard concentrated on Harvey Dent/Two-Face.[165] For Dent, whom Howard called "the emotional arc of the film," the composer used brass to evoke an all-American feeling. "Hans called me and asked how we would show that morally he is completely corrupted," said Howard. "The idea was to use the brass. It seemed like a good way to go, but it's so different from the rest of the movie. We took it and twisted it as the character loses ground."[166]

In composing music for Batman, they shied away from heroic-sounding fanfares. "I don't see Batman as a typical superhero, so I wanted to avoid anything 'super' in the music," said Zimmer. "I kept thinking about the Bat Symbol. It is the iconic representation of Batman, but at the same time, it is dark and unadorned."[167] The duo went for a sound that was even more experimental than what they had used previously. In the new film, Batman wouldn't have a theme, he would just have two notes. The Joker would only have one. "It's odd to put avant-garde touches on a blockbuster," said Zimmer. "It's tremendously enjoyable in an obsessive way. Once we stepped away from supplying a hero's theme, we spent most of our time getting rid of notes."[168]

Zimmer and Howard approached the scoring of the film in an innovative way. Usually, a film score is composed after the final edit is locked. For *The Dark Knight*, Zimmer and Howard composed ten hours of music based on the film's script. They presented it to Christopher Nolan on an iPod, which the director listened to on flights to and from Hong Kong.[169]

After recording the score at George Martin's Air Studios in London, Howard and Zimmer worked with the sound designers in the final mix. "We created a world from the left corner of the screen to the right rear of the theater. Every movie you score you hope is unlike anything you have done before. You are always trying to not sound like yourself. The vocabulary for this score, we really sweated over. It sounds simple but there were hundreds of choices."[170]

Warner Bros. began their advertising campaign with a teaser trailer released in December 2007, attached to the beginning of the Will Smith movie *I Am Legend*. Within hours of its release, copies of the trailer filmed from shaky camera phones were uploaded to the internet. The studio had already released a teaser poster showing Heath Ledger's Joker, and to quell fears that the new film, like Tim Burton's original *Batman*, would turn into a movie about the Joker with Batman as a guest star, another poster was released showing Batman looking out over the Gotham skyline.[171]

Besides being tied to the trailer for the new Batman film, *I Am Legend* contained a Batman in-joke. In one scene in the film, which was set in 2012, a billboard in the background had a giant movie poster with a composite Batman/Superman symbol and the release date "May 15, 2010." Though some comic book fans thought this was a marketing stunt hinting at a film to come, it was in fact just a sight gag to amuse *I Am Legend's* producer Akiva Goldsman, who at one time had been involved with the *Batman vs. Superman* film that had become mired in development hell.[172]

In December, Nolan screened a six-minute sequence from *The Dark Knight* to an audience of industry executives and journalists in Los Angeles. It didn't show a single frame of Christian Bale's Batman; it was all about Heath Ledger's Joker. "The bold decisions that Heath has made with this performance are fascinating to watch," said Nolan. "I think he's done something quite exceptional."[173]

But just as the film was taking shape, tragedy struck the production again. On January 22, 2008, seven weeks to the day after Nolan screened footage for industry executives and journalists, Heath Ledger was found dead in his New York apartment.[174] Ledger had only been in the city for a week, having just returned from London, where he was filming Terry Gilliam's *The Imaginarium of Doctor Parnassus.* A masseuse who had a 3 PM appointment with the 28-year-old actor arrived at his Broome Street apartment in the Soho district and, when Ledger didn't answer the door, went to the housekeeper.[175] The two discovered Ledger's nude body face down on the bedroom floor at 3:26 PM.[176] The masseuse tried to wake him. When she realized he was dead, she first placed three calls to actress Mary-Kate Olsen, who she knew to be a friend of Ledger's, before dialing 911. Olsen sent over private security agents, who arrived at about the same time as the emergency medical personnel.[177] The medical personnel immediately pronounced the actor dead.[178] Police said a bottle of prescription sleeping pills was found in the room.[179] There were other pills in containers in the bathroom.[180]

Just minutes after the news broke, fans began gathering by the hundreds outside Ledger's apartment building, where he had been living for about five months, since his split with actress Michelle Williams. An ambulance pulled up to the building entrance around 6 PM, and police cleared the crowd away so they could bring out Ledger's body. Fans on scaffolding and ledges across the way captured the event with their cell phone cameras.[181]

Professional accolades began pouring in. In a statement, Warner Bros. president and chief operating officer Alan Horn and president of Warner Bros. Pictures Group Jeff Robinov said in a statement, "The studio is stunned and devastated by this tragic news. The entertainment community has lost an enormous talent. Heath was a brilliant actor and an exceptional person. Our hearts go out to his family and friends."[182] Mel Gibson, who worked with Ledger in *The Patriot,* in which Ledger played his son, said, "I had such great hope for him. He was just taking off, and to lose his life at such a young age is a tragic loss." Lasse Hallstrom, who directed Ledger as *Casanova* (2005) said, "I am just shocked. He was a wonderful talent and smart. He was an old soul."[183]

Writing in *Newsweek,* Christopher Nolan said that he had Ledger very much on his mind as he was supervising the editing of *The Dark Knight*: "I would visualize the screening where we'd have to show him the finished film—sitting three or four rows behind him, watching the movements of his head for clues to what he was thinking about what we'd done with all that he'd given us. Now that screening will never be real. I see him every day in my edit suite. I study his face, his voice. And I miss him terribly."[184]

The day that Ledger was found dead was the same day that Academy Awards nominations were announced.[185] In early February, Ellen Borakove, a spokeswoman for the New York City medical examiner, said that Ledger's death was accidental. The actor overdosed on six kinds of painkillers, sleeping pills and anti-anxiety drugs; the medical examiner attributed his death to "acute intoxication."[186] "It's the combination of the drugs that caused the problem, not necessarily too much of any particular drug," Borakove told *The New York Times*. "All these drugs have a cumulative effect on the body."[187] Ledger's father, Kim, released a statement saying, "We learned today the combination of doctor-prescribed drugs proved lethal for our boy. Heath's accidental death serves as a caution to the hidden dangers of combining prescription medication, even at low dosage."[188]

For days after Ledger's death, the internet was ablaze with speculation that in playing the Joker the actor had plumbed so deeply into the dark depths of his soul that he was unable to find a way back, and committed suicide. It was all nonsense but it made for good tabloid fodder. In fact, when Ledger completed work on the film, he told an interviewer that playing the Joker was "the most fun I've ever had, or probably ever will have, playing a character."[189]

Christopher Nolan paid tribute to Ledger, and to the special effects man who had been tragically killed, with a title card in the closing credits of *The Dark Knight*, reading "In memory of our friends Heath Ledger & Conway Wickliffe."[190]

Ledger's death caused great concern at Warner Bros., where the marketing campaign of *The Dark Knight* was built partially around the grotesque images of Ledger as the Joker.[191] One poster showed the Joker writing "Why So Serious?" and drawing a clown's smile on a mirror with red lipstick.[192] The last thing the studio wanted was for the "Why So Serious?" tag line to be seen as a bad-taste comment on coverage of the actor's passing. Consequently, after Heath Ledger's death, Warner Bros. began focusing its marketing campaign more on Batman and less on the Joker. But just weeks before the film was due to open, they unleashed a new round of billboards, bus-stop ads and TV spots centering on the Joker's creepy countenance.[193] They even unveiled an online viral campaign in which the character took over websites with his maniacal laugh and revealed clues about the film to fans.[194] *The Times of London* called *The Dark Knight* "perhaps the most successful example of viral marketing ever." Besides a deal with Dominos Pizza that would allow pizza consumers to see an online trailer, the studio put up the entire $36,000 production budget for the first five episodes of a small Web series called *Kyle Piccolo: Comic Shop Therapist*, set in Manhattan's Midtown Comics.[195]

It was important to Nolan that no one connected with the film make a crass or maudlin misstep in promoting it. The director set the tone by writing an appreciation of Ledger for *Newsweek* in which he praised the actor's talents without ever mentioning *The Dark Knight's* release date. Aaron Eckhart said, "To have this film be successful and to have people see Heath's great work in it—to appropriately honor that performance by bringing the film to the audience—that became the goal for Chris and everyone involved. Chris gave us a set where the actors felt very secure, they felt they could take risks. And Chris has continued to protect Heath and his performance."[196] In an interview with Geoff Boucher of *The Los Angeles Times*, Nolan said, "I think we've said as much as we can about Heath. We want to do right by him. I'm proud of his work in this film, and I'm excited to have it seen, but I think in respect to him and his family, perhaps it's best to just let the film have the final word."[197]

Nolan was still hard at work at Warner Bros. Burbank studios in mid-May 2008, supervising the sound mix and overseeing the last stages of post-production.[198] Even then, before the film's release, buzz was building in Hollywood that Ledger's performance might win him a posthumous Oscar.[199]

With anticipation building for *The Dark Knight,* on July 8, 2008, Warner Bros. released *Gotham Knight,* a DVD with six animated Batman stories meant to fill in the timeframe between *Batman Begins* and the upcoming film. The brief stories, written by David S. Goyer, Greg Rucka, Jordan Goldberg, Alan Burnett, Brian Azzarello, and Josh Olson, were directed by seven top Japanese anime directors: Yahuhiro Aoki, Yuichiro Hayashi, Futoshi Higashide, Toshiyuki Kubooka, Hiroshi Morioka, Jong-Sik Nam, and Shoujirou Nishimi. Each of the six segments had a unique look unlike that of the animated *Batman* TV series.[200]

In May of 2008, well before the release of *The Dark Knight, Los Angeles Times* columnist Geoff Boucher was already speculating about who would be the villain in the eventual third film in Christopher Nolan's Batman series. "In public comments, Nolan has said he isn't a fan of the Penguin character," wrote Boucher, "and Catwoman was declawed not too long ago in the Halle Berry film fiasco. Maybe that means Gotham's protector will be solving dangerous riddles a few summers from now."[201]

THE DARK KNIGHT OPENS

Having made a cameo in the film, Sen. Patrick Leahy arranged for *The Dark Knight* to have a premiere screening at the Kellogg-Hubbard Library in Montpelier, Vermont on July 12, 2008, with the proceeds from the 350 screening tickets sold at $50 each and a reception going to the institution.[202]

On July 14, Christian Bale flew from the Albuquerque, New Mexico set of *Terminator Salvation,* on which he had begun work almost immediately after *The Dark Knight,* to go to New York for the *Batman* film's premiere. Michael Caine, Gary Oldman, Aaron Eckhart and Maggie Gyllenhaal also appeared, along with director Christopher Nolan, composers Hans Zimmer and James Howard Newton, Warner Bros. executives Alan Horn and Jeff Robinov, Legendary Pictures' Thomas Tull, and actors Emile Hirsch and Josh Hartnett. The premiere was held at the Imax theater at Broadway and 68th, with an after-party at the Mandarin Oriental, where a spacious lounge appeared to have been spray-painted by the Joker.[203]

For executive producer Michael Uslan, the highlight of the New York premiere was meeting two guests invited to the premiere by DC president Paul Levitz—Jerry Robinson, co-creator of the Joker, Alfred, Two-Face and other classic Batman characters, and Athena Finger, whose grandfather co-created the Dark Knight himself. As he began to go down the red carpet, Uslan yelled to the assembled press and fans, "Ladies and gentlemen! This is Jerry Robinson, co-creator of the Joker." With that, the newspapermen and photographers descended on Robinson, allowing him to finally gain recognition for characters he'd help to create nearly 70 years earlier. At the after-party, Uslan introduced Robinson to Michael Caine, and introduced Athena Finger to Christian Bale. In his autobiography, *The Boy Who Loved Batman,* Uslan described the night of *The Dark Knight's* premiere as "beyond special."[204]

After the New York premiere, Bale flew on to London to begin an around-the-world promotional tour.[205] But on July 22, he was arrested for allegedly assaulting his mother, Jenny James, and sister, Sharon, the previous night, before the London premiere of *The Dark Knight*. He was questioned at a police station in central London about the incident, which allegedly took place at the Dorchester Hotel.[206] It was reported that the cause of the altercation was money; after Bale snubbed his sister's request for a £100,000 loan to help bring up her three children, and Bale's wife was insulted, Bale "pushed and shoved" his sister and mother.[207]

The two women, who both lived in Dorset, filed formal charges against Bale at a Hampshire police station. The complaint was then passed on to the Metropolitan Police for more investigation. Despite the proceedings, police allowed Bale to attend the European premiere of *The Dark Knight* at the Odeon Leicester Square.[208] A source told *The Times of London*, "It would have been wrong to wreck the premiere over a complaint which we do not yet know is founded in truth."[209]

Bale, like all the other cast members who attended the London premiere, wore black in homage to Heath Ledger. Despite the domestic drama he had endured earlier in the evening, Bale posed for photos with his wife, Sibi. Attendees at the premiere were unaware of Bale's predicament, which wasn't revealed in the press until the following day. Some of the fans in the crowd were dressed as Batman and some as the Joker.[210] After walking the red carpet with Sir Michael Caine, Maggie Gyllenhaal and Aaron Eckhart on Sunday night, Bale voluntarily went to Belgravia police station on Monday, where he was arrested and questioned for four hours before being released on bail.[211] He denied his sister's and mother's allegations.[212]

On July 23, when he was in Barcelona to promote the film, Bale appeared at a press conference and was asked about the altercation. He responded, "It's a deeply personal matter. I would ask you to respect my privacy in the matter." The press conference was followed by a premiere with thousands of fans lining the red carpet; Bale signed autographs for nearly half an hour.[213]

The Times of London reported on August 14 that no charges would be filed against Bale over the alleged assault. A spokesman for the Crown Prosecution Service said, "There is insufficient evidence to afford a realistic prospect of conviction, and accordingly the police have been advised that no further action should be taken against Mr. Bale."[214]

The same month that Bale was accused of assaulting his mother, he lost his temper with director of photography Shane Hurlbut on the set of *Terminator Salvation* in New Mexico. Hurlbut had distracted Bale while the actor was filming a scene, and Bale unleashed a profanity-laced tirade that was soon posted on YouTube.com. Bale later apologized to Hurlbut, though he resented the outburst being leaked to the internet. Bale's managers urged him to release a statement, but he refused to do so, preferring to allow the incident to fade into obscurity.[215]

As its release date neared, *The Dark Knight* received mostly positive reviews, celebrating the riveting performance of Heath Ledger. Manohla Dargis of *The New York Times* wrote that Ledger's death, "might have cast a paralyzing pall over the film if the performance were not so alive. But his Joker is a creature of such ghastly life, and the performance is so visceral, creepy and insistently present that the characterization pulls you in almost at once."[216]

Peter Travers of *Rolling Stone* was also effusive in his praise, writing: "How can a conflicted guy in a bat suit and a villain with a cracked, painted-on clown smile speak to the essentials of the human condition? Just hang on for a shock to the system. *The Dark Knight* creates a place where good and evil—expected to do battle—decide instead to get it on and dance...I can only speak superlatives of Ledger, who is mad-crazy-blazing brilliant as the Joker. Miles from Jack Nicholson's broadly funny take on the role in Tim Burton's 1989 *Batman*, Ledger takes the role to the shadows, where even what's comic is hardly a relief...If there's a movement to get him the first posthumous Oscar since Peter Finch won for 1976's *Network*, sign me up."[217]

In *The Times of London*, Tim Teeman gave the film a five-star review, saying, "Ledger is so terrifying and unpredictable that his very presence on screen makes you horribly nervous—the atrocities he visits on his victims are bloody and vile-minded, and when he arrives at a party at the Wayne penthouse you feel sick as he observes the guests. He preys on our fear and sense of violation; what can Batman do to save us from that?... *The Dark Knight* will stun and surprise, delight and terrify, and it won't be the special effects, gizmos and bat-heroics that will keep you pinned to your seat, but the moral force of the script and an ending that takes our hero, unbelievably and brilliantly, to even darker realms."[218]

In yet another five-star review appearing in *The Times of London*, James Christopher wrote, "You will feel utterly numb after the screening of *The Dark Knight*. The film is bleak and brilliant. Batman is Hamlet and Heath Ledger is a sensation as the Joker. The late legend doesn't just steal the film, he murders it in style...He certainly makes Jack Nicholson's Joker in *Batman* (1989) look like a badly drawn cartoon. The chill realization that Ledger has calmly laid ethical mind-traps under every gothic frame is what makes Christopher Nolan's film, and the actor's performance, so powerful. The parameters of the comic book blockbuster have shifted forever."[219]

Justin Chang, in *Daily Variety*, called the film a "heroic reinvention of the iconic franchise. An ambitious, full-bodied crime epic of gratifying scope and moral complexity, this is seriously brainy pop entertainment that satisfies every expectation raised by its hit predecessor and then some...Utterly indifferent to simple criminal motivations like greed, Ledger's maniacally murderous Joker is as pure an embodiment of irrational evil as any in modern movies."[220]

Not every critic was bowled over by the film, however. In *The London Sunday Times*, Cosmo Landesman gave the film only 2 stars, writing, "People mistakenly think that if you give a character a 'dark side,' he must be interesting, but this Batman manages to be dark and boring...Of course, there's the Joker. There's nothing jokey about this Joker; he's a grungy, greasy psychopath who will leave his signature smile carved on your face. He provides the element of the fantastic and freakish that the film needs. Uncoupled from the confines of realism, Ledger is free to let rip and give us a character who is scary because you can't hurt him. He is in a place beyond good and evil, human and 'other.' Suddenly, the screen comes alive in what is a one-man show of verbal play and sadistic theatre. Yet when Ledger isn't on screen, *The Dark Knight* goes on for so long, it should be called *The Long Dark Knight of the Soul*."[221]

History began repeating itself when parents found the film too intense for small children, a reaction similar to what *Batman Returns* had encountered fifteen years earlier. Producer Charles Roven said, "Every parent needs to be their own guide on a PG-13 movie. I certainly wouldn't recommend it to anybody under 10."[222] In the U.K., *The Dark Knight* received a 12A certificate, comparable to a PG-13 rating in the

U.S.—children 12 years of age or older could attend unaccompanied by an adult. However, the British Board of Film Classification (BBFC) received 70 complaints about the certification, based on the film's violence. Scenes of the Joker describing how he enjoys killing people with a knife were found particularly objectionable.[223] Labour MP Keith Vaz, chairman of the Commons home affairs committee, said he would summon the BBFC to its October hearings on knife crime. "The BBFC should realize there are scenes of gratuitous violence in *The Dark Knight* to which I would certainly not take my 11-year-old daughter," Vaz said after seeing the film. "It should be a 15 classification." The BBFC admitted that Warner Bros. asked for *The Dark Knight* to be classified as 12A. They also admitted that they were under pressure from Hollywood studios to keep the classifications low so that as many people as possible could see films unrestricted.[224]

On August 5, *The Times of London* reported that Iain Duncan Smith, the former leader of the Conservative Party known as "the Quiet Man," was anything but quiet after taking his 15-year-old daughter to see *The Dark Knight*. By that point, the film had received 82 complaints. Smith wrote a letter to *The Times* saying the film was "relentlessly violent," adding, "I was astonished that the board could have seen fit to allow anyone under the age of 15 to watch the film. Unlike past *Batman* films, where the villains were somewhat surreal and comical figures, Heath Ledger's Joker is a brilliantly acted but very credible psychopathic killer, who extols the use of knives to kill and disfigure his victims during a reign of urban terrorism laced with torture." On its website, the BBFC defended its decision by writing, "*The Dark Knight* is a superhero movie and the violence it contains exists within that context, with both Batman and the Joker apparently indestructible, no matter what is thrown at them."[225]

THE DARK KNIGHT SOARS

With anticipation building to a fever pitch, the studio allowed theaters to begin selling tickets at midnight, a ploy designed to help pump up the opening weekend box-office numbers. When tickets for the July 18 midnight showings of *The Dark Knight* quickly sold out, 3 A.M. screenings were announced. When those sold out, theaters scheduled 6 A.M. screenings. Online ticket sales service Fandango.com reported that there were well over 1,500 late-night/early morning screenings of the film scheduled at theaters that normally didn't open their doors until 10 A.M. In a Fandango survey, about 38 percent of ticket buyers said they planned to take some or all of Friday, July 18 off from work to see *The Dark Knight*.[226] A week before the film opened, it had already sold out the entire first week's showings at New York's Lincoln Square Imax theater, save for some 6 A.M. screenings.[227] One patron listed his two $16 tickets to the Imax theater's midnight showing on eBay. When bidding was finished, the tickets went for $122.50, including shipping.[228]

The 2-1/2 hour film was scheduled to open at 4,366 theaters nationwide. With Fandango.com and Movie.com reporting the strongest advance sales they'd ever seen, industry pundits were anxious to see if the film would enter the record books.[229] Of the $67.85 million earned on Friday, $18.5 million came from midnight shows, beating the previous midnight record set by 20th Century-Fox's *Star Wars:*

Episode III—The Revenge of the Sith, which grossed $16.9 million from 3,663 theaters in 2005.[230] Overall, during its opening weekend, the film racked up $158.4 million in ticket sales.[231] That was enough to edge out the previous box-office champion *Spider-Man 3,* which had opened a year earlier with $151.1 million. $67.85 million of *The Dark Knight's* revenues came from its opening Friday, beating the $59.8 million *Spider-Man 3* had taken in on its opening day. *The Dark Knight* also broke *Spider-Man 3's* record for best Imax debut, earning $6.2 million at 94 Imax theaters around the country, as compared to *Spider-Man 3's* $4.7 million.[232] The film had already opened in Australia, beginning a day earlier than usual to take advantage of a local holiday. On Wednesday and Thursday alone—its first two days of release down under—it brought in a respectable $4.45 million.[233]

The same day that it opened in the U.S., it launched in 20 international markets in the first phase of its international roll-out, including Asia, Brazil, Hong Kong and Mexico. In Latin America, it debuted on 4,400 screens,[234] earning $41 million.[235] Mexico brought in $6.6 million, and Brazil $4.3 million.[236] In Hong Kong, the film grabbed 64% of the local box office with $2.12 million at 37 theaters.[237] After the phenomenal opening weekend, Warner Bros. knew they had a potential monster hit on their hands. "It just took on a life of its own," said Dan Fellman, Warner Bros.' president for theatrical distribution. "You never expect anything like this."[238]

Even with its astounding success, Warner Bros. feared that the film's theatrical debut would be undermined by unauthorized copies leaking to file-sharing sites on the internet. To combat this, the studio had employees patrolling the aisles of theaters wearing night-vision goggles, on the lookout for hand-held camcorders. The first copy to leak to the internet, 38 hours after the film's debut, was traced to a theater in the Philippines. Warners had tried to discourage pirates by flooding file-sharing sites with fake copies of the film after the first pirated copies surfaced. The studio was thought to have saved several millions in lost ticket revenue through such tactics.[239]

Nonetheless, despite Warner Bros. anti-piracy efforts, by the end of 2008 illegal copies had been downloaded more than seven million times around the world, according to BigChampagne, a media measurement firm. With the economic downturn, it appeared that more and more people were turning to illegally downloaded movies, contributing to shrinking DVD sales; in 2008, DVD shipments dropped to their lowest levels in five years.[240] Moreover, not all of the illegally watched copies were downloaded; streaming sites, many located in countries like China with lax piracy enforcement, allowed people to watch movies on their computers without transferring a full copy to their hard drives. Since streaming was hard to monitor, media companies didn't have a clear idea of just how much content was being stolen. Eric Garland, the chief executive of BigChampagne, said, "It is becoming, among some demographics, a very mainstream behavior."[241]

The Dark Knight continued to burn up the box office in its second week, when it was scheduled to open in the U.K., Italy, Belgium, Holland, Scandinavia and several Eastern European markets.[242] From Friday to Sunday of its second weekend, it grossed $75.6 million, delivering the best second-weekend gross in recent history. In analyzing its success, studio executives felt it was because of a confluence of factors. First was the expert promotional campaign headlined by marketing chief Sue Kroll that built anticipation for Ledger's performance as the Joker. Secondly, the morose film fit the mood of the nation. And lastly, in the bad economic climate, movies were still a relatively cheap form of entertainment. "We are starting to see a lot of repeat business," said Warner Bros. president of theatrical distribution Dan Fellman. "Older audiences are also starting to turn out in big numbers." The publicity surrounding Christian Bale's alleged assault of his mother and sister may also have boosted the box-office.[243]

In its first ten days of release, *The Dark Knight* grossed a record-setting $314.2 million domestically.[244] After twelve days, its worldwide gross was $440 million. The 8.5 million tickets it sold overseas exceeded the combined grosses of the next four highest grossing films—*Hancock, Kung Fu Panda, Mamma Mia!* and *X-Files: I Want to Believe*—even though Warner Bros. had yet to launch the film in key markets such as France, Germany, Japan, South Korea and Spain, where it was to open in August.[245]

It was thought that *The Dark Knight* might actually overtake *Titanic* as the number one box-office success of all time. *Titanic* was the number one film domestically for an astounding 15 weeks, remaining in theaters for nine months and collecting $600.8 million. "You can't compare this movie to *Titanic*. That was a different time, and a different genre," said Warners president of distribution Dan Fellman. Yet for four consecutive weeks, *The Dark Knight* remained the number one movie in America. In its fourth week, it pulled in $26 million at the box office. By that point, it had earned $441 million in 24 days.[246] It was finally knocked off the number-one position by Paramount Pictures and Dreamworks' *Tropic Thunder*, which took in $26 million in its first week of release, as compared to *The Dark Knight's* second-place $16.8 million in its fifth week of release. After five weeks, its total domestic gross reached $471.5 million,[247] enough to put it past *Star Wars* to become the second-highest-grossing film of all time. Paul Dergarabedian, president of the box-office tracker Media by Numbers, said, "It's a film that is rewriting the record books every day, redefining our notions of what a blockbuster can be."[248] Warner Bros.' Fellman said, "There's never been another movie like this that has done $500 million in business. That's a gross that will be remembered for eternity."[249]

By mid-August, *The Dark Knight* was playing on 7,700 screens internationally, and was still the top money earner. The cumulative box-office overseas had reached $328.6 million, nearly double what *Batman Begins*—the top grosser of all the films internationally, with $166 million—had earned. *The Dark Knight's* combined domestic and international gross grew to more than $800 million, making it only the 19th film to ever cross that mark. And that was before the film opened in Germany.[250] Conventional wisdom held that a dark superhero like Batman was a tough sell to foreign markets, but *The Dark Knight* proved the exception. During the final weekend of August, the film was still number one internationally, earning $19 million on 6,580 screens in 62 markets, bringing its international total to $417 million.[251]

Over the Labor Day weekend, *The Dark Knight* became only the second film in history to cross the $500 million mark in domestic grosses. Warner Bros. predicted that it would eventually earn $530 million, putting it second only to *Titanic*.[252] It also set a record for Imax, grossing $42.6 million in that format.[253] The success of *The Dark Knight* gave Warner Bros. a narrow lead in market share over Paramount at the summer box-office, despite Paramount having two heavy-hitters in *Iron Man* and *Indiana Jones and the Kingdom of the Crystal Skull*.[254]

The stellar performance of *The Dark Knight* led Time Warner to report better-than-expected third-quarter results on November 5, 2008.[255] By mid-December, as it was ending its international runs, *The Dark Knight* had grossed $530.6 million domestically and $466 million abroad for a worldwide total of $997 million, more than double the $371.8 worldwide gross of *Batman Begins*, making it hands-down the most profitable *Batman* film ever released and, for a short while, making it the second highest-grossing film in history, after *Titanic*.[256]

While the film burned up the box office, Morgan Freeman made headlines when he was involved in an accident on Sunday, August 3, 2008. Freeman was driving a Nissan Maxima on Mississippi Highway 32 in Tallahatchie County around 11:30 PM with passenger Demaris Meyer. The car apparently went onto the shoulder and Freeman overcorrected. The car left the road, became airborne, and flipped several times before landing upright in Lisa Hudson's front yard. Hudson ran over to the car to help and grabbed Freeman's hand. He asked her to help him get out, but he was pinned. More bystanders arrived, and when one tried to snap a photo of Freeman with a cell phone camera, Freeman said "no freebies, no freebies." Emergency crews soon arrived on the scene and, using the jaws of life, removed Freeman and Meyer, both of whom were wearing seat belts, from the wreckage. Both were airlifted to the Regional Medical Center in Memphis.[257] The accident left Freeman with a broken arm, broken elbow and minor shoulder damage; the injuries to his left arm left his hand paralyzed. Meyer, who suffered a broken left wrist, broken right scapula and a torn labrum in her right shoulder, was released the next day, but Freeman remained in serious condition.[258] Mississippi Highway Patrol spokesperson Ben Williams said there was no indication that either alcohol or drugs were involved.

In February 2009, Meyer's attorney, Gloria Allred, filed a lawsuit against Freeman, claiming that the actor had been drinking the night of the accident at the Bayou Bend Golf and Country Club and later at a friend's house, and that he was negligent when the car ran off the road. Meyer also complained that she was wrongly labeled "the other woman" and accused of having broken up Freeman's marriage; in fact, Freeman and his wife separated in December 2007 and were already in the process of getting a divorce when the accident occurred. On the night of the accident, Freeman had offered to let Meyer stay at one of the three houses on his property after they attended a party. Meyer sued for medical expenses, pain and suffering, lost wages, permanent disability and property damage. Freeman settled the lawsuit in November 2009.[259] He still often wears a tan glove to soothe the pain in his left hand. Some journalists attributed Freeman's accident to "The Curse of Batman," coming as it did within a year of the death of Conway Wickliffe, the accidental overdose of Heath Ledger, and the assault allegations against Christian Bale.[260]

AWARD KNIGHT

In mid-November 2008, the executive committee of the Academy of Motion Picture Arts & Sciences music branch disqualified the score of *The Dark Knight* from Oscar contention—just as *Batman Begins* had been disqualified in 2005—because five names were listed as composers on the music cue sheet, an official studio document that lists every piece of music in the film, along with its duration and copyright owners. Hans Zimmer told *Daily Variety's* Jon Burlingame that listing the multiple names on the cue sheet was a way of making sure that everyone who contributed to the score would share in the financial rewards, since performing rights societies like ASCAP and BMI use the cue sheets to distribute royalties to composers.[261] Besides Hans Zimmer and James Newton Howard, the cue sheets also listed music editor Alex Gibson, ambient music designer Mel Wesson and composer Lorne Balfe. Gibson, Wesson and Balfe reportedly signed an affidavit stating that the score was primarily the work of Zimmer and Howard, but that wasn't enough to sway the committee's decision.[262] At least not until December when, after he and Howard had written a pointed letter to Academy executive director Bruce Davis, Zimmer appeared at the music branch's executive committee meeting to make his case in person. The Academy reversed its decision.[263]

When Golden Globe nominations were announced on December 10, 2008, Heath Ledger was nominated in the Best Performance by an Actor in a Supporting Role category for his role as the Joker in *The Dark Knight*.[264] The following month, Christopher Nolan was nominated for the 61st annual Directors Guild of America award, the first time a director of a superhero movie had received such recognition from the DGA. By that time, *The Dark Knight* had already earned nominations from the Producers Guild of America, the American Society of Cinematographers and the Writers Guild of America. Commenting on the DGA honor, announced just one day after *The Dark Knight* swept the People's Choice Awards, winning for Favorite Action Movie, Favorite Cast, Favorite Movie, Favorite On-Screen Match-Up (for Christian Bale and Heath Ledger), and Favorite Superhero, Nolan said, "It's been a good week for us. I have always felt that the grand-scale blockbuster is the thing that Hollywood does best, and that was one of the reasons I was excited to take it on. It was really enjoyable to look at the iconography and the concept of who Batman is and who the Joker is and try to immerse yourself in their world."[265]

On January 23, 2009, one year to the day after his death, Heath Ledger earned an Academy Award nomination for his role as the Joker. Ledger's performance had already won awards from the Los Angeles Film Critics Association, a Critic's Choice Award, and a Golden Globe (as Best Screen Match-Up with Christian Bale). He was also nominated for Screen Actor's Guild and BAFTA Awards—both of which he would eventually win.[266] *The Dark Knight* was nominated for a total of 8 Academy Awards; besides Ledger's nomination, it nabbed honors for Film Editing, Sound Editing, Art Direction, Cinematography, Makeup, Sound Mixing and Visual Effects. On awards night, Richard King took home the statuette for Sound Editing, and Ledger won Best Supporting Actor. His father, Kim Ledger, mother, Sally Bell, and sister Kate Ledger jointly ascended the stage to accept the Oscar statuette, while the audience joined in a standing ovation. "This award tonight would have humbly validated Heath's quiet determination to be truly accepted by you all here, his peers, within an industry he so loved," said Kim Ledger. Kate Ledger said the family was accepting the award on behalf of Heath Ledger's 3-year-old daughter, "beautiful Matilda."[267] Betsy Sharkey in *The Los Angeles Times* commented, "Though it may be, it should not be said that Ledger's death last year at 28 won him the Oscar. His passing added layers of emotion, yes, but his is a performance that stands alone in its power and humility, a brilliant interior piece for a character who could have been little more than a series of vaporous expressions."[268]

For the following year's 2009 Academy Awards, the Academy of Motion Picture Arts & Sciences expanded the Best Picture category from five nominees to ten. Some industry observers felt that one of the reasons behind the move was because *The Dark Knight* failed to get a Best Picture nomination. Allowing for ten nominees, it was thought, would widen the field so that worthy blockbusters might get nominated along with the usual array of art-house films. Some in the industry called the expansion "The *Dark Knight* Rule."[269]

AFTERMATH

Long after its release, *The Dark Knight* continued to generate controversy. The success of the film was attributed to interest generated by the studios highlighting of the late Heath Ledger in almost all of the publicity, Ledger's mesmerizing performance, and the way that the film went beyond being just another superhero adventure to exploring the ethical issues of America's war on terror. In the online *Slate* magazine, Dana Stevens wrote, "Nolan turns the Manichean morality of comic books—pure good vs. pure evil—into a bleak post-9/11 allegory about how terror (and, make no mistake, Ledger's Joker is a terrorist) breaks down those reassuring moral categories." In *Time* magazine, Richard Corliss called the Joker "the Bin Laden of movie villains".[270]

Some bloggers saw *The Dark Knight* as a commentary on President George W. Bush's war on terror. As *The New York Times* pointed out, the Joker was a terrorist in the Osama Bin Laden tradition who damaged the free society of Gotham by instilling fear in the public. The Gotham Police Department represented conventional law enforcement. Batman was the dark response to the threat, perhaps going overboard by using people's cell phones to create a form of domestic surveillance and using torture to uncover details of an ongoing plot. But while the film seemed sympathetic to the Bush Administration's anti-terrorist approach, Lucius Fox is presented as the voice of reason, arguing against the intrusion on citizens' civil liberties. And in the end, Batman's methods make him almost as much a villain as the bad guys.[271]

In *The Wall Street Journal*, conservative novelist Andrew Klavan wrote, "There seems to me no question that *The Dark Knight* is at some level a paean of praise to the fortitude and moral courage that has been shown by George W. Bush in this time of terror and war...Like W., Batman is vilified and despised for confronting terrorists in the only terms they understand. Like W., Batman sometimes has to push the boundaries of civil rights to deal with an emergency, certain that he will re-establish those boundaries when the emergency is past."[272]

However, the way the film explored the issues was ambivalent enough that not only conservatives but also liberals claimed that it validated their beliefs. For instance, in *The New York Post*, film critic Kyle Smith wrote, "Batman is not charming. He isn't popular, partly because he's a zealot and partly because he doesn't bother to explain himself to the press. He is independently wealthy, having spent years as the head of an industrial company. His methods are disturbing, his operations bathed in darkness.

He is misunderstood, mistrusted, endlessly pursued by the attack dogs of the night... And he lives in an undisclosed location. Isn't it obvious? Batman is Dick Cheney with hair."[273]

On the liberal website *AlterNet*, Michael Dudley of the Institute of Urban Studies wrote that *The Dark Knight* "takes the viewer on a sometimes traumatic but ultimately redemptive and humanistic journey towards a post-9/11 ethic." Dudley noted that most of Batman's extra-legal actions—like beating up the Joker in jail in what the CIA might have called an "enhanced interrogation technique," or using a computerized tracking system to plug into every Gotham City citizen's cell phone, similar to Bush's proposed "Total Information Awareness" system—backfired on him and Gotham City, the metropolis he was trying to protect. Dudley concluded that the film "warns against abandoning our principles out of fear, grief and hatred, as well as abdicating our moral agency to external authorities—both of which comprised the hallmark moral syndrome of the years following 9/11...What Batman is doing is heroic, but it can be seen as vigilantism, as a dark force outside the law. That's a very, very dangerous road to go down. He's always riding a knife edge in moral terms."[274]

Christopher Goodwin in *The Times of London* wrote that Nolan touched a raw nerve in all of us by confronting his own deepest fears, quoting the director as saying, "Anarchy and chaos—even the threat of anarchy and chaos—are the most frightening things society faces, especially in this day and age." Goodwin continued, "it's possible that, with the Joker, Nolan is exploring his own most radical fear (and, it seems from the film's success, ours, too): the fear of psychological chaos, of madness, the unraveling of firm mental grounding, the complete loss of psychological control. Read in this way, the Joker represents nothing as banal as Bin Laden, but the id, 'the dark, inaccessible part of our personality,' as Freud put it, the base human instincts, unconscious, amoral and utterly selfish."[275]

The Dark Knight was used to comment on other political issues besides the lingering debate on appropriate responses to terror after 9/11. In September of 2008, when TV and newspapers were filled with news of a government bailout of banks, an enterprising satirist at Overthinkingit.com created a mash up video of the Joker and Gotham City's criminals watching President George W. Bush's speech.[276]

The image of Heath Ledger's Joker was so indelible that it was used for political commentary after Barack Obama's election as president of the United States. In early 2009, posters began appearing in Los Angeles and other U.S. cities that showed Obama with white face, black eye sockets and red joker smile and the word "socialism." Some viewed it as a right-wing critique of Obama's efforts to reform health care, others thought it racist. *The Los Angeles Times* tracked down the poster's creator: Firas Alkhateeb, a 20-year-old senior history major at the University of Illinois. Alkhateeb told *The Times* he didn't create the Obama/Joker portrait to express a burning political ideology, but that he had just been tinkering around during the holidays with Photoshop digital imaging software and was following an online tutorial about how to "Jokerize" portraits. The word "socialism," he claimed, had been added by an unknown person who downloaded the Obama/Joker image from the photo-sharing website Flickr and circulated copies of the image. He knew when the theft occurred. In the first two months the image was on Flickr, it logged around 2000 hits. After it was stolen, the hit counter suddenly ticked into the tens of thousands. Alkhateeb said he was alarmed and slightly ashamed of what happened, but remained silent because of Obama's popularity in Chicago and because he was afraid of being sued for copyright infringement. The person who added the word "socialism" and distributed the posters was never tracked down.[277]

A potential international political incident arose in early November 2008, when Batman was sued by Batman. Huseyin Kalkan, the pro-Kurdish Democratic Society Party mayor of Batman, an oil producing city in southeastern Turkey, sued Christopher Nolan and Warner Bros. for royalties from *The Dark Knight* for using the city's name without permission. Kalkan said, "There is only one Batman in the world. The American producers used the name of our city without informing us." Mayor Kalkan said the psychological impact that the film's success had on the city's populace was responsible for a number of unsolved murders and a high rate of female suicide. Warner Bros. shrugged off the suit, saying in a statement, "We are only aware of this claim via press reports and have not seen any actual legal action."[278]

The release of *The Dark Knight* on DVD and Blu-ray in mid-December 2008 highlighted the decline in DVD sales, and the rising popularity of Blu-ray. On the day it was released on Blu-ray, *The Dark Knight* set a new record, selling 600,000 copies in one day. The combined sales for DVD and Blu-ray were 3 million copies; the second day, the total number had risen to 4.4. million sales. However, just two years earlier, Warner Bros. sold 5 million copies of *Harry Potter and the Goblet of Fire* on its first day in DVD and Blu-ray release; the all-time best sales record was set in 2003, when *Finding Nemo* sold 8 million DVDs its first day out.[279]

As sales of DVDs declined, industry watchers looked at *The Dark Knight* sales as a test of the new Blu-ray format in a depressed economy.[280] Previously, *Iron Man* had sold 260,000 Blu-ray discs in its first day, with sales topping 500,000 before the end of the first week. In its first week on the shelves, *Iron Man's* combined Blu-ray and DVD sales hit 7.2 million units. *The Dark Knight* outsold *Iron Man* on the first day, and its sales were expected to climb through the Christmas holiday.[281]

On February 15, 2011, Warner Bros. found a unique way to offer *The Dark Knight* along with Christopher Nolan's follow-up film, *Inception*, to consumers in 23 countries where it wasn't offered through iTunes. The solution: make the films into iPhone apps. When the free apps were downloaded to an iPhone, iPad or iPod touch, users were able to see the first five minutes of the movie along with tie-in games, trivia, and other material. They could then access the full movie within the app for the standard iTunes price of around $10. The idea allowed Warner Bros. to offer the movies in markets where Apple had yet to launch a full digital movie store, such as China, Russia, Greece, Hungary, Portugal and the Czech Republic.[282]

A month later, Warner Bros. became the first Hollywood studio to make films available for rent or purchase on Facebook. The first film they made available to the website was *The Dark Knight*, which could be rented for $3.[283] Making the film more available online was Warner Bros.' way of boosting the digital distribution business, which the studio hoped to grow to offset losses from the diminishing DVD market.[284]

As the American economy began to crumble in 2009, collectibles suddenly seemed to be better investments than stocks. In the auction market, rare issues of

Superman and Batman comics battled for the record of most money paid for a comic book. On Monday, February 23, 2009, a rare 1938 copy of *Action Comics* No. 1, featuring the first appearance of Superman, sold for $1 million in a private sale arranged by the New York auction site ComicConnect.com.[285] But Superman's supremacy didn't last long; by Thursday, a 1939 copy of *Detective Comics* No. 27, with the first appearance of Batman, was sold in Dallas by Heritage Auctions for $1,075,500.[286] Malcolm Phillips, of the leading British seller Comic Book Auctions Ltd, said, "What it tells you is that high-end comics are going into collections which have become like an extension of the equities market. They are going into a very wealthy person's investment portfolio."[287] Fewer than 100 copies of each comic were believed to still exist.[288] But Superman bounced back. On March 29, a 1938 *Action Comics* No. 1 sold for $1.5 million on the auction web site ComicConnect.com.[289]

Christopher Nolan was contracted for a third *Batman* film, but after the success of *The Dark Knight*, he wanted to take some time away from the character and pursue other projects.[290] In October 2008, when asked about the inevitable third film in his *Batman* trilogy, and whether or not he would be involved in making it, Christopher Nolan told *The Los Angeles Times*, "There are two things to be said. One is the emphasis on story. What's the story? Is there a story that's going to keep me emotionally invested for the couple of years that it will take to make another one? That's the overriding question. On a more superficial level, I have to ask the question: How many good third movies in a franchise can people name?"[291]

The Times of London speculated that if Christopher Nolan were unwilling to return to the series, Warner Bros. might find another director for the next *Batman* film. The paper asked Christian Bale if he would appear in a third *Batman* movie if someone other than Nolan were to direct it. Bale said, "I don't even want to think about that, I don't know if there will be a third."[292]

Speaking to *Daily Variety's* Michael Fleming, Christopher Nolan looked back on *The Dark Knight* and summed it up by saying, "We weren't trying to make people think as much as feel, using the operatic quality of these iconic characters. Batman is appealing because of his human nature. He's not a guy with super powers, he's relatable because he has suffered greatly and tried to channel that into something positive. He is a perfect blend of the elemental qualities and romanticism found in such stories as *The Count of Monte Cristo, The Prisoner of Zenda* and *Zorro*."[293]

Zorro. It all began with Zorro....

---

1   Moran, Michael, "Dark Knight, 'I Believe Whatever Doesn't Kill You Simply Makes You Stranger,'" The London Times, March 14, 2008

2   Barnes, Brooks, "A Studio Head Slowly Alters the 'Warner Way,'" *The New York Times*, Feb. 9, 2010, http://www.nytimes.com/2010/02/10/business/media/10warner.html?scp=405&sq=batman&st=nyt, accessed Aug. 16, 2011

3   *Ibid.*

4   McClintock, Pamela, "Warner's Men in Tights: 'Batman,' 'Superman' to See Sequel Action," *Daily Variety*, Feb. 23, 2006, p. 17

5   Miller, Neil, "Interview: The Dark Knight Scribes David S. Goyer and Jonathan Nolan," *FilmSchoolRejects.com*, July 17, 2008, http://www.filmschoolrejects.com/news/interview-the-dark-knight-scribes-david-s-goyer-and-jonathan-nolan.php, accessed Aug. 27, 2011

6   Brevet, Brad, "'The Dark Knight' Writers' Desk With David Goyer and Jonathan Nolan," *RopeOfSilicon.com*, July 16, 2008, http://www.ropeofsilicon.com/article/the_dark_knight_writers_desk_with_david_goyer_and_jonathan_nolan, accessed Aug. 27, 2011

7   Miller, Neil, "Interview: The Dark Knight Scribes David S. Goyer and Jonathan Nolan," *FilmSchoolRejects.com*, July 17, 2008, http://www.filmschoolrejects.com/news/interview-the-dark-knight-scribes-david-s-goyer-and-jonathan-nolan.php, accessed Aug. 27, 2011

8   —, "The Dark Knight: Production Notes," © 2008 Warner Bros. Inc., SciFiJapan.com, http://www.scifijapan.com.articles/2008/07/13/the-dark-knight-production-notes/, accessed Aug. 20, 2011

9   Brevet, Brad, "'The Dark Knight' Writers' Desk With David Goyer and Jonathan Nolan," *RopeOfSilicon.com*, July 16, 2008, http://www.ropeofsilicon.com/article/the_dark_knight_writers_desk_with_david_goyer_and_jonathan_nolan, accessed Aug. 27, 2011

10 Miller, Neil, "Interview: The Dark Knight Scribes David S. Goyer and Jonathan Nolan," *FilmSchoolRejects.com*, July 17, 2008, http://www.filmschoolrejects.com/news/interview-the-dark-knight-scribes-david-s-goyer-and-jonathan-nolan.php, accessed Aug. 27, 2011

11 *Ibid.*

12 *Ibid.*

13 McClintock, Pamela, "Warner's Men in Tights: 'Batman,' 'Superman' to See Sequel Action," *Daily Variety*, Feb. 23, 2006, p. 17

14 Miller, Neil, "Interview: The Dark Knight Scribes David S. Goyer and Jonathan Nolan," *FilmSchoolRejects.com*, July 17, 2008, http://www.filmschoolrejects.com/news/interview-the-dark-knight-scribes-david-s-goyer-and-jonathan-nolan.php, accessed Aug. 27, 2011

15 Boucher, Geoff, "Christopher Nolan's 'Knight' Vision," *The Los Angeles Times*, July 6, 2008, http://www.latimes.com/entertainment/la-ca-nolan6-2008jul06,0,522026.story

16 Brevet, Brad, "'The Dark Knight' Writers' Desk With David Goyer and Jonathan Nolan," *RopeOfSilicon.com*, July 16, 2008, http://www.ropeofsilicon.com/article/the_dark_knight_writers_desk_with_david_goyer_and_jonathan_nolan, accessed Aug. 27, 2011

17 —, "The Dark Knight: Production Notes," © 2008 Warner Bros. Inc., SciFiJapan.com, http://www.scifijapan.com/articles/2008/07/13/the-dark-knight-production-notes/, accessed Aug. 20, 2011

18 Miller, Neil, "Interview: The Dark Knight Scribes David S. Goyer and Jonathan Nolan," *FilmSchoolRejects.com*, July 17, 2008, http://www.filmschoolrejects.com/news/interview-the-dark-knight-scribes-david-s-goyer-and-jonathan-nolan.php, accessed Aug. 27, 2011

19 Brevet, Brad, "Thomas and Roven, the Producers Talk 'Dark Knight,'" *RopeOfSilicon.com*, July 15, 2008, http://www.ropeofsilicon.com/article/thomas_and_roven_the_producers_talk_dark_knight, accessed Aug. 27, 2011

20 Tanner, "His Name is Wayne, Bruce Wayne: James Bond and *The Dark Knight*," *Double O Section blog*, http://doubleosection.blogspot.com/2008/07/his-name-is-wayne-bruce-wayne-james.html, July 17, 2008, retrieved Sept. 24, 2011

21 McClintock, Pamela, "Justice Prevails for Warner Bros.," *Daily Variety*, Feb. 23, 2007, p. 1

22 *Ibid.*, p. 54

23 McClintock, Pamela, "Big 'League' Play," *Weekly Variety*, June 18-24, 2007, p. 4

24 Garrett, Diane, "WB Makes Way for 'Justice,'" *Daily Variety*, Sep. 21, 2007, p. 1

25 *Ibid.*, p. 20

26 *Ibid.*, p. 1

27 Siegel, Tatiana, "Biel's Working Wonder at WB," *Daily Variety*, Sept. 25, 2007, p. 1

28 Fleming, Michael and Diane Garrett, "Warner Sticking Pin in 'Justice,'" *Daily Variety*, Jan. 17, 2008, p. 42

29 *Ibid.*, p. 1

30 *Ibid.*, p. 42

31 Garrett, Diane, "WB Seeks Swift 'Justice,'" *Daily Variety*, Feb. 27, 2008. p. 4

32 Malcom, Shawna, "10 Actors to Watch: Arnie Hammer," *Daily Variety*, Oct. 27, 2008, p. A12

33 Graser, Marc, "Hero Hunt Heats Up...and Taps Into Ties at DC Comics," *Weekly Variety*, Aug. 18-24, 2008, p. 7

34 *Ibid.*

35 Goldman, Michael, "Wally Pfister: The Prestige," *Daily Variety*, Jan. 4, 2007, p. A7

36 Halbfinger, David M., "Batman's Burden: A Director Confronts Darkness and Death," *The New York Times*, March 9, 2008, http://www.nytimes.com/2008/03/09/movies/09halb.html?ref=heathledger, accessed July 3, 2011

37 Carpetbagger, The Hollywood Blog, "Jake Gyllenhaal, Superhero," *The New York Times*, Feb. 7, 2006, http://carpetbagger.blogs.ny times.com/2006/02/07/jake-gyllenhaal-superhero/?scp=408&sq=batman&st=nyt

38 Lawrence, Will, "Memories of the Joker: Heath Ledger," *The London Times*, July 16, 2008

39 *Ibid.*

40 —, "The Dark Knight: Production Notes," © 2008 Warner Bros. Inc., SciFiJapan.com, http://www.scifijapan.com/articles/2008/07/13/the-dark-knight-production-notes/, accessed Aug. 20, 2011

41 Boucher, Geoff, Matea Gold and Paul Lieberman, "Ledger's Death is a Shock to Hollywood, Fans," *The Los Angeles Times*, Jan. 23, 2008, http://www.latimes.com/news/printedition/asection/la-et-ledger 23jan23,0,2933344.story, accessed July 2, 2011

42 *Ibid.*

43 Wells, Dominic, "Dark Knight Marks New Chapter in Batman's Seven Decade Screen Career," *The (London) Sunday Times*, July 12, 2008

44 McNary, Dave, "Ledger Joins Bat Pack," *Daily Variety*, Aug. 1, 2006, p. 16

45 —, "Brokeback Star to Play Batman Joker," *The London Times*, Aug. 2, 2006

46 —, "The Dark Knight: Production Notes," © 2008 Warner Bros. Inc., SciFiJapan.com, http://www.scifijapan.com/articles/2008/07/13/the-dark-knight-production-notes/, accessed Aug. 20, 2011

47 *Ibid.*

48 Fleming, Michael, "Inside Moves: Thesps 'Mad' About Indie Heist Pic," *Daily Variety*, Jan. 26, 2007, p. 5

49 McClintock, Pamela, "Batman Adores New Leading Lady," *Daily Variety*, March 9, 2007, p. 4

50 Brevet, Brad, "Maggie Gyllenhaal Opens Up About Her Role in 'The Dark Knight,'" *RopeOfSilicon.com*, July 14, 2008, http://www.ropeofsilicon.com/article/maggie_gyllen-haal_opens_up_about_her_role_in_the_dark_knight, accessed Aug. 27, 2011

51 —, "The Dark Knight: Production Notes," © 2008 Warner Bros. Inc., SciFiJapan.com, http://www.scifijapan.com/articles/2008/07/13/the-dark-knight-production-notes/, accessed Aug. 20, 2011

52 Brevet, Brad, "Maggie Gyllenhaal Opens Up About Her Role in 'The Dark Knight,'" *RopeOfSilicon.com*, July 14, 2008, http://www.ropeofsilicon.com/article/maggie_gyllen-haal_opens_up_about_her_role_in_the_dark_knight, accessed Aug. 27, 2011

53 —, "The Dark Knight: Production Notes," © 2008 Warner Bros. Inc., SciFiJapan.com, http://www.scifijapan.com/articles/2008/07/13/the-dark-knight-production-notes/, accessed Aug. 20, 2011

54 *Ibid.*

55 Abrams, Corinne, "How the Dark Knight Got a Makeover," *The London Times*, Aug. 28, 2008

56 —, "The Dark Knight: Production Notes," © 2008 Warner Bros. Inc., SciFiJapan.com, http://www.scifijapan.com/articles/2008/07/13/the-dark-knight-production-notes/, accessed Aug. 20, 2011

57 *Ibid.*

58 *Ibid.*

59 Abrams, Corinne, "How the Dark Knight Got a Makeover," *The London Times*, Aug. 28, 2008

60 —, "The Dark Knight: Production Notes," © 2008 Warner Bros. Inc., SciFiJapan.com, http://www.scifijapan.com/articles/2008/07/13/the-dark-knight-production-notes/, accessed Aug. 20, 2011

61 *Ibid.*

62 Brevet, Brad, "Batman Speaks, Talking 'The Dark Knight' With Christian Bale," *RopeOfSilicon.com*, July 15, 2008, http://www.ropeofsilicon.com/article/batman_speaks_talking_the_dark_knight_with_christian_bale, accessed Aug. 27, 2011

63 Halbfinger, David M., "Batman's Burden: A Director Confronts Darkness and Death," *The New York Times*, March 9, 2008, http://www.nytimes.com/2008/03/09/movies/09halb.html?ref=heathledger, accessed July 3, 2011

64 Abrams, Corinne, "How the Dark Knight Got a Makeover," *The London Times*, Aug. 28, 2008

65 *Ibid.*

66 —, "The Dark Knight: Production Notes," © 2008 Warner Bros. Inc., SciFiJapan.com, http://www.scifijapan.com/articles/2008/07/13/the-dark-knight-production-notes/, accessed Aug. 20, 2011

67 Abrams, Corinne, "How the Dark Knight Got a Makeover," *The London Times*, Aug. 28, 2008

68 —, "The Dark Knight: Production Notes," © 2008 Warner Bros. Inc., SciFiJapan.com, http://www.scifijapan.com/articles/2008/07/13/the-dark-knight-production-notes/, accessed Aug. 20, 2011

69 Abrams, Corinne, "How the Dark Knight Got a Makeover," *The London Times*, Aug. 28, 2008

70 *Ibid.*

71 —, "The Dark Knight: Production Notes," © 2008 Warner Bros. Inc., SciFiJapan.com, http://www.scifijapan.com/articles/2008/07/13/the-dark-knight-production-notes/, accessed Aug. 20, 2011

72 *Ibid.*

73 *Ibid.*

74 *Ibid.*

75 *Ibid.*

76 *Ibid.*

77 *Ibid.*

78 *Ibid.*

79 Boucher, Geoff, "Christopher Nolan's 'Knight' Vision," *The Los Angeles Times*, July 6, 2008 http://www.latimes.com/entertainment/la-ca-nolan6-2008jul06,0,522026.story

80 —, "The Dark Knight: Production Notes," © 2008 Warner Bros. Inc., SciFiJapan.com, http://www.scifijapan.com/articles/2008/07/13/the-dark-knight-production-notes/, accessed Aug. 20, 2011

81 *Ibid.*

82 *Ibid.*

83 *Ibid.*

84 *Ibid.*

85 *Ibid.*

86 *Ibid.*

87 *Ibid.*

88 Carpenter, Susan, "Wholly High-Tech, Batman. It's the Batpod!" *The Los Angeles Times*, June 18, 2007, http://www.latimes.com/classified/automotive/highway1/la-hy-throttle18jun18redo,0,6121661.story

89 Verini, Bob, "Dystopian Designs Dominate," *Daily Variety*, Dec. 12, 2008, p. A2

90 *Ibid.*, p. A5

91 —, "The Dark Knight: Production Notes," © 2008 Warner Bros. Inc., SciFiJapan.com, http://www.scifijapan.com/articles/2008/07/13/the-dark-knight-production-notes/, accessed Aug. 20, 2011

92 *Ibid.*

93 Verini, Bob, "Dystopian Designs Dominate," *Daily Variety*, Dec. 12, 2008, p. A5

94 *Ibid.*

95 —, "The Dark Knight: Production Notes," © 2008 Warner Bros. Inc., SciFiJapan.com, http://www.scifijapan.com/articles/2008/07/13/the-dark-knight-production-notes/, accessed Aug. 20, 2011

96 *Ibid.*

97 *Ibid.*

98 Brevet, Brad, "Thomas and Roven, the Producers Talk 'Dark Knight,'" *RopeOfSilicon.com*, July 15, 2008, http://www.ropeofsilicon.com/article/thomas_and_roven_the_producers_talk_dark_knight, accessed Aug. 27, 2011

99 —, "The Dark Knight: Production Notes," © 2008 Warner Bros. Inc., SciFiJapan.com, http://www.scifijapan.com/articles/2008/07/13/the-dark-knight-production-notes/, accessed Aug. 20, 2011

100 Brevet, Brad, "Thomas and Roven, the Producers Talk 'Dark Knight,'" *RopeOfSilicon.com*, July 15, 2008, http://www.ropeofsilicon.com/article/thomas_and_roven_the_producers_talk_dark_knight, accessed Aug. 27, 2011

101 Halbfinger, David M., "Batman's Burden: A Director Confronts Darkness and Death," *The New York Times*, March 9, 2008, http://www.nytimes.com/2008/03/09/movies/09halb.html?ref=heathledger, accessed July 3, 2011

102 —, "The Dark Knight: Production Notes," © 2008 Warner Bros. Inc., SciFiJapan.com, http://www.scifijapan.com/articles/2008/07/13/the-dark-knight-production-notes/, accessed Aug. 20, 2011

103 *Ibid.*

104 *Ibid.*

105 *Ibid.*

106 *Ibid.*

107 *Ibid.*

108 *Ibid.*

109 *Ibid.*

110 *Ibid.*

111 Brevet, Brad, "Batman Speaks, Talking 'The Dark Knight' With Christian Bale," *RopeOfSilicon.com*, July 15, 2008, http://www.ropeofsilicon.com/article/batman_speaks_talking_the_dark_knight_ with_christian_bale, accessed Aug. 27, 2011

112 Lawrence, Will, "Memories of the Joker: Heath Ledger," *The London Times*, July 16, 2008

113 Fletcher, Alex, "Caine: 'Ledger's Joker is Stunning," *DigitalSpy.com*, Nov. 30, 2007, http://www.digitalspy.com/movies/news/a80845/caine-ledgers-joker-is-stunning.html, accessed Sept. 24, 2011

114 —, "The Dark Knight: Production Notes," © 2008 Warner Bros. Inc., SciFiJapan.com, http://www.scifijapan.com/articles/2008/07/13/the-dark-knight-production-notes/, accessed Aug. 20, 2011

115 Boucher, Geoff, "Christopher Nolan's 'Knight' Vision," *The Los Angeles Times*, July 6, 2008 http://www.latimes.com/entertainment/la-ca-nolan6-2008jul06,0,522026.story

116 —, "The Dark Knight: Production Notes," © 2008 Warner Bros. Inc., SciFiJapan.com, http://www.scifijapan.com/articles/2008/07/13/the-dark-knight-production-notes/, accessed Aug. 20, 2011

117 *Ibid.*

118 *Ibid.*

119 *Ibid.*

120 Halbfinger, David M., "Batman's Burden: A Director Confronts Darkness and Death," *The New York Times*, March 9, 2008, http://www.nytimes.com/2008/03/09/movies/09halb.html?ref=heathledger, accessed July 3, 2011

121 —, "The Dark Knight: Production Notes," © 2008 Warner Bros. Inc., SciFiJapan.com, http://www.scifijapan.com/articles/2008/07/13/the-dark-knight-production-notes/, accessed Aug. 20, 2011

122 *Ibid.*

123 *Ibid.*

124 *Ibid.*

125 *Ibid.*

126 Belluck, Pam, "A Bigger Stage for a Senator," *The New York Times*, Jul 12 2008, p. A.9

127 *Ibid.*

128 *Ibid.*

129 —, "The Dark Knight: Production Notes," © 2008 Warner Bros. Inc., SciFiJapan.com, http://www.scifijapan.com/articles/2008/07/13/the-dark-knight-production-notes/, accessed Aug. 20, 2011

130 *Ibid.*

131 *Ibid.*

132 *Ibid.*

133 Brevet, Brad, "Batman Speaks, Talking 'The Dark Knight' With Christian Bale," *RopeOfSilicon.com*, July 15, 2008, http://www.ropeofsilicon.com/article/batman_speaks_talking_the_dark_knight_with_christian_bale, accessed Aug. 27, 2011

134 Pringle, Gill, "On the Move: Christian Bale—Terminator and Batman Star Has Dirt Bikes, Pick-up Truck and a Triumph TR6 Roadster But Wasn't Allowed to Ride the Bat Pod," *The London Times*, May 17, 2009

135 Brevet, Brad, "Batman Speaks, Talking 'The Dark Knight' With Christian Bale," *RopeOfSilicon.com*, July 15, 2008, http://www.ropeofsilicon.com/article/batman_speaks_talking_the_dark_knight_with_christian_bale, accessed Aug. 27, 2011

136 *Ibid.*

137 *Ibid.*

138 Lawrence, Will, "Memories of the Joker: Heath Ledger," *The London Times*, July 16, 2008

139 —, "The Dark Knight: Production Notes," © 2008 Warner Bros. Inc., SciFiJapan.com, http://www.scifijapan.com/articles/2008/07/13/the-dark-knight-production-notes/, accessed Aug. 20, 2011

140 *Ibid.*

141 *Ibid.*

142 *Ibid.*

143 *Ibid.*

144 *Ibid.*

145 *Ibid.*

146 —, "Crew Member Killed on Set of New Batman Film," *The Los Angeles Times*, Sept. 25, 2007, http://www.latimes.com/entertainment/news/movies/la-wi-batman25sep25,0,3370258.story

147 Zoe Blackler, Zoe, "Batman Crew Member Died in Stunt Accident," *The London Times*, Nov. 4, 2008

148 *Ibid.*

149 *Ibid.*

150 *Ibid.*

151 —, "Special Effects Guru in Court Over Batman Death," *Uxbridge Gazette*, UK, March 8, 2011, http://www.uxbridgegazette.co.uk/west-london-news/local-uxbridge-news/2011/03/08/special-effects-guru-in-court-over-batman-death-86289-28298871/

152 —, "Crew Member Killed on Set of New Batman Film," *The Los Angeles Times*, Sept. 25, 2007, http://www.latimes.com/entertainment/news/movies/la-wi-batman25sep25,0,3370258.story

153 —, "Special Effects Guru in Court Over Batman Death," *Uxbridge Gazette*, UK, March 8, 2011, http://www.uxbridgegazette.co.uk/west-london-news/local-uxbridge-news/2011/03/08/special-effects-guru-in-court-over-batman-death-86289-28298871/

154 *Ibid.*

155 Itzkoff, Dave, "Effects Man Cleared In 'Dark Knight' Case," *The New York Times*, March 15, 2011, http://query.nytimes.com/gst/fullpage.html?res=9A05E2DD133BF936A25750C0A9679D8B63&scp=59&sq=batman&st=nyt, accessed Aug. 17, 2011

156 Halbfinger, David M., "Batman's Burden: A Director Confronts Darkness and Death," *The New York Times*, March 9, 2008, http://www.nytimes.com/2008/03/09/movies/09halb.html?ref=heathledger, accessed July 3, 2011

157 Boucher, Geoff, Matea Gold and Paul Lieberman, "Ledger's Death is a Shock to Hollywood, Fans," *The Los Angeles Times*, Jan. 23, 2008, http://www.latimes.com/news/printedition/asection/la-et-ledger23jan23,0,2933344.story, accessed July 2, 2011

158 —, "The Dark Knight: Production Notes," © 2008 Warner Bros. Inc., SciFiJapan.com, http://www.scifijapan.com/articles/2008/07/13/the-dark-knight-production-notes/, accessed Aug. 20, 2011

159 Brevet, Brad, "Thomas and Roven, the Producers Talk 'Dark Knight,'" *RopeOf Silicon.com*, July 15, 2008, http://www.ropeofsilicon.com/article/thomas_and_roven_the_producers_talk_dark_knight, accessed Aug. 27, 2011

160 Fleming, Michael, "The Groundbreakers: Chris Nolan," *Daily Variety*, Oct. 29, 2008, p. A30

161 Cohen, David S., "Add Reality, Then Stir," *Daily Variety*, Dec. 11, 2008, p. A5

162 King, Richard, "Sound Editing: Richard King, 'The Dark Knight,'" *The Los Angeles Times*, Feb. 23, 2009, http://www.latimes.com/entertainment/la-et-oscarsoundediting23-2009feb23,0,5340814.story, Accessed June 17, 2011

163 —, "The Dark Knight: Production Notes," © 2008 Warner Bros. Inc., SciFiJapan.com, http:/www.scifijapan.com/articles/2008/07/13/the-dark-knight-production-notes/, accessed Aug. 20, 2011

164 *Ibid.*

165 *Ibid.*

166 Gallo, Phil, "A Different Kind of 'Knight' Music," *Daily Variety*, July 15, 2008, p. 2

167 —, "The Dark Knight: Production Notes," © 2008 Warner Bros. Inc., SciFiJapan.com, http://www.scifijapan.com/articles/2008/07/13/the-dark-knight-production-notes/, accessed Aug. 20, 2011

168 Gallo, Phil, "A Different Kind of 'Knight' Music," *Daily Variety*, July 15, 2008, p. 2

169 *Ibid.*

170 *Ibid.*

171 Moran, Michael, "The Dark Knight Hype Begins," *The London Times*, Dec. 14, 2007

172 Moran, Michael, "The Hidden Secrets of I Am Legend," *The London Times*, Jan. 8, 2008

173 Boucher, Geoff, "Christopher Nolan's 'Knight' Vision," *The Los Angeles Times*, July 6, 2008 http://www.latimes.com/entertainment/la-ca-nolan6-2008jul06,0,522026.story

174 *Ibid.*

175 Boucher, Geoff, Matea Gold and Paul Lieberman, "Ledger's Death is a Shock to Hollywood, Fans," *The Los Angeles Times*, Jan. 23, 2008, http://www.latimes.com/news/printedition/asection/la-et-ledger23jan23,0,2933344.story, accessed July 2, 2011

176 Gold, Matea and Paul Lieberman, "Actor Heath Ledger Found Dead," *The Los Angeles Times*, Jan. 23, 2008, http://www.latimes.com/news/nationworld/nation/la-na-ledger23jan23,0,7950900.story, Accessed June 17, 2011

177 Barron, James, "Medical Examiner Rules Ledger's Death Accidental," *The New York Times*, Feb. 7, 2008, http://www.nytimes.com/2008/02/07/nyregion/07ledger.html?ref=heathledger, accessed July 3, 2011

178 Gold, Matea and Paul Lieberman, "Actor Heath Ledger Found Dead," *The Los Angeles Times*, Jan. 23, 2008, http://www.latimes.com/news/nationworld/nation/la-na-ledger23jan23,0,7950900.story, Accessed June 17, 2011

179 Boucher, Geoff, Matea Gold and Paul Lieberman, "Ledger's Death is a Shock to Hollywood, Fans," *The Los Angeles Times*, Jan. 23, 2008, http://www.latimes.com/news/printedition/asection/la-et-ledger23jan23,0,2933344.story, accessed July 2, 2011

180 Gold, Matea and Paul Lieberman, "Actor Heath Ledger Found Dead," *The Los Angeles Times*, Jan. 23, 2008, http://www.latimes.com/news/nationworld/nation/la-na-ledger23jan23,0,7950900.story, Accessed June 17, 2011

181 *Ibid.*

182 *Ibid.*

183 Boucher, Geoff, Matea Gold and Paul Lieberman, "Ledger's Death is a Shock to Hollywood, Fans," *The Los Angeles Times*, Jan. 23, 2008, http://www.latimes.com/news/printedition/asection/la-et-ledger23jan23,0,2933344.story, accessed July 2, 2011

184 Carpetbagger, "Waving Goodbye From a Distance," *The New York Times,* Jan. 29, 2008, http://carpetbagger.blogs.nytimes.com/2008/01/29/waving-goodbye-from-a-distance/?scp=364&sq=batman&st=nyt, accessed Aug. 16, 2011

185 Boucher, Geoff, Matea Gold and Paul Lieberman, "Ledger's Death is a Shock to Hollywood, Fans," *The Los Angeles Times,* Jan. 23, 2008, http://www.latimes.com/news/printedition/asection/la-et-ledger 23jan23,0,2933344.story, accessed July 2, 2011

186 Barron, James, "Medical Examiner Rules Ledger's Death Accidental," *The New York Times,* Feb. 7, 2008, http://www.nytimes.com/2008/02/07/nyregion/07ledger.html?ref=heathledger, accessed July 3, 2011

187 *Ibid.*

188 *Ibid.*

189 Halbfinger, David M., "Batman's Burden: A Director Confronts Darkness and Death," *The New York Times,* March 9, 2008, http://www.nytimes.com/2008/03/09/movies/09halb.html?ref=heathledger, accessed July 3, 2011

190 Bloom, Julie, "Dark Knight Pays Tribute," *The New York Times,* June 28, 2008, http://www.nytimes.com/2008/06/28/arts/28arts-DARKKNIGHTPA_BRF.html?adxnnl=1&ref=heathledger&adxnnlx=1309716217-OB8etOLMp/2schQGRMQLAw, accessed July 3, 2011

191 Garrett, Diane, "Truly Tragic End to a Promising Career," *Daily Variety,* Jan. 23, 2008, p. 1

192 *Ibid.*, p. 24

193 Graser, Marc, "Joker Glows in 'Dark,'" *Weekly Variety,* June 30-July 13, 2008, p. 4

194 *Ibid.*, p. 4, 57

195 Steele, Francesca, "The Web Watcher: Batman; The Dark Knight; Kyle Piccolo; Fred Loses His Meds," *The London Times,* July 10, 2008

196 Boucher, Geoff, "Christopher Nolan's 'Knight' Vision," *The Los Angeles Times,* July 6, 2008 http://www.latimes.com/entertainment/la-ca-nolan6-2008jul06,0,522026.story

197 *Ibid.*

198 *Ibid.*

199 *Ibid.*

200 Morant, Michael, "Batman: Gotham Knight, " *The (London) Sunday Times,* Feb. 17, 2008

201 Boucher, Geoff, "Movie Sneaks: Summer 2008: Batman's Next Villain: Is This a Clue?" *The Los Angeles Times,* May 4, 2008, http://www.latimes.com/entertainment/la-ca-eckhartbox4-2008may04,0,3781728.story, accessed July 2, 2011

202 Belluck, Pam, "A Bigger Stage for a Senator," *The New York Times,* Jul 12 2008, p. A.9

203 Thielman, Sam, "A 'Knight' To Remember,'" *Daily Variety,* July 17, 2008, p. 15

204 Uslan, Michael E., *The Boy Who Loved Batman,* © 2011 Chronicle Books, San Francisco, p. 230-231

205 Cieply, Michael, "'Dark Knight' Star Denies Assault," *The New York Times,* July 19, 2008, p. E.2

206 Brown, David, "Batman Star, Christian Bale, Arrested After 'Attacking His Mother and Sister in Hotel Suite'" *The London Times,* July 23 2008

207 —, "Profile: Christian Bale—The Brooding Star of Batman Has Shades of His On-Screen Persona; But Last Week He Was Unable to Escape the Spotlight," *The London Times,* July 27, 2008

208 Hines, Nico, "Batman Star Christian Bale Arrested by London Police on Suspicion of Assault," *The London Times,* July 22, 2008

209 Brown, David, "Batman Star, Christian Bale, Arrested After 'Attacking His Mother and Sister in Hotel Suite'" *The London Times,* July 23 2008

210 Cusick, Casey, "Hard Day's 'Knight,'" *Daily Variety,* July 24, 2008, p. 23

211 Hines, Nico, "Batman Star Christian Bale Arrested by London Police on Suspicion of Assault," *The London Times,* July 22, 2008

212 Bloom, Julie, "Batman Actor Seeks Space," *The New York Times,* Jul. 25, 2008, p. E.2

213 Byers, David, "Batman Star Christian Bale Asks for Privacy in First Comments Since Arrest," *The London Times,* July 24, 2008

214 Hines, Nico, "Batman Star Christian Bale Will Not Be Charged With Assault," *The London Times,* Aug. 14, 2008

215 Pringle, Gill, "On the Move: Christian Bale—Terminator and Batman Star Has Dirt Bikes, Pick-up Truck and a Triumph TR6 Roadster But Wasn't Allowed to Ride the Bat Pod," *The London Times,* May 17, 2009

216 Dargis, Manohla, "Showdown in Gotham Town: Movie Review 'The Dark Knight,'" *The New York Times,* Jul. 18, 2008, p. E.1

217 Travers, Peter, "Review: The Dark Knight," *Rolling Stone,* July 18, 2008, http://www.rollingstone.com/movies/reviews/the-dark-knight-20080718, accessed Aug. 12, 2011

218 Teeman, Tim, "The Dark Knight: the First Review," *The London Times,* July 15, 2008

219 Christopher, James, "The Dark Knight: Heath Ledger's Posthumous Oscar Looks in the Bag as The Dark Knight Rewrites the Comic-Book Thriller Genre," *The London Times,* July 24, 2008

220 Chang, Justin, "'Knight' Plays Darker Card," *Daily Variety,* July 7, 2008, p. 16

221 Landesman, Cosmo, "Christian Bale's Batman is a Costume With No Content: it's Heath Ledger's Joker Who's the Fantastic Freak," *The (London) Sunday Times,* July 27, 2008

222 Graser, Marc, "Joker Glows in 'Dark,'" *Weekly Variety,* June 30-July 13, 2008, p. 57

223 Brooks, Richard, "Batman 'Too Violent' for Children: The Dark Knight Has Sparked Record Complaints," The London Times, Aug. 3, 2008

224 *Ibid.*

225 Malvern, Jack, "Batman Faces the Quiet Man as Iain Duncan Smith Complains About Violence," *The London Times,* Aug. 5, 2008

226 Cieply, Michael, "Many Movie Theaters Decide to Leave the Bat Signal On Till Dawn," *The New York Times,* Jul. 9, 2008. p. E.1

227 *Ibid.*

228 Thielman, Sam, "Screenings All 'Knight' Long," *Weekly Variety,* July 21-27, 2008, p. 38

229 McClintock, Pamela and Dave McNary, "B.O. Turns on 'Knight' Light," *Daily Variety,* July 18, 2008, p. 24

230 McClintock, Pamela, "Batman Goes Pow!: 'Knight,' 'Mamma' Rock Weekend," *Daily Variety,* July 21, 2008, p. 23

231 McClintock, Pamela and Dave McNary, "B.O. Turns on 'Knight' Light," *Daily Variety,* July 18, 2008, p. 24

232 —, "No joke! 'Dark Knight' Makes a Killing," *The Los Angeles Times,* July 20, 2008 http://www.latimes.com/entertainment/news/movies/la-et-boxoffice21-2008jul21,0,3066584.story, accessed June 17, 2011

233 McClintock, Pamela and Dave McNary, "B.O. Turns on 'Knight' Light," *Daily Variety,* July 18, 2008, p. 24

234 *Ibid.*

235 Cieply, Michael, "'Dark Knight' Star Denies Assault," *The New York Times,* June 19, 2008, p. E.2

236 Cieply, Michael, "Batman Rules the Night, and the Whole Weekend," *The New York Times,* Jul 21, 2008, p. E.1

237 McClintock, Pamela and Dave McNary, "Batman, the B.O. Wonder," *Daily Variety,* July 22, 2008, p. 17

238 Cieply, Michael, "Batman Rules the Night, and the Whole Weekend," *The New York Times,* Jul 21, 2008, p. E.1

239 Arango, Tim, "Holy Cash Cow, Batman! Content Is Back," *The New York Times,* Aug. 10, 2008, p. BU.1

240 Stelter, Brian and Brad Stone, "Digital Pirates Winning Battle With Studios," *The New York Times,* Feb. 4, 2009, http://www.nytimes.com/2009/02/05/business/media/05piracyhtml?scp=311&sq=batman&st=nyt, accessed Aug. 17, 2011

241 *Ibid.*

242 McClintock, Pamela and Dave McNary, "B.O. Turns on 'Knight' Light," *Daily Variety,* July 18, 2008, p. 24

243 Barnes, Brooks, "Batman Weekend 2: $75 Million, Still Ahead," *The New York Times,* Jul. 28, 2008, p. E.1

244 *Ibid.*

245 McNary, Dave, "O'seas B.O.'s Batty Too," *Daily Variety,* July 28, 2008, p. 22

246 Bosman, Julie, "Dark Knight Stays On Top," *The New York Times,* Aug. 11, 2008, p. E.2

247 Cieply, Michael and Brooks Barnes, "'Thunder' Dethrones A Batman Blockbuster," *The New York Times,* Aug. 18, 2008, http://query.nytimes.com/gst/fullpage.html?res=9F03E5DB163AF93BA2575BC0A96E9C8B63&scp=25&sq=batman&st=nyt, accessed Aug. 16, 2011

248 Christopher Goodwin, Christopher, "How Batman Became Cinema's Top Trump," *The London Times,* Aug. 17, 2008

249 McClintock, Pamela, "Titanic Task: How Far Will 'Knight' Soar?" *Daily Variety,* July 30, 2008, p. 1

250 McNary, Dave, "Fruit of the 'Tomb,'" *Daily Variety,* Aug. 18, 2008. p. 9

251 McNary, Dave, "O'seas Flies With Batpic," *Daily Variety,* Sept. 2, 2008, p. 1

252 McClintock, Pamela, "Summer Cum Laude: B.O. on Par With Hot '07," *Daily Variety,* Sept. 2, 2008, p. 20

253 *Ibid.*

254 *Ibid.*

255 Boyle, Catherine, "Time Warner Picked Up By Batman," *The London Times*, Nov. 5, 2008

256 McClintock, Pamela, "2008: Year That Broke the Rules," Weekly Variety, Dec. 15-21, 2008, p. 8

257 —, "Actor Morgan Freeman hospitalized at The MED after accident," WMCTV.com, Aug. 4, 2008, http://www.wmctv.com/story/8783679/actor-morgan-freeman-hospitalized-at-the-med-after-accident?redirected=true, accessed Sept. 7, 2011

258 *Ibid.*

259 —, "Records Show Freeman Settles Car Crash Suit," *MSNBC.msn.com*, http://today.msnbc.msn.com/id/33683095/ns/today-entertainment/t/records-show-freeman-settles-car-crash-suit/, accessed Sept. 8, 2011

260 Zoe Blackler, Zoe, "Batman Crew Member Died in Stunt Accident," *The London Times*, Nov. 4, 2008

261 Burlingame, Jon, "'Knight' Score's Nixed," *Daily Variety*, Nov. 13, 2008. p. 4

262 *Ibid.*

263 Goldstein, Patrick and James Rainey, "Hans Zimmer to Academy: I'm no Liar!" *The Los Angeles Times*, Dec. 9, 2008, http://latimesblogs.latimes.com/the_big_picture/2008/12/hans-zimmer-to.html, accessed Sept. 7, 2011

264 Chang, Justin, "'Wall-E' Booted Up," *Daily Variety*, Dec. 10, 2008, p. 1

265 King, Susan, "'Dark Knight' Swoops Into DGA Nominations: Superhero Movie Continues to Perform Well Among Guilds," *The Los Angeles Times*, Jan. 8, 2009, http://theenvelope.latimes.com/entertainment/env-et-dga-noms2009jan8,0,1602939.story, accessed Aug. 17, 2011

266 —, "Oscar Nominations: Supporting Players," *The Los Angeles Times*, Jan. 23, 2009, http://www.latimes.com/entertainment/la-et-oscarssupportingactors23-2009jan23,0,2572291.story, accessed July 2, 2011

267 Johnson, Reed, "For Heath Ledger, A Bittersweet Salute," *The Los Angeles Times*, Feb. 23, 2009, http://theenvelope.latimes.com/entertainment/la-et-oscarledger23-2009feb23,0,3072313.story

268 Sharkey, Betsy, "Supporting Actor: Heath Ledger—Yes, Absolutely," *The Los Angeles Times*, Feb. 23,2009, http://theenvelope.latimes.com/entertainment/la-et-oscarsupportingactor232009feb23,0,3045958.story, accessed July 2, 2011

269 Boucher, Geoff, "Christopher Nolan: All His Altered States,"*The Los Angeles Times,* Dec. 9, 2010, http://www.latimes.com/entertainment/news/la-en-chris-nolan-20101209,0,54088.story, accessed June 17, 2011

270 Christopher Goodwin, Christopher, "How Batman Became Cinema's Top Trump," *The London Times*, Aug. 17, 2008

271 —, "Batman and the War on Terror," *The New York Times*, July 21, 2008, http://theboard.blogs.nytimes.com/2008/07/21/batman-and-the-war-on-terror/?scp=28&sq=batman&st=nyt, accessed Aug. 16, 2011

272 Christopher Goodwin, Christopher, "How Batman Became Cinema's Top Trump," *The London Times*, Aug. 17, 2008

273 *Ibid.*

274 *Ibid.*

275 *Ibid.*

276 Rampell, Catherine, "The Joker's Bailout Plan," *The New York Times*, Sept. 26, 2008, http://economix.blogs.nytimes.com/2008/09/26/the-jokers-bailout-plan/?scp=634&sq=batman&st=nyt, accessed Aug. 16, 2011

277 Booth, Jenny, "Author of 'Shocking, Racist' Obama Joker Image Unveiled—as a Bored History Student," *The London Times*, Aug. 18 2009

278 Jaafar, Ali, "Bat Spat: Turk Kicks Caped Crusader," *Daily Variety*, Nov. 12, 2008, p. 26

279 Garrett, Diane, "Pressure on 'Knight': Huge Blu-Ray Bow Can't Ignite DVD Biz," *Daily Variety*, Dec. 12, 2008, p. 8

280 *Ibid.*

281 *Ibid.*

282 Fritz, Ben, "Warner Bros. Launching 'Dark Knight,' 'Inception' as iPhone Apps," *The Los Angeles Times*, February 15, 2011, http://latimesblogs.latimes.com/entertainmentnewsbuzz/2011/02/dark-knight-inception-iphone-apps-warner-bros.html, accessed Aug. 17, 2011

283 Fritz, Ben, "First Movie on Facebook: Warner Bros.' 'The Dark Knight,'" *The Los Angeles Times*, March 8, 2011, http://latimesblogs.latimes.com/entertainmentnewsbuzz/2011/03/the-dark-knight-first-movie-available-on-facebook.html, accessed July 2, 2011

284 *Ibid.*

285 Smyth, Chris, "Batman Scores $1m Knockout Against Superman in Comic Wars," *The (London) Sunday Times*, February 27 2010

286 Gustines, George Gene, "Batman's First Appearance at a Bruce Wayne Price," *The New York Times*, Feb. 26, 2010, http://arts beat.blogs.nytimes.com/2010/02/26/bat mans-first-appearance-at-a-bruce-wayne-price/?scp=43&sq=batman&st=nyt, accessed Aug. 17, 2011

287 Smyth, Chris, "Batman Scores $1m Knockout Against Superman in Comic Wars," *The (London) Sunday Times*, February 27 2010

288 Gustines, George Gene, "Turning a 10-Cent Comic Book Into a Million Bucks," *The New York Times*, February 27, 2010, http://www.nytimes.com/2010/02/28/weekinreview/28 gustines.html?scp=66&sq=batman&st=nyt, accessed Aug. 17, 2011

289 —, "Rare Comic Book Sells For $1.5 Million," *The Los Angeles Times*, March 29, 2010, http://www. latimes.com/entertainment/ktla-superman-comic-record-sale,0,6704702.story, accessed July 2, 2011

290 Graser, Marc, "Hero Hunt Heats Up...and Taps Into Ties at DC Comics," *Weekly Variety*, Aug. 18-24, 2008, p. 7

291 Moran, Michael, Chris Nolan on Dark Knight, on Heath Ledger, and the Possibility of Batman 3," *The London Times*, Oct. 28, 2008

292 Moran, Michael, "Christian Bale to Kill Batman AND Terminator?" *The London Times*, June 25 2009

293 Fleming, Michael, "The Groundbreakers: Chris Nolan," *Daily Variety*, Oct. 29, 2008, p. A30

AFTERWORD

So, what happened to the man who, in 1979, saw that Batman had the potential to rise out of the dustbin of television history and become one of Warner Bros. biggest corporate assets? How does he feel about how the franchise evolved? Interviewed in 2009, Michael Uslan summed up his view of the *Batman* films, saying, "If you look at the comics in the '30s all the way on up, there have been so many radically different interpretations of Batman in tone and appearance and story, in every way, shape or form, completely different. And, to me, the first *Batman* movie captured a lot of the tone of the Batman of 1939. The second one, I thought, was very much like the Batman comics of the '90s, where Batman was just about as dark as he had ever been, sometimes soulless, almost vampiric in a sense, very cold. With *Batman Forever*, with the exception of the way Val Kilmer interpreted Bruce Wayne, I think it was really, truly the Batman of the late '40s through the '50s—the typical Bill Finger scripts, Batman and Robin punning their way through, jumping across giant typewriters against a rogue's gallery of grotesque supervillains. And I always thought that that was played with such darkness and a looseness by Val Kilmer in the third one, *Batman Forever*, that his performance evoked, to me, my experience of seeing Frank Langella play Dracula on Broadway. I always thought that *Batman and Robin* was the '60s TV show regurgitated, and the less said the better. And then with Chris Nolan's genius, brilliant work, I think it is the definitive Batman that works for every generation no matter which Batman you grew up with, which one you read or which one you saw in the media. It just absolutely nails it for everyone."[1]

But how do audiences today react to the various films? What would happen if an informal group of Bat-fanatics congregated to watch all of the *Batman* theatrical films back-to-back? How would they rank the individual films on a 1 to 10 scale? Would the *Batman* films of Tim Burton outrank those of Joel Schumacher? And would an audience comprised mostly of viewers born well after the release of the Adam West movie appreciate its campy take on the character?

On Saturday, August 6, 2011, Brad Hansen and Athena Stamos of Los Angeles, California hosted a Bat-marathon, starting at 8 AM in the morning and ending at 2 AM the following morning. The couple had previously hosted a 3-day James Bond marathon and an all-day *Star Trek* marathon, both of which garnered international recognition.

For the Bat-marathon, they screened eight theatrically released *Batman* films, beginning with the 1966 *Batman* (they skipped over the two Batman serials, which together would have added an additional eight hours to their viewing time). They screened both of the Tim Burton movies, the animated *Batman: Mask of the Phantasm*, both Joel Schumacher films, and both Christopher Nolan epics. The number of attendees fluctuated throughout the day, with a low of 8 and a high of 20, so the survey was hardly scientific. However, after each film was screened, each viewer was asked to rank it on a scale of zero to 10, 10 being best. So how did the films fare? Here's the breakdown:

Film	# of Viewers	Highest Vote	Lowest Vote	Average Score
Batman (1966)	8	7	6	6.75
Batman (1989)	14	8	1	6.71
Batman Returns (1992)	18	9	3	5.56
Batman: Mask of the Phantasm (1993)	17	10	5	9.17
Batman Forever (1995)	20	9	0	4.05
Batman & Robin (1997)	18	4	0	0.83
Batman Begins (2005)	19	10	5	8.63
The Dark Knight (2008)	16	10	7	9.50

The clear favorite was *The Dark Knight*, but interestingly, the second-runner up was *The Mask of the Phantasm*, the animated Batman film from 1993. The lowest ranking, to no one's surprise, was 1997's *Batman & Robin*. But it is interesting that the Adam West *Batman* of 1966 scored higher than Michael Keaton's *Batman* (1989) and *Batman Returns* (1992) or Val Kilmer's *Batman Forever* (1995). Apparently, while this small group clearly preferred the darker Batman, they still appreciated the humor of the Bright Knight. And why not? Adam West has himself become a contemporary cult hero, apart from his interpretation of *Batman*. And echoes of the TV show can still be seen in pop culture, as in the on-screen POWS and WHAMS that punctuate the fight scenes in *Scott Pilgrim Vs. the World* (2010), or Nicolas Cage's Adam West-style line delivery as Big Daddy in *Kick-Ass* (2010).

As I write this, Christopher Nolan and company are filming *The Dark Knight Rises*, which Nolan promises will bring his *Batman* trilogy to a close. Warner Bros., having budgeted the film at $250 million, expects it to be a gargantuan hit, perhaps big enough to dislodge *Avatar* as the highest-grossing film ever made.

After *The Dark Knight Rises*, it is anyone's guess what the next Batman film will be. Perhaps we'll get the long-delayed *Batman Vs. Superman*, or see Batman in a *Justice League* movie. Or perhaps another director with a unique vision will put his or her own personal stamp on a new, rebooted *Batman* series. But one thing is certain—as long as *Batman* remains Warner Bros.' biggest corporate asset, there will always be a *Batman* on film and television.

Index

Numbers in **bold** refer to photographs

ABOUT THE AUTHOR

Photo by Alejandro Arjona

BRUCE SCIVALLY, a pop culture historian with an encyclopedic knowledge of film and television, teaches screenwriting, film production and cinema history and theory courses at the Illinois Institute of Art-Chicago and Columbia College.

Scivally is the author of *Superman on Film, Television, Radio & Broadway* (McFarland, 2006), the most comprehensive history of Superman in popular media. He also co-authored *James Bond: The Legacy* (Abrams, 2002) with John Cork, which sold over 200,000 copies worldwide and was featured on *The Today Show,* CNN, Fox News Network and *Headline News,* and was highlighted in magazines as diverse as *Glamour, Entertainment Weekly, New York Magazine, The New Yorker* and *Playboy.* His first book was *The Special Effects and Stunts Guide* (Lone Eagle, 1989), co-edited with Tassilo Baur.

Scivally co-produced documentaries and other features for Special Edition DVD releases from MGM, 20th Century Fox and Sony, including documentaries on the making of the *James Bond* films, the *Charlie Chan* series, *Pink Panther* movies and many others.

For more information on Batman, to keep up with Bruce Scivally's book signing appearances, or to order autographed copies of his books, please visit www.BruceScivally.com.